# THE ARTS & MEDIA IN AMERICA:
Freedom or Censorship?

# THE ARTS & MEDIA IN AMERICA:
# Freedom or Censorship?

An Editorials On File Book

Editor: Oliver Trager

**Facts On File**
*New York • Oxford*

303.3
ArT

# THE ARTS & MEDIA IN AMERICA:
## Freedom or Censorship?

Published by Facts On File, Inc.
© Copyright 1991 by Facts On File, Inc.

All rights reserved. No part of this book nay be reproduced in any form without permission of the publisher except for reasonably brief extracts used in reviews, which retain their copyrights.

---

Library of Congress Cataloging-in-Publication Data

The Arts and media in America : freedom or censorship / edited by Oliver Trager
   p.  cm. — (Editorials on file book)
Includes index.
   Summary: a compilation of newspaper editorials and cartoons concerning censorship and related issues.

  ISBN 0-8160-2578-9
  1. Censorship—United States. 2. Arts—Censorship—United States.
3. Mass media—Censorship—United States. 4. Freedom of speech—
United States.  [1. Censorship. 2. Freedom of speech.]
I. Trager, Oliver. II. Series

Z658.3'1'0973—dc20                                       90-37445
                                                                   CIP
                                                                   AC

---

Printed in the United States of America
9 8 7 6 5 4 3 2 1

# Contents

**Preface** . . . . . . . . . . . . . . . . . . . . . . . 1

**Part I: Television, Movies & Radio** . . . . . . . . . . . . . . . . 2
The Fairness Doctrine, The FCC & Indecency, Supreme Court Rules on Obscenity, *Amerika* TV Movie Controversy, Children's Broadcasting Debate, Talk Shows Spark Debate, Andy Rooney's Suspension, Senate 'Live' on TV, High-Definition Television, Screenwriter's Strike in Hollywood, Directors Protest 'Colorization' of Films, *The Last Temptation of Christ* Opens Amid Protest, Televangelist Jim Bakker in Sex Scandal, Jimmy Swaggart Loses Pulpit, Garrison Keiller Leaves *A Prarie Home Companion*, Computer Virus Sweeps Nation

**Part II: Art, Performance, Flag Burning & Censorship** . . . . . 90
Helms & the NEA, Bush & the NEA, NEA Grant Rejections, The Robert Mapplethorpe Photography Debate, 'Miss Saigon' Broadway Debate, Supreme Court Flag Burning Decision '89, Supreme Court Flag Burning Decision '90, House & Senate Reject Flag Burning Bills, Van Gogh paintings Fetch Record Price, Gardner Museum Robbed

**Part III: Publishing & Pornography** . . . . . . . . . . . . . . . 150
Meese Vows Pornography Crackdown, Meese Pornography Panel Releases Report, Pornography Debated Across U.S., 'Dial-A-Porn' Legislation Passed, Supreme Court Rules on Satirization, 'The Satanic Verses' Controversy, Murdoch Forced to Sell Newspaper

**Part IV: Music in America** . . . . . . . . . . . . . . . . 196
Ratings Urged For Rock Music Recordings, Rap Music Group Arrested, Heavy Metal Band on Trial, 20th Anniversary of Woodstock Marked

**Index** . . . . . . . . . . . . . . . . . . . . . . . 210

# THE ARTS & MEDIA IN AMERICA:
## Freedom or Censorship?

# Preface

The arts have been an integral aspect of the human experience since the first paintings appeared in the caves of our earliest ancestors. Indeed, music, art and stories distinguish Man.

Likewise, the arts and media have helped define the identity and character of the United States and much of the world for the better part of the 20th Century. The influence of both the fine and popular arts especially when combined with the technological developments in film, video and audio has been profound. Hollywood, television, radio and the long-playing record shape the aesthetic, political and social orientation of millions.

In modern times the arts and their transmission by technological media have sometimes veered into the political realm. At the heart of the controversy in the U.S. is the constitutional right of free speech artists cite to express themselves versus society's moves to limit that expression.

Censorship is nothing new and is not confined to the arts. All modes of expression whether defined as "art," "news" or "pornography" have been subject to scrutiny for centuries. The tug-of-war between the arts and media and the political, religious, social and business interests that attempt to regulate their dissemination has continued into the 20th Century.

One of the masterworks of modern fiction, James Joyce's *Ulysses*, was banned in the U.S. for years following its French publication in 1922. But the battle has not ended there. J.D. Sallinger's books, most notably *Catcher in the Rye*, are still subject to periodic legal challenge. Most recently, Sen. Jesse Helms has caused heated debate by seeking to limit the nature of the grants awarded by the National Endowment for the Arts.

But the questions of free expression are not confined to the arts. Mass media and the culture they generate, both high and popular, have presented complex topics of controversy. The backlash against rock music and MTV, for instance, have been particularly acute.

*The Arts & Media in America: Freedom or Censorship?* examines these issues and the questions that provoked them. Should pornography be illegal? Does rap music promote racism? Was *The Last Temptation of Christ* blasphemous? Was Sen. Jesse Helms justified in condemning the photography of the late Robert Mapplethrope? How did the U.S. artistic and business community react to Iran's death threats against Salman Rushdie, author of *The Satanic Verses*? Should rock music albums be labled if they are deemed to contain offensive lyrics?

In *The Arts and Media in America: Freedom or Censorship?* the nation's leading editorial writers and cartoonists evaluate the the controversies and stories that call the very essence of American culture and society into question.

November 1990

Oliver Trager

# Part I: Television, Movies, Radio & Theatre

When the inventor Thomas Edison demonstrated his kinetoscope for the first time on April 14, 1894 he had no inkling that by the end of the month, the first recorded protest against a film would come. The protest was directed at *Dolorita in the Passion Dance*, a peepshow running in Atlantic City. In 1913, the first instance of official film censorship on a state level came when the state of Ohio passed a statute to establish a board of censors to precensor all films proposed for showing in the state. The basis of its judgment was a clause stating that "only such films as are in the judgment and discretion of the board of censors of a moral, educational or amusing and harmless character shall be passed and approved..." This law was tested in 1915 and upheld by the Supreme Court in the case of *Mutual Film Corporation v. Industrial Commission of Ohio*. As far as the court was concerned, film was simply just another business; the concept of free speech did not enter into the matter. Not until the 1950s did this federal approval of local censorship begin to dwindle. In 1952 the court overruled its earlier decision, and the power of local censorship was weakened.

In the meantime the range of such censorship was substantial. Depending on local sensibilities films were often barred from using even the most restrained references to sex, violence, race relations, veneral disease, communism, divorce, abortion and a number of other topics deemed too sensitive for the population.

It was only when the courts began to consider film as a medium of communication and artistic expression rather than simply as a commercial enterprise did local censorship begin to vanish. The changing attitudes of the 1960s made it possible to produce and screen films on topics that would have been unthinkable in Hollywood's "golden age." Although there were no attempts to to abandon local licensing, a series of court decisions weakened the grounds upon which permits might henceforth be refused.

Based on the premise that all such censorship would be in violation of First Amendment freedoms, it was no longer possible for local authorities to ban films on the grounds that they were sacriligious, prejudicial to the best interests of the people of a community, tending to corrupt morals, harmful rather than educational, or undermining confidence that justice can be carried out. The tenor of such judgments, taken as a whole, was to emphasize that films might be made about real life, rather than being the optimistic, sentimental fare that seemed safer to many local censors. It is for the return of those "positive, wholesome values" that conservative groups such as the Moral Majority currently campaign.

However, by the time the film industry began gaining control of its output, television had secured itself as perhaps the most important and influential social and cultural force in the United States. Since it emerged in the late 1940s as a nationally available medium of mass entertainment and information, commercial television has been the principal window through which Americans have viewed the world. What was new or popular or influential in American life came now through TV. The medium made nationwide events out of local happenings; and it transformed national, even international, events into neighborhood concerns. It made celebrities and toppled leaders. And as it described and interpreted the recent movements of humankind, it revealed the strengths and foibles of ourselves and others. It has shown us to be neither fully moral nor invincible: through TV we have realized our limitations.

Television rapidly became the cutting edge of social, political, economic and cultural developments in the U.S. It seemed to deliver the fullness of which the Great Depression and World War II had robbed earlier generations. It represented a reward for years for forbearance. TV was the ultimate American medium, requiring no physical labor, offering wonderful diversion, reaffirming the reliance on technology that Americans had developed in the 20th Century, and symbolizing a victory over deprivation that cut across class lines.

But as the medium was controlled by the capitalist ethic from its inception, it has operated as a commercial billboard pitching everything from cars and junk food to presidential candidates. Still, the splashy spectacle has never ceased to fascinate the audience. Indeed, its commercial announcements have become enduring cultural artifacts viewed for their nostalgic and artistic qualities.

In this regard, American television has always been equated with network TV, that is the CBS-NBC-ABC trinity that has beguiled the public with its mysteries and miracles since the medium's earliest days. Critics have suggested that if television played a role in the Vietnam War, the Watergate scandal or civil rights movement, it was because of what the networks programmed. Further, they point out that if there has been a controversy about excessive violence, the manipulation of children through materialistic messages or sexual permisiveness on TV, it is because of what the networks have provided.

The question of censorship has periodically affected broadcast media. Perhaps the key incident that has affected this issue occured in October 1973 when the American comedian George Carlin recorded a 12-minute long monologue entitled "Filthy Words." In it said the words in question. On the afternoon of October 30, 1973, a New York radio station broadcast the monologue. A man who had been driving with his young son complained to the Federal Communications Commission (FCC). The FCC referred to its own regulations regarding indecency and obscenity and stated that while the monologue was not obscene, it was certainly indecent and "patently offensive." It stated that it would make a note of the broadcast on the station's license file and would decide in due course whether to take further action. The station appealed against this ruling. In a decision in 1978, the Supreme Court examined the context of the broadcast and stated that it was not obscene, but that it was indecent and that the FCC, under its own stautory regulations, had the right to make the relevant note in the licensee's file.

These are confusing times for network television. Through cable TV and satellite dishes, many new channels have appeared, and further advances in delivery promise even greater selection. The video revolution is, however, costing a lot of money. Americans are spending billions of dollars on recorders, camcorders, blank and recorded tapes, cable services, and pay-per-view programming. Once heralded as "The Greatest 'Free' Show on Earth," the full spectrum of American television is no longer affordable or available to a sizeable part of the citizenry. The egalitarian implications of a medium that was mass and free have been subverted by expensive monthly cable bills and costly electronic paraphenalia. Because of this, critics argue that the American television experience is increasingly being denied to those with insufficient cash, turning the U.S. into a country of TV-haves and TV-have-nots.

## FCC Rescinds 'Fairness Doctrine'

The U.S. Senate June 23, 1987 effectively sustained President Ronald Reagan's veto of a bill that would write into law the "fairness doctrine," a long-standing federal policy that required radio and television broadcasters to present balanced coverage of controversial issues. In a 53-45 vote, the bill was returned to the Commerce Committee.

The Senate April 21 had approved the legislation by a 59-31 vote. The House had passed it June 3 by a 302-31 vote. Arguing that the doctrine violated broadcasters' First Amendment rights, Reagan had vetoed the measure June 20. The bill would have become law had both houses voted to override the veto by a two-thirds margin.

Congress had approved the bill to prevent the Federal Communications Commission (FCC) from dismantling the fairness doctrine, which dated from the 1930s, when federal regulators sought to guarantee that all sides of an issue were presented by the broadcasting industry, which then consisted of only a few radio stations on the AM band.

However, the FCC, under former chairman Mark Fowler, a Reagan appointee, had gone on record as opposing the doctrine as an unnecessary infringement on broadcasters' freedom to program.

In 1985, the FCC had issued a report saying that the fairness doctrine was unnecessary and probably unconstitutional because more stations were broadcasting now than in 1969, when the U.S. Supreme Court, relying heavily on a "scarcity rationale," had upheld the constitutionality of the doctrine.

The inability of Congress to enact the fairness doctrine into law over the president's veto appeared to leave the FCC free to repeal the regulation.

The FCC Aug. 4, voted, 4-0, to abolish, as an unconstitutional restriction of free speech, the "fairness doctrine," which for 38 years had required U.S. radio and television broadcasters to present balanced coverage of controversial issues. The FCC action followed a congressional effort to write the doctrine into law, a drive that failed in June when President Ronald Reagan vetoed such action.

The FCC's decision did not affect the equal time rule, which dealt solely with the air time allotted to competing federal political candidates. Nor did it deal with such other FCC rules as the one mandating programming designed to meet local needs as a condition for holding a license.

The decision was immediately hailed by the U.S. broadcasting industry, whose spokesmen said the doctrine often did the opposite of what the FCC originally intended by making stations avoid controversial issues altogether.

But various civil rights and other advocacy groups expressed dismay at the decision.

Consumer advocate Ralph Nader, for one, called the decision a major setback to those seeking to advance minority views.

Several members of Congress, including Senate Commerce Committee Chairman Ernest F. Hollings (D, S.C.) and House Commerce Committee Chairman John Dingell (D, Mich.) vowed to renew their efforts to enact the doctrine into law.

## The Hutchinson News

*Hutchinson, KS, June 29, 1987*

President Reagan does wield a mean veto pen.

In that, he's frequently right.

He certainly was right last week when he vetoed Congress' infatuation with what it liked to call the "fairness doctrine" in broadcasting. Under the guise of making certain that broadcasters and other TV hucksters use the airwaves "responsibly," Congress had overwhelmingly written a law to require them to do so.

The law would have required broadcasters to report on controversial issues of the day, but in doing so, ensure that those reports would be balanced by an airing of all other sides of the issue.

This sounds like a vote for motherhood, apple pie and the flag. Who could be against fairness?

You should. The "fairness" the politicians were talking about is their fairness. Any time government is called upon to regulate news and information you receive, you need not guess how that news and information will be slanted to favor government.

Certainly there are broadcast hucksters who are patently unfair. However, you need only count the options you have these days in supporting hucksters who abuse their rights.

Hutchinson has so many radio and TV stations at its disposal that the diversity of opinion long ago passed the clutter stage, even without government dictation of programs.

Mr. Reagan's veto should stand. Congress should be content with its exercise in equating "fairness" with apple pie, and move on to something important. Like honesty in budget making.

## THE BUFFALO NEWS
*Buffalo, NY, June 27, 1987*

PRESIDENT REAGAN put his veto pen to good use in rejecting legislation to write into law the "fairness doctrine" that requires broadcasters to air all sides of controversial public issues.

No one is opposed to fairness in broadcasting, but as the president declared in his veto message, "this type of content-based regulation by the federal government is ... antagonistic to the freedom of expression guaranteed by the First Amendment" and would be "unthinkable" in any other medium.

The president also pointed out that because of changing technology, there is no longer a problem of limited numbers of broadcasting outlets, as there was when the Federal Communications Commission first set forth the fairness doctrine.

In practice, the doctrine often works against itself by encouraging broadcasters to shy away from controversial topics, lest they trigger objections and license challenges.

The central question here is not the need for fairness — which all responsible stations accept — but the unacceptability of governmental control over journalistic judgments by the nation's broadcasters.

It is to Reagan's credit that he recognizes the true issue at stake in this matter. Fortunately, it does not appear that the Senate will be able to override his veto. If ever a presidential objection deserved to be sustained, this one does.

## THE TAMPA TRIBUNE
*Tampa, FL, June 24, 1987*

President Reagan's veto of a bill writing into law the "fairness doctrine" imposed on the electronic media was for the best possible reason: The doctrine violates the First Amendment rights of radio and television broadcasters.

"This type of content-based regulation by the federal government is, in my judgment, antagonistic to the freedom of expression guaranteed by the First Amendment," he wrote in his veto message.

The U.S. Supreme Court in 1969 ruled the doctrine then imposed by the Federal Communications Commission legal on the theory that broadcast frequencies then available were extremely scarce. Under that circumstance, requiring broadcasters to present both sides of controversial issues was seen as promoting diverse and vigorous debate on public issues.

Even then, the court indicated it would be willing to reconsider the appropriateness of the fairness doctrine if it reduced rather than enhanced broadcast coverage. Through the years, that has been its effect. Many broadcasters have avoided controversial subjects lest they be required to give "equal time" to all sides, however frivolous.

The FCC has so concluded, and in addition in 1985 found that the huge increase in the number of broadcast outlets, including cable, clearly made the doctrine unnecessary. It was to counteract that FCC finding that Congress sought to mandate the doctrine through law.

Mark Fowler, former FCC chairman, charged the doctrine "helps incumbents (members of Congress) on the Hill, and that's what this is all about." Other opponents noted that today there are more than 10,000 radio stations, 1,600 television stations. and more than 7,700 cable systems, many of which offer a hundred or more channels.

The Tribune has long maintained that the fairness doctrine violated the First Amendment even in the face of the argument that the electronic media use a limited public resource, the electromagnetic spectrum, and the doctrine is necessary to ensure that minority viewpoints be aired. It is one thing to guarantee access to a public forum, but another to require a government agency to intrude "into the function of the editorial process," as President Reagan described the way the fairness doctrine works. He also noted that the "obvious intent ot the First Amendment" is "to promote vigorous public debate and a diversity of viewpoints in the public forum as a whole, not in any particular medium, let alone in any particular journalistic outlet."

Supporters of the bill may try to override the veto but will have a hard time achieving a two-thirds vote to do so in the Senate. That body's vote for the bill was 59-31, eight short of the number needed to override. Should the proponents fail, they may attach the fairness doctrine mandate to another bill.

That effort, too, should fail. The doctrine itself failed because it brought not free discussion but blandness to the airwaves. Fairness in the public forum is far more likely to develop from the freedom of each medium of expression than from governmental edict.

## The Wichita Eagle-Beacon
*Wichita, KS, June 24, 1987*

PRESIDENT Reagan was right last week to veto Congress' misguided attempt to elevate the Fairness Doctrine for broadcasters to federal law. Congress should let the matter go at that.

The Fairness Doctrine is a collection of Federal Communications Commission rules requiring broadcasters to present both sides of controversial issues and to let viewers and listeners reply, on air, to broadcast editorials. The doctrine supposedly attunes broadcasters more closely to their communities.

In reality, the doctrine stifles broadcasters. That's one reason the FCC earlier this year proposed rescinding the doctrine. Congress, with little forethought and a lot of goading from interest groups believing the doctrine is all that stands between broadcasters and gross irresponsibility, leapt into the breech, sending the now-vetoed bill to Mr. Reagan in a matter of weeks.

The irony is that most broadcast news operations these days routinely cover controversial issues, from all sides. As for editorializing, many TV and radio stations don't do it often; when they do, the stances they take often are less than bold, hence have diminished value to listeners and viewers. Better that, some stations' executives reason, than be forced to set aside air time every time a listener or viewer disagrees with them.

Broadcasters who incline toward responsibility would perform responsibly without government interference; for those who don't, the doctrine has made little difference. Broadcast journalism shouldn't deteriorate without it, and well might improve.

Broadcasters deserve a chance to test that proposition, which is why Congress should let the veto stand. Instead, the FCC should go ahead with its plan to rescind the Fairness Doctrine, which always could be be reinstated in the unlikely circumstance that disastrous consequences should ensue.

6 – Fairness Doctrine

# The Des Moines Register

*Des Moines, IA, June 24, 1987*

President Reagan made an important contribution to preservation of the First Amendment by vetoing a bill that promised "fairness" in broadcast journalism but which would in fact mock the constitutional guarantee of freedom of the press.

Congress recently passed legislation trying to engrave into law a Federal Communications Commission rule — known as the Fairness Doctrine — that requires broadcasters to report on controversial issues of public import. The hooker is that the rule requires that "all sides" of the issue be given.

Instead of the "Fairness Doctrine," this Catch-22 rule should be called the "Timidity Rule." The threat of an FCC complaint or license challenge causes broadcasters to duck important controversies rather than report on them.

The FCC, after thoroughly studying the practical effect of the rule, was moving toward abolishing it. But Congress, looking to take network television executives down a notch or two, hurried the rule into law. Aside from practical problems with the rule, it is preposterous that Congress would consider itself an arbiter of "fairness" in journalism.

President Reagan, in his veto message, said, "The framers of the First Amendment, confident that public debate would be freer and healthier without [this sort] of interference . . ., chose to forbid such regulations in the clearest terms." His words are a ringing endorsement of the First Amendment rights of broadcasters.

The old "spectrum scarcity" argument that separated broadcasting from the printed press for constitutional purposes should be discarded.

With more than 20,000 radio, television and cable systems in the country, versus fewer than 2,000 daily newspapers, it's no longer accurate to characterize the broadcast medium as "scarce."

# Arkansas Gazette

*Little Rock, AR, June 25, 1987*

President Reagan vetoed a bill writing the fairness doctrine into law Saturday, and the 52-year-old rule requiring radio and television stations to air both sides of controversies will soon end, presuming that the Congress fails to override. With his right-wing chorus divided between the ideological purists and those who hate the media more, Mr. Reagan made the right choice.

The president may have been moved by the desire to relieve one more powerful business interest of government restraints on the abuse of its public duty, but he gave the right reasons for vetoing the bill. The doctrine impinges on the First Amendment, and it does the opposite of its purpose. It restrains rather than encourages debate.

"History has shown," his message said, "that the dangers of an overly timid or biased press cannot be averted through bureaucratic regulation, but only through the freedom and competition that the First Amendment sought to guarantee." Well said, Mr. President.

When Congress established the Federal Communications Commission (the radio industry wanted regulation), it charged the agency with regulating broadcasting "in the public interest, convenience and necessity." The FCC adopted the fairness doctrine, which says stations should discuss public issues and give all sides equal time. The shaky underpinning of the doctrine was that the First Amendment didn't apply to radio and television in the same way it did to printed journals because stations used a limited public resource, the electromagnetic spectrum, and that the government had to require equal time to assure a voice for minority or controversial views. The United States Supreme Court took that stance in the last legal challenge to the doctrine, in 1969, in a case in which a radio station broadcast a program critical of a journalist, who demanded free time to respond.

Now, the FCC is proposing to abandon the rule, and Congress stepped in to protect the rule by embedding it in the law. The FCC's reasoning is that since the 1969 ruling technology has drastically changed conditions in the broadcasting media. The number of radio stations has increased from 6,595 to about 10,000 and the number of television stations from 837 to about 1,300. Competition and diversity of ownership assure the range of viewpoints on public issues will be heard.

But the case for abandoning the doctrine need not rest on technology and the proliferation of stations or even on the constitutional freedoms, though heavens knows that is sufficient, but on the sound practical reason that the doctrine has been a failure. The FCC hasn't jerked licenses for fairness violations, but it has not been because stations always entertain vigorous and evenhanded debates of public issues.

The doctrine intimidates stations rather than invigorates them. If government meddled it ought to be for the latter purpose. The doctrine has helped to make radio and television insipid. Rather than entertain the views of minorities on public issues or of those whose opinions abrade community leaders or powerful interests, stations often skirt the issues. Better to be safe and avoid the hassle.

President Reagan is right.

"EVICT HIM? ABSOLUTELY NOT! HE'S THERE FOR THEIR BENEFIT!"

## The Seattle Times
*Seattle, WA, June 23, 1987*

THE so-called "fairness doctrine" — a Federal Communications Commission policy requiring broadcasters to air all sides of controversial issues — is unfair, archaic and arguably unconstitutional.

President Reagan was absolutely right to veto a wrongheaded effort by Congress to write the fairness doctrine into law. Congress probably won't have enough votes to override the veto. Good.

Fairness shouldn't be subject to federal laws or government regulations, but a matter of policy at individual TV and radio stations — as it is for newspapers, magazines and other media.

But broadcasters have been subject to an unfortunate double standard since the FCC adopted the fairness doctrine in 1949. When the number of broadcast outlets was relatively small, perhaps it made some sense. But now that there are hundreds of TV stations and thousands of radio stations around the country, it's no longer necessary or justified.

The FCC has been considering scrapping the doctrine in recent years. Last fall, a U.S. District Court of Appeals ruled that the FCC could do so without congresssional approval.

That's when the move began in Congress to make the fairness doctrine law. But the First Amendment clearly states that "Congress shall make no law" abridging freedom of the press. There's no need for asterisks on the Constitution.

Most broadcasters make a conscientious effort to cover major public issues, reflect contrasting opinions, and provide time for opposing views — as the doctrine requires. Most will continue to do that with or without federal regulation. Granted, some won't. But that's what freedom of the press is all about.

As Reagan said in his veto message, "In any other medium besides broadcasting, such federal policing of the editorial judgment of journalists would be unthinkable." Precisely.

## WORCESTER TELEGRAM
*Worcester, MA, June 26, 1987*

In the absence of overwhelming necessity, government should not interfere with the bedrock freedoms of speech and of the press: That is the unmistakable message of President Reagan's veto of the so-called Fairness Doctrine bill.

The president's enthusiasm for the First Amendment is not, unfortunately, shared by a majority in the House and Senate. Last week, Congress passed a bill that would have enshrined the Federal Communications Commission Fairness Doctrine in federal law. The regulatory policy, adopted by the FCC in 1949, requires broadcasters to provide "equal time" to "all sides" of "controversial" issues. Reagan vetoed the bill over the weekend.

That notion of "fairness" has a nice ring, and the FCC regulation may have had a limited justification in the early days of television, when many sections of the nation were served by only one station. The equal time requirement provided a safeguard against potential abuses in monopoly television markets.

Even then, broadcasters — and their supporters in the print media, which are not regulated — opposed the Fairness Doctrine on First Amendment grounds; the doctrine has remained palatable only because the FCC has used the utmost of discretion in applying it. Now — with half a dozen or more television networks, satellite transmission and a multiplicity of local outlets on the UHF and VHF bands — any fear that a legitimate candidate or a cause might be frozen out of the public airwaves is ludicrous.

The Fairness Doctrine law would not broaden news coverage, as its proponents in Congress suggest, but would tend to make stations shy away from reporting on certain issues. For instance, the Fairness Doctrine, if applied rigorously, would open the possibility that all of the 100-plus avowed presidential candidates in the current race would have to be included in any televised debate. The same dampening effect would be felt in every hotly contested issue, from international nuclear disarmament to municipal trash disposal.

Such content-based government regulation, which would police the editorial judgment of journalists, is unthinkable in any other medium. It certainly goes counter to the Founding Fathers' belief that a free, unhindered public debate of issues is vital to democracy. The Fairness Doctrine, instead of making TV news more responsible and broadening public debate, would tend to make broadcasters shy away from controversy. It would also give the force of federal law to an anachronistic infringement on First Amendment freedoms.

President Reagan was correct to veto the bill, which may soon come up for an override vote. Our congressmen should rethink their position and vote to sustain the president's veto.

## CHARLESTON EVENING POST
*Charleston, SC, June 23, 1987*

Even if some court eventually decides he was wrong on the constitutional question, President Reagan did the right thing the other day. His veto of a bill that would write into law a rule of the Federal Communications Commission known as the "fairness doctrine" will at least make it tougher for Congress to deny editorial freedom to broadcasters.

The president says the 38-year-old rule, which authorized the Federal Communications Commission to police the editorial fairness of radio and television broadcasters, is unconstitutional. We think he's correct even though we concede there's some room for argument.

The fact is that the FCC finally had accepted the broadcasters' contention that dictating what stations should air violates their First Amendment rights. Last year, a federal appeals court ruled that the FCC could lift the regulation without congressional approval.

But Congress wasn't about to stand still for that. Small wonder. The rule, according to Mark Fowler, a former Reagan administration FCC chairman, "helps incumbents (members of Congress) on the Hill, and that's what this is all about."

In his veto message, the president noted that in any other medium beside broadcasting, "such federal policing of editorial judgment of journalists would be unthinkable. History has shown that the dangers of an overly timid or biased press cannot be averted through bureaucratic regulation, but only through the freedom and competition that the First Amendment sought to guarantee."

The counterargument is that print and electronic journalists really aren't the same. Policing proponents contend that radio and television stations are using a limited public resource — the electromagnetic spectrum — and the doctrine is necessary to ensure that minority viewpoints are aired.

But that leads us back to the president's point about competition. Since the fairness doctrine was promulgated, the airwaves have gotten a lot more crowded. There now are more than 10,000 radio stations, nearly 1,600 TV stations and about 7,700 cable TV systems.

Congress, however, is composed mostly of politicians who plan to run for re-election and have a special interest in monitoring the media. If they could, many would dictate to the print media what, in their view, constitutes "fairness." There's not much question that the House, which agreed by a vote of 302-102 to write the rule into the law, will vote to override the veto. The Senate's another matter. While the bill passed there by 59-31, some 67 votes would be needed to overcome the president's objection.

But even if the president wins this round, the sponsors say they'll keep on reintroducing the proposal. And, if they can't win with this president, they are sure to test the next one. This is one of those fights that ultimately the courts are going to have to decide.

## Wisconsin State Journal
*Madison, WI, June 16, 1987*

In the 1920s, when radio was in its infancy, some people in government decided it might be a good idea to control this technological marvel before it got out of hand. The solution was something called "The Fairness Doctrine," a harmless-sounding piece of regulation that was later extended to television as well.

The Fairness Doctrine says that broadcasters must cover matters of public importance and that the coverage must fairly reflect different viewpoints. To the casual observor, that doctrine sounds . . . well, fair.

Fair, that is, unless you take into account the First Amendment and its guarantees of a free press. Just because the founding fathers couldn't envision Dan Rather, CNN and the "drive-time" newscast is no reason to believe they would have drawn up exceptions to the First Amendment's protections against government interference.

The theory behind the Fairness Doctrine has been that the "scarcity" of broadcast airwaves and channels demands licensing and licensing permits regulation. For years, courts and some broadcasters bought that argument and swallowed their doubts about its constitutionality.

There is no reason to accept the "scarcity" argument today, and there is even less reason to accept the "Fairness in Broadcasting" bill passed by Congress and sent to President Reagan. The president should veto this attempt to institutionalize censorship of the airwaves.

For starters, the argument about "scarcity" doesn't fly. There are now about 10,000 radio stations and 1,800 TV stations not even counting cable. Nearly three-quarters of U.S. households with cable can get more than 10 signals. By way of comparison, there are 1,650 daily newspapers in the United States and most of them are in "one-paper" towns.

The agency that enforces the Fairness Doctrine, the Federal Communications Commission, thinks it's a bad law. The FCC has said the doctrine often inhibits rather than encourages debate — particularly on local matters — because broadcasters tend to steer clear of controversy.

Also, the doctrine has been used effectively to intimidate an industry terrified of challenges to its licenses; Democratic and Republican presidents have done so in the past. Reagan, a former broadcaster, has a historical understanding about how the Fairness Doctrine was used for political purposes by the Kennedy, Johnson and Nixon administrations.

There is nothing fair about the Fairness Doctrine. Reagan has shown himself to be a firm believer in deregulation; here is a chance to prove it anew.

## The Register-Guard
*Eugene, OR, June 24, 1987*

It is passing strange how some radio and television station owners can work themselves into a lather over the fairness doctrine.

They have Ronald Reagan on their side. He vetoed a bill that would make the doctrine a federal statute — which everybody thought it already was until last year when a federal appeals court decided that its status is only that of a Federal Communications Commission regulation.

But the broadcasters have not persuaded Congress. The House and Senate approved the bill by large margins, although there may not be quite enough votes in the Senate to override the veto. Oregon's Sen. Bob Packwood, the broadcasters' most devoted friend on this issue, will help muster votes against an override.

The rule in question says two things: First, radio and TV licensees must cover matters of public importance. Second, their coverage of those issues must provide "reasonable opportunity for the presentation of contrasting views . . ."

What self-respecting broadcaster would disagree with those principles? None. They all say they want to practice what the doctrine preaches. They just don't want to be *ordered* to do so by the federal government. That, they complain, violates their rights under the hallowed First Amendment.

The Supreme Court disagrees. It decided in 1969 in what is known as the Red Lion case that the scarcity of broadcasting airwaves permits government regulation.

Nonetheless, President Reagan bought the broadcasters' argument, declaring in his veto message, "This type of content-based regulation by the federal government is . . . antagonistic to the freedom of expression guaranteed by the First Amendment. In any other medium besides broadcasting, such federal policing of the editorial judgment of journalists would be unthinkable."

That's just the point. Broadcasting is unique, with special characteristics, one of which is that the operators don't own their physical medium, the airwaves. The public does. Station owners are not called "licensees" by accident. They must get a federal license to use a specific portion of the electromagnetic spectrum. In return, they must abide by certain regulations intended to protect the public interest.

This grates on many broadcasters. They would like to have the same status under the First Amendment as the print media. Legislation to amend the Constitution to grant them that status has been proposed but has never gotten anywhere. The basic reason relates to obvious physical differences between using airwaves and using paper and ink. The finite number of broadcast "channels" in the broadest sense makes governmental allocation and regulation a practical necessity. It was, after all, broadcasters themselves who originally demanded regulation to bring order out of chaos, pushing through the basic law, the Communications Act of 1934.

Today's broadcasters, chafing under the little federal regulation that is left after a decade of deregulation, pounce on the notion of scarcity of outlets as a rationale for the fairness doctrine. They say that in the last so many years the number of radio stations and television stations has grown to so many thousands. How, they ask, can anyone claim scarcity when such a plethora of outlets provides opportunity for every possible view to be aired in virtually every community?

In truth, that's not a bad argument. The situation *has* changed since 1934 to the point where we wouldn't really worry about elimination of the fairness doctrine for radio stations, and wouldn't worry too much about the same for TV if it weren't for the fact that the latter is still dominated by only three major networks. Even there, the presence of a good public broadcasting quasi-network is reassuring, although curiously some opponents of the fairness doctrine also would like to get rid of public broadcasting.

This is not an earth-shaking issue. We do not expect the republic to fall if Congress fails to codify the fairness doctine, or if the FCC finally carries out its threats to repeal the rule.

But neither do we believe that the yoke of regulation is so tight that broadcasters desperately need relief. They are more likely to choke on the profits that a license often guarantees than they are to suffocate under the burden of rules like the fairness doctrine.

## The Duluth News-Tribune
*Duluth, MN, June 27, 1987*

Regulation, or lack of it, of television programming for children is an area that cries out for review.

A U.S. Circuit Court of Appeals paved the way for that Friday when it orderd the Federal Communications Commission to review its decision deregulating the content of children's television.

Since the 1984 ruling, opponents of deregulation, who brought the suit, contend that much of children's TV programming has become "toy-based." In other words, characters and props portrayed in the programs are the self-same dolls and other toys available on the market for home use and shown in commercials.

Judge Kenneth Starr, speaking for the court's three-judge panel, said the FCC must explain *why* it deregulated children's television. Starr said prior regulation of children's television by the FCC had been based on the premise that the television market does not function adequately when children make up the audience.

We approve of the court's decision, and await the FCC's review. It is difficult to imagine how normal marketplace pressures which, for example, dictate how much time is devoted to commercials in adult programming, could apply to children's programs — especially if the material in the commercials is indistinguishable from that in the editorial content of the shows.

Our strong support of marketplace control in these areas is well established. But children's programming is an exception. Children are an exception throughout our society, throughout our legal system. The FCC has been asked to respond, and we await with interest its justification for deregulation of children's programming.

## Honolulu Star-Bulletin
*Honolulu, HI, June 23, 1987*

President Reagan deserves applause from defenders of the First Amendment for his veto of the Fairness in Broadcasting Act. This measure would have given the status of law to the so-called "fairness doctrine," which requires broadcasters to present differing views on controversial subjects.

As Reagan stated in his veto message, the measure "would be inconsistent with the First Amendment and with the American tradition of independent journalism."

In the past the Federal Communications Commission applied the "fairness doctrine" to radio and television on the theory that opportunities for differing opinions to be heard on the air were limited. The policy was upheld by the Supreme Court in 1969.

But the FCC now wants to abandon the fairness doctrine because it "chills and coerces speech." Moreover, it's no longer needed because more stations are operating, creating more outlets for differing opinions.

Under the American system of limited government, decisions regarding programing content should be made by broadcasters, not by bureaucrats. Official efforts to impose "fairness" may actually reduce the range of opinion by discouraging broadcasters from airing controversial subjects.

The president pointed out that "In any other medium besides broadcasting, such federal policing of the editorial judgment of journalists would be unthinkable." We in the print media are free of such government interference and resist attempts to impose it. Broadcasters are entitled to similar treatment.

## The Charlotte Observer
*Charlotte, NC, June 23, 1987*

Since 1949 the Federal Communications Commission (FCC) has imposed a Fairness Doctrine on American broadcasters. The rule requires radio and television stations to give equal time to all sides of any controversial issues on which they comment. Now Congress has passed legislation that would make the Fairness Doctrine the law of the land. On Friday, President Reagan vetoed it, noting that "in any other medium besides broadcasting, such federal policing of the editorial judgment of journalists would be unthinkable." The president is right.

Broadcasters have long contended that the Fairness Doctrine violates their First Amendment rights. Advocates of the doctrine argue that it is justified because broadcasters, unlike publishers, are using a limited and publicly owned resource — the public airways. They say the rule is needed to assure that unpopular views get a fair hearing on those airways.

But far from encouraging a robust airing of opposing views on controversial issues, the Fairness Doctrine has had the practical effect of inhibiting such dialogue and making broadcasters understandably timid. Rather than risk violations of the doctrine and challenges to their licenses, radio and television stations tend to avoid commentary on controversial issues.

The rule is particularly chilling during elections. For example, if a television station endorses a candidate for office in a contest in which there are three candidates, it must give each of the other two candidates equal time — meaning the station must provide twice as much time for candidates it doesn't support as for the candidate it supports. Also, the rule, as widely interpreted, requires stations to provide as much coverage to fringe candidates who aren't serious contenders as to major candidates. Considering the large number of names on most election ballots and the limited amount of air time available, it's understandable that few broadcasters endorse political candidates or comment extensively on elections.

Not only does the Fairness Doctrine not work the way its framers intended, it is also unnecessary. Most broadcasters would be fair to all responsible points of view even without an FCC rule, just as most editors in the print media are. And although the public airways are a limited resource, the number and diversity of radio and television outlets have increased dramatically. Today there are more than 10,000 radio stations, almost 1,600 television stations and some 7,700 cable television systems — more than enough to assure the exposure of a wide range of viewpoints.

The president's veto doesn't eliminate the Fairness Doctrine, of course. If the veto holds, it will be up to the FCC to decide whether to maintain the doctrine. If Congress overrides the veto, the doctrine will become law. Either way, the nation's broadcasters are increasingly inclined to find a way to get the issue into the courts, where they hope to have the Fairness Doctrine declared unconstitutional. We wish them well in that effort.

## The Washington Times
*Washington, DC, June 24, 1987*

President Reagan was right on target Saturday when he vetoed legislation (S. 742) enshrining into law the so-called Fairness Doctrine. The regulation, compelling broadcasters to air opposing views of issues of the day, was enacted administratively by the Federal Communications Commission in 1949. The U.S. Court of Appeals for the District of Columbia ruled last year that the FCC could repeal the rule — which had been written without congressional participation or approval — without first seeking congressional permission.

As one might expect, this did not sit well with political activists inside the Beltway. Liberals like Massachusetts Rep. Edward Markey and Energy and Commerce Committee Chairman John Dingell savaged the court's decision. Outspoken conservatives like Phyllis Schlafly and Reed Irvine's Accuracy in Media also promoted the doctrine, which they consider a useful tool for "neutralizing" liberal dominance of the electronic media.

This unholy alliance helped Congress draft and pass what amounted to a Yanqui version of the United Nations' ill-fated "New World Information and Communications Order." That initiative, recall, was criticized because it would have given governments worldwide the power to "review" for fairness any news reports originating from their soil. The only difference between NWICO and the Fairness Doctrine is that the latter applies only to American broadcasters, working on American networks.

After the Senate approved the measure by a 59-31 vote and the House passed it by a 302-102 margin, the president — for once allied with the media — issued his veto. The bill's sponsors say they will override the president or, failing that, extort "fairness" by trying to attach the doctrine to every new piece of legislation passed by Congress, until it becomes law.

This is more than a little frightening. The premise behind S. 742 — that the 11,000 radio and television stations in America will lose their sense of "fairness" if the doctrine expires — is ludicrous. As broadcasters long have known, the doctrine's threat of government intervention has not made the media more fair, it has made them more timid and mediocre.

Besides, the doctrine seems marginally constitutional at best. As the president noted in his veto message, "In any other medium besides broadcasting, such federal policing of the editorial judgment of journalists would be unthinkable. The framers of the First Amendment, confident that public debate would be freer and healthier without the kind of interference represented by the 'Fairness Doctrine,' chose to forbid such regulations in the clearest terms."

## THE DAILY HERALD
*Biloxi, MS, April 13, 1989*

The Federal Communications Commission rightly killed its fairness doctrine two years ago, correctly noting that it was not necessary and that it hindered broadcast coverage of important issues.

But the doctrine simply won't stay dead.

Congress turned right around and passed legislation containing essentially the same requirements as the FCC's fairness doctrine. President Ronald Reagan vetoed it and the Senate upheld the veto. Now the House Energy and Commerce Committee has approved another fairness doctrine bill and the full House is expected to pass it again.

Forty years ago, there was some justification for attempting to assure that minority opinions and viewpoints running counter to those of media owners were heard. The number of stations was limited. Radio and television air time was scarce.

Today, the situation is completely opposite. Radio and television stations abound. Cable television and satellite dishes have ushered in a period of virtually unlimited air time.

More important than the practical considerations is the Constitutional principle involved. The fairness doctrine's compliance with the free press guarantee of the Constitution has always been suspect since the doctrine dictated that stations that air opinions must seek out opposite viewpoints.

If the House passes a new fairness doctrine, the Senate, which upheld the last veto, should stand on that previous position and kill this bill.

## The Burlington Free Press
*Burlington, VT, April 1, 1989*

When Congress returns from spring break next week, the House will consider an attempt to revive the "fairness doctrine," which for 35 years unfairly forced broadcasters to present contrasting views on issues of public consequence.

The doctrine, which infringes on the discretion and freedom of broadcasters, is even less legitimate now than when it was first formally drawn in 1949. Back then, the government worried that the number of voices in the public so outnumbered the number of broadcast outlets that radio and television stations had to be compelled to give equal time to varied positions.

The Supreme Court agreed. In 1969 the justices unanimously upheld the fairness doctrine, contending that "... there are substantially more individuals who want to broadcast than there are frequencies to allocate."

In 1985 the Federal Communications Commission decided that the proliferation of radio and broadcast stations in the previous 16 years rendered the fairness doctrine an outdated regulation that no longer served the public interest.

Scarcity is no longer an issue. There are now nearly as many television stations (1,300) in the United States as newspapers (1,600). With more than 10,000 radio stations also broadcasting, there's a diversity of views coursing through the air at the touch of a button. The proliferation of cable televison has brought even more voices into American homes.

Still, some members of Congress are not content. Rep. John Dingell, D-Mich., is using his powerful position as chairman of the Energy and Commerce Committee to bring back the fairness doctrine and make it law. His efforts should be defeated.

The framers of the the constitution were farsighted. Despite their vision, they could never have foreseen the advent of television or radio. The concerns that prompted protections for freedom of speech and freedom of the press are no less appropriately applied to broadcasting. Congressmen should have that in mind when they take up the fairness doctrine, and they should reject it for what it is — an unfair constraint on freedom.

## The Birmingham News
*Birmingham, AL, April 3, 1989*

The "fairness doctrine," correctly buried by the Federal Communications Commission, should not be resurrected by Congress.

That policy had for many years required radio and television stations regulated by the FCC to present contrasting views on "controversial issues of public importance." Its effect was to discourage expression of opinion on the airwaves.

Although the artifical balance required by the policy was a far cry from fairness, it has its supporters. Among them is Rep. John Dingell, D-Mich., who has introduced a bill to make the fairness doctrine law.

The notion that government should have any control over the expression of opinion is counter to the Constitution, which clearly states that "Congress shall make no law ... restricting freedom of speech, or of the press." By placing bureaucratic requirements on those who express opinions over the air, Congress would be doing exactly what the First Amendment prohibits.

Also, the fairness doctrine is out of tune with today's media environment. It was conceived in a time when it was thought only a few voices would be heard on television, so those who governed access to the airwaves needed to ensure that they would use that power fairly. Today, the variety of voices is so great that it is unlikely any point of view is shut out.

There are more than 1,600 daily newspapers, more than 1,300 television stations and more than 10,000 radio stations in the country. The typical cable television subscriber may have access to 30, 40 or even 50 channels. There is plenty of diversity in the media.

Fairness is not something the government can measure or define. Congress has no business telling the media what they can or must say.

## LAS VEGAS REVIEW-JOURNAL
*Las Vegas, NV, April 14, 1989*

Congress refuses to let the outdated, unconstitutional "fairness doctrine" molder peacefully in its grave. They keep trotting out the rotting thing, trying to breathe new life into it.

Two years ago, the Federal Communications Commission scrapped this doctrine, which had required radio and television broadcasters to air programs that provide opposing points of view. The fairness doctrine was conceived half a century ago, at a time when there were few broadcast outlets and the airwaves were indeed a limited public resource. The doctrine was designed to ensure that a single point of view did not come to dominate the airwaves, that a variety of opinions would be offered the listening (and later viewing) public.

But the doctrine has long since outlived its usefulness. Today, there are a huge number of broadcast outlets. In Las Vegas alone, we count no fewer than 10 AM and 17 FM radio stations, six local television stations, not to mention 30 or more cable channels — and dozens more available to owners of satellite dishes.

At the same time, there are only two local daily newspapers — and Las Vegas is unusual in that regard; few American cities have more than one daily. Yet newspapers have never been covered by any fairness-type doctrine — such government interference with the content of newspapers is a clear violation of the First Amendment, which mandates that Congress shall make no law abridging freedom of the press.

Well, radio and television are "the press," too. Radio and television broadcasters should enjoy the same freedom from government meddling with their news content as do newspapers. With the wealth of broadcast outlets available in this day and age, a diversity of views will be available simply by virtue of the demands of the marketplace.

This week, the House Energy and Commerce Committee voted to turn the outmoded and discarded fairness doctrine into federal law. Congress simply cannot resist tampering with the free press when it sees an opportunity. President Bush should — and probably will — veto the fairness measure. Afterward, Congress should let the thing rest in peace and not try to resurrect this hoary corpse again.

## AKRON BEACON JOURNAL
*Akron, OH, February 7, 1989*

THE SO-CALLED "fairness doctrine" for U.S. broadcasters never was fair. It was a policy of the Federal Communications Commission — now discredited and abandoned by the FCC — which required radio and TV stations to give equal time to opposing views on "controversial issues of public importance."

It may sound fair, but the result was that broadcast news simply shied away from not only expressing opinions but from covering controversial subjects. Since a majority of Americans get part or most of their news from broadcast sources, the fairness doctrine resulted in a less well-informed nation.

Unfortunately, there is now another attempt to revive this discarded doctrine. Rep. John Dingell, D-Mich., has introduced a bill in Congress to make the fairness doctrine law. A similar attempt last year was vetoed by President Reagan, and for good reason.

It would be bad law. For one thing, it's not needed. If broadcast journalists are free to cover controversial issues and express opinions, there would be enough diversity of opinion in the nation's 1,300 TV stations and 10,000 radio stations — not to mention 1,600 daily newspapers.

People in markets served by cable TV have access to dozens of channels and probably a similar number of radio stations. It's hard to believe all would have the same views on every subject.

For another thing, the fairness doctrine raises troubling free speech issues. Comment in print journalism is protected by the Constitution. Broadcast opinion should be also. And it probably is.

In 1974, the U.S. Supreme Court ruled unconstitutional a Florida right-of-reply law. The case involved newspapers, but the principle is the same. The First Amendment protections for "the press" logically would include forms of "the press" not invented when the Bill of Rights was written.

The fairness doctrine is not needed nor desirable in a free society. President Bush should follow the lead of his predecessor and make clear he would veto such a law. Hopefully, it won't get that far this time around.

## The Charlotte Observer
*Charlotte, NC, March 31, 1989*

Like a vampire in a horror movie, the so-called "fairness doctrine" just won't stay buried.

The doctrine, which long required radio and television stations to air both sides of controversial issues, was abolished by the Federal Communications Commission in 1987. When Congress tried to revive it with legislation, President Reagan drove a veto through its heart. Earlier this year, a federal appeals court refused to overturn the FCC's decision to abandon the 40-year-old rule.

But Congress is trying once again to resurrect the doctrine. While President Bush has warned that he has his veto ready should the doctrine come his way, how much better for Congress to let this bad idea rest in peace.

The fairness doctrine is only superficially about fairness. It is really about government regulation of broadcast speech, about government intimidation of the broadcast media. The product is not a fair debate, but a vapid one. As the FCC said in abolishing the doctrine, "The record reflects that broadcasters from television anchors to small radio station journalists perceived the fairness doctrine to operate as a demonstrable deterrent in the coverage of controversial issues. Indeed, the record is replete with descriptions from broadcasters who have candidly recounted specific instances in which they decided not to air controversial matters of public importance because such broadcasts might trigger fairness doctrine obligations."

While the airwaves are a finite resource, the country is rich in media voices: more than 1,600 daily newspapers, 1,300 television stations, 10,000 radio stations plus a vast array of magazines, newsletters and cable services. Far better to let the debate flow than to try to ensure fairness with a bureaucrat's stopwatch or a congressional checklist.

American government rests on the idea that the people, empowered with the vote, are the best arbiters of their own debate. As FCC General Counsel Diane Killory put it in 1987:

"The Founding Fathers sought to insure vigorous debate by guaranteeing free speech and free press — and by restraining the government from interfering. They had faith that people could distinguish truth from fiction; that the people's interest would best be served by the unrestricted debate that would follow. The commission, by contrast, in adopting a policy to regulate 'fairness,' evidently assumed that the people's interests would best be served by a restricted debate in which the government served as referee. What this commission now concludes is that the Founding Fathers had it right."

She was right. The FCC was right. The Founding Fathers were right. Congress should let the fairness doctrine stay buried.

## The Washington Post
*Washington, DC, April 15, 1989*

STAND BY for a rerun of the old, misnamed "fairness doctrine"—the one that sets up the government as a monitor of programming on public interest issues and the time allotted to opposing views. Again, the supporting cast includes Ralph Nader, armed with statistics purporting to prove that broadcasters have been starving their issues-hungry audiences of public affairs programming ever since the Federal Communications Commission voted unanimously in 1987 to abolish the doctrine. The assumption of the revivalists, now as before, is that Americans need government-prescribed doses of ideas on radio and TV.

The latest report, from a group started by Mr. Nader and called Essential Information, attempts to compare programming aired on commercial stations in 1988 with that of a similar period in 1979. It concludes that there has been a 51 percent decrease in the amount of time devoted to "issue-oriented public affairs" material and that stations now give less time to this kind of programming than they did before the rule was thrown out. But even ignoring the judgments of what programs may or may not qualify in the eyes of the researchers, the idea of measuring quality by the clock is even sillier than assessing it by government-inspected content.

The study examined TV listings for programs at 217 stations in 50 markets on seven days in early 1988. These listings were compared with FCC-required program logs from various earlier years. The study did not include cable channels, computer information networks, videotapes, audio cassettes or other sources of information that have become available to the public since the old days of limited AM radio when the fairness doctrine came into being. Today, these and still other methods of disseminating information have eliminated situations in which a community's access is limited to the whims or designs of a single broadcaster.

A truly free flow of ideas is one without the U.S. government playing program manager or public affairs director. As always when we discuss this issue, let us note that the company that owns this newspaper also owns broadcast facilities in other cities. But with or without stations, the journalistic First Amendment implications remain the same: free, independent and fair communication of points of view isn't improved by government proctoring and punishing. On the contrary, it's undermined.

## The News and Courier
*Charleston, SC, February 9, 1989*

When it comes to diversity, today's broadcast media offer a real smorgasbord. With more than 1,300 TV stations and a variety of cable choices competing with commercial networks, plus 10,000 radio stations, there is scarcely a shortage of diverse programming and opinions.

Yet despite this historic proliferation of choices, the federal government is once again trying to resurrect its completely discredited role as every broadcaster's Big Brother. Rep. John Dingell, an ultra-liberal Michigan Democrat, wants to roll back the clock to the 1950s and has introduced legislation to restore the old "fairness doctrine" in broadcasting.

On the face of it, who could object to something called the "fairness doctrine"? It required broadcasters to provide equal time for any and all opposing views to programs of opinion. But the doctrine not only threatened broadcasters with economic ruin if they violated its tenets, it was counterproductive to the serious coverage of matters of public importance. Worse, it was an assault on the First Amendment rights of all Americans.

The Federal Communications Commission wisely repealed the "fairness doctrine" in 1987, and during the 16 months since its elimination the broadcast industry has demonstrated its ability to once again wade into controversial topics to the benefit of the public.

Broadcasters are not perfect any more than the publishers of the country's 1,600 newspapers, but like print journalists they share the obligation to report the truth as they see it. In practice, the "fairness doctrine" operated to deter the exercise of that responsibility by acting as a prior restraint on a broadcaster's decision to report the news.

The government has absolutely no business telling the news media what is and what is not "fair" comment. That is enough reason to put the "fairness doctrine" to rest for all time.

## The Des Moines Register
*Des Moines, IA, April 4, 1989*

Whatever good might have come from the recent ruling by a federal appeals court upholding the Federal Communications Commission's repeal of the Fairness Doctrine quickly evaporated when Congress moved to resurrect the discredited broadcasting rule.

The U.S. Court of Appeals for the District of Columbia ruled that

### Government can't decide what's news.

the FCC was on solid legal footing in 1987 when it repealed the 40-year-old Fairness Doctrine, which required broadcast stations to cover important public issues and to present contrasting views.

The appeals court did not, however, address whether this federal regulation of news is constitutional under the First Amendment.

That opened the door for Congress to make the rule into law without fear of constitutional ramifications, and the ink was barely dry on the court decision when Hawaii Senator Daniel K. Inouye introduced a bill to do just that.

This legislation has been resurrected often because it sounds so good to make the news media "fair." In fact, the misleading title is like creating open season on bald eagles and calling it the "Endangered Wildlife Preservation Act." Rather than ensure fairness, the FCC's research showed that the doctrine had the effect of causing radio and television to shy away from wading into some controversial subjects.

The rule requiring that all contrasting points of view be aired meant some fringe group could demand free air time, and the federal government had the power to punish broadcasters who refused.

The only hope is that President Bush will follow through on his vow to veto the Fairness Doctrine law, as his predecessor did.

Broadcasters ought to strive for fairness at all times, and to present news of controversial and pressing public interest, but the framers of the Constitution never envisioned the government deciding what's news.

## Pittsburgh Post-Gazette
*Pittsburgh, PA, February 7, 1989*

Like a bad penny, a proposal to legislate "fairness" in the way television and radio cover public issues has turned up again in Congress. Rep. John Dingell of Michigan has introduced a bill to reinstate the so-called Fairness Doctrine, which, until its repeal by the Federal Communications Commission in 1987, required broadcasters to present opposing views on "controversial issues of public importance."

Congress tried to write the Fairness Doctrine into federal law, but then-President Ronald Reagan vetoed the legislation on the grounds that it violated the First Amendment. President Bush also should make it clear that he will veto any revival of the Fairness Doctrine.

In taking that position, the new president need not endorse his predecessor's view that the doctrine amounted to unconstitutional censorship, a controversial thesis that the U.S. Supreme Court may or may not be ready to accept. A less sweeping argument against the doctrine's revival is that its absence has not banished opposing views from the airwaves.

Actually, the electronic marketplace of ideas is more diverse than ever. And even the rare viewer who keeps his television set tuned to one station is liable to hear a cacophony of views about various controversies. Coverage of local news is still balanced (if often superficial), and station managers still follow their editorials with appeals for "responsible opposing views" — even in the absence of a Fairness Doctrine.

Given that fact, why the agitation in Congress and elsewhere to restore the doctrine? To a great extent, the dispute over the doctrine is a kind of proxy war over the more general question of whether the federal government should have the right to regulate the content of broadcasting.

The Reagan administration, supported by the broadcasting industry and press groups, argued that changes in electronic communications had undermined the traditional justification for imposing requirements on broadcasters that the courts would never allow to be imposed on newspapers or magazines.

The traditional justification is that radio and television outlets are a scarce resource. Yet today there are almost as many television stations (1,300) as there are daily newspapers (1,600). Radio stations are even more numerous — 10,000. And the growth of cable and satellite television means that viewers no longer are confined in their viewing habits to what a handful of local stations serve up.

One can still argue, however, that the lack of a Fairness Doctrine allows a single radio or television station to shut out opposing views — say, about a local election campaign. But that is largely a theoretical objection. In the real world, the problem is not that radio and television stations are aggressively trying to manipulate public opinion, but rather that they shy away from taking controversial stands at all — especially on local issues.

Technological changes may well be on a collision course with the legal theory that broadcasters do not enjoy the same First Amendment rights as newspaper publishers. One needn't resolve that issue definitively, however, to regard resurrection of the Fairness Doctrine as a bad idea. If Congress doesn't tune it out, President Bush should.

## DAYTON DAILY NEWS
*Dayton, OH, March 3, 1989*

A liberal organization has accused ABC's *Nightline* program of political bias.

FAIR (Fairness and Accuracy in Reporting) says, "A narrow range of guests makes *Nightline* a fundamentally conservative program." FAIR points out, for example, that of the 20 most frequent guests on the program, the only one who is a liberal politician or professional liberal advocate is the Rev. Jesse Jackson. Others on the list include Henry Kissinger, Alexander Haig, the Rev. Jerry Falwell, Elliott Abrams, Pat Buchanan, William Safire, Arthur Laffer and Jeane Kirkpatrick, all professional conservatives.

The criticism is, at best, suggestive. A more telling way to examine *Nightline's* alleged biases would be to look at individual programs and ask how often the liberal view got a fair airing. Maybe the reason the conservatives seem to be doing better is that just a few conservatives dominate the conservative slot on the program, while the liberal slot is spread out among more people.

A top of the head judgment: *Nightline* does a pretty conscientious job of balancing.

However, this FAIR report is a good thing.

Throughout the 1980s, the people doing most of the complaining about the media's political biases have been the conservatives. Their campaign is relentless; it includes the issuing of reports, the organizing of efforts to have people phone call-in talk shows, and every other form of complaining known to right-wing man.

Many media outlets practice a modified form of squeaky-wheel journalism. They respond to criticisms they are receiving. If all the noise that comes at them is from the right, then they will worry most about the right. The liberals need to start squeaking, too.

It is true that the political leanings of journalists tend to be liberal, and the reason is not — as is often said — that journalism makes one a liberal. Studies show conclusively that journalists tend to start out as liberals.

One of the more interesting studies done on the subject shows that one of the best ways to guess the political affiliation of a college student is to ask what his or her major is. The people in the humanities, social sciences and journalism tend to be liberals; the people in business and engineering tend to be conservatives, and the people in the natural sciences are harder to peg.

However, reporters (not editorial writers) are trained to and expected to — and most honestly try to — keep their political views out of their writing. Most generally have little trouble doing that, because their professional values are more important to them than their political values.

The problem with the constant harping of the political right on journalists' liberalism is that it ignores so many other possible sources of bias in reporting: Journalists — like judges — notice election returns and tend not to fight tides of public opinion; they tend also to be comfortable middle-class white people; they tend to work for companies that are part of the power establishment; they like some people and not others; and, perhaps most important, they and their bosses tend to react — in some degree at least — to the pressures on them.

## The Atlanta Journal AND THE ATLANTA CONSTITUTION
*Atlanta, GA, April 19, 1989*

Oh, no. Congress is plagued once again by that awful nervous tic: the Fairness Doctrine. Every now and then, it takes time out from serious business to obsess on this useless and unconstitutional idea.

Last week, the House Energy and Commerce Committee voted to reimpose the doctrine on broadcasters. When a station airs controversial issues, the measure would require it to broadcast opposing views as well. Until a few years ago, the Federal Communications Commission (FCC) enforced this practice by means of a rule. Happily, it came to its senses. The doctrine violates the First Amendment, the agency decided, and isn't needed in an age when airwaves are jammed with diverse views.

Some members of Congress have been in a dither ever since. It's not clear why — except that, as politicians, most have been stung by broadcast criticism and may view the measure as a shield. They could be right. With the doctrine in place again, many broadcasters will try to dodge trouble by dodging controversial issues altogether.

After the FCC dropped the doctrine in 1987, Congress tried to write it into law. President Reagan vetoed the measure, to the consternation of many on Capitol Hill. Now Congress wants to test President Bush. On the campaign trail last year, Mr. Bush promised to veto any new measure, and the Justice Department today is advising him to do just that.

Should the measure become law, the Supreme Court would surely overturn it. As Rep. Tom Tauke (R-Iowa), an opponent, told his colleagues last week: When our founders added the Bill of Rights to the Constitution two centuries ago, the nation's communications outlets were very limited.

"Then, as today," he explained, "some of those media outlets sometimes engaged in activities which ... may actually have been unfair. But the Founding Fathers said there was a greater risk in attempting to control the media by imposing fairness than there is in permitting a free media to perhaps occasionally be unfair."

Congress should stop wasting time on this lost cause and save the court and the president the trouble of killing it.

## THE BUFFALO NEWS
*Buffalo, NY, February 11, 1989*

A NEW ATTEMPT is being made in Congress to restore the old "fairness doctrine" for radio and television. The doctrine requires broadcasters to offer opposing views on controversial public issues.

On the face of it, that sounds like something everybody would strongly favor. And responsible stations do make every effort to be fair.

But the trouble with the fairness doctrine is not the goal it sets forth, but the fact that it allows government officials to regulate the public affairs content of radio and television. That's not a proper role for the government in a democratic society dedicated to freedom of speech and rejection of official censorship.

The fairness doctrine was first proclaimed by the Federal Communications Commission in 1949, when there were relatively few broadcasting outlets. Today, especially since the advent of cable television, there is a wide diversity of broadcasting outlets, offering an equally wide diversity of information and opinion.

The vast proliferation of stations and channels was an important consideration in the FCC's decision to drop the fairness rule as no longer necessary. But the commission also was aware that the requirement had had a counterproductive effect, because it often caused broadcasters to play it safe by avoiding coverage of controversial topics.

Nevertheless, there have been misguided efforts in Congress to put the fairness doctrine back on the books through legislative action. A bill was, indeed, passed in 1987 but it was wisely vetoed by former President Reagan, who pointed out that "this type of content-based regulation by the federal government is ... antagonistic to the freedom of expression guaranteed by the First Amendment."

The American Society of Newspaper Editors, recognizing the indivisibility of the First Amendment, is currently campaigning against an attempt in the new Congress to revive the fairness requirement.

"ASNE strongly believes in full First Amendment rights for all news media," said the society's president, John Seigenthaler, editor and publisher of the Nashville Tennessean. "Fairness is subjective. It cannot be legislated. Congress should stay out of the business of telling the news media what they can and cannot say."

That's good advice, and the nation's legislators should heed it.

## FCC Indecency Debate Rages

The Federal Communications Commission (FCC) April 16, 1987 adopted major new restrictions on the broadcast of obscene and offensive material, warning radio and television station owners that they faced fines or even loss of their licenses if they broadcast sexually explicit language or song lyrics.

The FCC voted, 5-0, to start enforcing a policy applicable to a wide range of broadcasters that had been upheld by the U.S. Supreme Court in 1978 but had never been used to penalize a license holder. Going beyond a narrow "seven dirty words" yardstick, the FCC's broader definition of "indecent" programming would encompass "language or material that depicts or describes, in terms patently offensive as measured by contemporary community standards for the broadcast medium, sexual or excretory activities or organs."

The FCC also said that broadcasters risked prosecution if they aired shows of questionable taste regardless of the hour of the broadcast. Previously the agency had not objected to broadcasts that included sexually suggestive material if the shows were aired after 10 p.m., when it was assumed that hardly any children would be listening. The agency said it had decided against setting any time that indecent language would be acceptable, arguing it was concerned that teen-agers listened to the radio at all hours.

The FCC action stemmed from the 20,000 or so complaints the commission had been receiving annually about indecent material on radio and TV broadcasts. Its April 16 decision focused on three radio stations – Infinity Broadcasting Corp.'s WYSP-FM in Philadelphia, the University of California's KCSB-FM in Santa Barbara and Pacifica Foundation Inc.'s KPFK-FM in Los Angeles. Finding that all three had made indecent broadcasts, the FCC April 16 voted to warn them that continuing the conduct in question could subject them to harsher actions.

The Philadelphia station was warned because complaints had been received from local listeners about broadcasts made by talk-show host Howard Stern, whose nationally syndicated call-in show originated in New York City. Stern had developed a large following for shows that blended salaciousness and scatology, racial and ethnic insults, weather and traffic reports.

The Santa Barbara station was warned because it had played a sexually explicit song, *Makin' Bacon*, late at night.

The Los Angeles station was warned because it had broadcast excerpts from a play called *Jerker* that included homosexual sex fantasies.

In the Los Angeles case, the FCC actually went a step further, referring the matter to the Justice Department for possible prosecution under obscenity laws.

The FCC voted to expand the scope of its indecency standard at the 201st and final meeting presided over by Mark S. Fowler as chairman. Fowler April 17 vacated the post, making way for Commissioner Dennis R. Patrick to succeed him.

The FCC Nov. 24 voted, 4-0, to permit radio and television stations to broadcast "indecent" programming between midnight and six a.m. without fear of FCC action. At all other times, however, the agency said, such programming would be prohibited because "there is a reasonable risk that children may be in the audience."

The ruling clarified an April decision in which the agency had affirmed its intention to apply a broader definition of indecency to the broadcasting industry than the "seven dirty words" standard previously applied.

In its original ruling, the FCC had said that broadcasters risked prosecution if they aired indecent material regardless of the hour of the broadcast.

A Washington, D.C. federal appeals court panel July 29, 1988 rejected a FCC ruling that limited "indecent" programming to broadcasts between midnight and 6 a.m.

### St. Petersburg Times
*St. Petersburg, FL, November 28, 1987*

(It's after midnight. Do you know where your $#&*%¢@!& children are?)

Listen up, kids! The members of the Federal Communications Commission (FCC) know what's best for you, and they want you to pay attention to their new rule for watching television and listening to the radio:

From now on, you have to go to bed every night before midnight, and you cannot wake up until after 6 a.m. No exceptions. Otherwise, you might accidentally stumble upon the special programing that stations can now offer only during the FCC's new "indecency hours," and there's no telling what harm that might do to your impressionable eyes and ears.

You may continue to watch and listen to whatever you want between 6 a.m. and midnight. The FCC won't allow any "indecent" programing during those hours, because "there is a reasonable risk that children may be in the audience."

Okay, kids, any questions?

*What's to prevent us from staying up until 11 p.m., or waking up at 7 a.m., and tuning in a broadcast from a station in another time zone?*

The same thing that's going to prevent you from staying awake between midnight and 6 a.m.: The FCC and I expect you to give us your scout's honor that you'll obey the rules.

*Doesn't the FCC have anything better to do than try to dictate morality for the whole country?*

Not anymore. For about 50 years, the FCC spent almost all of its time regulating the financial and technological aspects of mass communications. With rare exceptions, commissioners didn't attempt to influence regular programming. Now, though, the commissioners have gotten so carried away with financial and technological deregulation that they have plenty of free time that can be used to guard against indecency.

*What is indecency, anyway?*

That's an easy one: It's "something that, taken as a whole, appeals to the prurient interest; that depicts or describes in a patently offensive way sexual conduct, and that lacks serious artistic, political and scientific value."

*No, Dad. That's the Supreme Court's 1973 definition of obscenity. It's banned all the time, not just between 6 a.m. and midnight.*

Oh, you're right. The FCC said "indecent" material "depicts or describes, in terms patently offensive as measured by contemporary community standards for the broadcast medium, sexual or excretory activities or organs."

*But if "indecent material" isn't legally obscene, what gives the FCC the right to ban it 18 hours a day?*

Uh, well. . . stop asking so many questions. And go to bed — it's almost an indecent hour.

## THE ANN ARBOR NEWS
*Ann Arbor, MI, November 30, 1987*

As if conscientious parents don't have enough to worry about with their children, now the government is going to make the full-time job of parental supervision even more difficult.

Last week the Federal Communications Commission gave radio and television stations permission to broadcast indecent material between midnight and 6 a.m. In the process, the FCC gave its impersonation of Pontius Pilate, washing his hands of any guilt which may be imputed to him later.

So now if the kiddies want to tune in or fiddle with the dial after midnight, long after weary parents have switched out the light and called it a day, the station broadcasters themselves are the only protection children have against filth on the airwaves.

"The broadcasters should make a judgment and exercise discretion," said Diane Killory, FCC general counsel. "That's what we would recommend."

In effect, the FCC is putting the onus on parents to supervise what their kids listen to on the radio and watch on TV after midnight. For two-parent families, that's no hardship — one parent can stay up all night while the other one sleeps and the next night they can trade off.

Or one can sleep while the other does bedroom checks for six hours to make sure Johnny and Jane aren't becoming after-hours communications majors.

We're being only slightly facetious. Admittedly, most kids aren't up after midnight turning dials and flipping channels. But what a copout for the FCC to say, through counsel Killory, that "we would expect after midnight that we could rely on parents to supervise any children in the audience."

That's funny. Most parents probably thought they could "rely" on their regulator-protectors in government, the FCC, to control what is euphemistically called "adult programming" and to jerk the license of any station or broadcast house that aired filth.

And what does the Reagan administration, which is so solidly identified with traditional values and family issues, have to say about the FCC decision? So far, nothing.

Obscenity is, of course, outlawed on the public airwaves. But is the line between obscene material and indecent material clearly understood by broadcasters? The FCC, in its 4-0 decision, offered broadcasters little detail about what the commission considers indecent.

Now that the FCC has spoken, will the airwaves turn blue overnight? Probably not overnight, but broadcasters *can* expect their judgment and sense of good taste to be tested more often. And the tendency to let "anything goes" post-midnight programming go unchecked because "children aren't listening anyway" is a strong one to oppose.

The point is that there has been a national standard for radio and TV, so why change it? The FCC is only sowing confusion with its burst of permissiveness. What groups or sources are advocating the airing of indecent material?

Remember those public service spots on TV aimed at parents and saying "It's 12:00 — do you know where your children are?" Now apparently, it's not enough any more that parents do indeed know where their children are. They may be under the same roof and safely in their bedrooms, but they may also be getting an earful and an eyeful of government-approved filth.

But not in prime time, of course, and only if broadcasters and "lazy" parents aren't doing their jobs. As we said earlier this year, in connection with dial-a-porn on the telephone, there's more than enough pornography and titillating material around without having more of this stuff just a phone call away. Who is government allying itself with anyway, decency-minded parents or the smut lobby?

## The Idaho STATESMAN
*Boise, ID, November 30, 1987*

So, the Federal Communications Commission has found a "safe harbor" for indecent radio and television programming.

How decent of them.

Now comes the tough question: What belongs in the graveyard shift of American broadcasting?

In clarifying its April ruling setting standards for indecent programming, the FCC told broadcasters they may air such fare between midnight and 6 a.m.

Sometimes it seems that indecent programming airs on prime time now. But that, of course, depends on your definition of indecent. Our dictionary defines indecent as "not proper and fitting, unseemly, morally offensive" — which pretty well describes how many feel about what's shown between 7 p.m. and 10 p.m.

One can't watch five minutes of TV anymore without seeing sexual allusions, sexual jokes and sexual advances. Is that "proper and fitting" fare?

The commission's intent was to corral the really raunchy stuff into the late-night hours to protect young children. David Letterman's show already has the TV time staked out, but it was naughty radio that the commission had in mind. The FCC's April decision involved two California FM stations and a Philadelphia FM station.

We're not aware of any dirty TV shows that would be shunted to the midnight hours, other than the heretofore mentioned fare.

The FCC is to be commended for thinking of the children, although defining what constitutes indecency might prove a headache. And one wonders whether creating a special dirty time zone will encourage more dirty shows.

Nonetheless, the FCC has begun the fight to protect our young ones from indecency on the airwaves and that's good.

## The Duluth News-Tribune

*Duluth, MN, April 18, 1987*

The Federal Communications Commission seems to be marching boldly into the same legal, moral and semantic quicksand that has claimed others who tried to draw up a neat and tidy solution to the issue of obscenity.

Commission member Dennis Patrick, who becomes its chairman next week, said Thursday the panel intends to "correct an altogether too narrow interpretation of decency."

His comments came as the federal agency warned radio and TV broadcasters they will soon face problems for using more than just the "seven dirty words" that have been the basis for federal action in the past.

Though the agency has yet to spell out its broader limits, commissioners would be wise to remember problems others have had in trying to write broad rules on "decency".

Patrick stressed his agency's support for First Amendment rights of free expression. But we don't know of anyone who's been able to accomplish the hard task of writing broad limits on public comment while allowing constitutionally protected free expression.

Indeed, the commission said its new rules will be based on the 1978 U.S. Supreme Court ruling which allowed limits on words or pictures which offend community standards.

But we're not aware of even one successful effort — and many have tried — to write *broad* restrictions based on the high court's community standards definition.

The big problem, of course, is figuring out what community standards are. One reason it's so hard is that, whatever those standards are, they're constantly changing.

A recent poll indicates most Americans are not offended by sexual references in movies, advertising, books and television — and don't believe pornography is generally harmful.

All this is not to urge no limits on what is said or shown on radio or TV — only to say regulators should go slow and not write too broadly in handcuffing broadcasters.

## The State

*Columbia, SC, April 16, 1987*

THE U.S. Supreme Court has sanctioned the use of "community standards" in defining obscenity, but the General Assembly, now considering tough anti-obscenity legislation, could cause a lot of mischief by narrowing that geographic area too much and thus spawning a confusing hodgepodge of standards.

The measure has the virtue of cracking down on those who sexually exploit minors. Pornographers who prey on children most certainly deserve stiff punishment. But the bill is flawed in charging county juries to set "community standards" and decide what's "harmful to minors."

Such provision puts a heavy burden on book sellers who, failing to peruse some magazine or book, might learn too late that the content of a quality publication is found to be "harmful to minors." Certainly, no vendor can thumb through and evaluate all of the publications in stock.

In fact, such legislation might remove from the book shelves much quality literature that could offend only the bluest of blue noses.

On a broader front, the "community standard" concept could create a sea of confusion, and that problem has not been lost on some legislators.

Rep. John Bradley, a Charleston Republican, argued, "A person may not know he's committing a crime until the jury decides he's committed a crime.... How can I commit a crime in Charleston and not commit the crime in Horry? Am I to check out every town I go in?"

Some complain the bill imposes more restrictions on sexually explicit materials than the United States Supreme Court permitted in its "community standards" ruling.

Steven Bates, executive director of the S.C. American Civil Liberties Union, claimed the bill will discourage the sale of any sex-related material, including educational literature and PG-rated movies. He said it "effectively denies people under 18 the right to exercise their First Amendment right to free inquiry."

Indeed, one standard would seem appropriate for a small state like South Carolina, where the population is relatively homogenous.

We admit the difficulty of framing anti-obscenity legislation that will be constitutional and yet protects our people, particularly our children, from the grossest kind of pornography. But this legislation needs a great deal of fine tuning and maybe some fine pruning before passage is considered.

## The Miami Herald

*Miami, FL, April 20, 1987*

THE NATIONAL Federation for Decency (NFD), a conservative religious group, criticizes the Federal Communications Commission's decision to adopt a stricter obscenity standard for broadcasters. The NFD said that Thursday's decision didn't go far enough.

The Media Access Group, a liberal-minded free-speech advocate, was equally unhappy with the FCC's finding that, according to this standard, three radio stations produced indecent broadcasts. The FCC went too far, it complained.

When opponents in an issue both criticize a decision that affects them equally, it's likely that that decision is evenhanded. This one was.

In the complaints brought against three radio stations (the NFD lodged one), the FCC found that the programs' contents fell within a broader legal interpretation of obscenity than its "seven dirty words" guideline, upheld by the Supreme Court in 1978.

The Court also endorsed then the FCC's broader definition: "language or material that depicts or describes, in terms patently offensive as measured by contemporary community standards for the broadcast medium, sexual or excretory activities of organs." The FCC until now has enforced only the narrower "seven-word" rule.

The broadcasts dealt with scatological commentary and explicit descriptions of sexual intercourse through song lyrics and programming. Unlike cable television, whose content the FCC does not regulate, radio is a free-access medium. Cable TV can provide any programming that the subscriber is willing to pay for — and rightly so — although some localities require lockout devices to prevent children from tuning in without parents' knowledge.

But any child can turn the radio dial and listen in. What he hears is the business of the FCC, which made clear that what it considered indecent is specific to these broadcasts. Scatology and overly bawdy programming have little in common with, say, Dr. Ruth Westheimer discussing sexual activities and the risk of AIDS. While the FCC expects court tests of its decision, there is no reason to think that the broadened definition will have a chilling effect on the free broadcasting of information or entertainment. But perhaps it will help define the bounds of good taste.

## AKRON BEACON JOURNAL
*Akron, OH, April 25, 1987*

THE SILLY maneuvering in Congress over the so-called "fairness doctrine" for broadcasters shows how little even informed citizens understand the role of a free press in a democracy.

Under the fairness doctrine, imposed by the Federal Communications Commission in 1949, a broadcast station must offer equal air time for opposing viewpoints when covering or, especially, commenting on controversial topics. The print media are under no such restraints. Even the FCC indicated it might drop the doctrine after a 1985 FCC report found it to be unnecessary and probably unconstitutional.

The fairness doctrine should be dropped because it is clearly unfair to the broadcast media and because it restrains the free flow of information to the public by discouraging aggressive reporting and commentary. This is intolerable in a society based on an informed citizenry.

Yet now the Senate has passed a bill that would make the fairness doctrine law. The bill, which passed 59-31 Tuesday, would head off FCC attempts to drop the doctrine and would require broadcasters to report on controversial issues and present opposing views. The one good result of making the fairness doctrine law would be that it could finally be declared unconstitutional and buried forever. But the logic behind the legislation is tortured.

A sponsor, Sen. John Danforth, R-Mo., argues: "It does not seem . . . unreasonable to say if a broadcast station holds a license, it has an obligation to this country to inform the people." Fair enough. And it's true that many local TV and radio stations do poor job of covering essential issues. The best way to encourage better coverage, however, is to remove the restraints, not by telling the broadcasters what to cover.

Mr. Danforth also argues that television is a special case because it is "so important" to public officials in influencing public opinion.

By that reasoning, national newspapers such as the New York Times should be subject to greater regulation than, say, the Stow Sentinel, whose influence is more limited. That's not only absurd. The different standards of regulation, said an opponent of the bill, Sen. Bob Packwood, R-Ore., "stands the First Amendment on its head."

All media — broadcast and print — can at times be imperfect in their coverage and in granting access to minority viewpoints. But the system of free and unfettered media coverage is far better than goverment control of what is often the only independent voice that will question governmental power.

If the Senate doesn't understand that distinction, it doesn't understand the protections in the Constitutions or the needs of a free society.

## Pittsburgh Post-Gazette
*Pittsburgh, PA, April 6, 1987*

Newspaper and magazine publishers in America are under no legal obligation to provide balanced news coverage, or to devote their pages to matters of public importance as opposed to sports scores or the doings of Hollywood celebrities. Indeed, a law requiring newspapers to afford a right of reply to politicians they criticize editorially has been struck down by the U.S. Supreme Court.

Yet the journalists who ply their trade in radio or television *are* regulated by government. The Federal Communications Commission, established by Congress to police the broadcasting industry, not only requires that operators of radio and television outlets operate in the public interest; it also has promulgated a "Fairness Doctrine" requiring broadcasters to cover both sides of public controversies.

Broadcast journalists chafe under the FCC's rules, and complain about a double standard that allows them less freedom under the First Amendment than their colleagues in print journalism. The broadcasters have received powerful support from President Reagan's appointee as chairman of the FCC and from historians who point out that the original justification for federal regulation of broadcasting — the scarcity of radio and television outlets — has been rendered meaningless by innovations like cable television and all-news networks.

It is a fascinating and important debate, but now some in Congress would short-circuit it. Fearful that the FCC, which devised the Fairness Doctrine, might repeal it, the Senate Commerce Committee has voted to codify the Fairness Doctrine in federal law. Similar legislation is expected to be introduced in the House of Representatives.

Supporters of this pre-emptive move talk in terms of the public interest, but self-interest may also play a part. Rep. Henry Hyde of Illinois conceded that, in this era of television politics, "we're all terrorized by the power of the electronic media. It can destroy you."

Actually, it is doubtful that a television industry liberated from the Fairness Doctrine would suddenly become partisan, any more than most American newspapers risk alienating their readers by becoming the organs of particular political parties. As for the general utility of the Fairness Doctrine, broadcasters make a plausible case that federal regualtion actually results in *less* public-spirited TV journalism because broadcasters are fearful of offending special-interest groups that might challenge the renewal of a TV station's license.

Whatever the merits of that argument, Congress should not rush to moot the discussion by enacting the Fairness Doctrine into law precisely at the time it is being intelligently challenged.

## THE DAILY OKLAHOMAN
*Oklahoma City, OK, April 18, 1987*

IN a move that caught broadcasters and free-speech zealots off guard, the Federal Communications Commission announced a tough new enforcement policy against indecent programming.

The agency voted 5-0 to warn three stations — in Philadelphia, Los Angeles and Santa Barbara — that they had carried unacceptable material and would be subject to fines if they don't clean up their acts. The FCC said it didn't levy fines this time because it wanted to alert broadcasters to the change in enforcement policy.

The only individual singled out was a New York radio personality whose nationally syndicated show features bawdy humor and double entendres. Apparently this is a growing trend, especially late at night. Most folks in these parts probably are not aware of these things, although their kids might be.

A lawyer for the National Association of Broadcasters expressed concern his people might not know what they can and can't do. That's silly — a radio talk-show host knows a dirty word when he hears it.

Previously broadcasters figured they could get by with sexually suggestive material if the shows were aired after 10 p.m., when children wouldn't be listening. But the FCC decided against a time limit, arguing teen-agers listen to the radio at all hours. Then again, most teen-agers have heard all the dirty words by now.

## Supreme Court Clarifies Obscenity Rules

The U.S. Supreme Court May 4, 1987 specified that one of its three standing tests for obscene material should be based on a national standard, one upon which reasonable people would agree, not on local community values.

The other two tests, whether the material appealed to "prurient interest" or depicted sex in a "patently offensive" way, were based on community standards. The three-test standard was established in a 1973 ruling.

The 1973 ruling left unclear whether the third test, a determination that the material lacked "serious literary, artistic, political or scientific value," should be based on a local community standard.

Now, in *Pope v. Illinois*, the court opted for a uniform and national standard. "The proper inquiry," Justice Byron R. White wrote for the majority, "is not whether an ordinary member of a given community would find [some] value in allegedly obscene material but whether a reasonable person would find such value in the material, taken as a whole."

The value of a work, he said, may not "vary from community to community based on the degree of local acceptance it has won."

The dissenters, in the 6-3 decision, were Justices John Paul Stevens, William J. Brennan and Thurgood Marshall. They said the First Amendment prohibited criminalizing possession or sale of obscene materials to consenting adults.

The ruling involved a trial judge's instructions to a jury in the case of two Rockford, Ill. men convicted of selling obscene material. In its decision, the Supreme Court did not reverse their convictions. It instead returned the case to the state courts for a ruling on whether the convictions should be sustained because the trial judge's instructions to the jury involved nothing more than a harmless error.

## THE BUFFALO NEWS
*Buffalo, NY, May 10, 1987*

THE U.S. SUPREME COURT took a step away from narrow censorship last week in holding that a community may not suppress sexually explicit material simply on the basis of local community tastes.

A broader, less restrictive standard must be used in making such a judgment, the court held in a 6-3 decision.

Specifically, the court said, a disputed work is entitled to constitutional protection under the First Amendment's guarantee of free expression if "a reasonable person" would find that, taken as a whole, it has literary, artistic, political or scientific value.

This means that material could be protected from criminal prosecution under obscenity laws even if most people in a particular locality saw no redeeming social value in it.

In the view of some lawyers, the decision clears the way to have literary critics, art scholars and scientists testify to assist jurors in obscenity trials.

The publishing industry hailed the ruling, and understandably so. To welcome the decision is not to condone or want to encourage pornography, but to recognize the importance of protecting free expression from arbitrary acts by overzealous officials.

There is legitimate concern about the growing volume of sexually explicit material in this country, and citizens have every right to speak out against it. But there is a difference between public condemnation and government censorship, which sooner or later leads to serious abuses. As everyone knows, some works now accepted as literary classics were once banned.

Even the court's "reasonable person" test leaves a wide margin for disagreement, as the three dissenting justices noted. They attacked the constitutionality of laws making the sale of obscene literature to consenting adults a crime, "absent some connection to minors, or obtrusive display to unconsenting adults."

Given the high court's inability over 30 years to devise a satisfactory definition of obscenity, the dissenters' view may offer the most viable alternative.

Meanwhile, the present ruling should prove useful in refining the court's obscenity guidelines and reducing the danger of unwarranted censorship. The important point is that there are better ways for a free society to fight filth and smut than by resorting to government suppression, with its risks of eroding vital First Amendment principles.

## Los Angeles Times
*Los Angeles, CA, May 6, 1987*

Thirty years ago, in the case of Roth vs. United States, the U.S. Supreme Court held that obscenity was not protected by the First Amendment guarantee of freedom of speech. Since then the court has returned time and again to the troubling question of what obscenity is after all, each time digging itself deeper into a philosophical and legal morass. This week it tackled the question again, with results that are no more enlightening, though they may make it harder for prosecutors to obtain a conviction for selling obscene material.

In 1973, in the case of Miller vs. California, the court established a three-part test for obscenity. In order to be judged obscene, the court said, a book, film or other work must meet all three parts: (1) its dominant theme, taken as a whole, must appeal to prurient interest; (2) it must depict sexual conduct in a patently offensive way, and (3) the work, taken as a whole, must lack "serious literary, artistic, political or scientific value."

The question then became by what standard each of the three parts of the Miller test was to be judged. In Roth, Miller and subsequent cases, "contemporary community standards" appeared to be what the court had in mind, and that was the test applied to parts 1 and 2. But there was a question as to whether community standards could properly judge whether a work had serious value.

This week, in the case of Pope vs. Illinois (No. 85-1973), the court held 5 to 4 that community standards were not the right test for value. Instead, the justices said, a "reasonable person" test should be applied. That is, never mind what the community standards are. Would a reasonable person viewing this material think it lacked value? As a result, defendants in obscenity trials may call expert witnesses to testify about the value of a work, and the jury may take that testimony into account regardless of what the community standards are.

So obscenity convictions should be harder to obtain, which is all to the good. But it would have been even better if the minority view in this week's case had prevailed. The dissenters—Justices John Paul Stevens, William J. Brennan Jr., Thurgood Marshall and Harry A. Blackmun—argued that the "reasonable person" test was subject to all the flaws that plagued the "community standards" test, and that juries could still find material obscene just because it offended them.

Stevens wrote that the four dissenting justices would declare unconstitutional all laws that "criminalize the sale of magazines to consenting adults who enjoy the constitutional right to read and possess them."

This is the view of this matter that we prefer, and someday, perhaps, a fifth justice will see the light and make the minority opinion the majority view. In the meantime, we'll have to settle for any decision that makes it harder to convict people for selling obscene material. Every adult should be free to read what he or she wants to.

## The Register
*Santa Ana, CA, May 11, 1987*

The Supreme Court sure can complicate things. In 1973, the justices strove mightily to conceive a definition of obscenity that would allow prosecutors to seek convictions of pornographers without violating constitutional protections of free expression. They seemed to find one. Now, 14 years later, the court has decided we need a new definition.

The key to the 1973 ruling was that juries should use "community standards" in judging whether material had redeeming qualities or was simply prurient. In a democracy, that sounded right to a lot of people: let the community decide. Indeed, there have been a handful of celebrated obscenity convictions under that standard.

Now the court has taken away that criterion, ruling last week that jurors in obscenity cases should not look to the community at large, but rather consider what a "reasonable person" would think of the material in question.

Under the old rule, juries at least could arrive at a vague definition of "community standard." Were enough people outraged by the material to warrant labeling it pornography? But who qualifies as a "reasonable person"? The court left this definition wide open.

This is, many will say, so slippery a standard as to make obscenity prosecutions impossible. But it *should* be very difficult, if not impossible, to prevent the expression of ideas in America, no matter how offensive they might be to some people.

The Supreme Court may well have complicated matters for prosecutors looking for headlines by hauling pornographers into court. It may cause some uneasiness in communities that are honestly fearful of an onslaught of dirty book stores or dirty movies.

But American democracy is a fragile thing that should not come easy. It has never been as simple as enshrining the wishes of the majority. In many ways, it has been something of the opposite; that is, protecting the rights of the minorities against the power and force of the majority, whether held by a mob, or by government, or, yes, even by good people who find some ideas offensive or sinful or degrading.

Those people, some of whom have been the target of scorn for their religious and personal beliefs, ought to know how precious the right of free expression is. The Supreme Court last week made it more difficult for the majority to abridge that freedom.

That's an expression that deserves to win in the marketplace of ideas.

## The Philadelphia Inquirer
*Philadelphia, PA, May 9, 1987*

It is somewhat ironic in this conservative Age of Reagan that the U.S. Supreme Court, composed largely of Republican-appointed senior citizens, is narrowing the legal boundaries of what constitutes obscenity, but that's what the jurists did on Monday.

Ruling 6-3, they made it much more difficult for local prosecutors to outlaw sexually explicit material as "obscene." Not the least of the attendant ironies is that the three dissenters did not object to the new standards on obscenity, as one might expect, but felt that the majority hadn't made its argument strongly enough.

The court refined the standard it set in the 1973 case, *Miller v. California*, by which a book, magazine, film or other creative work might be deemed legally obscene and thus outlawed. The 1973 standard imposed a three-part test. The first two were whether a jury — applying local community standards — determined that the work in question appealed to a "prurient interest in sex" in a "patently offensive way." The third part required that the work be found not to have "serious literary, artistic, political or scientific value."

What the court did Monday in *Pope v. Illinois* was make it explicit that local community tastes are not the criterion by which to apply the third part of the test. The applicable standard in reaching those judgments, in the words of the majority opinion by Justice Byron R. White, "is not whether an ordinary member of a given community would find serious literary, artistic, political or scientific value in allegedly obscene material, but whether a reasonable person would find such value in the material, taken as a whole."

"The ideas a work represents need not obtain majority approval to merit protection" under the constitutional guarantee of free speech, Justice White observed. Similarly, the value of creative work may not "vary from community to community based on the degree of local acceptance it has won."

The dissenters, led by Justice John Paul Stevens, make a good point in arguing that Justice White's "reasonable person" standard is worrisomely vague. Reasonable people can and do disagree, obviously, on what constitutes obscenity, which is after all a subjective concept, not unlike beauty dependent upon the eye of the beholder. The dissenters fear that juries "might well believe that the majority of the population who find no value in ... a book are more reasonable than the minority who do find value."

If that happens, clearly it would be contrary to the intent of the Supreme Court as emphasized here in both majority and minority views. Lawyers involved in the case, however, expect this ruling to substitute more sophisticated national standards as the operative criterion of judgment, making it harder to outlaw creative works. Thus it expands intellectual freedom, and that's to the good.

## The Dallas Morning News
*Dallas, TX, May 6, 1987*

The U.S. Supreme Court may have had good intentions by ruling Monday that the view of a "reasonable person" must be applied when judging obscene materials rather than the vague notion of "community standards." But the "reasonable person" test may prove even more elusive, ambiguous and difficult to apply.

The court's continuing division on the issue of how to determine whether sexually explicit materials are obscene was reflected in the closeness of the vote — 5 to 4 — and the fact that five separate opinions were rendered.

In the landmark 1973 Miller vs. California case, the high court had stated that a book, film, magazine or other work might be found obscene if it met each element of a three-part test. Local standards were to be used to determine, first, whether the dominant theme appealed to lascivious interest and, second, whether it depicted sexual conduct in an offensive way. What was unclear was whether a national or community standard should be used to determine the third criteria, whether the work lacked literary, artistic, political or scientific value.

The case in question involved two clerks in an adult bookstore who sold magazines containing graphic descriptions of sexual practices. The court majority said this week the ideas in the work should not have to have the support of the majority of a community to warrant constitutional protection. Instead, the court said judges and juries should consider whether "a reasonable person would find such value in the material, taken as a whole."

The question now is whether this makes things more clear, or less? The new definition may discourage prosecutors from pursuing obscenity convictions. Or, as one dissenting justice pointed out, it could mean that once banned or misunderstood classics such as James Joyce's *Ulysses* might be at risk again because juries "might well believe that the majority of the population who find no value in such a book are more reasonable than the minority who do find value."

A reasonable person indeed might conclude that the court's ruling isn't . . . well, a reasonable improvement.

## AKRON BEACON JOURNAL
*Akron, OH, May 8, 1987*

THE U.S. SUPREME Court has again wrestled with the obscenity issue. In essence, the court revised the standard for declaring materials obscene. The old guideline relied on the prevailing community standard to judge any materials obscene; the new standard would judge from the standpoint of a "reasonable person."

This doesn't put obscenity laws any closer to resolution, however, because the court failed, as always, to define what is obscene and who is qualified to render such a judgment.

It's hard to fault the court, of course. Those questions cannot be resolved, at least not in a free society in which many different ideas of what is acceptable can be found, even within one community.

In this case, *Pope v. Illinois*, the issue was the sale of sexually explicit works, the arguments over whether such materials have any higher social or literary value, and whether the yardstick should be "community standards" of what is acceptable.

The court is right in indicating that the community standards measure is unconstitutional. A book or play or movie is not necessarily obscene just because a majority of a community says it is.

But the "reasonable person" yardstick is little better. "Reasonable" is hard to define. Even professional literary critics, for instance, often disagree on what is literature and, hence, what should be protected against obscenity laws.

As Justice John Paul Stevens wrote in dissent, the new standard still puts legitimate art works at risk because jurors "might well believe that the majority . . . who find no value in such a (work) are more reasonable than the minority who do find value."

It may take years for the new standard to be refined into local law and custom. But the larger issue of what constitutes obscenity will always be in doubt. Maybe it should be since the disagreement reflects the wide range of ideas and opinions that can only be found in a free society.

## THE ARIZONA REPUBLIC
*Phoenix, AZ, May 8, 1987*

THE U.S. Supreme Court continues to punch at the issue of obscenity, but like tangling with the tar baby of Uncle Remus' tale, the high court succeeds only in becoming increasingly stuck. The latest ruling has left legal experts scratching their heads. On a 5-4 decision in a case involving two proprietors of an Illinois adult bookstore, the court struck down its 1973 "community standard" test in favor of a more "objective" criterion.

In *Miller vs. California* in 1973 the court held that descriptions or depictions of sexual behavior may be banned as obscene if the works "taken as a whole appeal to the prurient interest in sex . . . and which, taken as a whole, does not have serious literary, artistic or scientific value" according to the prevailing standards of the community.

In this week's ruling, the majority expressed concern that the community-standards test might lead to some works being banned in one locale while being found acceptable in another. Justice Byron White, writing for the majority, noted that ideas do not necessarily require majority approval to merit First Amendment protection, and that the intrinsic value of works do not vary from one community to another.

In this ruling, the court held that in determining obscenity juries should consider materials from the standpoint of a "reasonable person," and not just prevailing community norms. Thus, some materials may meet with the disapproval of the majority of a local community, but be deemed not to be obscene if a "reasonable person" could find social value in them. Because a majority of, say, Possum Hollow, Tenn., might find James Joyce's works obscene doesn't mean a "reasonable person" would.

Clear? Not exactly. How all this clarifies obscenity, or how this aids juries in making that determination, is clear only in the minds of the five justices of the majority opinion.

Writing in dissent, Justice John Paul Stevens observed that the new standard is too vague and fails to accomplish what the majority ascribes to it. In many cases, "reasonable" people will disagree about whether particular materials have any redeeming social value. Moreover, the majority failed to provide guidelines instructing juries how to decide such cases.

The reasonable-person test suffers from the same subjectivity as the community-standard yardstick. Instead of juries having to find materials obscene because they are deemed without value by a majority of the community, juries now will have to make their decision on what some mythical "reasonable person" might think. How is this a step toward objectivity, or a correction of the potential abuse of geographic disparities in the 1973 ruling? Juries in Americus, Ga., and San Francisco might well have very different ideas of what a reasonable person finds obscene.

The court is hopelessly enmeshed in this tar baby, and how deeply the justices are divided on this sticky issue is illustrated by the fact that five written opinions were issued in this ruling.

The dissenters generally believe any restrictions on what materials consenting adults choose to read are unconstitutional. While those in the majority have the feeling there ought to be some standards governing obscenity, they have no real idea of how to go about establishing such a yardstick with any degree of objectivity and uniformity.

## The Washington Post
*Washington, DC, May 12, 1987*

WOULDN'T YOU want to read a Supreme Court opinion titled *A Book Named "John Cleland's Memoirs of a Woman of Pleasure" v. Attorney General of Massachusetts*? Does the name itself arouse prurient interest? Perhaps. But if you went to the trouble of digging up the 1966 opinion, you'd probably be more confused than titillated. The case is one of a series in which the court has struggled over the past 30 years with the question of obscenity. What is it and to what extent can it be regulated without violating the First Amendment? In the 1966 case, the nine justices wrote seven different opinions. Last week, in a case involving obscenity, there were only five different views.

That is where the law now stands: a jury may find material to be obscene if it 1) appeals to prurient interest, 2) is patently offensive, and 3) lacks serious literary, artistic, political or scientific value. The first two determinations should be made by applying "community standards," but in judging whether material has redeeming social value, the test is different and somewhat more difficult to prove. The question for the jury here is whether a reasonable person would find such value in the material. All three elements must be present for a finding of obscenity.

The case decided last week was an appeal of a criminal conviction under the Illinois obscenity statute. Two salesmen in a Rockford adult bookstore were found guilty of violating this law. Keep in mind the critical importance of clarity in a criminal statute so that ordinary people can understand what conduct is prohibited. Now put yourself in the position of the bookstore employees and try to define with certainty the terms "prurient interest," "patently offensive," "community standards," "literary, artistic, political or scientific value" and "reasonable person."

The late Justice Potter Stewart once wrote that he couldn't define hard-core pornography but that he knew it when he saw it. That view was expressed in a case in which a motion picture was found *not* to be obscene. But in fact, criminal convictions are based on evaluations that are essentially so subjective that even Supreme Court justices can't agree on their meaning. In a dissenting opinion last week, Justice John Paul Stevens wrote that "the difficulties inherent in the court's 'reasonable person' standard reaffirm my conviction that government may not constitutionally criminalize mere possession or sale of obscene literature, absent some connection to minors, or obtrusive display to unconsenting adults." He is right. There is no room for subjective standards in criminalizing behavior that is otherwise protected by the First Amendment.

# The Chattanooga Times
*Chattanooga, TN, May 1, 1987*

Several years ago, comedian George Carlin came up with a routine entitled "Seven Dirty Words," in which he repeated scatalogical words over and over. The intent was to show that repetition robbed the words of their shock value and that they became just — words. But when a California radio station broadcast the routine one afternoon and a listener complained to the Federal Communications Commission, it responded by barring as indecent the use of the words on radio or television. But where that rule at least had the virtue of clarity, the FCC's latest effort to clean up radio programming is so vague that it could threaten free speech.

The FCC says expansion of its so-called "decency code" has been prompted by public complaints about offensive talk-shows on radio and sexually explicit song lyrics, and that its new measures are aimed at restricting such explicit language on radio and television. Accordingly, the agency says that station owners could be fined or lose their licenses if it is found they have broadcast "indecent" material.

Given that authority, it is reasonable to ask how far the government could go in imposing censorship. Whether or not you approve of such material — and most Americans do not, although the "raunch radio" shows do have high ratings — you ought to be concerned about how much the government can define and control information, including entertainment. Another point: If you accept the dubious argument that an announcer's on-air offensiveness is such a grave threat to the nation's collective morality that it requires government intervention, then who should determine what you or your community may or may not hear? How much authority should they have? You can see the possibility for abuse implicit in such a proposed enforcement.

The FCC's standards of decency were adopted in 1976 and upheld by the Supreme Court two years later, but enforcement has been sporadic. However, the standards explicitly forbid the seven dirty words, require broadcasters to warn audiences that some material might be objectionable and say they may only air such programs after 10 p.m., when most youngsters, presumably, have gone to bed.

Now, however, the FCC intends tougher enforcement of the heretofore loosely enforced policy. It says that certain stations' shows "did not merely consist of an occasionally off-color reference or expletive, but consisted of a dwelling on sexual and excretory matters in a way that was patently offensive as measured by contemporary community standards for the broadcast medium." The application of that standard demands a couple of reasonable definitions. "Contemporary," for starters; what does that mean? Ditto for "community." Which community are we talking about? What plays to huge audiences in New York or San Francisco might be rejected out-of-hand in Boise.

Such vagueness recalls the Supreme Court's narrowly drawn ruling on the FCC standards. It did not, for example, get into the agency's authority to control radio and television programs' content. Nor did it involve the agency's power to censor scripts or prohibit the use of certain words. The issue merely focused on the FCC's right to tell broadcasters they could have re-licensing problems if they aired "patently offensive" material at a time when children might be listening. The court pointed out that it was not ruling on the propriety of broadcasting the same material at, say, 2 a.m. Implicit in the decision was the argument that wider latitude is permissible for cable-TV material and late-night programming.

The thrust of the FCC's latest foray, however, is that its definition of indecency is not merely limited to Carlin-like material, although it will permit material it considers indecent to be broadcast during hours when children are least likely to be listening. So, does that mean that sex and sex-related issues — AIDS, contraception, abortion — can't be discussed if they offend anybody. Absent clear guidelines on what's permitted and what's not, what are broadcasters to do?

Ironically, many of those who usually criticize federal regulation are the chief proponents for regulation in this matter. Clearly, however, this is an area better controlled by the public than the government. With all the legitimate functions of government, do you really think it ought to have the power to decide what we should be allowed to see or hear on the television or radio? One doesn't have to be a fan of "raunch radio" to believe that if government gets its nose into this area, it's not likely to stop.

# DESERET NEWS
*Salt Lake City, UT, May 6/7, 1987*

Unhappily, the U.S. Supreme Court has once again handed down a verdict making it more difficult for states to control pornography.

The court ruled this week that community standards could not be used to judge the "artistic merit" or "value," if any, of an allegedly obscene book, film, or other material.

Instead of being able to use what states or communities consider as local standards, the court decreed that the standard now must be that of a "reasonable person."

The high court's ruling amounts to near total retreat from common sense. It's hard enough to get a legal grip on "community standards," but what does "reasonable person" mean? The court, probably seeing the swamp it was getting into, refused to elaborate on what a reasonable person is, or how to define one. Even so-called experts often disagree on whether or not a particular book or film has artistic merit or value.

Previous Supreme Court decisions have laid down three points that must all be met in determining pornography: (1) material that appeals to prurient interest, (2) patently offensive sexual conduct, and (3) whether as a whole, the material lacks literary, artistic, political, or scientific value.

Failure on even one of these points means that the material cannot be labeled as pornographic. It is in connection with the third item that the court dumped community standards as a way to decide.

As dissenting Justice John Paul Stevens pointed out in the 6-3 verdict, the court has only made things worse, further muddying the already murky legal waters surrounding obscenity. Lower courts are going to have an even tougher time deciding such cases, and as a result, prosecutors may be more lenient on pornography.

What the ruling means is that a place like Utah, with its own values and standards, may be forced to accept the New York or Los Angeles definition of obscenity and social value. That can be pretty low.

The case on which the Supreme Court ruled arose in Illinois, where officials argued that it is impossible to establish nationwide standards for what is obscene.

They declared that it is not constitutionally sound to require ". . . that the people of Maine or Mississippi accept public depiction of conduct found tolerable in Las Vegas or New York City."

That makes a lot more sense than what the Supreme Court decided.

# The Charlotte Observer
*Charlotte, NC, May 6, 1987*

To the extent that it moved a step further from the notion of majority rule in obscenity cases, the U.S. Supreme Court's ruling in an Illinois case Monday was welcome. But the 6-3 decision failed to clarify the murky issue of what constitutes obscenity. If anything, it made a legal definition of obscenity even more difficult to establish.

In 1973 the high court established a three-part test for obscenity. First, a work's dominant theme had to appeal to lascivious interest. Second, it had to depict sexual conduct in an offensive manner. Third, it had to be without literary, artistic, political or scientific value. Until Monday it was generally accepted that "community standards" could be applied in testing those three points. But the court majority said Monday that community standards are not the relevant test on the third point. Instead, a "reasonable person" rule should apply.

Justice Byron White wrote that "the ideas a work represents need not obtain majority approval to merit (constitutional) protection." Instead, White wrote, there should be protection if "a reasonable person would find such value in the material, taken as a whole."

We've always been uncomfortable with the idea of using community standards to determine whether something is obscene because, as Justice White suggested, community standards could be construed as simply representing the majority view. One purpose of the First Amendment is precisely to protect the right to express a point of view even if it clashes with majority opinion.

For that reason, we agree with the court majority that a reasonable person test is preferable to a community standards test in determining whether a work has redeeming value. But we don't envy lawyers, prosecutors, judges or juries who have to apply this new test. If there is one true thing that can be said about obscenity, it is that reasonable people can and do disagree over what it is.

## Children's TV Bill Vetoed

The House of Representatives by a vote of 328-78, June 8, 1988 passed legislation aimed at restricting the commercialization of children's television.

The bill would require broadcasters to "serve the educational and informational needs of children" in order to get their licenses renewed. Licenses had to be submitted to the FCC for renewal every five years.

The National Association of Broadcasters had lobbied against stronger versions of the legislation, so that by the time the bill reached the House floor, it had been stripped of such features as a provision mandating an hour a day of educational programming for children.

The legislation then moved to the Senate, where two companion bills were under consideration.

The Senate cleared and sent to the White House Oct. 19 a bill to restrict commercials telecast to children and to make children's television fare a factor in license renewal.

Congress did not specify any content for children's programming, but it required the FCC to consider, when station owners sought license renewal, whether the station had served "the educational and informational needs of children in its overall programming."

The basic communication law called only for a general consideration of whether the public interest had been served.

The bill would limit commercial advertising on children's programs to no more than 10.5 minutes each on weekends, and no more than 12 minutes per hour on weekdays. Currently, there were no limits.

The bill would limit commercial time during children's shows to a total of 10.5 minutes an hour on weekends and 12 minutes an hour on weekdays. The Federal Communications Commission (FCC) had repealed similar limits in 1984.

The legislation would take effect in 1990.

President Ronald Reagan Nov. 5 vetoed the bill.

The President said this "simply cannot be reconciled with the freedom of expression secured by our Constitution."

Such provisons, he said, "would inhibit broadcasters from offering innovative programs that do not fit neatly into regulatory categories and discourage the creation of programs that might not satisfy the tastes of agency officials responsible for considering license renewals."

The veto was a pocket veto, meaning the measure expired without the president's signature at a time when Congress was not in session, after the 10-day period allowed for presidential consideration.

The House Aug. 1, 1989 voted, 399-18, to approve a bill that would waive the Sherman Antitrust Act in order to allow broadcast and cable television representatives to meet and discuss voluntary guidelines to curb violent programming.

The Senate had approved a similar measure May 31 that included curbs on sexually explicit programming or depictions of illegal drug use.

Although antitrust exemptions had been granted in the past to insurance companies, newspapers and other industries in specific instances, this would be the first time such an exemption had been approved for television broadcasting.

Officials of the three major broadcast networks said they would be willing to discuss the issue, but they said they doubted an agreement would be possible because competitive pressures would force programmers, particularly cable systems, to continue carrying violent fare.

Viewer complaints about violence on television had increased in recent months, prompting cancellation of some programs and withdrawal of sponsor advertising from others.

Television executives cited several factors behind the rise in viewer complaints, according to the *New York Times* April 23. Those factors included a cutback in network censorship staffs, technically known as "standards and practices" departments, to save money. They also included the television writers' strike of 1988, which had gave networks less time to censor potentially offensive material.

### AKRON BEACON JOURNAL
*Akron, OH, November 8, 1988*

THERE ARE FEW places where the description of television as a "wasteland" is more accurate than in programming for children. The waste is all the greater for the potential television has for education.

Yet for every children's program that enlightens as well as entertains, there are several that are devoid of intelligence and of any worthwhile message or content. Particularly disgusting are those TV characters created merely to hawk a product aimed at the children's market.

The question is what to do about it. And President Reagan was right last week in deciding that bending the Constitution was going too far to correct the problem.

The President vetoed legislation that would have imposed advertising limits on children's TV programs (10.5 minutes an hour on weekends; 12 minutes an hour on weekdays) and would have required that stations offer certain educational and informational programming for children as a condition of license renewal.

Tne goals of the legislation are laudable, and it enjoyed solid support in Congress. Even the networks supported it as better than a more stringent original bill. More dedicated proponents of the legislation called the Reagan veto "ideological child abuse."

But Reagan, correctly and rather surprisingly, believes the bill's restrictive provisions could discourage the networks from providing quality programming for children, and that the bill would violate constitutional free speech guarantees.

"The Constitution," Reagan said, "simply does not empower the federal government to oversee the programming decisions of broadcasters in the manner prescribed by this bill."

The Reagan veto doesn't end the matter. The Federal Communications Commission is continuing a study into programming practices (though it may be reluctant to act because of the constitutional questions). Congress is threatening to come back after recess with an even tougher measure.

The most positive aspect, however, is the increased public attention to problems with TV for children — public pressure that can be brought to help improve programming. This pressure can be as effective as legislation, and much less burdensome on free expression.

# DAILY NEWS
*New York, NY, November 8, 1988*

President Reagan's pocket veto of a bill that would help enrich children's television programing was ill-advised. Current TV fare for kids—much of which is schlock containing excessive amounts of advertising—simply does not serve the public interest, as mandated by the Federal Communications Commission.

The bill, which was overwhelmingly approved by Congress, would have limited advertising during children's shows and required broadcasters to provide educational and informational programs as a condition of license renewal. The President, who failed to act on the measure within 10 days and thus killed it, said it infringed on the constitutional right of freedom of expression.

Although free speech, as guaranteed under the First Amendment, must be protected, information sent out over the public airwaves for the consumption of impressionable children serves a special purpose. It must be sifted so as to be acceptable as well as palatable. The proposed legislation would have helped do that by reverting to the sensible FCC rules that were in effect before the commission opted for marketplace determination in 1984.

Said Sen. Timothy Wirth (D-Colo.), who favors the bill: "As a result of the FCC's neglect of this problem, a troublesome situation has grown much worse." And he's right. With kids spending an inordinate amount of time in front of the TV set—especially on weekends—it's vital that better programing be encouraged. This bill is a welcome step in that direction, and it's good to know supporters in Congress have vowed to reintroduce the measure next year.

## LAS VEGAS REVIEW-JOURNAL
*Las Vegas, NV, November 8, 1988*

Despite the expressed outrage of children's-television activists, President Reagan did the right thing in nixing a bill that would have limited advertising during children's shows. It was a clear First Amendment issue and Reagan came down on the right side of it.

Now, few parents relish having their children subjected to the sustained barrages of commercials for toy weapons and sugary cereal while the youngsters are planted in front of the tube Saturday mornings. The bill Reagan pocket-vetoed this week would have restricted advertising during children's programming and also would have required TV broadcasters to provide educational and informational programming for children or risk punitive action from the Federal Communications Commission.

While this bill was well-intentioned, it flew in the face of the First Amendment's guarantee of free speech.

It should be noted that those who wanted this bill written into law are not the only ones who have some ax or other to grind with commercial television. There are groups that would like to ban beer and wine advertising. There are groups that would like to see violence eliminated from the TV airwaves. There are groups that would like to see a ban on advertising for war toys, and so on. If all these groups were successful, the free speech rights of broadcasters would be effectively eliminated.

It has been argued that because the airwaves are a limited resource broadcasters enjoy fewer First Amendment rights than do publishers, and that the federal government has a legitimate role in regulating what appears on the airwaves. That argument might have been valid 25 years ago. But today, with the advent of cable television, satellite reception and home videotape, the airwaves can no longer be considered a scarce public resource. In light of the new technologies, the federal government should be backing away from regulation of the airwaves, not seeking more control over them. Ideally, broadcasters should enjoy the same unfettered First Amendment rights as newspapers.

Parents who dislike what their children watch on TV and who want to take issue with broadcasters and advertisers have several options, outside of federal regulation: They can boycott products whose ads they find offensive; they can make their concerns known to the broadcasters through protests. Most effective of all, they can hit the "off" button.

# The Idaho STATESMAN
*Boise, ID, June 11, 1988*

Should television advertisers be restrained from bombarding children with their messages?

The House of Representatives thinks so, voting overwhelmingly – 328-78 – Wednesday to reinstate restrictions on the number of minutes of advertising allowed during children's programming. The need for congressional action came about because the Federal Communications Commission dropped its limits in 1984. A court challenge to that action still is pending.

It should be noted that the limits proposed by Congress are more liberal than the policy dumped four years ago by the FCC. Congress would limit advertisements during children's programs to 10½ minutes per hour on weekends and 12 minutes per hour on weekdays. The old FCC rules provided for 9½ minutes and 12 minutes, respectively.

The reasons for the rules are self-evident. Whereas adults can filter advertisements through their own judgment and make consumer decisions accordingly, children are more vulnerable. They rarely make purchasing decisions, so advertisements beamed at them are really aimed at getting children to prevail upon the parental decision makers.

Advertising has increased about 30 seconds per hour since the FCC ban was lifted, according to a FCC spokesman. There have been no efforts by the networks to voluntarily limit children's advertising.

That's too bad, because ideally parents and the networks should be limiting agents. Government intervention shouldn't be needed.

How much TV children watch and what shows they see can and should be regulated by parents. Programs, whether they be undesirable because of too much violence, too much advertising or too much inanity, can be switched off. Easily.

But as long as government holds a watchdog position over broadcasting it has a responsibility especially to younger viewers. The advertising limits are not excessive and not new. They are just appropriate.

# THE TORONTO SUN
*Toronto, Ont., November 8, 1988*

One of the last marks of the Ronald Reagan's presidency may be his rejection of regulations that would provide some protection for children against hucksterism and violence on television.

Mr. Reagan, just before the election of his successor, refused to sign a bill passed by wide margins in the U.S. Congress; because Congress is adjourned, that means the legislation dies. Even broadcasters supported the new rules, which would have marginally limited commercials to 10½ minutes an hour on weekends (12 minutes weekdays) and would have required at least some educational or informational broadcasting as a condition of a station's licence.

Mr. Reagan's excuse was that the legislation was an unconstitutional infringement on freedom of expression. Does he feel the same way about obscenity and pornography?

There is no doubt that television exploits children, commercially and in content. Mr. Reagan is its ally. But a new Congress, next year, will get another chance, with another president who might be a better actor.

## The Grand Rapids Press
*Grand Rapids, MI, November 9, 1988*

With his veto of a bill promoting quality television for children, President Reagan has tuned out a disturbing reality of his old business.

The shows currently being pushed at children are not entertainment so much as series of commercials. Some of them are even full-length advertisements — programs built around characters or games which the kids are induced to buy.

The bill just vetoed would have forced the Federal Communications Commission, before renewing a television station's license, to determine whether the outlet was serving the educational needs of children in its programming. In addition, stations could not air more than 10.5 minutes per hour of commercials on weekends, 12 minutes on weekdays.

The approach is hardly revolutionary. Prior to 1981, and Ronald Reagan's arrival in Washington, the FCC routinely limited advertising on children's shows and it had a formal policy of pushing broadcasters to air programs of "educational and informative value." Under Mr. Reagan, the FCC began backing off — treating children's television as just another form of business. Four years ago, the quality policy and the advertising caps were dropped altogether.

After that, programming went downhill like kids tumbling down a sandpile. Within two years, CBS has pushed Captain Kangaroo into a weekend corner, laid off the entire children's programming staff and eliminated 156 hours a year of children's TV. ABC and NBC did much the same. Award-winning dramas, news-magazines and educational programs were out; video comics and commercials were in. They are "in" now more than ever, with program-length commercials — shows whose characters can be bought as toys — having become an industry staple.

The vetoed bill, sponsored by Rep. Edward Markey, D-Mass., was thus an attempt to restore a prudent and responsible FCC policy. Not even the television industry's trade group, the National Association of Broadcasters, was objecting.

The logic of the government involving itself in this area should be overwhelming. Youngsters spend long hours in front of television screens and they are particularly vulnerable to the sly pitches of TV hucksters. Maintaining some quality standards for what the children see is in the national interest, a fact reflected in the rigorous children's programming standards existing in other countries.

Mr. Reagan, in vetoing the Markey bill, rationalized that it violates the Constitution's freedom of expression guarantee. The airwaves, though, are unlike the public sidewalk. They are a national resource. Licenses to use them are parceled out to a favored few who use them to turn whatever profits their skills and consciences allow. No contradiction is involved in government insistence on some modest show of broadcaster responsibility, particularly in the field of children's television. The NAB's acquiescence in the bill is evidence that Mr. Markey wasn't expecting too much.

This legislation was long in coming. Various lawmakers, and children's interest groups, had been urging it for years. This year they won large votes of support in both the House and Senate. In 1989, with Mr. Reagan out of the picture, they should try again.

## The Honolulu Advertiser
*Honolulu, HI, November 12, 1988*

President Reagan has defied Congress and made others angry by vetoing a bill that would have limited commercial time during children's TV shows and required stations to show evidence of educational programming when seeking license renewal.

The president's rationale, that "this bill simply cannot be reconciled with the freedom of expression," is dubious. Even the National Association of Broadcasters recognizes — as have the courts — "the unique position of children in the television audience."

All the bill would have done is reimpose by statute the voluntary guidelines in effect until 1984. That year, the Federal Communications Commission lifted all restraints on broadcasting for children.

Actually, the bill would have brought only minimal improvement, and not until 1990. It would have limited advertising on children's shows to 10½ minutes per hour on weekends and 12 minutes per hour on weekdays. Now a whopping 22 percent of total TV air time allotted to children consists of commercials — 13 minutes per hour. Some shows are "program-length commercials," which would not have been affected by the legislation.

Congress could revive the measure next session, and it might still go into effect in 1990. Or the FCC could act. It is under court order to consider reimposing the guidelines administratively.

And the first and last resort — the On-Off knob — is still available to all parents who agree with Congress that TV's glut of "insipid cartoons" and commercials for war toys and oversweetened cereals has a negative effect on young viewers.

## THE BUFFALO NEWS
*Buffalo, NY, November 8, 1988*

ROCK-HARD MONSTERS, sorcerers, crooks and various space weirdos mix it up in the too-often violent world of children's television. Mom and dad get a break from the routine of child-rearing while the little ones watch chases and fights to their heart's content.

Children's TV is a part of Americana that many deplore and they have good arguments. The television industry — with a chance to do something constructive — too commonly falls back on violence and scary stuff.

Periodically, the focus turns to legislative answers — that is, to governmental intervention. The latest effort came as the 100th Congress wrapped up its business.

It placed in President Reagan's lap a bill that would reimpose limits on the time that could be devoted to commercials on TV programs aimed at children. There would be a limit of 10.5 minutes an hour on weekends and 12 minutes an hour on weekdays. Another provision would rather vaguely require stations to "serve the educational and informational needs of children."

For all its obviously good intentions, it was a questionable bill, and Reagan was justified in vetoing it.

It conflicted with the Constitution's First Amendment guarantees of freedom of expression and would get the government involved in TV programming and advertising. For better or for worse, the marketplace — not politicians and bureaucrats — should determine such matters.

As the president said in his veto announcement: "While I applaud efforts to increase the amount and quality of children's television programming, the Constitution simply does not empower the federal government to oversee the programming decisions of broadcasters in the manner prescribed by this bill."

Parents who object to some of the children's TV fare can and should move in and control what their children watch. When they have to rule certain programs off limits, it would be a good idea to let the offending television stations and its advertisers know about it in no uncertain terms.

Enough parents landing on a single program should give broadcasters a clue that it is time to find something else to present. They should be sensitive to such complaints.

The bill has been hailed as a "landmark victory for parents and children" by the head of Action for Children's Television, a group that has lobbied for 20 years for such legislation. But even from an advocate's viewpoint, that would seem to exaggerate the measure's worth.

The bill was actually compromise legislation that the broadcasting industry played a role in developing. Industry spokesmen said they could "live with" the outcome and contended that they share Congress' interest "in assuring the provision of programs that serve the needs of the child audience."

To which we say: Good. Go ahead and provide them then.

# The Houston Post
*Houston, TX, August 3, 1988*

Last year, in a further effort to shield children from inappropriate programming, the FCC ruled that radio could broadcast so-called "indecent" material between midnight and 6 a.m. only.

The decision brought yelps of protest. Some voiced First Amendment concerns, others were confused by the vagueness of "indecent," and still others wondered why the cutoff — which had been 10 p.m. for nearly a decade — was pushed back to midnight.

Now a federal appeals court has struck down portions of the controversial FCC ban. But the situation remains distorted by static. The FCC had *not* shown a large number of unsupervised children would be exposed to this material between 10 p.m. and midnight, said the court. The FCC's role is to *assist* parents in choosing what their children will hear, chided the court, not to act as censors.

However, the court did let stand the FCC's broad definition of "indecent" and its warnings to two morning radio shows. In effect, this confirms the agency's right to exercise such restraints — just not as arbitrarily. This remains a perplexing issue, but the court's decision to safeguard the right of free, even if "indecent," speech was necessary and commendable.

## FORT WORTH STAR-TELEGRAM
*Fort Worth, TX, November 8, 1988*

Network television's idea of "children's programming" is appalling. Trusted with policing themselves and providing children's shows that are educational as well as entertaining, TV executives have, instead, turned the airwaves over to the hucksters since the Federal Communications Commission eased its regulatory grip.

Saturday morning TV fare is little more than one long, hard-sell commercial for toys. Most of the cartoon shows offer little of redeeming social value for children and a vast amount of redeeming dollar value for toy manufacturers.

Entire shows are built around animated characters of toys manufactured by the shows' sponsors, and that represents a shameless pitch to youngsters to pressure their parents into buying the toys.

As if that were not bad enough, many of the shows feature violent, mindless action that could have a lasting impact on the children watching them. If any TV offerings perfectly fit former FCC Chairman Newton Minnow's description of television as a "vast wasteland," it is the Saturday morning kids' cartoon shows.

Despite all that, President Reagan was justified in vetoing a bill that would have limited advertising in children's programs and would have required TV broadcasters to provide a certain amount of educational and informational programming for children as a condition of license renewal.

As bad as children's programming is, the "big brotherism" advocated by supporters of the vetoed legislation could be worse. The First Amendment not only protects what people can say but it also protects people from being told by the government *what* to say. And that, in effect, is what the bill would have done.

Basing a station's license eligibility on its acquiescence to what the government deems to be suitable programming would establish a dangerous precedent, philosophically akin to closing down newspapers because they do not print what the government wants printed. That is a practice that the lawmakers who passed the vetoed bill condemn vigorously in totalitarian nations.

Reagan's veto does not close the book on this issue, nor should it. The bill was approved overwhelmingly in both houses of Congress, and its supporters have vowed to introduce an even more stringent measure during the next session. The next president, whoever he may be, might be more inclined to sign it than Reagan was.

The responsibility for forestalling such action lies with the television networks themselves, which are abusing their First Amendment rights. While pleading for deregulation, TV executives pledged to police themselves. They have reneged on that pledge, and the result has been irresponsible, exploitative TV for children.

Parents also bear a great deal of responsibility for the current situation. Many of them do not know — or do not care — what their children are watching. That is a none-too-subtle form of child abuse in itself. Many of those parents who *do* know or who *do* care apparently are not aware of how to deal properly with the problem.

In the first place, parents should learn the location of the on-off switch on the television set and use it responsibly. No matter how demanding they may be, children do not have a constitutional right to watch Saturday morning cartoons. A generous ration of parental discipline could go a long way toward eliminating the problem.

Other ways parents can respond include notifying the networks of their displeasure and/or boycotting the advertised products.

The gravest threat inherent in prolonging the status quo is that complaints will grow so loud that First Amendment rights will be ignored. The American people are already losing their tolerance for liberty because of continued abuse of freedoms by those who put profit ahead of integrity.

The TV networks are guilty of doing exactly that when it comes to children's programming.

## The Chattanooga Times
*Chattanooga, TN, June 16, 1988*

The House of Representatives voted overwhelmingly last week to reassert regulatory control over children's television programming. By a vote of 328 to 78, the House passed a bill to limit the amount of advertising time during children's programs, and, perhaps more important, to require broadcasters to serve the educational needs of the young as a condition of license renewal.

The legislation signals that the deregulation fever of the Reagan years is beginning to break. Its broad bipartisan support in the House reflects widespread concern over the commercialization of children's television since 1984, when the Federal Communications Commission removed longstanding restrictions on children's programming.

Then-FCC chairman Mark Fowler successfully pressed for deregulation on grounds that the open marketplace would determine what was best for America's youth. But experience suggests children's programming has suffered from the marketplace's overriding interest in what is best for the sponsors' bottom line. Since 1984, toy manufacturers have become heavily involved in children's television programming. They have developed entire programs based on the "adventures" of toys manufactured and sold by the sponsor. These shows amount to little more than program-length commercials, and there have even been extreme cases in which broadcasters were enticed to air them in exchange for a cut of the profit from toy sales.

Another point that illustrates concerns about the declining quality in children's television was made recently by Peggy Charren, president of the Boston-based Action for Children's Television. Before deregulation, she said, CBS News "had 20 people in its news department working on children's programs; now they have none."

The National Association of Broadcasters says the bill's time limit on advertising — 12 minutes an hour on weekdays and 10.5 minutes an hour on weekends — will make little difference. The organization maintains children's programs now carry an average of only eight and one-half minutes of advertising per hour on weekdays and about eight minutes per hour on weekends.

The more significant element of the House bill is the provision that requires broadcasters to provide programming that serves the developmental and educational needs of children. It is not too much to require in exchange for the federally licensed right to use the airwaves. Considering the amount of time American children spend in front of the television, it serves the national interest for broadcasters to offer them programs that are not only entertaining, but also enriching.

Experience indicates that broadcasters need some regulatory incentive to provide what Americans have a right to expect in programming for their children. The House bill would provide that incentive. It deserves passage in the Senate as well.

## The Boston Globe
*Boston, MA, November 1, 1988*

A bill requiring television broadcasters to do better by children – set time limits on commercials and improve the quality of children's shows – is languishing on President Reagan's desk. Though the bill is the most important statement on children's television in 20 years, it will die unless Reagan signs it by Saturday.

The administration has opposed the bill for reasons that have nothing to do with children. Rather, the bill is seen as an intrusion of government into private broadcasting and commercial advertising decisions; thus, it goes against the tide of deregulation that the White House has fostered.

Actually, limits on children's TV commercials are not new. From 1969 to 1984, the Federal Communications Commission accepted the idea that children are more vulnerable than adults to commercial pitches on TV. The FCC limited commercials on children's TV programs until 1984.

The bill would require that television broadcasters develop programs that inform as well as entertain. How well a television broadcaster lived up to that commitment to better programs for children would become a condition for license renewal.

Rep. Edward Markey, a co-author of the Children's Television Act of 1988, said the bill was carefully balanced. Not only would it ensure that children learn more from TV than "the wonders of the latest cereal or toy," but it also accommodated those market interests.

Peggy Charren of Action for Children's Television had envisioned that the bill would signal a change in the way broadcasters and the FCC operate on children's behalf. She was encouraged by the support from the television industry; the National Association of Broadcasters had worked with Congress and children's organizations on the bill.

No one disputes that children spend too much time – 30 hours a week – in front of television sets. Given that, however, Reagan, an ex-broadcaster, should sign this bill to at least make some of that time worthwhile.

## The Christian Science Monitor
*Boston, MA, November 8, 1988*

PRESIDENT REAGAN has killed a bill that would have limited the commercial content of television programs for children. He saw an affront to the First Amendment that the 378 members of Congress who voted for the measure somehow failed to perceive.

Mr. Reagan's pocket veto stops, for now, an attempt to restore needed balance. Four years ago the Federal Communications Commission dropped longstanding rules regarding children's programming, and product-based TV shows started to dominate Saturday mornings.

Lawmakers wanted to set limits on the proportion of children's programming time allowed for pitching products. They also wanted the quality of children's shows to be weighed in renewing a station's license.

Explaining his veto, the President argued that the bill would "inhibit broadcasters from offering innovative programs that do not fit neatly into regulatory categories." If what we've seen over the past four years is an example of "innovative" programming, a degree of inhibition may be needed. More likely, the bill would encourage broadcasters to meet the needs of children.

A few months back the FCC was bent on banning "indecent" programming from TV. That effort raised a First Amendment storm. An effort to limit the commercial exploitation of young viewers does not. Its backers should, and probably will, try again next year.

## The Seattle Times
*Seattle, WA, November 11, 1988*

THE Senate and House had approved it by overwhelming margins. It received strong backing from such respected groups as Action For Children's Television. It even was supported by the National Association of Broadcasters.

Yet President Reagan, citing an evidently newfound interest in the First Amendment, has pocket-vetoed a much-needed bill to improve children's television. This from an administration that has trumpeted its support for education and family values.

By restricting the amount of advertising messages during children's program periods (to up to 12 minutes an hour), as the bill proposed, Reagan said the government would be infringing on constitutionally protected freedom of expression.

Ridiculous. The issue involves material broadcast on publicly owned airwaves. And, as pointed out by Rep. Al Swift, D-Bellingham, an expert on broadcasting issues, the bill merely would have reinstated rules long in effect until their repeal by the Federal Communications Commission four years ago.

Rather than requiring broadcasters to provide educational and informative children's programs and to limit the number of commercials in them, the FCC said in 1984 that such matters should be determined by the "marketplace."

Well, the "marketplace" has worked just fine for the marketeers, but has not done much to improve the content of children's programs. The New York Times reports, for example, the heavy involvement of toy manufacturers in kids' programs featuring the manufacturers' products. Some broadcasters were promised a share of the profit on toy sales in exchange for scheduling the toymakers' programs.

Reagan's veto rightly outraged the bill's advocates. "Another example of ideological child abuse in the Reagan administration," said Patty Charren of Action For Children's Television." Rep. Edward Markey, D-Mass, a bill co-sponsor, said the veto was "a victory for the toy and cereal hucksters, but a major defeat for our nation's children."

What comes next? Fortunately, Reagan soon will be out of office and proponents can make a new try. Rep. Matthew Rinaldo, R-N.J., said Reagan's veto was based on "bad advice." But next year, said Rinaldo, "a new president will be faced with a tougher bill and a more determined Congress."

## The Hutchinson News
*Hutchinson, KS, November 9, 1988*

Ronald Reagan backhanded the kids again last week.

He quietly vetoed a modest federal law that would have put lukewarm restrictions on the manner by which TV networks and produce peddlers stick to the youngsters.

"The Constitution simply does not empower the federal government to oversee the programming decisions of broadcasters in the manner prescribed by this bill," Mr. Reagan claimed. Limitations on the number of commercials "may well undermine its stated purpose by discouraging commercial networks from financing quality children's programming."

The bill would have limited advertising in children's shows to 10½ minutes per hour on weekends and 12 minutes per hour on weekdays. Some limits, eh?

The Reagan standard is clear: Nothing is too good for the hucksters on TV, and nothing is too bad to dump on the kids.

His decision is vulgar.

The nation owns the airwaves. TV moguls don't. The nation should impose requirements on the TV moguls. Especially when the moguls dump the stuff they're dumping on kids, in their frantic efforts to peddle stuff no matter how lousy their programming may be.

## THE TENNESSEAN
*Nashville, TN, November 13, 1988*

PRESIDENT Reagan has angered parents and politicians alike with his last-minute veto of a bill concerning children's television. The parents' motives were right — but so was the President's veto.

The bill sought to curb the Saturday morning deluge of 30-minute toy commercials that are masquerading as children's TV programs. The bill would have limited advertising during children's programs to 10½ minutes per hour on weekends and 12 minutes per hour on weekdays. It also would have required broadcasters to provide educational and informational programs to their children's lineup.

There is no doubt at all of the sincerity on the part of Congress and the groups that lobbied for this legislation. Many caring parents rallied behind the bill because they observed their children being mesmerized by TV mush that has a single purpose — selling a toy line. Finally, those parents stood up and declared, "There ought to be a law."

But that's where their efforts are misguided: there shouldn't be a law. The First Amendment says specifically "Congress shall make no law...abridging the freedom of speech." Note that the amendment doesn't protect only political speech, or religious speech, or education speech, or nice speech. It just says speech.

As tempting as it may be, Congress does not need to be in the business of dictatiing programming decisions to broadcasters. Television is a powerful medium; it is also an extremely varied medium and is, for the most part, a responsible medium.

The parents have a legitimate concern about what their children are watching on the tube. But the best, most efficient, and most direct way for them to make their displeasure known is to call their local station managers, write to the networks, and tell the advertisers.

If parents would turn the channel, turn off the set, and refuse to buy the products, the offending programs would disappear. ■

## ST. LOUIS POST-DISPATCH
*St. Louis, MO, November 12, 1988*

When the Federal Communications Commission limited the broadcasting of so-called indecent TV programs earlier this year to between midnight and 6 a.m., its rationale was that few children would likely be watching at those hours. Now, in another case concerning broadcasting and children's interests, President Reagan has used his pocket veto to kill a bill to limit the amount of advertising on children's shows. The government's actions are inconsistent.

The president argued in the most recent case that the First Amendment prevents him from signing any legislation regulating the nature of programming, no matter how beneficent the purpose. He took care to point out that the bill also would have required broadcasters to provide educational programs for children as a condition of license renewal. In his view, the public interest is defined exclusively by the market; government has no role in promoting the public interest in the licensing of TV stations.

But when it came to obscenity, the government felt it had a mandate to protect children. It is clear, then, that the administration's argument that children's TV cannot be regulated because of the First Amendment isn't really sincere.

Where the moral standards of the community would clearly be outraged — as they would be were so-called obscenity programming permitted in prime time — the community's interest is undoubted, and the First Amendment is no bar to action. So the same rationale should apply in evaluating TV stations' license-renewal applications partly on the basis of how they have furthered children's interests, not merely refrained from damaging them.

## THE SACRAMENTO BEE
*Sacramento, CA, November 9, 1988*

President Reagan has refused to sign a bill, passed by overwhelming majorities in both houses of Congress, that would have restored limits on the number of commercials that can be jammed into television programs aimed at children. He did so on the ground that such limits infringe on broadcasters' constitutional right of free expression. That view is either obtuse or disingenuous; in either case, Congress should waste no time next year in re-enacting a measure that would be law had Reagan not resorted to the pocket veto, a device that enables a president to invalidate legislation by ignoring it when Congress is not in session.

What's so troubling about the president's decision is that the bill was but a pallid corrective to television programmers' neglect of their responsibility, under the law, to broadcast educational material. Essentially it would have limited commercial time to 12 minutes per hour on weekdays and 10½ minutes on weekends, in effect restoring a rule junked in 1984 by the free-market fanatics on the Federal Communications Commission. This year's measure was watered down, under pressure from broadcasters, to delete an injunction against what critics call "program-length commercials" in which products being sold — mostly toys — are incorporated into program content.

What the bill usefully did, however, was to put broadcasters on notice that fidelity to their obligation to "serve the educational and informational needs of children" would be considered at license-renewal time. Without even that modest admonition, the kids are left entirely to the mercy of the Saturday morning hucksters.

Broadcasters would still be well advised to clean up their act, as some, commendably, have done. Many in Congress favored a much tougher crackdown that would have mandated, for example, one hour of educational programming each day. Now, with the FCC having abandoned its responsibility and Reagan having evaded his, it's up to Congress to once again find the right balance between the rights of broadcasters and those of children. If the lawmakers lean even further toward the kids next time, who could blame them?

## *Amerika* TV
## Film to Proceed

The ABC television network Jan. 22, 1986 announced that it would proceed with the production of a controversial television miniseries. The 12-hour miniseries, *Amerika*, was to be broadcast in 1987.

*Amerika* was to depict life in the U.S. after a Soviet takeover. ABC had announced a production delay Jan. 8, a few days after the planned miniseries was denounced by Moscow. Brandon Stoddard, the president of ABC Entertainment, indicated that the Soviet criticism would be taken into account in a decision on whether to proceed with production.

At the time of the announced production delay, the network disclosed that Soviet officials in December 1985 had hinted of a possible retaliation against the ABC News bureau in Moscow if *Amerika* was produced.

The postponement was assailed by U.S. Education Secretary William J. Bennett Jan. 11 during a speech in New York City. Bennett asserted: "What this means is that the American people's television fare is in jeopardy of being censored by Soviet officials."

Stoddard issued a statement Jan. 22 saying that ABC would proceed with the miniseries because of the "inherent dramatic quality of the material. There was never any lack of faith in the concept or the script for *Amerika*."

John B. Sias, the new president of ABC Television, Jan. 22 maintained that the decision to go ahead with *Amerika* was "supported by the top management with the full understanding of what pressures this decision might bring to other areas of our company."

*Amerika* aired in six episodes Feb. 15-20, 1987 in the U.S. Portraying the U.S. 10 years after a Soviet takeover, *Amerika* starred Robert Urich and Kris Kristofferson. (Ironically, Kristofferson, who played an anti-Soviet patriot in the program, was attending the Moscow peace forum when the program debuted.)

The 14-hour miniseries, produced by Capital Cities/ABC Inc., cost a record $40 million to make.

Based on preliminary ratings, about 70 million Americans watched the opening episode Feb. 15.

The Soviet Union and peace groups in the U.S. denounced the miniseries as anti-Soviet propaganda. On the other side, some American conservatives argued that the program did not accurately reflect the horror of a Soviet occupation.

ABC Television offices in several U.S. cities were picketed by peace activists Feb. 15.

In related developments:

■ Chrysler Corp. Jan. 27 withdrew the commercial advertising, valued at about $5 million, it had planned to run during *Amerika*. In a statement, Chrysler explained that its "upbeat product commercials" would be "inappropriate" for the program.

■ Kristofferson Feb. 12 taped a 30-second public service announcement praising the United Nations. The action was taken to partly offset the U.N.'s strong objections to *Amerika*. (In the program, the Soviets used soldiers, identified as U.N. peacekeeping troops, to subjugate the American populace. The U.N. symbol was incorporated into the flag of the occupying forces.)

### Pittsburgh Post-Gazette
*Pittsburgh, PA, March 12, 1987*

One of the most dramatic examples of media hype — and anti-media hype — was the controversy earlier this year about the television mini-series "Amerika."

The ABC drama, which depicted life in a future Soviet-occupied America, was savaged by critics on the left who seemed to believe that it would foment hatred against the Soviet Union, with God knows what consequences for world peace. At least during its production, some right-wingers seemed to attribute similarly miraculous powers to a mere piece of entertainment. Now Americans would finally wise up about the Evil Empire!

Well, we can all breathe a sigh of relief. According to a survey by a professor at George Washington University, "Amerika" came, was seen but did not conquer any attitudes. The poll conducted by Prof. William Adams showed that the series had no measurable effect on attitudes toward the Soviet Union, the United Nations or U.S.-Soviet relations.

Concluded Prof. Adams: "It takes more than a television mini-series to shift longstanding opinions on fundamental issues." No kidding.

### The Augusta Chronicle
*Augusta, GA*
*February 18, 1987*

It ended.

The long years of resistance to Communist takeover of a free people simply folded like a collapsed deck of cards.

**That's the haunting basis of the week-long ABC-TV miniseries, "Amerika," and it's no wonder the Soviet Union and its domestic apologists are screaming foul.**

This drama about life in the United States under Soviet occupation is striking a responsive chord among many Americans because a stark lesson is there for all to learn.

The fall of America in "Amerika" reminds us of those dark days in April 1975, when South Vietnam fell to Communist slavery — one of the most shameful pages in U.S. history.

We do not belabor the matter of recriminations, since what is past is past. We note, only because the record speaks so clearly, that Vietnam was lost because of astoundingly naive and stupid policies, and because of unabashed failure to realize that Communist "peace" agreements aren't worth the paper they are printed on.

And these things were compounded then due to a U.S. Congress which lost its determination to resist the spread of a communistic New Dark Ages over Southeast Asia.

"Amerika" focuses on this same U.S. collapse of will which resulted in slavery for the Vietnamese people.

The series subtly asks how a free people can allow their freedom to be taken away without a fight.

**That's excellent food for thought, especially for young people often subjected to leftist propaganda in our high schools and colleges.**

We must ask again: Will a free America fall in the real world, as "Amerika" suggests, because complacent men and women have grown tired of defending anything?

We hope not, but we wonder.

## The State
*Columbia, SC, February 18, 1987*

THE RECENT moderation of some heavy-handed Soviet domestic policies and the "new look" of Mikhail Gorbachev were unthinkable two years ago. Today the prospects for the future under his leadership are intriguing.

The general secretary, however, wants Soviet citizens and the world to know that they should not expect socialism to be abandoned or that the government will be like that of any other country.

What he wants, he says, is "Soviet-style" democracy with one-party elections — but a more efficient, creative Communist state. The changes have nothing to do with criticism from Western nations of the Kremlin's human and civil rights policies, he declared.

Speaking Monday to an international peace forum in Moscow, he asserted that "our new approach to the humanitarian problems is there for all to see. And I must disappoint those who think that this has been the result of pressure on us from the West, that we want to gain somebody's fancy in pursuit of some ulterior motives. No, we do not."

Early in his new role as leader of the superpower, Mr. Gorbachev pleasantly surprised Europeans by traveling to their capitals with his wife and pulling off Western-style public relations coups. Clearly, he was not like the previous hulking, ponderous Soviet leaders we've come to expect.

He enjoyed another P.R. triumph recently when a group of former U.S. government officials, including President Reagan's ex-Ambassador to the United Nations, Jeane Kirkpatrick, talked with him for three hours in Moscow. They came away from that audience impressed with him, and several are now saying the United States should deal more seriously with him.

Mrs. Kirkpatrick wrote an article saying Mr. Gorbachev's view of the United States was distorted by stereotypes and "it would be useful if Mikhail Gorbachev knew us better." She might have said the same of an American official whose rhetoric labels the Soviet Union an "evil empire."

The appearance of changes under Mr. Gorbachev's regime is impressive, although Kremlin watchers advise care in appraising them. Nevertheless, dozens of dissidents have been freed, among them Nobel prize winner Andrei Sakharov who has been allowed unusual freedom to criticize Soviet policies on human rights. He was put in internal exile for years for doing that.

A Russian-made film which is critical of Josef Stalin's purges has been released for public viewing. Artists, writers and actors are getting a taste of freedom for the first time in 20 years. The Kremlin has announced more humane emigration rules, although Western observers say there's only a slight increase in the numbers leaving.

The Soviet press is reporting more national "news," notably disasters such as the Chernobyl reactor melt-down and a passenger ship's sinking. Soviet authorities are now holding news briefings for foreign newsmen, and American talk-show host Donahue has been doing his thing with Soviet audiences.

But there are contradictions in this trend to openness. Soviet security men broke up a peaceful demonstration in a Moscow mall on behalf of a Jewish activist named Josef Begun. American newsmen were roughed up as uniformed police looked the other way, and a woman demonstrator was knocked to the pavement and kicked in the stomach while passersby watched.

Perhaps we should regard the treatment of Sakharov as the litmus test of Mr. Gorbachev's actions to "democratize" the country. The internationally famous scientist and human rights activists spoke at the same forum in Moscow, declaring that "an open and democratic" Soviet Union would be an important step toward international trust and disarmament. He would have been thrown into a psychiatric hospital for that two years ago.

## Roanoke Times & World-News
*Roanoke, VA, February 18, 1987*

MIKHAIL GORBACHEV is going to put a lot of Kremlinologists out of work. For years, experts on Soviet politics have been scanning entrails and coming up with the sage revelation that the U.S.S.R. needs a period of quiet on the global scene so it can work on domestic problems. Now the Soviet party leader comes right out and frankly says so.

"Before my people, before you and before the world," Gorbachev declared in a televised speech Monday, "I state with full responsibility that our international policy is more than ever determined by domestic policy, by our interest in concentrating on constructive endeavors to improve our country.

"That is why we need lasting peace, predictability and constructiveness in international relations."

The Communist Party's general secretary was speaking to an international forum on peace and disarmament, so one could expect words about the need for lasting peace. On similar occasions, his predecessors have said similar things. The cynics could note that when a Soviet leader says his country wants peace, he's also saying that it wants the world: In Russian, the words happen to be the same.

Still, it is refreshing to hear from Gorbachev an implicit admission that his country needs a breather from international friction and conflict; that all is not peachy-keen with the New Soviet Man as he labors daily to build communism. It is one more bit of evidence that Gorbachev is what he seems to be: a reformer, a man who wants to let some light and air into the moribund Soviet system, who is ready to ease some of the repressive controls that bind the human spirit in that great land.

Those bits of evidence add up to a fairly impressive whole. Gorbachev is the first Soviet leader since the 1917 revolution who is not, in some way, a child of those times. He is less bound by ideology, less paranoid about the outside world, less fearful of technological and other change. When he took the Soviet helm nearly two years ago, it would have been easiest for him to hold the ponderous, barnacle-encrusted ship on its same course, keeping its crew of apparatchiks content with their usual perks and blandishments.

Instead, Gorbachev has rocked the boat alarming many of the people with whom he must work in governing the U.S.S.R. He has tried to remove deadwood from the party's Central Committee, to decentralize control, to relax some of the rigidities that prevent change and growth in the economy. He is not, of course, out to junk the entire system — he is still a communist, and the Soviet Union is not turning into a democracy. But he has freed many political prisoners and eased other oppressions, recognizing that innovation and progress demand more freedom of the mind.

Of course, some of this change is meant to court good opinion elsewhere. How should the West react? There are those — Ronald Reagan may still be among them — who believe that the only good Russia is a weak and beleaguered Russia; that the bear should be run until it drops by forcing an all-out race in armament and technology. Others see that as a dangerous course; they would suggest that the United States, for one, is itself starting to pant a bit from the weight of its own budgetary and trade deficits.

There is also a misperception that the Kremlin is happiest when it can fish in troubled waters. There are definite limits to the amount of trouble the Soviets want to stir up. It is not mere propaganda for Gorbachev to say that his country needs predictability. Every great power wants that; the more it has at stake, the more important does stability become.

Every great power will also pursue its own interests first. Whoever is its leader, count on the Soviet Union to do that. But it is also very much in the West's interest to work toward broader arms-control agreements, to welcome and encourage change and openness in the U.S.S.R., and to cooperate — through trade, technology and the like — in that country's economic development.

Especially where technology and the fruits of economic growth can reach the common people. The better informed, the more capable and the more comfortable ordinary Soviets become, the less malleable will they be to their masters' orders, and the less willing to support any form of adventurism abroad.

## THE SAGINAW NEWS
*Saginaw, MI, February 25, 1987*

Poor "Amerika." Nobody loved it and a lot of people left it.

This was the television series with a minimum guaranteed audience — everyone who just "knew" what it ought to say, or was going to say.

As this fictional world turned out, not often did those preconceived notions coincide with the vision of Donald Wrye, who did the actual writing and directing. What he had in mind, said Wrye, was an exploration of how Americans might react to losing their freedoms under foreign domination. Russia? Well, as it was pointed out on the "Viewpoint" post-mortem, would anyone have believed Bermuda?

It is also a little hard to believe Wrye and the ABC network could not have predicted that the show would be viewed through glasses colored in tones of individual political beliefs. For different reasons, that audience would have been satisfied only if "Amerika" had indulged in 14½ hours of Russian-bashing.

Then the left, which seems to forgive any Soviet transgression, including the original alliance with Hitler, on the grounds of "peace," could say, see, we told you so. The other side could, conversely, cheer a portrayal of Soviet monstrosity.

Well, Wrye had other literary ambitions. "Amerika" began in lethargy and concluded in ambiguity, with a whimper, not a bang-up victory for liberty or, alternatively, brutal crushing of it. The show people were looking for, said network chief Brandon Stoddard, is "another show."

Maybe America needs a sequel. "Amerika" got lost in rhetoric — sometimes its own, but mostly that of people who refuse to respect an artist's intentions.

## The Hutchinson News
*Hutchinson, KS, February 17, 1987*

Not to worry, komrades. "Amerika" won't get them aroused.

Those Amerikanskes could be more of a threat to international kommunism if they really got serious about demokracy. They've been getting lazy about demokracy lately.

As kommunists know, demokracy works only when the people make it work, and will fail when the people don't bother to get informed, get involved and get with it.

So relax, komrades. The Amerikanskes won't get any revolutionary message from "Amerika." It's so boring the only message those Amerikanskes are going to get watching "Amerika" is from their bladders.

## THE CHRISTIAN SCIENCE MONITOR
*Boston, MA, February 18, 1987*

WHAT is real? In the United States we are asked to look at a television series, "Amerika," and imagine that Americans have handed over to fictitious Russians the democratic freedoms that Americans fought a revolution, a civil war, numerous civil rights wars, and continuous other legal and personal battles to ensure. As if to mock the fiction, the Miss America pageant goes on amid a controversy over whether contestants should parade in real furs or fake.

Meanwhile, in Moscow with a "c," Mikhail Gorbachev stages a "peace pageant" of his own, to which Gregory Peck and Kris Kristofferson were invited. We are finding it hard to discern whether dissident Iosif Begun has been released or is still detained – much as outsiders are straining to perceive whether the release of 140 other detainees, the publishing of long-banned books, and other signs of "freedom" within the Soviet Union are real or imagined.

In Washington, again, the latest reports in the Iran scandal are of a dark side to Project Democracy, the undertaking President Reagan announced in London during his first European tour in 1982. Project Democracy was advertised as a kind of free-enterprise foreign policy effort, with older democracies supposedly leading the way in by fostering free institutions like the press, political parties, and universities. Billionaires were invited to support it. Unfortunately, the undertaking apparently soon acquired a secret side – a covert network of communications, emissaries, arms suppliers, and transportation facilities, under the direction of the National Security Council's former employee Oliver North. Such an operation, designed to circumvent the established foreign policy apparatus with its legislative and judicial review, mocks the true meaning of democracy. What fantasy land must officials and their colleagues inhabit when they determine that a democracy's tasks are too urgent to be decided openly and left to the elected representatives of the people?

Another irony: Today marks the 40th anniversary of the first Voice of America broadcast to the Soviet Union. The Voice seems like an almost quaint institution, now that television satellites bring Moscow and Washington spokesmen together for instant discussion or confrontation. Yet the Voice has played a long and useful role in reporting on world affairs. The daily Voice dispatches, heard by millions of Soviet citizens, help build a foundation for democratic freedom there by broadcasting an independent view of world affairs.

Times change. Mr. Gorbachev can see that the Soviet Union needs to release some of the creativity of the Soviet intelligentsia, its scientists and managers, if his state is ever to meet its economic and cultural goals. With every inch of freedom comes the risk of greater expectations, which if not realized can lead to bitterness and dissent. Given the strains within the Soviet system and the history of repeated repressions, the West should be cautious in expecting either too much or too little of Gorbachev's *glasnost*. When he contends that peace with the West is requisite for his freedom experiment to succeed, he is probably right. He may be about to give up on the Reagan administration, which wants to reinterpret the ABM Treaty to permit "star wars" deployment.

In Washington, the Reagan administration's credibility comes under daily review. Does it mean what it says about democratic idealism, or is it secretly and willfully pursuing a separate agenda?

Freedom is a process that West and East cannot afford to trivialize.

## Richmond Times-Dispatch
*Richmond, VA, March 5, 1987*

Liberal critics of ABC's "Amerika" have indignantly denounced the miniseries, charging, among other things, that it would poison relations between the two superpowers and give viewers a bad impression of the Soviet Union. It turns that out they had nothing to worry about. Americans, it seems, already had a bad impression of the Soviet Union, and "Amerika" did little to change it.

According to a George Washington University poll of 1,110 adults before and after last month's showing of "Amerika:"

• An "overwhelming majority" of those surveyed believed there would be mass executions, concentration camps and less freedom of speech if the Soviets took over.

• Sixty-three percent said they believed the Soviets would like to take over the United States.

• Before "Amerika" aired, 69 percent said they would rather be dead than red. After it aired, the figure was 72 percent.

• Forty-five percent of those surveyed believe that the grim portrayal of life in "Amerika" is an accurate depiction of what life would be like under Soviet occupation. Another 25 percent said it would be even worse.

Maybe the real problem here is not a TV program. Maybe, just maybe, it's the Soviets themselves.

## The Charlotte Observer
*Charlotte, NC, March 1, 1987*

The congressional hearings on nuclear testing were open and the answers from administration officials perfectly public — until the official transcripts appeared with gaping deletions, edited questions and, in one case, an altered answer.

The censoring was presumably done to keep the Russians from taking over. But such Orwellian rewriting of the public record is enough to make us wonder if perhaps they already have.

## THE INDIANAPOLIS STAR
*Indianapolis, IN, February 25, 1987*

Most Americans by far would rather fight an all-out nuclear war than live under communist rule, according to a national survey directed by Professor William Adams of George Washington University. The survey was taken before the showing of the ABC-TV miniseries, *Amerika*, which dramatized a Kremlin-directed occupation of the country.

Of 1,110 adults polled, 72 percent said they would prefer to fight a nuclear war; 19 percent said they would rather be Red than dead.

"Almost two-thirds believe that the Soviet Union would like to take over the United States — although 85 percent believe this is not likely to happen," Adams said.

Most Americans have realistic ideas about what happens when the communists take over. They should. Hundreds of thousands of Americans came here when communists took over their countries — Russia, Latvia, Lithuania, Estonia, Poland, East Germany, Hungary, Bulgaria, Yugoslavia, Romania, Albania, Czechoslovakia, China, Cuba, Vietnam.

Millions have read *I Chose Freedom, Doctor Zhivago, Out of the Ice, The Gulag Archipelago* and hundreds of other books giving first-hand accounts of life under communism.

Americans are the best-informed people in the world. Their knowledge is one of the benefits of their freedom. They know it.

## THE RICHMOND NEWS LEADER
*Richmond, VA, March 11, 1987*

"Amerika." Everything about it stirred controversy. The Left saw red; many on the Right saw pink (the game was given away when a Soviet overlord said reflexive anti-Communism helped do America in).

The film jostled the memory. A similar theme was explored by Oliver Lange in his novel *Vandenberg*. An artist and iconoclastic rebel, Gene Vandenberg fights back against the Soviet oppressors, and is destroyed by them.

He rails against the "post-invasion spirit of co-operation that infected the country." And he fights.

About the evolution of American character under Soviet domination, he says: "Supplied with the perquisites of material symbolism (it was, perhaps, the first time a subjugated country was permitted to retain nearly all the hedonistic bric-a-brac that contributed to its downfall), who, after all, cared to tackle the messy problem of self-determination, a philsophical Gordian knot [Americans] were not equipped to unravel?"

And Vandenberg's version of Amerika was published in 1971.

"Remember, son... this series about a foreign takeover is purely fictional..."

## TV Talk Shows Raise Debate

Reality-based talk shows, particularly prevalent in first-run syndication, brought adult topicality to the weekday adult audiences in 1980s. Sometimes poignantly but more often in an exploitative and tawdry manner, long-standing taboos against sexual frankness were broken on *The Oprah Winfrey Show*, *The Morton Downey Show*, *Donahue* and *Geraldo*. TV with the gossipy values of supermarket tabloids appeared in *A Current Affair* on the Fox Network and on the syndicated shows *Inside Edition* and *Entertainment Tonight*.

In a related format, the role of television as promoter of constructive public debate also gave way to the hyperbole and bombast of show business. Adopting a shrill rhetorical style, men with distinguished records in public service and journalism verbally lashed at one another.

Some of the more infamous incidents involving these programs or their hosts included:

■ TV talk-show host Geraldo Rivera had his nose broken Nov. 3, 1988 in a fracas that erupted during the taping of a show on "teen hatemongers." Punches began to fly after White Aryan Resistance Youth member John Metzger called Roy Innis, chairman of the Congress of Racial Equality, an Uncle Tom. Innes grabbed Metzger in a choke hold, other panelists and audience members joined in, chairs were thrown, and the host found himself with a broken and bloody nose.

■ Controversial television host Morton Downey Jr. claimed that he was attacked April 24, 1989 by a group of neo-Nazi youths in a restroom at the San Francisco airport. Downey said the youths had beaten him up, cut his hair and drawn swastikas on his face and clothes. Airport police said April 25, however, that the attack had not occurred the way Downey said it did. They noted that witnesses had not seen any confrontation and that there was no evidence that a fight had taken place in the restroom.

■ Television talk show host Oprah Winfrey drew protests from Jewish groups following the May 1, 1989 broadcast of a show in which a woman claimed that she had taken part in the ritual Jewish sacrifice of babies. The anonymous woman, who appeared on an "Oprah Winfrey Show" devoted to cult murders that had recently been discovered in Matamoros, Mexico, was identified on the show as someone who was undergoing long-term psychiatric treatment for multiple personality disorders. She claimed that when she was young, she had been forced to participate in ritual infant sacrifice and that "there's other Jewish families across the country [engaged in the same practice]. It's not just my family." Jewish groups criticized the show's use of the mentally ill woman saying her remarks could reinforce anti-Semitic stereotypes. They also complained that Winfrey did not do enough to challenge her statements.

### The Augusta Chronicle
*Augusta, GA, August 26, 1988*

Regardless of what you might hear on TV's "Donahue" show, men — at least married men — are contributing more and more to their wives' happiness. Or at least it seems that way, thanks to a recent Gallup poll. Why? Because its results point clearly to married women being much more satisfied with their lives than unmarried women.

Sadly, money was right up there (along with marriage and part-time employment) as one of the three most common factors in the satisfaction equation. But that's just human nature. A man would probably like his spouse to be well paid while he holds down a part-time job.

By the way, of those with children, 46 percent said they were very satisfied with their lives. Of those with no children, only slightly fewer, 39 percent took that choice.

It's doubtful, but perhaps a well-known cigarette ad will seize on the latest poll findings to change its slogan, which lauds the emancipation of women (we want cancer too!) at the expense of lampooning stuffy, chauvinistic Victorian males.

The ad writers could switch the slogan to something more modern, say "I can't get no — Sa-tis-fac-tion."

In the meantime, you've come a long way buddy.

### Omaha World-Herald
*Omaha, NE, August 31, 1988*

Television practices are partly to blame for the fact that two former Omaha actors slipped onto three talk shows and played fictitious characters, apparently without the producers and hosts realizing what was happening. The push for more salacious and bizarre topics for talk-show treatment has reached the point where producers aren't screening their guests closely enough.

There was a time, not too many years ago, when television interview programs consisted of lively, literate discussions with hosts such as Edward R. Murrow, Steve Allen and Dave Garroway. Now the airwaves are crowded with the likes of Phil Donahue, Geraldo Rivera, Oprah Winfrey, Morton Downey Jr. and Sally Jessy Raphael, whose programs lean to the sensationalistic, the shocking and often the sexually oriented to attract audiences.

In their search for ever more bizarre topics, the new daytime, syndicated talk show producers ran the risk of setting themselves up for deception. The two actors went on the Rivera, Raphael and Winfrey shows playing the parts, variously, of a sex therapist and people with sexual problems. The routine differed from show to show but was essentially a variation of the kind of material the new talk shows thrive on.

A former Nebraskan and a distinguished Lutheran theologian, Martin E. Marty of the University of Chicago, recently pointed out that normal, everyday religious life is almost never reflected in American movies, but that a sensationalized, distorted version of American religious life often is.

Much the same could be said of the syndicated talk show approach to sex. Relatively normal Americans, discussing the routine problems of marriage and child-raising, are rarely seen. Instead, there is a steady procession of sexually abused, sexually bizarre, transvestite, sex-changed or otherwise unusual guests who never seem too embarrassed to discuss their situation with Geraldo or Sally in front of an audience.

This time, the push for ever more peculiar topics and guests apparently has backfired. More balance and caution in selecting guests and topics might have prevented the bright red faces in the television industry.

# The Houston Post
*Houston, TX, November 11, 1988*

It's tempting to say that controversial television host Geraldo Rivera got what he deserved when his nose was broken during a mini-riot that erupted on the set where he was taping a program entitled "Teen Hatemongers."

The skirmish began when black activist Roy Innis put a stranglehold on a member of the White Aryan Resistance Youth who had hurled a racial slur at Innis. The audience joined in, folding chairs and fists flying.

Sadly, anything goes on American television these days, as long as it draws an audience. Television's self-hype that followed Rivera's clubbing assured a large viewership for the program.

Rivera and his ilk, which includes Morton Downey Jr. and Maury Povich, have struck a disconsonant note that has a macabre appeal to the American public. A public that finds it difficult to make sense of the world as it flies by turns toward things that it understands — confrontation, sensationalism, violence and hate. Rivera's recent program on devil worship, described as "dirty-minded teleporn" by the Washington Post, was the highest rated two-hour documentary in history.

That's a bit of social commentary that speaks poorly of the American public.

# TULSA WORLD
*Tulsa, OK, September 5, 1988*

PARDON us a small, smug chuckle over the flap that currently consumes the TV talk show circuit.

It seems that an actress and actor from Chicago, using different names, disguises and stories, appeared on the syndicated shows hosted by Geraldo Rivera, Sally Jessy Raphael and Oprah Winfrey to talk about S-E-X.

She claimed to be either a "sex surrogate" or a sex-hating housewife. He pretended to be either a sex surrogate's client or an adult virgin.

The victim-hosts were outraged; "spitting mad" in Rivera's words. He complained that the hoax compromised his show's integrity. He threatened to "go after" the actors in court. This from the man who brought you Al Capone's vault and other glowing moments in TV journalism.

Ms. Raphael administered the ultimate TV punishment — she invited one of the perpetrators back on her show and unloaded on her before the studio audience.

Really, what's the beef? Geraldo and the others, communications-age carneys who garb themselves in sociological newspeak, got their money's worth and more. The guest-hoaxers were paid to titillate viewers with tales of offbeat sexual activities. They told their stories and the viewers got titillated.

Does it matter that their stories were as phony as Al Capone's closet?

# Houston Chronicle
*Houston, TX, November 6, 1988*

Physical violence directed by one person against another is in most settings, including television studios, lamentable. But Geraldo Rivera seems to have been asking for a punch in the nose for a long time. Something similar finally happened during the fiming of his program, modestly called *Geraldo*.

The on-camera ruckus involved a black civil rights leader and white supremacists. It was an example of how sensational, confrontational television journalism brings out the worst in people, especially people like white supremacists who aren't too stable anyway. It drives away sponsors, too, but, alas, not viewers. Rivera's recent program on satanic religions was a ratings success.

We're sorry Rivera's nose was broken, almost as sorry as we are that he still appears all too frequently on television.

# The Burlington Free Press
*Burlington, VT, August 21, 1988*

The rich and famous aren't the only ones exposing themselves these days.

The proliferation of kiss-and-tell books, gossip magazines and confessional television programs like "Donahue," "Geraldo," and "The Oprah Winfrey Show" is part of a disturbing trend in American society.

Americans are routinely revealing to acquaintances, colleagues and strangers what were once considered intimate, private parts of their lives to be shared with spouses, family members, close friends and therapists only.

Letting it all hang out has become a virtue, and the more said, the better.

"Somewhere down the line the whole gospel of confession got perverted," argues the author of the book "Psycho-babble." Richard Rosen says, "People began believing that expressing a problem was tantamount to curing it. Now they can't stop talking."

Talk of relationships is like talk of the weather. It is now considered a neutral topic of conversation suitable for strangers.

Few are surprised when someone sitting next to them on a short flight plunges into details of his wife's affair, their subsequent divorce, and his new husband-in-law (i.e., ex-wife's spouse). Conversations like this routinely take place between individuals who part without ever finding out one another's name.

Given what's being discussed daily before millions on "Donahue," "Oprah," and "Geraldo," what's the surprise?

Nudists, adulterers and anorexics have become passe on the talk show circuit.

Today nymphomaniacs, self-mutilators, multiple-personalities, the occasional menage a trois ("Look at them. She's married to one, and she's holding hands with the other," an insightful Geraldo remarks), suicide attempters and women who stay loyal to men who commit sex crimes are all too ready to spill their guts.

Gays talk about how they conceived children with lesbian friends. Women discuss having affairs with the husbands of their best friends (caption for the television audience: "Man stealer"). Others explain why they are suing former lovers who gave them sexually transmitted diseases.

The proclivity for self-exposure should not be dismissed as a low-brow preoccupation.

The "About Men" column in the Sunday New York Times is starkly revealing. "Why I go for women half my age" is a popular theme here. In a Times column several weeks ago one man explicitly described how he and his partner decided to have a child (right down to what contraceptive they gave up and when), and how she subsequently decided singlehandedly to have an abortion.

The paradox of all this is that Americans are both fiercely private and fiercely public people.

A colleague will not hestitate to ask, "How's your relationship going?" Yet rarely will you hear, even between friends of longstanding, "So, how much do you make?"

Salaries and age, the grist of conversation in many other cultures, remain verboten in the United States.

Americans are also very private about their homes. The man who will lament his child's drug addiction or his own marital problems for anyone willing to listen is completely taken aback if a close friend drops in without calling first.

All this public confessing may breed tolerance of different lifestyles. However, it also helps to trivialize or sensationalize problems and to cheapen what was once considered precious and private.

# The Kansas City Times

*Kansas City, MO, November 5, 1988*

Roy Innis is so predictable. That is probably why he is a favorite guest on schlock talk shows. He's good for a ratings share.

Innis, national chairman of the Congress of Racial Equality, should wear boxing gloves if he continues to appear on sensational programs hosted by people like Mort Downey Jr. and Geraldo Rivera. The civil rights activist has brawled on each man's show.

On Downey's show it was Innis vs. the Rev. Al Sharpton, the civil rights activist of Tawana Brawley infamy. Sharpton insulted Innis, so Innis shoved him out of his chair. Ironically, the black men were debating black American leadership.

On Rivera's program, it was Innis vs. the white supremacist Skinheads and White Aryan Resistance Youth. Innis allowed himself Thursday to be lured into violence by the name-calling of these people at a studio taping of Rivera's program.

Is it any wonder this man with the gift of jab insisted in 1983 that heavyweight champion Larry Holmes had a "sacred mission" to fight Gerrie Coetzee, the white South African boxer?

The civil rights movement in the tradition of the late Rev. Martin Luther King Jr. is non-violent. Many times was Dr. King insulted, assaulted and threatened. Yet he retained his dignity. And in so doing, he revealed the true identity of the bigot as an ignorant coward lacking maturity and whose only pleasure is to encourage separatism through violent means.

Had Dr. King succumbed to the taunts of white racists, he would not have become the great leader who is remembered today. His was a greater purpose. Does Innis think the Rev. Jesse Jackson has not been called names? Innis, for that matter, has been insulted by other black civil rights activists. Did he think the white racists were going to call him Mister?

No civil rights group should be led by someone with such a hair-trigger. And no decent television format should deliberately enlist characters who guarantee this sort of performance.

# The Seattle Times

*Seattle, WA, November 17, 1988*

PREDICTION: Before the end of the year, NBC News anchor Tom Brokaw will pop commentator John Chancellor in the nose.

On local TV, KIRO point-counterpointers John Carlson and Walt Crowley will be counterpunching while chained together inside a boxing ring.

Television programming lives and dies by the ratings, and soft-porn journalist Geraldo Rivera has proven in a video prelim that violence pays off with big numbers.

One of his docu-voyeur theme shows, "Young Hatemongers," erupted into a chair-tossing melee in which Rivera's nose was broken.

By the time the program tape actually aired, the nation was primed to put that episode of "Geraldo" into talk-show ratings history.

Naturally, any responsible television person deplores this debasement of Edward R. Murrow's noble medium. They all want to revive "Omnibus" and concentrate on high-quality broadcasting. But, hey, the schmuck couch potatoes want only this sleazy stuff. And, well, don't forget about advertisers.

If fistfights bring in the viewers, then expect a hearty serving of knuckle sandwiches. Who knows where this ugliness will lead? Someday, don't be surprised if Oscar the Grouch sucker-punches Mr. Rogers.

**Geraldo Rivera** — Taylor Jones

---

*Seattle, WA, August 31, 1988*

IN NOVEMBER 1986, Tani Freiwald told Oprah Winfrey's national television audience she hated sex. She now says that was a lie, she was faking it.

So was Wes Bailey. He told Geraldo Rivera he was a 35-year-old virgin, and later confessed to Sally Jessy Raphael he was an impotent husband. On that show Tani pretended to be his sexual surrogate. That is someone who, when asked to help a person with a sex problem, reclines to do so.

Turns out that Tani and Wes have the same normal, boring sex lives as everybody else. Indeed, they are part-time actors recruited by a psychologist, whose real patients and surrogates were not sufficiently telegenic or chatty.

This whole tawdry episode has made Geraldo feel cheap and dirty. He says he is really upset. Lawyers may get involved.

It's no wonder. Geraldo says the very integrity of the television talk-show industry is at stake.

Absolutely. Suppose Geraldo is hosting a typical show: A glimpse inside a support group for nude skydivers with a proclivity toward aerial congress with barnyard animals. Geraldo masterfully referees a raucous studio debate between educators, counselors, aviation authorities and book publicists.

What if no one took any of this electronic intercourse seriously? That's right; Geraldo would be back scratching for the secrets of Al Capone's vault, and "Wheel of Fortune" would be shown three times a day.

If sexual impudence isn't put back in the closet, no topic will be safe from mockery on afternoon television.

Strike now while the irony is hot.

[Cartoon: TV showing caricature of Morton Downey Jr., with speech bubble: "OBNOXIOUS TALK SHOW HOSTS WHO EXPLOIT THE TRAGIC AND BIZARRE FOR GOOD RATINGS...AND LIVE TO TELL ABOUT IT!... ON THE NEXT "GERALDO". — Rogers ©1988 The Pittsburgh Press, United Feature Syndicate]

# TULSA WORLD
### Tulsa, OK, May 5, 1989

THE giants of trash TV are circling the wagons.

Morton Downey Jr.'s "credibility" (if the use of that word in the context isn't ludicrous) is falling. Police, and apparently most everyone else, doubt his story that Nazi skinhead punks attacked him in a restroom at the San Francisco airport, cut off locks of his hair and drew a swastika on his face with Magic Marker.

Downey, who's gained a measure of notoriety as the uncivil, foulmouthed host of a syndicated talk show, reportedly is in trouble even with some advertisers and TV station operators who believe his tale was nothing more than a ratings-boosting ploy.

Now comes Phil Donahue, dean of the trash TV school, who says, on a show broadcast this week in Tulsa, that he believes Downey's tale. Donahue says he doesn't want to see Downey's show leave the air. "We'd have to find someone else," Donahue says. "He not only keeps us honest, he keeps us more aggressive."

If Donahue and the other trash TV folks need Downey it is only because their shows seem less putrid by comparison. Downey's show treats the most emotional issues in the basest possible way. His guests, who represent extreme positions, scream at each other, fangs bared. Sometimes they even push and shove one another.

The show provides absolutely nothing in the way of useful or enlightening discussion. Its appeal is on the lowest emotional and intellectual levels.

Notwithstanding Donahue's fawning support, if Downey's show disappeared tomorrow the world would be a better place.

# The Houston Post
### Houston, TX, July 22, 1989

AT A TIME WHEN television is under fire for crudeness and violence, it's refreshing to see Morton Downey Jr. put to pasture.

Discussion is one thing, and intelligent discussion can even be dull at times, but Downey's gift for insults, abrasiveness, incitement to riot and other forms of mayhem hardly become the medium, to which he added a new and ugly dimension.

The show has been canceled — for good, we hope. Downey may be as smart as they come, but he injected something quite the opposite into public broadcasting — a substandard that might be called "UQ," or short for Unintelligence Quotient.

## The Hutchinson News
*Hutchinson, KS, June 19, 1989*

There must be limits, after all, to TV moguls' affection for trash.

Morton Downey Jr., has admitted publicly in New York that his nationally syndicated TV talk show is getting flushed.

"It's my guess that it'll be all over in September," Downey told the New York Daily News in Friday's editions.

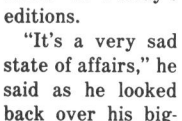

"It's a very sad state of affairs," he said as he looked back over his big-mouth show that appears to viewers to have been arranged to out-trash all the trash on otherwise abundantly trashy TV.

His latest broadcast type hype for his ailing show came two months ago when he claimed that he was attacked by a bunch of neo-Nazis in San Francisco.

The well-publicized (naturally) episode was politely called a stunt by those who routinely expect such things from radio or TV hucksters.

"I feel bad that this will mean the end of this type of talk show," Downey said. "No one will take a chance on it anymore."

Not to fear.

Given the track record of trash TV and trash radio, even if he gets the treatment he expects and deserves, the ghost of Morton Downey will surely survive and inspire future broadcast loudmouths.

## The Charlotte Observer
*Charlotte, NC, March 12, 1989*

First, let's make some distinctions. Perhaps there are, across the Carolinas, a few demented misfits who worship Satan, with obscene rituals and blood-drinking and a lust for evil that would make even Geraldo Rivera tremble. Rumors of such activity abound. There's no indication, however, that Satanic cults are more than a disturbing oddity here. There is reason for vigilance, but not for alarm.

There also is a lot of youthful rebellion going around, a hormone-induced tendency to push against barriers. As surely as young birds will try their wings, young humans will try their elders' patience. In an area where religion is a strong force, some of that youthful rebellion will naturally be directed against religion. In its mildest form that involves cutting Sunday school; in a more radical form it may involve tinkering with symbols of Satanism. There's one reassuring thing about that sort of rebellion. It has a natural duration: Kids grow up.

The most dangerous Devil worshipers here and elsewhere don't wear "I ♥ Satan" T-shirts. The really dangerous ones are those who look like everyday, honest folks but in fact are eager to subvert morality and trample their neighbors in pursuit of those treasures with which Satan buys souls: power, money, fame.

Weirdos who blaspheme and drink animal blood are scary, all right, but they are merely Satan's way of showing off. The real menace is the multitude of ordinary folks who do Satan's work without calling his name or wearing his uniform.

## SYRACUSE HERALD-JOURNAL
*Syracuse, NY, July 24, 1989*

When Morton Downey Jr. burst upon the national scene some 15 months ago, his instant popularity worried some people. The TV talk-show host specialized in vulgarity and personal abuse. He pandered to Americans' basest instincts as he bullied his guests and promoted simplistic approaches to complex social problems.

What was in store for America, critics wondered, if this anti-intellectual trend were to continue?

Well, Downey is on his way out and America is still here. He was a very hot match that burned brightly for a short time, but he is flickering out as quickly as he flared. His program has been canceled for lack of ratings and advertiser support.

Good riddance. Screaming and blowing smoke in people's faces is an act that grows old in a hurry. Some folks who initially were fascinated by Downey have wised up. The ones who thought he was profound have short attention spans in any case.

Chalk one up for intellect — and for Americans' good taste.

## The Hartford Courant
*Hartford, CT, July 23, 1989*

It probably does not represent the beginning of the end of all trash TV, but it is a good start — "The Morton Downey Jr. Show" has been canceled.

Mr. Downey is the host who shouts down guests and sets them against each other, as well as against pit bull audiences. The shame of his program is that it found enough of an audience to get on the air and that for a time Mr. Downey was celebrated as being famous for being famous. As obnoxious as his performance was, it was more obnoxious that his attempt to find and exploit ignorance and bigotry was considered credible when the ratings were high.

The good news is that the market took care of him. Ratings and advertising fell. Hate sells, but only for a time. Other trash jockies should bear this in mind. Morton Downey Jr. is unlikely to turn up on the "Hollywood Squares."

Talk is an odd form of entertainment, and the idea of conversation as show business may say something about the superficiality of much contemporary human interaction. It may also be an indicator of loneliness. Certainly the radio talk shows capitalize on loneliness in America.

Yet in the hands of an interviewer such as Bill Moyers, talk is not at all cheap. It can be enlightening as well as entertaining.

It is good to know that we don't find hateful talk so entertaining. Morton Downey Jr. is nearing the end of his treadmill to oblivion, and gentle interlocutors like Dinah Shore and Dick Cavett are making comebacks.

## THE CHRISTIAN SCIENCE MONITOR
*Boston, MA, May 1, 1989*

THE rap on television used to be that it was a wasteland. The current charge is that TV is becoming a swampland.

Critics point to such developments as "tabloid" or "trash" TV — "infotainment" programs that treat sensational topics in lurid ways (Geraldo Rivera), and talk shows whose hosts seem bent on infuriating (Morton Downey Jr.), titillating (Phil Donahue), or offending (both hosts) the studio and viewing audiences.

Whether it's to compete with such programming, or simply from a lowering of their own standards of taste and what they perceive to be the public's interests, network executives are also allowing more and more offensive material into the sitcoms and dramatic shows they air, including on prime time.

Various reasons are given for this descent into bad taste. One is that, for budget reasons, the networks have cut back their own standards (i.e., censoring) departments. Another reason is that, in the aftermath of last summer's writers strike, the networks are scrambling to recapture audiences put off by reruns.

Some observers believe that deregulation of the airwaves has furthered the slide to lowest-common-denominator programming.

Whatever the reasons, some viewers, like the star of the movie "Network," are fed up and aren't going to take it anymore. Their ire is aimed at both the networks and, more effectively, corporate advertisers. As a candidate for heroine of the year, we nominate Terry Rakolta. She's a Michigan homemaker and mother who, unaffiliated with any organized protest group, shamed several major sponsors into pulling their support of the Fox Broadcasting series "Married . . . With Children," which traffics in sexual innuendo.

In response to letters from other angry viewers, such major sponsors as Coca-Cola, McDonald's, Chrysler, General Mills, and Sears have also cancelled commercials.

Such protests don't violate the First Amendment, as some media defenders imply. The Constitution protects the media from government intrusion, not public indignation. Television, advertising, and corporate execs who live by the market must be prepared to perish by the market.

Messrs. Downey, Rivera, Donahue, and other purveyors of trash TV say their detractors are "elitists" and that they are just "democratizing" the medium.

Well, to use their term (which we don't buy), count us with the "elitists." Of course, the protesters aren't truly elitists at all. They are simply typical men and women ("I'm not a prude," Mrs. Rakolta said), many of them parents, who wish to protect their families and communities from media pollution and who recognize that the empathy, tolerance, and goodwill that make democracy possible are not enhanced by epithets, shouting, sensationalism, and appeals to base emotions.

TV today is neither a wasteland nor a swampland. It offers hours of serious, amusing, and enriching programming. But it also includes some growing toxic dumps whose poisons, in the absence of public alertness, threaten to seep into the cultural ground water.

## The Hutchinson News
*Hutchinson, KS, February 5, 1989*

The unequaled arrogance and venality of television stars could cause an otherwise calm and cool observer to erupt in a rage of noise.

But let's remain calm.

The wife of Geraldo Rivera, purveyor of broadcast nonsense, tells readers of TV Guide that her man slept around, but she's coping with things and old Geraldo has really calmed down in the past few years.

Oprah Winfrey, on the other hand, recently introduced her viewers to her new beau during sweeps week, telling one wire service: "I want people to meet Stedman (her beau) for themselves and get a feel for what our relationship is about."

Such invitations to romantic voyeurism should ignite a chorus of "Who cares?" from the masses, but the mere fact that these TV bozos thrust their private nonsense on their viewers ought not be tolerated.

The fact that the Riveras and Winfreys of TV flail their public with their private moments says a lot more about the people who make them popular than it does about the personalities who sell private matters for public consumption.

## DAYTON DAILY NEWS
*Dayton, OH, July 31, 1989*

Flag burning, yes; but Morton Downey Jr.?

There are those who would make the case that if any form of political expression should be made illegal, it's the form practiced by this fading talk show host: mean, personal, hyperbolic, hyperemotional, televised and way too loud.

For the past 15 months, some local viewers could find this former Dayton disc jockey going toe-to-toe with the likes of the equally obnoxious Rev. Al Sharpton of Tawana Brawley fame on a talk show that started in New York and caught on nationally overnight.

Mr. Downey's product was conflict. He was a master at working an audience — his kind of audience, anyway — into a rabid and violent mood. He would taunt, he would yell, he would spit, and he would occasionally seek refuge behind a studio bodyguard.

His "reality programming" — about as realistic as professional wrestling — eventually started to lose advertiser support, apparently as much because of the host's behavior (on and off screen) as because of ratings. So now he' going.

It seems like only last year that Ted Koppe was hosting a *Nightline* edition that aske whether the likes of Morton Downey Jr. wer going to replace the likes of Ted Koppel. Som guests answered that Mr. Downey was proba bly just a fad. They turned out to be more righ than they probably thought.

Ultimately, provocation for the sake c provocation is boring. Once people knov you're just trying to provoke them, they can' be provoked.

[Cartoon: A TV showing Geraldo Rivera with speech bubble: "OBNOXIOUS TALK SHOW HOSTS WHO EXPLOIT THE TRAGIC AND BIZARRE FOR GOOD RATINGS... AND LIVE TO TELL ABOUT IT!... ON THE NEXT 'GERALDO'." A woman watches from an armchair. Signed Rogers ©1988 The Pittsburgh Press, United Feature Syndicate.]

# THE BLADE

*Toledo, OH, November 2, 1988*

HAS Geraldo Rivera no shame? This would-be newsman whose specialty is a kind of made-for-TV yellow journalism has done it again. This time the issue was satanic cults, a subject guaranteed to horrify and titillate TV viewers — and Mr. Rivera did everything he could to exploit it.

There are reasons, at times, to provide a great deal of blood and graphic accounts of violence on television if an important point is to be made.

But the undiscerning viewer who made the mistake of tuning in the gory and explicit "Devil Worship: Exposing Satan's Underground" might be led to believe that devil-worshipers who commit human sacrifice are all around us. Everyone that Mr. Rivera interviewed seemed to be suggesting that there are far more of these folks around than one would imagine.

The truth is that devil worship does not have wide appeal, and there are devil worshipers around who are not bloodthirsty ghouls. The subject deserves careful handling, even when a visual medium like TV is dealing with it. But a clue as to what Mr. Rivera had in mind was the timing of the program — a week before Halloween. That kind of tie-in suggested that all he was after was sensationalism and high ratings, which he got.

A balanced, cautious treatment, with all opinions being considered, was in order — but that is not what Mr. Rivera supplied. If some people are now panicked, they can thank Mr. Rivera — an entertainer who provided none of the balance needed to put this isolated phenomenon in perspective.

# The Burlington Free Press

*Burlington, VT, May 17, 1986*

Anyone in the public eye has to get used to having his or her privacy invaded; it comes with the territory. Or, as Harry Truman put it, "If you can't stand the heat, stay out of the kitchen."

Whether entertainer, politician, athlete or in any other occupation that attracts media attention, the person is likely to be hounded by autograph seekers and others who want to be close to a celebrity.

Most of the people who write, phone or chase celebrities are decent folks. Some, however, are kooks, so every once in a while there is an incident that causes a celebrity to lose his or her cool. In most cases, there is no undamaged party. If the celebrity displays emotion or hauls off and whacks the offender, the celebrity often is viewed by the public as being mean-spirited. After all, says the public, the celebrity gets paid well so he or she should ignore even the most objectionable person.

Celebrities understand the price they pay for fame; on occasion, however, they do make mistakes. It's happened at least twice recently: first, Reggie Jackson, the future Hall of Fame baseball player, reportedly pounded an obnoxious fan who threw a ripped autograph in Jackson's food while the ballplayer was eating; second, Phil Donahue, the popular talk show host, got into a fight with a protester who shouted that Donahue and his wife, actress Marlo Thomas, "ought to be murdered."

The circumstances in the Jackson incident are sufficiently muddy that it's hard to argue with certainty that Jackson's behavior was justified; that's not the case in the incident involving Donahue.

The kook, a disciple of political extremist Lyndon LaRouche, confronted Donahue and Thomas as they were walking through New York's LaGuardia Airport. Following an exchange of words, a fight ensued.

No doubt Donahue on another occasion would have ignored the heckler; this time Donahue chose not to turn the other cheek. Harry Truman would have understood; he, too, was known to lose his temper on occasion.

## The Providence Journal
*Providence, RI, May 28, 1986*

When last heard from, TV personality Phil Donahue was punching out a follower of Lyndon LaRouche at La Guardia airport. He had been insulted, he said.

Now he's back in the news, with last week's announcement that he is to join Soviet propagandist Vladimir Pozner in a televised "citizens' summit" that will bring 200 women from Boston and 200 women from Leningrad together to discuss issues of common concern. The meeting will be edited to one- and two-hour shows and available for syndication throughout the United States.

Without speculating about what those issues of common concern might be, we would remind readers of an earlier Donahue-Pozner production, broadcast last December, which featured children in Seattle and children in Moscow, joined by satellite, discussing issues of common concern. The Soviet children asked the sort of questions Mr. Pozner tends to ask when he appears on American television to defend Kremlin policies. The American children posed the sort of questions Mr. Donahue likes to pose when he is interrogating State Department officials on his popular morning program. Mr. Pozner told a press conference that the program was watched by Mikhail Gorbachev himself, and "according to information I have, he liked it." We have no doubt that he did.

And he will probably like the second one, too. While the Boston participants may prove unpredictable on camera, it does not take much imagination to guess what the women from Leningrad will say. They were not chosen by lottery; ordinary citizens in the Soviet Union tend to have extraordinarily uniform opinions — in public, anyway. Phil Donahue may put this down to sensibility, but we can think of other reasons.

Yet what would induce Americans to watch such a program? There is one possibility. Vladimir Pozner, who speaks impeccable colloquial English, has a gift for virulent language and broad accusations. Perhaps even Phil Donahue will take umbrage at one of Mr. Pozner's provocative remarks, and repeat his La Guardia airport performance.

It's a long shot, but it could make television history.

## The Boston Herald
*Boston, MA, May 30, 1986*

THERE is freedom of speech in the Soviet Union, insists emigre Russian comedian Yakov Smirnoff. The difference between there and here, he says, is that in America, people have freedom *after* they speak.

Indeed, talk is not cheap in the Soviet Union. Some kinds of talk can be very expensive, say, about 20 years in a Siberian chrome mine. Now talk show host Phil Donohue plans to team up with KGB mouthpiece Vladimir Pozner to exchange a lot of hot air between Boston and Leningrad.

Donohue says the audiences, "will be able to discuss anything they are interested in." That may certainly be true, and we strongly suspect that the Soviet women (carefully selected by the KGB for reliability) will have been well-briefed ahead of time as to what subjects to be "interested" in.

We can see it now. Some American leftist/pacifist/holy roller will earnestly proclaim her desire for peace and her opposition to the U.S. building of a missile defense system. A Russian woman will nod her head understandingly, for she too opposes the U.S. building a missile defense system.

Pozner, of course, is that smooth-talking American-accented Russian who shows up on "Nightline" every now and then. In fact, he grew up in Brooklyn, where the kids in the schoolyard were calling him "a dirty Commie" when he was only 15. They'll get no argument here.

When will people like Donohue realize that it is Pozner's job, not to enlighten us on Soviet intentions, but to sell us their usual bill of goods. Meanwhile, the KGB gets a couple of hours of free propaganda on network television.

## THE SAGINAW NEWS
*Saginaw, MI, May 14, 1986*

What hope is there now for peace? Phil Donahue, rivaled as "Mr. Sensitive" only by Alan Alda, slugged someone at New York's LaGuardia Airport.

Of course, there was some provocation. Police said a follower of Lyndon LaRouche shouted an obscenity and made other threats against Donahue and his wife, feminist actress Marlo Thomas, also known as Ms. "Free to Be You and Me." In this instance, Thomas did not feel free to be macha. Reportedly she "stood by horrified," although recovering quickly enough to cite the incident as another argument for nuclear disarmament.

And so the idols fall. What can be done to help them out here? New York authorities have a nearly ideal solution. Donahue and pronuclear demonstrator William Ferguson agreed to talk it over at the city's Conflict Resolution Center.

Still better, though, would be to put the session on the air. Donahue could then explain, perhaps to Marlo's benefit, under what circumstances it's OK to use violence in your own defense. And it would be appropriate, if somewhat cruel and unusual, treatment for a LaRouchite to be forcibly mellowed out in full view of millions.

## ST. LOUIS POST-DISPATCH
*St. Louis, MO, May 12, 1988*

Twenty-five years ago last week, Newton Minow, the chairman of the Federal Communications Commission, called television "a vast wasteland." Those who believe that it should always be dedicated to stimulation and education would say it still is. They are wrong.

The growth of public television, almost nonexistent in 1961, has greatly increased the availability of serious drama, sophisticated comedy, documentaries and educational programs. The advent of cable has provided yet more diversity; there are now special channels for children, old movies and a host of other special interests. While not everyone is yet able to receive them, that time isn't far off. Even networks offer more news and have made some strides in children's programs compared to 1961.

Thus television has improved. But prime-time network entertainment hasn't changed much; it is still marked primarily by low comedy and crime shows filled with sex and violence that are often badly done. But does this make television a wasteland?

Audience research indicates many seek relaxation and entertainment, not stimulation. A medium that can offer either one, but rarely the two together because of the exceptional talent required to combine them continuously in the volume the schedule demands, can legitimately opt for entertainment if the audience wants it.

To term television a wasteland because it doesn't dedicate itself solely to stimulation as opposed to entertainment is a failure to understand limits of artistic production. It is also the worst kind of snobbery.

## The Burlington Free Press
*Burlington, VT, November 11, 1988*

Being nasty and rude, and winning — or at least getting even — at all costs are no longer taboo. In fact, such traits are downright chichi these days.

The evidence is overwhelming that we are becoming a less civil society.

The negative campaigning and mudslinging that made this election infamous were not aberrations. Politicians recognized an ugly strain that has been creeping into American society, and they exploited it instead of rising above it.

Bashing is fashionable — verbal bashing, physical bashing, and sometimes a combination of the two. Late night talk show host David Letterman did not get so popular because of his sense of humor and his stupid pet tricks. It's his audacity. He has no compunction about mercilessly mocking and humiliating his guests.

Morton Downey Jr. has gone a step further. "Talk show host" is a misnomer for him. Enthusiastic cheerleader — and occasional referee — as the Christians are served up to the lions is a more apt description of what he does on his nightly television show. He tries to see how far he can incite his audience without having them riot in the studio.

Downey has become a cult figure because of his outlandish statements, which are invariably anti-something or anti-someone. He's racist. He's sexist. He's explicit and profane. His remarks are so spiced with profanities that his language is bleep-speak.

His behavior is equally outlandish. Downey's trademark is the burning cigarette he waves in the faces of the guests/gladiators who appear on his show.

Violence on stage is not only acceptable, but also expected. Earlier this year civil rights activist Roy Innis got into a shoving match with Al Sharpton, the flamboyant lawyer who represented teen-ager Tawana Brawley in a controversial New York case, when the two appeared on Downey's show.

Geraldo Rivera went one better early this month. He had to pay with a broken nose, but he probably thought the sacrifice worth it for the spectacle he choreographed. In a show on "hatemongers" he brought together Innis and white supremacist "skinheads," who stormed the stage during a taping on the show and busted Geraldo's nose in the ensuing melee.

In an atmosphere like this, it's no wonder that a Newton, Mass., entrepreneur started a business specializing in revenge. "Enough is Enough" is billed as "creative revenge for today's world."

For a price, it will send a dead bluefish to a philandering husband or deliver a burned and messy suit to a man who described his girlfriend as "unsuitable." Twenty-five dollars gets you a box of 13 dead roses festooned with a black ribbon. Thirteen black balloons cost five bucks more.

Examples of the new nastiness abound in everyday life. Any driver knows that more people are running red lights and cutting off other vehicles. Any handicapped person will tell you that the able-bodied are not shy about taking their parking spaces.

When was the last time a door was shut in your face? Did you get even by slamming it on someone else — or did you vow not to degenerate into such Downeyism?

And, be honest, did you get at least a tinge of satisfaction when Geraldo's nose was busted?

## THE SACRAMENTO BEE
*Sacramento, CA,
December 26, 1988*

Geraldo Rivera, of the broken nose and the unshatterable ego, has attacked his critics for deploring what he does on television. In a piece published in the New York Times the other day, Rivera, whose recent TV specials have dealt with such topics as AIDS, drug abuse, kids in crisis and satanic worship, says those who accuse him of being a sleaze merchant don't understand that television is changing, thanks to "increasingly hard-edged" syndicated programs like Donahue, Oprah Winfrey, USA Today: The Television Show, Crimes of Passion, "the indomitable Morton Downey Jr." and, of course, Geraldo himself.

In fact, Rivera's critics do understand that the networks' stranglehold on TV audiences has been broken, that there's now a multiplicity of things to choose from on the box, that some of it is of good quality and that such diversity is a good thing. Competition can concentrate creative minds wonderfully. What's troubling, however, is that the sensationalist route taken by Rivera and some others threatens to further erode what remains of good taste on American television.

Rivera says TV has become "more interesting, vital and less pretentious." Maybe so, but that doesn't necessarily make it better. Public hangings in Victorian England may have been interesting, and few doubted Al Capone's vitality. As for "less pretentious," that's a howler coming from Rivera, whose dramatizations of the acts of his bizarre subjects and his too-righteous indignation over their perversities reek of hypocrisy.

"Face it," says Geraldo, "the old-style news documentaries had become boring." Perhaps, but so are a lot of things that an enlightened society needs to deal with soberly, not sensationally, if it is not to lose its bearings. "At some point," he went on, "even the ivory tower elite will recognize that an audience numbering in the tens of millions is not a lunatic fringe nor a gullible cult. It is America, and it is watching."

Indeed, but it's equally arguable that most Americans are quite capable of responding to less visceral treatment of unpleasant subjects. Like so many hustlers before him, Rivera has found his metier and made the most of it by targeting an audience that savors the salacious. Too bad so many TV stations — including, most recently, one of the networks nervous about the challenge of "trash TV" — have gone along by giving him so visible a platform.

## MILWAUKEE SENTINEL
*Milwaukee, WI, November 5, 1988*

Fans of All-Star wrestling better start tuning into the Geraldo Rivera show.

The brawl Thursday that ended up with a broken nose for the provocative host provided more real action and venom than a tag team match without a referee.

The busted proboscis, in Rivera's view, might have been a small price for the ratings hike and notoriety he will enjoy.

And he might deserve them if his purpose in bringing together elements of the neo-Nazi "skinheads" and civil rights leaders was to have a sensible discussion of the issues that so widely divide the two.

But the fracas truly filled the bill for Rivera who is really running a news-entertainment operation of the genre commonly called "TV-tabloids."

For those who missed the controversial event, the fight broke out when a skinhead called civil rights leader Roy Innes an "Uncle Tom."

Innes charged the offender and ultimately wound up choking a man who interfered. Someone from the audience clobbered Rivera and at least one chair was hurled in the melee.

This kind of exploitation is hardly in keeping with the concept of giving vent to opposing ideas or good journalism and is an abuse of the right of free press and speech.

So are the countless programs being aired by people like Rivera and others involving disgustingly explicit discussions of every type of sexual perversion imaginable.

Such things should be left on the police blotters and in the notes of social welfare workers where they belong.

## THE KANSAS CITY STAR
*Kansas City, MO, November 23, 1988*

Little did we know that the movie "Network" would be a portent of the fate of television news. To recall, the film showed how American viewers grew tired of the news of the day and developed an appetite for the unusual.

Weather forecasters were replaced by soothsayers and astrologers. An anchorman who later committed suicide on the air made famous the line "I'm mad as hell and I'm not going to take it anymore."

Cast in the "Network" role this year is Geraldo Rivera, formerly of ABC's weekly "20/20" news program and currently host of his own daily dose of schlock and various syndicated specials.

Not only did a fight break out during a "Geraldo!" taping which featured white supremacists and black civil rights activists, but Rivera's nose was broken photogenically in the melee. Either 13 million households tuned in this week to watch the host get punched in the face or to watch a race war live and in living color. Ratings watchers only tell how many tuned in, not why.

Regardless, this could be the dawning of the "Network" days, as evidenced by the high ratings the Rivera show received. It's no wonder that evening news programs, the ones that offer real news, are secondary to game shows with wheelers and dealers and pretty women in evening gowns. The soothsayers must not be far behind.

## THE TENNESSEAN
*Nashville, TN, November 24, 1988*

THE man has no shame.

Mr. Geraldo Rivera has been described as being the P.T. Barnum of TV talk show hosts, the Jerry Lewis of investigative journalists, and a purveyor of teleporn.

In his latest TV outrage, he orchestrated matters so that a brawl erupted during the taping of his show. Mr. Rivera got a broken nose; his show, *Geraldo*, got terrific ratings.

TV ratings are what the shenanigans of Mr. Rivera are all about. And TV viewers who enjoy this type of juvenile goings-on are excused; no one ever said the viewing audience had to have good taste.

Mr. Rivera, meanwhile, realizes he's onto a good thing. The title of his next show: *Has TV Gone Too Far?* The answer, if anyone cares, is "Yes!" ■

## "60 Minutes" Commentator, Andy Rooney, Suspended

CBS News Feb. 8, 1990 suspended satirical commentator Andy Rooney of the popular news magazine program "60 Minutes" for three months without pay. The suspension came in response to remarks that Rooney allegedly made that were derogatory to blacks and homosexuals. Rooney was quoted in the Feb. 27 issue of the *Advocate*, a newspaper based in Los Angeles, as saying. "I've believed all along that most people are born with equal intelligence, but blacks have watered down their genes because the less intelligent ones are the ones that have the most children. They drop out of school early, do drugs and get pregnant."

The *Advocate* did not tape Rooney's comments. The paper had sought an interview with Rooney after he made what many homosexuals considered to be offensive remarks in a television special, "The Year End with Andy Rooney," broadcast on Dec. 28, 1989. In the program, Rooney said, "Too much alcohol, too much food, drugs, homosexual unions, cigarettes. They're all known to lead quite often to premature death." Rooney denied making the comments quoted in the *Advocate* and said he "abhorred" the racist sentiment expressed.

## The Phoenix Gazette
*Phoenix, AZ, February 10, 1990*

Andy Rooney, the Emmy-winning columnist and commentator on CBS-TV's "60 Minutes," has been suspended for three months without pay for allegedly making racist remarks during a telephone interview with a reporter for a gay magazine.

We can hear him now when he returns to "A few minutes with Andy Rooney:" "Didja ever wonder about interviews?"

"I wonder about them. I wonder about their accuracy, especially if there is no electronic record of them. Thanks to Richard Nixon, of course, we never had to worry about what really was said in the Oval Office.

"But, suppose you are a prominent fellow, a bit rumpled and overweight, perhaps, but prominent in the sense that you appear on a weekly news show. A good news show.

"And then this reporter calls you up, says he is doing an interview for *The Advocate* — a magazine for . . . well, a magazine for those with an 'alternate lifestyle.'

"When the article comes out, it has you making absurd racial remarks about blacks that you, in fact, never said. It is your word against the reporter's. You lose.

"Your boss, CBS News President David Burke, takes the side of the reporter and suspends you.

"Is that fair?

"I don't think so. But, it beats getting fired. And I'll tell you one more thing about interviews. I'll bet *The Advocate* never interviewed Richard Nixon. And you don't have to wonder why."

## DAYTON DAILY NEWS
*Dayton, OH, February 11, 1990*

It's not like CBS's Andy Rooney didn't have precedent to warn him. Former sports analyst Jimmy "the Greek" Snyder proved that uttering seat-of-the-pants comments on racial genetics can be dangerous for one's career.

Both of these men got in trouble making off-the-cuff public remarks about black Americans. The black who interviewed Mr. Snyder said Mr. Snyder was being complimentary rather than insulting (ascribing black athletic prowess as a survival-of-the-fittest result of slavery). But the remarks were widely interpreted as racist or insulting. So Mr. Snyder lost his job as sports commentator.

Mr. Rooney has been suspended as a commentator on *60 Minutes* for his alleged comments in an interview with a Los Angeles magazine. He is quoted as saying about blacks: " . . .(They) have watered down their genes because the less intelligent ones are the ones that have the most children. They drop out of school early, do drugs and get pregnant."

Mr. Rooney has furiously denied making the remark.

Assume, though, that he said it. The first rule to remember is to be careful about making assumptions about genetics. Because history has been so loaded with the idiotic and hateful effects of racial-genetic theories and slanders, one must be sensitive in discussing genetic distinctions that do exist, between and within races, even between sexes.

Avoiding all that, Mr. Rooney could have said that disadvantages often perpetuate themselves. Blacks are disproportionately dropping out of school, abusing drugs and having children at early ages. The children born into these poor environments end up deprived.

NAACP leader Benjamin Hooks would have said, "Amen." And the remark would have never been front-page news.

## THE BLADE
*Toledo, OH, February 14, 1990*

CHALK up another apparent case of foolish insensitivity and ignorance regarding racial stereotypes. This time it's CBS News humorist Andy Rooney, who has begun a three-month suspension from his job for loose talk.

A gay magazine that interviewed Mr. Rooney quoted him as saying that "most people are born with equal intelligence, but blacks have watered down their genes because the less intelligent ones are the ones that have the most children. They drop out of school early, do drugs, and get pregnant."

Mr. Rooney protested that he didn't say that at all, but no matter. His comments created a furor, with ritual denunciations by black leaders and politicians. Mr. Rooney was suspended without pay for three months from his job on "60 Minutes." Apparently CBS felt the network had to make a statement even though Mr. Rooney's absence from the show may adversely affect the ratings.

If one takes Mr. Rooney's words at face value, they indicate an astounding insensitivity — the same exhibited by Al Campanis and Jimmy (The Greek) Snyder in recent years. Blacks have good reason to be outraged by commentators who resurrect — from a forum of national prominence — old racial stereotypes. Too often such individuals simply do not understand how times and attitudes have changed.

Mr. Rooney denies making the remarks attributed to him, and the reporter has only his notes, not a tape recording, to sustain his quotation.

But whether he uttered them or not, we are reminded that a need exists for thoughtful analyses of the problems that blacks must deal with in this country. And whites and blacks alike should be encouraged to participate in such discourse. What is regrettable is that grossly inappropriate attitudes still prevail, and that the occasional racial diatribe continues to get in the way, even though the perpetrator often wonders what all the fuss is about.

# The Oregonian
*Portland, OR, February 13, 1990*

CBS News has given us a few months without Andy Rooney. The humorist for "60 Minutes" has drawn a three-month suspension without pay for ... well, here it becomes a little unclear, but it has to do with offending somebody.

Whether Rooney will be missed depends on the beholder. Whether he should have been suspended raises an important question of where legitimate, even if perhaps disagreeable, opinion becomes bigotry.

Rooney's suspension, CBS said, was due to a remark attributed to him by a publication oriented toward the gay community. He is quoted as saying that "most people are born with equal intelligence, but blacks have watered down their genes because the less intelligent ones are the ones that have the most children. They drop out of school early, do drugs and get pregnant."

Rooney denies saying that and vehemently denies any imputation of racism.

Earlier, Rooney had drawn the wrath of gay activists when he said on a broadcast that "many of the ills which kill us are self-induced," and then cited "too much alcohol, too much food, homosexual unions, cigarettes." He apologized later for giving offense and said he should have referred to unsafe sex rather than homosexual unions.

We take our text from one of CBS News' most hallowed figures, Walter Cronkite, who happens also to be a friend of Rooney's. Cronkite said he knew Rooney was no racist, though some of the commentator's more outspoken comments may offend some people. But, Cronkite added, "Any suggestions that such a rare journalistic voice should be silenced indicates a dangerous weakness in our pluralistic society."

Exactly.

That weakness shows itself when those controlling the channels of comment — certainly including the television networks — impose a public orthodoxy on the very people hired to say what they think. Or when they seek to sanitize commentary to render it inoffensive. Or when they show undue timidity when offense is taken.

CBS hasn't explained itself well, especially in the face of Rooney's denial that he said what he was suspended for saying. As matters stand, CBS looks like it backed down under pressure when it should have advanced the case for vigorous public debate.

# The Register-Guard
*Eugene, OR, February 10, 1990*

The suspension of CBS commentator Andy Rooney is both unfortunate and encouraging. Unfortunate, because Rooney is a likable character one would not expect to make slighting remarks against blacks or homosexuals. Encouraging, because the action by CBS shows appropriate corporate sensitivity.

The picture is muddled because Rooney flatly denies saying the worst thing he is reported to have said. He is quoted this way in The Advocate, a national gay newspaper based in Los Angeles: "I've believed all along that most people are born with equal intelligence, but blacks have watered down their genes because the less intelligent ones are the ones that have the most children. They drop out of school early, do drugs and get pregnant."

That's pretty bad. But Rooney claims he never said it and doesn't think that way. Perhaps a tape recording of the interview can settle the dispute.

On a TV special in December, Rooney said, "There was some recognition in 1989 of the fact that many of the ills which kill us are self-induced. Too much alcohol, too much food, drugs, homosexual unions, cigarettes. They're all known to lead quite often to premature death." That understandably outraged gay activists, and Rooney later apologized, saying he should have said "unsafe sex" instead of "homosexual unions." That did not placate the activists, but at least it was an attempt to set things right.

Ironically, while this controversy was breaking out in New York, in Washington the Senate was passing, 94 to 2, a bill requiring the federal collection of data on "hate" crimes — offenses motivated by race, religion, sexual orientation or ethnic roots.

Voting against the bill was Sen. Jesse Helms, D-N.C., who described it as "the flagship of the homosexual and lesbian legislative agenda" and a bill that "fans the fires of the homosexual movement." He objected to provisions requiring the gathering of data on crimes motivated by "sexual orientation."

All things are relative. On a scale of bigotry, Andy Rooney might deserve a 2. Jesse Helms would get a 10.

# THE INDIANAPOLIS STAR
*Indianapolis, IN, February 13, 1990*

Chris Bull, a reporter for *The Advocate*, a Los Angeles-based magazine for homosexuals, has stirred up a nationwide furor by saying that humorist and social commentator Andy Rooney made a racist remark in an interview.

It is easy enough to see why the statement ascribed to Rooney, that "blacks have watered down their genes because the less intelligent ones are the ones that have the most children," is considered racist and offensive.

But Rooney insisted that he is not a racist and that he did not make the remark.

In spite of Rooney's denial, CBS News President David Burke suspended Rooney for three months without pay from the *60 Minutes* television show, on which his humor spot is a weekly feature.

Burke said Rooney's future with CBS would be discussed when the suspension ends.

One extremely curious thing about this episode is that the *Advocate* issue containing the controversial remark pinned on Rooney was not due on newsstands until the day after the suspension was announced. Yet somehow the remark reached the National Association for the Advancement of Colored People and prominent blacks, bringing strong denunciations of Rooney.

Another curious thing is that Rooney was already under fire from homosexual rights organizations for saying, in a CBS-TV special in December, that in 1989 people had recognized that many self-induced ills, such as "too much food, too much alcohol, drugs, homosexual unions, cigarettes ... (are) all known to lead quite often to premature death."

Rooney said: "I am guilty of what I said about gays, and I deeply regret having offended them. But on the other charge, I am absolutely innocent. I never made any remark about blacks having 'watered down' their genes. I never made or thought the statement attributed to me. I am just infuriated by the notion that I am being called a racist. Anyone who knows me knows that is not true."

Rooney has been with CBS since 1959. He has been a regular on *60 Minutes* since 1968. He has written eight popular books. He also writes a column that appears on the editorial page of *The Indianapolis Star*.

Former CBS anchorman Walter Cronkite came to Rooney's defense, saying: "I've known Rooney for almost half a century, and I know he's not a racist. He is an independent thinker and a courageous social critic. His more outrageous comments are bound to offend one element or another of the population from time to time, but any suggestion that such a rare journalistic voice should be silenced indicates a dangerous weakness in our pluralistic, democratic society."

Cronkite is right. Stifling of freedom of expression is a standard tool of tyranny. It has no place in a free society.

## Senate Goes 'Live' on Television

The Senate Feb. 27, 1986 voted to allow live television and radio coverage of its proceedings on a trial basis from June 1 to July 15, 1986. After a two-week review period, the Senate would then vote in late July on whether to make the coverage permanent.

Proceedings on the House floor had been televised since 1979.

The 67-21 vote approving the measure came after days of debate and negotiation. The agreement included some changes in Senate rules aimed at tightening procedures and speeding debate, including limits on filibusters. Debate following a vote of cloture would be limited to 30 hours, down from 100.

The rules also prohibited using the broadcast material in campaigns, camera-panning around the chamber to reveal dozing senators and empty seats, and noting senators' absence from committees. (According to a *Washington Post* story Feb. 11, "committee cameos" had become popular among senators sensitive about their attendance records. A senator would make a brief appearance in the hearing room, say a few words for inclusion in the record, and depart; an aide would then whisk away the senator's nameplate so that his absence would be less obvious.)

The U.S. Senate June 2 began the six-week experiment with live television broadcasts of its proceedings. A one-month trial on closed-circuit TV had begun May 1.

Coverage began at 2 p.m. on a new channel of C-Span, the public affairs cable television network that already covered House proceedings.

## WORCESTER TELEGRAM
*Worcester, MA, May 19, 1986*

Politics and show business share some common characteristics. They will be even more evident next week when live television coverage of the U.S. Senate begins on a test basis.

People in every part of the country can judge whether the Senate is "the world's greatest deliberative body." At the very least, the presence of the cameras might remove another label attached to the upper chamber — the "world's most exclusive club."

For many viewers, televised Senate debates will seem anticlimactic. The Cable Satellite Public Affairs Network (C-SPAN) has provided gavel-to-gavel House coverage since 1979, producing a number of "C-SPAN junkies," a small but devoted band of cable TV subscribers hooked on unedited public affairs programming. But the Senate operates by different rules, at a more leisurely pace than the House. Some members are leery of TV cameras in the chamber. Says one senator: "It doesn't work efficiently. It's a messy, untidy spectacle." The Senate will vote July 29 on whether to make the telecasts a permanent fixture.

When the telecasts start Monday, the Senate will be operating under a rules change. An amendment reduces from 100 hours to 30 hours the time allowed for debate, procedural moves and roll calls after members have voted for cloture. Cameras will be operated by Senate staffers and will be fixed on the speaker — a senator, the presiding officer, chaplain or clerks. During roll-call votes, but only then, the camera may pan the chamber. There is no coverage during closed sessions and quorum calls, which are used to stall for time while senators confer on or off the floor.

The Public Affairs Network, which now reaches about 23 million American households, says it does not know how many people watch the House sessions, which last year accounted for 10 percent of its programming. By all accounts, the show is not particularly exciting for general audiences used to soaps or action-filled crime dramas. But those devoted to politics may find Senate telecasts worth watching.

The presence of cameras may alter the personal style of some lawmakers, but they are not likely to substantially change the political process. A politician's first instinct on confronting the risky or the unknown is to play it safe. That is why the Senate's first brush with television coverage is an experiment. If the ratings are poor, the show might be canceled.

## THE BLADE
*Toledo, OH, May 7, 1986*

THE Senate often prides itself on its reputation as the world's greatest deliberative body, although more irreverent observers sometimes refer to it as the Cave of the Winds. Now the chamber of Daniel Webster and Strom Thurmond has succumbed to television.

The camera vantage points are tightly controlled so as to avoid showing the usually empty Senate chamber or the random dozing lawmaker. They zoom in on only the presiding officer or the speaking senator. Some lawmakers are suspected of primping a bit for the cameras, although gray-maned Sen. John Warner of Virginia said, "I remain unchanged, defiantly unchanged."

The House of Representatives has been broadcasting its televised debates since 1979. Under House rules debate tends to be more trenchant than in the Senate, home of the filibuster, a means of talking legislation to death or calling attention to a legislative or procedural point. The filibuster has lost a good deal of its clout in recent years.

However, the Senate has not given in easily. The decision to proceed with a television experiment came only after many months of deliberation, three weeks of debate, albeit by a 67-to-21 vote. The broadcasts are over closed-circuit television until June 1, after which they are scheduled to be carried on C-SPAN, the network that carries House debates and goes to 23 million homes.

Nobody knows just how much of an audience congressional proceedings have, although the GOP minority in the House has taken advantage of TV to try to reach beyond the floor of the chamber where the Democrats are firmly in control.

It is doubtful that the televising of the Senate will make much difference in the long run. Some senators may try to grandstand for the cameras, but other observers think it will speed up matters by causing the senators to dispense with some of their more arcane procedural debates and time-consuming quorum calls. The only question is, does the nation want the Senate to be more efficient or less efficient than it now is?

One could argue that question convincingly both ways.

## The Seattle Times
*Seattle, WA, May 26, 1986*

FOR a body that 199 years ago wouldn't permit citizens into the viewing gallery above its chamber, the U.S. Senate has undergone dramatic changes in attitude about public exposure. Starting a week from today, senators will experiment with live TV of floor debates via the Cable Satellite Public Affairs Network (C-SPAN).

While the coverage will be mostly dullsville, viewer discretion is advised. As Sen. J. Bennett Johnston, D-La., has observed, "The Senate doesn't work efficiently. It's a messy, untidy spectacle to watch." The public will never understand, Johnston added, "why it's important . . . for the Senate to play the role of the saucer where the political passions of the nation are cooled."

Mindful that TV could create unfavorable impressions, the Senate has adopted a few changes in its procedures — reducing time for debate, for example — that one member described as "cleaning up our act." A raucous debate in February over the rule changes was cited by TV opponents as a good example of why Senate sessions are unsuitable for viewing.

And several members fear that some of their colleagues will duck tough votes and posture for the cameras (which will be controlled by the Senate staff). Said Sen. Russell B. Long, also a Louisiana Democrat: "Statesmanship is all too scarce a commodity now. It will be even more scarce with television."

These concerns explain why the TV coverage is being tried only as an experiment. The Senate has scheduled a vote July 29 on whether the telecasts should continue on a permanent basis.

## Las Vegas Sun
*Las Vegas, NV, June 1, 1986*

The nation's most reflective, deliberative body made its television debut last week, with members demonstrating bits of wit, nervousness and showbiz savvy.

The concept of television in the U.S. Senate has been kicked around for a while and, for whatever reason, senators have decided to allow the presence of cameras. The House brought television into its chambers in 1979.

Public looks into the Senate are essential, and this year's Senate members must be lauded for allowing at least a trial view of their professional lives.

### Shows naked effectiveness

Television has become the average Joe's eye on politics. Most of us can't rub elbows with senators, assemblymen or U.S. congressmen, getting glimpses of their performances. We depend on the media to show us the naked effectiveness of men and women in public office. Television is the greatest undresser of them all.

Even if senators approved the televising of their proceedings for nothing but self-serving political reasons, benefits go to voters as well as public servants.

Watching our own Sens. Paul Laxalt and Chic Hecht on the tube — for those who can sit in front of it for a while — can prove nothing but insightful for Nevadans as well as for voters in every state in the union. Hecht was no supporter of the live coverage.

Senators may argue that the real work is done in committee and on the tennis courts, but they owe voters a look at their performances among their peers.

True, the Senate floor is the site of over-worded, poetry-filled speeches in which orators rely on quotes from our forefathers. But the floor also is the place that separates average politicians from great ones. It singles out sincere senators from those who haven't bothered to study the governmental process.

### Weeding through the chaff

Despite television executives' thoughts that the average viewer has no more mental capacity than a 10-year-old child, the audience watching the Senate proceedings does not fit into the same category. Most Americans aren't dumb. They easily see through stupidity, inconsistency and insincerity in politicians.

The average cynical C-SPAN viewer will look at the Senate through informed eyes and will see senators for what they are. We sincerely hope the good senators decide to keep the television eye on themselves after their one-month TV test period ends. It will be especially enlightening for the whole nation to watch the impeachment trial of U.S. District Judge Harry Claiborne so that injustice can receive a proper airing.

Television in the U.S. Senate will bring out the ham in senators for a while, but our elected officials eventually will settle down and understand their everyday work is more important than the camera's eye.

Politicians are most responsive to their constituents. Sometimes the most frightening sentence from a voter's mouth starts with, "I saw you on TV the other night..."

We'll be watching you, senators, but don't think you have to do anything different than you did before your television debut. We'll judge you on your on- and off-air performances. We hope they'll show enough similarities to prove we can still trust you as a person as well as a politician.

The public's ratings are more scrutinizing and more determined than the Nielsens, senators. It's up to you to keep your show on television and in Washington, D.C.

## Chicago Tribune
*Chicago, IL, June 1, 1986*

Hushed, the audience awaits. The curtain rises. The spectacle begins. That there will be a potential audience of millions for the U.S. Senate's debate on an historic tax bill is somehow dramatically and democratically right. Alexis de Tocqueville would marvel at such a country.

For the first time in its sometimes august history, the Senate is allowing cameras to televise its proceedings, beginning Monday. On Wednesday, according to Senate Majority Leader Robert Dole, debate on a tax bill that promises to touch the lives of everyone will begin.

This gives senators two days in which to rid themselves of opening-day jitters and to polish their oratory. Ideally, the cameras would focus not on the inflexible spots that have been carefully chosen in advance by the Senate but on what is happening outside those narrow confines. In the lobby, for instance.

But that is probably asking too much on the day of the Senate's video debut.

The as-yet-unwritten script of "Live from Washington—it's the U.S. Senate" is a motherlode of potential. This bill that came flying out of Sen. Bob Packwood's Finance Committee isn't perfect but it does do some remarkable things:

● It drastically lowers marginal tax rates, In the process, it removes entirely some six million of the working poor from the tax rolls

● It simplifies the tax code, meaning millions of middle-income people no longer will have to trek to experts every spring for assistance in translating their 1040s. Given the fact that even today many go to tax consulting firms for help in preparing their 1040EZ forms, this simplification should not totally devastate that particular business enterprise.

● It improves the chances that those with similar economic conditions will be treated similarly by ridding the tax code of its surfeit of sometimes obscure shelters and deductions and credits and exemptions that are subject to various interpretations: yours and those of the IRS.

● It ensures that corporations—and wealthy individuals—will pay some taxes. The fact that often they don't because they take advantage of perfectly legal loopholes has been one reason the current system has been perceived as being so unfair. Those drafting this bill in the Senate Finance Committee reminded themselves in a morning ritual of what came to be called the Grace Report: that W.R. Grace & Co. had paid taxes to Libya last year but received a $500,000 tax refund from the U.S.

There are people and industries and groups and causes out there complaining about this bill, mostly because they are due to lose a particular advantage. But as Roger Smith, the chairman of General Motors Corp., pointed out, "You've got to look at the whole elephant." And beginning this week, you will have that chance.

## Rockford Register Star
*Rockford, IL, June 8, 1986*

The cameras are rolling on the U.S. Senate, but don't expect "Candid Camera."

There will be silliness, that's for sure, but don't look for it to be spontaneous, at least not for a while. There will be too much powdering and posturing going on initially for the public to get a candid picture of how the Senate works.

We suspect the public eventually will discover that the actual lawmaking goes on outside the Senate chamber. Votes may be taken on the floor, but the action is elsewhere.

Nevertheless, televised Senate sessions are a good first step toward helping the American people understand how laws are made.

Even the filibuster, a favorite Senate ploy to slow some bills, could be instructive. Senate Minority Leader Robert Byrd, D-W.Va., said television could force both sides of an issue to present their cases publicly during filibusters. Previously, one side could sit out the long, boring debate and watch the opponents pontificate. Now, everybody will pontificate, but that's not necessarily bad if it helps public understanding of an issue.

C-Span's coverage of the Senate sessions also could give coverage to diligent, but little-known Senators who are passed over by network TV in favor of Senate "stars." They, too, deserve recognition (or blame) back home and nationally for what they do.

The Senators are expected to formally approve television coverage of their sessions once the six-week trial period ends. We hope they do. More than ever before, the public needs to understand the crucial issues and make decisions at the voting booth based on that knowledge

Television in the Senate ensures that a politician who runs for election can't hide for long once he gets to the U.S. Senate.

## Wisconsin State Journal
*Madison, WI, June 4, 1986*

The U.S. Senate has been described as "the world's greatest deliberative body." Some have suspected that was a title bestowed by the members themselves, or at least those who fancied being carried into those august chambers on sedan chairs.

Now, from the safety and comfort of their own living rooms, people in every part of the country have a chance to see just how great this "deliberative body" is or is not.

Live telecasts of Senate proceedings began this week on the Cable Satellite Public Affairs Network (C-SPAN), which has provided gavel-to-gavel coverage of the House of Representatives since March 19, 1979. It is an experiment that was approved, 67-21, by Senate members in February. Members will vote July 29 on making the telecasts permanent.

So what was the first day of live telecasts like? One Chicago writer likened it to Mindinao tribesmen happening upon an electric toothbrush.

Senate Majority Leader Robert Dole of Kansas dropped his microphone with a resounding thud. Sen. John Glenn of Ohio showed that he still has the right stuff when he patted down his balding head with makeup powder, explaining to his amused colleagues that it cuts down on glare from television lights.

Sen. Edward Kennedy of Massachusetts got a haircut. Sen. Robert Stafford of Vermont said he was too old to try to cover up "the bags under my eyes." Sen. Alan Dixon of Illinois joked about being "out of uniform," a reference to the notion that dark suits would contrast nicely with the chamber's mustard-yellow walls.

Sen. William Armstrong of Colorado last week mailed out a press pamphlet called "Glossary of Senate ... A Guide for TV," complete with a Senate seating chart. Armstrong, who is being mentioned as a Republican presidential candidate, holds down seat No. 45. He just thought he should point that out.

"The novelty will wear off; it's not a big deal," said Senate Minority Leader Robert Byrd. This, of course, was the same Sen. Byrd who faced the cameras and rambled through a history of the upper house, as if to bemoan the fact that Henry Clay and Daniel Webster were born before television.

Sen. William Proxmire of Wisconsin, a telecast opponent, basically ignored the presence of cameras and spoke on the subject of arms control. Once a maverick, always a maverick.

The real test for television begins today, when the Senate begins debate on the tax-reform bill passed by its Finance Committee. Will senators again play to the cameras (i.e., voters), or will they pay attention to the serious business at hand?

## The Hartford Courant
*Hartford, CT, July 17, 1986*

"Television," remarked Senate Majority Leader Robert Dole, R-Kan., the other day, "is here to stay."

It's an observation the rest of the world had pretty much embraced more than three decades ago. That tells us something about the readiness of the Senate to accept modern reality.

In this case, Dole was referring to broadcast coverage of Senate proceedings, which has just come through an eight-week trial period without toppling the republic. Ironically — predictably, actually — the Senate has imposed a three-day television blackout while it debates whether to make the experiment permanent.

The blackout is little more than a courtly gesture toward never-say-die senators who still can't reconcile themselves to the notion that television is here to stay — or that it has any place poking its electronic nose into the world's most exclusive debating society.

Nobody — not even the die-hards — believes that the plug can be pulled on broadcast coverage of Senate proceedings once begun. Indeed, even the three-day blackout represents a retreat from the original plan for a full two-week halt in coverage while the experiment is debated in secret.

Senate Minority Leader Robert C. Byrd, D-W.Va., put it in properly baroque senatorial phrases: "I want to express not just the belief — but as a certitude that it is bound to happen — that the Senate will go forward with permanent television coverage; now the Senate galleries have been extended from sea to shining sea."

In other words, television is here to stay.

Welcome to the 20th century, senators. With the 21st century just around the corner, we'd say you got here none too soon.

## The Burlington Free Press
*Burlington, VT, June 3, 1986*

What happened yesterday afternoon in the Senate represented a belated recognition by that body's lawmakers that the time had come to put their act on television.

They joined their House colleagues, who have been on home screens for seven years, in giving people throughout the country a view of their deliberations. Millions of Americans probably will never have the opportunity to sit in the gallery and watch the proceedings. Using television surely may be the best way of reawakening the public's interest in government.

During a month-long trial period before Monday's debut, many of the problems that lawmakers feared did not materialize. Some thought that there would be long speeches, grandstanding and posturing by the better media stars. That it did not happen seems to have persuaded some senators that televised sessions were not such a bad idea after all.

But many lawmakers appeared to be afflicted by self-consciousness, a fact which Sen. Thad Cochran, R-Miss., said might not be "necessarily bad." As evidence of the change, one senator is said to have dyed his hair. Another was warned by his staff to stop scratching his nose because he was appearing on television while another senator was speaking. Some members with thinning hair have moved from front seats to the back of the chamber. Sens. John Kerry, D-Mass., John D. Rockefeller IV, D-W.Va., and Albert Gore Jr., D-Tennessee, complained that the color of the wall behind them resembles a bus terminal. Many are wearing red ties and blue shirts.

Even so, the public now will be able to make intelligent judgments about the ability of the people who are elected to Congress.

In that sense, live broadcasts from both chambers will be a plus for television viewers and a way of involving them in the processes of representative government.

## The Idaho Statesman
*Boise, ID, June 5, 1986*

President Reagan predicts it will outdraw *Wheel of Fortune*. Sen. Bennett Johnston, D-La., fears the show's new stars will "speak too much, too often, too long ... " Others say it will become dismissable daytime drama, mundane minutes that never will threaten the soaps.

Still, it's all for the good that daily television coverage of the U.S. Senate is now reality. One hundred ninety-seven years after its first session, and seven years after TV came to the House, the Senate is on the air for a trial period that is all but certain to become permanent.

Change comes glacially to the World's Most Exclusive Club. However, the cameras do not presage ruin. Senators waxed rhetorical long before cathode ray tubes dominated living rooms. As Sen. Wendell Ford, D-Ky., said, the only changes television will bring to the Senate are more blue shirts and red ties. And as Sen. Howell Heflin, D-Ala., noted, Capitol Hill sales of hair spray, styling mousse, Grecian Formula and Ultra-Brite toothpaste should skyrocket.

Despite the heady debates over whether a televised Senate will lead to grandstanding or just Sominex, the real questions appear to be practical. For example, should props such as Wisconsin cheese be allowed on the floor during debate? Should speaking senators be shown up close or as part of the larger, usually empty, Senate chamber? Should there be a clock at the bottom of the picture during roll calls, and should the clerk calling the roll be shown? Sound silly? "Never underestimate the insignificant," cautions Sen. Ford.

When the novelty has worn off, the Senate will go on with its business as always — slowly, carefully, with just a touch more makeup. The public will tune in twice a year for selected big debates. *Days of Our Lives* and *As the World Turns* should be safe for another season.

## The Ann Arbor News
*Ann Arbor, MI, June 6, 1986*

The greatest deliberative body in the world — the U.S. Senate — has finally taken to television. Now senators are "deliberating" what color shirts and ties to wear and what makeup aid will take the glare off shiny bald pates.

How unfortunate the televising of Senate sessions arrived too late for Sen. Everett Dirksen. What great theater it would have been, for organ-pipe Ev to rise majestically before the TV cameras and then to launch into one of his stemwinders on the beauty of the lowly marigold and why this hardy flower should be enshrined.

One of the worries in televising Senate sessions may be that Americans will take what they see seriously; they shouldn't. When it seems as though nothing is happening on the Senate floor, Americans should simply accept the fact that nothing really is happening.

Another worry is that presidential hopefuls in the Senate — which means about 100 people — will use their new entree into American living rooms to speechify in favor of — who else? — themselves.

That seems a trifling concern. The ratings for "Live from the Senate" aren't likely to be high anyway, and the prospect of Sen. Foghorn rising to pontificate on why he should be elected president is certain to be accompanied by the sound of television sets either clicking off or over to the soaps.

## High-definition TV Guidelines Set by FCC

The Federal Communications Commission (FCC) Sept. 1, 1988 announced unanimous approval of initial technical guidelines for high-definition television (HDTV) that would gradually bring the new technology to the market by the 1990s.

The FCC decision was analogous to that made in the early 1950s introducing color television into a black-and-white market. The color system had been designed then to ensure that existing black-and-white sets were able to receive color broadcast signals and display them as black-and-white images.

HDTV technology promised to deliver high-resolution video images as clear as 35-millimeter film – images twice as clear as those provided at present. Viewers wishing to receive the clearer images would have to purchase a new HDTV set (at an estimated cost of at least $1,000), because the old sets would not have the ability to display the pictures of superior quality.

The initial FCC guidelines would require broadcasters to transmit high-definition signals on existing VHF and UHF frequencies, thereby enabling viewers to continue to use their old television sets once the HDTV system began to operate. The guidelines would also bring the new system to the public as swiftly as possible.

In addition, according to the FCC, the HDTV signal would have to be suitable for cable, satellite and broadcast television while offering viewers quality comparable with that of other HDTV systems.

With the new guidelines, the FCC hoped to make sufficient spectrum for HDTV technology available. While insuring that no exisiting television set would be made obsolete, the guidelines would also provide direction to researchers and equipment managers making design decisions.

Because the U.S. system would continue to use terrestrial broadcasting as the primary carrier unlike the satellite systems proposed by Japan and the European Community, the world faced the prospect of three distinct sets of HDTV standards competing for leadership in the world market. Both the existing Japanese high-definition production system – MUSE Hi Vision, developed by Japan Broadcasting Co. – and a rival system being developed by a European manufacturing consortium under the Eureka program would be excluded under the new FCC standards.

Industry analysts regarded the sales potential of HDTV as greater than that of any other single consumer electronics product, with the market for HDTV sets in the U.S. expected to be worth as much as $20 billion annually by 1997. As a result many saw the new technology as the best opportunity for the U.S. to regain competitiveness in a consumer-electronics market now dominated by Japanese producers.

The FCC based its guidelines on reports and recommendations offered by its Advisory Committee on Advanced Television Service and the Office for Engineering Technology. It would be at least a year before the FCC chose its final standard. The International Radio Consultative Committee, an advisory body, would not decide on a global standard untiil 1990.

Sixteen leading U.S. electronics competitors Jan. 12, 1989 agreed to form consortia to develop HDTV technology that would enable U.S.

The *Wall Street Journal* Nov. 16, 1989 reported that the Bush administration planned to cut off all federal aid for HDTV development in the fiscal 1991 budget.

The government had earmarked $30 million for HDTV research in 1990.

Spending on HDTV and several other high-technology programs had been favored by the Commerce Department and by the Pentagon's Defense Advanced Research Projects Agency (DARPA). DARPA had awarded five contracts for HDTV research, it was reported June 14.

But critics charged that direct federal involvement was tantamount to an official industrial policy, where the government and not the marketplace decided on the allocation of the nation's financial and technological resources.

## Newsday
*New York, NY, July 2, 1989*

Again the technology race is on, this time to create the next generation of television broadcasting systems: high-definition TV. Will the United States get there first, or Japan? If we lose this one, some say, we'll fall behind in all kinds of related technologies.

But as the U.S. electronics industry tries to stampede the federal government into $1.3 billion worth of support for HDTV, nobody is asking the key question: Is high-definition TV really so good a deal that Washington must shell out for it? The answer isn't in yet.

HDTV sounds like a marvel. By doubling the density of the TV image, it will give television pictures the sharpness of a movie screen. It will open a $10-billion market just for TV sets, its backers assert, and make new industrial and medical applications of TV possible.

Maybe so, but it's no sure thing. HDTV receivers will be expensive — probably no less than $1,000. People who have seen it on home-sized screens say, yeah, it's nice, but they wouldn't pay much for it. And U.S. industry hasn't had much success in producing TV sets against foreign competitors anyway; maybe that's just not what we're good at.

Two groups of U.S. companies have come up with a pilot version of the technology, and the Federal Communications Commission plans to set a U.S. standard in 1992. But the international body that sets worldwide broadcast guidelines plans to come up with an HDTV standard in 1990 and both Japan and Europe, which are farther along with development, are angling to get there first.

It would be a mistake to end up with more than one HDTV standard. Not only does the world benefit from a free flow of communications, this country benefits commercially: Just as Japan thrives on making cheap TV receivers, Americans excel at TV programing; Japanese and European love our shows. If the United States has a unique HDTV technology, it could crimp foreign distribution of our programs. And since HDTV sets will be costly and buyers scarce, it is better to have a single, worldwide market, not several local ones.

So it makes far more sense to agree to an international HDTV standard than to have America establish a unique system. Before Washington even thinks of lavishing subsidies on this new technology, it must have some idea where the race is going to end up.

## WORCESTER TELEGRAM
*Worcester, MA, September 14, 1988*

Television pictures twice as sharp as today's — so they can be twice as large — could well revolutionize home entertainment in the 1990s as color TV did in the 1970s.

But whether or not Americans take to high-definition television — HDTV, in industry jargon — they will be able to watch all programming on today's sets as well as on the expensive new HDTV sets. HDTV will be compatible with regular TV, just as color has been with black-and-white.

That is the most significant provision of the HDTV guidelines made public last week by the Federal Communications Commission. We suppose it would have been politically impossible for the FCC to rule otherwise. Even so, the decision took spunk, for none of two dozen HDTV systems that have vied for the FCC go-ahead is compatible. And that includes the system Japan has adopted as standard for its market and had hoped would become standard in the United States.

Since America's compatible HDTV system has yet to be invented, it's just possible that one of the many American companies sidelined by Japanese consumer electronics in recent years will do the inventing and get the United States back into TV manufacturing. That opening for U.S. industry is another reason to applaud the FCC decision.

But electronics industry analysts believe it is much more likely that one of the Japanese or European companies that have kept their hand in will solve whatever problems need solving before any American company can get up and running.

Even so, the FCC decision ensures that Americans will be the winners in one way. Everybody in Japan will have to buy an expensive new TV set when Japan goes HDTV. In contrast, anybody in America who cares can ignore HDTV — and go on watching their old Sony. The American way — if not the American consumer electronics industry — seems to be the winner.

## THE TENNESSEAN
*Nashville, TN, May 28, 1989*

IT might be called something like the dialogue for the deaf that has come up in the Congress over high-definition television which is billed as the technological future.

The U.S. electronics industry has released a plan proposing more than $1.3 billion in government aid to help America catch up with the future. But Commerce Secretary Robert Mosbacher said U.S. firms shouldn't depend on Uncle Sam to be their "Uncle Sugar" in bankrolling the effort.

The Japanese are well into development of the new television, which offers the promise of sharper, brighter and wider pictures. The U.S. has barely begun testing the technology.

A billion dollars in research aid is quite a chunk of money in a time of budget constraints. The question here is what is at stake. A spokesman for the electronics industry said if the U.S. fails to catch up the "effects on our economy will be drastic" and would adversely affect a range of industries, including semiconductors, software and automated manufacturing equipment.

IBM Corp. Vice Chairman J. D. Kuehler said the HDTV issue "has become the symbol of, or the last bastion of, or the best opportunity...to put this country in a role of a provider of consumer electronics."

There are a range of estimates about the potential market for HDTV. Some say it could represent from $40 billion to $50 billion in sales of televisions alone over a decade. It is pointed out that the application would spread to other fields such as defense, aviation, research and retrieval of information. Such estimates depend on several things: acceptance of the public, cost of the equipment and the like. People with conventional TVs are hardly likely to discard them in favor of a new and more expensive toy.

Yet Mr. Mosbacher is hardly advancing any new ideas by falling back on the administration's plans on the capital gains tax and tax credits for research and development. He says the private sector has to take the lead in HDTV. He could have suggested the idea of a possible compromise.

Without some kind of help for home industry, the answer about who will supply high technology electronics in the future is easy. It will be Japan.

## THE LINCOLN STAR
*Lincoln, NE, April 5, 1989*

While not easily understood, high-definition television (HDTV) is an electronics advancement with huge potential. Congressional Quarterly reports that the American Electronics Association estimates the U.S. market for HDTV receivers to be about $1.5 billion in the year 2000 and more than $6 billion 10 years later.

Jerry K. Pearlman, chairman and president of Zenith Electronics Corp., has reported that to convert just 15 percent of today's U.S. television market to Zenith HDTV reception would cost $500 million. Pearlman maintains that Zenith, the only major TV set producer left in the United States, has based its research on a superior HDTV system of reception directly to a picture tube.

**JAPAN AND** most others in this market are working on a more costly system involving a projector and a picture tube, Pearlman explained. The Zenith president testified recently before the House Committee on Science, Space and Technology. The U.S. Department of Defense has announced a series of grants totaling $30 million to develop an American HDTV industry because of its potential as image sensors for missiles or spy satellites.

Pearlman favors the grants but adds that they need to be $100 million a year for three or four years and matched by an equal or greater amount from industry. The potential swing in world trade, he said, could be billions of dollars annually for the United States.

There are other considerations. An Associated Press story reported that HDTV tied together a variety of advanced technologies, including digital image processing, high-capacity satellite transmission, fiber optics and micro-electronics.

Admittedly, Zenith has a selfish interest in this matter. But that is not a prime consideration.

**SOME NEWS** reports claim Japanese HDTV research has been financed almost totally by private industry. But Congressional Quarterly reports that up to half of its $700 million in HDTV research has been paid for by the government.

With the United States losing so many markets, especially in advanced electronic technologies, the loss of another highly promising market should be viewed with concern by Congress. Unfair protection of U.S. markets is discouraged, but it is imperative that Congress make sure that U.S. electronics firms are on an equal opportunity footing with foreign competitors.

In the areas of transmission, broadcasting, production and sales, HDTV already has earned sufficient attention to warrant thoughtful concern by Congress and the administration. Zenith's Pearlman said in his testimony that $1 billion was scheduled to go into HDTV equipment for the Federal Aviation Administration's air traffic control system in 1992 and 1993.

That lends further credibility and currency to the technology.

## TV, Movie Scriptwriters Strike 22 Weeks

A 22-week strike by 9,000 movie and television writers ended Aug. 7, 1988 with ratification of a new four-year contract with producers.

The strike, the third longest in Hollywood history, disrupted fall television programming and posed a threat to studio and network revenues. Layoffs in allied services were widespread.

Members of the Writers Guild of America began the strike March 7. A resultant drought of new material forced television networks to focus on sports, special events, movies and reruns. The critically important fall opening of the new television season, normally in mid-September, was pushed back months. Most new shows were not expected to appear until November, if then. Half-hour situation comedies could be resumed by November, but one-hour dramas would most likely not make it back to the screen until 1989.

The strike was longest ever for the Writers Guild, which ran into an impasse with the Alliance of Motion Picture and Television Producers over residuals, a form of royalties, and the amount of say the writers would have over disposition of their scripts.

Reportedly, the settlement provided some improvements in creative rights of the writers, and only a very modest financial plus in the residuals area, a perennial bone of contention.

Under the new plan, the writers would have the option of keeping the existing arrangement or switching to a new plan that would give them a percentage of the producer's foreign sales.

Among the three major commercial television networks, CBS was facing the bleakest immediate prospect until the new scripts and new shows were available. NBC was scheduled to broadcast the 1988 Summer Olympic Games in the fall, followed by the World Series. ABC had an 18-hour series, *War & Rememberance*, set for November.

In 1987 television news writers, editors and other employees went on strike against CBS Inc. in New York for six weeks and against ABC News in New York for eight weeks in March and April.

The settlement at CBS April 16 called for salary increases of 3% annually over the three-year life of the contract and preserved an employee's right to seek arbitration if dismissed.

The network won more flexibility in hiring temporary employees, in ignoring seniroity in layoffs (for 25% of the shop; seniority would apply to 75%) and in using managers and on-air reporters to write stories.

The settlement at ABC, along similar lines, was reached April 26. The union involved at both networks was the Writers Guild of America. The contracts covered 325 employees at CBS and about 200 at ABC.

---

## The Star-Ledger

*Newark, NJ, August 9, 1988*

The nation's television viewers—a staunchly loyal lot—can breathe a little easier now that the screenwriters' strike has been settled after 22 weeks of hard-nosed negotiations. They no longer are faced with the unsettling possibility of a winter of discontent, with tired old retreads instead of new shows.

With the strike over, those avid TV viewers are assured they will once again have their fantasies and dreams fulfilled by newly minted sitcoms that no doubt will bear a striking resemblance to the dreary fare they have been watching for too many years—programs spiced up with laugh tracks that are supposed to cover up limp, unfunny lines.

The fall season will be delayed, waiting on the writers to begin churning out new scripts that are supposed to enhance our culture. The strike hiatus should have given TV producers a creative respite that now can be usefully deployed, devising situations that will brighten prime-time viewing. Hopefully, the refreshed, eager writers now should be able to turn out scripts with witty dialogue that has been lacking for too many years.

Don't count on all this happening, but television audiences can always hope for the best—and settle for the least, as they have been doing for so long. In the strike-caused interim, there will be the Olympics as fill-in, which could be better than the programs that would have been on line if the writers didn't stage a walkout to get a bigger piece of the lucrative TV action—a large share of the lucrative residuals that producers, naturally, did not want to give up because that would dilute long-term profits.

Autumn is a crucial period for the television industry. It is the opening of a season when the networks put their best creative foot forward, counting on new programs that will catch the viewers' fancy, that will appreciably increase ratings. That's the name of the game in television, the vital bottom-line key that producers look for every year, the exciting, profitable potential of another "Bill Cosby Show," or a long-running soap opera like "Dallas."

With all its shortcomings, television is still a prime source of recreation for millions of Americans. It is a medium that has taken the pre-eminent status that films once held. Television has the obvious advantage of at-home convenience—and it is, of course, less pricey, even with cable, which has been steadily cutting into commercial television.

---

## THE RICHMOND NEWS LEADER

*Richmond, VA, March 6, 1987*

Early morning tube addicts owe striking network writers a favor.

The other day Senator Daniel Patrick Moynihan was scheduled to appear on one of the cutesy morning news-entertainment shows. He didn't make it.

The writers — why would anyone willingly take the blame for scribbling the stuff anchors and anchorettes recite? — have called a strike for one reason or another. Moynihan doesn't cross picket lines, so the show went on without him. Instead, the interviewer probably swapped lo-cal recipes with a dancing rhino.

Thus viewers were spared the agony of another ritual hosing of the President. We take no sides in the teevee strike. But the picket lines have performed at least one public service.

## Chicago Tribune
*Chicago, IL August 9, 1988*

Well, it's finally over after a record 153 days. And they're back! But then, you probably never noticed they were gone. Let alone wondering about where they went. Or who they are, wherever they were.

You remember all that talk about how we might miss our whole blessed fall television season? And how the moguls might trot out remakes of old "Mission Impossible" scripts and all that? No such luck.

You've got it. The writers have been on strike. And now they're not. And the fall season will be saved. More's the pity. It will just be pushed back about six weeks till late October or early November—not over the edge as it most likely will deserve.

It may sound as if they're just making up most of the stuff as they go along, but the production companies really do pay people who claim to write TV scripts. Sure, it defies belief that anyone would confess to most of them.

But try to be forgiving. If people get hungry enough, there's no accounting for what they'll do. And it's been a generation since Playhouse 90 was commissioning the likes of "Requiem for a Heavyweight" and "Days of Wine and Roses."

Makes you wonder, though, when you find that the screen writers have 9,000 members. Go figure how many of them are writing down words for Vanna White to put up on "Wheel of Fortune" or some such. Of the 7,500 who were eligible to vote on the new contract, only 2,523 participated. Maybe the others' crayons were broken so they couldn't mark their ballots. More likely it was just writer's block, an occupational hazard that may yet save the season.

## The Dallas Morning News
*Dallas, TX, August 6, 1988*

A tentative agreement has been reached in the 22-week television producers' and writers' strike.

Darn it.

We were just getting used to life without "fresh" sitcoms.

Oh, we'll admit to occasionally sneaking a peek at a rerun of *Perfect Strangers* or *Full House*. But for the most part these past 22 weeks, we managed to do without.

And guess what: It wasn't so bad.

There is life after laugh tracks.

To be more precise, we discovered that there are books to be read, leisurely walks around the neighborhood to be taken, vegetable gardens to be harvested, trips to the ice cream shop to be enjoyed.

All in all, it was an experience we wouldn't mind repeating.

Network executives are predicting that many of their comedy series will be back on the air with new shows by the end of October. After that, we suppose, we'll be chuckling to their stupid jokes again.

Or will we?

## MILWAUKEE SENTINEL
*Milwaukee, WI, August 9, 1988*

The true victors in the Hollywood writers' strike are the viewers who learned there are alternatives to sitcoms and cop shows.

The settlement in the 5-month-old strike against television and movie producers means production can be resumed on shows for the the fall TV season. But the audience impact may be longer lasting.

Endless reruns from last season drove many viewers to cable channels, movie theaters — even to non-video activities. The strike may well hasten the end of the Couch Potato Era.

Now, will the returning writers and their producers give us better shows than the dull drivel that permeates so much television programing?

## THE PLAIN DEALER
*Cleveland, OH, August 11, 1988*

Oh, lucky us. After a 22-week reprieve, we'll return to "normalcy" in a few months. The Hollywood writers are going back to work. Back to silly sitcoms, canned laughter and formula writing. Back to brilliant comedy, sensitive drama and well-crafted plots. Back to that mish-mash of inconsistent entertainment that gives television and film-making such fascination and frustration.

Considering that so many actors, directors and producers were making big bucks on reruns, the writers who made so many successes possible deserved a cut of the pie. There were legitimate concerns, too, about who gets to rewrite a work and other professional issues. None of that mattered to the tube junkies who were tired of plots and characters getting confused on the soaps and tired of reruns of the reruns on night-time series.

Now that the fall television season approaches, and later the November sweeps that determine future advertising revenue, fantasyland has seen the future. Much of America may not have cable services yet, or VCRs that can play movies not long out of the theaters. But the threat of non-network viewing is sufficient that the network must fight back. NBC thinks it's in the best position to recover quickly because it has rights to the Olympics and World Series. ABC has miniseries, including the epic "War and Remembrance." CBS has, well, internal struggles that would make a movie script. As for feature-length film fare, the future was bleak without the scriptwriters, which means next year could be lean at the box office.

America may have been better off when people got more exercise and read books and family members talked to each other and no hypnotic box sat in the corner. But that was then and this is now. Is ALF on tonight? Oh, lucky us.

## THE SUN
*Baltimore, MD, August 5, 1988*

The threat of fall without our quota of hope, dreams, fantasy, special-effect thrills and canned laughter is over. The apparent settlement of the television writers' strike after 22 omen-filled weeks is reassuring. This season's start will be delayed, but they won't have to stretch the summer (autumn, really) Olympics till Christmas. Nor does the American public have to reassess its evening habits. The two sides went to the brink, but then stepped back as they are meant to in strikes. American culture as we know it will survive.

Autumn, when networks normally roll out new shows, is the season of hope. It is when Americans yearn for a discovery as stimulating as Archie Bunker and the Cosby family and "Dallas" in their first years. Or a cult show that attracts a self-defined slice of the population while befuddling the rest. Mostly, the hopes are unrealized. What we get are pale imitations of the previous season's gimmicks, faceless new cop shows, outtakes of old auto chases, as well as the proven series progressively shopworn. What the writers strike threatened was not quality — the networks can always drag out reruns or buy British series — but the hope of finding a gem in the fluff, the hope that greets all creativity.

The threat of deprivation once again honored television as the most important art form in the aesthetic lives of Americans. It is what movies once were and, before them, theater and books. It is the vicarious drama, beauty, fantasy and thrills of more lives than any other medium provides. Comic books don't come close.

The strike also highlights television's potential as an export, helping to right the U.S. balance of payments. That provided the strike issue. Union writers were striking against the producers to get a share of the fees for television rights sold overseas. The U.S. may be a net importer of shirts and automobiles but the world thirsts for our sitcoms and soap operas. Many countries have added domestic television networks and channels and cable systems beyond their ability to produce, and need our creative genius. Some strikes come from the distress of shrinking industries; others, such as this, from the promise of market expansion.

It would be nice to think that in 22 weeks the television producers had nothing better to do than store up crisper situations, and the writers wittier dialogue. Then the quality of our lives would improve in prime time as a direct byproduct of the strike. Fat chance.

## The Register-Guard
*Eugene, OR, August 9, 1988*

The recently concluded writers' strike gave television viewers a behind-the-screen glimpse of their favorite industry. The strike showed what most viewers probably knew anyway: TV's engines are fueled by money — and, to an ever-increasing degree, foreign money.

The 22-week-old strike, one of the longest labor disputes in Hollywood history, was primarily over foreign residuals. The networks are seeing their American markets gradually erode as viewers opt for cable or satellite television, movies, outdoor activities and other forms of entertainment. (There's even a rumor that Americans have rediscovered that reading is fun.)

While the domestic TV markets are eroding, foreign markets are booming. For example, until recently France had only two government-run TV stations. It now has six, each competing for a share of France's growing TV audience. Similar things are happening in New Zealand, Spain, Belgium, Italy, West Germany and other countries. These markets constituted the battleground for the writers' strike.

The writers saw the foreign bonanza and wanted a piece of the action. The producers declined, claiming that their foreign sales made up for losses — especially on hour-long, prime-time dramas — on the domestic side. Details of the final agreement are sketchy, but it seems that both sides, as they often do in these situations, won some and lost some.

While the strike will delay the start of the networks' fall schedules by about a month, most viewers probably won't notice. NBC had already planned to fill a big chunk of its early prime-time season with, first, the Olympic Games (from Sept. 17 to Oct. 2), followed by the World Series (beginning Oct. 15). ABC will jump in with the baseball playoffs in early October, followed by 18 hours of its mini-series, "War and Remembrance." CBS, with no big sports events or miniseries on hand, will simply plug its shows into the schedule as they become available.

There are far more important things in the world to worry about than a strike by TV writers. But, ever so briefly, this one did hold out the intriguing possibility of an autumn filled with busy libraries, strolls in the parks, dinner parties and that grandest of human art forms — conversation.

## LOS ANGELES HERALD EXAMINER
*Los Angeles, CA, August 5, 1988*

"The time was right to make a deal." Those were the words of Brian Walton, chief negotiator for the Writer's Guild of America, in announcing a tentative settlement to the 150-day strike. The statement has an ominous ring for guild members, considering that the agreement came shortly after a group of dissatisfied writers turned up the heat with their threats to resign unless a settlement came quickly. What's more, producers said they'd go ahead with new shows with or without the union.

The conventional wisdom says no one wins a strike. But if the settlement sticks, producers will have lost much less than the writers. Under the terms of the new pact, the writers pretty much settled for the producers' offer on the crucial issue of residuals on shows sold for syndication overseas. "It was no home run," said one official. "Damage control," said another.

Long labor strikes, painful as they can be for all concerned, do offer clarification on exactly what a particular labor market can demand. And the writers have learned that right now, they can't get a whole lot more than what they had. The Hollywood entertainment industry seems willing to replace its writers, one way or the other, rather than make them partners in the business — particularly the expanding areas such as sales to international audiences.

Dedication and devotion to craft, long experience and years of low pay are a necessary part of becoming a success for many TV or film writers who don't have a well-connected father, mother or sister-in-law. But those dues won't guarantee a piece of the Hollywood action. For every seasoned writer, there are hundreds desperate for the chance. Producers know that.

True, there aren't a lot of people who could pen an episode of the more inspired TV offerings, like "St. Elsewhere," "Frank's Place," "Hooperman" or "The Tracey Ullman Show." But many, many TV programs are stale, trite ideas being trotted out for the umpteenth time.

Likewise, not all movie scripts reflect real talent, style and originality. Indeed, everyone in L.A. *does* seem to be working on a screenplay. Considering all this, there's only so much leverage a writers' union can generate.

## THE GOOD NEWS / THE BAD NEWS

THE TELEVISION WRITERS ARE COMING BACK.

THE TELEVISION WRITERS ARE COMING BACK.

## The Washington Post
*Washington, DC, July 2, 1988*

With the television writers' strike in its fourth month and the possibility of its lasting into the fall season, NBC has a contingency plan – a "writerproof" schedule that will include foreign shows, revivals and pilots for series that never made it into a season's schedule.

Whatever the merits of the writers' strike – and whatever the merits of not-ready-for-prime-time shows that will now be on prime time – the notion of something writerproof is distressing (and should be, even for people who are not professional writers).

There is a question whether the stuff now on TV is writerproof already, but that is a matter left to the discretion of the viewer with a channel-flipper in hand.

In announcing the contingency schedule, NBC listed a fourth type of writerproof program, along with the imports, revivals and pilots – most of which (having already been written by someone) clearly will not require the services of a str ing writer.

This programming is something NBC calls "reality programs" – events cheaply and easily photographed *cinema verite*. The question for NBC is whether "reality" can have any meaning for the viewer without the shaping and guiding that a writer has brought to it.

The reports in every day's Globe are reality, but they come to the reader not as entries in a police blotter or a governor's schedule, a box score or a stock table, but shaped and placed into context by a writer.

The excitement of being present at an event is illustrated by baseball fans who stay at the game until the final out, then read a news story and several columns about it the next morning – realizing that reality sometimes needs a helping hand. The political junkie who will get cable, if necessary, to watch the national conventions gavel-to-gavel eagerly reads every pundit's observations the next morning. Reality still needs its interpreters. The world is not ready to be writerproofed.

## Lincoln Journal
*Lincoln, NE, August 8, 1988*

In the end, even columnist Georgie Anne Geyer admits elsewhere on today's Opinion Page she was spinning a fanciful wish, i.e., that because of the 22-week strike by Hollywood writers of "entertainment" television programs, overseas victims would be granted a brief period of relief from seeing warped, distorted images of the United States.

Not to be, as Geyer knows. There are about as many boatloads of trashy U.S. commercial television re-runs for sale in distant "markets" as there are barge shipments of U.S. toxic ash and waste readily available for dumping off Africa's west coast, if the Africans will bite.

Geyer is only the latest voice to protest the false and wicked perception daily presented to millions of people in Africa, Asia, the Pacific Basin and Latin America by U.S. television programs keyed to violence and sex, especially urban violence. This is an old story. The international harm such programs do is palpable.

One need not step out of Lincoln, either, to grasp such distant reality. Local citizens active in the Mayor's Committee for International Friendship who host foreign visitors quickly learn from their guests of the cheapening and brutal images many U.S. television programs leave on other cultures.

A recent visitor from Guinea, on his first journey to the United States, admitted that for his first two days in Lincoln, he was constantly afraid of being mugged and robbed by street hoodlums. That fear was the pre-conditioning he had received from seeing American television.

It may be that Lincoln is a favored spot on the itinerary of foreign guests sponsored by the State Department just because it so solidly reflects what is basic and best in our national life — not what makes for agitated and agitating television programs, later destined for years of overseas viewing. And damage.

Incidentally, the Guinea radio journalist was charmed by Nebraska's Capital City.

## 'Colorization' of Films Sparks Wide Controversy

Film director Woody Allen appeared before a U.S. Senate subcommittee May 12, 1987 to protest the computerized coloring of black and white movies, a practice he called "sinful." The reclusive director, who rarely left New York City, was joined in his Capitol Hill protest by a number of directorial colleagues and by actress Ginger Rogers. In videotaped testimony, ailing director John Huston, an early and vocal opponent of what had come to be known as "colorization," called the coloring of his classic film *The Maltese Falcon* "bushwacking."

The villain of their complaints, was broadcaster Ted Turner, who in 1986 had announced plans to color 100 black and white films from the massive film library he acquired as part of his purchase of Metro-Goldwyn-Mayer.

The hearing room was packed with spectators, but only one lawmaker attended, Sen. Patrick Leahy (D, Vt.), who had convened the hearing under the mandate of his subcommittee on technology and the law. Proponents of colorization also testified. Young people, said Roger L. Mayer, president of Turner Entertainment Co., "simply cannot be persuaded, cajoled or bullied into watching [old movies] in black and white."

Computer-colored films would be granted copyright status if those tinted versions revealed a certain degree of human creativity and were produced by existing computer-coloring technology, the U.S. Copyright Office of the Library of Congress ruled June 19, 1987.

The ruling came after months of debate surrounding the "colorization" process, a debate that had reached all the way to the U.S. Senate.

The copyright office ruled that computer-colored versions of black-and-white films were entitled to copyright protection as "derivative works." Such protection gave a studio the right, generally for 75 years, to distribute a colored version of a movie through broadcast and cable-TV outlets and to sell videotape copies. The studio could also collect damages from companies that copied the colored films.

Films would not be eligible for copyright protection if the tinting "consists of the addition of only a relatively few number of colors to an existing black-and-white motion picture."

## The Register
*Santa Ana, CA, May 17, 1987*

Woody Allen says the issue of coloring black-and-white films is a matter of morality. If so, Congress should stay well away from it; politics and morals simply don't mix.

Truth to tell, the colorization controversy seems more about money. Which is no doubt why Congress, not to mention presidential hopeful Richard Gephardt, is so attracted to this issue. There are a lot of contributions to be had from the Hollywood set.

Indeed, the stars were out in force last week. Allen joined actress Ginger Rogers and directors Sidney Pollack, Milos Forman and Elliott Silverstein in putting on a show for the Senate Judiciary subcommittee on technology and the law — which had no colorization legislation pending at the time.

They all came to testify about the recent trend to use a computer to add color to black-and-white movies. The practice was variously described as "sinful" and "morally unacceptable," but the real sin would be for Congress to outlaw the practice.

No matter how much blood, sweat, and creative juice an actor, actress, or director puts into a film, the finished product ultimately belongs to the person (or persons) who made the whole thing possible by paying the bills. If the owner wants to change the work, that is his or her prerogative, plain and simple.

There is no reason the owner of a painting cannot change its colors. The painting may not be worth nearly as much as it was before, and it certainly would be unethical to pass the work off as an original — but the act of altering personal property should not be a concern of Congress.

No one suggests that colored versions of films will supplant the original black-and-whites. But a host of studies do show that viewers respond better to color. Colored films sell better on TV and in the video stores, which means at least a part of the work is seen by a much wider audience. That should be heartening, not "sinful."

Nevertheless, the day after the subcommittee hearing, Gephardt introduced a bill to outlaw colorization. What's next — a bill outlawing the practice of cutting films to fit into prime-time television slots?

Surely that's just as "sinful" as colorization. And just as silly an issue for a Congress that needs to first figure out how to balance a budget.

## Roanoke Times & World-News
*Roanoke, VA, May 20, 1987*

PARDON OUR Philistinism, but what's so dastardly about "colorizing" black-and-white movies? What's so dastardly about it, anyway, that a federal law is needed to protect underprivileged film directors from seeing their products altered by the ogres who have paid — handsomely, as a rule — for the exhibition rights?

To hear the directors tell it, "colorization" is on a par with taking a switchblade to the Mona Lisa. It is the moral equivalent, they seem to believe, of razing the Notre Dame de Paris. It is tampering with *art*, for God's sake, and by people only interested in a buck.

As if the directors aren't. If all they were interested in were the integrity of their movies, then no exhibition rights ever would be sold to television — which "squeezes" dialogue, edits out entire scenes, and interrupts the film every 10 or 15 minutes for commercials. The Directors Guild of America isn't seeking a ban on "colorization." What the directors want is a federal law to improve their bargaining position to get extra money from exhibitors who want to "colorize."

Is "colorizing" bad for movies? The only intelligent answer is: It depends on the movie. Some black-and-white films are masterpieces that, artistically speaking, should be left alone. Others are dogs that nothing can help. Most, though, are somewhere in between, and it would be foolish to say in advance whether "colorizing" would help or hurt them.

But whatever the artistic merits of fiddling with black-and-white movies, the analogy to paintings or Gothic cathedrals is weak. There is only one Mona Lisa, only one Notre Dame de Paris. By contrast, movies — like books — come in multiple copies. To abridge "War and Peace" may be to commit a literary travesty, but you can always read the full version. To turn "The Maltese Falcon" into a color movie may be to commit a cinematic travesty, but you can always see the black-and-white version.

And in another important way, movies are different from books, too. A book customarily is the product of one creative intellect, the author's. But for movie directors to claim a similarly exclusive kind of authorship is absurd. The degree of a director's influence varies with the director and with the movie, of course, but the director never works alone. Also involved are the creative talents of actors and screenwriters, of cinematographers and, often, book authors — whose work, once rights to it are bought, is subject to far more manipulation than anything the "colorizers" are doing.

Director Woody Allen, who hasn't exactly grown poor making movies, says "the justness of this cause will prevail over avariciousness." Missouri Congressman Richard Gephardt, a Democratic presidential candidate and author of a bill to ban (via federal copyright law) unsanctioned "colorizing," says film-makers "should not be second-guessed by entrepreneurs in search of a quick buck."

But Gephardt's bill should be seen for what it is: a piece of special-interest labor legislation, perhaps politically inspired, to give film-makers an edge when they negotiate exhibition rights. That doesn't necessarily make it a bad bill. But, please, spare us the sanctimonious rhetoric.

## The Duluth News-Tribune
*Duluth, MN, May 13, 1987*

The congressional hearing room was crowded. Witnesses were assembled. Testimony poured forth.

Iran-contra hearings? Yes, but also the hearing on computer colorization of movies where some luminaries associated with Hollywood — actor-director Woody Allen and actress Ginger Rogers among them — appealed Tuesday to a Senate subcommittee to do something to prevent American films produced in black and white from being turned into color movies through computer technology.

It's already been done to several popular black-and-white movies such as "Yankee Doodle Dandy" and "Casablanca," and Allen and company want it stopped by making it illegal. Those who own or control many of the films defend the practice, saying colorization makes them more salable for use on television and in the home video market.

Who should prevail here? Most agree it's an issue of art vs. money and most often when art and money are pitted against each other, money wins. We believe that, ideally, works of art should not be tampered with, although it will be difficult to enact legislation that would define which films are art and which are not — if art is going to be the criterion. Hollywood has produced plenty of black-and-white trash, the colorization of which might improve the product, if only to the eye.

We agree art should not be tampered with but suspect that the directors of many Hollywood potboilers over the years would not object to the colorization of their movies. A question: Were the private owner of a different kind of visual art — say a great painting — to markedly change it and put it on display, would the owner be prosecuted?

This is not a black-and-white issue.

## THE BUFFALO NEWS
*Buffalo, NY, June 28, 1987*

SOME MOVIE stars and others connected with filmmaking have been vigorous in condemning the colorization of old black-and-white movies. Woody Allen has used words like "desecration," "mutilation" and "sinful" in commenting on the new process, which has been used to color about 25 movies so far. The public response to colorization has been generally good.

Rep. Richard A. Gephardt, D-Mo., has gone even further, proposing to Congress a "moral right" measure that would allow directors and screen writers to forbid the coloring of movies, even if they did not own the copyrights. Those opposing color had a setback recently when colorized versions of movies were ruled eligible for copyright protection.

Well-meaning as these opponents are, they are off base in seeking federal regulation of these artistic — or nonartistic — activities.

Granted that black and white was used with great creativity by the old film makers and granted that it may be dismaying for many to see their work tampered with, it is not the government's role to intrude on such decisions by owners of old films.

It seems clear that the television audience for black-and-white movies is limited, no matter how artistically that medium has been used. Use of the new colorization process is thus bringing these old movies to much wider audiences than would otherwise view them.

Woody Allen says he is fighting "to protect American movies from mutilation." But the original black-and-white movies still exist; all that is happening is that new versions are being created. It is not like drawing a moustache on the Mona Lisa; at worst, it is like drawing a moustache on a reproduction of the Mona Lisa. It would be foolish to enact a statute forbidding that.

It would be even more foolish when one considers that movies shown on television today are already mutilated — cut to fit a time slot like so much sausage and interspersed with commercials that disrupt the mood of the film.

Indeed, most movies are not made for the TV screen, and their artistic effect can be distorted simply by the cramped nature of the medium.

Attempts to legislate public taste in the matter of colorization are misguided and probably unconstitutional. One might as well try to make it illegal to view a color film on a black-and-white set or to broadcast it in installments. Or to make movies out of books, which, after all, are often seriously distorted when transferred to the screen.

For better or worse, colorization appears here to stay. But connoisseurs of old films will still have recourse to art theaters, specialized television channels or videocassettes to see Mona Lisa without a moustache.

## The Star-Ledger
*Newark, NJ, June 3, 1987*

Green and red are the traditional colors of Christmas, but there is no hint of that seasonal good cheer in the controversy over the reissuing of tinted versions of memorable black-and-white films. Green, as in money, is the motivation, for the people pressing ahead with what has come to be known as "colorization." Red, as in anger, is what colorization has provoked among people who are vehemently opposed to tampering with classic movies.

The pro-color crowd argues that it's sitting on mountains of films that nobody wants to see because they're in old-fashioned black-and-white. Jazzing them up with color, they claim, will enhance their value. And they insist they have a right to make as much money as they can on movies because they have bought them and own the rights to them.

Not so, respond the purists. The films in question are works of art and no one has a right to alter a work of art. How right they are! "Casablanca" is a film classic which can only be butchered by colorization. The same is true of "Yankee Doodle Dandy," which loses dramatic impact and artistic subtlety when wrapped in red, white and blue.

Ginger Rogers, Woody Allen and a lot of other talented people who respect creativity and appreciate artistry want Congress to put a stop to the colorization nonsense by amending the copyright laws.

Mr. Allen, who writes, directs and often stars in his own films, was most persuasive in a recent appearance before a Senate judiciary subcommittee considering legislative changes. He spoke of a moral issue and maintained, quite correctly, that "You can't have a culture where people can go in at will and mutilate an artist's work." Miss Rogers provided a personal touch by noting it was embarrassing and insulting to see herself "painted up like a birthday cake" in a tinted-version of "42d Street."

They could have added that the colorization process is far from perfected, that the tints often detract and distract from the film. But that would have been gilding the lily. On the issue of artistry alone, Congress should act to preserve the authenticity and appeal of the black-and-white classics.

## The Dallas Morning News
*Dallas, TX, May 25, 1987*

With Gary Hart having departed the field as a result of his guest problems, Rep. Richard Gephardt is coming up fast on the outside in the Democratic primary sweepstakes. As he showed the other day, he has a firm grasp of candidate mathematics.

Ginger Rogers, Woody Allen and a cast of thousands have been crusading against colorization of old black-and-white movies, a melodrama in which the villain is portrayed by the cable TV baron, Ted Turner. Turner, known in his sailing days as "Captain Outrageous," apparently enjoys the cape-and-top-hat role, for he declares that he may just color up *Casablanca* for the controversy's sake.

But the other day, Gephardt stepped forth dramatically with the film stars and promised a federal law — "the Film Integrity Act," no less — to prevent dastardly doings with old movies. Thus Gephardt proved he understands the numbers that are so important to those who wish to offer their services to the public at a higher level of elected office. As any serious candidate can see, there are more voters who are not Ted Turner than voters who are Ted Turner.

## Honolulu Star-Bulletin
*Honolulu, HI, June 26, 1987*

The people who want to color old black-and-white movies have won an important victory. The Copyright Office of the Library of Congress has decided to grant copyright protection to some color-enhanced versions of classic films.

The Copyright Office said copyrights of the original black-and-white films will not be affected, but it will allow copyright protection for the modified versions of movies, provided they "reveal a certain minimum amount of individual, creative, human authorship" in the coloring process. A computer artist may select from nearly 4,100 hues for each movie.

The decision is important because it will eliminate uncertainties about the rights to many films and make colorization a better financial bet.

The opponents of colorization aren't giving up. They have gotten legislation introduced in Congress that would stop unauthorized coloring.

Colorization does seem like a sleazy idea, particularly when it is done without the consent of the people who made the films. But the tinted versions may reach audiences that wouldn't look at the originals in black and white. The approval of the Copyright Office could be the green light the proponents of coloring needed.

## Chicago Tribune
*Chicago, IL, May 17, 1987*

Some pretty high-profile people from the film industry are trying to get Congress to forbid anyone from displaying in color movies originally filmed in black and white. They think the process, which Ted Turner has announced he would use on 100 films he owns, is a crime against artists.

Maybe Congress should pass a resolution that says Ted Turner has abysmal taste for putting a dull paint job on such masterpieces as "The Maltese Falcon." But otherwise, it ought not be meddling.

In the future, film-makers by contract can restrain anyone from putting color on their black and white films. It might mean their films are slightly less marketable, but it is up to them to decide whether purity is worth it.

As to films made before the colorization process was developed, the thing to remember is that the original is not destroyed. All that happens is that audiences are given the opportunity to see a bastardized version—just as they see a bastardized version of wide-screen films whenever they watch television, and often see a truncated version because TV stations cut the films to fit their time slots.

The film-makers say that showing a colorized black and white film is like displaying a copy of Picasso's "Guernica" painted over in harlequin shades. Maybe so, but they ought to ask themselves whether they really want Congress to legislate taste. They might find that Congress' taste is not quite as fine as their own.

## The Philadelphia Inquirer
*Philadelphia, PA, May 16, 1987*

Should owners of black-and-white film classics such as *Casablanca*, *Citizen Kane* and *The Maltese Falcon* use computers to "colorize" them?

"Sinful," says Woody Allen.

It sells, answer businessmen.

Both, of course, are right, but what, if anything, should be done about this latest eruption of Hollywood's eternal conflict between art and commerce? The issue is joined because Ted Turner, the gaudy Atlanta entrepreneur, owns the cinematic archives of RKO, MGM and everything Warner Bros. produced before 1950. He intends to "colorize" 100 black-and-white films, which outrages directors and actors, but which, indeed, evidently does give new commercial life to old movies.

Item: Jimmy Stewart, who starred in *It's a Wonderful Life*, says he cannot bear to watch it in its new colorized version. "The artificial color was detrimental to the story, to the whole atmosphere and artistry of the film ...," he said in written testimony submitted to Congress. Every real American knows Jimmy Stewart wouldn't lie.

On the other hand, Hal Roach Studios couldn't market the old film in black and white, but within weeks of its colorization, stations in 96 percent of the nation's television markets bought it, and color videocassette versions of it outsold black-and-whites by 6-1 at Christmas.

To artists, it's a matter of moral respect for artistic integrity. To businessmen, it's a matter of markets, money and ownership. Thus as ever. Complicating this neat dichotomy, unfortunately, is the reality that movie-making is an inherently collaborative process, which often muddies the question of precisely who deserves credit as a film's artistic creator. That's especially true for movies made prior to the 1960s, when even directors often were ordered about by studio bosses like errand boys, and films were made as if on assembly lines.

Even so, there can be no mistaking the distinctive artistry in films directed even under those conditions by *auteurs* such as John Huston, and there is no question that work such as his *Maltese Falcon* is art, as surely as is a sculpture or a painting.

Although black-and-white originals continue to exist, the intensely marketed colorized versions remain assaults on how the artist intended to present his vision. Suppose that some (but not all) of the owners of the 19 castings of Auguste Rodin's sculpture *The Thinker* painted a dozen of them purple?

Ultimately, the law must resolve such conflicts. The best answer is for filmmakers to emulate Woody Allen, whose contracts stipulate that his films will not be colorized or otherwise altered without his consent. To protect artists less able to dictate their own terms, as well as to protect works from the past, Congress should consider amending copyright law to strengthen claims by creative artists, or their heirs, to protect their work. European filmmakers have such rights; why not Americans?

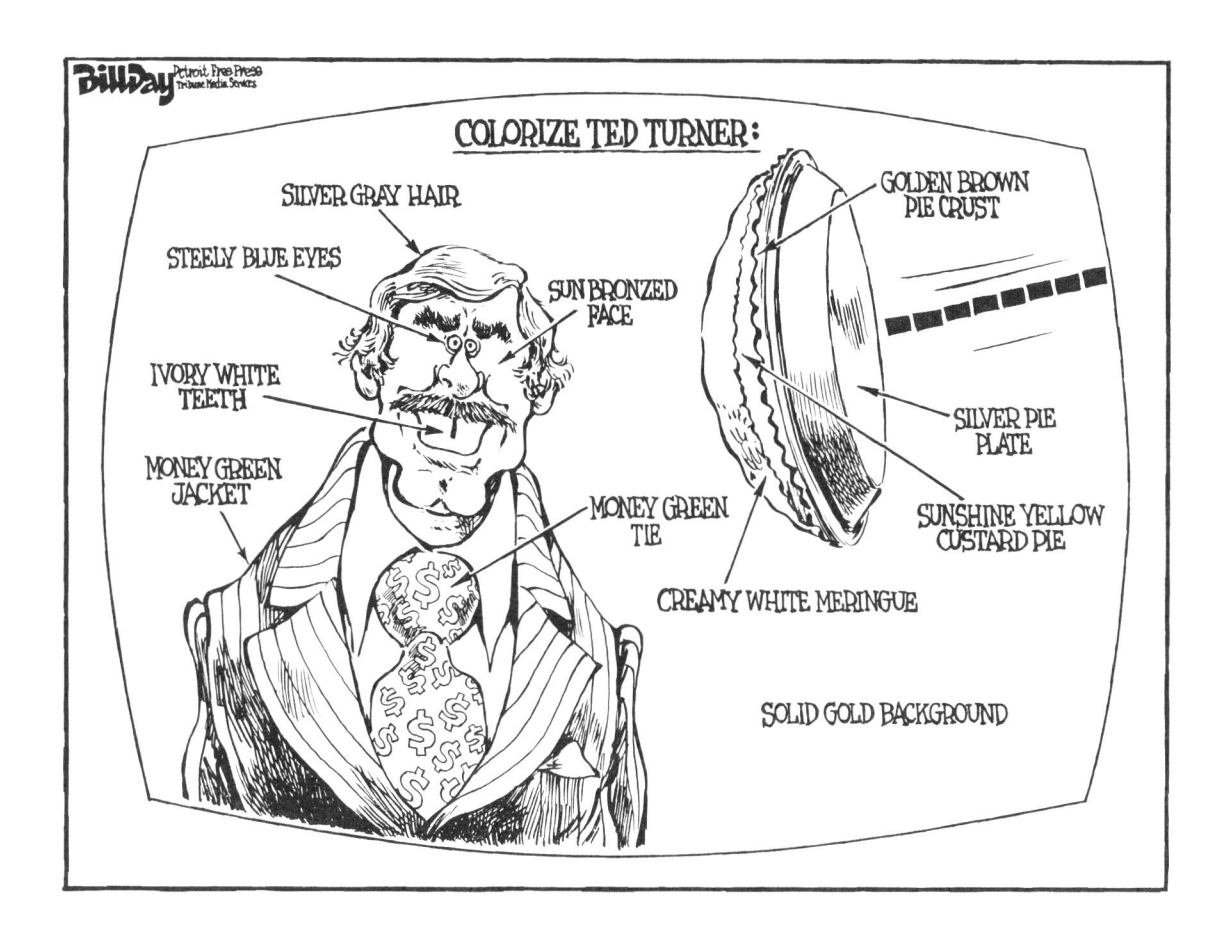

## COLORIZE TED TURNER:

- SILVER GRAY HAIR
- STEELY BLUE EYES
- SUN BRONZED FACE
- IVORY WHITE TEETH
- MONEY GREEN JACKET
- MONEY GREEN TIE
- GOLDEN BROWN PIE CRUST
- SILVER PIE PLATE
- SUNSHINE YELLOW CUSTARD PIE
- CREAMY WHITE MERINGUE
- SOLID GOLD BACKGROUND

*Bill Day, Detroit Free Press, Tribune Media Services*

# DAILY NEWS
*New York, NY, May 26, 1987*

Woody Allen calls it sinful. And so it is, though some may snort that movie "colorization" is not a moral debate. They're wrong. Just like it's wrong—wrong as it can be—to color-by-computer a movie made in black and white. No matter *what* Ted Turner says. But esthetically, even morally wrong doesn't always mean it should be illegal.

Turner knows that lots of viewers would *prefer* to see the old classics in color. In fact, color may be the only way to get some people to watch at all. And he wants to make money. Lots. Turner bought the entire MGM film library, intending to color at will—or, as he says, to "color-enhance."

Woody Allen and Ginger Rogers went to Congress to say that's sacrilege. That movies are works of art. That they should be left the way they are. That Congress has a duty to protect them from the lurid touch of the commercial brush.

It's a sympathetic argument, but it doesn't quite wash. After all, a version of a movie that has been "colorized"—the nonword used by what director John Huston calls the "coloroids"—is just one version. The original remains intact. No matter how many jazzed up, punked out, low-down variations on the theme are trundled out in pursuit of the almighty buck. And viewers have a choice. Turn the dial. Don't watch. Buy, rent or demand the original.

Behind the congressional hearings are various rumblings—led by Rep. Richard Gephardt and Sen. Patrick Leahy—about possible legislation to beef up the copyright laws to allow less tampering after the fact. Fine! As importantly, let all this be a lesson to artists from every field to protect their future rights—and the integrity of their work—with as tight and tough a deal as they can forge.

But despise as any movie lover might the "colorized" versions of "Miracle on 34th Street" or "It's a Wonderful Life" or "The Maltese Falcon," it is hardly fair—or constitutionally sound—to try to legislate the debate in retrospect.

# The Hutchinson News
*Hutchinson, KS, December 27, 1987*

Few people could do absolutely nothing and win the acclaim of a grateful nation. Ted Turner has just done it.

Mr. Turner, who owns rights to 3,000 MGM movies, has bought exclusive world rights to 800 RKO Pictures movies. One of those 800 is the classic "Citizen Kane."

Turner, who loves to botch up good black and white movies by slopping pastel colors over them, has made a solemn promise about his new "Citizen Kane," however. He says he won't "colorize" it.

Civilization escapes again. But this is rather like congratulating Attila the Hun for letting one village stand while he levels the rest of the countryside.

# THE COMMERCIAL APPEAL
*Memphis, TN, May 25, 1987*

ONCE more Rep. Richard Gephardt, presidential candidate, has come roaring to the rescue. He wants to stop "colorization" of old black and white movies.

Missouri's Gephardt wrote the protectionist "Gephardt Amendment" to a trade bill, which would bash several U.S. trading partners. His amendment is a favorite of organized labor.

He also is sponsoring a farm bill designed to appeal to voters in Iowa, an important first stop along the nomination trail.

Why is Gephardt against colorizing old films? Well, Woody Allen says it's "sinful," and assorted other actors and directors told a congressional hearing that it is "morally unacceptable." There's also a lot of campaign money to be picked up in Hollywood, especially now that Warren Beatty's best political friend, Gary Hart, has given up the race.

The Gephardt anti-colorization bill is unlikely to go far. For one thing, it would infringe on the property rights of those who own the films. Second, Congress has more important things to do, such as draw up a national budget and see to the country's defenses.

But the issue got Gephardt and several Hollywood types on the evening network news, which probably was a major objective of this frivolous undertaking.

## THE SACRAMENTO BEE
*Sacramento, CA, July 18, 1988*

Surely you've seen them: Those grainy, out-of-focus, often black-and-white TV commercials that seem less like a sales pitch than a slice of life or, as they're called in one case, a "slice of death." Others feature real people (as opposed to "real" people impersonated by actors) at work, playing softball or just schmoozing in an artful facsimile of home movies. And that's the idea: Welcome to "reality" advertising.

This rage for reality was born in the minds of Madison Avenue's creative folks who, a couple of years ago, began to sense a souring, distrustful public mood generated by things like the space shuttle disaster, the spread of AIDS, Wall Street insider-trading scandals and last October's stock market collapse, Irangate and the nation's growing trade and budget problems. Suddenly, slickness and the upbeat "Morning in America" theme of a few seasons back rang false.

"Reality" ads have done more than just turn simulated amateurism into a new pop-art form: They're making money for John Hancock, which pioneered the genre with its "Real Life, Real Answers" insurance commercials, and AT&T, which offers a series of grim morality tales built around some executive's disastrous failure to buy the right communications system, a message guaranteed to chill any aspiring young MBA. Others are less forbidding and, in some cases, barely mention the name of the product being touted. Was reality ever this daring?

Still, one shouldn't confuse this "reality" with real life. Madison Avenue, like its creative counterpart in Hollywood, is presenting a synthetic authenticity no less fanciful than the rosy-hued world at the other end of the spectrum. No matter how skillfully art imitates life, it's still art. Soon, people will tire of pseudo-realism and the hucksters will rediscover Technicolor fantasy as quickly as you can say bottom line. There's no business like show business.

## The Register-Guard
*Eugene, OR, June 29, 1988*

It's been nearly 50 years since James Stewart, as the idealistic hero in the movie classic, "Mr. Smith Goes to Washington," battled *governmental* corruption. Last week, the legendary actor revived memories of "Mr. Smith" when he returned to the nation's capital to do battle with *artistic* corruption.

Stewart's target was the "colorizing," re-editing or otherwise altering of classic black-and-white movies. Only those films on which the original copyrights have expired and new copyrights have been obtained can be transformed from black-and-white to color.

Supporters of the colorization process argue — with a straight face — that they're actually helping preserve the movie classics by providing them with a new generation of enthusiasts. They say that today's film market is dominated by TV-watching, video-renting young people who simply won't watch anything in black-and-white. They contend that by colorizing such black-and-white classics as "The Maltese Falcon," "It's a Wonderful Life" and "Yankee Doodle Dandy," they're building a brand new audience for some of Hollywood's greatest motion pictures.

Purists, among whom we count ourselves, view the colorization process as artistic desecration. The artists who created those old films in black-and-white did so intentionally. Adding color to a film such as "Mr. Smith Goes to Washington" demeans the artistic process. That film's director, Frank Capra, said of the colorization of another of his and Stewart's collaborations, "It's a Wonderful Life": "They splashed it all over with Easter-egg colors and ruined it . . . Even the villain looks pink and cheerful."

That brings us back to why "Mr. Smith" returned to Washington. He went in support of a bill now before Congress to establish a national film commission. The nine-member commission would designate certain films as "a significant part of our nation's historical and cultural heritage and ones that uniquely reflect the spirit of their times." No designated film could be colorized or otherwise changed unless it was given a new title and carried a label detailing all changes from the original.

The anti-colorization proposal is a worthy attempt to preserve or slow down the debasement of movie classics. The proposal has been approved by the House Appropriations Committee as a rider to a $9.7 billion appropriations bill for the Interior Department and related agencies. That alone may cause it trouble later on. It would be better for the measure's sponsors to present it as a separate legislative entity. Attaching it to an appropriations bill circumvents the committee process and needlessly increases the potential opposition.

## DESERET NEWS
*Salt Lake City, UT, July 27/28, 1988*

If there's anything this country does not need, it is a new federal agency to tell the public which motion pictures are classics and "part of our nation's historical and cultural heritage."

Yet that is exactly what will happen if the Senate goes along with the House and creates a 13-member National Film Preservation Advisory Board, which would be under the Secretary of Interior.

The drive to put a federal quality-seal on old movies grows out of the conviction among some film directors, writers, and actors that it is sacrilegious to "colorize" a movie originally was made in black and white.

These folks tried to get Congress to ban the coloring of films, but failed. So, as an interim step, the preservationists are willing to accept the advisory board, which could choose up to 25 films a year for protection as classics. Once so honored, Scripps Howard News Service reports, a movie would be included in a National Film Registry and given a seal that could be used to promote it.

And if the film were altered or colored, it would have to be labeled as "materially altered" or "colorized" and carry a disclaimer that "certain creative contributors did not participate." This information would appear at the beginning of the film and on videotape packages.

The thought among the Hollywood types is that fewer persons would view or buy tapes of altered films. What nonsense! Cable network mogul Ted Turner and others are rich because they tried out both black and white and colorized films, saw there is a larger audience for the tinted versions, and gave the public what it wants. If citizens like viewing colorized old movies, fine. Devotees of black and white can see the "pure" examples at art theaters and film festivals.

Creating a bureaucracy to decree what is and isn't a classic film would be paternalistic, elitist, and meddlesome. If the busybodies prevail, what next? Maybe a board to designate classic books and to issue an official seal of approval?

## MILWAUKEE SENTINEL
*Milwaukee, WI, June 22, 1988*

The debate over the colorization of masterpiece black-and-white movies is far from over as the result of action by the House Appropriations Committee.

There was nothing conclusive about the committee vote (it was a close 25-20) to come to the rescue of movie directors and others who are angry at the process of colorizing their films.

The vote signified that anything can still happen.

The question is: What?

Should there be a commission to determine what movies are so artistically significant that those who colorize films, such as TV cable magnate Ted Turner, cannot get at them? Should there be another level of bureaucracy? What standards would be developed for artistic significance?

Frankly, a commission to reduce some color films to black-and-white makes a lot more sense. It could signify the absence of artistic value.

And Congress probably would be willing to set up that commission, too.

## The Hutchinson News
*Hutchinson, KS, March 19, 1988*

Ted Turner's destruction of classic American movie films by "colorizing" them should not be an issue for the federal government.

But, all else having failed, bringing it to Washington at least makes sense.

Film actors and directors took the stage last week in Washington in their campaign. Some of the big actors went to the National Press Club first to make their pitch that "moral rights" of the artists were being violated by the "colorization" and that somebody ought to do something.

The actors and directors asked for national legislation to protect those "rights" or provide some protection with adoption of an international copyright treaty.

In a just universe, Ted Turner's cultural atrocities would be handled in the only way that he can understand. That would be with color and money.

After what Turner has done by schlocking up classic black and white movies with Easter-egg colors, the only appropriate punishment would come when every one of his millions of dollars suddenly changed color and looked like an Easter egg, too.

He would understand that. Suddenly the idea of changing the color of a classic document would not seem so neat.

## The State
*Columbia, SC, November 12, 1988*

This week, multimillionaire media mogul Ted Turner did something useful.

He released a "colorized" videotape of the black-and-white film classic "Casablanca."

Thanks to the computer colorizing process, film fans can see a pink-cheeked Humphrey Bogart, Ingrid Bergman attired in a series of gaudy dresses and Dooley Wilson sing "As Time Goes By" while wearing a blazer that looks like the aftermath of a small nuclear disaster.

The elegance that made "Casablanca" so special may be gone, but it definitely looks more modern. And it gives us ideas about how Ted might "improve" other works of art.

For instance, the gown on the Statue of Liberty looks somewhat passe'. Perhaps Ted could hire a team of sculptors to chip a miniskirt out of the Statue's copper and steel. That also would give tourists a chance to check out the grand old lady's gams.

Then there's the really old-fashioned chair they have Honest Abe sitting in at the Lincoln Monument. How about sculpting a Lazy Boy for the 16th president to rest upon, Ted? The least America can do for the man who won the Civil War is give him the chance to recline.

Let's not forget the Washington Monument. Perhaps a revolving restaurant atop it would make a nice addition.

What, Ted?

You say you have some ideas about improving and modernizing Mount Rushmore?

You think maybe Thomas Jefferson would look "more '80s" wearing a Mohawk?

We couldn't agree more. It's a good idea, Ted — almost as good an idea as colorizing "Casablanca" was.

## THE BUFFALO NEWS
*Buffalo, NY, March 26, 1989*

THE BATTLE over whether old black-and-white movies should be "colorized" for showing on television has flared up again, in spite of a House subcommittee's decision last year that there was no need for any legislation.

The subcommittee asked the U.S. Copyright Office to study the matter, and the agency, an arm of the Library of Congress, has now issued a report declaring that the new colorization technique "has an adverse effect on the esthetics of black-and-white motion pictures."

The agency favored laws protecting future films from colorization, as well as other alterations of the films.

The Copyright Office's dislike of colorization, right or wrong, is in line with the views of many Hollywood celebrities, including Woody Allen, who feels that it is a "desecration" to color movies shot in black and white. Most people don't appear to agree. The reason dozens of old films are being colorized is that there is a much broader market for the colored versions.

But no matter who is right, the colorization of old films should not be a matter for the law. It is simply a matter of preference and taste, and the government has no business legislating in such matters.

We agree with the movie and recording industry whose spokesman, commenting on the new report, said: "We are deeply troubled by an agency of government making esthetic judgments about the quality of creative works."

There is no doubt that some of the film industry's finest work was done in black and white in the 1940s and 1950s before the use of color became almost universal. Film buffs might be understandably distressed and offended at seeing such films as Hitchcock's "Rebecca" or the Alastair Sim version of "A Christmas Carol" offered up in color.

But it goes too far to denounce this as "desecration" or "mutilation," — as if someone had taken an ax to Michelangelo's Pieta. These black and white film classics have not been destroyed. They still exist. The owners of the films have simply made new versions to appeal to a new audience.

If purist logic were followed, the old films could not be shown on television at all, since the small screen, editing for time and the frequent interruptions for commercials make the presentations quite different from what they were originally.

Similarly, films could not be based on novels, since there is inevitably some distortion and shortening in the transference to the screen. Reproductions of works of art through lithographs, silkscreen and needlepoint or on ornamental dishes and souvenirs could also not be tolerated.

While it may be annoying to see an old film favorite in the colorized version or to see the Mona Lisa reproduced on cheap souvenirs, this is something for the public to decide on.

The government should not get involved in telling us what is esthetic and what is not. People may not know much about art, but they know what they like.

## Newsday
*New York, NY, September 5, 1988*

Care to see "Casablanca" — the classic Humphrey Bogart-Ingrid Bergman movie — in color? Yes? No? Maybe?

You might get a chance, the way owners of some classic old films are adding color to what were once plain old black-and-white movies.

You might not, if Congress steps in.

We think the choice should be up to you, not Congress.

Colorizing, as it is called, has only become practical in the past few years, thanks to contemporary computer technology. It doesn't destroy the original; it just results in copies in color. But some motion picture figures — notably New York's own Woody Allen — oppose it vehemently. Colorizing distorts the filmmakers' original vision, they say. Often enough, that's true.

But wait, say the owners of those old films. Some people (the young in particular) will not watch an "old-time" black-and-white film. Colorizing can make those old movies acceptable to a whole new audience. Besides, they say, we bought and paid for those films, and we can colorize them if we want to.

That's just where Congress proposes to step in, with a law designed to protect classic movies against colorizing — even though somebody other than the orginal director now owns them.

The notion that someone might apply color to a black-and-white classic such as Orson Welles' "Citizen Kane," whose brooding monochrome is as important as any prop or dialogue, is horrifying. But should the government be setting or promoting an artistic standard? And if Congress can legislate the color of a film, what about the content?

Lawmakers shouldn't muck around with artistic judgments and must have a compelling reason to legislate away film owners' (or anybody else's) property rights. Colorizing isn't reason enough.

## The Tennessean
*Nashville, TN, July 19, 1989*

COMPATIBLE people who usually agree on everything else often disagree on movies.

That is why the National Film Commission, which meets for the first time today, has a tricky job ahead. The commission, which is composed of representatives from 13 movie organizations, is scheduled to select 25 American movies as national treasures.

This all began when Mr. Ted Turner and other entrepreneurs began buying the copyrights of old films to show on television. In order to make the black-and-white movies more acceptable to modern audiences, color was added. In order to make them compatible with TV, longer films were cut and commercials were added.

The coloring and cutting angered film devotees, who pressured Congress to stop the slaughter of American films. So Congress passed the National Film Preservation Act, which designates certain films as national treasures.

The designated films may still be bought, colored, and chopped to shreds. All the designation means is that those films will carry a label that they have been altered "without the participation of the principal director, screenwriter, and other creators of the original film."

Henceforth, (or more appropriately, From Here to Eternity) the Librarian of Congress may designate up to 25 films a year as national treasures. But this year, the commission must select the first 25 films to be protected by law.

This should be some debate. A majority of the commission may be able to agree that such classics as *Citizen Kane*, *Casablanca*, and *The Best Years of Our Lives* will be included in the 25. But having 13 people trying to decide what the 23rd, or 24th, or 25th best American film is will be a nightmare. Was *The Godfather* better than *Snow White and the Seven Dwarfs*? Was *The Maltese Falcon* better than *To Kill a Mockingbird*? Wars spring from such discussions.

The whole issue might seem trite because the new law won't stop the altering of films. As long as people pay to see them, someone is going to provide them.

But as meaningless as the new law may seem, it does require the government to assume a new role — that of film critic. And that is most definately a role that the government doesn't need. ■

## The Register
*Santa Ana, CA, July 22, 1988*

The House Rules Committee will debate later this week what should be a black-and-white issue: the colorization of films. Directors and actors are using a full spectrum of arguments to support their view that films should be unretouchable. These artists, however, lack proper standing. Actors and directors help make films, but they do not own them.

All this would be much ado about nothing except that a star-studded line-up of whining and sniveling Hollywood hands has garnered a lot of publicity and created more than a little pressure on Congress to do something. But what?

The folks who are adding color to black-and-white movies aren't defacing the originals. They're simply making color copies that seem to have won overwhelming favor from television audiences and video-rental patrons. Those who want to see the original still can, and those who want to see the color copy in black-and-white have only to turn off the color on their television sets.

That should be the end of the argument. Instead, lobbyists are trying to convince the politicians that larger principles are at stake here than property rights. It's a battle for the preservation of a "national treasure" argues director Fred Zinnemann ("From Here to Eternity" and "High Noon") in a letter to Rules Committee Chairman Claude Pepper. Others argue about "moral rights" and protections for artists.

Searching for a compromise that would make everyone happy, the politicians have hit upon a scheme that should scare the living daylights out of filmmakers and film-owners alike. The House Appropriations Committee last week endorsed a proposal to create a National Film Commission. The Rules Committee this week will decide whether to send that proposal to the full House. The proposal would establish a needless bureaucracy; it deserves an early death.

The proposed nine-member commission would be authorized to designate as classics those films that form "an enduring part of our national heritage." These films would then be listed on a national registry and could not be colored without first changing their titles and providing an on-screen notice that the film originally was produced in black-and-white.

Imagine the confusion that would result. Those who saw the color version of "The Maltese Falcon" would know it by a different name — even though it was essentially the same movie. This would enhance our national heritage? Hardly. "Miracle on 34th Street" is a wonderful movie whether in black-and-white or color. Why confuse the issue by calling the color version something else?

The Rules Committee can put an immediate stop to a debate that, while colorful, is mostly a waste of time.

## the Charleston Gazette
*Charleston, WV, May 24, 1987*

WHAT A SCENE in U.S. Senate chambers the other day: creative funnyman Woody Allen deploring the "immorality" of coloring classic black and white movies; still glamorous Ginger Rogers saying how embarrassing it is to see her 1934 self "painted up like a birthday cake" in "42nd Street."

But tough as it may be to tell attractive entertainers to take a hike, lawmakers should tell Hollywood's anticoloring crowd to take a hike. Congress has better things to do than to recast copyright law to cover TV titan Ted Turner's "Colorization" of classic black and white movies.

Sure, coloring of achromatic film is crass. It rates in the same class as turning out digital grandfather's clocks and glass Buddhas with clocks in navel. Besides, the product isn't really color; it's a computerized overlay that literally pales beside Technicolor. Even the contrived, overlong name, *Colorization,* is offensive in the awful tradition of "prioritize" and other "ize" abominations.

But the key issue, as far as Congress is concerned, is not taste, or even morality. It is *legality*. And there is no question but that Ted Turner has the legal right to alter the look of films that he now owns. Curiously, though, Rep. Richard Gephardt has gone so far as to introduce a bill outlawing film coloring, except in cases where director and screenwriter have approved.

Ironically, relatively little has been said about two TV desecrations more offensive than movie coloring. One is commercial interruption of films of poetic quality ("All Quiet on the Western Front," "A Place in the Sun"). Another is the presentation of Cinemascope pictures on the 4-3 ratio TV screen; more than a third of the original picture is lost. Nothing can be done about either problem, of course. It's the ads that make the movie broadcasts possible, and a wide TV screen has never been marketed.

Ted Turner can't do much about his coloring binge, either. Having bought fewer MGM pictures than he thought he was getting — at a higher price than he thought he was paying — he has little choice but to milk the prints for all they are worth. And oldtime directors' artistic intent aside, what young viewers want today is color, even if it's a tacky latter-day paint job.

## The Register
*Santa Ana, CA, May 14/15, 1987*

Forget about the Iran arms scandal. Forget about Star Wars. Forget about the federal deficit, too. Some people in Washington — and Hollywood — seem to have higher priorities on their minds these days.

One of those people is Sen. Patrick J. Leahy of Vermont. This week, with the fate of the arts if not of the republic ostensibly hanging in the balance, his Senate Judiciary Subcommittee on Technology and the Law held a hearing on what must be one of the paramount issues of the day judging by the luminaries it attracted, including Woody Allen, Ginger Rogers, and John Huston.

The issue: Should TV mogul Ted Turner be allowed to keep on using computers to turn classic old black-and-white films into colorized movies? Or should Congress, in its superior wisdom, step in and outlaw the practice?

Never mind that Turner isn't just renting them but owns the movies involved, that computer colorization doesn't destroy the black-and-white originals but merely provides an alternative, that the artistic merit of colorized films is a matter of individual taste, or that modern audiences have become conditioned to looking at movies in color. Never mind that if Washington can tell television to stop colorizing films, it could also tell TV to stop interrupting movies with commercials. Whenever there's any kind of a controversy, Washington must get into the act — right?

Wrong! This is one issue that should be decided not along the banks of the Potomac but in the marketplace. If colorization offends enough viewers, it will soon follow such film gimmicks as 3-D, cinerama, and smellevision into oblivion. If not, doesn't Hollywood usually try to defend its own forays into bad taste on the grounds that it's merely giving the public what it wants?

Sorry, Woody and Ginger. But if the public wants colorized versions of old black-and-white films, so be it.

## The Providence Journal
*Providence, RI, July 17, 1988*

Is "Who Framed Roger Rabbit" timeless art or just another good movie? Soon, only the government may know for sure.

Legislation sponsored by Rep. Robert Mrazek, D-New York, and Sidney R. Yates, D-Illinois, would set up a National Film Preservation Board that would name up to 25 films a year "that represent an enduring part of our nation's historical and cultural heritage."

Both the artistic and political cognoscenti will recognize this at once for what it is — a sop to the anti-colorization *artistes* who have been frustrated by Ted Turner's penchant for colorizing every black-and-white film of the past he can get his hands on.

Until now, their battle with the Philistines (as Woody Allen calls the owners who dare to touch old films) has been handicapped by copyright and First Amendment laws. Thus, the proposed legislation is highly circumspect. No such board could prevent the legal owners of films from doing exactly what they like with them — be it colorization, time compression or other distorting alterations. It would only require the specially designated films to bear warning labels. But it would add another costly bureaucracy in an area where it is absolutely unworkable.

In its quest to keep art pure, Congress seems to have ignored the ludicrous side effects of giving government the power to dictate the proper method of enjoying "art," a controversial topic that is best defined in personal, not national, terms. Taken to its extreme, the quest to keep "art" in unadulterated forms would soon limit readers to hard-bound editions, ban translations, and prevent acting companies from performing Shakespearean plays in modern settings.

If these aren't reasons enough to kill the idea, it augers poorly to learn that the proposed 13-member board would be appointed by the Secretary of the Interior. We've had bad artistic experiences from that direction before. Recall that infamous music critic, James Watt, who found the Beach Boys too offensive to play on the Fourth of July.

So much for our confidence in the government's artistic taste.

## The Hartford Courant
*Hartford, CT, July 17, 1988*

Every heart beats true for the — salmon, eggshell and azure?

"It's a softening of the blatant red, white and blue — a more acceptable look to the eye," said Hollywood designer Rene Lagler in explaining why he's abandoning America's traditional patriotic colors in favor of something more "interpretive" with which to decorate Atlanta's Omni Coliseum for the upcoming — or should we say yupcoming? — Democratic National Convention.

Plain old red, white and blue looks too garish on TV, apparently.

Also, the Hollywood production team preparing the convention hall and attendant proceedings for television has decreed that there should be no balloons, bunting or cardboard signs — too old-fashioned, Mr. Lagler sniffs. Instead of balloons, what the Democrats are going for is mylar confetti.

Good grief! The flag Betsy Ross designed and stitched together more than 200 years ago wasn't salmon, eggshell and azure.

The flag hoisted at Iwo Jima wasn't some yuppie-looking thing from a boutique. The banner that waves over schools across America, over the nation's Capitol — over the dead at Arlington National Cemetery — doesn't have some washed-out, bloodless, "interpretive" look. It's the real thing.

## The Boston Herald
*Boston, MA, June 26, 1988*

THE PROPOSED National Film Preservation Act now wending its way through the U.S. House of Representatives has to rank as one of the smarmiest ideas we've encountered in a long time.

The bill is being pushed by those who are offended by the "colorizing" of old black-and-white movies. These opponents, led by Rep. Robert Mrazek (D-N.Y.) and actor Jimmy Stewart, are incensed at cable titan Ted Turner's efforts to broadcast such Hollywood classics as "Casablanca" or "It's a Wonderful Life" in color. They denounce colorizing as a violation of a movie's artistic integrity — and to keep Turner from doing something they disapprove of, they've cooked up this bill.

Under its terms, a federal commission (what else?) would identify those movies so valuable that they must be protected for all time from technological changes such as colorizing. It would be illegal to broadcast, under its original title, a colorized version of any movie so designated. Thus, Turner Broadcasting could colorize "Citizen Kane"... but it could never use the words "Citizen Kane" in marketing it.

We concede we weren't too thrilled either with the beige Bogart who starred in the colorized version of "The Maltese Falcon." But this legislation is so off the wall it deserves to be laughed out of Congress.

First of all, colorizing one print of "Bringing Up Baby" doesn't permanently alter *anything*; thousands of other prints remain untouched.

Second, any TV viewer who prefers to watch a colorized movie in black-and-white has only to reach over and turn off the color control — a substantially easier solution than passing a federal law.

And how are we to take the notion of a government commission passing on what constitutes a true masterpiece? It's absurdly silly. But it's also, in a way, chilling.

What *really* takes the cake, hypocrisy-wise, is hearing movie directors bleat about the artistic integrity of their work. It is directors, after all, who routinely mangle, spindle and mutilate the work of the authors they base their films on. Directors think nothing of taking a movie out for a sneak preview — and then changing the ending, based on the audience's reaction, without giving two hoots about "artistic integrity." Nor do they balk at distributing movies for TV broadcast, even though that means their work will be broken up for commercials and edited for prime-time.

We're not fans of Ted Turner, but we are turned off far more by congressional provisions aimed at putting one man, or one enterprise, out of business. Congress ought to leave Turner and his colorizing alone and return to the nation's business.

## The Gazette
*Cedar Rapids, IA, March 22, 1988*

OLD-TIME ACTORS Jimmy Stewart and Burt Lancaster were in Congress the other day pleading movie-makers' case against computerized coloring of classic black and white films. They want lawmakers to expand federal copyright laws to give actors and directors perpetual "moral rights" over what can be done to their works.

The Directors Guild sent the right guys. Stewart, 80, is America's most beloved movie star. Lancaster, 74, still looks fit enough to clean up Dodge City and Tombstone. But Capitol Hill isn't the place to stage the battle. Congress seems legally powerless to help. Atlanta cable super-station owner Ted Turner may be an insensitive boor. And he may be dead wrong in his assumption that you have to splash color into a film classic to draw young viewers. As the owner of the movie rights, though, Turner can do anything he pleases with the prints. Ordered to desist, he could file suit, claiming abridgment of his right to make a living.

Two other factors weigh against the actors' and directors' anti-coloring campaign. First, other than Hollywood oldtimers and a few movie buffs, nobody seems to care. Second, as epic-scale changers of classic books and plays to fit their needs, moviemakers are hardly in a position to talk about "the integrity of original works."

The "nobody cares" element could change, though. Seeing "Casablanca" on the list of Ted Turner colorations, this newspaper called AP to question the reference. AP reported "Casablanca" indeed is set for color release later this year.

Anybody who'd do that would give the Mona Lisa a moustache. "Casablanca," profoundly powerful after 45 years, is the ultimate black and white classic. Its stark photography captures the spiritual desolation of refugees trapped by the Third Reich. The anti-coloring lobby should pick up supporters, as time goes by.

## The Seattle Times
*Seattle, WA, March 13, 1988*

FOR the average viewer, the conversion to color of an old black-and-white movie — "The Maltese Falcon" or "Casablanca," to cite only a couple of numerous examples — may not be a big deal. But film purists and creative people in the motion-picture industry are making a very big case for congressional action to protect the artistic integrity of some fine old films.

Computer technology for adding color to black-and-white films was developed primarily because of the voracious demand for movies in the television marketplace. TV programmers say films without color simply don't draw big enough audiences.

Forty years ago, films often were without color because of prohibitive costs and/or limited technology. Decisions about camera angles, costumes, and sets were made according to the kinds of film available. But through the years, many movies also have been produced in black and white for artistic reasons.

Congress is being asked to adopt international copyright standards that give creators — not financial backers — "moral" rights over their work and to pass a law protecting films from unauthorized colorization and/or alteration.

The people whose earlier work has been tampered with, or who face that possibility in the future, are on solid ground in urging a congressional response.

**Bogart and Bergman in 'Casablanca'**

## The Evening Gazette
*Worcester, MA, July 13, 1988*

The Hollywood debate over whether television moguls should be allowed to "colorize" old black-and-white movies for today's TV audiences has led us to what comic Oliver Hardy would describe to Stan Laurel as "another fine mess."

The Directors Guild has gone whining to Congress, and the House has approved creation of a National Film Preservation Board. If the Senate agrees with the idea, government appointees will soon be deciding which Hollywood films have artistic merit and deserve at least limited federal protection.

As the provision is now worded, the board would simply select up to 25 old or new movies each year as representing "an enduring part of our nation's historical and cultural heritage." This would not stop the colorization of those films, but colorized versions would have to be labeled as such, with a disclaimer that the original makers did not participate in the changes.

The limitation of the board's powers may make the panel seem innocent. But a government film board with any powers at all to "protect" movies is a foot in the door for all manner of ills, including artistic or even political censorship.

It is surprising that the Directors Guild, of all organizations, fails to understand this. Back in the witch-hunting McCarthy era of the 1950s, when a congressional subcommittee searched for subversives under every desk, few professionals suffered more than movie directors for alleged communist leanings. Evidently, memories are short.

To his credit, Jack Valenti, president of the Motion Picture Association of America, fully understands the danger. "It is desperately wrong for the government to get involved in the motion-picture business," he told a hearing the other day.

He is right. Little good has ever come of the government messing into entertainment and the arts.

There is a simple way for concerned studios to keep their films from being colorized — or chopped up to fit TV time slots, screen shapes and morality codes. They can resist the huge profits and stop selling their movie rights to television.

## The Oregonian
*Portland, OR, September 14, 1988*

Say this about the current efforts of film makers and actors to get Congress to enact legislation to guard against the colorization of old black-and-white movies: They beat the usual Hollywood lobbying on Capitol Hill since the celebrities at least know what they're talking about.

In an age when a former B-movie actor presides over the U.S. government, Tinsel Town eminences have increasingly trooped before committees to testify on the great issues of the day.

Their qualifications: They might have starred in a movie on the topic. A special favorite was the day three actresses who had starred in "farm films" enlightened one congressional committee on U.S. agricultural policies. Some cameos!

But if anti-colorization lobbyists have some knowledge of the issue, they don't necessarily have an issue that should concern Washington at all. Yet a House-Senate conference has found time to do the final editing on the National Film Preservation Act. Expected to be signed by the president, the bill would establish a national film commission to designate which films must be labeled if colorized.

But there's still more. Hollywood artistes are after so-called moral-rights legislation that would give creators rights over their work, regardless of who owns the copyright.

Such a law would protect against what the Directors Guild of America labels colorization's "technological assaults on our film heritage." Even old-movie watchers who would recoil in horror at seeing Humphrey Bogart and Ingrid Bergman painting the town of Casablanca in color should question these dramatic claims of celluloid violence.

These old black-and-white movies are preserved in the process of colorization. They're still available in black and white. Moreover, modern audiences like the colorized version, which actually expand the audiences for our film heritage. Video representatives report that the gussied-up renditions outsell and outrent the originals.

Colorization rights should be an issue in individual or collective bargaining. But surely Congress has weightier issues to ponder — like passing resolutions establishing National Dairy Goat Awareness Week.

## Last Temptation of Christ
### Opens Amid Protests, Sell-Outs

Martin Scorsese's film *The Last Temptation of Christ* opened Aug. 12, 1988 to angry protest rallies by groups that considered the film blasphemous as well as to long lines and sold-out theaters. Ticket buyers greatly outnumbered the protesters in all nine cities where the movie opened. Though more than 500 people, many of them Greek Orthodox, turned out to protest at New York City's Ziegfeld theater, the number of pickets in other cities remained small.

Several prominent film directors Aug. 12 held a news conference in Los Angeles, Calif. to defend Scorsese and the companies that financed the project, Cineplex Odeon and Universal Pictures.

People waiting in line to see the movie were defiant about their right to see the film. In one instance, when one picket at the Century Club Complex in Los Angeles admonished ticket buyers, many of the 150 people who were waiting in line yelled back that they had the right to see the movie if they wanted to. One man waiting in the ticket line waved a sign that said, "It's only a movie" in response to the placards with the word "Blasphemy."

While *The Last Temptation of Christ* was condemned by evangelical Protestants and conservative Catholics for its revisionist portrait of a Jesus with human doubts and frailties who struggles against his divinity, the movie was praised by some liberal Catholic and Protestant ministers for showing the full humanity of Christ.

Reviews of the film, starring Willem Dafoe, Harvey Keitel and Barbara Hershey, were mixed, with the balance tilted to the favorable side.

## The Hartford Courant
*Hartford, CT, August 16, 1988*

More heat than light has been shed in the controversy over the Martin Scorsese film "The Last Temptation of Christ."

The movie, based on a book by Nikos Kazantzakis, purports to examine the human nature of Jesus. Conservative Protestant and Roman Catholic church leaders nationally have rated the movie as objectionable, and Hartford Archbishop John F. Wealon concurred.

Many Christians believe that the film is blasphemous, or at least offensive. Proponents counter that the film's detractors are intolerant and practiced censorship through intimidation when they tried to stop the film's distribution or harangued moviegoers at theaters, as they did last week.

Incredibly, considering the feverish emotions "The Last Temptation of Christ" aroused, few people had seen it.

Among the most rational and appropriate responses to the film came from a spokesman for the Hartford Archdiocese of the Roman Catholic Church.

The Rev. John Gatzak, director of the office of radio and television of the Hartford Archdiocese, said he was "against any kind of petition or negative efforts. I would like to see more of our Catholics in support of good-quality Catholic radio and television that will show Jesus as he existed." Condemning a film without seeing it first is "irresponsible," Father Gatzak said. He also observed that paying a lot of public attention to the film will only help it attract more viewers.

Father Gatzak's approach was positive. He spoke of the need for good-quality productions and suggested that the movie might not fit that description. But he was not censorious or heavy-handed. He noted that responsible criticism should be informed.

Most detractors overlook the benefit that could come from the distribution of the movie. Mr. Scorsese is a major film maker and many film critics say his work, while not entirely successful, is a profound, sincere examination of an important subject.

Such films don't just confirm beliefs; they question. They make people re-examine their beliefs. The result is usually stronger beliefs — stronger because they've been tested.

## The Wichita Eagle-Beacon
*Wichita, KS, August 31, 1988*

Now that the controversy over the movie "The Last Temptation of Christ" has died down somewhat, it's time to focus on the real issue — money.

Indeed, a skeptic may wonder whether the fuss over the Martin Scorsese film on the life of Jesus wasn't a plot between the movie's producers and the fundamentalist Christians who tried to prevent its showing.

Before the conservative Christians drew worldwide attention to the movie, studio executives figured it would play in a few theaters and make little, if any, money. At best, they thought it would become an art film, noticed only by cinema afficionados.

Then the Christians launched their protests and what was expected to be a minor film has become a box office smash. After its third week of release, "The Last Temptation" had grossed more than $2.6 million and, on a per screen basis, was the top draw in the country.

The fundamentalists, however, also saw a silver — and gold — lining in the film. The Rev. Jerry Falwell is using outrage over "The Last Temptation" to push videotapes of another life of Jesus movie that he says accurately depicts the biblical Christ (available for $30, major credit cards accepted). Other ministers have cited the movie to plea for money. In fact, it may become one of the fundamentalists' best fundraising gimmicks of recent years.

Actually, it all seems to have worked out well. Large audiences are seeing a critically acclaimed movie that otherwise would have been ignored. The studio is reaping profits. The fundamentalists and televangelists have a new crusade to fill their financial coffers.

But that's show business.

## Arkansas Gazette
*Little Rock, AR, August 14, 1988*

Everyone has a right not to see a movie that he or she believes would be offensive to him. In fact, great pleasure can be derived from avoiding a particular film — so much, you'd think people would be satisfied. But some are more demanding. They insist that *no one* be allowed to see it.

They have a right to argue that point, too, as long as their protests are nonviolent. And theater owners, in business to make a profit, have a right to note objections to a particular film and to not show it as a result. Yet when all this occurs, the community is diminished — less enlightened, more intolerant, its members more suspicious of one another. Not a good place to have a thought of one's own.

And this ungenerous attitude can lead to worse. A Pine Bluff theater has been damaged by fire, apparently arson. Notes were sent to the theater and a newspaper said the fire was set as a warning not to show or advertise the film "The Last Temptation of Christ." If true, this is a crime for which religious beliefs can be no defense.

Those objecting to "Last Temptation" seem to have carried the day in Arkansas, at least for the moment. Major theater chains operating in the state say they won't show it. But it will be shown elsewhere, and the publicity surrounding it will swell the attendance. Eventually, it will be shown in Arkansas too, after enough people around the country have seen it and reported that there's really not much to get worked up about. And there won't be; there never is. Ignorance of what's actually in a movie or book is essential to the kind of fury the protesters are stirring.

Malice has a place too. Arkansans may not be aware of how much anti-Semitism is involved in the organized opposition to the film. It is very large. In California, fundamentalist Christians have demonstrated in front of the home of the head of the company that made the film, charging that he, a Jew, is encouraging anti-Semitism by allowing the film to be shown, that he is inviting retaliation against the Jewish community and endangering support for Israel. These accusations are really more in the nature of promises, and those who make them are itching to carry through. "It's all the Jews' fault" is a familiar line, after having been around a couple of thousand years. It helps to get a feel for the California protests to know that one of the leaders is the same preacher who prayed for the death of Supreme Court justices. The creative forces behind the film are not Jewish, incidentally. It is based on a novel by a man who was a member of the Greek Orthodox Church. The director is Roman Catholic and the author of the screenplay grew up in the Dutch Reformed Church.

While the storm rages, there is consolation in knowing that in the long run, no group will be able to impose its own view of Jesus Christ on everybody else, wiping out all other opinions, all other speculations, all other faiths. The Romans couldn't do it, and the Moral Majority can't either.

About 10 years ago, there was a commotion over a television mini-series, Franco Zefferelli's "Jesus of Nazareth." It proved to be perhaps the most beautiful of all the cinematic versions of Christ's story. Television stations show it around Christmas and Easter. The controversy is all but forgotten.

---

In former times, suffering was supposed to be an essential training experience for writers. Now the agony is more likely to be reserved for those who attempt to read some of the writings of authors who obviously felt no pain.

## Buffalo Evening News
*Buffalo, NY, August 17, 1988*

SOME PEOPLE like the new film, "The Last Temptation of Christ," and some don't. In view of its controversial theme, this is understandable. What would not be understandable or acceptable in a free society would be any moves to suppress it.

While the film (which we have not seen and which has not yet been shown in the Buffalo area) is controversial, reviews indicate that it cannot be considered in the category of exploitative movies that seek sensationalism through pornography or other means. It was directed by Martin Scorsese, a renowned and serious filmmaker, and based on the 1955 novel by Nikos Kazanztakas.

Many religious leaders say the movie is immoral, even blasphemous, because it depicts Jesus Christ as sometimes confused and uncertain about his divinity. He faces a struggle between the human and spiritual before going to his death in an affirmation of the divine purpose. On the other hand, other clergymen have praised the movie for showing the humanity of Jesus, and they insisted that the film, while provocative, is not blasphemous.

There are other reasons why some might find the film offensive. There is nudity in the baptism and crucifixion scenes, as well as graphic, bloody episodes.

But whether one finds the film too bloody, tasteless or offensive on religious grounds, this could not justify any attempts to suppress it. More than two centuries ago, Voltaire declared: "I disapprove of what you say, but I will defend to the death your right to say it." The same principle is enshrined in our First Amendment guarantees of freedom of speech.

That freedom extends equally to the right of people to protest the film and urge that it be boycotted. It is ironic, however, that the protests have generated free publicity for the film and created sellout crowds at the initial showings around the country.

If it had not been for the protests, the film might have flopped. Movie critics gave it mixed reviews, some of them feeling that the film was boring and, at two hours and 40 minutes, much too long.

## The Boston Globe
*Boston, MA, August 12, 1988*

"The Last Temptation of Christ" opens at movie houses across the country today (but not in Boston). The film is considered blasphemous by some religious lobbying groups that seek to ban its showing. Blasphemy is not the issue here, but censorship.

Those heading the censorship drive – the television evangelists who have been discredited by the blasphemy and hypocrisy within their ranks – have another political agenda.

When cornered by perfidy, the fundamentalist mullahs seek to make scapegoats of others, even injecting anti-Semitism into their complaints against the movie. They do so by the most insidious means, piously proclaiming their fear that the movie's release, not their censorship drive, will feed anti-Semitism.

Directed by Martin Scorsese, the movie – at two hours and 45 minutes – may be more boring than controversial. "Taxi Driver" and other Scorsese movies combined the pretentious and the sensational to little effect. The fundamentalist fulminations may change that box-office equation.

It is doubtful that any movie can weaken the faith of a committed Christian. The late Mayor Jimmy Walker of New York skewered censorship by observing that he never knew of a girl ruined by a book.

But complaining of a heathen plot against the faith is good box office for the television pulpit. The would-be censors seek to shift attention away from the capers of Jimmy Swaggart and Jim and Tammy Bakker. The television preachers need to clean up their own blasphemous act first.

The Constitution grants rights that cannot be taken away by zealots, even zealots who neglect the New Testament lessons in the seventh book of St. Matthew:

"Judge not, that ye be not judged.... Why beholdest thou the mote that is in thy brother's eye, but considerest not the beam that is in thine own eye?... Thou hypocrite, first cast out the beam out of thine own eye; and then shalt thou see clearly to cast out the mote out of thy brother's eye."

## THE SAGINAW NEWS
*Saginaw, MI,*
*August 12, 1988*

A movie called "The Last Temptation of Christ" will open in Los Angeles and New York today — but in Saginaw, maybe never.

Some people want to buy up all the copies and burn them. Others want it never to be shown. Still more want it boycotted if it is shown.

Not having seen the movie, we won't review its content. Nor do we intend to debate the theology of suggesting, as director Martin Scorsese has, that the Son of God, in his agony, may have been subject to human fantasies.

But those negatives do define the nature of the debate.

The strongest criticism is coming from those who almost proudly declare that, no, they haven't seen the film, they won't see it, and what's more, no one else had better see it, either. At least when it comes to defining obscenity, would-be censors can say they know it when they see it. In this case, judgment is rendered from blindness and hearsay.

And the legitimate question of the interpretation of the church raises others: Which church? Which interpreter?

Those issues, of course, have been around since the dawn of Christianity. Matthew, Mark, Luke and John told the same story, but in different ways. Today, Christians are divided into dozens of theologies, sharing a basic belief, but assuredly varying in their practice of that belief.

Director Scorsese has quietly defended his film as a work of reverence. Numerous church leaders — after viewing the film — agree. Some others don't. Yet that is one of the functions of art: To take a perception of truth and prompt us to see it in new ways — ones that may be uncomfortable and, possibly, inaccurate.

Clearly, "The Last Temptation of Christ" presents such a challenge. How should it be regarded?

Entertainment Editor Janet I. Martineau gave her personal position in a column on Page C-3 in Thursday's News. We repeat the invitation for readers to offer their own views. The address is: Letters to the Editor, The Saginaw News, 203 S. Washington, Saginaw 48605.

## The News and Courier
*Charleston, SC, August 17, 1988*

"The Last Temptation Of Christ" is not such a bad movie, some reviewers are saying. We have read several reviews in the last few days which find artistic merit in a film whose release has scandalized Christians from one end of the country to the other and brought unprecedented pressure on theater chains to prevent its showing.

Good, bad or indifferent (and we wouldn't know which because we haven't seen it), it is a movie which appears to justify fears of Christians — not all of them fundamentalists. They perceive a concerted effort in Hollywood and in television studios to undercut their beliefs by suggesting that the words of the Bible are empty words in that the character of Jesus as portrayed in the Gospels is more fiction than fact.

The Christian position with regard to films which undertake to rewrite the Bible *a la* Hollywood can only be, of course, that such films are more fiction than fact. In terms of art, which is what interests movie reviewers, that may be perfectly acceptable. As it relates to true belief, it is a grave offense.

Compared to other people in the world who resent persistent offenses against belief, Christians in this country have been slow to anger and mild in ways in which they have expressed their anger. They have complained, but they have launched no holy wars.

Until now, anyway. A massive boycott, which spokesmen for outraged Christians are calling for, is a break with the "turn the other cheek" attitude, which Jesus preached two thousand years ago and many Christians continue to regard as fundamental to Christian behavior.

Condemnation awaits those Christians who support holy war against the sanctified economics of the movie business. Already they are being called bigots and (as in a letter printed on this page today) hypocrites and threats to free speech. Worse awaits them, no doubt.

It can be said in defense of Christians, however, that they have been recklessly provoked into their present state of mind. In a country where anti-Semitism is viewed as a virulent disease and jokes about Hindus, Moslems and Buddhists are in bad taste, Christians are fair game.

Partly, that is their own fault. The tolerance they have extended to false prophets, like Jim Bakker, has made them the butt of jokes from coast to coast and an excuse for every conceivable gripe against prayer, chastity, demands for clean speech, etc. As viewed by the non-prayer, the unchaste, the foul-mouthed, etc., Christians and their attitudes have a lot to answer for.

The shortcomings of Christians, real imaginary, do not justify mockery of their beliefs. The shortcomings of Christianity, real or imaginary, do not justify rewriting its history for box office appeal. It is unreasonable to expect Christians, who rely upon history to shape their beliefs, to forever bow their heads to jibes and taunts. Neither should they look placidly on while their beliefs and their history are lampooned. We are not surprised to see Christians roused up about this movie.

Neither are we critical of them. It may be open to debate whether Christians are in strict accord with their beliefs if they go to war against producers, actors and movie theaters to protest what they regard as a scandalous attack on their religion. There is no room, however, for debate about whether they are un-American, as some of their critics allege. They are not. Never a day passes in this country but somebody hits the streets to protest something.

There is room in that parade for Christians. If anybody is being hypocritical about talk of boycotts and demonstrations that makes movie moguls and theater operators sweat, it's not the Christians. It is those who want to deny them freedoms accorded without reserve — and often to ridiculous extreme — to anybody and everybody else with a cause or a grievance — good, bad or indifferent.

## THE SUN
*Baltimore, MD, August 14, 1988*

"The Last Temptation of Christ" was denounced when it came out as a novel a generation ago, and it is being denounced now, as the movie version appears. Both the book and the movie present Jesus as much human as divine, as much flesh as spirit. He has human yearnings and fevers. This is deeply offensive to many Christians. So it is understandable, even to those who are not offended by the movie, why outrage is now being expressed.

But to understand is not to accept or condone the statements of some of the offended. The intensity of the opposition to this movie verges on the dangerous. Picketing, protesting, boycotting are legitimate reactions. But resorts to anti-Semitism and implied threats of violence have no place in this debate. Christians who are upset have no right to try to deny to Christians who are not upset — or to non-Christians — the right to see, hear and think about the message this movie offers.

Most reviewers believe the film would be a box office flop but for the furor.

There are many, many devout Christians who believe that a true understanding of Jesus requires pondering his human as well as his divine characteristics. And there are Christians who believe that a true understanding of God requires contemplation of a Jesus other than just the Jesus of the Scriptures. Theologians, historians, philosophers, novelists and, yes, movie directors through the ages have offered new interpretations of who Jesus was and what his life meant. This is neither blasphemy nor heresy.

We believe such Christians constitute the majority and that they either do not find the movie offensive or would not try to impose their values and sensibilities on others. Regardless, a free society must never, ever tolerate book-burning in any of its manifestations.

## The Record
*Hackensack, NJ, August 21, 1988*

"The Last Temptation of Christ," Martin Scorsese's new film, has tempted too many people into hasty denunciations and, in some cases, into blatant anti-Semitism. Mr. Scorsese invited controversy, to be sure, by offering highly unconventional views of some of the most hallowed areas of Christianity. But in a free society, that is his right.

"The Last Temptation" is nothing like "The Greatest Story Ever Told" or other Bible movies packed with conventional piety. Mr. Scorsese opens the film by presenting a Jesus who is bewildered and fearful in the face of his divine mission. Gradually he comes to accept his destiny. But as he is dying on the cross, he suffers one last agonizing temptation: He sees the life he could have had by rejecting his divinity and living as an ordinary man. In a dream fantasy, he sees himself marrying Mary Magdalene and having sex with her. After her death, he marries again and commits adultery. Christ is shown nude on the cross. This is strong material, designed to jolt the viewer into a fresh awareness of Christ by smashing familiar clichés.

Even if Mr. Scorsese's movie were blasphemous and exploitive, he would have every right to make and exhibit it. The United States is not a theocracy such as Iran, where government censors enforce correct theology. Many of Mr. Scorsese's critics weakened their case by proudly admitting that they hadn't bothered to see the movie before venting their wrath.

And some of the opposition has been vicious. The Rev. Donald Wildmon, a conservative Christian fundamentalist, wrote to MCA, parent company of the film's distibutor, Univeral Pictures, and demanded to know how many Christians sit on its board or hold top management positions. Rev. R.L. Hymers, of the Fundamentalist Baptist Tabernacle in Los Angles, staged a vile little scene in which Lew Wasserman, chairman of MCA, was depicted taking part in Christ's crucifixion. This is far more anti-religious than anything in Mr. Scorsese's thoughtful movie.

There's also an instructive lesson here for those who scrambled to denounce the movie without having seen it. Many theologians and critics who took the trouble to watch the film found it has the power to deepen understanding of the life of Christ, not diminish it. Part of the power of the Christian message lies precisely in the point being made by Mr. Scorsese and Nikos Kazantzakis, the Greek author who wrote the 1955 novel upon which the film was based.

Christ chose to take on the suffering and doubts and temptations of ordinary men and women, and nowhere in the Bible does it suggest that the temptation of sex might be excluded. "That part of Christ's nature which was profoundly human helps us to understand him and love him and to pursue his Passion as though it were our own," wrote Mr. Kazantzakis in the introduction to his book.

Mr. Scorsese's film has its weak points. It has some clumsy dialogue and poorly realized scenes, and it gets tangled on some points of theology. But that doesn't detract from Mr. Scorsese's evident sincerity.

Last year, when a television mini-series called "Amerika" depicted life under a Russian occupation, right and left alike denounced it without having seen a single inch of film or having read a script. In this year's replay, "The Last Temptation of Christ" has brought out a streak of intolerance, and, in some cases, raw hatred directed at people who don't share Christian views. But America stands for open discussion of a variety of viewpoints, no matter how unpopular they may be to some. And before people rush to condemn something, they should at least take the time to find out what it is they're condemning.

## Los Angeles Herald
*Los Angeles, CA, August 14, 1988*

Few modern works of fiction have ignited the kind of response "The Last Temptation of Christ" fired up, with 25,000 Christians and others pouring into the street last week to protest it. Despite all that heat, little light has been generated around the most interesting issue of all: Who was Jesus, and does this movie add anything to our understanding of him?

The theological vision presented in filmmaker Martin Scorsese's adaptation of the 1955 novel by "Zorba the Greek" author Nikos Kazantzakis is a fascinating, though not new, look at the figure who changed human history forever. Ever since Jesus Christ walked the earth, his followers have debated whether he was as human as he was divine.

Some, like Kazantzakis, have claimed Jesus understood us and our frailties intimately because he felt them, and fought them in himself. Thus, when he is faced with temptation, he struggles with it — and eventually conquers it. Others have argued that Jesus was beyond temptation, because he was, after all, God.

Few who have actually seen the film can doubt the sincerity of its creators in searching for an original way to dramatize the basic Christian tenet: belief in Jesus as the son of God in human form who resists temptation, lives a sinless life, yet suffers and dies on the cross to redeem the rest of mankind.

Beyond the theological debate, however, it's clear that as Kazantzakis wrote in his book, and as Scorsese has said in discussing his film, the depiction of Jesus in this fictional interpretation of his life are intended to affirm Christian faith, not undermine it. After all, in this version of Christ's life, he makes the ultimate sacrifice. He resists Satan's last temptation to forsake his appointed role and live out his life as an ordinary mortal with wife and family — instead, consciously choosing to die in the agony of crucifixion.

There is much in this work to challenge conventional portrayals of Jesus and to make viewers think about his life and times. But it cannot fairly be said the film attempts to disparage his dignity or divinity. Unfortunately, it seems too many of the protesters haven't had the patience to sit through to the film's faith-affirming conclusion.

*FATHER, FORGIVE THEM... THEY KNOW NOT WHAT THEY DO.*

*NOW SHOWING THE LAST TEMPTATION OF CHRIST*

## TV Evangelist Bakker Resigns in Sex Scandal

Rev. Jim Bakker, one of many popular television evangelists in the United States, resigned his ministry March 19, 1987 after admitting to an extramarital sexual encounter seven years before. Bakker charged that he had been blackmailed subsequently as part of a "diabolical plot" to gain control of his PTL enterprise, which reported $129 million in revenues in 1986.

Bakker's lawyer, Roy Grutman, identified rival television evangelist Jimmy Swaggart as the one behind the hostile takeover attempt (but not the blackmail effort). Swaggart denied the charges but delivered disparaging remarks about the Bakker operation, as well as about Oral Roberts's drive to raise $8 million by March 31 or be called home to heaven. Other television evangelists took sides as a "holy war" broke out in headlines across the nation.

Bakker, 46, an Assemblies of God minister, had run the PTL Club in Fort Mill, S.C. – the letters stood for "Praise The Lord" and "People That Love." He and his wife, Tammy Faye, were co-hosts of a daily talk program going out over hundreds of stations around the country, through the PTL network. As part of the operation, PTL ran a 2,300-acre religious theme park, Heritage USA, sometimes called the "Christian's Disneyland." It included boutiques, a wave pool, water slides and a swimming pool the size of a football field. On a March 6, 1987 broadcast, Mrs. Bakker revealed that she was undergoing treatment at a Palm Springs, Calif. clinic for drug dependency. The habit was formed, reportedly, with prescription drugs taken after the birth of her daughter, now 17.

Bakker disclosed his wrongdoing in a statement to the *Charlotte Observer*. It said he had been "wickedly manipulated by treacherous former friends" who "conspired to betray me into a sexual encounter in 1980." The encounter was reported to have taken place in a Clearwater Beach hotel. The blackmail followed, Bakker said, and he "succumbed" to it to protect his ministry and family. The newspaper reported that $115,000 had been paid to the woman involved, who was identified as Jessica Hahn, who was 21 years old at the time and a church secretary from Oklahoma. The newspaper said that Hahn acknowledged the incident but denied any blackmail.

Jerry Falwell, the fundamentalist preacher who conducted the Old Time Gospel Hour on television, was called in by Bakker to run the PTL in the interim.

The evangelical dispute over the PTL ministry heated up May 26-27 with personal charges traded between Falwell and Bakker. Bakker broke seclusion at his Palm Springs, Calif. home May 26 for an interview on ABC's *Nightline* television program, where he accused Falwell of attempting to "steal Heritage USA and my ministry." Heritage USA had become the country's third most popular amusement park, after Disneyland and Disney World. The 2,300-acre complex had an assessed value of $178 million. The PTL cable television network was valued, by investment analysts, at $20 million to $50 million.

Bakker said Falwell had met with him, just before the sexual escapade became public, and urged a "caretaker" leadership of PTL, by himself (Falwell), as necessary to avert a hostile takeover by Swaggart. "He said he wanted to save his own ministry, which he felt would next be destroyed by Swaggart," Bakker said. "He wanted to help me and that he would never touch my ministry, he would not manage it."

---

### The Globe and Mail
*Toronto, Ont.,
March 25, 1987*

Welcome to the Holy Wars of the airwaves, where the Lord's self-appointed agents move in mysterious ways.

First, evangelist Oral Roberts told the faithful that God had given him an ultimatum: if viewers did not send him $8-million by March 31 for his good works, the Lord would call him home. The battle lines were drawn. Evangelist Rex Humbard stood up for Mr. Roberts. Evangelist Jimmy Swaggart said, "God is not a terrorist."

Then Jim Bakker, host of the TV show The PTL Club, claimed that a "well-known individual" had attempted a "hostile takeover" of his ministry, which last year took in $129-million (U.S.) in revenue. This corporate raider, he said, was using as ammunition details of a "sexual encounter" between the married Mr. Bakker and a church secretary seven years earlier, and his subsequent blackmail payments of $115,000. Mr. Bakker's lawyer alleges that Mr. Swaggart was behind the threatened takeover; Mr. Swaggart told the Charlotte (N.C.) Observer earlier this week that "nothing like that has ever been considered."

Meanwhile, Oral Roberts, who went on TV to defend the Bakkers and to receive a $1.3-million cheque saving him from uncertain death on March 31, was cut off in mid-broadcast by a thunderstorm. (Nice one, Lord.) And Mr. Bakker, in what he called a move to counter the takeover, resigned to recuperate with his wife and co-host Tammy, who broke the news two weeks ago that she was being treated for drug addiction. Pat Robertson, former TV evangelist and Republican presidential hopeful, had this charitable reaction: "I think the Lord is house-cleaning a bit. I'm glad to see it happen."

Mr. Bakker handed his ministry to Moral Majority leader Jerry Falwell — white knight or poison pill? — whose first act was to appoint seven new members to the PTL board, including Mr. Humbard and former U.S. interior secretary James Watt. Readers may remember Mr. Watt as the man who, when asked whether he favored preserving wilderness areas for future generations, said he wasn't sure "how many future generations we can count on before the Lord returns."

Given the nonsense of the past weeks, the Lord may well be advancing His plans.

# The Morning News
*Wilmington, DE, March 24, 1987*

WHEN ALL other considerations are put aside for a moment, it still is sad to think that any Christian ministry is dominated by thoughts of money.

Money is needed to get some jobs done. A worker is worthy of his hire. All such notions acknowledged, it was upsetting to hear the new leader of a major religious organization urge followers to dig deeper for dollar donations so as to "Let the world know this ministry is going to stay strong."

That was the weekend message of Richard Dortch, now president and chief evangelist of PTL.

The evangelical organization, whose initials are taken both as "People That Love" and as "Praise the Lord," had been headed by Jim Bakker. Mr. Bakker had disclosed that he had been blackmailed in connection with a sexual incident years ago. Then he yielded the PTL pulpit to Mr. Dortch.

Mr. Dortch has vowed to his congregants that the full story about Mr. Bakker is yet to be told, and he has urged them to be charitable toward offenders, as is a Christian tenet. Mr. Bakker is human, as all of us are, and who is qualified to throw the first stone?

But can some way be found to show that a ministry is going to stay strong other than having its supporters dig ever deeper for dollars?

Certainly Mr. Dortch knows, as all Christian leaders should know, the message of Matthew 19:24: "And again I say to you, it is easier for a camel to go through the eye of a needle than for a rich man to enter the kingdom of God."

Mr. Dortch, we might concede, is not concerned with amassing personal wealth. He is concerned, we will say, with the needs of his ministry, including the need that the world be shown that its followers remain faithful to it.

We'd accept that if they kept contributing at their present level. They don't have to increase that level to show us.

# The Evening Gazette
*Worcester, MA, March 27, 1987*

The recent fall from power, if not from grace, of some leading television preachers is a sad episode in the American evangelical movement. One has to feel deeply for the millions of believers who showed their trust and faith by taking the words of some evangelists into their hearts and by supporting with hard-earned dollars the ministries of these television personalities.

Non-believers may find glee in the downfall of these electronic preachers, shake their heads and say, "I told you so." Scoffers are having a field day over the "religious civil war" between Jim Bakker of PTL and television evangelist Jimmy Swaggart. But true believers put their faith in God, not in men. Believers are saddened, but not shaken in their heart of hearts.

Television evangelism in this country is the direct descendant of the old-fashioned revival movement. Back when the West was being settled and the population was thinly spread over vast areas, traveling revival meetings were a source of faith and inspiration for many hard-working rural Americans. There were charlatans in the revival movement even then; they just didn't reach as many people as the television evangelists do today.

The thing that is so staggering to the casual observer is the vastness of the financial empires built up by these national evangelical personalities. Their corporate structures and marketing techniques make them vulnerable to the economic vagaries affecting any business enterprise. The hypocrisy that played a part in amassing those fortunes makes the evangelists' financial kingdoms the ultimate in "unfair trade."

What hurts the most in this unfortunate affair is the fact that the trust of so many believers was betrayed. The selfless giving of the thousands who respond to televised solicitation for spiritual causes deserves a better accounting than can be offered by the religious soap opera now playing on the nation's TV screens.

# TULSA WORLD
*Tulsa, OK, March 26, 1987*

WILL Jim and Tammy Bakker confess, repent and hit the television equivalent of the sawdust trail again? Will Jim's "encountress" show up on television and in magazines to "tell all?" Will Oral Roberts survive God's threats to live to plead for even more money?

Is the Pope a Catholic? Do Baptists have buses? Do preachers like fried chicken?

Forgive the frivolity. There are times when it's better to laugh than cry.

The Bakkers, who played a key part in merging old-time fundamentalist religion with show-biz, soap opera techniques, are in trouble. Tammy admits to a bit of a drug problem. Jim has resigned over what he said were attempts to blackmail him and take over his show by threatening to reveal his sexual "encounter" of seven years ago.

Jerry Falwell, the famous Moral Majority pastor, is standing in for Jim at the Praise The Lord operation. Jimmy Swaggart, the Louisiana preacher who's at the top of the electronic ministry business, is heaping coals of fire on his brother fund-raisers.

The Bakkers see a diabolical plot involving the "secular" press and other shadowy figures. Oral Roberts has his usual explanation. It's the work of Satan. Oral also has given his followers his usual prescription for Satanic meddling: send money.

Having already reached his highly publicized goal to raise $8 million for missionary work or be killed by God by March 31, Roberts has reconsidered, much like the fellow who sets a price on his old car and then starts quibbling when you accept. Oral's decided he might need a bit more than $8 million, so he's in the prayer tower fighting Satan.

The electronic preachers of all stripes are wringing their hands that the Bakker and Roberts tribulations will harm the cause of Christianity.

They overestimate themselves.

True, there will be followers of the television soaps who will be disillusioned. But that surely happens in a wholesale way every day.

The Christian church and the millions of believers who regularly and faithfully practice their religion in a quieter and less flamboyant way than the electronic church will survive and thrive.

Meanwhile, stand by for the next development in the tawdry and gauche lives of our heroes of the prime time religion's equivalent of "Lifestyles of the Rich and Famous."

It is, after all, show business.

# The Sun
*Vancouver, B.C., March 25, 1987*

It is difficult to imagine anything more blasphemous than the Oral Roberts caper. Here's a man who claims God set a deadline — an appropriate word — for him to raise $8 million for His works. The penalty of shortfall: death.

The last $1 million to put the evangelist over the top came from — did Evelyn Waugh script this? — a greyhound racing magnate. So the fruits of gambling have been utilized to keep Mr. Roberts from the bosom of Abraham.

Abraham must be weeping, his head buried in his hands, and not because he lost a heavenly roll on a slow canine in the fifth.

A thunderstorm interrupted Mr. Roberts's live broadcast the other day. He should indeed be wary of thunderbolts.

## The Grand Rapids Press
*Grand Rapids, MI, March 31, 1987*

Toppling the pedestal of a television preacher is no great feat. Basic human weaknesses become sins of prime-time magnitude when committed by dispensers of divine wisdom like Jim Bakker. For that reason alone, skeptics should resist the temptation to gloat.

Many in the media and elsewhere already have given into that temptation. Jim and Tammy Bakker, and others who spread piety through the airwaves, seem to live in a shadeless world where one is either bathed in God's light or lost in darkness. When an absolutist like Mr. Bakker gets stuck in reality, the ensuing media stories have a vindictive air.

The Bakker family's problems are not minor, by any means. Jim Bakker's sexual liasion with a female acolyte was, given his religious position, hypocritical. But that, and Tammy Bakker's drug dependency, are essentially personal, family problems. What's more difficult to accept is the apparent effort by Mr. Bakker and the PTL ministry to use cash payments to shut up the woman involved. Either the arrangement was a legally sanctioned out-of-court settlement of a civil suit, or it was a private arrangement akin to extortion. A grand jury or district attorney's investigation could help with the answers.

Also unsettling is the willingness of Mr. Bakker's fellow TV ministers to dance around his toppled pedestal. Jimmy Swaggart, who has been heard to preach forgiveness and the healing power of grace, has shown no mercy to Jim Bakker. Mr. Swaggart seems to be concerned that a sinful Mr. Bakker was hoodwinking his followers, taking money under false pretenses. But Mr. Swaggart and Mr. Bakker are of the same ilk: if the followers of Mr. Bakker have been hoodwinked, then shouldn't Mr. Swaggart's congregation, which has built his ministry into a $100-million-a-year business, be similarly concerned about their leader?

Differences in theology aside, the television evangelists should recognize their common ground. They employ the power of rhetoric and oratory, combined with the great traditional appeal of the Biblical and Christian messages, to move people to follow, to pray and to part with their money. Much of that money is put to altruistic purpose; some of it goes to improve the preacher's lifestyle. This episode, and the subsequent unearthing of ill feelings among popular TV ministers, should warn those in search of divine guidance to choose their human signposts carefully. The wrong one can mean an expensive detour.

Which preacher to follow is an individual choice, the kind the framers of the Constituion had in mind when they insisted on freedom of religion. One may like or dislike Jim and Tammy Bakker, or Jimmy Swaggart, or Rev. Jerry Falwell, but we all should realize this religious soap-opera is peculiarly American. That Jim and Tammy Bakker could rise, and fall, and rise again some day, at least reinforces our faith in freedom of religion.

## The Hutchinson News
*Hutchinson, KS, March 24, 1987*

TV evangelist Jim Bakker's sexual activities may be more properly judged by his own religious denomination. But the financial activities of his big TV show should be of interest to all denominations.

As Bakker ran for cover last week under a brotherly umbrella provided by Jerry Falwell, Bakker's lawyer cited the real reason for the startling demise of his PTL reign.

The reason: Bakker was trying to avoid a "hostile takeover" by yet another of the big TV evangelists.

And why not? Hostile takeovers have been the rage on Wall Street the past few years, as one big corporation after another is gobbled up by yet other corporations in the race for greater and greater profits.

Until now, nobody had paid much corporate attention to the big religious money makers, but there's no reason why the religious empires should be expected to stand on the outside while other enterprises are swallowed, devoured and regurgitated into more efficient money machines.

The religious money machines should be, as they say on Wall Street, in play these days as typical examples of corporate profit centers open to expansion.

The TV evangelists prey on the unsuspecting or naive with the notion that religion is paramount. But as the evidence mounts for those willing to notice how the TV supersalesmen invest the money, there should be no doubt that the bottom line is more important than the upper room.

## Winston-Salem Journal
*Winston-Salem, MA, March 31, 1987*

It is now being labeled the "holy wars", or "biblegate" and having been raised to cover status on at least one of the news weeklies, the PTL scandal may push the White House ransom for hostages and illegal gunrunning deal off the front pages.

There are similarities. Once the personal scandal begins to die down, the PTL affair, like the Iran-Contra episode, may boil down to mostly futile attempts to follow the money. One senses that someone lined his pockets but who? And where are those trousers stashed anyhow?

The PTL revelations may settle in a short while into legal maneuvers and a flurry of public confessions, just like Irangate. And that would be a shame. That would mean that we have lost sight of the fundamental issue.

In Iran-Contra, the focus should be the president's governance. Much more than style is involved. The president said he likes to pick the best people and let them go, doing good work within the parameters he sets. But the point is that he did not set clear parameters and he did not get good people. The issue is competence, and more, responsibility.

The president has a responsibility to his office and his people, the American voters. Similarly in the PTL scandal, the true issue is responsibility. Bakker says he is accountable to God. But as with the assignments in the basement of the Reagan White House, that's rather free-wheeling duty.

Accepting that Bakker is on his own with his maker and can square himself there, what about his flock? What does he owe them?

There is a marked similarity between Col. North and the likes of Jim Bakker and Jimmy Swaggart. They each seem to be persons who operate along Nietzschean lines of narcissistic heroism while cloaking themselves in the mantle of St. Paul. For the higher cause that coincides conveniently with personal gain, it is permissible to make one's own rules.

Such men (Norths and Bakkers) become nations or religions unto themselves, and the trouble with that kind of patriot or believer is that they aren't answerable, finally, to anyone or anything but their own fantasies of grandeur. That adds up only to singular tragedies or instances of pathos, except that more people are involved.

Just as North's gambits would ultimately involve the lives of persons he doesn't now imagine on his chess board — the Nicaraguan peasant, or the 18-year-old American Midwesterner unfortunate enough to have enlisted — Jim Bakker's pinball theology may most powerfully affect the elderly shut-in who listens to him and wants to believe in his work.

It is not Bakker or his wife who will suffer. Professionals in their game have a way of landing on their feet. It is not religion itself either. It is the lonesome American, who wishes to believe in something greater than the emotionalism and materialism that seem to be suffocating us, that seem to have suffocated the Bakkers.

The great sin is not money, it is not sex and not finally the debasing of religion, which had to be debased before it came to this (television) and has been debased off and on from the beginning of time. Faith endures.

The real scandal, the sin of the holy warriors, is that many ordinary Americans who desire rectitude, and the sanity of the Christian ethic will find that their seeking has been ridiculed. This, when what they were seeking was something noble.

Somehow to con such people with such a product is not the same as selling swampland condos or even a better tax code. Perhaps North can mock Jefferson. But God is not to be mocked.

## The Cincinnati Post
*Cincinnati, OH, March 24, 1987*

Some followers of the Rev. Oral Roberts may be troubled by the big donation that allowed the preacher to meet his much-publicized deadline for raising $8 million in aid of medical missionaries. They shouldn't worry.

It's true, the $1.3 million gift that put Roberts over the top did come from a dog-track owner. But in accepting gambling proceeds to support good works, Roberts is only following in the practical tradition of a certain Kentucky mountain preacher who was offered a donation by a notorious bootlegger.

"I have just sold a gallon of moonshine and would like to give you this dollar, Brother Thompson," the reprobate said in a loud voice, with a wink to his friends.

The old preacher grabbed the bill without missing a step, saying, "Thank you, neighbor. This dollar has been in the devil's service long enough. Now I will put it to work for the Lord."

## The Charlotte Observer
*Charlotte, NC, March 22, 1987*

More than anything else, the moment was sad. Television evangelist Jim Bakker resigned last week from his ministry at PTL, acknowledging a sexual encounter with a young woman in Florida and substantial payments to her after she and her representatives threatened to sue for damages.

His more than 14 years in the Charlotte area have been stormy and controversial, and for many of his followers, profoundly inspirational.

All of that is understandable. Mr. Bakker is a man of almost childlike faith, seeing the hand of God in every corner of life and declaring with a conviction there is no reason to doubt that God can transform pain into happiness, suffering into triumph.

That message — delivered with such exuberance on his Christian talk show and at personal appearances at Heritage USA, his Christian retreat center in York County, S.C. — has touched the lives of millions. It has stirred their faith, and for many of them, provided hope and purpose where none existed before.

In a number of different ways, Mr. Bakker gave touching substance to his message of faith. He is a man frequently given to great compassion and kindness — impulses that led to such projects as the establishment of a home for unwed mothers and another for handicapped children at Heritage USA.

### 'A Rollercoaster Ride'

But despite the volume of Mr. Bakker's good works, there was always another side to his life at PTL. He used to declare quite frequently that God had him on "a rollercoaster ride," and he and his wife Tammy were "doing our best to hang on."

The image is appropriate in ways that Mr. Bakker probably didn't intend. It suggests a kind of fast-lane, out-of-control quality to the activities at PTL, which in fact was too often the case. Mr. Bakker was not a good manager, and there were moments of introspection when he admitted as much. He built new structures at an astonishing rate, governed frequently by his whims, rather than by sober calculations of cost and resources.

On several different occasions, carefully documented by this newspaper, Mr. Bakker's ambitions for Heritage USA pushed him toward misleading solicitations of money from his supporters. The controversy and the managerial chaos sometimes coincided with — and probably exacerbated — marital problems that Mr. Bakker blames for the sexual infidelity that led to his resignation.

### Obsessed By Glitter

All of that taken together is a sad and tragic story — the story of a man of decency and faith, overtaken, for now, by his less noble qualities. In his autobiography, "Move That Mountain," Mr. Bakker paints a portrait of himself as a person embarrassed by the humility of his origins, obsessed by the glitter of his PTL kingdom.

That obsession — and the hectic, fishbowl life it thrust upon the Bakkers — has had bitter consequences. But Jerry Falwell, the conservative evangelist who has now taken over PTL, has suggested that God is not finished with Jim and Tammy Bakker.

That is almost certainly the truth. The Bakkers are still young. Their vigor is undeniable, as is their faith. They are both in therapy at a California treatment center, and if they can come to terms with their tendencies toward materialism and excess — their own difficulties in accepting responsibility for the problems they face — then it seems very likely that they will reenter the world of Christian evangelism.

Perhaps the next time they will be even more effective, less inclined to trip themselves up or to become embroiled in pointless controversies. That is the hope, and it ought to be the prayer of Christians everywhere.

## THE BLADE
*Toledo, OH, March 27, 1987*

LET'S see now. Jim Bakker of the PTL Club (Praise the Lord, People That Love, Pass The Loot) has resigned, confessing tearfully to sexual indiscretions with a secretary some years ago. His wife Tammy is in a detoxification center.

Oral Roberts, who said God would call him home unless he raised $8 million, reached his goal, in large part because of a racetrack owner who decided to turn some of his cash to supposedly more uplifting purposes.

Jimmy Swaggart, one of the more flamboyant television preachers, admits he blew the whistle on Mr. Bakker, and in turn he is accused of being the diabolical force that tried to take over the PTL Club.

The lawyer for Mr. Bakker had the nerve to call the current upheaval "a holy war." He is off-base there. This is the religious equivalent of one of those classic bar fights in an old Hollywood western where one drunk throws a chair through the expensive mirror and starts a free-for-all in which everybody starts slugging everybody else.

We don't pretend to know the merits of these allegations or care much about them, except to the extent that some television evangelists prey upon elderly and lonely individuals who send in contributions that they can ill afford, often in desperate hope of finding some kind of solace.

Ministers of churches all across the country must surely grit their teeth in frustration as they watch tens of millions of dollars pour into the hands of these smooth-talking snake oil salesmen on the tube. This is money that would not only help keep their own church doors open but also enable them to reach out and provide real assistance to the folks who are mesmerized by television religion's flashy cathedrals, rapid-fire delivery, large and photogenic choirs, and unctuous appeals for money — always, appeals for money.

Some of the more restrained TV preachers like the Rev. Jerry Falwell and the Rev. Robert Schuller profess to be pained by the theatrics of Oral Roberts and the mean-tempered street fight between adherents of Mr. Swaggart and Mr. Bakker. They are careful, though, to muffle those criticisms lest such opinions reduce the inflow of money.

Mr. Swaggart even has the effrontery to say that the church of Jesus Christ has been hurt by the headline revelations of the past few days. What does he think the church is, a presidential administration that can be hurt by a pulpitgate scandal? Two millenia of Christian history and religious traditions cannot be seriously affected by the lawsuits, angry exchanges, money lust, and headline grabbing of a few televangelists whose lifestyles apparently have gone to their heads.

The secular press is slow to criticize men of the cloth, whatever their activities, because of the special place clergymen occupy in our society. As far as Mr. Swaggart, Mr. Bakker, and others of their ilk are concerned, the public should by now know that they, like other mortals, put their pants on one leg at a time. It should lead to a healthy clearing of the air — and possibly the airwaves.

## 72 – Jim Bakker

*THE FIRST HOSTILE TAKEOVER*

### Roanoke Times & World-News

*Roanoke, VA, March 24, 1987*

THE BIG-TIME evangelist pays for the glory and adulation he receives. When you're Jim Bakker, shepherd of a television congregation spread among 250,000 households, mogul of a 2,500-acre park devoted to religious recreation, and husband of a flamboyant wife who keeps the jewelers, furriers and cosmetic manufacturers in business, you learn that the fast lane runs through a glass tunnel. It keeps you constantly on display and the glass threatens to shatter around you at the first missed turn.

Somewhere back there, Jim Bakker missed a turn. In surrendering his position as chairman of PTL, the evangelistic organization he led to national prominence, Bakker admitted that he had tripped over the Seventh Commandment. He had an affair with a church secretary.

The indiscretion should not shock those who believe that clergymen are cut from the same imperfect mold as other sons of Adam. It should be even less shocking in the light of Bakker's flamboyant lifestyle.

Jim Bakker led the life of a show-business celebrity. When he wasn't tending to his religio-commercial business in Charlotte, he could relax at his Palm Desert home. He didn't have to do his traveling in a parsimonious Chevy; he could tool around in a Rolls. When he wished to wash his hands of something, he didn't have to contaminate them by touching brass or chromium. He ordered gold plumbing fixtures for his Florida condo. His wife didn't have to wear strait-laced black. She could dress like a showgirl and still be lauded as a model for Christian women to follow. They were living proof that you didn't have to take vows of poverty to follow the Gospel Trail.

But with all these luxuries, Bakker lacked one that other performers take for granted: the luxury of fooling around. A one-night stand that would be a minor footnote in the career of another media star becomes a fatal dalliance for the electronic preacher.

The Seventh Commandment constantly invites the unwary clergyman to honor it in the breach. The mature pastor knows about the pitfalls and knows how to avoid them. He knows that he will be dealing with persons of the opposite sex in particularly intimate ways and at particularly vulnerable times. He knows how to deal with such situations with a combination of pastoral empathy and professional detachment.

But Bakker is something besides a mature minister. He is a performing artist of considerable skill. He is a bold entrepreneur. He is a poor boy who learned how to garner wealth and fame before he quite learned what to do with them. His enthusiasm sometimes got ahead of his practical judgment

His freewheeling methods kept him on the edge of legal difficulties. The feds wondered whether the money he received in response to his televised appeals was going where he said it would go. After one investigation, three members of the Federal Communications Commission wrote that PTL "was under a cloud of serious misconduct, including substantial and material questions of fraudulent use of the airwaves, breach of fiduciary duty, and false testimony." But their charges were never proved.

His ministry prospered in spite of reports of marital discord, in spite of his wife Tammy's treatment for drug dependency, in spite of the lavish lifestyle they enjoyed while pleading with PTL supporters to send in their checks and money orders. The Assemblies of God, the denomination with which he was affiliated, grew by more than 50 percent during the 10 years in which his ministry flourished.

In stepping down "for the good of my family, the church and of all our related ministries," Bakker put the blame on "treacherous former friends" who "wickedly manipulated" him and "conspired to betray me into a sexual encounter."

He is turning his empire over to Jerry Falwell of Lynchburg, a less flamboyant, though highly successful, evangelistic performing artist who differs with Bakker on theology but shares his enthusiasm for ambitious projects financed by the faithful.

If it seems strange that a preacher of one denomination should turn his ministry over to a preacher of another, it might help to regard this as a business merger, on the order of Piedmont merging with USAir but keeping the old names on the airplanes.

The move will no doubt enhance Falwell's religious stature and fund-raising clout, though it isn't likely to increase his national political influence. To improve himself politically, Falwell would have to break out of the narrow circle of right-wing fundamentalists and join the American mainstream. PTL lies well outside the American mainstream.

Those who scorn Bakker's style and methods should reserve judgment on the cause of his downfall. Religious men of enduring fame have similarly succumbed. Reuben violated his father Jacob's concubine. Judah was seduced by his daughter-in-law disguised as a harlot. David bedded Bathsheba after sending her husband to certain death in battle. Popes have sired illegitimate children while publicly advocating priestly celibacy. The Rev. Martin Luther King Jr. was not known for marital fidelity.

Heaven handled each case with varying degrees of tolerance, but none of the offenders was struck dead on the spot. That fate was reserved for Annanias, who played false with the church when it came to money and property.

## Post-Tribune
*Gary, IN, March 26, 1987*

**Our opinions**

Some television evangelists, it has been revealed, are just like ordinary people. Imperfect, maybe even acquainted with greed. That is the unmistakable perception created by the recent fall of Jim Bakker, who quit as chairman of the PTL (Praise the Lord) organization. It's a $174 million empire.

In the beginning, it was reported that he resigned over a sexual indiscretion several years ago that had been kept quiet because of $150,000 in "blackmail" payments from Bakker. And it was revealed that his wife had a drug problem.

But Bakker says the real reason was to prevent a "hostile takeover" of his organization by another evangelist. That clearly gives this story a soap opera touch. What would a "hostile takeover" of an evangelistic program involve? Is TV evangelism that competitive?

Then evangelist Jimmy Swaggart denied that he was the takeover threat. Evangelist Oral Roberts did not mention a name, but it was clear he was talking about Swaggart as part of an "unholy alliance." Roberts said Satan was involved.

Should the press and televison news continue to reveal the developments in this controversy, or is it a religious matter that deserves privacy? The answer is easy. Television evangelists have become entertainers. They are show business people — that is not a bad thing, but it lifts them beyond pure religious status. Their salesmanship allows some to live in grand life styles. That is not bad. But they must be judged like other entertainers who use the airwaves and publicity to expand their fame.

The evangelical purity of this episode becomes more diluted with almost every statement. A Bakker lawyer says that "he," meaning the evangelist who wants to take over PTL, will find that he has dirtier laundry in his closet than was found in Bakker's. Is this a contest?

And the church secretary involved in the sex encounter says she got only a little of the $150,000 allegedly paid. Who got the rest? A traveling evangelist reportedly set up her meeting with Bakker.

There is no doubt that the Bakker case and subsequent public exchanges will damage the television ministry movement. Some of the people involved deserve their comeuppance. If someone is out there waiting to take over the PTL goldmine, he too has fallen from the pedestal paid for by believers who watch and support the shows.

It is easy to be judgmental of people with such unusual skills, people who hit the pinnacle of success. But when evangelists drive around in Rolls Royces, they do not exhibit much humility.

This unpleasant and revealing series of events may have a cleansing effect on the television ministry phenomenon. It is time for that.

Swaggart insists that he did not reveal the story of Bakker's sexual indiscretion, but had talked to church officials about "other matters" relating to Bakker's behavior.

Jerry Falwell has temporarily taken over the PTL organization, in an attempt to save it. Falwell is controversial because of his political views, but he has not been overcome with self-importance and the need for living in grandeur. There is considerable virtue in that.

This clash has been labeled a holy war, a civil war and a war over ratings. Swaggart says he is disgusted with the state of televised religion. He is not alone. It is fair to say that some of the evangelists are reaping what they have sown.

There is an incongruity in mixing opulence and service to people. The issue here is accountability. People who pass the offering plate in person or via the airwaves must be held accountable for use of the gifts and for their conduct. It is elementary.

## The Seattle Times
*Seattle, WA, May 19, 1987*

THE $265,000 in "hush money" paid by PTL (Praise the Lord) founder Jim Bakker to hide his motel tryst with former church secretary Jessica Hahn pales in comparison with the $92 million now reported to have disappeared in a "black hole."

Adding cosmic mystery, PTL accountants said that same "black hole" also swallowed up a $62,000 vintage Rolls-Royce that had been used as an ornament outside the PTL's Heritage USA theme-park hotel in Fort Mill, S.C.

The "black hole" description given by Jerry Nims, PTL chief executive officer, might not satisfy federal investigators looking into several questions, including possible tax fraud.

Nor will it help Jerry Falwell, who had pledged not to "beg for money on the air," in his effort to raise $7 million by the end of this month and about $25 million within 90 days if PTL is to survive. Falwell took over the TV ministry after the disgraced Bakker and his wife Tammy stepped down.

Nor will Falwell's fund-raising effort be helped by a tour Nims gave newsmen of the opulent 3,000-square-foot hotel suite the Bakkers had occupied — ranging from seven bathrooms with 14-karat-gold faucets to an air-conditioned and heated doghouse. Friends said it was too opulent even for the dog, which declined its use.

What continues to emerge is not a comforting mosaic for even the most fervent of PTL followers, who gave their money in heavenly faith — not to have it frittered away in earthly disregard.

## The Honolulu Advertiser
*Honolulu, HI, May 29, 1987*

Think politics is rough? Think corporate takeover battles are savage? Try the Jim and Tammy Bakker saga for sheer verbal brutality.

The latest episode has Bakker charging that Jerry Falwell duped him into giving up his PTL ministry and Falwell responding in lurid detail, accusing Bakker of lying about his tryst with a young woman and looting the PTL treasury, among other things.

The spectacle makes the Iran-Contra hearings and the Wall Street insider-trading scandal seem tame by comparison. Here are two of the nation's most visible TV preachers trading the most sensational sort of allegations against each other.

Beyond the charges of immorality lies a power struggle for control of the PTL empire, with Bakker apparently hoping for a comeback, unlikely as it seems, and Falwell in the role of the good Samaritan whose motives are being unjustly impugned.

Whoever wins this unseemly battle may be less important than the damage it is doing to the Christian fundamentalist cause. The television evangelists who are not directly involved in this incredible scandal may find themselves tarred with the same brush in the public mind.

## THE ATLANTA CONSTITUTION
*Atlanta, GA, May 24, 1987*

There's been quite a bit of talk about singer Pat Boone taking over as host of the PTL television show. It's certainly not up to us to address the question of his suitability in theological terms.

We can say this about the image question, however They shouldn't rule out a Hollywood celebrity, because some of them are in fact accustomed to a somewhat more modest lifestyle than Jim and Tammy Bakker

## Edmonton Journal
*Edmonton, Alta., May 20, 1987*

The latest episode in the sordid PTL saga strains credulity to the breaking point.

You'd think that viewers of the ministry's TV show, after being told that $92 million (US)in contributions can't be accounted for, would be just a little skeptical at being asked to fork out another $25 million to tide the ministry over. Surely their eyebrows must have risen slightly over revelations that Jim and Tammy Bakker, the now discredited founders of the PTL Club, were fond of spending church money on such perks as gold-plated toilet plumbing, a $600,000 retreat in Palm Springs, silk underwear, diamond earrings, and a Jacuzzi for the office.

You'd think they'd question whether new leader Jerry Falwell's plea for $25 million within 90 days to ensure the ministry's existence puts them in the incongruous position of being held hostage by their religious leaders.

But PTL followers remain faithful followers. How else to explain that Falwell's cry for cash was greeted by 22,000 letters more than triple the number the ministry received a week earlier and even more than the ministry normally received before Bakker's sex scandal was revealed in March?

Pass The Loot, indeed.

## The News and Courier
### CHARLESTON EVENING POST
*Cincinnati, OH, May 31, 1987*

With their new unbeatable formula — sex plus religion Jim and Tammy Bakker seem certain to make prime-time television. Already they've earned ABC's Nightline its highest rating ever. There were 20 million people tuned into their Wednesday night interview. That's a 15.4 rating, better by far than Nightline's previous record, a 12.3 for a program on the U.S. bombing raids on Libya.

## The Houston Post
*Houston, TX, May 20, 1987*

It cannot be encouraging to the creditors of the PTL ministry, who collectively are owed nearly $67 million, to learn that $92 million of the organization's funds have disappeared into what PTL Chairman Jerry Nims terms a "black hole."

Apparently this also left a negative impression on federal agents, who are preparing to investigate the ministry. Nims says the questions raised include "wire fraud, tax fraud, possible extortion, fraud and non-compliance with various state and federal statutes."

In their rags-to-riches-to-ousted saga, evangelists Jim and Tammy Faye Bakker seem not to have learned from 1 Timothy 6:7 about the consequences that flow from the love of money. It was a lesson they needed badly, judging from revelations of gold-plated bathroom fixtures, chandelier-lit closets and shelves full of shoes — to say nothing of the mysterious $92 million.

It is true that some of that money probably will turn out to represent day-to-day PTL expenses. It is also true that the PTL ministry has done some good: Its Heritage USA park in South Carolina includes shelters for the poor and homes for handicapped children and unwed mothers.

But it also should cause concern that the Bakkers' lust for material wealth, along with a penchant for loose bookkeeping, may have opened the door to a showdown between tax agents and the religious establishment in America. Given churches' longstanding tax exemptions and the Constitution's ban on laws "respecting an establishment of religion," we have entered a touchy and worrisome area.

Perhaps the biggest concern now should be that more conventional religious bodies — ones that hew much closer to their vows to minister to the poor and troubled than PTL ever has — are at growing risk of being punished for PTL's transgressions.

## The Hartford Courant
*Hartford, CT, May 31, 1987*

The feud among the TV preachers continues to degenerate, and it is a sorry spectacle.

Seldom has religion been so badly used. And seldom has a fight among well-known figures been so vicious or so public.

Last week the Rev. Jim Bakker charged that he was tricked by the Rev. Jerry Falwell into giving up the PTL ministry. Mr. Bakker raised the interesting possibility that the leader of the Moral Majority secretly coveted the PTL ("Praise the Lord") television network. Mr. Bakker's programs reached 10 times as many homes as Mr. Falwell's "Old Time Gospel Hour."

Mr. Falwell denied hoodwinking Mr. Bakker, and suggested that the deposed Pentecostal minister took "millions" from the PTL, was greedy, self-centered, avaricious, a homosexual, an adulterer and possibly a rapist. He said Mr. Bakker has a terrible memory or is dishonest or mentally ill.

Mr. Bakker denounced Mr. Falwell as a liar.

The name-calling, which began shortly after Mr. Bakker resigned the PTL leadership in March, has been punctuated with angelic smiles and unctuous protestations of love. At week's end, both promised to stop the invective, but that's been promised before.

Political rivals or business competitors don't measure up to the TV preachers when it comes to airing one another's dirty laundry in public. The soap opera called Holy Wars or Gospelgate is unique in its animus. America has never seen anything quite like this sanctimonious guttersniping.

Why the intensity? If it were only a matter of sexual misadventures, or the high-living habits of Mr. Bakker and his wife, Tammy Faye — the fat salaries and bonuses, the air-conditioned doghouse, the Palm Springs mansion — disapproval might be muted. The sinner wouldn't be flogged — or fight back — so conspicuously. When Mr. Bakker's one-day affair with church secretary Jessica Hahn was first revealed, remember, the evangelical community tended to rally around him, even when shunting him aside.

But this is much more than a fight over Jim Bakker's soul; it is a fight over turf and money as well as moral authority. That became more and more apparent as Mr. Bakker sought a comeback.

Mr. Bakker's sin, it seems, was not so much marital infidelity as it was embarrassing the brotherhood and jeopardizing the good will of the devoted followers who keep evangelical empires afloat with hundreds of millions of dollars in donations. The stakes are high. Mr. Bakker wants to recapture his following; Mr. Falwell wants to enlarge his.

Before Gospelgate, those who run the electronic ministries were among the most powerful people in the country. They commanded vast audiences: The PTL alone reached 15 million homes. They were politically influential, and, perhaps most important, were unaccountable. The government — or anyone else — hardly ever asked any questions about their multimillion-dollar operations and they rarely volunteered answers.

The rise of the Rev. Pat Robertson as a Republican presidential aspirant and the downfall of Mr. Bakker have focused the public's attention on the television ministers as never before. The PTL scandal, regrettable and tawdry as it is, will have done some good if it makes people question the substance and value of religion-as-entertainment, and results in the TV ministers' coming clean about their finances.

But the scandal has taken a toll. The hypocrisy, lust for power and avarice exhibited by the major players in the PTL scandal have tarred not only the affected ministries, but legitimate evangelism and the traditional churches. The name-callers have, in their well-publicized fight, confused and deeply hurt many devout people.

The "cause of Christ" has suffered a terrible setback, Mr. Falwell lamented recently. He, Mr. Bakker and the other brawlers ought to consider who's responsible.

## News-Tribune & Herald
*Duluth, MN, May 18, 1987*

It's little wonder that the public gets skeptical with institutional and political fund-raising.

Ploys being used to separate people from their money in the form of donations have become cynical to the point of insult. The most infamous, of course, is preacherman Oral Roberts' scam in March in which he told supporters of his ministry that God would take him (meaning he would die) if they did not send millions by the end of the month. He was spared by gullible followers.

Supporters of Rep. Jack Kemp's Republican presidential candidacy appeared to have adopted a form of that ploy last week when they sent a telegram to potential donors to his campaign saying: "If we don't raise $212,900 in the next 17 days, our whole campaign could be in serious trouble."

When a newspaper reported the contents of the telegram, a Kemp spokesman admitted the campaign is financially sound, but that the campaign was using the standard "if you don't send us $10.11 by midnight, we'll shoot this puppy school of direct mail." The spokesman said the campaign of Sen. Robert Dole "is using the exact same ploy."

Whew! But that's not all. Also late last week, the Rev. Jerry Falwell, who took over the PTL ministry amid scandals and charges of possible improper use of contributions of the faithful, asked the ministry's supporters to send $1 million by today, $7 million by the end of the month and about $25 million within 90 days or the ministry won't survive. "I know Satan is against us," Falwell told a TV audience.

Yes, and the puppy will be shot at midnight.

Such methods are insulting and callous, and should prompt people to turn their backs on those who use them. But people won't.

## The Charlotte Observer
*Charlotte, NC, May 31, 1987*

Billy Graham, the Charlotte-born world-renowned evangelist, hasn't said much about the recent backsliding and backbiting in the world of television evangelism, but one thing he did say contained a lot of wisdom: "How the Lord has ever put up with His church, I'll never know."

Some of the stuff the Lord is putting up with in the brouhaha at PTL prompts these observations:

• To us, the wrangling over the theological implications of having a fundamentalist take over the ministry of the charismatic Bakkers at PTL has, if you'll pardon the expression, an other-worldly quality to it.

Theology? Under the Bakkers PTL was not a church, it was an entertainment and fund-raising enterprise that used religious themes and spent some of its money on humanitarian projects. Whatever theology the ministry had was rooted as much in television as in the Bible — a mixture of Norman Vincent Peale, "Wheel of Fortune" and a Jerry Lewis telethon, with a peculiar brand of happy-talk Christianity in the role of sponsor.

• Jerry Falwell's recent comments about Jim Bakker make us wonder what the Rev. Falwell would say about Mr. Bakker if they *weren't* loving brothers in Christ. Is there anything left?

Some time ago the Rev. Falwell said there wouldn't be any "holy war" between him and the Bakkers because it takes two sides to make a war. For a noncombatant, he certainly has fired some withering barrages at Jim Bakker.

• Jim Bakker may well be, as he tells us, a well-meaning man who has sought and obtained forgiveness for his sins, but his capacity for shunning responsibility is beyond belief. Consider the record:

He admitted sexual misconduct and paying hush money to cover his misdeed. The Assemblies of God church stripped him of his ministerial credentials. While being paid an annual salary that exceeded the lifetime earnings of many of his supporters, he professed poverty in the service of PTL and begged them for money. And with brazen mismanagement and profligate living he squandered millions of the dollars they sent in.

And now Jim Bakker wants people to see him as the victim of a Jerry Falwell power grab and help him regain control of PTL. Amazing.

## The Kansas City Times
*Kansas City, MO, May 19, 1987*

The revelation that as much as $92 million in contributions to the PTL ministry could have vanished without a trace staggers the imagination. It also makes it abundantly clear that some federal guidelines and tax controls are urgently needed. They are long overdue.

Under the rules now in place, gifts to religious and eleemosynary organizations are tax deductible, and properly so. In theory, their mission is to do good works. In practice it is becoming increasingly clear that the PTL ministry was a handy vehicle to promote the lifestyle of Jim and Tammy Bakker which, at least in the later years, approached the scale of a Middle East potentate.

At this point, no one knows what happened to the $92 million and the chances seem excellent a good deal of it will never be determined. Vast sums appear to have been dispensed without any records at all.

Enough is known to indicate that an enormous amount of money — in addition to millions in salaries and bonuses — went to the Bakkers and their top aides. The new PTL board is saying it financed their standard of living. One official calls this "mind-boggling," which puts it mildly.

There is no way to predict the conclusion of the federal and state investigations now under way. They are looking at things like tax fraud, mail fraud, extortion and the like. But surely enough has already been revealed to prompt Congress to require full and open accounting of contributions, how the money is spent and who gets it. The FCC should also take a look to see how the airwaves are being manipulated.

All of this is revolting to those who never sent PTL a penny. Pity the tens of thousands of Americans who dipped into their savings and Social Security checks — and in good faith — to keep the ministry and its version of the gospel on the air. The sad part is that so much of the money went for other purposes. It is high time for Congress to write some new rules in an attempt to get a firm handle on such abuses.

## ARGUS-LEADER
*Sioux Falls, SD, May 28, 1987*

**Editorial**

The holy war of the past two months has made it clear that TV evangelists are ordinary people. Like the rest of us, they are not perfect.

Basic human weaknesses become amplified in preachers of the airwaves, especially the pious who fail to meet the standards they impose on others. But the more the Rev. Jim Bakker talks, the more he appears to be driven by greed, power and lust rather than a sense of duty.

The fallen PTL leader has shown little remorse since a disclosure in March about a seven-year-old extramarital sexual encounter with a church secretary. More charges have followed that revelation, including accusations that Bakker, his wife, Tammy Faye, and other PTL leaders misspent ministry funds.

The thought of some evangelists driving around in Rolls Royces, living in excess and fighting for power has, understandably, turned some donors off. The PTL, estimated to be $70 million in debt, is struggling to survive. Yet, Bakker, who turned his ministry over to the Rev. Jerry Falwell, continues to describe himself as the victim of a diabolical plot to gain control of his empire.

Just this week, Bakker accused Falwell of pretending the takeover was necessary to forestall a hostile takeover by another TV evangelist, the Rev. Jimmy Swaggart. Bakker said Falwell had promised him he could return to PTL at any time.

"He said he wanted to save his own ministry which he felt would be next destroyed by Swaggart," Bakker said. "He wanted to help me and that he would never touch my ministry, he would not manage it."

Bakker said it was under those conditions that he agreed to step down during a meeting days before the sex scandal broke.

Falwell, meantime, said he initially believed that Bakker had engaged in one brief and incomplete sexual encounter, but that he has since learned that Bakker's misbehavior went beyond that. Knowing what he does now, Falwell thinks it would be a disservice to God to allow Bakker to come back.

Allowing Bakker back would indeed be a disservice, especially to contributors who did not intend for their money to be used for blackmail payments.

Items like Bakker's gold-plated toilet fixtures and air-conditioned doghouse have captured a lot of the public attention, and Bakker still wants the PTL to pay him $300,000 a year for life. But not all of the millions raised by television ministries are wasted. Contributors also pay for missions that have helped many people.

For the sake of those worthy programs and other TV ministries, Bakker should look for a new line of work. He should fade quietly away. For now, at least, the nation would be better off if he would join a congregation rather than lead one.

## ST. LOUIS POST-DISPATCH
*St. Louis, MO, May 30, 1987*

The sordid fight among evangelists over the future — and future earning rights — of the PTL television ministry is captivating melodrama. But the important public policy issues remain the soliciting and investing of tax-exempt dollars from hundreds of thousands of private donors. Unexciting though the thought is compared to sensational charges and countercharges ringing across the airwaves, what should most concern the public and public officials are the uses to which money raised by TV evangelists is put and the evangelists' accountability for it.

Evangelism through TV is obviously big business, with the accompanying temptations that such flows of cash and benefits induce. That is what appears to motivate the present conflict between the Rev. Jerry Falwell and Jim Bakker, who has been stripped of his ministry by his sponsoring faith, the Assemblies of God.

The disturbing fact about the ostentatious lifestyle of Jim and Tammy Bakker is not only that it contrasts so sharply with the teachings of Jesus, but that it was made possible by exploiting the religious devotion of tens of thousands of believers, many of whom make genuine sacrifices to support the PTL ministry.

TV evangelists, after all, are using public airwaves and enjoy a tax-exempt status. This gives the government both the right and the responsibility to make certain the evangelists keep faith with their congregants through strict financial reporting requirements. True, a government presence risks state intrusion into church matters, but the multimillion-dollar abuses found in the PTL operation, along with suspicions about some other TV ministries, demand that the risk be taken.

## THE PLAIN DEALER
*Cleveland, OH, May 29, 1987*

The intelligence services are riddled with holes. The White House is besieged by the Iran-contra scandal. Leading presidential contenders face questions of fidelity and truthfulness. Wall Street is shaken by what seems like wholesale participation in illegal trading activities. Yet what tawdry news event seizes the national imagination? The Jim and Tammy Show.

You probably know that Jim and Tammy Faye Bakker were the founders of the PTL Club, a charismatic tele-ministry that seemed remarkably successful until, like the walls of Jericho, its facade of wholesomeness came tumbling down. First, it was disclosed that Jim had engaged in an adulterous liaison with a young camp follower in Florida. Two out of three versions suggest that the incident came close to rape. Amid fears that his "ministry" was under attack by a covetous fellow evangelist, Jim and Tammy called in fundamentalist Jerry Falwell to temporarily shepherd their flock.

During subsequent audits of the PTL Club, Falwell discovered that Jim and Tammy had lived a life of grotesque high luxury. They spent millions of dollars on opulent houses, cars, clothes, chandeliered dressing rooms. They even built an air-conditioned doghouse. The residents of a PTL project called Kevin's House, built with money donated to build a home for terminally ill children, were three children and several Bakker relatives.

Neither the charges of sexual misconduct nor the evidence of fraud have abated. After weeks of silence, Jim showed up on television to charge that Falwell was expropriating his ministry. Falwell returned fire, saying that he had heard testimony that alleged that Jim had a "homosexual problem" dating back to 1956 and that he would not allow Jim, now defrocked, to resume his pulpit. In a subsequent interview, Jim denied the charge, his wife admitted that shopping was her "hobby," and neither could say how much they earned. It was implied that Falwell had conspired to seize the PTL ministry right from the start. In order to fade away, the Bakkers asked Falwell to assure them a joint income of $400,000 a year for life.

The Jim and Tammy Show has attained a certain cultural perfection. You have your defrocked minister accused of promiscuity, homosexuality and adultery; his giggling, overpainted wife given to weeping on cue and shopping; not-so-dim allegations of narcissism, mismanagement, fraud, greed and plain old bad taste. It is, in short, a drama that contains the juiciest bits of Gary Hart's indiscretions, Wall Street's avarice, the intelligence community's insecurities and the Iran-contra scandal's secret payments.

The PTL Club scandal has proven as inexorably gripping as a melted lemon lollipop. As the sordid affair escalates, it continues to provoke the nation's prurient interest. The fact that thousands, perhaps hundreds of thousands, of the PTL Club's followers are witnessing the destruction of the conduit of their faith should be more appalling. But it isn't, because the perversity that is being played out in public is overwhelming. Alas, there can be neither compensation nor satisfaction for those of the Bakkers' flock who have been cheated and abused and manipulated. The money can never be returned, the faith can never be fully restored. And unlike scandals of finance or politics or treason, public humiliation and disgrace are no punishment. If they were, the Bakkers wouldn't perpetuate this disgusting display in the first place.

## The Philadelphia Inquirer
*Philadelphia, PA, May 29, 1987*

Jim Bakker is gone now, exiled with Tammy to the couple's $450,000 digs in Palm Springs, Calif. He has become the evangelical equivalent of Ferdinand Marcos mulling over nibbles to guest-host *The Late Show with Someone Besides Joan Rivers*. Of course, the PTL Club he once hosted isn't gone — yet — and its savior-designate, the Rev. Jerry "Bishop Tutu is a phony" Falwell has put out the word that the ministry needs $3.2 million by today or "we go out of business."

That means no more Mercedeses, no more gold-plated bathroom faucets, no more shopping sprees for Tammy, no more air-conditioned doghouses. What it could mean, also, old PTL hands fear, is "a situation where this ministry ends and Jerry Falwell goes home with our mailing list and satellite in his hip pocket."

There certainly seems to be a scent of value-free religion wafting from this business. That and the faint chortling of P.T. Barnum — wherever he is.

## Evangelist Jimmy Swaggart Loses Pulpit in Scandal

Television evangelist Jimmy Swaggart admitted to an unspecified "sin" Feb. 21, 1988 in a tearful confession to an overflow crowd of more than 6,000 at his ministry's Family Worship Center in Baton Rouge, La. He said no one was to blame but himself and begged forgiveness. He said he would step down from his pulpit for an "indeterminate period of time." News reports said the incidents involved the hiring of prostitutes for sexual acts.

Swaggart's local denomination leaders, members of the Assemblies of God, met in Alexandria, La. Feb. 22 and decreed a two-year period of rehabilitation for Swaggart and a three-month absence from the pulpit, aside from foreign commitments.

The incident recalled the unfrocking in 1987 of another television evangelist, Jim Bakker, also affiliated with the Assemblies of God, after he acknowledged a sexual episode with a female church secretary.

In a related development, presidential candidate Pat Robertson, a former television evangelist, accused Vice President George Bush Feb. 24 of bringing about the disclosure involving Swaggart just to tarnish him by association. Robertson, at a news conference in Columbia, S.C. Feb. 23, said Bush had been behind the Swaggart revelation to embarrass Robertson before the Super Tuesday voting. Super Tuesday was the name given to the 20-state presidential election primaries which were held March 8, 1988. Asked for specifics, Robertson said, "The evidence is that two weeks before the primary...it suddenly comes to light."

Robertson went on to attack Bush's campaign staff as "sleazy." Bush dismissed the charges later Feb. 23 as "crazy" and "absurd." On the campaign trail Feb. 24, Bush said, "If somebody is going to make a scathing allegation of that nature, they ought to prove it. If they can't prove it, they ought to apologize for it."

### The Times-Picayune / The States-Item
*New Orleans, LA, February 26, 1988*

Christianity has attracted religious rascals since the beginning — Acts mentions one by name, Simon Magus. And in America, scattered through a long and fruitful history of evangelist and revivalist movements and leaders, there have been a notorious few who entered American folklore as less than savory characters.

But the power of television has created modern "televangelism," whose potential for accumulating power and riches poses a danger both to religion and to the religious. Its attraction to con men is obvious, and the corruptive power of adulation and money even over the originally genuine cannot be discounted.

We now have Jimmy Swaggart, one of the most successful of the type. He stands as a confessed sinner — a yet to be elucidated "addiction to pornography" — and a demonstrated hypocrite begging forgiveness only after having been caught at it. The whistle was reportedly blown by fellow evangelist Marvin Gorman, who was forced from his pulpit two years ago for sexual misconduct. It was Mr. Swaggart who blew the whistle on evangelist Jim Bakker, also ousted from his church, for similar behavior.

This is, on the surface, buffoonery of Rabelaisian proportions. But below it lies a troubling social and religious tragedy. Recent studies have shown that while the public is becoming suspicious of television evangelists themselves, it is tuning in to televised evangelical programs in increasing numbers. Clearly the yearning for a return to clearcut, Scripture-based religion and morality engages many minds and emotions regardless of the particular spokesmen of it.

The pull toward fundamentalism is doubtless a reaction against secular, technological, pragmatic modernism and a perceived failure of mainline religious organizations to bridge what many must feel is a discontinuity between religion and modern life. We might remember that the early successes of Christianity itself were in some part due to a reaction against the sterile traditional religions of the time.

The Constitution rightly prevents government from interfering in religious matters except when there are violations of criminal and civil laws based on secular governmental powers. So there may be little that can be done legally against rapacious profiteers who hide behind the First Amendment. Regulation must lie with the churches the evangelists represent and the individual members of their congregations, including their television congregations.

In the case of Mr. Swaggart, the penance his church leadership has so far required of him is so light that it is bringing demands from the congregation for sterner measures. In earlier, even more fundamentalist times, he would, at best, have never been allowed to preach again. Personal atonement is one thing; public leadership and ministry as representative and role model of the congregation are another.

Individuals must recognize that along with the true stewards who take the call to lead the faithful there may be others who themselves have gone astray. The believers' knowledge of Scripture should warn them to be vigilant against false prophets "which come to you in sheep's clothing, but inwardly they are ravening wolves."

### THE ASHEVILLE CITIZEN
*Ashville, NC, February 23, 1988*

So one more television evangelist falls. Jimmy Swaggart is one of the biggest, but the country has become accustomed to seeing TV ministers stumble because of worldly pleasures.

The only remarkable thing about the Swaggart case is the extent to which everyone is focusing on his physical sin, that of consorting with a prostitute. In the eyes of his church and his followers, that was his greatest offense, and they already have begun forgiving him.

Give Swaggart credit: He knew what he had to do. He prostrated himself before the elders of the Assemblies of God denomination, his congregation, his TV audience and God himself. Swaggart blamed no one else. He admitted sinning, took full responsibility and begged forgiveness. Most of his sympathizers were not just touched, they were overwhelmed.

Amid all this glorious healing, it seems almost unkind to note that Swaggart did not admit his sin until he had no choice — until it was reported by a fellow TV evangelist and competitor whom Swaggart had helped discredit and drive out of business. He did not confess until his worldly empire was at stake. Where were Swaggart's humility and repentance during all those months or years before he was found out?

Swaggart spent most of those months condemning in the harshest way possible TV evangelists whom he thought unworthy of Christ — all the while indulging in the same physical sins for which they were accused.

Many Christians, and especially those who lean toward a rigid view of the faith, elevate sins of the flesh above all else. They see these as the worst offenses against God.

The Gospels teach us otherwise. Christ viewed sins of the flesh as minor transgressions compared to sins of the spirit. Among the latter are greed, jealousy, hardness of heart, hatred and hypocrisy.

Swaggart is fortunate that most of his followers and contributors see things the opposite. Perhaps he himself does not, or one day will not, and will come to seek other forgiveness as well.

## The Virginian-Pilot
*Norfolk, VA, February 23, 1988*

Little wonder that presidential candidate Pat Robertson abhors being called a televangelist. These are not the best of times for TV preachers.

Jimmy Swaggart is the latest to be humbled. Not everyone in the evangelical movement will be dismayed. Mr. Swaggart was in the forefront of those who accused other televangelists of betraying their flock by straying from the houses of prayer into the dens of iniquity. Now we find that he, too, is human, and not immune to the sins of the flesh.

According to news accounts (which change daily), Mr. Swaggart was attracted to pornographic literature. That does not make him unique; pornography is a booming business in America. But Mr. Swaggart made his living denouncing the evils of such literature. That's hypocrisy, which is another sin.

Mr. Swaggart's dramatic confession Sunday may hasten his return to the pulpit. Unlike some other fallen TV preachers of recent vintage, he didn't attempt a cover-up but admitted his mistakes. That fits in with the time-honored Southern tradition of raising Cain on Saturday night but 'fessing up and seeking forgiveness on Sunday morning. Soon he will be back on TV, railing against the problems that pornography can cause. Speaking from experience. And making a good living at it, too.

## Roanoke Times & World-News
*Roanoke, VA, February 23, 1988*

**When a preacher of the Gospel falls, and he is known quite well, then it's naturally a scandal and it really ought to be, because the minister of God is a moral yardstick.**
— **Evangelist Jimmy Swaggart**

WHEN those words were spoken, the fallen preacher was Jim Bakker of PTL, the initials standing for "Praise The Lord" or "People That Love."

Today it's Swaggart's turn. The Baton Rouge televangelist has confessed to succumbing to temptations of the flesh. Marvin Gorman, an evangelist he once fingered for sexual dalliance, apparently has fingered him in turn, with photographs of Swaggart entering a motel with a known prostitute.

It was Swaggart who passed the word to Assembly of God church officials that Bakker had been involved in sexual misconduct. After Bakker's sins had become public knowledge, Swaggart declared, "Today, the most filthy, the most rotten, the most diabolical, the most hellish of sin is covered with 'Praise the Lord.' God deliver us from these pompadour boys, hair done, nails done, fresh from the beauty shop, preaching the Gospel."

Even then, his enemies had hinted at retribution. Roy Grutman, Bakker's attorney, said that if Swaggart kept up his intrigues against Bakker's former ministry, "We're going to be compelled to show that there's a smellier laundry in his hamper than the laundry that he thought was in the Rev. Bakker's."

When it comes to mud-slinging, politicians can take lessons from evangelists.

"The credibility crisis is unbelievable," said Jerry Falwell of Lynchburg, who described his Old Time Gospel Hour as "the last television ministry." Falwell added, "The last thing America needs is another credibility crisis."

Wrong, Jerry. It's about time the American public visited a credibility crisis on an industry that makes celebrities of people who live like millionaires off the charity of honest, hard-working people.

The televangelist is more than an ordinary preacher. He is at once a show-business personality and a business tycoon. He is the custodian of tens of millions of dollars. His contributors send him the dough in complete trust. That kind of money conveys power. And power can be an aphrodisiac. The celebrity feasting on the adulation of his followers finds that the forbidden fruit is readily available. And it takes fortitude to resist.

But "Thou shalt not commit adultery" is only one of the rules of conduct laid down in the book the televangelist waves before his audience. There are other passages that deal with greed and deception and the worship of material goods.

Swaggart's ministry has netted him contributions by the mailbag — upwards of $120 million a year. It takes a lot of money just to keep him on the air. His television programs have been broadcast into 193 of the 212 television markets in this country, on numerous cable television systems, and into 145 foreign countries.

A large portion of the annual millions must go to support his 257-acre headquarters complex in Baton Rouge. This includes a 12-building world-ministry center and a Bible college. In addition, the Swaggart organization provides 20 school buses to pick up poor children on Saturdays and provide them with hot meals and religious programs. And his Child Care International builds schools and sponsors feeding programs in the Third World.

This highly visible charity hasn't impoverished the evangelist and his family. Compared to their annual gross, their salaries are modest — $19,000 a year for Swaggart, about $50,000 for his wife, Frances, and about $56,500 for their son, Donald. But the perks are superb.

Jimmy and Frances drive his and hers Lincoln Town Cars. They live in a home with a swimming pool on a 20-acre site assessed at $1.5 million. Their only son, Donald, lives on a more modest four-acre estate valued at $750,000. They have the use of a Palm Springs retreat owned by the ministry.

"We could be millionaires ... but we're not," said Frances. "I could be dripping in luxury ... " She doesn't say what it is she's dripping in now.

Explained Swaggart: "Our people in the church, all the people that we minister to, they don't take the position that when a person becomes a Christian ... he moves into a tent and wears sackcloth and ashes. They believe that God blesses you, if you live for God and you serve God."

Swaggart has gone through the ritual of repentance and will attempt, no doubt, to return to his lucrative empire. The earnest worshiper must be left wondering where to look for a reliable religious leader. Swaggart himself provided some good advice in the context of the Bakker scandal: "I'm not the judge, God is. But you do see what kind of fruit a tree bears. If it's thorns, it's obvious."

## Wisconsin State Journal
*Madison, WI, February 23, 1988*

Evangelist Jimmy Swaggart's tearful confession that he had "sinned" by consorting with a prostitute comes while the charismatic religious movement is still reeling from the antics of the Rev. Oral Roberts ("Give me $8 million or God will call me home) and former TV preacher Jim Bakker, whose downfall was linked to disclosures of sexual and financial improprieties.

The initial reaction will be public ridicule and a fresh supply of one-liners for stand-up comedians, but the real story behind Swaggart's admission is less humorous than profoundly sad. That sadness was evident Sunday when Swaggart, hauled on the carpet three days earlier by the Assemblies of God denomination, made an emotional 20-minute appearance before more than 7,000 of his stunned and weeping congregants at the World Faith Center auditorium in Baton Rouge, La.

These were people who had obviously invested a lot of their time, energy and money in a religious leader who, to one degree or another, let them down. And their pain was not eased by the knowledge that it was Swaggart who less than a year ago stridently criticized fellow Assemblies of God clergyman Bakker for essentially the same kind of behavior.

Swaggart then called Bakker "a cancer that needs to be excised from the body of Christ" and urged him to step down. Today, Swaggart is begging forgiveness and fighting to retain a role in the $150-million evangelistic empire he helped to build.

Perhaps many or even most of Swaggart's followers will forgive him, but now they, too, have learned a powerful lesson about elevating a single leader to near-icon status. The higher they are, the harder they fall. That law of charismatic gravity seems to apply equally in the religious and secular worlds.

There are other TV evangelists who are untainted by scandal of any kind, but the troubles of Swaggart, the Bakkers and Roberts should renew a sense of caution among those people who believe unquestionably in a single leader. That should apply to the political world, too, where two candidates for president have built their campaigns on different but moralistic foundations.

One need not feel sorry for Swaggart to feel compassion for his followers, because their disappointment was real. Perhaps too real.

## Los Angeles Times
*Los Angeles, CA, February 23, 1988*

Human nature being what it is, there are probably two prevailing responses to the news that the Rev. Jimmy Swaggart, a highly successful television evangelist, has been compelled to confess publicly to unspecified but almost certainly spicy moral transgressions. Some, warmly remembering Swaggart's past ministerial services, will probably react to his tearful confessional candor with a generous readiness to forgive his slip from grace. Others are more likely to find the revelations of his alleged trysts with prostitutes utterly hilarious.

There is no way to measure which of these responses may be dominant across the land. Our guess is that the laughers likely have the edge, for nearly everyone is cheered by seeing hypocrisy exposed and—the other side of the coin—by perceiving that moral justice has to some extent been done. Is there something cruel in this? Of course, as there always is whenever we take pleasure from the misfortunes of others. But there is also something perfectly understandable.

Swaggart has made what from all accounts is a lucrative career preaching about the wages of sin to millions of followers in 142 countries. He was also instrumental in leading the charge that unseated and defrocked the Rev. Jim Bakker, formerly the well-paid and rich-living head of the PTL television ministry. Swaggart could feel no charity for Bakker; he called his confessed sexual lapses "a cancer on the body of Christ." Now Swaggart himself has been forced to ask his wife, his congregation and his church to pardon his own weakness of the flesh.

This seems to have been something less than a spontaneous outburst of repentance. Apparently Swaggart was nailed by another ministerial adversary, the Rev. Marvin Gorman, who is reported to have got hold of—in some unexplained way—pictures of Swaggart entering and leaving a New Orleans motel room with a reputed lady of easy virtue. Gorman, also defrocked with Swaggart's help after admitting to unsanctioned sexual encounters, says that—whatever role he may have played in Swaggart's exposure—his heart for now is deeply saddened by the affair.

It is a sad business certainly for all who may find comfort and consolation in the preachings of a Swaggart, a Bakker, a Gorman or any of the other evangelists who reach millions and who reap millions through their television ministries. Repentance, no matter how lachrymose, cannot easily wash away the dark stain of hypocrisy. Others, though, are likely to appreciate the matter more for its unambiguous but certainly not unfamiliar irony. The guy who scared the hell out of a lot of people crusading against sin got caught Doing It. The human comedy goes on, with the fallibility of others providing endless opportunity for moral instruction.

## The Des Moines Register
*Des Moines, IA, February 26, 1988*

Another television evangelist has taken a spectacular fall from grace: this time the Rev. Jimmy Swaggart, the very same man who rose to such high dudgeon over the sexual indiscretions of former cable-TV preacher Jim Bakker.

Swaggart has confessed his sin of hiring a woman of the night, resigned his pulpit and will go through a two-year rehabilitation.

The rest is predictable: extensive news coverage fueled by a steady stream of new revelations to be followed by a gut-spilling best-seller and his resurrection with a new passion for reforming others' lives after having salvaged his.

Of course, his television congregation will forgive him. That should come as no surprise, because forgiveness is a generally accepted Christian concept.

What is difficult to fathom, though, is the seemingly endless reservoir of toleration for the huge piles of cash it takes to support these TV ministries, not to mention the TV preachers themselves.

Swaggart's $142 million ministry has afforded him a lifestyle that could guarantee him a regular slot on TV's "Lifestyles of the Rich and Famous." Swaggart is not alone, though. Jim and Tammy Bakker's conspicuous consumption bordered on the obscene, and some contributors might wonder about the wisdom of helping postpone Oral Roberts' appointment with his Maker if they knew how the money was spent.

The television ministries, with their spinoff theme parks, hotels, colleges and seminaries, have enormous appetites for cash. Raising money becomes a near obsession, and the twin themes of giving (money) and receiving (redemption) become blurred.

Many mainline Christians find it hard to believe that Swaggart, et al, are reading the same gospels that used to be taught, for if they did they would recognize the inconsistency of their own ministries and the life of Christ, who rejected the temptation of wealth and power to take his wisdom to the poor, unwashed and outcast.

No, it's not difficult to forgive Jimmy Swaggart for his sin(s). It is not so easy, though, to overlook the signs of lust for power, fame and wealth that surround his ministry.

"REV. SWAGGART, YOU WERE HIRED HERE TO PLAY THE PIANO!"

## THE ARIZONA REPUBLIC
*Phoenix, AZ, February 23, 1988*

IN Baton Rouge they wept and shouted and spoke in tongues, and when the Rev. Jimmy Swaggart cried out, "Oh, I have sinned against you, and I beg your forgiveness," they wept some more and fell on their knees and forgave.

"I think he is a man of integrity," said the district superintendent of Swaggart's Pentacostal denomination, the Assemblies of God. He conceded Swaggart's mistake — it was hard to deny — but was quick to add, "I don't think it's a fatal mistake."

Another church official said he was impressed that Swaggart had accepted responsibility for going astray, which is trimming the truth a little. If the reports are to be believed, Swaggart did not simply go astray. He stayed astray, all the while belting out those imprecations about other evangelists ("pretty little boys with their *hair* done and their *nails* done who call themselves *preachers*") and, of course, sin.

What Swaggart has admitted, insiders disclose, is a lifelong obsession with pornography, leading to his now-publicized motel-room rendezvous with a prostitute. Some will find it perplexing in the circumstances to hear him described as "a man of integrity." Yet for some reason, his superiors seem to take it as a mark of valor that, finding his sins laid bare, he disdains to blame anyone else, though it is unclear exactly who else he might have blamed.

Swaggart's hypocrisy is especially striking. When Jim Bakker's sexual adventures became known last March, Swaggart denounced the errant evangelist as "a cancer on the body of Christ." Viewed in the context of his own shortcomings, Swaggart's exuberance about Bakker, another Assemblies of God performer, is especially hard to stomach.

What is it about the "television ministry" that seems to attract so many Elmer Gantrys or, if you prefer, corrupts so many giants of the faith? Perhaps it is the money, perhaps it is the power, and perhaps it is the nature of the medium, with its capacity for exalting the ego. If Christian charity "vaunteth not itself, is not puffed up," as St. Paul preached, then television is surely its antithesis.

Jimmy Swaggart's stumbling descent from the heights of power and glory must elicit compassion, however deep-dyed his sins. But even more to be pitied are the thousands who believed in him, who enabled him to pile up $140 million a year in donations and who, much more costly, invested so much faith in his power to steer them to salvation.

Far more than his obsessive lechery, this studied deception is the crime for which Jimmy Swaggart and other such humbugs will have to atone.

## Omaha World-Herald
*Omaha, NE, February 23, 1988*

Jimmy Swaggart, who thundered with condemnation last year when sex scandals forced fellow television evangelist Jim Bakker to leave the ministry, has acknowledged that he, too, has strayed. Swaggart's confession didn't come as a voluntary act of conscience and contrition. He got caught. Church officials had pictures.

Photographs surfaced showing Swaggart entering and leaving a motel room with a prostitute. Swaggart's tearful confession Sunday to his 6,000-member congregation in Baton Rouge, La., left a strong impression that he was ashamed of his behavior.

Remember that Swaggart has made a career of issuing harsh, withering judgments. In installment after installment of his internationally televised sermons, he condemned clergymen and other Christians who he said didn't speak out strongly enough against sin. "Mealy-mouthed" was one of the more gentle adjectives he used to describe them.

And lust, as Swaggart repeatedly declared from the pulpit, is one of the seven deadly sins.

It was this same sanctimonious condemner of sins of the flesh who helped bring down Bakker. Swaggart passed rumors about Bakker and Jessica Hahn to officials of the Assemblies of God Church, the church to which both Bakker and Swaggart belong. Swaggart, speaking of Bakker's behavior, said: "I'm ashamed. I'm embarrassed." He said Bakker was "a cancer that needs to be excised from the body of Christ."

Admittedly, Swaggart didn't look for scapegoats, as Bakker did, when confronted with evidence of his hypocrisy. His confession and plea for forgiveness from the pulpit Sunday seemed sincere.

Nevertheless, Swaggart let a lot of people down. He has been one of the more popular television evangelists. Millions of people in the United States and other countries tuned in to his television programs, including many older people and shut-ins who counted on Swaggart for moral guidance, spiritual comfort and religious music. They have been betrayed by a man who did not practice what he preached.

Some of Swaggart's congregation said that they have already forgiven him. Perhaps prompt forgiveness is a feature of the faith Swaggart preached, although it wasn't reflected when Swaggart called Bakker a cancer. But forgiveness for Swaggart's sexual misbehavior can't erase the fact that he displayed two conflicting standards of behavior: one in the pulpit and another in the motel room. If he returns to his ministry now, his fire and brimstone will be out of place. His condemnations of "sins of the flesh" will ring hollow.

## The San Diego Union
*San Diego, CA, February 23, 1988*

Mark Twain recalled a businessman, notorious for his pomposity, who announced with great fanfare, "Before I die I will go to the Holy Land, climb Mount Sinai, and read the Ten Commandments aloud at the top."

"I have a better idea," said Twain. "You could stay home and keep them."

The story comes to mind while digesting the latest twist in the career of the Rev. Jimmy Swaggart, the flamboyant TV evangelist who stepped down from his pulpit Sunday after a tearful confession of "moral failure." He declined to be more specific than that, telling his congregation only that "incidents" had led to his confession to church officials last week.

Reports are circulating that the one-time backwoods Louisiana preacher, whose evangelistic ministry ultimately brought in more than $140 million annually in donations, was seen leaving a New Orleans motel in the company of a reputed prostitute.

Ironically, a year ago Mr. Swaggart insisted that the Assemblies of God investigate charges of sexual immorality against fellow Assembly minister and TV preacher, Jim Bakker. Mr. Swaggart publicly condemned Mr. Bakker as "a cancer on the body of Christ."

Two mainstays of the fiery Swaggart repertoire were his relentless attacks on other Christian denominations, particularly the Roman Catholic Church, and his withering denunciations of fellow TV evangelists. "Hypocrites" and "false prophets," he called them, "pompadoured pretty boys with their hair done and their nails done who call themselves preachers." Millions are deceived and duped by such people, he would say.

Even a stopped clock is correct twice a day, and Mr. Swaggart was right about a few TV ministers. Not all, by any means. In stark contrast to Mr. Bakker and Mr. Swaggart, there is the Rev. Billy Graham, the Rev. Robert Schuller, the venerable Dr. Norman Vincent Peale. And laughable would be the comparison of Mr. Swaggart with the luminescence of the late Bishop Fulton J. Sheen.

The common denominator between Mr. Swaggart, Mr. Bakker, Oral Roberts, and others, is their preoccupation with the things that are Caesar's. The money that fills their coffers comes from tens of thousands of people who dutifully send in their offerings, often at great sacrifice. Too many cases have been documented in which people have signed over their pensions, property, and life's savings to TV evangelists.

The tragedy of Jimmy Swaggart is not the fall of a dynamic, yet flawed, preacher. It is the bitter disillusionment that will be felt most deeply, and painfully, among Mr. Swaggart's faithful followers. Mr. Swaggart ought to think about that while he is taking Mark Twain's advice.

## Garrison Keillor Leaves
*A Prairie Home Companion*

Humorist and best-selling author Garrison Keillor Feb. 14, 1987 told listeners to his National Public Radio variety show, *A Prairie Home Companion*, that June 13 would be his last broadcast as host of the show. Keillor, 44, had hosted the show since its inception in 1974 on Minnesota Public Radio. The show, which revolved around a fictional Minnesota community known as Lake Wobegon, had been heard throughout the U.S. since 1980.

### THE SACRAMENTO BEE
*Sacramento, CA, June 20, 1987*

Four million people tuned in last week to listen to Garrison Keillor's last report from Lake Wobegon. That's pretty small potatoes for mass entertainment. But after 13 years on the air, Keillor's program *A Prairie Home Companion* leaves behind a lot of happy memories and a string of accomplishments — including a new radio network (American Public Radio), at least one best-selling book (with a new book soon to appear) and innumerable Powdermilk Biscuit T-shirts.

Much of the program's charm lay in its seeming determination to be out of step with the 1980s and the rest of popular culture. It was on radio, for one thing, and a variety show to boot at a time when that format has all but disappeared. It pitched snowbound, Midwestern themes to a nation that's moving to the Sun Belt. And it sang of small-town virtues for an audience that in large part has probably never lived anywhere except along the fringes of big cities.

But Keillor was wiser than the apparent contradictions of his success might suggest. He knew how to mock the sentimentality he dished up in such abundance while still savoring all its sweetness. This was a program for the Baby Boomers, not the Yuppies, and it tapped into that same collective memory that saved Classic Coke and made Golden Oldies the *leitmotif* for contemporary advertising.

Even if his listeners had never known a place like Lake Wobegon, his stories always touched on familiar moments everyone recalls: those large family gatherings at Thanksgiving where the conflict between the generations becomes so intense that you don't know whether to pass the mashed potatoes or throw them; the sense of growing older when you no longer sing in the shower and begin to think instead about putting down some rubber treads to keep from slipping.

Over the years, Keillor talked a lot about love and envy and loss. But mainly his program dealt with longing — for youth, for simplicity, for understanding. To that long list of things to wish for, add another: just one more visit someday to the Chatterbox Cafe and the little town that time forgot but the decades can never improve.

### The Wichita Eagle-Beacon
*Wichita, KS, February 18, 1987*

THE news from Lake Wobegon this week saddened us: Garrison Keillor, host of the popular radio show "Prairie Home Companion" and sole proprietor of mythical Lake Wobegon, Minn., has announced his resignation after 13 years. His many fans wish him all the best.

Keillor says he wants to spend more time with his new wife, and perhaps live in her native Denmark for awhile. He also wants to quit while the show is still fresh. That's understandable and wise, but fans nevertheless will miss hearing about Lake Wobegon, where "all the women are strong, all the men are good-looking and all the children are above-average."

In this literal-minded age, Mr. Keillor's "Prairie Home Companion" offered a refreshing alternative of homespun whimsy and song. Its entertainment was truly radical — humor that laughs with people, not at them, and music that is participatory. It breathed new life into the golden tradition of radio variety programs and helped renew Middle America's faith in its values and humor.

What will not be missed is Mr. Keillor's singing, which was atrocious. But his talent for stand-up comedy as well as prose — a rare combination — has established him as one of America's truly gifted humorists.

The airwaves won't be quite the same without the news from Lake Wobegon.

### The Hutchinson News
*Hutchinson, KS, February 19, 1987*

Minnesota will never be quite the same without Lake Wobegone.

Neither will every place else.

Garrison Keillor, host of National Public Radio's "Prairie Home Companion" and creator of the mythical Minnesota community and its galaxy of interesting characters told his audiences through Hutchinson's KHCC Saturday that he's hanging it up June 13.

No more Powdermilk Biscuit ads. No more Bertha's Kitty Boutique. No more reports from a town where "all the kids are above average." No more news from Lake Wobegone, because he wants to do something else, he says.

Too bad. The show was one of the best things public radio had going for it. If it had been on commercial radio, it would have been the only good thing going for it.

But Mr. Keillor will leave town as a hero, which is certainly a better way to go than in the middle of the night. Going this way, at a peak in popularity, just might encourage him to find some other place to park the talent that has given so much pleasure these past few years.

## San Francisco Chronicle
*San Francisco, CA, June 2, 1987*

GARRISON KEILLOR is about to move away from Lake Wobegone and many Americans are going to be wondering what to do with a major part of their weekends. Keillor's remarkable imagination, his gentle humor and great grace made him almost a cult figure in millions of homes where his public radio creation, the Prairie Home Companion, was required listening.

Keillor gave his 90-minute radio show its life, its style, its laughter and its wistfulness. He captivated his followers, many of whom would not tolerate any interference of their Sunday listening addiction.

In discussing his departure, Keillor explained that no one should fear change. It was a welcome and reassuring bit of homespun philosophy from a man who made us laugh at ourselves, made all human foibles our own and truly captured, gently and elegantly, the ironies of life.

## DAILY NEWS
*New York, NY, June 12, 1987*

Ralph's Pretty Good Grocery is locking its doors. The Chatterbox Cafe is turning off the grill. Lake Wobegon—that wonderful town where all the women are strong, all the men good-looking, all the children above average—is about to vanish into the mists of memory. The Wistful Vista where beloved radio shows go when they die. The great good place in the sky where Jack Benny and Vic and Sade and the flaky residents of Allen's Alley hang their hats.

"A Prairie Home Companion" is closing down tomorrow night. Garrison Keillor is calling it quits.

Native New Yorkers thought Keillor's soft-spoken "News from Lake Wobegon" monologues a lovely, improbable fantasy. But the city-dwelling nomads who hail from America's small towns knew Lake Wobegon was a *real* place—just like the ones back where they came from. And so they listened, week after week. To be gently reminded of home.

All is not lost. There are 13 years' worth of reruns available to give "Prairie Home Companion" fans everywhere the strength to get up and do what needs to be done. But there will be no more new news from Lake Wobegon. No more "Hello, Love." No more Raw Bits commercials. Saturdays will never be the same again.

## TULSA WORLD
*Tulsa, OK, February 17, 1987*

GARRISON Keillor is making it official. On June 13 America must say goodbye to Lake Wobegon and its delightful population.

The ficticious Minnesota community — "the town that time forgot and the decades cannot improve" — was created by Keillor in his affectionate, rambling monologues on "A Prairie Home Companion," produced by Minnesota Public Radio.

Thirteen years ago, Keillor took the video generation by surprise with his two-hour radio show filled with his personal musings, skits, music and commercials for imaginary products such as powdermilk biscuits or Wobegon merchants like Bertha's Kitty Boutique.

But millions learned the old-fashioned joy of tuning in, sitting back and listening.

Keillor could bring tears with a monologue about visiting a great-Aunt's house at Christmas and finding traditions, smells and sights carefully preserved from his youth; or bring laughter with a rollicking account of the first snowfall of the year in Lake Wobegon.

Saying he is going to "resume the life of a shy person," Keillor's immediate plans are to live in his wife's native Denmark and pursue a career as a writer.

He will be missed on American radio.

## AKRON BEACON JOURNAL
*Akron, OH, June 12, 1987*

FOR MANY Americans, something will be missing after tomorrow night, when Garrison Keillor and his friends broadcast the last weekly radio show of *A Prairie Home Companion*.

There has been something friendly and wholesome about these 13 years of weekly broadcasts, something delightfully homespun and touching about Mr. Keillor's mythical Midwestern town, Lake Wobegon, and its wonderful characters.

Whether you listened each Saturday evening, or only occasionally, Garrison Keillor caught the flavor, the pathos and the humor of much that many of us tend to think of as the real roots of Americans — simple, hometown virtues; human frailties that do little harm to others; and a youngster's appreciation of such verities as the first warm day of spring, the lazy delights of summer when school is out, or the small but important dramas of the classroom.

In the process, whether down at the Chatterbox Cafe or visiting Bertha's Kitty Boutique in the Dales, Garrison Keillor helped restore the good name of humor. His has not been the slapstick humor of television, but the gentle humor of James Thurber, Ring Lardner, Mark Twain and George Ade.

In the course of its 13-year weekly broadcast, *A Prairie Home Companion* has also restored luster to the medium of radio. Mr. Keillor gave radio intimacy with its audience once again, and the show's popularity over National Public Radio — in this area over WKSU-FM — attested to the appeal of quality, good writing and broadcasting on subjects other than just violence and glitz.

In his second book, *Lake Wobegon Days*, Garrison Keillor said the idea for the show came from a short story he had written but had lost and forgotten, a story titled *Lake Wobegon Memoir*. "Somehow the radio show kept going," he wrote, "perhaps because I had no illusion that I was good at it, and I brought in Lake Wobegon as the home of a weekly monologue, hoping that one Saturday night, standing on stage, I would look into the lights and my lost story would come down the beam and land in my head. . . . I am still waiting for it."

After the last broadcast tomorrow night, he and we may still be waiting, but it has been a delightful wait, punctuated by the graceful musings of a talented writer and story-teller. His 4 million listeners on 275 public stations will miss his monologues and hope that he eventually finds the lost story, or some variation of it, and that we all get to share in the discovery.

## Computer 'Virus' Shuts Down Networks Across Nation

More than 6,000 computers across the country shut down Nov. 2-3, 1988 after being sabotaged by a computer "virus." It was the worst incident of computer tampering reported to date.

A "virus" is a set of instructions hidden in a computer system. Viruses are designed to copy themselves while jumping from computer to computer via shared disks or computer networks. Some viruses are relatively harmless and merely passed along humorous messages. Other, however, causes malicious damage by wiping out previously stored information.

The latest virus worked by filling up the memory capacity of the computers it attacked. Eventually, each computer ran out of available memory and became inoperable. The virus did not destroy any information. Computer experts Nov. 4 estimated that the main damage consisted of thousands of hours of lost work time and thousands of additional hours spent by computer scientists trying to clear the virus out of their systems.

The affected computers were linked to the 60,000-member Internet network, whose subscribers included universities and military and corporate research departments. The virus had taken advantage of known security flaws in the operating systems of some computers hooked up to the network. Several computer operators had saved their systems from invasion by shutting down their connection to the network once word of the virus began to spread.

The Defense Department's Milnet and Arpanet (Advanced Research Projects Agency Network) were linked to Internet and were also invaded. However, Pentagon officials said Nov. 4 that the virus had not affected restrcited-access computers that handled classified information.

The *New York Times* reported Nov. 5 that the virus had been planted by a Cornell University graduate, Robert T. Morris Jr.

The Federal Bureau of Investigation (FBI) Nov. 4 launched an investigation into whether the Internet virus had violated federal law. A bureau spokesman said that the inquiry would hinge on whether the virus had harmed the government's computer network. The Defense Communications Agency and the National Security Agency's Computer Security Center had also began their own investigations.

Prior to the Iternet virus, one of the worst reported instances of computer sabotage had been the so-called "Brain" virus. That virus had eventually been tracked to two brothers in Lahore, Pakistan who had sold infected software to American tourists. *Time* magazine had reported the incident in a Sept. 26 that brought the issue of computer viruses to wide public attention.

## MILWAUKEE SENTINEL
*Milwaukee, WI, November 9, 1988*

The virtual computer plague reportedly loosed when a 23-year-old Cornell graduate student sent a so-called "virus" filtering through a computer network once again revealed a disturbing vulnerability in these complex systems that impact on the lives of millions of Americans.

Obviously, enough safeguards are not in force. But even as that problem is addressed, the FBI appropriately has decided to upgrade the probe of this computer infiltration to a full-scale investigation. It cannot be taken for granted that this was merely an irresponsible prank.

Robert T. Morris, a graduate computer student at Cornell University, is believed to be responsible for the problem. Morris tapped into a Defense Department computer network and, inadvertently, according to reports, paralyzed 6,000 computers.

An attempt by a friend of Morris to remedy the situation after the error was detected fell flat.

Things finally got straightened out after Morris reportedly told his father about the difficulty. To make the story more bizarre, the elder Morris is chief scientist at the National Computer Security Center in the division of the National Security Agency that focuses on computer security.

If there ever was justification for taking a son to the woodshed, this was it! The younger Morris apparently not only caused nationwide havoc but his actions reflect on his father's reputation.

Also due for some criticism is Eric Allman, a computer programer who designed the system that was exploited, who said he created a "back door" into the system to get around administrative red tape while working on the project and then forgot to close it.

Carelessness with computers is a cardinal sin when people such as the younger Morris are around.

## The Providence Journal
*Providence, RI, November 11, 1988*

Robert Morris Jr., the Cornell graduate student who conceived and deployed the famous virus that disabled thousands of computer systems across the country last week, is now reported to be the subject of a criminal investigation. The Federal Bureau of Investigation has been put on the case, and young Mr. Morris has retained an attorney.

It may be some time before we know, or even understand, very much about this extraordinary incident — the statutes governing computers are not especially precise, and the world of computers is not inviting to the layman — but this case could set important precedents in the law.

In the recent past, "hackers" have been convicted of felonies committed with the aid of their computers. But charges have never been pressed against anyone accused of sending a virus — for whatever reason — into a nationwide network. If a case is assembled against Mr. Morris, it will be interesting to see what happens.

Interesting for two reasons. First, it will be useful to learn how a graduate student, even a "brilliant" one with a Harvard degree in computer science, could so readily penetrate the defenses of computer systems at such places as the Lawrence Livermore Laboratory, NASA's Ames Research Center, the Los Alamos National Laboratory, the Princeton mathematics department, and the University of Michigan.

Second, if an inspired tinkerer could accomplish such a feat, what about somebody determined to do harm? This virus merely filled storage space in different systems; another virus could eradicate data, close down computers, cause inestimable damage. Imagine such a weapon in terrorist hands.

Many of the systems affected by this virus are important to the nation's security and defense. And computers are now critical components of bank transactions, manufacturing plants, airline traffic control and telecommunications. It seems evident that the capacity of viruses to do dangerous mischief is considerable indeed.

Two questions, therefore, need to be answered. First, what can be done to protect computer systems from malicious intrusions? Nationwide networks that are interconnected will always be vulnerable to subversion such as viruses. But can such networks be better protected? The window of vulnerability is serious enough for our economic health; it could be catastrophic for defense-related systems.

And what about those who perpetrate these viruses? The law should reflect our legitimate concern about incidents like this. Nobody has the right to penetrate private channels of communication, destroy information, disrupt the orderly processes of civil society, and endanger our security. The law's responsibility seems clear enough to us; prevention and deterrence are the cures for this virus.

## Omaha World-Herald
*Omaha, NE, November 12, 1988*

The story has been heard before: A brilliant young computer hacker gums up thousands of computers across the country. Computers continue to be vulnerable to such meddling, either because of the carelessness of computer owners and operators or because state-of-the-art computer security can't quite keep up with the hackers.

Computers are becoming increasingly important in American life. They are, in effect, electronic filing cabinets as well as calculators, typewriters and high-speed processors of information. They store everything from the data of day-to-day business transactions to vital national defense secrets, from public library listings to personal medical records.

A lack of adequate security allows hackers or disgruntled employees to violate privacy and alter or destroy irreplaceable information through the telephone lines that connect computers with others around the country.

In a recent incident, the FBI is investigating the activities of a young man whose father is a computer security expert at the National Security Agency. The young man told associates that he intended to slip a short and innocuous program into computers tied to a nationwide network. He apparently made a programming mistake that changed the program into a computer virus, which replicated itself rapidly and disabled thousands of computers.

It was relatively easy to get access to the network of computers. The person who designed the network's program apparently created a special electronic entryway for his own personal use, then forgot to restrict access after his work was done.

That kind of problem is not uncommon among computer systems. It isn't unusual for programmers to create personal "back doors" for themselves. Computer users, too, are often sloppy in their habits — personal passwords are sometimes simple dates or names that hackers can determine by trial and error.

There is no substitute for computer security. It is vital for the federal government, which has crucial secrets to safeguard. But it is also necessary for any individual, agency or company that stores information using a computer. Every incident emphasizes the need for security and more security. Wise managers will heed these warnings.

## Rockford Register Star
*Rockford, IL, November 8, 1988*

As was perhaps inevitable, the first great nationwide epidemic from a single computer virus has arisen with the infection of military, corporate and university data systems from coast to coast —and at a potentially staggering cost.

The incident calls for swift and concerted action by the federal government to remedy the immediate problem and to develop the means of safeguarding everybody's computers from such vandalism.

Computer viruses are maverick instructions deliberately planted on software disks to create mischief or havoc with a computer's operations. Viruses can infect the internal operating system of a computer and can spread to other machines by way of computer networks or on software that has been used on an infected computer.

The current case, according to experts, arose from an experiment by a graduate student who apparently had intended to infect a federal military computer system with a relatively harmless virus. The student reportedly miscalculated, resulting in the spread of a harmful virus all along a vast network of systems. At this writing, it is not known if the virus has destroyed valuable data, but it certainly has messed up numerous operations.

The potential for disaster from computer viruses is mind-boggling. The nation's military defenses and economy could be dealt crippling blows by such computer contamination. Computers now keep our modern society humming along; business and government are ever more reliant on these increasingly sophisticated machines. Obviously, serious glitches can have serious consequences.

The Arpanet virus, as this current case is known, dramatizes the need for the federal government to redouble intensive research into preventive and curative measures that will safeguard the nation's millions of computers. Stricter and sterner laws against the creation of viruses should also be adopted.

Computer viruses are more than mere pranks and more than mere vandalism. They are potentially deadly to the social, military and economic health of the country.

## 86 – Computer Virus

[Cartoon: Two military generals view a large screen displaying "RED ALERT! RED ALERT! INCOMING SOVIET MISSILE! TYPE: ICBM, NUCLEAR WARHEADS: 10 TARGET: BEAT EGG WHITES TO FLUFFY CONSISTENCY, ADD NUTMEG AND SIMMER." One general says, "I THINK WE'VE GOT A COMPUTER VIRUS!" Signed Miami News 1988 Wright.]

## AUGUSTA HERALD
## The Augusta Chronicle
*Augusta, GA, November 9, 1988*

Remember Mathias Rust, the West German teen who flabbergasted the world a few years ago when he flew a light plane through Soviet air defenses and landed in Moscow?

**It was considered a remarkable stunt. But according to Paul Graham, a Harvard computer science graduate, Rust's success was positively primitive compared to the electronic virus unleashed by Cornell computer doctorate student, Robert T. Morris.**

"It's as if Mathias Rust had not just flown into Red Square, but built himself a stealth bomber by hand and then flown into Red Square," Graham said.

The analogy is neither far-fetched nor inappropriate. Just as Rust's flight exposed the weaknesses in Soviet air defenses, Morris' virus exposed the vulnerabilities of the U.S. government's computer networks.

To be sure, the Pentagon denied Morris' virus got into its sensitive defense and intelligence networks. That may be true. (If it weren't, would the Pentagon admit it?) But skeptics inside and outside the government rejected the military's blanket reassurances.

As one former expert on military communications noted, methods of protecting software have not "met the test yet. If there's online communications between any two computers...then I think it's pretty difficult to stop a virus."

**If the unclassified computers, which were affected by the virus, were hooked up to a classified computer, then the classified computer would be affected, too.**

We suspect Morris' mischief-making has set off a lot of worries in the Pentagon. Hopefully, those worries will produce a secure classified network system before another computer genius — whose intent may not be benign — finds a way to emulate Morris.

## WORCESTER TELEGRAM
*Worcester, MA, November 12, 1988*

The "virus" that infected computers at U.S. military installations and major corporate and university research centers last week presented the scariest scenario yet for this bedeviling problem of the high-tech age. Still, we can be thankful that the latest tampering showed where the vulnerabilities are and where safeguards are needed.

A computer "virus" is essentially a rogue computer program that acts like a real virus. Surreptitiously introduced, it replicates itself and hops from one computer to another, doing whatever damage its inventor designed. The inventor might only want to have a little fun — or cause serious harm.

The creator of this latest virus, a 23-year-old graduate student, apparently was not motivated by any malice. Although he may not have planned for the program to go out of control, he should be held accountable. The damage the virus caused was in the millions of dollars.

People who knowingly tamper with computer software are committing a serious offense. In this day and age, when computers govern so much of everyday life, infecting a system with viruses could be disastrous, particularly if national security is involved.

The latest "bug" did not infect supersecret defense computer systems but still managed to interfere with and jam some 6,000 computers nationwide, and that's unforgivable.

In addition to calling for new electronic safeguards against future inavasions, this ill-advised prank underlines the need for a whole set of legal and punitive procedures against those who deliberately spread a computer "disease."

## TULSA WORLD
*Tulsa, OK, November 9, 1988*

A COMPUTER wizard has struck again. This time it was a "bored" young man who planted a "virus" in a Cornell University computer terminal.

It brought down the Department of Defense Arpanet computer network for a day and a half last week. The damage is still being assessed. An estimated 60,000 computers are directly or indirectly tied to the defense computer network, and 6,000 of those were thought to have been brought to a complete standstill.

Incredibly, there is a question if a crime has been committed and if it was a misdemeanor or a felony.

Destruction of computer files by a wizard 1,000 miles away is just as criminal as the actions of a burglar.

The hacker's defenders praise him for showing American ingenuity and blame the computer networks for not being more secure. That is like thanking the burglar for showing you how easy it is to get into your house and then letting him off scot-free.

It's time to recognize these criminals for what they are — thieves.

## LOS ANGELES HERALD
*Los Angeles, CA, November 8, 1988*

The young hacker who brought the nation's computers screeching to a halt last Wednesday night has taught everyone who depends on the machines — and that's all of us — an important lesson. Computers run our banking systems, store credit histories, coordinate transportation systems, record academic marks, operate hospital equipment and control nuclear weapons. Just when society thinks everything is secure and running smoothly, a 23-year-old wise-guy graduate student like Robert Morris Jr. creates a rogue program and systems nationwide go haywire.

What to do? For starters, use the incident to help prevent sequels. In the past, the more ingenious lawbreakers have often ended up consultants to the industries they plundered. Police once learned most of what they knew about safe-cracking from master thieves. Railroad companies hired robbers to advise them on secreting valuable shipments. More recently, the phone company hired "phone freaks," who were adept at defrauding the Bell network, as security advisers. Even today pickpockets and con men lecture at police academies.

When it comes to computer security, a key part of making a system safe is finding every possible way to break into it. The computer whiz who screwed up everything so thoroughly last week was toying with a "virus," a program that can be slipped into the operating instructions of a system to change how it works.

His virus, unlike others that have infected systems, did not erase memory or lock up information. But it did instruct computer networks to stop what they were doing, make copies of the virus and send it to other accessible mainframes. With the help of phone links, it spread in minutes throughout the country, halting operations in 6,000 computers at universities, government offices and laboratories.

The young perpetrator, who friends say loosed his creation by mistake, turned himself in to one of the federal government's top security experts — who just happened to be his father. The actual havoc wrought might have been accidental, but the complex series of steps needed to create the virus and get it past numerous security systems and restrictions were very purposeful indeed. Perhaps the hacker, due to his training and his father's profession, has been part of the world of hacking so long that he lost his sense of where solving a puzzle ends and committing a crime begins.

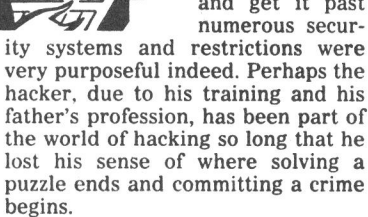

As long as mischievousness is part of the human character, there will be people trying to break into computer systems. The public has to hope that security firms can employ hackers who will stay one step ahead of expert criminals out to make money or do damage. To help keep the balance on the side of law enforcement, it's essential that the old adage, "Crime doesn't pay," be made to carry weight in regards to renegade computing, just as with more traditional crimes.

That means the young virus perpetrator shouldn't get off lightly. Brilliant as his accomplishment was, it was dangerous. While we're at it, though, let's be sure that part of his punishment includes teaching security personnel how he did what he did. Payment for his prank should include helping to prevent it from happening again.

## THE TENNESSEAN
*Nashville, TN, November 8, 1988*

LAST week computer networks across the U.S. had an unwelcome visitor, a so-called "virus" that coursed through them, constantly multiplying itself and devouring the space that computers use to store information.

A virus is a self-contained program which can attach itself to a computer, instruct the host computer to make multiple duplications and thus slow down or overload a computer. The infection spread rapidly through a low-security computer network called InterNet, which is designed to let researchers easily exchange messages.

Attention has focused on a young Cornell University graduate student who simply wanted to enter computer systems that were off-limits to him. Somehow, he found a "secret" back door to the network and gained entry. His experiment went awry in that it wasn't supposed to copy itself but once when moving to another computer. Instead it copied itself over and over.

The back door that was left open happened because of human error. The programmer who designed the network system had left himself a secret door to enter and work on the system. When he finished his work, he forgot to close it. Someone else found it.

The invading virus seems to have been benign in the sense that it didn't seek to destroy files and information. But some such infections are designed to lie dormant in a system and then do their damage later.

While no information seems to have been lost, the cost of battling the virus will be in the millions of dollars. Although computer "hackers" — those with expertise in entering systems — have been around for a while, this is the first large scale system virus.

It means that computer system managers are going to have to take new looks at access; business and research centers are going to have to do backup programming daily, not once in a while and access codes will have to be changed frequently. System vulnerability has been exposed all too dramatically. ■

# THE INDIANAPOLIS STAR

*Indianapolis, IN, November 13, 1988*

The 23-year-old hacker whose "virus" disabled thousands of computers may have done the country a favor unintentionally with his prank. But those who willfully spread such havoc deserve a penalty, not a reward.

By demonstrating how open computer networks are to mischief-making, he also showed how vulnerable they may be to military, terrorist or criminal sabotage.

How easy would it be for a deadly enemy hacker to invade computer networks that control the nation's defense systems including strategic weapons, networks that run railroads and control communications, electricity generation and transmission?

Or how easy would it be for a hacker, acting out of greed or pure malice, to destroy records of hospitals, research centers, insurance companies, banks, brokerage houses, schools, universities or other institutions relying heavily on computers?

The latest virus was not a destroyer but a nuisance, using up empty storage space. But it spread through networks used by the Defense Department and research institutions and shut down thousands of computers. It also cost hundreds of thousands of dollars in labor costs to cure.

The FBI is investigating the motives and actions of the hacker, Robert T. Morris, a first-year graduate student in computer science at Cornell University and son of a computer expert at the National Security Agency.

Computer defense systems are numerous, varied and readily available. Some experts say that if the right defenses had been operating, last week's virus attack could have been prevented. Vigilance and regular maintenance procedures, they say, can catch a virus before it can do serious harm.

The experience strongly suggests that deliberate, periodic "hacker exercises" be made to test computer security.

It also strongly suggests that special anti-hacker legislation should be considered as soon as possible by Congress and recommended penalties be well-publicized to discourage temptations to play serious computer pranks or commit computer crimes.

# The Salt Lake Tribune

*Salt Lake City, UT, November 15, 1988*

It may be that the initial alarms raised about a "virus" afflicting computer systems nationwide in the United States were overstated. But the implications in the matter can't be taken too seriously.

The reports were substantially correct: Someone managed to crack computer codes sufficiently to place interfering instructions in various systems from coast to coast. While the news accounts spoke of "havoc" done, national security data banks "broken into" and expensive "antidotes" for the virus, the damage appears mostly confined to finding and exorcising the intrusion.

According to genuinely concerned authorities, the virus creator acquired no sensitive information, nor were valuable, crucial computer programs ruined, nor did machinery sustain costly malfunctioning. Loss and inconvenience resulted from time taken to divert systems from normal functions while they were cleansed of alien instructions.

Not that the interruptions shouldn't be a matter of grave concern. They impose a price in lost work and "repair" that are both tangible and needless. More conspicuous, however, is computer vulnerability.

At this point, the chief suspect of the spectacular "infection" is said to have merely been demonstrating his knowledge, that he meant only to "send a message" to the infiltrated systems, but by mistake he included instructions which made the impact far more troublesome. In any case, he certainly demonstrated what someone might do if they fully intended a malicious or venal act.

Experts have been assuring ever since last weekend's "computer virus" story broke that this sort of "break-in" can occur only to systems linked in a network. Moreover, federal authorities insist all defense information included in established network is perfectly protected against unauthorized computer "hackers." But other equally knowledgeable people say candidly that "all the advantages are with the hackers."

One line of defense, of course, is criminal law. Right now, it is a misdemeanor to intentionally enter without permission any federal government computer and cause damage to programs or operations. It's a felony to gain unauthorized access to computers in two or more states and deliberately cause a malfunction which could cost as much as $1,000 in corrections. Of course, it's a crime to filch classified national defense information under any circumstances.

Systems are routinely designed for exclusive use by authorized personnel. The sophistication of that security is apt to increase as incidents such as the latest "virus attack" recur. Because, however, those determined and clever enough to solve the codes can, with enough ingenuity, do precisely that, the ultimate advantage, as experts claim, is with the "hackers."

Clearly, more and tougher laws will be passed on this subject, and the technicians will continually change, update and adapt their security procedures. Perhaps the value of last week's computer virus episode is its demonstration that constant attention must be paid to "inoculation" against such electronic age "illnesses," since the marvel of computerization, no less than any other advent of the modern age, is accompanied by concurrent malevolence.

## THE CHRISTIAN SCIENCE MONITOR

*Boston, MA, November 8, 1988*

ANYONE who has taught a "dumb" computer or pocket calculator to solve a complex problem knows the exhilaration of successfully meeting that challenge. It truly is fun.

The quest for complex programming challenges, however, never justifies unauthorized entry into someone else's high-tech home. That ethical lapse lies at the bottom of last week's clogging of a nationwide computer network, apparently by a Cornell University graduate student, Robert T. Morris Jr.

Some may view Mr. Morris as a folk hero. That would be inappropriate. True, he displayed technical finesse in discovering a "back door" in Internet, which links defense and university computers to speed the exchange of unclassified research information. He allegedly inserted onto the net's electronic mail service a program designed to mask its origin, to multiply and slowly spread, and then to use up vacant memory in computers tied to the network – without damaging data files. (It wound up spreading much faster than he had anticipated.) The network's designer left the door open so he could get back in to fine-tune it over time.

Technical elegance, however, does not compensate for the time computer specialists spent trying to unclog an estimated 6,000 computers affected, as well as the time lost to researchers.

More important, unauthorized entry into a computer system is no different in principle from breaking and entering a home. Society rejects the excuse that a suspected housebreaker was only trying to meet the challenge of picking a new type of lock, or that "no harm was done, I only filled the living room with confetti." Similar responses are unacceptable in the field of computers.

So is the notion that Morris might have been trying to point out the network's security weaknesses to its sponsors. The proper approach is to contact the sponsors after discovering the loophole, not exploit it.

Where gaps in federal and state computer-crime laws exist, they should be plugged and sanctions strengthened, without unduly hampering the flow of information vital to a democracy. Society needs to put itself on record as rejecting such intrusions.

Computer users have responsibilities, too: to be alert to the technology's potential for abuse and take common-sense precautions; and to accept with that new computer box or computer science class the moral obligations that accompany the key tool of the information age.

## BUFFALO EVENING NEWS
*Buffalo, NY, November 8, 1988*

LIKE A DANGEROUS new disease running through a community, the new phenomenon of computer "viruses" is striking fear throughout the far-flung communities composed of computer networks.

Computers across the country were brought to a standstill last week by the introduction of a program that automatically reproduced itself and clogged the system.

While apparently no permanent harm was done, the ability of a clever "hacker" to penetrate the system demonstrates the potential danger to all participants in such a network.

In this case, the network was a scientific and academic one, uniting thousands of computers at nearly all American universities, corporate offices, national defense laboratories and the National Aeronautics and Space Administration.

Classified national defense data, such as information controlling the nation's nuclear weapons, does not move on this network, but the ease with which the scientific network was invaded suggests that more stringent safeguards are needed to guard against hostile access to defense secrets.

The culprit in the present case reportedly was a graduate student in computer science who was merely experimenting and had no intention of creating chaos in the system he had penetrated. Apparently a small programming error caused his program to multiply itself hundreds of times and travel through the system. The virus was reported detected, not only across the United States, but in Canada, West Germany and Australia."

When such spectacular results can flow from a mere academic exercise, imagine what damage could be done if the system had been penetrated with malicious intent.

Instead of merely clogging the system, a destructive virus could systematically erase academic, scientific or corporate records. One expert said that "if it had been malicious, it would have destroyed many, many systems."

Even now, computer experts are not sure whether all traces of the virus have been eliminated. Conceivably it could be reactivated at some later point by instructions in the programming.

Computers can do wonderful things, but by their nature they can also go wonderfully awry, as was demonstrated by the rapidity with which this computer program streaked across the nation and around the world.

Aware of the danger from hackers, the federal government has a program to develop more safeguards for computers in federal agencies and in the private sector. The laxity revealed in the current spectacular episode shows that much more needs to be done.

## Birmingham Post-Herald
*Birmingham, AL, November 8, 1988*

The vulnerability of the nation's computer networks was dramatically exposed last week when a "virus" infected a maze of Department of Defense data banks.

A computer "virus" is an injurious program, or set of instructions, that can spread rapidly through a computer system. In this instance, it contaminated thousands of computers at university and defense research centers thoughout the country.

This particular one attached itself to the nation's largest unclassified military computing network. It jammed the network by causing computers to overload themselves through continuous reproduction of the virus program.

Had the virus been introduced in a network containing secret national security information, or if it had been designed to systematically destroy data rather than simply clog computers, the damage could have been infinitely worse. Even so, some officials said the cost of ridding some 6,000 infected computers of the virus could run into millions of dollars.

The New York Times reported Saturday that the rogue program was created by a computer science graduate student at Cornell University.

Someone who called the Times said the virus was intended to be harmless but went awry because of a small programming mistake. Whether done maliciously or simply as a prank, the perpetrator deserves severe punishment.

Government officials are trying to determine exactly what happened and whether the invasion of the data network violated the 1986 Computer Fraud and Abuse Act passed by Congress. Violators of that law can draw a year in jail and heavy fines for the first offense.

Legislation was introduced this year to strengthen the 1986 law. This would make it a federal crime to insert unauthorized information or commands into an interstate data system. Obviously, Congress should broaden computer abuse laws at the first opportunity.

In additon, computer scientists need to get busy devising better protection against the invasion of computer systems by saboteurs or spies.

In one sense, what happened last week may prove beneficial. Geoffrey Goodfellow, an expert on computer communications, said: "This was an accident waiting to happen ... We needed something like this to bring us to our senses. We have not been paying much attention to protecting ourselves."

## THE SACRAMENTO BEE
*Sacramento, CA, November 14, 1988*

The obvious response to the "virus" that crippled some 6,000 interlinked research computers for a couple of days last week is to increase security, either by making access to the network more difficult or by creating anti-viral programs — "vaccines" — intended to make it harder for such programs to run amok from one computer to another. But the harder it becomes for researchers to get into such a system, and the more controls there are on communication between computers, the less useful the network will be.

Thus there's always conflict, especially in a system such as Arpanet, the unclassified Defense Department network linking universities, industry and the military, in which the virus created by young Robert T. Morris Jr. went on a rampage recently. As security becomes tighter in such systems, it will inevitably represent a still greater challenge to test it. Morris, the son of one of the country's leading computer security experts, was just looking for a more or less harmless challenge — a program that would spread slowly from computer to computer in the network without crippling them — but which, because of a programming error, instantly turned malignant.

There seems to have been no serious damage done in this case, other than the loss of thousands of hours of valuable time, but still there is a warning here, particularly to managers of systems that could be highly sensitive to tampering, either by hackers like Morris or by more malicious saboteurs: bank, election, health and criminal justice data systems and any other network that requires access from many sources. Security for non-classified multiuser systems will always require compromises, which means it will never be perfect.

There is a federal statute that appears to cover the kind of computer tampering involved in the Arpanet case, but since it's not been used in this kind of situation it, too, may require some tightening. At the same time it ought to be reassuring that so far most hackers and tamperers are Americans trained in American universities, most of them interested in nothing more sinister than their own pernicious amusement.

# Part II:
# Fine Arts, Performance & Flag Burning

A war over culture in the U.S. is being waged. With the clergy, irate taxpayers and outraged parents one side and painters, gallery owners and performance artists on the other, the place of the arts in society and what role government should assume in supporting them is quickly reaching a flash point. As old-fashioned moralists and the avant-garde collide many issues and the questions that provoke them are being raised for the first time, who is to judge what art is worthy and what is not? How are conflicts between decency and free expression to be sorted out? What role should the governmment assume in supporting the arts?

Since the National Endowment for the Arts (NEA) was established in 1965 these questions were not much cause for concern. But the as furor over the NEA and its grants to a handful of controversial artists arose, disputes over morals and free expression, the First Amendment and the Ten Commandments are spilling onto a broad cultural terrain. Everything from the homoerotic works of the late photographer Robert Mapplethorpe to the onstage antics of performance artists such as Karen Finley to the burning of the American flag seems likely to bring out strong opposition.

If the concerns expressed by civil libertarians might not be unjustified or surprising, it might be because the arts have never been a full partner in America. Certainly the recent sense of purge that the artistic community is experiencing is nothing new in the U.S. During the 1930s, the House Un-American Activities Committee (HUAC) closed the Federal Theatre Project, staffed with the likes of Orson Wells and John Houseman, charging that it was filled with subversives. After World War II, HUAC focused much of its work on Hollywood, resulting in the blackballing of dozens of actors, directors and others for their alleged communist affiliations. "You've got a fight going on today that is just as emotional as the fight that took place then," said Rep. Sidney Yates (D, Ill.), a 20-term House veteran and defender of the arts. "Except communism isn't the bogeyman. This time it's pornography and obscenity."

Supporters of the arts argue that by current standards, the work of Mapplethorpe and Finley is not obscene. It does, however, disgust many ordinary Americans all the same. Detractors of these and other artists and performers charge that those who delight in shocking conventional people with their medium have no right to cry foul when these people kick back.

A Gallup poll released in July 1990 suggests that the art crowd has more public backing than their detractors might want to admit. Though the poll showed that while 71% of Americans believed obscenity has increased in the arts and that 78% think parents should do more to protect their children from it, 75% don't want anyone imposing laws on what they can see or hear. In addition, the fact that more people now go to arts events than live sports events indicates that the arts should be able to put up a good fight.

Perhaps their main opponent in this

aesthetic and ideological tussle is Sen. Jesse Helms (R, N.C.), Capitol Hill's point man against obscenity. Insisting that he is not a censor, Helms has been bent on preventing the NEA from spending tax money on art that might offend God-fearing Americans. "If America persists in the way it's going, and the lord doesn't strike us down," he says, "he ought to apologize to Sodom and Gomorrah."

The Mapplethorpe photos have been a boon for Helms's direct-mail fund-raising operation. By suggesting that "perverted art" is just a half-step away from a homosexual takeover, he raised several million dollars in mostly small donations from across the country.

But on Capitol Hill, Helms is often a strike force of one as he harrangues his colleagues and threatens to portray them as pro-obscenity. In turn, the Democrats question whether Helms can make Mapplethorpe a metaphor for discontent about cultural values. They point out that though people might be concerned about the state of American morality, it may be Hollywood rather than the NEA that is the focus of their concern.

To make matters even thornier, the NEA is caught in a cross-fire between their political opponents such as Helms and detractors from their own ranks. These detractors are members of the artistic community who, though they have no problem with the work of Mapplethorpe, Finley or their ilk, faullt the Endowment's cosziness with big museums and the power brokers of the New York/Los Angeles art establishment as well as the cronyism that periodically mars the peer-review panels authorizing grants.

NEA Chairman John E. Frohnmayer conceded that the endowment has "let its relationships with Congress and the American people go fallow." President George Bush initally supported no restrictions on the NEA. But as the heat turned up under the issue, he edged back to see what Congress had to say.

Though Congress has yet to enact any legislation regarding the nature of the grants the NEA awards or the methodology that its bureaucratic apparatus employs in making such decisions, the notion that a compromise agreement to restructure elements of the peer-review panels and restate restrictions on grants in the language of the Supreme Court seems likely. No doubt the First Amendment will bar draconian restrictions. There will, however, be pressure for tougher limits even if they invite challenges in court.

## 'Obscene' Art Ban Rejected

The Senate July 26, 1989 voted to accept the House's $45,000 cut in funding for the National Endowment for the Arts (NEA) and approved additional restrictions that would prohibit any federal funding of "obscene or indecent" art works.

The budget cut and restrictions were contained in an amendment to the Interior Department appropriation, which was passed by a voice vote. The amendment had been proposed by Sen. Jesse A. Helms (R, N.C.).

It specifically barred the NEA from using federal funds to "promote, disseminate or produce obscene or indecent materials, including but not limited to depictions of sadomasochism, homoeroticism, the exploitation of children, or individuals engaged in sex acts; or materials that denigrates the objects or beliefs of the adherents of a particular religion or nonreligion; or material which denigrate, debases, or reviles a person, group, or class of citizens on the basis of race, creed, sex, handicap, age or national origin.

The Senate also voted to cut off all federal grants for the next five years to the two institutions that had sponsored the controversial exhibits – the Institute for Contemporary Art at the University of Pennsylvania (which had sponsored a retrospective of photographs by Robert Mapplethorpe) and the Southeastern Center for Contemporary Art in Winston-Salem, N.C. (which had supported an exhibit by photographer Andres Serrano).

In addition, the Senate measure called for a cut of $400,000 in the endowment's grants to visual artists and increases of $200,000, respectively, in its budget to local projects and folk art.

A House and Senate conference committee Sept. 29 rejected the amendment.

Instead, the committee unanimously approved a series of compromise measures that had been passed earlier in the day by the Senate. The strongest of the proposals would bar the NEA from funding art work that was obscene as defined by the standards of the Supreme Court's 1973 *Miller v. California* decision. Under the *Miller* ruling, a work was judged to be obscene if it appealed to prurient interest, contained patently offensive portrayals of specific sexual conduct and lacked serious literary or artistic value. The NEA would decide for itself whether a particular work met the definition.

In addition, the compromise allocated $250,000 to establish a 12-member commission that would review the NEA's grant-making procedures and decide whether those procedures should be revised. The measure also cut the agency's total budget by $45,000 – the amount the NEA had spent to support two controversial photography exhibits by Mapplethorpe and Serrano.

The committee dropped the Senate proposal that had called for a five-year ban on federal funding for the Institute on Contemporary Art at the University of Pennsylvania and the Southeastern Center for Contemporary Art in Winston-Salem, N.C. Instead, the committee adopted a compromise that would put both organizations on probation for a year and would require the NEA to "notify" Congress if it wished to provide grant money to either group.

Lastly, the compromise reinstated $400,000 that the Senate had shifted from the NEA's visual arts program to other projects.

The adoption of the compromise followed a Sept. 28 vote in which the Senate had reversed its previous position and voted down the original Helms amendment, 62-35. The Senate then voted Sept. 29 to adopt a revised version of the amendment, by a vote of 65-31, and the revision was sent to the conference committee.

## The Washington Post

*Washington, DC, July 30, 1989*

THE SENATE, like the House, has been struggling to decide whether to restrict the sort of art the federal government should be allowed to fund and, if so, how. Now comes Sen. Jesse Helms (R-N.C.) to provide guidance. No federal money, the senator proposed, should be used to "promote or disseminate: 1) obscene or indecent materials, including but not limited to depictions of sadomasochism, homoeroticism, the exploitation of children, or individuals engaged in sex acts; or 2) any "material which denigrates the objects or beliefs of the adherents of a particular religion or non-religion; or 3) material which denigrates, debases, or reviles a person, group, or class of citizens on the basis of race, creed, sex, handicap, age, or national origin."

To this array of injunctions upon the content of future artwork the government might fund—not only in the visual arts, where recent controversy has arisen but also in publicly supported plays, poetry readings, films and TV documentaries—the Senate responded unequivocally. It passed the Helms amendment by voice vote.

The two barely cloaked assumptions underlying the vote are that the amendment is unlikely to survive to the final bill and that nobody could be expected actually to *oppose* a measure that proclaims such high sentiments. A bare handful of lawmakers—among them Sens. Howard Metzenbaum (D-Ohio) and John Chafee (R-R.I.)—did express misgivings over whether this kind of proscription would really advance the National Arts Endowment's stated mission of fostering the arts, let alone, as the authorizing legislation puts it, the "encouragement of free inquiry and expression."

Freedom of expression, artistic or otherwise, is not, we stress, censored or suppressed by this sort of legislation. The government as arts patron is within its rights to fund or refuse to fund anything it chooses. But whether it is exercising this right in a way that makes any sense is a different question, and in this case it is not.

The Helms amendment was proposed to a near-empty chamber with little or no advance warning, and with no examination of its implications for the existing peer review system of awarding grants. There was no scrutiny of what previously funded artworks the newly expansive language would cover. Would it have ruled out support for the National Gallery's Gauguin show? For Rodin's sculpture "The Kiss"? For a community Shakespeare series that included "The Merchant of Venice"? On such a matter the senators' hasty, cross-your-fingers-and-look-the-other-way acquiescence to the Helms amendment does not make sense except as a flight from responsibility. The way to debate issues of congressional arts funding is to debate them. The conference committee should delete the Helms amendment, not just for the arts' sake but for the sake of its own dignity.

## THE ARIZONA REPUBLIC
*Phoenix, AZ, July 14, 1989*

IN a mild rebuke of public subsidies for questionable "art," the House of Representatives this week trimmed $45,000 from its appropriation for the National Endowment for the Arts. This was out of a total budget of $171 million. And though some were heard to gasp "censorship," such modest pruning seems unlikely to touch off the Dark Ages.

What it does do — or so we may hope — is send a warning to those who suppose that the taxpayers are required by the Constitution to dig into their pockets so that kinky "artists" may flaunt their indecencies.

With few exceptions, House members were offended by two government grants in particular. One went to the Southeastern Center for Contemporary Art in North Carolina, which paid Andres Serrano $15,000 to submerge a crucifix in a jar of urine. The other provided $30,000 to the Philadelphia Institute of Contemporary Art, which used the money to exhibit the "homoerotic" photographs of the late Robert Mapplethorpe, who died of AIDS last March.

"The Mapplethorpe show," *The New York Times* reported delicately, "was criticized by many for its sexual content." In fact, the photographs were grossly pornographic. *Washington Post* ombudsman Richard Harwood revealed their character in response to a reader's facetious suggestion that the photographs be published.

"There is not the slightest possibility that this newspaper today or on any other day in the 20th century would publish any of the photographs in question," he wrote. "The storm created would make life in the newsroom difficult and likely would cause certain vacancies in the executive ranks."

If private organizations wish to patronize such "artists" at their own expense, that is their business. But it is indefensible for the government to use its coercive authority to extract money from the public for such purposes.

The law has to be considered as well. Under a 1985 statute, the National Endowment for the Arts is specifically prohibited from funding grossly offensive projects — a category that, by even the most permissive standards, would include the works of Messrs. Mapplethorpe and Serrano. The National Endowment, which nevertheless authorized the funding of these projects, ought to have been flogged much more severely than the House could bring itself to authorize.

Even so, the message may have gotten through. Though it may howl about censorship, what really concerns the art establishment is money. The chances are reasonably good that when the next starving "artist" turns up with a crucifix to dunk, he will be advised to go soak his head.

## THE COMMERCIAL APPEAL
*Memphis, TN, July 18, 1989*

ART may be in the eye of the beholder, but most citizens can recognize trash when they see it. And it's a sure thing they don't want their tax dollars used to subsidize it.

The U.S. House of Representatives acted appropriately the other day when it rebuked the National Endowment for the Arts for contributing $45,000 to help finance two exceedingly distasteful photographic productions palmed off as art.

One is a photograph by Andres Serrano of a crucifix submerged in a container of the photographer's urine. This piece of filth was subsidized to the tune of $15,000 by the Southeastern Center for Contemporary Art in Winston-Salem, N.C., which gets federal money from the NEA.

The other is a collection of photographs by Robert Mapplethorpe that have a homosexual and sadomasochistic orientation. Mapplethorpe, an acknowledged homosexual, died recently of complications from AIDS. The NEA provided $30,000 to the Philadelphia Institute of Contemporary Art for a traveling exhibit of his work.

There was some sentiment in the House to give the NEA a very heavy whack. Rep. Dick Armey (R-Texas) wanted to cut the agency's $171 million by 10 percent. A few who don't believe in government subsidization of the arts would like to wipe out the entire budget.

In the end, the House voted 361 to 65 to cut NEA funding by $45,000, the amount the agency gave to the two controversial exhibits.

Rep. Charles Stenholm (D-Texas), who introduced the compromise measure, called it a "shot across the bow" that sends an "appropriate message without shooting everything in sight."

Some arts supporters complained of censorship and said the action sets a disturbing precedent for congressional interference in the NEA's grant procedure. That's hogwash.

Members of Congress are sent to Washington to represent the people, and in this instance the House undoubtedly did. This wasn't censorship of art. The Serranos and Mapplethorpes of the world can photograph whatever they want.

The House simply passed notice, as Armey said, that the taxpayers shouldn't be called on "to fund whatever outrage or trash some artists dream up."

## THE PLAIN DEALER
*Cleveland, OH, July 30, 1989*

Politicians make lousy art critics, but that hasn't stopped meddlesome moralists in Congress from injecting politics into the process of aiding America's cultural institutions. With a series of mean-spirited swipes at the National Endowment for the Arts, Congress has overstepped its oversight role and endangered the NEA's rightful independence in making artistic judgments. By trying to condemn points of view it finds offensive, Congress intrudes intolerably in the freedom of expression.

It was bad enough when the House last week slapped the NEA on the wrist, cutting $45,000 from its budget as punishment for granting money to two controversial recent exhibitions. That cut would offset $45,000 in grants to two groups—the Southeastern Center for Contemporary Art in Winston-Salem, N.C., and the Institute of Contemporary Art at the University of Pennsylvania—that mounted artworks by Robert Mapplethorpe and Andres Serrano.

Those artists' works may indeed be shocking, manipulative and outrageous. We don't presume to pre-empt each viewer's right to judge their artistic merit; neither should Congress. Those works were chosen through the long-standing NEA grantmaking policy of "peer review," designed to insulate artists from the very type of pressure Congress now exerts.

The Senate this week compounded the error, cutting the NEA budget and imposing a punitive, five-year ban on all NEA grants to the Winston-Salem and Philadelphia institutes. But that didn't appease the Senate's self-appointed scourge, Jesse Helms of North Carolina. The Senate approved his amendment to ban all grants for "obscene or indecent materials"—offering a broad-brush denunciation of many topics that are central to great art.

If the Bible Belt bluenose would ban any denigration of religion, presumably the NEA would bar any aid for groups that include Shylock in Shakespeare's "Merchant of Venice." Forbidding any offense to the handicapped, congressional censors would demand that the hunchbacked king in "Richard III" be bowdlerized; if ageism is taboo, there'll be no more grants to depict the addled "King Lear." To avoid any explicit depiction of sex, perhaps the NEA would deny aid to colleges that study classic paintings like "The Rape of the Sabine Women," the erotic poetry of Sappho or bawdy novels like Vladimir Nabokov's "Lolita."

Congress should remove its appalling gag order on art, which reflects a narrow-minded attack on free inquiry and "highbrow" culture. America's commitment to supporting the arts requires sensitivity to the creative process and imaginative viewpoints—a standard that this Congress apparently holds in contempt.

CREATION OF ADAM
By Jesse 'Michelangelo' Helms

Bill Day, Detroit Free Press, Tribune Media Services

## The Register-Guard
*Eugene, OR, July 31, 1989*

We don't expect Sen. Jesse Helms to know any better, but other members of Congress should. Lawmakers have no business deciding what is or isn't art, or who is or isn't an artist.

But that's just what the Senate and House are trying to do in the legislative backlash to a couple of artistic exhibitions that some senators and representatives found objectionable.

At the center of the hubbub were photographic exhibitions by Andres Serrano and the late Robert Mapplethorpe. Both exhibits were supported by arts groups that received funds from the National Endowment for the Arts. The works of both artists are highly controversial, being variously described in terms ranging from "bold" to "disgustingly obscene." The politicians responded because some $45,000 of the NEA's annual $171 million (congressionally approved) budget found its way to the Serrano and Mapplethorpe exhibitions.

While the endowment can be second-guessed for its financial decision, its artistic judgment is specifically designed to be screened from political interference. Congress itself approved a peer-review process by which members of the arts community pass on grant applications in their respective fields. The process is designed to prevent precisely the kind of meddling now going on in the Senate and House.

The two chambers expressed their unhappiness with the NEA in different ways. Neither is acceptable, but the House's approach is far preferable to the Senate's. The House opted for a slap on the wrist; the Senate — led by Helms' righteously indignant harrumphs — chose a firing squad. The House simply cut the NEA's budget by $45,000 — the amount of endowment money that went to the Serrano and Mapplethorpe exhibitions — but the chamber placed no restrictions on the rest of the NEA budget.

In the Senate, Helms obtained voice-vote approval of an amendment to 1) prohibit for five years any NEA grants to the two regional arts groups — one in Pennsylvania, the other in North Carolina — that helped fund the Serrano/Mapplethorpe exhibits; 2) prohibit the use of federal funds to promote, produce or dissiminate "obscene or indecent" art works, and 3) prohibit federal funds for works that denigrate "the objects or beliefs of the adherents of a particular religion or non-religion."

Helms' definitions would cast a wide net — wider even than the South Carolina senator might prefer. But as columnist Tom Wicker points out on the opposite page, Helms' main intent probably was less to pass restrictive legislation than to send a message to the arts world that Congress has become the country's arts arbiter and will quickly jerk the NEA's tether if the agency's grants offend congressional sensitivities.

We suspect that Wicker is right about Helms' intent. If so, the message is chilling indeed, for it could lead the NEA to turn down grant applications for art works that some politician might consider controversial. That in turn could have a stifling effect on artists dependent upon NEA largess. That mustn't be allowed to happen, for as The New York Times says, it would drain art of creativity, controversy — and life.

Art, by definition, involves the artist's imagination and perception, and is inherently a *personal* statement. The NEA's mission, through the peer-review process, is to help visual and performing artists reach the full extent of their potential and, in the process, to help elevate not only the beauty but the spirit of the nation. The peer-review process works in the pursuit of that mission. Congressional interference won't.

## The News and Observer
*Raleigh, NC, July 28, 1989*

The old adage that "one man's meat is another man's poison" applies to food, clothes, houses, cars and jobs. It speaks to the individual's freedom to make a choice, even though the next-door neighbor and everyone else on the street may think that choice is bad, even horrible. It speaks to all matters of taste, especially art and music, where the spectrum is broad.

But North Carolina's Senator Helms doesn't respect that freedom. He wants to narrow people's choices when it comes to works of art. And he wants to do it by writing his own tastes into law.

A Helms-sponsored move by the Senate to censor projects supported by the National Endowment for the Arts would do just that. Mr. Helms proposes to bar the arts agency from supporting work that is deemed "obscene or indecent," as well as "material which denigrates the objects or beliefs of the adherents of a particular religion or nonreligion." And what sort of ayatollah would make those kinds of judgments for Americans?

There's no question that freedom in art sometimes offends. But art that repulses one person may strike another as innocuous, or even beautiful. So long as the government is committed to subsidizing art, it ought not try to limit what artists can create. The public would be shortchanged.

Mr. Helms, always quick to tell other people what's good for them, leaps to hamstring the arts endowment after it provided financial help to two exhibits that included deliberately shocking works. Most people would agree that a photograph of a crucifix submerged in urine, for example, is in abominably poor taste. But who is Mr. Helms, or the Senate, or any federal bureaucrat to say whether that photo has artistic merit? That decision varies from viewer to viewer, depending on their own values and experiences.

Practically speaking, the Senate ventures on treacherous ground in voting to bar the endowment's support for material that might be offensive to a "religion or nonreligion." What about separation of church and state? And "obscene or indecent" has many interpretations. Michelangelo's nude "David" might be indecent to some. Others might find the violence in "Rambo" obscene.

The endowment, as it disburses public funds, cannot be immune from scrutiny. Artists receiving support ought to meet some level of professional standing. But they should not be chosen on the basis of taste or philosophy — just as in politics, public funds finance the Senate offices of both Jesse Helms and Ted Kennedy. There is room on the political spectrum, and there must be room on the spectrum of the arts.

The Senate's action, although it speaks to a single public agency, amounts to putting a heavy hand across the right of free speech and expression. Authors, who also are artists, might understandably be shaken by the fear that books would follow paintings and sculpture and photographs onto Mr. Helms' personal blacklist. The Senate has tolerated Mr. Helms' vendettas before — but it should not have voted to write this one into the law.

## Minneapolis Star and Tribune
*Minneapolis, MN, July 31, 1989*

When Truman Capote read Jack Kerouac's renegade novel "On the Road," he remarked: "That's not writing — it's typing." Now the U.S. Senate has offered a similar assessment of the iconoclastic photography of the late Robert Mapplethorpe: The stuff isn't art, say the lawmakers — it's trash. Senators are as entitled as ordinary folk to spout off about such matters. But in voting last week to ban federal support of "obscene or indecent" artwork, they have done more than blow off steam. They have clipped the wings and narrowed the horizons of both artists and audiences.

The immediate objects of senatorial ire are two exhibitions funded by the National Endowment for the Arts (NEA). The first is a traveling retrospective of Mapplethorpe's homoerotic photos; the second a show featuring an Andres Serrano photo of a crucifix submerged in the artist's urine. Both have sparked debate about the propriety of spending tax money to support projects that many people consider malignant. Last week, the House expressed its view on the matter by cutting the NEA's annual $171 million budget by $45,000 — the amount spent on the two projects.

In making the cut, the House took a small but perilous step toward shackling the NEA. Now the Senate has finished the job: Urged on by North Carolina Sen. Jesse Helms, it barred NEA grants to the sponsors of the offending exhibits for five years and sharply limited the kinds of grants the endowment can make. The measure would bar the use of NEA funds to "promote, disseminate or produce obscene or indecent materials, including but not limited to depictions of sadomasochism, homoeroticism, the exploitation of children or individuals engaged in sex acts; or material which denigrates the objects or beliefs of the adherents of a particular religion or nonreligion." Also forbidden would be grants to artwork that "denigrates, debases or reviles a person, group or class of citizens on the basis of race, creed, sex, handicap, age or national origin."

That spacious definition might very well prevent federally subsidized display of centuries of honored art — from Michelangelo's "Leda and the Swan" (which portrays a coupling between a woman and bird) and Rubens' "Rape of the Daughters of Leucippus" (which depicts exploitation) to Bronzino's "Venus, Cupid, Folly and Time" (which shows a nude Venus being fondled by a prepubescent Cupid) and Goya's "Witches' Sabbath" (which ridicules a religion). The definition might encompass all art that explores the territory of eroticism, belief, violence and depravity.

Proponents of the Helms measure insist that barring federal support of the "indecent" really isn't censorship, since people who want to show such stuff remain free to do so. But by whatever name, the Senate's action is a grave mistake. It sabotages the system Congress set up nearly 25 years ago to nurture artistic creativity in all its forms. Relying on panels of artists to award grants, the NEA has populated galleries across America with the elegant and folksy, the abstract and the outrageous. And since art often provokes as well as inspires, the process has always been insulated from congressional second-guessing.

No longer. The Senate measure would hogtie the endowment. It could not give away a single dollar without scrutinizing a project for traces of "indecency." It would be obliged to perform that task without any clear notion of what is permissible. Its panels would be haunted by the thought that art that seems splendid to some might strike others as merely salacious. The NEA thus might steer clear of anything remotely spicy and settle for pablum. Such timidity ultimately might dampen the development of a future O'Keeffe or Wyeth or Stieglitz; it might just deprive arts-starved communities of lively and exotic exhibits.

There are risks in cultivating a wide range of aesthetic expression, just as there are risks in tolerating free speech. But the alternative is conformity and small-mindedness. In forcing art into the vise of politics, the Senate has sadly scorned originality in favor of orthodoxy.

## The Kansas City Times

*Kansas City, MO, July 29, 1989*

The Senate was wrong in trying to combat obscenity by cutting off funds through the National Endowment for the Arts. It's a little like the flag furor. To strike at a couple of silly, horrible examples, frightened politicians want to do away with the Bill of Rights and impose prior censorship.

The Senate hardly is qualified to leap into the business of defining art. The politicians are simply out of their field. Moreover, the ragtail amendment to a multibillion-dollar Interior Department bill goes far beyond even the complicated matter of obscenity, though that would be enough to cross the line of censorship.

The restriction proposed by Sen. Jesse Helms not only would cut off funds but would set new standards for federal support of arts projects through the National Endowment. Prohibited, in addition to "obscene or indecent" works, would be those which "denigrate the objects or beliefs of the adherents of a particular religion or non-religion" (religion or non-religion?) and material that "denigrates, debases or reviles a person, group or class of citizens on the basis of race, creed, sex, handicap, age or national origin." It is difficult to imagine criteria that might be more inclusive or subjective.

As a representative of the American Arts Alliance observed, many of Shakespeare's plays would be outlawed under such rules. Art galleries that receive federal funding might have to dispose of their religious art. Aren't those old martyr paintings awfully violent? Some of them depict kinky abuse to women. What about those lascivious nudes? Nymph, indeed!

Frankly, the particular productions that triggered the fuss are not what advocates of constitutional freedom of expression would like to take a stand about. They're pathethic. But just as traditional peer and professional review winnow out most junk from competition for federal and state subsidies, the good-sense judgment of the public usually shortens the lives of such materials. That's where censorship questions should be settled.

Shallow material would have less of a lifespan if the objectors and resulting media attention didn't inflate its worth.

Nontheless, the principle is wrong. Cooler heads expect the Senate's rashness to be corrected in an upcoming Senate-House conference. Far too much is threatened beyond Helms' red herrings.

## Wisconsin State Journal

*Madison, WI, July 28, 1989*

A good example of why government should be wary of involvement with the arts is the current Congressional flap over the National Endowment for the Arts.

At the center of the controversy are works by two photographers: Robert Mapplethorpe, who photographed, among other things, gay men engaging in erotic and sado-masochistic behavior, and Andres Serrano, who photographed, among other things, a crucifix submerged in a jar of urine. The Philadelphia Institute of Contemporary Art spent $30,000 of NEA money to organize an exhibit of Mapplethorpe's work, while the Southeastern Center for Contemporary Art in Winston-Salem, N.C. awarded $15,000 in NEA money to Serrano as a fellowship.

Enter, stage left, a passel of art critics masquerading as congressmen. The House of Representatives voted a punitive cut of $45,000 from the NEA's $171-million budget. The Senate added insult to injury by including a five-year ban on NEA funds to the two museums.

That's changing the rules in the middle of the game. Certainly the subject matter of the Mapplethorpe and Serrano photographs is in questionable, if not execrable, taste. Certainly the museums showed questionable, if not execrable, judgment in requesting public money to pay for art that could reasonably be expected to offend public sensibilities. Certainly the NEA showed equally bad judgment in approving the requests.

But it is patently unfair for Congress to levy after-the-fact penalties on the two museums, which jumped through all the proper NEA hoops en route to receiving the money. The Honorables are within their purview when they order an outside review of NEA grant-making procedures, but when they enact punitive budget cuts, they stray dangerously close to the line separating artistic freedom and government censorship.

What's next? Individual congressmen reading into the Congressional Record lists of banned body parts? Sen. Jesse Helms, R-N.C., persuaded his Senate colleagues to include an amendment prohibiting the NEA from granting money for any project considered obscene or offensive to any particular religion, race, sex or nationality. That raises the Big Question: by whose standards? It's not a great leap of the imagination to envision the day when government support for the arts is limited to velvet paintings of big-eyed waifs and statues of dead war heroes.

If a little good sense had been shown at the beginning, this sorry episode would never have come to pass. But the horse is already out, and if Congress tries to shut the barn door now, the Honorables risk slamming it on their own feet.

## Tulsa World

*Tulsa, OK, July 29, 1989*

THE Senate has overwhelmingly approved Sen. Jesse Helms' amendment that orders the National Endowment for the Arts not to use tax money to "promote, disseminate or produce obscene or indecent materials."

The vote was prompted by understandable outrage over NEA subsidies to an exhibition of homoerotic photographs and a photograph that pictures a plastic crucifix submersed in urine.

Helms' amendment may or may not be the answer to the problem. Perhaps all that's needed is somebody in charge at NEA who has a sense of responsibility and taste.

One thing is certain: It is not censorship when the government fails to subsidize any artist's work or exhibitions of it.

If Congress, which represents the people, is going to spend public tax dollars on art and art exhibits, there is no reason why that art shouldn't reflect accepted standards of public decency.

Withholding a tax subsidy is not the same as the government telling an artist he can't produce whatever he wants. If he wishes to paint, photograph or construct something that deliberately provokes by offending public decency, he may do so. He also may exhibit it and attempt to sell it without benefit of public tax dollars.

Government may not restrain artists. It may legitimately restrain the public officials who pass out publicly funded art subsidies, if they don't show some restraint themselves.

## The Atlanta Journal AND THE ATLANTA CONSTITUTION
*Atlanta, GA, September 15, 1989*

Push is coming to shove in Congress over federal arts funding as House and Senate conference-committee representatives prepare to work out milewide differences in the bills passed by the two chambers. Actually, no legislation at all is called for, but Congress has let itself become embroiled in the flap over a handful of controversial photographs.

The result in the House was legislation giving a slight financial rap to the National Endowment for the Arts, certainly the most that can be justified by the incidents. The Senate, however, suckered for a Jesse Helms bill that would rip major funding away from the two respected art institutions that exhibited the work and would bar federal aid for work that is obscene or indecent, or, for that matter, simply cheeky.

Note the two words. "Obscene" has specific legal standing. Works falling within the definition are illegal, and any congressional prohibition against their funding is thus unnecessary.

"Indecent," however, has no legal meaning. Its adoption in law would allow every on-the-make politician, crusading bluenose or free-form demagogue in the country to raise the charge against even garden-variety nude paintings or plays with salty language. Enactment of the legislation would set legitimate art up for harassment and would have a deeply chilling effect on artists.

Nor is that the end of it. The Helms law also bans funding for art that "denigrates the objects or beliefs of ... a particular religion or non-religion or denigrates, debases or reviles a person, group or class of citizens on the basis of race, creed, sex, handicap or national origin." That would effectively bar aided art from any social controversy, even from unpleasant if apt commentary.

The South in particular has an interest in keeping the prudish Helms cloak from being dropped over arts support.

Traditionally starved for major private funding for the arts, the region has seen a remarkable burst of creativity, especially in drama but in the visual arts as well, as a result of even the relatively modest amount of federal support that has become available. Even small grants have gone a long way n this region. The South's landscape artists and the playwrights of historical givens would have no trouble with the Senate's legislation, but then, such work never wants. The artistic yeastiness of recent years would be flattened.

Presumably the conference committee will have a difficult time rejecting the Helms law. Members fear that a vote against it will set them up for re-election challenges claiming they are thus in favor of obscenity. Already, cynically, Republican candidates have used that charge in some special elections.

Is it too much to ask, however, that for once the members simply do what is right? Or has Congress lost the knack altogether?

## The Washington Post
*Washington, DC, September 16, 1989*

OPPONENTS OF Sen. Jesse Helms's amendment to restrict federal arts funding had feared that a recorded vote in Congress would be hard to win. The senator's allies, they believed, would depict any vote against the measure as a declaration in favor of pornography, and that would be hard to explain at home. This is exactly the tactic used when the question came up on the House floor Wednesday, but members of Congress refused to be intimidated and said no to the Helms amendment by a recorded vote of 264-153.

The amendment rose on the wave of controversy generated by two photography exhibits—including the work of Andres Serrano and Robert Mapplethorpe—funded by the National Endowment for the Arts. As passed by the Senate on voice (unrecorded) vote in July, it would prohibit spending to produce or disseminate material that is "obscene" or "denigrates" any religion "or nonreligion," or "reviles" anyone on the basis of race, creed, sex, handicap, age or national origin. The difficulty of defining such suggestive terms as "obscene" and "nonreligion" in a way that would leave the First Amendment intact is apparent at a glance. The sweep of the proposal, which applies, for example, to all museums that receive federal funds, is enormous. It would radically rewrite the necessarily uncertain and wary relationship between government and the arts.

In the House last Wednesday, Rep. Dana Rohrabacher (R-Calif.) asked that House conferees on the Interior appropriations bill, which includes the NEA, be directed to accept the Helms provision. He and his supporters repeated his earlier threat to characterize a vote on the procedural question of whether to take up his motion as a vote on pornography. Such an assertion is, of course, absurd. The issue was not whether to embrace pornography but whether to alter a procedure for subsidizing the arts that seems reasonable to most people and that has served both the government's interest in deciding what it should pay for and the arts' interest in maintaining a seemly independence.

The House, in turning down the Helms amendment, directed its conferees to address the issue of NEA grant-making. But House members, who over the summer had heard not only from Helms partisans but from home-town supporters of the current NEA system, did not see reason to order the peremptory replacement of peer review with a set of congressionally mandated standards—a dubious set at that. It's well that the Senate will have a chance in the currently calmer atmosphere to review its cave-in to intimidation and extremism of last July.

## The Philadelphia Inquirer
*Philadelphia, PA, September 15, 1989*

By a wide margin, House members have torn up Sen. Jesse Helms' invitation to attend the gala opening of his punitive campaign against public funding for nasty artwork. The preliminary vote this week on an appropriations bill for the National Endowment for the Arts looks like the death knell for Mr. Helms' demagogic attempt to impose a broad-based ban on federal funding for artwork judged obscene, indecent or denigrating to a religion or ethnic group. As Democratic Rep. Sidney R. Yates of Illinois said, the vote was "a resounding vote against censorship." Glad to say, most Philadelphia-area representatives joined Mr. Yates.

There's still bad news, however, in that the legislation as it now stands would ban federal funding for the University of Pennsylvania's Institute of Contemporary Art for five years. It was the ICA that organized one of the two exhibits that started the ruckus — a showing of photos of Robert Mapplethorpe, including the one of a man urinating into another's mouth. The other exhibit was one by artist Andres Serrano that included a photograph of a crucifix in urine.

It's also unfortunate that one other sanction seems sure to make it into law. That's the provision punishing the NEA with a $45,000 budget cut, an amount equal to the cost of the two controversial exhibits.

Both penalties are blatantly unfair. The photographs of Mapplethorpe and Serrano were cleared by the NEA's peer review process as required by law. No matter what anyone thinks of their taste in art, the institutions involved were playing by the rules. This sort of vindictive political punishment is excessive.

The Helms amendment, which was approved by the Senate in July (but now presumably will be omitted from the NEA legislation by House-Senate conferees), was as unworkable as it was unwarranted. It not would only have stifled NEA arts funding, but also more than 30 other federal agencies where public funds are doled out for artwork.

What's more, members of Congress already have transmitted their displeasure with public funding for this kind of artwork. The NEA has no doubt already gotten the message, and will be most unlikely to use tax dollars for such obviously offensive exhibitions in the future.

The admonitions to the art world are punitive enough, even if too bland for Mr. Helms' tastes.

## THE BUFFALO NEWS
*Buffalo, NY,
September 22, 1989*

IT CAME ON a parliamentary maneuver. But at least, given a chance where its members were protected from direct political exposure, the House of Representatives did decisively reject the Senate's effort to restrict federal money for art considered "obscene or indecent."

To have gone along with the Senate would have shamed the entire federal program of promoting vigorous art through the National Endowment for the Arts.

What many members of Congress worry about is being accused, however falsely, of supporting obscenity if they don't approve restrictions on the endowment aid. But the issue here is not obscenity. It is crude censorship of art by the government.

In its 264-153 vote, the House turned down a vague prohibition that would have diminished or ended federal grants for art that is deemed obscene or indecent or that "denigrates, debases or reviles a person, group or class of citizens on the basis of race, creed, sex, handicap, age or national origin."

As one House member remarked, that could be stretched to protect the Nazis from art that was a putdown of their creed.

The House vote does not end the struggle in Washington over federal aid to the arts. The question will still be asked: What is wrong, when art offends, about denying federal funds for its showing or to its creators? After all, can't the works be shown in private galleries and theaters?

There's a lot wrong.

Funds would be denied on the basis of social and political considerations. Does anyone believe that Congress is truly capable of evaluating the artistic qualities of this or that controversial art work?

Knowing controversy could kill funding would discourage artists from experimenting. The result could be only "safe" public art.

No one should want or expect art that never provokes or offends. That would convey an unreal perception of the world. If art is to mirror and comment on what is, it will sometimes show ugly truth.

Government often supplies the seed money that helps the new artist get started. It promotes individual insights and creativity, a task that should not be left only to private contributions.

Washington needs to step back from this flirtation with deciding what is naughty or nice in the art world. Decisions on what is fine art and what is indecent junk ought to remain with those who have the training and expertise to make informed judgments.

Of course there will be mistakes. But at least they won't result from some preconceived, legislative formula. Let artistic standards — not political ones — determine what projects receive those federal funds whose whole purpose is to stimulate what is creative and new.

## The Union Leader
*Manchester, NH, September 17, 1989*

Jesse Helms' attack on the National Endowment for the Arts for funding the work of Messrs. Mapplethorpe and Serrano has turned into one of the most interesting ideological battles of the summer. And once again, unapologetic conservative arguments are winning the hearts and minds of Americans, despite the sneers of academics and media commentators.

Even some politically-savvy liberals in the arts community are reported to be urging a compromise, fearing that the public's anger over federal grants to artists whose work is repellent to most taxpayers will endanger the subsidies of more "mainstream" artists across the country.

We think the left may understand the political question involved far better than do many of our allies on the right. The debate shouldn't be limited to federal funding of controversial or repellent art, but whether the government should be supporting 4,000 artists with your tax dollars. Conservatives ought to realize that Mapplethorpe and Serrano are to some degree a sideshow, an easy diversion from the real issue: Why are taxpayers funding (i.e. hiring) any artists at all?

Cutting the NEA's $171 million budget by $45,000 as punishment for its poor judgment would be a tiny step in the right direction. But we wouldn't be much happier if the dollars had gone to Andrew Wyeth or New Hampshire's Donald Hall.

We must demand results when tax dollars are spent, and there's no reason to believe that America's cultural and creative life is stronger today than it was before the artistic community was given a space at the federal feeding trough. Budget-cutters, turn off that money spigot.

## ST. LOUIS POST-DISPATCH
*St. Louis, MO, October 2, 1989*

The U.S. Senate has decided that the federal government should withhold financial support of art that offends people. This notion is philosophically and politically unsound, it may be unconstitutional, and what's more, it's unnecessary.

Two exhibitions of photographs, undoubtedly offensive to many people, prompted the Senate's action. One depicts homosexual and sadomasochistic acts, another shows a plastic crucifix submerged in urine.

Sen. Jesse Helms, R-N.C., sprang to the defense of the public's sensibilities. He offered an amendment to an appropriations bill funding the National Endowment for the Arts that would prohibit federal financing of organizations that exhibit art that is "obscene or indecent," denigrates the objects or beliefs of a particular religion or non-religion (whatever that is) or reviles people on the basis of race, creed, sex, handicap, age or national origin. Sen. Helms' measure passed the Senate last week.

The point of this legislation is to deny federal support to art that Sen. Helms deems offensive and to punish arts institutions that violate Sen. Helms' code of morals and artistic taste.

If the purpose of the legislation were to prevent obscenity in art, it would be legally superfluous. The Helms rider says that federal funding should not "promote, disseminate or produce obscene or indecent materials, including but not limited to depictions of sadomasochism, homoeroticism, the exploitation of children, or individuals engaged in sex acts . . ." Graphic depictions of this type already are illegal under local laws in most jurisdictions if they meet the legal definitions of obscenity. Recent legal history clearly shows that the best way to fight obscenity is through vigorous enforcement of local laws that pass constitutional muster, not through new federal legislation that is vague and overly broad.

On the other hand, indecency and other affronts to beliefs or ideas are matters of taste and personal conviction, and it is in this regard that the Helms law endangers constitutionally protected expression. Admittedly, the threat does not amount to direct censorship, since an institution could continue to support lawful art with or without federal funding, but galleries probably would be less likely to venture into controversial areas if to do so could jeopardize federal support.

In fact, most arts institutions already are careful not to offend large numbers of people. If they do, they threaten the private gifts and public good will that are far more important to their survival than the modest support the NEA provides. In fact, the art that has scandalized the Senate is notorious because it is an aberration.

In such a case, the artist, the exhibition curator and the sponsoring institution should take the heat of an outraged public. Museum boards aren't deaf to cries of protest, in fact, they tend to be sensitive to criticism and negative publicity.

The Helms proposal suggests the kind of government intrusion into art that occurs in totalitarian or authoritarian countries where the ruling power prohibits certain subjects or styles of expression. When the NEA was conceived some 25 years ago, a system of peer review was created to insulate the agency from such political pressures.

That was good thinking then; it remains a sound philosophical basis for federal arts policy now and into the foreseeable future.

## The Salt Lake Tribune
*Salt Lake City, UT, August 1, 1989*

House and Senate conferees have accepted a substitute for the Helms anti-arts amendment that the National Endowment for the Arts should be able to live comfortably with. Though the controversy over government-funded art is likely to erupt again down the road, for now the yahoos have been beaten back — assuming the full House and Senate accept the conferees' recommendations.

House and Senate conferees agreed to recommend that the endowment should be bound by the obscenity standard set out in 1973 by the Supreme Court, which held that a work must appeal to the prurient interest, contain patently offensive portrayals of sexual acts and lack literary, artistic, political or scientific merit. That should pose no problem for the endowment, which over the years has funded some 80,000 arts enterprises without finding itself involved in controversy — sexual or otherwise — more than a dozen or so times.

Before the conferees adopted that and other recommendations, the Senate voted 62 to 35 to kill Sen. Jesse Helms' proposal to prohibit endowment funding for "obscene or indecent" art or art that "denigrates" anyone's beliefs. Mr. Helms offered the amendment, which the Senate had adopted in July on a voice vote when few members were on the floor, in response to two controversial art exhibits that had received endowment funding.

One exhibit included photographs of men engaged in bizarre sexual acts and the other a photograph of a crucifix in urine. That the photographs were offensive and should not have been part of a taxpayer-supported art exhibit is not in dispute. What is in dispute is the sweeping, heavy-handed nature of the Helms proposal, which would have limited government-funded art to the bland. The function of art, however, is to stimulate and challenge, not to be the equivalent of elevator music.

Mr. Helms sought to portray those who differed with him as defenders of pornography. That is a cheap stunt. Pornography was not the issue, as Sen. John C. Danforth reminded his colleagues. "The issue is how good are we at defining whether something is suitable art or not suitable art, and how do we draw those definitions and should we write definitions on the floor of the Senate which cover "Godspell" and "Tom Sawyer" and "The Merchant of Venice" and "The Color Purple" and "The Godfather"? . . . . I think that the answer is no." He was right, and fortunately his view prevailed this time.

## The New York Times
*New York, NY, September 19, 1989*

Representative Sidney Yates has any number of well-chosen words — "incredible hodgepodge of administrative barriers," for instance, and "the start of George Orwell's age" — for the proposal by which Senator Jesse Helms would shackle the National Endowment for the Arts. Last week they fell on willing ears. The House rejected the punitive Helms amendment to the $10.9 billion appropriations bill. Would that the Senate had been as sensible; it passed the Helms amendment by voice vote six weeks ago.

The Senate was reacting to the Endowment's partial funding of a retrospective show of Robert Mapplethorpe's photographs, some of which depict sadomasochism, and its award of $15,000 to another photographer, Andres Serrano, whose work included an image of a crucifix submerged in urine. This is confrontational photography, and perhaps cruelly unsettling. But it's hardly a reason to destroy a process carefully legislated to insulate art from politics.

For a peer-review process that has worked very well for 24 years Mr. Helms would substitute clumsy censorship. He would bar use of Federal art funds to "promote, disseminate or produce obscene or indecent materials" and bar grants for artwork that "denigrates, debases or reviles a person, group or class of citizens on the basis of race, creed, sex, handicap, age or national origin."

Are Lautrec's depictions of prostitutes obscene? Does the way Willem de Kooning paints women denigrate, debase or revile? Should any publicly funded theater planning to produce Shakespeare first blue-pencil the play? Who's to decide what is art and what is pornography?

The only certain judge is time. In the end, the best invariably proclaims itself. In the interim the critics among us take chances and make guesses, and choices are made by peer review. But Senator Helms thinks his way is quicker, surer: Congress will dictate.

This week Senate and House conferees meet to agree on an appropriations bill. It's a chance for the senators to undo the original hotheaded response. The peer-review process has probably engendered a few mistakes. Cultural dictators make more.

copyright © The New York Times 1990

## Bush Opposes Obscene Art Censorship

President George Bush said March 23, 1990 that opposed legislation that would bar the NEA from supporting "obscene" artwork.

In 1989, at the urging of Sen. Jesse Helms, Congress had approved an annual appropriation for the NEA that prohibited the agency from funding artwork that was considered obscene as defined by a 1973 Supreme Court ruling. Subsequently, the NEA had required grant recipients to sign a statement promising that they would not use the funds to create obscene art.

The legislation had been prompted by a controversy over two exhibits sponsored in part by the NEA – a retrospective of photographs by Robert Mapplethorpe, which included scenes of homoeroticism, and a photograph by Andres Serrano that depicted a crucifix in a jar of urine.

Helms had recently introduced an amendment to the NEA's reauthorization legislation for 1990 (the NEA was reauthorized every five years) that would prohibit funding of obscene or indecent art.

Bush said that while he had been "deeply offended by some of the filth that I see into which federal money has gone," nevertheless, he remained opposed to censorship. "I will try to convince those who feel differently in terms of legislation that we will do everything in our power to stop pure blasphemy," Bush pledged.

## The Atlanta Journal AND THE ATLANTA CONSTITUTION
*Atlanta, GA, March 23, 1990*

It is a scene out of classic melodrama: Little Nell is lashed to the railroad tracks, the locomotive is bearing down and the villain stands to the side, stroking his waxed mustache and chortling at the prospect of Nellburger, when —

When President Bush, to his great credit, comes to the rescue, throws the switch that sends the train fading harmlessly down a spur and the villain, muttering "Curses!" behind his stage mustache, is revealed as Sen. Jesse Helms, the North Carolina Republican, foiled in his attempt to misuse public funding as an excuse for a national witch-hunt against the arts.

But don't applaud too soon. This play isn't over.

The president's sanity will be a huge help, particularly in bucking up the politically faint in Congress, but Mr. Helms very much intends to continue the demagogic campaign he unleashed last year against the National Endowment for the Arts after the flap over NEA funding for a couple of art shows whose sexual content and social commentary stirred controversies.

Mr. Helms tried to bar NEA funding for any art he and his friends would object to. The issue was finessed with a one-year legislative ban on obscene material "including but not limited to, depictions of sadomasochism, homoeroticism, the sexual exploitation of children or individuals engaged in sex acts; and which, taken as a whole, do not have serious literary, artistic, political or scientific value."

Despite its grandstanding language, the law in fact only bars federal aid for material that would be obscene under U.S. Supreme Court guidelines; it is little threat per se. That was the policy already.

Even so, the provision has had a chilling effect in the arts, producing hesitations that numb creativity, and it has provided an excuse for right-wing groups, particularly the religious right, to fly-speck NEA grants even for second-handed association with any project or artist the far right and fundamentalists find untoward. Suddenly, people whose only previous attention to art was the day they bought the day-glo Elvis on black velvet are now scouring art galleries, playbills and esoteric presses.

Mr. Helms has used the law to justify a formal request for the government's General Accounting Office to search for instances of wayward art, and he will be pushing Congress to make his prohibitions — or some more severe version — part of the five-year extension of NEA.

We were late among titularly civilized nations in providing public arts support. NEA was set up just 25 years ago. And we still do far less than most such nations. NEA's $170 million budget is small beer. Even this modest effort has helped to spark remarkable artistic activity, inspiring local-government support, too, and leveraging strong increases in private and corporate funding. And of the 80,000 grants NEA has given, only five have incited controversy.

Mr. Bush and his appointee as NEA chairman, John F. Frohnmayer, have drawn the right line in the sand: It is improper and self-defeating for Congress to start dictating the content of art, and nothing in NEA's responsible stewardship of public funding suggests there is any need for legislative intrusion.

Villain Helms and his black-hat gang ought to be booed off the stage.

## LEXINGTON HERALD-LEADER
*Lexington, KY, March 27, 1990*

The education president? The environmental president? It seems at least as likely that George Bush could well be remembered as the aesthetics president.

The president certainly earned some distinction for refusing to censor the content of federally supported art. That decision bucked the wishes of Sen. Jesse Helms, R-N.C., and others who would like to tell us what's art and what's nasty. The president correctly recognized that the National Endowment for the Arts and its community panels will be better judges of artistic merit than Helms and other self-appointed art cops.

Helms fueled this controversy last year when he proposed legislation to block funding for arts projects that denigrate the beliefs of religion or non-religion, or are found offensive to individuals on the basis of race, creed, sex, handicap, age or national origin. That large legislative fig leaf would have covered just about everything, which was the trouble.

Instead, Congress drew its own line, a softer one. It approved a ban on the use of federal money for one year for works that, in the judgment of the NEA and the National Endowment for the Humanities, "may be considered" obscene and that lack "serious literary, artistic, political or scientific value." That was more vague, but no more sensible.

When Congress began debating the NEA's future again last week, Bush made his stance clear. He is "deeply offended by some of the filth" that passes for art. But he is opposed to censorship and will oppose legislative restrictions on the content of federally funded art.

The president's message to the endowments is simple. Carry on. Let the process work. Let the panels that represent different regions of the country and community attitudes help award the art grants. Keep the politics out of the decisions.

And above all, leave the artists free to show us ourselves and the world around us in ways that are sometimes delightful, sometimes surprising, and sometimes shocking.

## THE ARIZONA REPUBLIC
*Phoenix, AZ, March 25, 1990*

SEEMINGLY unaware of what the National Endowment for the Arts has been doing with public money since the celebrated Robert Mapplethorpe exhibit of erotica, President Bush last week proposed giving the NEA carte blanche to fund whatever it likes.

Among the projects recently liked was porn queen Annie Sprinkle's New York stage show, which included an exhibit of autoeroticism, followed by "hands on" audience participation. It is hard to believe that Mr. Bush would have approved.

After last week's NEA proposal, the White House switchboard was "deluged" with protests, according to *The New York Times*, and NEA Director John Frohnmayer was shoved into the breach. "I will be diligent that obscenity will not be funded by the endowment," he declared in a prepared statement that did little to quiet the ruckus.

In fact, such guarantees from Mr. Frohnmayer are meaningless. He was equally reassuring last October, when Congress urged the NEA to avoid obscene and sacrilegious exhibits. Within 30 days an NEA-supported project distributed a catalog damning St. Patrick's Cathedral in New York as "that house of swastikas" (evidently because of John Cardinal O'Connor's stand on homosexuality) and fantasizing about setting Sen. Jesse Helms's "putrid a-- on fire" (deletion ours).

Mr. Frohnmayer briefly yanked the project's $10,000 grant, but a few weeks later yielded to cries of "censorship" and restored the money, on condition that the "too political" catalog be withdrawn.

The NEA and its defenders are entirely correct when they point out that the arts kitty is used for other purposes than to bankroll outrageous and salacious peep shows. But it is not enough to demonstrate that some of the public's money, or even most of it, is spent on worthwhile projects. The public is entitled to know that none of its money is being misspent. This is an assurance the NEA cannot truthfully provide.

Most Americans, to be sure, probably would look with disfavor on the appointment of Sen. Helms as keeper of the public morals. At the same time, probably an overwhelming majority also would be appalled to know how NEA funds are being squandered, and not simply on homoerotic exhibits. Here is a short list of NEA grants, as compiled by *Reader's Digest* writer Randy Fitzgerald.

- $10,000 to study thoroughbred racetracks.
- $8,000 to explore and map Newark, N.J.
- $10,000 to investigate "public uses of abandoned Atlas missile silos."
- $36,000 to examine whether the "urban baseball park" can endure past the 20th century.

The battle over NEA funding is not, as some like to pretend, a clash between the high-minded and the small-minded, freedom and censorship. The fundamental question is whether the people, acting through their elected representatives, have a right to determine how their money will be spent, or whether they are obliged, willy-nilly, to fund any project — however offensive or witless — once the NEA proclaims it "art."

## The Washington Post
*Washington, DC, March 29, 1990*

THE SENATE begins hearings today on the issue that was last summer's longest-running sensation: the matter of what restrictions, if any, should be placed on federally funded art. But the script so far has unfolded with one major difference—an explicit stance by the White House against any legislation that would impose such restrictions through Congress.

The president's budget first telegraphed this position when it offered no proposed restrictions—and a small budget increase—in its five-year reauthorization of the National Endowment for the Arts, which became the target of fierce attacks last summer for grants to artists Andres Serrano and Robert Mapplethorpe. When asked about the issue at a press conference last Friday, the president went further. He answered that he was "deeply offended by some of the filth that I see into which federal money has gone . . . but I would prefer to have this matter handled by a very sensitive, knowledgeable man of the arts, [NEA head] John Frohnmayer, than risk censorship or getting the federal government into telling every artist what he or she can paint or how she or he might express themselves."

This, together with the budget, stakes out a clear and measured position: to object to certain uses to which NEA money has gone, and to accept the government's right to make such objections, and also to believe that Congress is the wrong body and broad legislation the wrong vehicle through which to make them. There are better ways to make such distinctions, ways that do not threaten whole categories of subject area or drastically narrow artists' scope. The arts endowment's chairman, John Frohnmayer, has testified before a House subcommittee on ways in which the endowment itself can become more public and responsive in its decisions, including opening the deliberations of some selection panels to the public; several state councils do this already.

When the Senate last summer overwhelmingly supported a proposal by Sen. Jesse Helms (R-N.C.) to impose sweeping restrictions on federally funded art, passing it by voice vote without debate in a near-empty chamber, many lawmakers later said they had acted out of fear that any attempt to protect the endowment would be used to label them pro-pornography in attack ads at home. What they and their House counterparts lacked was credible political cover for voting their convictions, and that protection is what President Bush has now given them by his carefully modulated statement.

## The Hutchinson News
*Hutchinson, KS, March 25, 1990*

The Bush folks have decided to surrender to the hoity-toity "arts" crowd, after all.

The spokesman for the National Endowment for the Arts, John Frohmeyer, went before a congressional committee last week to announce that the Bush administration would oppose any restrictions placed on the taxpayers' money handed over to the arts crowd.

Federal arts subsidies were intended "to be free of political or cultural or content-based restrictions," Frohmeyer said as he suggested that restrictions against "sadomasochism, homoeroticism, or sexual exploitation of children engaged in sex acts" be removed from today's rules.

The modest restrictions were placed in the rule book last year, after two particularly obscene "arts" projects were revealed in Washington. One of the "arts" programs financed by taxpayer money was a crucifix immersed in urine and passed off as great art by the hoity-toity modern-art crowd.

The Bush folks and the NEA may try to hide behind a virtuous cloak of anti-censorship, but they shouldn't be allowed to get away with it.

Nobody is trying to censor those characters who create modern garbage and call it art. They can create as much garbage as muddle-headed buyers will finance.

What needs to be done is to force them to pay for their garbage themselves. They don't have any right to unrestricted handouts from American taxpayers, and the Bush administration is wrong to suggest they do.

Somebody better wave some broccoli at George Bush to get the adrenalin moving so that he'll be strong enough to withstand the selfish screams from the panhandling arts crowd.

## THE SACRAMENTO BEE
*Sacramento, CA,
March 31, 1990*

Both the White House and National Endowment for the Arts director John Frohnmayer are getting a lot of heat from social conservatives for failing to back restrictions on the content of federally funded art. The heat is not surprising, but the administration is right, and it should stick to its guns.

The conservative groups complain, correctly, that some federally funded works in the past have verged far enough into the obscene that they would offend the vast majority of those whose taxes helped support them. But writing formal restrictions into law, however worded, opens the door to endless disputes and uncertainty about what fits or doesn't fit the guidelines. One cannot read art like a formula in mechanics or a cookbook recipe. If the committees of artists and critics who evaluate grant requests can't make reasonable choices, they should be replaced.

What's particularly significant about this controversy now is that it marks the first time that George Bush, that most cautious of men, has departed on any significant social issue from the Republican Party's most conservative wing. Many people see that as a test of the party's flexibility and its ability to grow. But it's also a small sign that Bush may be willing to take some risks for the sake of leadership. If he's not turned to stone by the extreme right's protests about dirty pictures, maybe he'll decide he won't be turned to stone by conservative protests on other decisions. The possibilities are breathtaking to contemplate.

## THE INDIANAPOLIS NEWS
*Indianapolis, IN, March 24, 1990*

Behind the controversy over offensive art and the National Endowment for the Arts is the issue of whether the federal government ought to be in the business of subsidizing the arts.

The controversy is certainly not going to go away.

On one side, various organizations and artists seem to be itching to see how far they can go to come up with foul and obscene art that is guaranteed to prolong the controversy.

Along with them, some artists and their defenders keep whining about censorship and the First Amendment when the critics want to cut off funding to these offensive projects. Yet the First Amendment says nothing about anyone's right to get a subsidy from other taxpayers.

On the other side, Sen. Jesse Helms, R-N.C., proposed last year to cut off funding to obscene exhibits or art work. Other members of Congress, however, are horrified by his proposal on grounds that it will stifle creativity and threaten free speech.

Rep. Pat Williams, D-Mont., questioned the new NEA chairman, John Frohnmayer, demanding to know whether he thought "offensive" art ought to be funded by the government. Frohnmayer finally said yes in a recent hearing over whether the NEA ought to get a five-year renewal of federal funding.

"For a chairman to answer yes to that question in today's climate shows real determination that the NEA not be used as a censoring agency," Williams declared in triumph.

The issue, though, is not censorship. These artists can go ahead and put their crucifixes in bottles of urine or whatever else they want to call "art." Some of the junk is so bad that USA Today won't accept ads from the American Family Association citing specific art exhibits they don't like. USA Today officials say that the ads are in bad taste, which tells much about federally-funded art projects. Let the artists sell this junk on the open market, not through subsidies through the taxpayers and the federal government.

Philosophy Professor Steven Yates offers an easy way out, and it's so simple that it may not appeal to the bureaucrats in Washington D.C. He suggests just having the government stop the subsidies.

"If federal dollars support certain artists and exhibits, then these artists and exhibits will gain an advantage they would not have had in an open market, in the same way that government-subsidized automobile manufacturers will gain advantages they would not have had otherwise," he writes in The Freeman magazine. "The only satisfactory solution to the problem of censorship in the arts, therefore, is for the government to get out of the art business altogether, and allow people acting under free market conditions to support the kind of art they want."

His proposal makes sense, especially in light of a $150 billion annual federal budget deficit, which threatens the United States in an increasingly competitive world economic environment.

## FORT WORTH STAR-TELEGRAM
*Fort Worth, TX, March 24, 1990*

Conservative criticism of President Bush for not endorsing legislation to restrict federally funded arts programs is ill-founded.

Bush Wednesday supported National Endowment for the Arts chairman John Frohnmayer, who asked Congress for legislation extending the NEA's life for five years without restrictions on what it may support.

Sen. Jesse Helms and other conservative political and religious leaders have sought strict legislative controls — censorship — over what artistic projects can be supported by the NEA and its public funds.

Such legislation, however, is like using a howitzer to swat flies. NEA's defenders say that it has made more than 85,000 grants, of which fewer than 20 have caused any controversy.

The present squabble arose last year over NEA support of a museum showing of photographs by Robert Mapplethorpe and Andres Serrano. The pictures in question were definitely objectionable to most citizens and to most members of Congress.

That point was made, with soaring rhetoric.

NEA chairman Frohnmayer got the message. Frohnmayer was not appointed to administer obscenity, and he knows it. It comes down to whom you trust and whether Congress needs to be dictating specific standards of artistic merit.

Congress does not. Bush trusts Frohnmayer to keep the NEA's standards up. That should be good enough.

# THE INDIANAPOLIS STAR
*Indianapolis, IN, March 24, 1990*

The Bush administration wants nothing to do with controlling the content of art supported by federal tax dollars. In that, the administration is flat out wrong.

It should want nothing to do with using taxes to support art of any kind. But if federal money is going to be handed out in such a fashion, the people have the right not to be insulted, humiliated or outraged by recipients. Not so, says John E. Frohnmayer, chairman of the National Endowment for the Arts.

Frohnmayer told a House subcommittee this week that the administration wants the life of the endowment extended another five years and it wants no restrictions placed on the art that the endowment may support.

That was a kick in the teeth for Sen. Jesse Helms, R-N.C., and other lawmakers who have tried to ban federal support for such artistic obscenities as graphic homosexual photographs and crucifixes in urine and on-stage masturbation.

Maybe administration officials such as Frohnmayer see nothing wrong with subsidizing moral garbage. But every indication is that the average American taxpayer is offended and scandalized when his government uses his money to line the pockets of pretentious phonies and perverts parading as serious artists.

The administration has been bamboozled by a noisy clique that wants public money but no public say-so in how it is used. That is not the way the game is played. In this instance, the game should be called off.

# The Seattle Times
*Seattle, WA, March 22, 1990*

TOO much attention has been given to a few smutty pictures financed or displayed by tax dollars from the National Endowment for the Arts.

The NEA needs to clean up its act, but the issue is much more fundamental than a handful of offensive exhibits.

Would-be artists are turning out junk, and expecting Uncle Sam to be the patron of last resort. What truly frightens the arts community is exposure of this much more insidious decline.

Anguished cries against censorship are a smokescreen to distract attention from a vigorous discussion of whether the NEA has been reduced to a mediocre art enterprise.

Sadly, the debate is muddied by excesses on both sides.

Sen. Jesse Helms' legislative sensitivities were so aroused by one erotic display that the North Carolina Republican had a morality oath written into this year's NEA funding.

Legislation to renew the NEA charter for another five years is before Congress, and the Bush administration has decided not to seek extension of Helms' restrictions.

John Frohnmayer, chairman of the arts endowment, has pledged to improve the geographical and cultural representation in NEA grants, and diversify the membership of NEA selection panels.

Don't make the concept of quality a stranger to the review process, either. Why should the taxpayer finance work that would be hooted down by a private gallery or rejected by an art school's admission board? Encouraging excellence is not a totalitarian plot.

If integrity really were a central issue, there'd be a groundswell from the arts community to refuse all government funds, and simply paint, perform or write without fear of contradiction, or Big Brotherly judgment.

Oops, nevermind. This is about money, not censorship.

# The Gazette
*Cedar Rapids, IA, March 31, 1990*

DESPITE conservatives' concern over "obscene" and "indecent" art, the Bush administration has urged Congress not to define the types of projects the National Endowment for the Arts (NEA) may support. It is sound advice as far as it goes. Once you specify "no obscenity," you are forced to say which works are "obscene" and which are not. As the courts have found, the definition of "obscenity" is a will-o'-the-wisp.

But while they are mulling NEA funding reauthorization, congressmen should consider asking the arts community to do without the relatively small — $171 million a year — government support.

Initially, the proposal might seem ominous. The national endowment's relatively small role in arts funding has a ripple effect. It probably leverages far more corporate money than might otherwise go to the arts. But if patrons of the arts remain ardent toward their cause, they should have little trouble sustaining a private endowment organization. They are a resourceful, well-heeled group.

With the arts-funding umbilical finally cut, they probably would find it a relief to be free of Jesse Helms-style censorship.

We doubt the NEA will go private. Patrons of the arts are convinced that without federal funding, promising new talents will be stifled. And George Bush, working through NEA Chairman John E. Frohnmayer, does not wish to be the president who put the kibosh to cultural creativity.

A scene we would like to see, though, is that of Bush delivering a charge to the NEA: *"Freedom" and definitions aside, do not underwrite projects that are likely to offend taxpayers. In particular, do not endorse "artistic works" that are antagonistic toward Christ and other religious figures. And never support funding for live performances by porn film stars.*

We are not urging that the president imagine what projects NEA funding might support directly or indirectly. We are asking that he realize how far out NEA backing already has gone — Jesus in drag; a performance by "post-porn modernist" Annie Sprinkle, invoking the spirits of "ancient, sacred prostitutes"; a display of Sen. Helms nailed to a cross (these in addition to the publicized crucifix in artist's urine and the exhibit featuring homoerotic and sadomasochistic behavior).

There is hope. In a discussion with doubting congressmen, Frohnmayer stressed that the reality of pain in the world justifies the reflection of pain in art. "I don't think anybody wants elevator music."

But, said Rep. E. Thomas Coleman, R-Mo., "some people want to cut the elevator cords and record the screams of the people falling — as art."

Frohnmayer said he does not believe such a recording would be art. Nor (he said) would a recent proposal by an artist to show a rat being squeezed between two boards.

That discusssion, passed along by Congressional Quarterly, suggests what the taxpayers would stand for and what they wouldn't in their support of the arts:

Give the world a reflection of humankind's pain — hunger, ignorance, despair. But spare us the crushed rat.

## NEA Rejects Four Grants

The National Endownment (NEA) for the Arts June 29, 1990 rejected grant applications from four performance artists who had been recommended by one of the agency's review panels. The move came at a time when the NEA was embroiled in a controversy over funding of artwork that some critics considered to be obscene.

Performance art was a type of live performance in which the artist often addressed unusual subject matter. It often blended elements of other art forms, including theater, dance, storytelling and film.

The four performance artists whose grant requests were rejected were: Karen Finley, who used nudity in dealing with feminist issues; Holly Hughes, who addressed lesbian concerns; John Fleck, who had appeared nude and urinated on stage during his performances; and Tim Miller, whose work concerned homosexuality and AIDS. All four had previously received NEA grants.

Under NEA procedures, grant requests were first submitted to review panels made up of creative artists and arts managers from specific fields. Recommendations from the panels were then passed on to the 26-member National Council on the Arts and to the NEA chairman.

Finley, Hughes, Fleck and Miller had been among a total of 18 artists (out of 95 applicants) whose applications had been approved by the solo-performance review panel. On June 20, however, the National Council on the Arts had voted to recommend to NEA Chairman John E. Frohnmayer that only 14 of the 18 artists receive grant money. Frohnmayer acted on that recommendation June 29 in denying the grants to Finley, Hughes, Fleck and Miller.

Frohnmayer's reversal of the review panel's approval was considered unusual. In 1989, the NEA had calculated that, over the past seven years, the agency's chairman had reversed review panel approvals in only 35 cases out of a total of 33,700 grants.

### THE ARIZONA REPUBLIC
*Phoenix, AZ, July 13, 1990*

THE controversy in Washington and elsewhere over what is and is not "art" or, more pointedly, what kind of art should be tax-supported, rages on. The largely inept attempts by the chairman of the beleaguered National Endowment for the Arts to mediate the dispute have failed spectacularly.

In fact, if NEA chief John Frohnmayer had deliberately set out to inflame passions on both sides, he could not have done a better job.

It will be recalled that the endowment got itself into hot water in Congress and with the artistically unsophisticated for its funding last year of, among other things, the displays of the scatological homoerotica and kiddie-porn of the late photographer Robert Mapplethorpe and the sacrilegious works of Andres Serrano.

The latest troubles involve 18 grant proposals approved by an NEA peer-review panel. Mr. Frohnmayer's senior deputy, Alvin Felzenberg, thought it might be prudent to review the panel's recommendations, particularly the questionable works of four "performance artists."

When Mr. Felzenberg confirmed to syndicated columnists Rowland Evans and Robert Novak that one of the acts in the running for an NEA grant involved a certain Karen Finley, Mr. Frohnmayer fired him. So much for dedication to truth and freedom of expression at the NEA.

Ms. Finley, it should be noted, does rather unusual things with vegetables. It seems her performance consists of smearing chocolate laced with bean sprouts over her nude anatomy. She then proceeds to put the vegetables into, well, various and unmentionable body orifices. Some, doubtless, regard this as on par with Laurence Olivier's *Hamlet*. Others will be more skeptical.

Another of the four grants the cashiered Mr. Felzenberg flagged for attention was the "artistry" of John Fleck, whose *oeuvre* is urinating on a portrait of Christ painted on the inside of a toilet bowl.

With congressional hearings scheduled for later this month on NEA funding, Mr. Frohnmayer apparently reconsidered his fired deputy's advice, and suspended the approval of the four grants. The esteemed arts panel and the rest of the art world erupted in a predictable frenzy over "government censorship."

The issue, of course, has absolutely nothing to do with censorship. Ms. Finley is perfectly free to do anything she wants with vegetables, except demand that the taxpayers fund her act. The right of free expression, no matter what the arts community would have the rest of us believe, does not depend on public subsidy.

Not to be denied, Ms. Finley, who claims her vegetable performance represents the plight of women in America, says she is "being punished because I am a morally concerned artist." Another of the rejected *artistes*, Holly Hughes, whose act runs along the same line, said she was devastated by the decision. Without the NEA grant, she said, "I have to get a job." Pity.

## The Hutchinson News
*Hutchinson, KS, July 12, 1990*

The hoity-toity national arts establishment is simply beside itself again.

Now, the arts crowd is furious at the man who's chairman of the National Endowment for the Arts in Washington.

The poor fellow finally decided that he'd have to step forward and say what he believed was art and what he believed wasn't, before doling out tax money to four, ahem, artists.

In the four cases, John Frohmayer, the chairman, rejected the unanimous recommendation from his (hoity-toity) arts advisory board. Frohmayer decided that the four shows wouldn't meet the anti-obscenity rules for the use of taxpayer money.

One of the artists is known for her performances in covering her nude body with chocolate. Another urinates on stage as part of his, ahem, art.

The arts crowd is horrified. With it hangers-on in the press, the arts crowd is writhing in anguish at the idea that anybody dare question the great talents in these shows or allow untalented and common wretches like us to refuse to pay for the artistic virtues of stage-urinating or chocolate-covered nudes.

A news story in The Washington Post suggests that the arts crowd may be able to force Frohmayer, himself, out of his job.

Heavy drama this NEA flap isn't, no matter what Jesse Helms, John Frohmayer, the arts crowd and the chocolate-smearers may do.

It is, however, high comedy.

Watching a nude chocolate-covered dancer writhe on stage won't do much for anybody. But watching the hoity-toity arts crowd writhe in agony because the peasants don't understand that such high "art" is exhilarating.

# DAILY NEWS
*New York, NY, July 5, 1990*

WHERE'S SOLOMON when you need him? It's going to take someone with the wisdom of that king of ancient Israel to save the National Endowment for the Arts. The agency is at the center of an obscenity controversy. Some members of Congress want to gut the NEA, or at least place severe restrictions on its operations. Congress should be careful. Mortally wounding the NEA would be needlessly counterproductive.

The firestorm over the NEA started 18 months ago when attention turned to two controversial grants. One went to a Robert Mapplethorpe exhibition that contained several sexually explicit photographs. The other was given to Andres Serrano, whose work includes a photograph of a crucifix submerged in a jar of urine. Is this art offensive? Most certainly. Enough to justify hamstringing the NEA? No.

Those were two grants out of 85,000 the NEA makes every year. The controversial works total about 20 images out of millions the NEA has funded over its 28-year existence. The proposed "punishments" do not fit the "crimes."

THERE'S GENERAL AGREEMENT that the current NEA bill — a five-year, no-strings-attached re-funding — has only a slim chance of passage. President Bush, who originally backed the five-year extension, made a noble attempt at a compromise. His idea is re-funding for one year. But rather than soothe, the Bush idea only angered both sides. A compromise is needed. One that will take the NEA out of the political arena long enough for cooler heads to prevail and for outsiders to monitor the NEA's grant-making process.

A two or three-year extension would do the trick. No restrictions, but lots of observation. An already appointed presidential commission assigned to review the NEA could carry out this mission. And there is good evidence that the NEA can police itself. Agency head John Frohmayer proved that with his recent veto of grants to four performance artists. NEA opponents were impressed. But the art community unwisely bristled at the decision. If the NEA is to retain any independence, artists must get used to this kind of rejection. Government funding isn't a right. It's a privilege — with limits and responsibilities.

The federal government does have a role in supporting the arts. Without its help through the NEA, this nation's cultural life would certainly be much poorer. Oscar and Pulitzer winner "Driving Miss Daisy" might never have been written. Children's dance troupes in Queens and the South Bronx would never have been organized. Oscar Hijuelos might never have written his prize-winning novel on life and music in East Harlem. The list of artistic accomplishments funded by NEA is endless. A few missteps shouldn't put a stop to this agency's good works.

# LAS VEGAS REVIEW-JOURNAL
*Las Vegas, NV, July 3, 1990*

Last week the National Endowment for the Arts announced it would not continue to provide fellowship grants to four performance artists, among them New Yorker Karen Finley.

Finley's act includes segments in which she appears on stage naked from the waist up, smeared with chocolate syrup and covered with alfalfa sprouts, which she calls "sperm."

Upon hearing the federal arts agency would not renew her grant, Finley was outraged. "I am being punished because I am a morally concerned artist," Finley said. "We as a nation are now in an era of blacklisting as during the 1950s' McCarthyism. Today begins an era in American history not strong in its cultural diversity but weak in not allowing our cultural diversity a right to speak."

Holly Hughes, another New Yorker whose performance art takes a radical lesbian point of view and who was also denied an NEA grant this year, likened conditions in the United States today to Nazi Germany.

Hughes and Finley are dead wrong. No one would dream of denying their First Amendment right to express themselves through their "art." They have a right to perform as they wish; they do not, however, have a right to feed at the public trough. The NEA is entirely within its rights to deny funding for art of marginal value, or art it finds offensive.

# The Seattle Times
*Seattle, WA, July 13, 1990*

FEDERAL support for the National Endowment for the Arts should be extended by Congress for five more years, without malicious tampering or restrictions — or a lot of wasted time and debate.

Agitated critics with their well-thumbed examples of objectionable art have failed to make a case that America is headed straight to hell in a salaciously decorated, taxpayer-financed hand basket.

Likewise, the NEA budget ought to be reauthorized despite the self-righteous windbaggery from indignant corners of the nonprofit-arts complex.

The debate is about sponsorship, not censorship. No one has suggested that artists denied federal aid should not be able to display their works in galleries or perform in public.

Both sides use emotional appeals to rally support, and politicians wallow in the demagoguery. Brace yourself for unfettered ranting and raving on the floor of Congress.

NEA's opportunistic foes denounce sexual themes in art with a suspect, transitory relish. Something else will come along.

Meanwhile, the only thing more fun than ferreting out and condemning prurient material is cataloging and describing it over and over again.

*Benjamin Benschneider / Seattle Times*
**Outside the Seattle Opera House, protester Julie Johnson hands out leaflets to people on their way to see the Bolshoi Ballet July 2.**

Repetition is not only titillating but necessary. The political-performance artists badgering NEA cannot produce more than a handful of examples to rouse their followers.

After 25 years and 85,000 grants to famous and forgotten artists, plus major and minor chorales, troupes and ensembles around the country, NEA's opponents yammer about maybe two dozen works.

NEA is vulnerable precisely because it goes about its work in a quiet, modest fashion, handing out inconspicuous sums of money to a great number of people and communities.

Seed money and sustenance have been provided for the visual and performing arts, for novelists, poets and playwrights. Federal money has inspired an outpouring of corporate and private donations and matching grants.

The cultural life of this nation has been nurtured and enriched by the NEA through awards to artists and groups in places as diverse as the Big Apple and Yakima, where big apples come from.

Almost three decades of good work must not be destroyed by cynical zealots who will move on to another emotional target when NEA-bashing fails to bring in contributions.

Taxpayers should be proud of their patronage of the arts and NEA's stewardship of their hard-earned dollars.

106 – NEA Rejections

## THE BUFFALO NEWS
*Buffalo, NY, July 9, 1990*

NORMALLY, LEGISLATION to renew the National Endowment for the Arts doesn't stir up jumbo controversies on Capitol Hill. But because of last year's fiery dispute over federal funding of an exhibition of photographs that some members of Congress considered obscene, efforts to renew the NEA for another five years could run into obstacles this summer.

The House is expected to open debate on the NEA enabling legislation before the end of this month.

Regrettably, last year's hubbub over the photos of Robert Mapplethorpe also resulted in Congress placing the first limitations ever on grants awarded by the NEA. That was a distressing backward step that puts political and official preferences into the process of deciding artistic values.

The upcoming struggle in Congress will concern new restrictions on NEA grants rather than, primarily, how much money the NEA should get to distribute to artistic works, groups and institutions. In the last quarter-century, the NEA has supported the creative diversity represented in more than 80,000 cultural projects.

To take a local example, Buffalo's outstanding Albright-Knox Art Gallery received a $600,000 challenge grant for its 125th anniversary campaign last year and has received from the NEA other funds for 100 works of art over the last nine years.

Nationally, annual NEA budgets run about $170 million. For the next budget, President Bush recommends $173 million.

The president also wants the NEA enabling legislation renewed without any restrictions clamped over the content of projects applying for and receiving grants.

That's sound judgment. Mistakes will always be made in awarding the grants, of course. Overall, however, the present system under which panels of experts, knowledgeable in their field and independent of government, award the grants to the most promising projects from among all of those that applied offers the surest safeguard against artistic sterility and oppression.

This is a review process that guards against government censorship, or some officially approved government line in art. It's far from ideal. But if artists are to create and experiment and test the limits of human imagination, they must be free to make mistakes — which they surely will — and their peers who judge the worth of the applications must be free to use their best judgment as well.

That's certainly preferable to leaving the job up to some government bureaucrat, or to some member of Congress, who knows little or nothing about the orchestra or novel or series of paintings under review.

The House and Senate committees studying the Bush legislative proposal have not yet recommended, opposed or modified it. In the House, the administration plan is going directly to the floor for open debate.

Once there, efforts to restrict the content of works eligible for federal monies will be vigorous and sustained.

But Congress should follow Bush's lead and resist these temptations to dictate rigid rules on art.

## TULSA WORLD
*Tulsa, OK, July 9, 1990*

THE National Education Association has relented in its opposition to allowing professionals who did not follow the traditional education-school route into the classroom.

Reversing earlier opposition, the NEA at its Kansas City convention decided to allow engineers, scientists and others to teach if they are supervised by certified teachers and enroll in teacher accreditation courses.

The change in position is reasonable. One of the main obstacles to attracting prospective teachers has been the lock-step approach toward teacher training that has been formulated over the years by the teaching establishment.

Too often, that approach has put more emphasis on teaching techniques and the cant of education than on mastery of subject matter. This rigid approach is one of the reasons that most teachers today come from the bottom 25 percent of college classes.

Alternative certification of teachers isn't the whole answer for education's problems.

But it can be a part of it. Teachers are going to be in short supply in the future and it opens up a new career path for professionals who might be attracted to the classroom as a second career or as an adjunct to their chosen profession.

NEA delegates were wise in recognizing this.

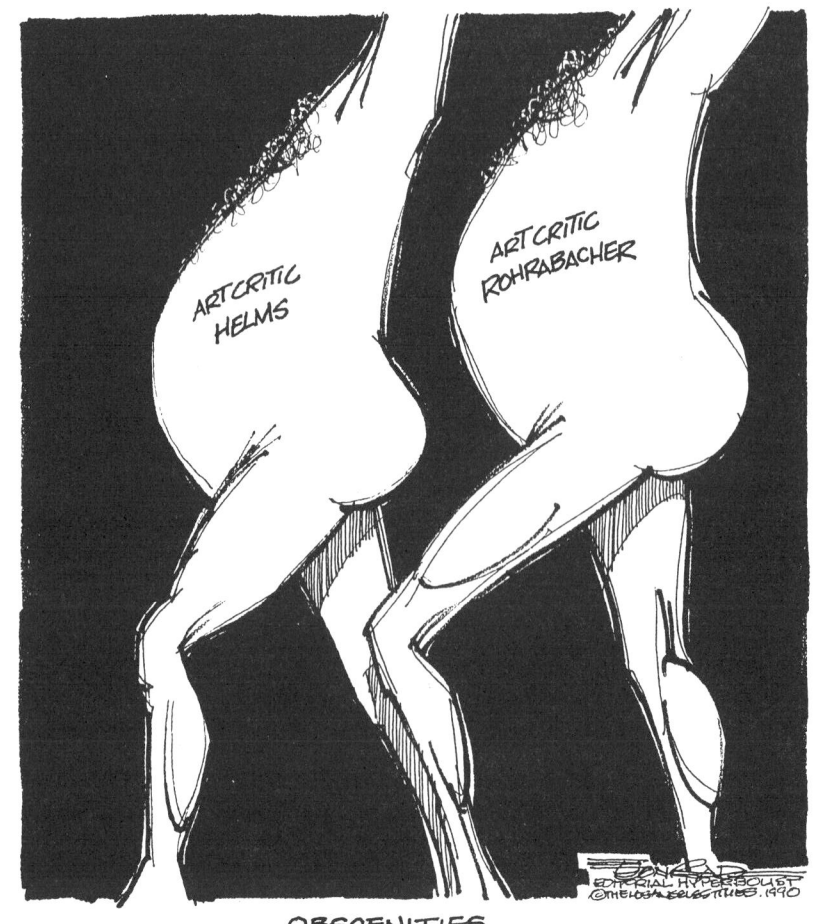

## The Philadelphia Inquirer
*Philadelphia, PA, July 5, 1990*

Consider the plight of Joe Kluger, executive director of the Philadelphia Orchestra, as he recently mulled the form he had to send back to the National Endowment for the Arts acknowledging receipt of a major grant.

The form required all grant recipients to promise to obey the NEA's "general terms and conditions," and this year one of the conditions is that none of the funds be used to "promote, disseminate, or produce" obscene materials. Mr. Kluger pondered that for a moment, before deciding to return a letter of protest.

Was the NEA fearful that Maestro Muti might add just a *soupcon* too much sensuality to a rendition of Ravel's *Bolero*? Perhaps it was terrified that the orchestra might choose some works from opera, thereby kindling impure thoughts in the audience's mind of, for example, the lovers living in sin in Puccini's *La Boheme*. It was ridiculous.

And clearly, this ridiculousness has to stop. The NEA deserves support, and the proposed restrictions put forward by Sen. Jesse Helms (R., N.C.) and others are unneeded, demeaning, and, perhaps worst of all, silly.

Even more ludicrous are the calls for abolishing federal funding for the arts. The NEA gets a tiny amount of money, about one one-hundredth of a cent out of every tax dollar. And, with it, it has probably done more good with less money than any other part of the federal government, with the possible exception of the National Park Service. More than 40 different organizations in Philadelphia received a total of more than $2.7 million from the NEA in fiscal 1989. Generally speaking, the money was well spent, greatly enriching the lives of people who attended the concerts, performances and exhibitions of the institutions that received the grants. In fact, out of the thousands of grants the NEA has made, its critics are succeeding in making an amazing amount of hay out of just a few.

We have refrained, however, from getting into too much of a lather over the controversy surrounding such matters as the NEA's support for exhibitions of Robert Mapplethorpe's photographs, some of which are homoerotic, and the work of Andres "Piss Christ" Serrano. The reason we've been holding back is that it has been hard to figure out who, if anyone, was getting unfairly hurt in this brouhaha.

After all, when you have a bunch of artists whose announced goal in life is to shock the ordinary folk, well, it becomes somewhat difficult to feel sorry for such artists when they succeed beyond their wildest imaginings. Wasn't it just a little while ago that we heard lots of whining over how contemporary American society ignores its artists? Now, suddenly, American artists and their work have become front-page news. Attendance is greater than anyone would have dared hope for the Mapplethorpe exhibition. Mr. Serrano, who only months ago seemed likely to live out his life in relative obscurity, has become (for better or worse) a Celebrated Artist.

Moreover, just because an artist is denied federal funds does not mean that his or her art is being suppressed. Consider the rap group 2 Live Crew: Its artistic expressions are even more vulgar than Mr. Serrano's or Mr. Mapplethorpe's, and yet it seems to get along quite well without a penny of federal assistance.

And we think it probably was a lapse in judgment to include, in a federally funded exhibition, pictures of such things as a man with a bullwhip handle stuck up his rear end. That, as the world now knows, is just exactly what our own Institute for Contemporary Art did when it assembled the Mapplethorpe photographs. The ICA has to expect that its subsequent grant applications are going to be greeted with something less than joy unconfined.

But this has all gone far enough now. Sometime after Congress resumes its deliberations after the July Fourth holiday, the saner, more clear-headed members of the House and Senate are going to have to sit down and have a talk with Sen. Helms, along with all the other yahoos and peckerwoods who have been calling for restrictions on, and cuts in, federal aid to the arts. What those wiser members will have to say is something like this:

OK, Jess babes, it's fine for you to be getting all this political mileage, but we're not going to let you turn the U.S. Congress into the laughingstock of the Western world.

## The Hartford Courant
*Hartford, CT, July 10, 1990*

The marriage between government and the arts is necessarily a strained one. In government, the creative impulse usually drives toward an orderly and rational end. In art, one begins with the rules but the drive is toward something chaotic, imaginative and new.

And yet art and power seem to attract one another. Artists have always sought the powerful as patrons, and the powerful have sought out the authenticity of the arts. Had the two been kept separate but equal down through the ages, J.S. Bach would have had to find a day job, and so would Michelangelo.

The rub comes when the patron begins to make demands and suggest restrictions. Here the historical record is clear. The response of the serious artist has been to resist all compromise and to tell the patron that he sponsors the artist not the art.

The patron is then entitled to withdraw support, and the artist must go find another aristocrat or members of the nouveau riche to back him. Or the patron may continue to harass the artist until the artist tells him to get lost and finds another patron. Patrons usually need artists as much as artists need patrons.

The U.S. government, through the National Endowment for the Arts, is playing picky patron these days thanks to the urgings of some members of Congress. The endowment now imposes guidelines with its grants that ask applicants to promise not to "promote, disseminate, or produce obscene or indecent materials, including but not limited to depictions of sadomasochism, homoeroticism, the exploitation of children, or individuals engaged in sex acts, or material which denigrates the objects or beliefs of the adherents of a particular religion or non-religion."

President Bush and the endowment's head dislike the restriction. They have recommended striking the clause from next year's authorizing legislation for the agency. But there has been much pious huffing on the part of both artists and moral majoritarians. The artists say that they are being censored. Sen. Jesse A. Helms, who is the patron of Comstockery, has said that at this rate God will have to apologize to Sodom and Gomorrah. Both claims are bunk.

In this tug of war, the artists must be willing to stand up for themselves, sometimes tell the patrons where to get off, and yes, go hungry. There is no serious possibility of government funding for the arts drying up any time soon. It won't hurt the most provocative artists to look for new patrons. We suspect that gifted actors, composers and painters won't go without for long.

Artists who expect never to struggle, never to make waves and never to be the victims of the controversy they create, are spoiled artists. Government officials who think they can control art — or even judge it — are naive.

Lately, art groups have been saying "no thanks" to the endowment's conditions, notably the theatrical producer Joe Papp and the editor George Plimpton. Others — like the Long Wharf Theatre in New Haven — have said they will take the money but protest the restriction. Still others have said they will do what they want with their grants and fight the government in court if it wants to enforce the tastes of the state. That sounds like the honorable artistic temperament of old.

## Cincinnati Museum Indicted Over Mapplethorpe Exhibit

Cincinnati's Contemporary Arts Center and its director, Dennis Barrie, were indicted by a grand jury April 7, 1990 on obscenity charges for displaying an exhibit of photographs by the late Robert Mapplethorpe. The exhibit, which opened at the arts center that day, contained 175 photographs, seven of which were targeted by prosecutors because they depicted naked children or homosexual acts.

The Mapplethorpe exhibit was the same one that had sparked a controversy over federal funding of the arts in 1989, when the Corcoran Gallery of Art in Washington, D.C. canceled a scheduled display, because of fear of a possible congressional backlash. (The exhibit was partially supported by funds from the National Endowment for the Arts.)

Barrie and the museum were each charged with two misdemeanor counts of pandering and illegal use of a minor. If convicted, Barrie faced a fine of up to $1,000 and six months in jail on each count, while the museum could be fined $5,000 on each count.

U.S. District Judge Carl B. Rubin April 8 barred local law enforcement officials from shutting down the exhibit. He told officials from Hamilton County that they could not "remove the photographs or close the exhibit or take action intimidating in nature to prevent the public from seeing the exhibit."

The museum reported that a record 23,000 people attended the exhibit as of April 17. In a poll conducted for the *Cincinnati Post*, 59% of respondents said they believed the museum had a right to display the photographs.

Cincinnati had had a reputation for many years as a city that did not tolerate pornography. The city was home to the National Coalition against Pornography, and local law enforcement officials, headed by Sheriff Simon Leis, had prosecuted numerous obscenity cases, including one against *Hustler* magazine publisher Larry Flynt. As a result, the city was reported to have no adult bookstores, no bars offering nude dancing and no stores in which pornographic magazines or X-rated videotapes could be obtained.

## THE BLADE
*Toledo, OH, April 10, 1990*

NOTHING should be more repugnant to citizens of a free society than the image of two dozen Cincinnati police officers storming the Contemporary Arts Center last weekend to shut down the Robert Mapplethorpe photography exhibit.

Members of a Hamilton County grand jury exhibited intolerable ignorance of First Amendment rights and arrogant abuse of the justice system by indicting the center and its director, Dennis Barrie, on obscenity charges in order to close the exhibit. Fortunately, at least one judge had the good sense to allow the show to continue while the court cases proceed.

It is no coincidence that this insult to the Constitution occurred in Cincinnati, which is home to the National Coalition against Pornography and a local group calling itself Citizens for Community Values, which earlier had tried to halt the show's opening.

Certainly these groups have the right to express their objections to the exhibit, which includes a dozen or so sexually explicit photographs, seven of which the grand jury decided to call obscene. But for them to pervert the right of free expression by denying the same rights to the gallery and to the people who paid to see the exhibit is hypocrisy, and it is contemptible.

Equally deserving of contempt are the law-enforcement and other officials who capitulated to the pressures of self-appointed censors by deciding it was a criminal matter and putting the issue before a grand jury.

Of course, we have only to thank GOP Sen. Jesse Helms of North Carolina for catapulting this issue to prominence last summer, when he tried to curtail funding to the National Endowment for the Arts for supporting the exhibition's showing at the Corcoran Gallery in Washington, D.C. The show brought no such outcry in Chicago before the Helms attack, and went on to other cities afterward to be shown with little dissent. It should be noted, too, that the Contemporary Arts Center went out of its way to consider community sensitivity by restricting the 175-photo exhibit to adults.

Toledo Museum of Art Director David Steadman likened treatment of the CAC and the Mapplethorpe showing to the repressions of Nazi Germany and the days of burning books. "Frankly, it has a horrible, chilling effect," he said. "We seem to have really forgotten what happened less than 60 years ago for all of western civilization. I think we'd all better start remembering it."

Mr. Steadman is right. How sad, when the Soviet Union and countries throughout eastern Europe are breathing fresh freedom for the first time in decades, when they restore citizenship to their exiled artists and, in the case of Czechoslovakia, call them to leadership, that some Americans whose rights so much of the world has envied would surrender them to the sheriff of Hamilton County and the Cincinnati police.

## AKRON BEACON JOURNAL
*Akron, OH, April 12, 1990*

ON SOME things about art most of us can agree:
- Not everyone likes all art.
- Not everyone can always agree on what is art and what is not.
- A painting or a photograph that seems a masterpiece to some may seem to be junk to others.

However, we each make up our own minds about art, and even whether we want to go and look at it or not.

In Cincinnati, the thought police, in the form of the local sheriff and prosecutor, have decided they should censor art based on their tastes and interfere with the free choice of people to see or not to see photographs by the late Robert Mapplethorpe.

The work is being shown in a current exhibit at Cincinnati's Contemporary Arts Center.

The exhibit contains 175 photos by the artist. There is no controversy over 168 of them. Most people who see those photos, such as Mapplethorpe's glorious photographs of flowers, will generally agree that he was a brilliant photographer.

Seven of the photos, set off in the exhibit from the others, are tough photos of tough subjects. Some call them erotic or homoerotic. The sheriff and the prosecutor contend they are obscene, have indicted the museum and its director and have sought to bar the public from seeing the show.

However, a federal judge has intervened, and it is likely the case will not come to trial until after the show closes.

Instead of criminal charges, why not let people make up their own minds if they even want to see the photos and then if they object to them? The museum is not forcing anyone to look at anything, and one person's definition of obscenity is not always another's.

Freedom is a wonderful thing, but it involves letting others see and read things some may disagree with. The thought police in Cincinnati do not understand freedom, but seek to censor art that they alone have decided others should not view. That is the way a totalitarian society operates.

## THE PLAIN DEALER
*Cleveland, OH, April 11, 1990*

The woman with the placard around her neck had it right: "Welcome to Censor-nati!"

A publicity-seeking prosecutor is taking advantage of the Supreme Court's milquetoast waffling on what obscenity is to try to shut down the Robert Mapplethorpe photography exhibit in Cincinnati. The misdemeanor indictments of the Contemporary Arts Center and its director are believed the first criminal counts against a museum merely for choosing to mount a photography display. Even when judged by the high court's ridiculously vague obscenity standards, the charges can't hold up: This is clearly an exhibit with redeeming social value and where the principal motive is not titillation, but illumination. The indictments are based on only seven out of 175 photos.

The artist, who died last year, portrayed flowers and people. Infrequently, he used his lens to capture a part of the spirit of the times — prurient and homoerotic though it was.

So, sure, this exhibit contains some rough stuff. You wouldn't want to take the kids. "Kids" aren't even allowed in. But to have nine grand jurors sneak a peak and then rush back to the grand jury room and indict the arts center and its chief for "pandering obscenity" and using minors in pornography (there are a few pictures of nude or semi-nude children) is pushing it a little far, even if the photos are vulgar or offensive to some. There's no rule that art must be lovely or soothing or socially irrelevent or blind. And where does the pandering come in? In charging admission?

The U.S. Supreme Court in 1973 came up with a three-part "test" for obscenity that included the ambiguous notion of "contemporary community standards." However one arrives at it in a diverse city, that standard appears tough in Cincinnati. The city's anti-obscenity statutes are as legendary as the councilman who paid by check for carnality across the river. Even before the Mapplethorpe exhibit opened at the arts center Saturday, that standard had made itself felt: Harassment against the museum and its principal benefactors was so intense the museum's board chairman resigned and the arts center itself pulled out of a communitywide fund-raiser.

Yet most constitutional scholars, however much they dislike the high court's shrugging off to localities a key part of its obscenity test, feel this case will be no test of that test; it's too obviously "art," not pornography.

Hamilton County Prosecutor Arthur Ney and Sheriff Simon Leis should quit while the quitting is good and leave this exhibit to stand or fall on its own merits, as photography and as a social statement that is often disquieting and, sometimes, disgusting.

But they won't. The free publicity is too great a temptation to politicians who have made careers out of pandering to public gullibility. If, as the court seems to have indicated, obscenity, like beauty, is in the eye of the beholder, then Ney and his fellow bluenoses could use a bucket of eyewash.

## The Hartford Courant
*Hartford, CT, April 10, 1990*

Hartford survived Robert Mapplethorpe's exhibition of photgraphs, which made a 10-week stop at the Wadsworth Atheneum last fall.

In fact, the show came and went with little fuss. There were no daily mass demonstrations, no publicity hounds masquerading as prosecutors, no police chiefs sniffing vice and no grand jurors sneaking a peek to determine if the pictures in the museum violated obscenity laws.

No one was forced to see the exhibition. Visitors had to pay an extra $3 and proceed to a speciallly designated, third-floor gallery. No tax money was involved to bring the exhibit to Hartford.

The people of Connecticut had an opportunity to determine for themselves whether they liked the 150 or so pictures. If they wanted to skip the few homoerotic and sadomasochistic photographs, they could do so easily. The show broke attendance records at the Atheneum.

So what's so different about Cincinnati, where a grand jury indicted the museum and its director on obscenity charges? Are there more bluenoses in the home of Procter & Gamble than in the Insurance City?

Perhaps the head of the Cincinnati Contemporary Arts Center, Dennis Barrie, is a devout student of P.T. Barnum's school of publicity. Mr. Barrie went to court even before the opening to seek a determination whether the exhibition was obscene. A judge predictably refused the request, and the show opened anyway.

Why Mr. Barrie sought to open the door to prior restraint is difficult to understand. In any case, his request further fueled the controversy, and therefore magnified national attention on Cincinnati. It also triggered huge demonstrations in support of First Amendment principles.

But zealots, who are not found only in Iran and Albania, rarely are swayed by arguments about freedom to view, read or write what one pleases. A self-appointed group called the Citizens for Community Values believes that the minds and eyes of Cincinnatians shouldn't be polluted by Mr. Mapplethorpe's pictures. The well organized Community Values brigade has been effective in intimidating public officials. Courage isn't found in abundance among officials faced with controversy.

Any prosecutor worth his law degree could find out that the Bill of Rights, as interpreted by Supreme Court decisions, protects the museum's right to exhibit the Mapplethorpe photographs. The court wisely has set tough tests of what constitutes obscenity. Something may be deemed obscene if, among other standards, "the work taken as a whole lacks serious literary, artistic, political or scientific value," according to the court's Miller vs. California decision of 1973.

Mr. Mapplethorpe's art isn't liked by everyone, or perhaps by most people. But any work that is accepted for exhibition by museums throughout the world can scarcely be regarded as lacking in serious artistic value.

It's sad to see so much energy wasted by people who want to impose their own values on others. If only the protectors of public morals were as determined to fight real crime. Cincinnati's police chief and prosecutor should rest assured that their community will "survive" Mapplethorpe.

## The Philadelphia Inquirer
*Philadelphia, PA, April 11, 1990*

When Robert Mapplethorpe's photographs — including the infamous X rated batch — were assembled and hung (without incident) at the University of Pennsylvania's Institute of Contempary Art, who'd have known that they'd soon be almost as familiar to the general public as Ansel Adams' naturescapes. That was in 1988, back before North Carolina's Sen. Jesse Helms popularized the exhibit he sought to punish, back before the late Mr. Mapplethorpe became a *cause celebre* in an art world that had sniffed — at least on occasion — at the photographer's self-promotion and ambitious commercialization.

And, now? If Cincinnati's ham-handed prosecutor gets his way, Mr. Mapplethorpe's occasionally homoerotic work will climb into yet another category — that charmed circle occupied by the repressed works of dissident playwrights, exiled composers and anti-apartheid poets.

Perhaps it doesn't merit such enshrinement — or warrant the surging curiosity that Cincinnati's censors have unwittingly unleashed. (At last count, more than 10,000 viewers had clamored to see the exhibit that Arthur Ney, the local prosecutor, had deemed obscene under local ordinances.) But it surely deserves protection against police with video cameras, gallery-emptying orders by plainclothes sheriff's deputies and all the rest of the jack-booted righteousness involved in this sorry episode.

We take note that a federal judge has already temporarily blocked Cincinnati's art police from interfering further with the exhibit, even under the guise of crowd control. So, we'll moderate the pitch of our protest. Perhaps the prosecutor will take political note of the humiliating rejection of his efforts to defend the public sensibility. Perhaps he'll re-read the Supreme Court's definition of obscenity, which would seem to favor any artwork deemed serious enough to be displayed in a local museum.

And perhaps, he'll recognize the choice available to Ohians who find Mr. Mapplethorpe's imagery offensive: They can just skip the exhibit. Unless the hysteria the prosecutor has whipped up has simply made it impossible to resist.

## St. Petersburg Times
*St. Petersburg, FL,
April 10, 1990*

Thousands of people showed up at the Contemporary Art Center in Cincinnati last weekend to view the exhibit of photographs by the late Robert Mapplethorpe.

That is a point being lost in the midst of the controversy over obscenity that Mapplethorpe's work once again has stirred: People came to the Contemporary Art Center because they chose to see the art work on display.

The freedom to do so is what art is about, just as much as is the freedom of artists to create works that may not have universal appeal. Indeed, some or even all of the 175 Mapplethorpe photographs, most of which depict subjects such as calla lilies and celebrities, are certain to be offensive to some people. The freedom to decide what is offensive should be left to the viewers.

Yet the principle of freedom was lost as sheriff's deputies and police officers converged on the museum Saturday after a grand jury indicted it and its director on charges of obscenity. Officers forced patrons out of the museum while they videotaped as evidence the photographic exhibit that includes seven homoerotic and other sexual images.

That Cincinnati has a reputation for intolerance does not lessen the impact of the indictments. The attitude that pressed for the show's cancellation is indicative of a growing repressive sense toward art in the United States. President Bush may have stated recently that he opposes the extreme requirements approved by Congress last year for artists seeking federal grants, but he still vowed to oppose strongly any federal grants for art he termed obscene.

Fortunately, for the sake of the arts and those who cherish the freedom to enjoy them, the director of the Contemporary Art Center also has remained strong in the face of pressure and legal charges.

It is also fortunate for museum-goers in Cincinnati that a federal district judge has ruled that the Mapplethorpe exhibit cannot be closed to the public before the obscenity trial.

Demonstrators' signs outside the museum last weekend proclaimed "Art is Freedom." The freedom in Cincinnati, however, is guaranteed only until a court attempts to decide what is obscene. That is a distinction history has struggled repeatedly to show is not clear-cut. To struggle over it again in this case is, sadly, to miss the greater implication of art censorship.

## The Register-Guard
*Eugene, OR, April 13, 1990*

During his lifetime, which ended a year ago, photographer Robert Mapplethorpe achieved modest fame with his homoerotic and controversial exhibitions. However, his work was relatively unknown to the general population. In death, and for all the wrong reasons, that has changed.

It was a planned Mapplethorpe retrospective exhibit last year in Washington, D.C., that led to an assault on the National Endowment for the Arts by Sen. Jesse Helms, R-S.C., a first-ever congressionally imposed content restriction on NEA grants, the resignation of the director of Washington's prestigious Corcoran Gallery and a mounting threat to the NEA's very existence.

If that wasn't enough, a Cincinnati, Ohio, grand jury has now indicted the director of a local arts center and the center itself on obscenity charges for presenting a Mapplethorpe exhibit. Police even temporarily shut down the Cincinnati exhibit last weekend in the midst of its opening day, so that officers could fan out through the center taking photographs of photographs. And you thought drugs were the No. 1 crime problem.

Threatened with either police closure of the exhibit or seizure of the exhibit's most controversial photographs, the center sought and won a federal court order prohibiting any city, county or law enforcement interference with the exhibit until a trial can be held on the obscenity charges.

While the judge's ruling was a welcome victory for artistic freedom as well as common sense, the indictment and the effort by city and county officials to shut down the exhibit did more to promote it than any advertising campaign ever could. More than 10,000 people — at $4 a pop — already have seen the exhibit and thousands more are expected to see it before it closes on May 26 and heads for Boston. The Mapplethorpe exhibit in Washington, D.C., which turned Helms into an instant art critic, was equally successful.

That's usually the way it turns out for self-appointed censors, be they Ohio prosecutors or U.S. senators. Had Helms and Hamilton (Ohio) County Prosecutor Arthur Ney Jr. simply ignored Mapplethorpe's photographs to concentrate on more important matters, it's likely that a few curious art patrons and some faithful fans would have attended the exhibits, leaving Mapplethorpe to rest in obscure peace.

By their misguided efforts, however, Helms and Ney have turned Mapplethorpe into a kind of folk hero, made themselves look ridiculous and called attention to the very thing they sought to suppress.

## The Courier-Journal
*Louisville, KY, April 7, 1990*

DON'T CONFUSE the Robert Mapplethorpe controversies. Last summer's flap was about public funding for the arts, while the one raging in Cincinnati concerns pure, raw censorship. Law-enforcement officials have indicated that they might keep viewers from the photography exhibition, which has been extremely popular elsewhere, by seizing pictures from the Contemporary Arts Center.

The show, which opens to the public today, represents the center's deliberate attempt to broaden the artistic horizons of a city with a history of caving in to censorship while maintaining its own integrity as an art institution. Director Dennis Barrie arranged for it before the uproar on Capitol Hill, and called it "the most stunning photographic show I'd seen in years."

Most of the 170 photographs are straightforward portraits of men, women and children that are made riveting by their emphasis on form and light as opposed to character. It's the 13 sexually explicit photographs that raised the ire of the Cincinnati posse. Even sophisticated viewers will find their haunting beauty disturbing, because they challenge the assumption that art ought not be overtly sexual. Also, they defy the notion that if one happens to love members of one's own sex, one is supposed to conceal that fact — not advertise it in artwork. This is what makes the pictures especially difficult for some to accept, as critic Ingrid Sischy noted in *The New Yorker*.

Sometimes what art reveals — be it photography, literature or drama — *is* difficult, even intolerable, for some persons. But a function of art is to express what otherwise might not be expressed — to stretch our sensibilities.

The controversy in Cincinnati isn't about whether the Mapplethorpe photographs are offensive. It's about the right of the artist to express himself and our right to see his work if we so choose. That right must be protected; otherwise, we will be diminished as individuals and as a nation.

## LEXINGTON HERALD-LEADER
*Lexington, KY, April 10, 1990*

Who decides? That's the question in Cincinnati these days.

The question is being asked because of an exhibition of photographs by Robert Mapplethorpe. A grand jury has decided that seven of the 175 photographs on display at the Contemporary Arts Center are obscene. The grand jury has indicted the center and its director on charges of pandering obscenity and illegal use of a minor in pornographic material.

The indictments are hardly surprising. Even before the exhibit opened, the Hamilton County sheriff and prosecutor were threatening museum officials with criminal charges.

These same pictures had been shown without incident in other cities. But authorities in Cincinnati clearly had decided in advance that citizens there needed to be protected from the pictures.

Why, then, are so many citizens of Cincinnati upset about this protection?

More than 2,000 people have marched in downtown Cincinnati to protest attempts to shut down the show. Thousands of people already have stood in line to see the exhibit. Crowds have been so large that the museum has had to strictly control entry.

Given the shocking nature of some of Mapplethorpe's work, it's not possible that all of these people have liked what they saw at the exhibit. But they all have one common view: They want to decide for themselves about the nature of the work. They don't want to be told what they can and cannot see.

That's the crux of the controversy in Cincinnati. And that's why what happens there is important to the rest of the country.

Mapplethorpe's comparatively few photographs of sadomasochistic and homosexual acts aren't easy to look at. They may not be great art or — to many — not art of any kind.

But in a free society, individuals have the right to make those judgments for themselves. They also have the right not to attend such exhibits, the right to march or picket peacefully, to denounce either orally or in writing.

A society that can take away individuals' rights to make such judgments for themselves can take away the rights to march, to picket, to speak freely. That's why the real issue in Cincinnati is one of freedom. In a free society, individuals can decide for themselves. If residents of Cincinnati can't do that, how free can that city claim to be?

## BUFFALO EVENING NEWS
*Buffalo, NY, April 11, 1990*

LIFE WOULD BE idyllic indeed if it prompted from artists only depictions of searing sunsets, serene seas and children playing ball in the pasture.

Unfortunately, that isn't the totality of human experience. The late artist Robert Mapplethorpe saw more and attempted to depict it — in admittedly graphic detail — in photo exhibits that include images of homosexual acts and nude children.

Now a Cincinnati art center and its director have been indicted for deciding that adults who want to see an exhibit that includes such photographs should have the opportunity to do so.

It is a frightening prospect. Even if that city's Contemporary Arts Center and its administrator are acquitted of all obscenity-related charges, the heavy-handed police action has to make art directors in Cincinnati and elsewhere fearful.

The likely result will be a shrinking from their mission of judging what is artistically significant — whether innocuous or upsetting — and providing the public a forum in which to view such works.

In place of that educated assessment will be a much more stultifying criterion: What can be shown that will not offend the police or the city council? When that becomes the standard, as it already has to some degree following Congress' plunge into the fray last year, this society will be culturally poorer.

The Cincinnati indictments followed a grand jury's viewing of the exhibit, and that will no doubt fuel prosecutors' efforts as they assert that such a panel is an adequate judge of what is acceptable. But using the grand jury as a shield for government regulation of artistic expression is no more defensible than is direct political control.

Art is a distinctly non-democratic medium. Much of its value derives from the fact that it challenges conventions, pokes holes in sacred cows or makes us ponder realities — such as sex and sexual exploitation — that we'd just as soon sweep under the rug.

It may make some uncomfortable, but it is one way change is precipitated. And change is hardly likely when those picked to represent the status quo are set up as arbiters of allowable artistic expression.

Experts at the Cincinnati center and others that have shown the Mapplethorpe exhibit apparently saw a statement in the sexually graphic photos included among images of calla lilies and famous faces.

Should those who are non-expert be allowed to stifle that statement so that no one else gets affected by it? And if the answer to that is "yes," where will it lead?

Not everything that results from letting the art community police itself will be pleasing. Nor should it have to be.

But that system — with patrons and donors setting outer parameters by making their feelings known — is far better than one in which police, prosecutors and grand juries determine which exhibits adults may or may not view.

## Los Angeles Times
*Los Angeles, CA, April 10, 1990*

If the wider implications of their actions were not quite so disturbing, it might be possible to muster a small stirring of sympathy for the would-be censors of Cincinnati. Their flinty little campaign to keep their city from seeing seven photographs by the late Robert Mapplethorpe has left the authorities there in a situation something like that of the cat Heine observed chewing its own tail: In the objective sense it was eating, but in the subjective sense it was being eaten.

Until last weekend, the 175 photographs—a few of which depict homoerotic and sadomasochistic images—probably were best known as Exhibit A in the mean-spirited, if politically potent, attack mounted against the National Endowment for the Arts by Sen. Jesse Helms (R-N.C.). Then Cincinnati got into the act. A county grand jury, acting under a local ordinance hailed by anti-pornography crusaders as a national model, indicted the city's Contemporary Arts Museum, where the exhibit is on view, and its director on two counts of pandering and using a minor in material involving nudity.

So far, all the grand jury seems to have accomplished is to give Mapplethorpe's work qualities he could not himself provide. During his life, serious critics frequently took the artist to task for a brittle self-preoccupation and slick technique that borrowed so heavily from the world of commercial advertising that even his self-consciously provocative images seemed like a kind of consumer kink. Thus, by making such art the center of a now unavoidable battle for freedom of expression, the Cincinnati censors have managed to drape the mantle of principle over a set of shoulders that themselves seldom managed more than a shrug of cold disdain. In the process, they also have secured Mapplethorpe's work a public it never found on its own. Openings at the Cincinnati museum usually are free and about 600 people show up. Friday, an estimated 6,000 people stood in line for hours and paid $10 apiece to get in. Thousands more streamed in over the weekend.

This shabby legal exercise is a reminder that what began as a campaign against a handful of vulgar photos has become an attempt to deprive Americans of the right to decide for themselves what kind of art they will enjoy. The events in Cincinnati represent more than tedious yahooism. They are an unacceptable blurring of the distinction between the indispensable right to live according to one's private convictions and the insupportable insistence that others must live by them, too.

### AKRON BEACON JOURNAL
*Akron, OH, April 9, 1990*

CINCINNATI is hosting the latest squabble over art vs. community standards.

Some citizens' groups say a planned exhibit of photos by the late Robert Mapplethorpe that includes some "homoerotic" photos violates community standards. The museum, the Contemporary Arts Center, has asked for a court ruling on obscenity so the photos can be exhibited.

Obscenity can be a murky concept. But one certainty results from such bickering: It gives the work in question more attention than it would normally receive or, perhaps, deserve.

If the photos are shown, expect a large crowd of the curious to swell the ranks of art lovers. You just can't buy that kind of publicity.

# THE INDIANAPOLIS STAR
*Indianapolis, IN, April 11, 1990*

It is good that the Robert Mapplethorpe exhibition went to Cincinnati. The legal fight now under way there about the late photographer's prints may produce more fog at first, but in the end it may clarify a few things.

This is a federally aided exhibit, through the National Endowment for the Arts. Members of a local grand jury individually viewed the exhibit with other visitors and promptly indicted the Contemporary Arts Center and its director on charges of pandering obscenity and illegally using a minor in photography. The grand jury objected to seven of 175 photographs.

The Mapplethorpe show became notorious in recent months because of disputes over certain of the pictures involving children, homosexual sex and controversial poses. Its showing at the Corcoran Gallery in Washington was canceled last June. The director who canceled it drew great criticism in artistic circles and resigned.

The exhibition originated in December 1988 at the University of Pennsylvania with three grants, two private and one from the NEA. Another D.C. gallery showed it after the Corcoran cancellation. It has been exhibited in other cities, including Chicago.

When the Cincinnati grand jurors acted Saturday, sheriff's deputies closed the show for about an hour while they videotaped the prints. Sunday the art center obtained a federal court order blocking further law enforcement action that would interfere with the exhibition.

So those insisting on their right to see these photographs without government intrusion will be satisfied. The prosecutor and others who feel part of the show is an affront to public decency will get their test.

And Congress will take note of the outcome. So will the serious, if not always circumspect, people who make up the NEA board. The sensibilities of Robert Mapplethorpe, such as they were, are meeting Middle America, where the public spending bills get paid.

Opponents of the Mapplethorpe view have given the exhibition a high publicity profile through the controversy. But America is learning where some of its money went, and as a result opponents of federal funding for the arts may be the principal gainers.

### The Atlanta Journal AND THE ATLANTA CONSTITUTION
*Atlanta, GA, April 13, 1990*

There's only one possible justification for going to the extreme of suppressing photographs such as the ones in a Cincinnati exhibition that have drawn criminal obscenity charges: That the average person, viewing them, will be driven to dangerously anti-social behavior. Otherwise, the law is simply being misused to enforce one group's taste — or distaste — on another.

Suppose the worry hadn't already been found unnecessary in practice (obscenity is de facto legal in many places, without dire consequence) and in serious studies both in the United States and Europe. Suppose it was still an open question. Even then Cincinnati presents a cute puzzle.

The authorities have filed charges but insist that the photos remain on exhibit even so, fearing their removal would moot the case and lead to the dismissal of the charges.

Either (a) authorities know perfectly well that no one will be harmed as a result of the exhibition or (b) authorities would rather endanger citizens than take the risk of losing their prosecution.

Not a pretty choice.

### RAPID CITY JOURNAL
*Rapid City, SD, April 11, 1990*

The late Robert Mapplethorpe's photographs continue to demonstrate how difficult it can be to define obscenity.

A Cincinnati grand jury has indicted an art center and its director for exhibiting the Mapplethorpe show, citing seven of the 175 photographs as obscene. The offensive photos depicted either homosexual acts or children with their genitals exposed.

A group named Citizens for Community Values also has opposed the show, which remains open to record crowds while everyone waits to see what happens in court. A trial date will be set Friday, and the show is scheduled to run through May 26. However, it's a safe bet that anyone who wants to see it will have seen it before jury decides whether Mapplethorpe's work is obscene, so the case is a moot point in regard to protecting Cincinnati adults from themselves. (No one under 18 is admitted to the show.)

The case is not moot in regard to free expression. It also is different from the first Mapplethorpe flap, which was over whether federal funds should be used to support the controversial show. The Contemporary Arts Center in Cincinnati is a private art museum. Director Dennis Barrie, who faces a year in jail and a fine of up to $2,000 on each of two counts, is not a public employee.

Cincinnati prosecutors and a group of citizens there have taken it upon themselves to decide what sort of art the rest of the adult community can or cannot see.

That's a dangerous proposition even under the broadest definition of obscenity — which is that it appeals to only to prurient interest and is "utterly without redeeming social value." Under the more restrictive "community standard" test of obscenity, it is clear that free expression could be limited to what the majority, or a politically powerful minority, deemed correct.

## The Cincinnati Post
*Cincinnati, OH, April 7, 1990*

Art vs. pornography. Freedom of expression vs. social responsibility.

Those issues remain unsettled today as the Robert Mapplethorpe photo exhibit opens to the public at The Contemporary Arts Center. They have been in the forefront of this community for nearly a month, ever since a local organization began making phone calls and sending letters criticizing the exhibit.

The controversy has put Cincinnati in the national spotlight. Some have found the attention embarrassing. They say it brands the city as an unsophisticated, hick town.

The fact is, Cincinnati provides a most appropriate forum for this debate — a debate that has been brewing for months nationally. Fortunately, up until today, it has not been decided by presumptuous value judgments of local police officials, or dominated by extremists.

This hasn't been narrow-minded religious zealots taking on fanatical activists. The representatives on both sides who have spoken out publicly have been intelligent, rational, respectable citizens. The letters to the editor written to this paper — both pro and con — have come mostly from sensible people who clearly care about their community.

It is precisely those strong sentiments that have made the city such a hotbed.

This is not Washington, D.C., where the Corcoran Gallery of Art buckled under and canceled the show when opposition heated up. The Contemporary Arts Center, from the beginning, has vowed to display Mapplethorpe's work in its entirety. The arts community and others have stood unified in its corner.

At the same time, Cincinnati has long been a national leader in organizing resistance against pornography, more so than Chicago or Philadelphia or Berkeley, Calif., or any other city where the Mapplethorpe exhibit has been shown without fanfare.

It is most appropriate, then, that this be the place where the national controversy over sexually explicit art is focused.

Robert Mapplethorpe had every intention of creating this furor. Among his stunningly beautiful photographs of portraits, still lifes, and figure studies, he deliberately incorporated images that express his homosexual orientation. Even the most liberal viewer would find a few of them violent, disturbing, perhaps revolting.

The Mapplethorpe exhibit has accomplished exactly what art sets out to do: challenge us to examine our attitudes and values. It has sought to push the community to new limits of tolerance and acceptance.

It is the community, then, that ultimately must decide where those limits are set. That is what Cincinnati has struggled with these past few weeks.

As long as we continue to do so in a spirit of open dialogue, where individuals are allowed to act freely on their convictions — without manipulation or government interference — we have no reason to be ashamed.

## The Miami Herald
*Miami, FL, April 12, 1990*

SO THEY arrested the museum director on smut charges in Cincinnati because photographs on display were porn by community standards. Sure. When the museum next opened, the lines of people waiting to see these feelthy pictures extended for blocks.

Prurient interest? Perhaps. Interest in photography? Perhaps. Interest in controversy? Sure. Fruit becomes more tempting when forbidden, a human reaction deepened by the fiercely American dislike of government censorship.

The photographs in Cincinnati are part of a retrospective of the late Robert Mapplethorpe. Earlier they aroused a congressional furor culminating in a redrafting of arts-funding laws. The show was assembled in part with Federal funds. Because it includes several homo-erotic pictures, many objected to such a use of public money.

Life would be much easier in Cincinnati, as well as in the halls of Congress, if there were a tidy definition of obscenity. The courts have wrangled with this for years.

But words in law that would cover the nasty sleaze sold in "adult" bookstores also would cover works considered by experts to be art. They'd even cover the anatomically correct doll that Vice President Dan Quayle bought as a gag on his last Latin American trip. While most sentient human beings can tell the difference between sleaze, art, and gags, deep divisions inevitably arise over specific examples.

Consider the controversy raging over 2 Live Crew, the rap group elevated in the public consciousness by Gov. Bob Martinez. Some of its songs are truly vile, explicitly describing sex acts in the rawest of terms.

Yes, that album and other explicit materials should be kept out of the hands of children. Yes, no one should be forced to see or hear material that offends them. But there is a huge difference between letting potential viewers and listeners make their own judgments about what is acceptable and having government make that choice for them.

## Chicago Tribune
*Chicago, IL, April 10, 1990*

On Sunday, in Cincinnati, deep in the heart of the land of the free, a federal judge had to issue a legal command to make sure local police would not do something normally associated with totalitarian governments: invade an art museum and confiscate forbidden works.

For Americans too young to remember when the authorities rode tight herd on what the public was allowed to see, hear and read, the legal battle over the exhibit of photographs by the late Robert Mapplethorpe dramatizes the dangers of government censorship. It is just another chapter in the long and ignoble history of government efforts to outlaw art that offends.

Like the efforts to ban "Tropic of Cancer" and "Carnal Knowledge," this censorship is likely to fail in the end. The city's effort to block the exhibit, far from keeping it from the public, has stimulated greater attendance than most artists ever dream of.

The director of Cincinnati's Contemporary Arts Center remains under indictment for showing the photos, which include depictions of homosexual acts and nude children. If convicted of pandering obscenity and using minors in pornography—an unlikely outcome—he could get 18 months in jail and $3,000 in fines. In any case, he faces the costly task of defending himself.

Cincinnati officials take seriously their commitment to barring graphic erotica. They have managed to keep out adult bookstores and movie theaters, escort services, pornographic videocassettes and all but the tamer men's magazines. The message to sellers and buyers of pornography is blunt: Not here.

But the local authorities show no grasp of the deep gulf between run-of-the-mill smut and art. When a local troupe planned a production of the critically acclaimed play "Equus," which features male and female nudity, police officers reviewed it before it could be presented. Now there is Mapplethorpe, whom prosecutors apparently can't distinguish from Larry Flynt.

The prosecution rests on a foundation of sand. The Supreme Court, true, has declined to extend the protection of the 1st Amendment to material that is obscene. But the chief prosecutor obviously needs to re-examine the court's definition—particularly the part that says a given specimen is obscene only if "the work taken as a whole lacks serious literary, artistic, political or scientific value."

Critics may disagree on whether Mapplethorpe's photos are good or bad, but few would argue that they are not art—and it is a foolish prosecutor who defies that judgment.

About the only redeeming value of the city's attempt to supress this exhibit is educational. When Congress last year voted to refuse federal funding to works that are obscene, the arts community denounced the legislation as reminiscent of the worst police states—as if there were no difference between declining to finance a particular book (or photo) with tax money and deploying the full force of the law to eradicate it.

For anyone who has trouble comprehending that vital distinction, the Cincinnati prosecutor has provided an unforgettable illustration. Declining to provide public money for works like Mapplethorpe's was censorship only in the crudest metaphorical sense. This outrageous attempt at suppression is the real thing.

## Miss Saigon on Broadway

Theatrical producer Cameron Mackintosh announced Aug. 8, 1990 that he was canceling the planned production of the British musical *Miss Saigon* in New York City, rather than accede to a demand by the American Actor's Equity union that he replace leading performer Jonathan Pryce with an Asian actor.

After Mackintosh announced plans to cancel the show, Actor's Equity received petitions signed by more than 150 of its members asking it to reconsider its decision. In a second vote, held Aug. 16, the union's council reversed its earlier decision and said it would allow Pryce to perform in New York.

However, Mackintosh said he would not reschedule *Miss Saigon* unless he received assurances from Equity that the union would allow him complete freedom in casting all of the roles in the show.

*Miss Saigon* was an updating of the Puccini opera *Madama Butterfly* set during the Vietnam War. It told the story of a young Vietnamese bar girl who is made pregnant and is then abandoned by a U.S. soldier. The musical had been a hit in London, and it had set a record for the highest advance ticket sale in the history of New York City's Broadway theater – $25 million.

Some Asian-American actors and playwrights had complained, however, about the casting of Pryce as a half-French, half-Vietnamese pimp. Responding to those complaints, the council of Actor's Equity Aug. 7 denied permission for Pryce to repeat his London role in New York because the union could not "appear to condone the casting of a Caucasian in the role of a Eurasian." Under international rules, both Equity and its British counterpart could deny foreign actors the right to perform in their respective countries. The only exceptions were for performers who were acknowledged to be "stars" of international stature. American Equity had previously allowed Pryce to perform in the U.S. in 1976, when he won a Tony Award for best actor in the play *Comedians*.

## The New York Times
*New York, NY, August 9, 1990*

Actors' Equity asserts that a British actor portraying a Eurasian in the musical "Miss Saigon" would be "an affront to the Asian community." But refusing to let him repeat his London role on Broadway is an affront to the essence of theater.

The union claims to be taking a moral stand in the interests of its minority members. The cause is just, but the effect is perverse. Understandably angered, the producer, Cameron Mackintosh, has now canceled the U.S. production. That means some three dozen Asian-Americans and other minority actors who would have had roles will instead be jobless. So will scores of other performers, musicians and stagehands in New York and on the road.

"Miss Saigon" stars Jonathan Pryce as the Eurasian owner of a bar and brothel in Saigon during the Vietnam War. Already established as a great actor on both sides of the Atlantic, Mr. Pryce has won a Tony award as best actor on Broadway and by all accounts gives an outstanding performance in "Miss Saigon." And what is greatness on the stage if not the versatility to star in many roles?

Legally, even morally, Actors' Equity has a weak case. It cannot dictate casting for any show, home-grown or imported. Rather it has an agreement with British Equity that allows stars to cross the ocean on a reciprocal basis. The union suggests that Mr. Mackintosh go to arbitration, and concedes that he would probably win. That's a cop-out; lacking the courage to offend a few members who object to Mr. Pryce, the union wants to pass the buck to an arbitrator.

Actors' Equity is right to promote minority actors, but wrong to promote stereotyping. Men and women have swapped roles for centuries. More recently there has been a healthy crossing of racial and ethnic lines. Must Shylock always be played by a Jew? No. Othello by a black? There was no outcry when Edwin Booth took that role. Right now in Mr. Mackintosh's Los Angeles production of "The Phantom of the Opera," a black star plays the phantom.

Let Actors' Equity focus on actors acting.

*copyright © The New York Times 1990*

## The State
*Columbia, SC, August 28, 1990*

ACTORS' EQUITY, recovering from a severe case of stupidity, has yielded in the face of a principled stand by British producer Cameron Mackintosh and given its permission for a white actor to portray a Eurasian character in the musical, "Miss Saigon."

British actor Jonathan Pryce performed the role of a pimp of French and Vietnamese extraction in the play, set in the last days of the Vietnamese war. Presumably a full-blooded white should be as acceptable as a full-blooded Asian in an Asian-Caucasian role. Mr. Pryce's performance was widely and critically acclaimed in London, and he won the British equivalent of the Tony for it.

But when Producer Mackintosh proposed to use him in a planned Broadway run of the play, the governing body of the actors' union, after receiving complaints from two Asian members, voted to bar Mr. Pryce. (It has veto power over foreign actors.) Mr. Mackintosh was having none of the tommyrot and canceled the New York production. He said he would return the $25 million advance ticket sale.

More than 600 Equity members signed a petition deploring the move, and the union eventually relented. The union's "moral" position, really nothing more than reverse discrimination and a denial of artistic freedom, may still have cost its members 50 acting jobs (including 34 minority parts), 129 jobs for musicians, stagehands, etc., and a payroll of $200,000 a week. Mr. Mackintosh has not yet decided whether he will stage the play in New York.

What we have here is a new form of racism that is currently in vogue, a racism that finds color-blind hiring offensive, that makes talent a secondary consideration.

When we first heard of this ridiculous ban, we couldn't help thinking that, if this kind of mindset had been in vogue a few decades ago, the world would have been denied the joy of seeing Yul Brynner cavort on stage and screen as the Siamese monarch in "The King and I." What a shame that would have been.

## Rockford Register Star
*Rockford, IL, August 24, 1990*

Faced with a firestorm of criticism for objecting to a white actor in the role of a Eurasian in a Broadway production, Actors Equity has wisely reversed its decision — and perhaps also has learned a lesson about racism. That lesson would be that you can't fight racism with racism.

The controversy arose when plans were made to bring the hit London musical, *Miss Saigon*, to Broadway with British actor Jonathan Pryce in the lead role of a pimp who is half Asian and half European. Actors Equity, the union of 39,000 stage performers, turned thumbs down on Pryce, arguing that the role should go to an actor of entirely Asian extraction.

That position seemed preposterous on its face. Racially speaking, a pure Asian would fit only half the role, just as Pryce would. Why did the union seem to recognize only the Asian half of the character? The implied answer to that question is that too often in the past Asian roles have been played by white actors, just as whites long ago used to play black roles in blackface, (which clearly would be unacceptable today).

That point might be valid if the role in *Miss Saigon* were that of a pure Asian. But it isn't. Besides, there is a long and admirable history of certain lead roles in stage productions being played by persons of other races who are made-up to look the part — Laurence Olivier in *Othello*, for example. These cases seem to be valid exceptions to the worthy principle of hiring only minority actors to play minority roles.

In a sense, the marketplace should make the determination. Audiences seem to buy Jonathan Pryce as a Eurasian. It isn't likely, however, that they would buy, say, Joel Gray as the male lead in *Porgy and Bess*.

## THE RICHMOND NEWS LEADER
*Richmond, VA, August 15, 1990*

In the growing animus generated by a racial spoils system, Actors Equity has lent a whole new dimension to hypocrisy parading as moral superiority. The actors union has forbidden a British actor, Jonathan Pryce, from starring in the hit musical, "Miss Saigon," scheduled to open on Broadway in April. The union says an Asian should be cast in the role of the Eurasian pimp that Pryce has been playing for two years in London.

And how, you may ask, does a union have a final say over what should be a purely artistic decision by the musical's director and producer? After all, with America's *artistes* in a snit over restrictions in funding by the National Endowment for the Arts, much is being made of artistic "integrity." If Pryce were a U.S. citizen, Actors Equity could do nothing. Because he is British, however, the union had to certify that he is a "star," so he could qualify for a visa. Equity had no trouble in finding Pryce "a star" for visa purposes in 1984 when he appeared on Broadway. But in 1990, he has become a non-star to satisfy Equity's egalitarian — some say racist — cravings.

To his credit, Cameron Mackintosh, the British producer of "Miss Saigon," promptly cancelled the musical's opening on Broadway. Said he, Equity's stand is "irresponsible and a disturbing violation of the principles of artistic integrity and freedom." Mackintosh thus rejects $50 million in advance sales and takes a loss of $600,000 that already had been spent on the Broadway production. Gone, too, are 34 supporting roles in which Asians would be cast and 125 other jobs in the production.

A mutiny in the rank-and-file has forced Equity to call a special meeting tomorrow to reconsider its decision — and well it should. If Equity wants to get technical, an Eurasian is half-Caucasian, and certainly Pryce half-qualifies for the role under Equity's suddenly pristine notion of typecasting. The union did not squawk when Morgan Freeman played Petruccio, nor did it raise questions about Yul Brynner as the King of Siam, Ben Kingsley as Gandhi, Robert Hooks as Henry V, or Laurence Olivier as Othello. It has been reported, by the way, that Equity president Colleen Dewhurst — who bleated that "this is the time. The time has arrived" to start racial stereotyping in Pryce's case — played the role of an Asian in a 1970 production.

For years, minorities complained of being excluded from many entertainment jobs. Anyone who follows the entertainment world today, from the popular to the sublime, would find that claim ludicrous. In fact, non-traditional casting has put minorities in many starring roles they would not get under Equity's new rule. If Equity's foolish experiment in social engineering stands, the play no longer will be the thing, but the least of it.

## ST. LOUIS POST-DISPATCH
*St. Louis, MO, August 19, 1990*

Actors' Equity has acknowledged that it erred in trying to prevent British actor Jonathan Pryce from recreating his role as the Eurasian "Engineer" in the New York production of "Miss Saigon." Stung by the adverse reaction to its decision, the actors' union reversed its earlier vote barring Mr. Pryce from appearing. Now the producer of "Miss Saigon," Cameron Mackintosh, should return the favor by rescinding his cancellation of the show.

All's well that ends well? Not quite. Certainly, Actors' Equity made a major blunder in how it handled the "Miss Saigon" controversy, and it was savant to recognize — and correct — its mistake. But the union's points about the dearth of roles for minorities should not be ignored. Non-traditional casting is meant to open the doors for all actors, not to provide a new name for the old practice of reserving leading ethnic roles for whites.

## DAILY NEWS
*New York, NY, August 11, 1990*

**B**EFORE THE FINAL CURTAIN goes down on "Miss Saigon," Cameron Mackintosh should know one thing: Broadway needs you. Broadway wants you. Actors' Equity is rethinking its misguided decision to ban Jonathan Pryce from appearing as the star of your show. If it backs down, you should bring "Miss Saigon" to New York — with Pryce.

Mackintosh, the producer of "Miss Saigon," did make some mistakes. Right from the start, he should have announced that he planned to bring Pryce, the star of the London production, to play the lead in the New York version. Period. Nothing wrong with that. It's been done a million times before.

Instead, he claimed that he had searched the world over for an Asian actor but "couldn't find one that was qualified." That statement was demeaning and insulting to Asian actors and the entire Asian community. It did much to trigger the present controversy. Mackintosh should apologize for it.

At the same time, Actors' Equity also owes Mackintosh an apology. Its hysterical reaction to the casting of Pryce has been an international embarrassment.

Equity is part of an arts community that is dead set against the government dictating which artists it will and won't fund by placing content restrictions on the National Endowment for the Arts. For months, artists have been crying: "Artistic freedom!" "No censorship!" "No outside control!"

But Equity is practicing exactly the same censorship it decries when it won't grant Pryce and Mackintosh the right to practice *their* artistic freedom in "Miss Saigon." The shameful irony of that position appears to be lost on the members of the Equity council who voted to bar Pryce.

**T**HE ARGUMENT OVER WHO SHOULD STAR in "Miss Saigon" has been muddied by frequent comparisons of the casting of a white man to play a Eurasian with the casting of a black man (like Morgan Freeman in this summer's Joseph Papp production of Shakespeare's "Taming of the Shrew") to play a role usually reserved for whites.

These comparisons may sound plausible on the surface. But they ignore the once-common practice of using white actors, with makeup to darken their skins, to play people of color — at the same time that other actors and actresses were barred from roles *because* of the color of their skin. And it remains disgracefully difficult for people of color to find work on the stage. Yes, a growing number of plays make use of "non-traditional" casting. But such productions are few and far between.

The one good thing to be said for Actors' Equity's heavy-handed conduct in the "Miss Saigon" controversy is that it may well have helped sensitize Mackintosh, as well as the general public, to the complexities surrounding ethnic casting decisions.

But now that the point has been made, it is essential that Equity get firmly behind the principle of truly color-blind casting. Equity's decision on Thursday to reconsider the ban on Pryce provides a perfect opportunity to let Mackintosh bring his production to Broadway with Pryce as the star. Jobs and livelihoods depend on it. Let the show go on.

## Los Angeles Times
*Los Angeles, CA, August 17, 1990*

Actors' Equity did the right thing. The union reversed its monstrous decision that would have barred the English star Jonathan Pryce from taking a role on Broadway because he allegedly wasn't the right race for the part. That move outraged theater lovers everywhere—and threatened to kill the show.

In now approving Pryce to play a Eurasian pimp in the U.S. version of the London hit musical "Miss Saigon," the union's council said the actor qualifies as a "star." Under an agreement between American and British unions, a star billing allows a foreign actor such as Pryce to perform in the United States.

The union had originally voted against Pryce in an effort to dramatize its campaign to open up more roles to Asian actors. This is a laudable and inarguable goal, and Asians have long struggled with the limited number of roles—and a great deal of stereotyping—in the entertainment industry.

But Actors' Equity's cure was worse than the disease. It was an assault on freedom of artistic expression and choice. It triggered widespread criticism and objections from within and outside entertainment circles. "Miss Saigon's" producer retaliated by canceling plans to bring the musical to New York. But now "Miss Saigon" could be back on track and headed for Broadway's lights. A decision will be made in a few days.

That's good. But let us not forget the very real and troublesome problem that the incident brought to light: continued racism in the entertainment industry against Asian actors.

## The Record
*Hackensack, NJ, August 9, 1990*

Long before the scheduled opening of "Miss Saigon" on Broadway next year, it looked like a sure-fire smash. Rave reviews in London, a producer with "Cats," "Les Miserables," and "The Phantom of the Opera" among his credits, and a lavish $10-million production all made "Miss Saigon" the hottest ticket of the coming season. That is, until the heavies from Actors Equity, the actors' union, came galumphing onto the stage and threatened to kill all the fun.

The leading character in the musical, a remake of "Madame Butterfly" set in Vietnam in the Seventies, is a Eurasian pimp. The union's executive secretary, Alan Eisenberg, complains that the part is played by an English actor named Jonathan Pryce, a Caucasian. And that's impermissible in New York, the union's council has decided.

"The casting of a Caucasian actor made up to appear Asian is an affront to the Asian community," Mr. Eisenberg said this week. "The casting choice is especially disturbing when the casting of an Asian actor, in this role, would be an important and significant opportunity to break the usual pattern of casting Asians in minor roles."

It's hard to know whether the actors' union is pursuing a kind of affirmative action gone mad, or just trying to keep out foreign talent to make life easier for its own members. Whatever the motive, the union is wrong.

Actors Equity has no right to be making delicate moral judgments about who is suitable for leading roles in "Miss Saigon" or any other play. An agreement between the British and American actors' unions clearly allows stars to perform in either country. Mr. Pryce's credentials as a star are impeccable. He won a Tony Award in 1976 as best actor for his performance in "The Comedians," and in England he has won an Olivier Award as best actor for his appearance in "Miss Saigon." Actors Equity has no legal grounds for blocking his appearance on Broadway.

In addition, Actors Equity's stand is an embarrassment that will undermine better-thought-out efforts to increase job opportunities for minority members on Broadway or anywhere else. The union, usually an advocate of non-traditional casting that emphasizes talent rather than race, certainly can't argue that characters of a particular race can only be played by actors of the same race. That would keep black or Asian actors from winning many desirable parts. Morgan Freeman never could have played Petruchio in "The Taming of the Shrew" in Central Park, for example. The union says it is just trying to increase employment opportunities for its minority members. That's an eminently worthy goal, but knocking an established star out of a hit production is the wrong way to pursue it.

Cameron Mackintosh, the producer of "Miss Saigon," canceled the New York production on Wednesday, saying he preferred to have no show at all rather than give in to the union's demand. So unless a compromise is reached, some 50 actors will lose jobs — including 34 minority union members already signed up for the production. And Broadway will lose the excitement of an international hit such as "Miss Saigon."

Actors Equity should reconsider and find a graceful way to back down. Broadway needs "Miss Saigon," and it needs a production in which the actors union doesn't interfere with casting decisions. That's also exactly what's needed by minority members that Actors Equity is trying to help.

## The Washington Post
*Washington, DC, August 15, 1990*

IT LOOKS as if Actors Equity, the New York-based actors' union, will have a chance to reverse itself tomorrow on last week's ludicrous decision to prevent the Caucasian actor Jonathan Pryce from playing the Eurasian lead character in the musical "Miss Saigon." The decision, which brought a prompt flood of ridicule, seems to have startled everyone involved; it demonstrated the silliness of taking an initially well-intentioned sentiment to absurd and legalistic extremes. The long-ago original motive of the union's policy is clear enough: ethnic minority actors have long suffered from the widespread refusal of directors to cast them in any but specifically minority roles. When specifically minority starring roles *are* written into musicals—such as the "Miss Saigon" character or, for that matter, his Asian female co-star—pressure mounts to give them to Asian actors. Casting more minority actors is a laudable purpose. But held rigidly, Equity's position would prohibit casting nonwhite actors in white roles, the very solution to the problem it addresses.

That solution, to which more and more directors are now turning, is the so-called "nontraditional casting": ignore the race of actors, cast the best ones and rely on their talent at creating illusion. Washingtonians have seen great successes in this vein at the Arena Stage, the Shakespeare Theater at the Folger and elsewhere; and Shakespeare in general has been a fruitful field for such efforts. (This is only fitting for plays whose female roles were written to be played by male Elizabethan actors and whose minorities, such as Othello, almost certainly were played by white ones.) The acclaimed British musical "Miss Saigon" is not in this league, but it fell afoul of the "protective" policies of the union, which also, for example, opposes any actors' appearing in blackface for any reason. The union, which admitted to "long and emotional debate" on the matter of Mr. Pryce, said in a statement last Thursday that it could not "appear to condone the casting of a Caucasian actor in the role of a Eurasian." Rather than back down, the British director, Cameron Mackintosh, canceled the show, turning an instance of mere silly thinking into one that would cost 50 actors jobs (including 34 minorities), forfeit $25 million in advance ticket sales and bite into the always precarious New York theater industry.

Mr. Mackintosh and Equity in fact have a history of friction, the director having threatened before to close shows when the union tried to keep him from importing his London stars rather than replace them with Americans. The union has also complained about his general record on casting minorities, especially in the large ensembles of his "Les Miserables" and "Phantom of the Opera"; but in the case of "Miss Saigon," with an Asian co-star and largely Asian ensemble, the showdown would seem misplaced even if it were not so wrongheaded. The union, to top it off, had also certified Mr. Pryce a "star" when he wished to recreate an Italian role in 1984. Equity's "long and emotional debates" evidently didn't cover much ground. Maybe it will straighten things out in this second run-through.

# TULSA WORLD
*Tulsa, OK, August 18, 1990*

ACTORS' Equity reversed its decision that forbade a prize-winning British actor to recreate his role in the smash hit "Miss Saigon" on Broadway. But not before the American stage actors' union made itself look foolish.

Jonathan Pryce portrayed a Eurasian character in the British stage production of "Miss Saigon," but Equity said he couldn't do it here. The union said it couldn't "appear to condone the casting of a Caucasian in the role of a Eurasian," and insisted the role be filled by an Asian.

The ruling, of course, was reverse racism at its worst. Further, it ignored the fact that the very nature of acting is to play someone who the actor is not.

Producer Cameron Mackintosh balked at the union's attempt to dictate who he could or couldn't cast in his play — an obvious infringement on his artistic freedom — and canceled the $10 million Broadway production. Thus the union's attempt to make work for an Asian actor led to 50 actors, including 34 minorities, losing their jobs.

Union board members voted to reverse their decision and announced that they had "applied an honest and moral principle in an inappropriate manner." The board members were too kind to themselves. The rule that minority characters must be played by appropriate minority actors is unfair. Would the union object if an Asian actor played a Caucasian role? Not likely.

Producer Mackintosh said he would decide over the weekend whether plans to stage "Miss Saigon" on Broadway can be resumed. Let's hope B'Wayites aren't denied the opportunity to see a popular show because of Equity's foolishness.

# St. Petersburg Times
*St. Petersburg, FL, August 27, 1990*

If black actors want to play English kings, and whites want to play Moors, and women want to portray boozing male blowhards, so be it. Let producers cast plays and movies, and let critics and audiences decide what works and what doesn't.

That's clearly the lesson that Actors' Equity should learn from the whole *Miss Saigon* debacle, wherein the 39,000-member union ran into a public relations buzzsaw over its refusal to permit English actor Jonathan Pryce to recreate on Broadway his lead role as a Eurasian pimp in the hit London musical. It was an unwise and potentially costly decision, and the union was right to reconsider and reverse itself.

But let's be clear about *what's* being reversed.

The union cannot presume to decide who gets to play what based on whose racial sensibilities might be offended; that is misguided and could backfire against the very people it's trying to help. But the union has every right to continue its efforts to see that Asians, blacks, women and other minority groups get better treatment and more opportunities in show business. Anyone who truly thinks such efforts aren't needed just isn't paying attention.

The union does need to get its equality act together, though. Its characterization of a white actor playing a Eurasian as "an affront to the Asian community" only drove a painful racial wedge between its membership. Worse, it created an opening for cheap shots from the kind of people who seem to resent any attempt at fairness for any minority group under any circumstances.

Columnist George Will lost no time denouncing "the union's weaselly position" as "the usual one of liberals running a racial spoils system;" he even managed to tag it to the "legacy" of retired Supreme Court Justice William Brennan. "Obscenely racist," harrumphed right-wing dilettante Charlton Heston, declaring his intention to resign from the union.

To hear them howl, you'd think white males were persecuted pariahs instead of the undisputed controllers of Broadway, television, movies or any other medium. That doesn't make any instance of unfairness to a white male performer any less unfair, but it hardly signals the end of Western civilization.

These same critics have been remarkably silent about the well-documented tradition of meaningless, demeaning or nonexistent roles for minority performers that Actors' Equity is at least trying to address. How those who pooh-pooh racism charges can so readily acknowledge the existence of "reverse" racism seems to be one of those unfathomable mysteries of the right-wing mind.

Actors' Equity erred, but only in an attempt to include the people who some seem to wish would just shut up and go away. That gives the union a lot more credibility than some of its critics.

WHERE WERE YOU, ACTORS' EQUITY, WHEN WE NEEDED YOU?

## Supreme Court Protects Flag-Burning

The Supreme Court ruled, 5-4, June 21, 1989 that burning the American flag as a political protest was protected by the First Amendment guarantee of free speech.

"We do not consecrate the flag by punishing its desecration, for in doing so we dilute the freedom that this cherished emblem represents," Justice William J. Brennan Jr. wrote in the majority opinion. "The government may not prohibit expression simply because it disagrees with its message," he said.

The majority consisted of an unusual alignment of liberal justices – Brennan, Thurgood Marshall and Harry A. Blackmun – and conservative Reagan appointees, Antonin Scalia and Anthony Kennedy. Kennedy, who praised Brennan's opinion, said in brief concurring statement that the case was a "rare" one where "we are presented with a clear and simple statute to be judged against a pure command of the Constitution." "It is poignant but fundamental that the flag protects those who hold it in contempt," he said.

Justice John Paul Stevens, a frequent ally of the liberals, joined the conservatives in dissent, Chief Justice William H. Rehnquist and Justices Byron R. White and Sandra Day O'Connor. Stevens, in a rare reading of his dissent, rebutted Brennan's earlier lengthy reading of his own opinion. If "the ideas of liberty and equality...are worth fighting for," Stevens said, then "it cannot be true that the flag that uniquely symbolizes their power is not itself worthy of protection from unnecessary desecraton."

Brennan's majority opinion extended protection to "expressive conduct" such as flag-burning as long as there was no danger of rioting or other breach of the peace. The ruling derived from a 1969 Supreme Court decision, *Brandenburg v. Ohio*, which said political speech was protected unless there was a clear danger of violence.

"The way to preserve the flag's special role is not to punish those who feel differently about these matters," Brennan said. "It is to persuade them that they are wrong."

In further demonstration of the emotion aroused by the issue on both sides, Chief Justice Rehnquist, in his turn, objected to the passage by Brennan as "a regrettable patronizing civics lesson."

The ruling evoked immediate reaction from the White House and in Congress. President George Bush called it "dead wrong."

## The Atlanta Journal
### THE ATLANTA CONSTITUTION
*Atlanta, GA, June 25, 1989*

Well, of course burning or otherwise desecrating the American flag "is wrong, dead wrong," as President Bush said in deploring the recent U.S. Supreme Court ruling. The court did not say otherwise, however. It did not welcome desecration. It only ruled that our Constitution's free-speech guarantee allows the surly, the sick and the silly to trash the flag if they insist.

The justices could hardly have done otherwise. (And it is worrisome that four would have.) The principle has long been established that "speech" in the Bill of Rights does not mean only literal speech but other forms of personal expression as well — symbolic speech, as the term goes. To hold differently would be to crimp the guarantee into a narrow literal-mindedness that would erode its protections, especially in an age when televised and other images are a large part of the nation's political and social semaphore.

For most of us, the flag is a potent symbol of what we love about this country. And it is precisely because the flag is so potent that dissidents can't properly be denied its misuse to make a point. (In the informal justice of such matters, however, the desecrations invariably repel rather than attract interest in the dissent; the abuses are self-indulgent and neatly self-defeating.)

The ruling surprised many, coming from a court that is now widely and correctly recognized as conservative. In fact, the furtherance of civil liberty is a profoundly conservative imperative, though it may be that this court was about lesser business. It begins to appear that the court's conservatism has a libertarian streak, of the sort that matches laissez-faire social policy to laissez-faire economics. The justices on Friday barred Congress from enacting an across-the-board ban on sexually explicit telephone services, the so-called dial-a-porn.

In both cases, the court gave the First Amendment its full due and left it up to individuals, not legislators, to make decisions about their own behavior. Where there is no potential harm to others, generally that is just the thing to do.

## THE PLAIN DEALER
*Cleveland, OH, June 23, 1989*

Americans' right to voice political dissent, even in ways that the majority of society finds abhorrent, is a cardinal feature of the Bill of Rights and must not be diminished by law. The First Amendment requires tolerance for even the most eccentric forms of free speech. The Supreme Court thus ruled correctly this week in a decision that upheld the right of free expression, even when it involves an act many citizens deplore: burning the American flag.

In a ruling that scrambled the court's usual voting patterns, a 5-4 majority struck down 48 states' laws against desecrating the flag. "If there is a bedrock principle underlying the First Amendment," the court ruled, "it is that the government may not prohibit the expression of an idea simply because society finds the idea itself offensive and disagreeable."

Remarkably, the majority included two justices—Antonin Scalia and Anthony Kennedy—whose votes usually reflect the rigid conservatism of Ronald Reagan, the man who appointed them; the most vigorous dissenter was John Paul Stevens, a Gerald Ford appointee who often votes as a liberal. If even Reaganite justices are willing to put the substance of the First Amendment above patriotic symbolism, then flag-waving traditionalists—like the architects of the flag-factory, pledge-of-allegiance 1988 Bush campaign—have no grounds to claim that activist liberals scheme to trample the national banner. As the votes of the two Reagan appointees showed, First Amendment absolutism is an eminently conservative position.

The sound reasoning of the majority opinion, written by Justice William Brennan, stands in sharp contrast to the emotionalism of Chief Justice William Rehnquist's dissent. Brennan wrote for the majority that "the flag's deservedly cherished place in our community will be strengthened, not weakened, by our ... reaffirmation of the principles of freedom and inclusiveness that the flag best reflects.... The way to preserve the flag's special role is not to punish those who feel differently about these matters. It is to persuade them that they are wrong."

Rather than offer a rebuttal based on constitutional law, Rehnquist's opinion was larded with popular odes to the flag: John Greenleaf Whittier's poem "Barbara Frietchie," Ralph Waldo Emerson's "Concord Hymn" and John Philip Souza's "The Stars and Stripes Forever." Moreover, Rehnquist's opinion voiced a presumptuous populism: "Surely one of the high purposes of a democratic society is to legislate against conduct that is regarded as ... profoundly offensive to the majority of people." Yet the court is the anti-majoritarian branch of government, acting as a brake on popular forces that may subvert the rule of law. If Rehnquist truly believes in a majoritarian judiciary, it will be interesting to see whether he sides with the popular majority in a ruling about to be announced: the Missouri case on abortion rights, in which the anti-choice Rehnquist—if he is to follow his own logic—would have to side with the pro-choice majority of Americans.

Understandably, those who revere the flag will be saddened by this week's ruling, but they should weigh the reasoning of the conservative Kennedy: "The hard fact is that sometimes we must make decisions we do not like. We make them because they are right—right in the sense that the law and the Constitution, as we see them, compel the result." The flag will remain an honored symbol of nationhood, but its symbolism must be seen as less vital than the values of the Constitution it represents.

## RAPID CITY JOURNAL

*Rapid City, SD, June 25, 1989*

Despite the public outrage and uproar over the Supreme Court's decision that burning the American flag cannot be outlawed, the Supreme Court decision was right.

The Supreme Court did not rule in favor of burning American flags. The majority opinion, as well as the dissenting opinions, made it absolutely clear that the justices individually find such actions reprehensible. In fact, treating our national emblem with such contempt is disgusting and highly offensive. But burning the flag was not the issue before the justices. The issue was whether such expressions could be outlawed under the Constitution.

The only possible answer is no.

The American flag is a meaningless symbol without our constitutional protections. Without free speech, freedom of religion, the right to keep and bear arms, the right to speedy and public trial, the right to assemble, etc., Old Glory has no glory. If the justices had ruled otherwise, the gunshots signaling the deaths of flag-burners in China eventually could echo in the streets of America.

The court's newest member, Justice Anthony M. Kennedy, said it well. "The hard fact is that sometimes we must make decisions we do not like. The case before us forces recognition of the costs to which (adherence to law and the Constitution) commit us. It is poignant but fundamental that the flag protects those who hold it in contempt."

When a person burns the American flag, he demonstrates that he does not hold the ideals of the United States of America in reverence. When he sets the match to the flag, he does so knowing how those of us who love our country will feel. Flag burners torch flags simply to get that reaction. To the burners, they are just brightly colored cloth. They cannot see the nation it symbolizes as do we who love that nation.

Justice William Brennan explained perfectly in his majority opinion: "The flag's deservedly cherished place will be strengthened not weakened by our holding today. ... We can imagine no more appropriate response to burning a flag than waving one's own, no better way to counter a flag-burner's message than by saluting the flag that burns.

"If there is a bedrock principle underlying the First Amendment, it is that the government may not prohibit the expression of an idea simply because society finds the idea itself offensive or disagreeable," Brennan said.

It was unfortunate that not one of South Dakota's three congressmen had the courage, wisdom and understanding to support the Supreme Court decision. They showed themselves politicians and not statesmen by their pandering to emotions, and not considering first the bedrock of the Constitution that protects us all. Unfortunately, these men fail to comprehend the meaning of the gunshots ringing across China. But when emotions subside and reflection takes over, most Americans will understand. Last week the Supreme Court stood up for the principles that brave men and women in China died for, and that millions of Americans have perished winning and preserving. If the justices had ruled otherwise last week, they would have ruled against the principles that the flag stands for.

Lose those principles, and we lose everything — including the meaning of our proud and noble flag. Those who despise it cannot diminish its glory by demeaning it. They lack the capacity to destroy its meaning, although they can revile and burn the banner. Only those of us who revere and love the emblem can diminish it by failing to live up to the high ideals it represents.

The Supreme Court did not fail those ideals, despite the personal feelings of those on the court. The difficult ruling was a national triumph, not a tragedy. The Supreme Court was spitting in the face of those who would spit on the flag.

The defilers didn't win. They lost.

We won.

Today the flag flies a little higher, shines a little brighter, proudly.

Free.

## THE INDIANAPOLIS STAR

*Indianapolis, IN, June 23, 1989*

Signs of the times that make patriotic blood boil: On the day that the Supreme Court ruled that desecrating the American flag is protected by the First Amendment, a man in Las Cruces, N.M., faced a 90-day jail sentence for flying the flag.

In Las Cruces, a man who flew a U.S. flag on a 40-foot pole at his home was prosecuted because a woman living next door said the flapping of the flag disturbed her. He said he would appeal.

The cases were not related, but they might as well have been. Old Glory is under the heaviest fire since Francis Scott Key wrote *The Star-Spangled Banner* during the War of 1812.

The Supreme Court affirmed a Texas Court of Appeals ruling of April 20, 1988, that the First Amendment guarantee of free speech protected the action of Gregory Lee Johnson, who burned a U.S. flag to protest Reagan administration policies, during the 1984 Republican National Convention at Dallas, while a crowd of 40 to 50 chanted, "America, the red, white and blue, spit on you."

Under Texas law, desecration of the U.S. or state flag is a crime. Johnson was convicted, fined $2,000 and sentenced to a year in prison. The appeals court overturned the conviction. Texas sought to reinstate it.

The Supreme Court voted 5-4. Conservative Justices Antonin Scalia and Anthony Kennedy joined Justices Thurgood Marshall, Harry A. Blackmun and William Brennan to affirm.

Brennan wrote the opinion, saying, "We do not consecrate the flag by punishing its desecration, for in doing so we dilute the freedom that this cherished emblem represents."

Chief Justice William Rehnquist and Justices Byron White, Sandra Day O'Connor and John Paul Stevens dissented, Rehnquist writing: "Surely one of the high purposes of a democratic society is to legislate against conduct that is regarded as evil and profoundly offensive to the majority of people — whether it be murder, embezzlement, pollution or flag-burning."

The court's ruling appears to nullify the laws of 48 states and a federal statute against flag desecration at peaceful protests. Only Wyoming and Alaska lack such laws. But it left open the possibility that flag-burning to incite a riot may be prosecutable as a crime.

That was wise. A great many Americans are strongly opposed to public burning of the flag, just as they would be to public burning of the Declaration of Independence and the Constitution. Even if such symbolic actions are, in the eyes of the law, words, to many they are fighting words, which can incite riots and other violence, and have done so often.

At present, the rights of protesters to destroy the symbols of American freedom are protected. Who will protect the rights of the millions who oppose destruction of the symbols of American freedom? Do they count for nothing in this supposedly enlightened age?

## Wisconsin State Journal
*Madison, WI, June 25, 1989*

*"If there is a bedrock principle underlying the First Amendment, it is that the government may not prohibit the expression of an idea simply because society finds the idea itself offensive or disagreeable."*
— **Supreme Court Justice William Brennan.**

That quote summarizes Brennan's majority opinion in the U.S. Supreme Court's 5-4 ruling that burning the American flag as a political protest is generally protected by the Constitution's free-speech guarantees. As much as it pains those who cherish Old Glory, and who would never willingly do anything to dishonor it, Brennan is correct.

The freedoms symbolized by the red, white and blue of the U.S. flag protect the very people who would burn it as a form of political protest. That's a hard lump to swallow for those who have seen the flag flown proudly from the mast of America's ships, waved defiantly from her battlements, or laid solemnly across her coffins.

But swallow we must, for the nation's 202-year-old symbol of democracy is cheapened if we forget the ideals it represents.

"We do not consecrate the flag by punishing its desecration, for in doing so we dilute the freedom that this cherished emblem represents," said Brennan, the most senior of the justices. Brennan, a liberal, was joined by four other judges — including two conservatives, Antonin Scalia and Anthony Kennedy.

The court's ruling does not say it's OK to burn flags, any time, any place. It does not condone flag burning that would incite a riot, and leaves untouched all state and local laws against breaches of the peace that outlaw incitement to riot.

The case before the court involved the burning of a flag at the Republican National Convention in Dallas in 1984, in which protesters chanted "America, the red, white and blue; We spit on you." As loathsome as those actions were, they were protected speech, and not punishable by the state of Texas.

Emblems cannot be held above liberty, or else those symbols stand for less than we dare hope.

Look back at Brennan's words and think not of flag burnings but of a Board of Regents proposal to outlaw certain types of objectionable speech on University of Wisconsin campuses. In principle, there isn't one whit of difference.

The UW rule would forbid uttering racial epithets at individuals, and allow the university ("the state") to punish those who do so. Again, the behavior in question is repugnant. But who judges what is an "epithet" and what is a legitimate expression of political or academic dissent? The UW's icon of sifting and winnowing is cheapened by such a rule, no matter how despicable the speech it seeks to police.

The way to punish flag-desecrators is to overwhelm them with honorable displays of the flag, and to live up to the ideals it represents. The same holds for those who would use racial slurs on college campuses. Educate them about why that's unacceptable in a multi-racial society, and reinforce the ideal by attacking the root causes of racism.

## THE INDIANAPOLIS STAR
*Indianapolis, IN, June 24, 1989*

The Supreme Court's ruling that burning the U.S. flag is a form of expression protected by the First Amendment shocked and dismayed the president, members of Congress, leaders of veterans' organizations, rank-and-file veterans and millions of other Americans.

Many asked why anyone would want to burn the American flag.

They got an answer Thursday when, outside the University of California at Berkeley, members of an outfit called the Revolutionary Communist Youth Brigade burned Old Glory and referred to it and the American Republic in profane language.

There are those among us who not only want to destroy the flag, which symbolizes our liberty, but would, if they could, destroy our liberty too.

## DAILY NEWS
*New York, NY, June 23, 1989*

THE DUMBEST THING ABOUT *Texas v. Johnson* is that it puts the U.S. Supreme Court in naked contempt of the overwhelming majority of Americans, expressing themselves through constitutionally sanctified legislatures.

The opinion overthrew Texas' criminal prohibition of "desecration of a venerated object." But it also cast onto the judicial junkheap a federal law — and the statutes of 47 other states. Only Wyoming and Alaska had *not* made it a crime to put Old Glory to the torch. Those windswept territories contain a total of 4,363,582 humans (but substantially more undomesticated animals). Almost, but not quite, 2% of the U.S. population.

The second dumbest thing: The decision was split as narrowly as possible, 5 to 4. To a lot of sound-minded people, that says this: "If the nine wisest heads in the Republic can't merge more closely than a hairsbreadth from deadlock, why not stay in bed and let the people speak?"

The third dumbest: That knife's-edge division was not based on any recognizable ideological, philosophical, geographic, historic, political or ethnic difference. Try as people will to brand the decision "liberal" or "left-wing," it isn't.

The majority included Justices Anthony M. Kennedy and Antonin Scalia — conservative to their bootstraps — and William J. Brennan Jr., Harry A. Blackmun and Thurgood Marshall, liberal to their earlobes. Dissenters: liberal John Paul Stevens and conservatives William H. Rehnquist, Sandra Day O'Connor and Byron R. White.

So now come tens of millions of befuddled Americans, bitterly wounded by the spectacle of their country licensing the foulest desecration of the most cherished of all their symbols. And what solace of authority can they find? None. So devoid of pattern are the majority and dissenting voices that the deciding force could as well have been a whim of weather on decision day, or an acid stomach, as anything else.

SO BURN THEIR ROBES — the physical symbol of the justices' presumed wisdom — along with the national banner that five of them cast down with ill-considered intrusiveness. But will their decision matter much? Yes, to those who find it difficult to stomach the anger that in many mature, reasoning people is a healthy reponse to the vision of their flag in flames. Finally, though, those Americans will rise above the dumbness of the court's chaotic act.

No sane, sober human will take any joy in the idea of desecrating the American flag. Still, does declaring such desecration a protected form of free expression constitute a grand threat to the Republic? Hardly.

Look, after all, at the brat-child whose pablum-throwing, highchair-banging tantrum brought the case to court. This nutbar — name of Gregory (Joey Boy) Johnson — babbles on about "repression" in the U.S. In between drooling and getting diaper changes, he claims to be a "Maoist." Just while genuine Maoists are gleefully massacring their own kids by the thousands for having picnics in their own town square. With that kind of enemy, sensitive Americans need worry less about mounting the defensive ramparts of the Republic than about toilet training.

But damn, it's annoying for the Supreme Court to set fire to its own robes and stand, dumb and naked, in pompous insensitivity to the most beloved symbol of the most benevolent form of government ever to appear on this Earth.

## St. Louis Review

*St. Louis, MO, June 30, 1989*

As our country celebrates Independence Day it is fitting that we consider certain freedoms guaranteed to us by our Constitution in light of recent Supreme Court decisions. These decisions challenge us to think carefully about our civic virtues as they also reopen many wounds inflicted on our society in recent history.

Does the freedom of speech guaranteed us in the First Amendment include the right to deface or burn our country's flag? Many veterans fought to defend our flag and our country in World War II, the Korean conflict as well as Vietnam. They and many others are rightly upset about the decision to permit such demonstration of disrespect and we share with their upset. Too many lives were lost and too many lives ruined in defense of the flag to ignore this challenge.

The Court's decision to allow courts to impose the death penalty on juvenile felons reflects our society's growing concern about juvenile crime. There are approximately 2,200 people currently awaiting execution in prisons around the country. Twenty-five of them are appealing their cases on the basis of their youthful age. We disagree with this decision because we disagree with the death penalty and extending it to younger people is not going to make any significant difference in public attitudes towards crime. There are just too many who escape justice these days to make the death penalty look like anything but arbitrary justice.

Those concerned with recent decisions regarding civil rights and affirmative action programs are rightly expressing disappointment and concern about a rollback of civil rights in this country. In so many ways we have grown beyond the 1950s. Victories won by black people must be preserved. As other minority groups such as Hispanics, Asians and East Europeans become a larger percentage of the American population, they will likewise expect and need special consideration to enable their full participation in American life.

While increasing numbers of immigrants are coming into this country it is good for us to remember that it is estimated that up to 15 million displaced people are currently wandering the globe searching for a new land. People from Afghanistan and mainland China are two of the most recent groups seeking asylum for whatever reason. Whether we agree or disagree with one another on the Supreme Court decisions, it is good to realize that this is what makes life in United States so precious at this time. Our constitutional guarantees on so many issues were hard won. They must also be preserved and guarded by all of us.

## FORT WORTH STAR-TELEGRAM
*Fort Worth, TX, June 28, 1989*

In their momentary passion to shield the flag of the United States from the repertoire of political expression in this country, the earnest and well-intentioned patriots who seek such hallowed consecration through constitutional amendment instead would reduce the banner to an unapproachable icon, a totem, embued with a greater sanctity than the difficult yet enduring principles that it represents.

No true patriot can help but recoil in anger and disdain for desecrations of the flag committed by those who demonstrate contempt and hatred for this country and all that it stands for.

Yet, if we are to take the Constitution at its word and in the fullness of its spirit, this nation stands for nothing if it does not stand for freedom, especially in matters of individual conscience. The Constitution protects the right to be wrong; it preserves the freedom for bitterly dissenting opinions to wage intellectual warfare unfettered by the dictates, coercion or proscriptions of the government.

That, after all, was the first principle on which the Founding Fathers ordained and established this nation and committed it to the continuing struggle for ordered liberty.

We who are approaching the 21st century should not lose sight of the fact that the original Constitution was ratified on the condition that the Bill of Rights be included — those 10 amendments that secured individual rights. Erecting a structure of government was not sufficient; protection of the civil rights of each individual was a *sine qua non* to the democratic republic they were creating. Those precious liberties could not be conditional upon the imprimatur of the government.

This country derives its strength from the strenuous, often petulant, diversity of opinions that animate the shared expectations and aspirations of a free people. Our flag is a beautiful symbol of the highest principles and values to which this nation aspires, and no act of desecration, no matter how offensive, can diminish those principles and values — unless the people have lost their faith in them.

The furor surrounding the Supreme Court's ruling that such repugnant expressive conduct as flag-burning is protected as political speech has opened to the country the opportunity to reflect on the proposition that America's commitment to freedom is more durable than the celebration of its symbols.

Despite the passions of the present moment, such freedom is the indispensable blessing that we must protect for ourselves and convey to our posterity.

## The Dallas Morning News
*Dallas, TX, June 23, 1989*

What occurred in front of the Dallas City Hall one day during the 1984 Republican Convention should have disgusted any American who holds this country dear. With 100 demonstrators looking on, Gregory Lee Johnson, a member of the Revolutionary Communist Youth Brigade, unfurled an American flag, doused it with kerosene and set it on fire.

Old Glory burned as any piece of cloth would, but to think of the flag in those emotionless terms would be much like thinking of a human being as little more than a container of chemicals. No, the flag is not just a piece of cloth. It is the most powerful symbol we have of our nationhood and of all the principles that make us Americans.

Old Glory has been with us since our founding. At the dawn of the American Revolution, it served to unify the 13 colonies. Later, as the young nation matured, it helped win worldwide recognition of our sovereignty. During our lifetime, Old Glory has fluttered over many foreign battlefields as thousands of our brave countrymen have died for the American cause.

Why then, many Americans ask, has the U.S. Supreme Court decided that what Gregory Johnson did was legal? Justice Anthony Kennedy probably best explained the court's thinking: "The hard fact is that sometimes we must make decisions we do not like. We make them because they are right, right in the sense that the law and the Constitution, as we see them, compel the result."

A majority of the justices — an unusual alignment of the court's most conservative members and its most liberal — justified the decision by saying, "If there is a bedrock principle underlying the First Amendment, it is that the government may not prohibit the expression of an idea simply because society finds the idea itself offensive or disagreeable."

It is difficult to dispute the justices' argument. When Americans pay respect to the flag, and fight for it, they also are paying homage to, and defending, the fundamental principles it represents, one of which is the freedom of expression. As Justice Kennedy noted, it is one of our nation's great ironies that the flag protects those who hold it in contempt.

What Gregory Lee Johnson did may be legal, but it still is despicable. And while five justices may have reaffirmed the man's right to engage in such extreme protest, that should not be taken to mean they were encouraging others to do so. To the contrary, the court said, the best way Americans could counter a flag-burner's message would be to salute Old Glory themselves.

## THE SUN
*Baltimore, MD, June 23, 1989*

Justice John Paul Stevens, whose very name evokes America's patriotic heritage, and who is himself a decorated Navy veteran of World War II, said this in his dissent to Wednesday's Supreme Court decision overturning laws against burning the U.S. flag: "The ideas of liberty and equality [were] an irresistible force in motivating . . . the Philippine Scouts who fought at Bataan and the soldiers who scaled the bluffs at Omaha Beach. If those ideas are worth fighting for — and our history demonstrates that they are — it cannot be true that the flag that uniquely symbolizes their power is not itself worthy of protection from unnecessary desecration."

We agree with Justice Stevens more often than not, but in this case we believe he is absolutely wrong. One idea worth fighting for, for which Americans have died over the centuries and all over the globe, is the right *not* to respect their national symbols. A World War II cliche was that men fought for "the right to boo the Dodgers." In fact, it was more for the right to boo the government and even the nation itself, whose history, organic documents and institutions are imbued with the confidence to guarantee that right.

The reaction to the decision has been surprise and outrage. But how could the court have ruled otherwise? The decision should have been unanimous, not 5-4. For as Justice William Brennan said for the majority of the court: "If there is a bedrock principle underlying the First Amendment, it is that the government may not prohibit the expression of an idea simply because society finds the idea itself offensive or disagreeable."

Once you start letting government outlaw the expression of ideas by such symbolism as desecrating the flag, there is no telling where you end up. As Justice Brennan also said, "Could the government, on this theory, prohibit the burning of state flags? Of copies of the Presidential seal? Of the Constitution?" That may sound unfeeling and legalistic to many who are disgusted by flag burners and the apparent condoning of flag-burning. They should contemplate these further words of Justice Brennan: "The flag's deservedly cherished place will be strengthened not weakened by our holding today... We can imagine no more appropriate response to burning a flag than waving one's own, no better way to counter a flag-burner's message than by saluting the flag that burns."

The pledge of allegiance to the flag speaks of it as a symbol of a republic in which there is "liberty and justice for all." As the news from Tiananmen Square reminds us, there are millions of men and women today who are willing to risk their lives for even a semblance of the freedom that that phrase suggests. This nation's ability and willingness (however provoked, however reluctant) to tolerate its citizens who hate, mock or defy it are the envy and the hope of the world.

## THE ARIZONA REPUBLIC
*Phoenix, AZ, June 23, 1989*

IN this week's 5-4 decision affirming the "precious right" to burn the flag of the United States, haul garbage in it or otherwise treat it with contempt, the U.S. Supreme Court relied heavily on the need to protect the thought we hate. But in so doing it went to extremes, appearing to hold that any behavior, however outrageous, is legitimate, provided it can be roped into a political context.

This is not a view of the First Amendment that is universally held. And while Justice Brennan's majority opinion was compelling — more so, in fact, than Chief Justice Rehnquist's dissent, with its quaint allusions to Barbara Frietchie and the Concord Bridge — it also reflected an absolutist view and consequently lacked moderation.

The facts of the case were simple enough. In defiance of a Texas law prohibiting desecration of the American flag, Gregory Lee Johnson and a group of demonstrators doused a flag with kerosene and set it on fire, chanting, "America, the red, white, and blue, we spit on you," as the flag burned.

The Texas law, said the court, was unconstitutional because, under the First Amendment, "the government may not prohibit the expression of an idea simply because society finds the idea itself offensive or disagreeable." Only if the flag-burning incident had created the danger of civil disorder — "imminent lawless acts," in the court's words — would the Constitution have allowed Mr. Johnson to be prosecuted, said the court.

It takes no legal scholar to see the fallacies here. Mr. Johnson and his colleagues were plainly at liberty to express whatever offensive or disagreeable ideas they wished, and in fact did so. Moreover, the court exhibits a strange set of values. Free expression may be curtailed to prevent a fist-fight, but not to protect a cherished national symbol that, in the words of Justice Kennedy's oddly concurring opinion, "holds a lonely place of honor in an age when absolutes are distrusted and simple truths are burdened by unneeded apologetics."

The sanctity of noxious political ideas is incontestable. To protect them was precisely, almost exclusively, the intent of those who incorporated free speech into the First Amendment. But laws protecting the flag against insult — laws adopted by 47 out of 50 states — in no way impede political discourse. Nothing could make this plainer than the circumstances of this Texas case, in which the protesters voiced their political discontents with impunity even as they burned the flag.

Some wise words of Judge Learned Hand come to mind. "I often wonder," he said, "whether we do not rest our hopes too much upon constitutions, upon laws and upon courts. These are false hopes; believe me, these are false hopes." A more moderate opinion from a more reliable court would simultaneously have protected the flag and Mr. Johnson's rights of free speech.

## The Pittsburgh PRESS
*Pittsburgh, PA, June 23, 1989*

The burning or desecrating of this country's flag inevitably stirs feelings of anger and even outrage in most Americans. That's perfectly understandable.

But no matter. Such acts, at least when they occur as political protest, are a constitutionally protected form of expression, the U.S. Supreme Court ruled this week in a landmark First Amendment case.

It was the right decision, in our view, however unpopular it may be.

The decision wasn't an easy one for the high court and the 5-to-4 vote showed the profound legal and philosophical differences among its members. For a change, there were no clear-cut liberal and conservative alliances.

Justices Antonin Scalia and Anthony M. Kennedy, two of President Reagan's appointees who are regarded as conservatives, sided with the majority. Justice John Paul Stevens, often found in the liberal camp, wrote a strong dissent and, in an unusual move, read it from the bench.

Justice William Brennan Jr. similarly had read parts of his controlling opinion in open court. Strong feelings, all around.

The case involved a flag-burning protest incident at the Republican National Convention in Dallas in 1984. The man who set the flag afire, Gregory L. Johnson, was convicted of violating the Texas flag-desecration law, fined $2,000 and sentenced to a year in jail.

All but two states have similar laws. So does the federal government. All such restrictions apparently have been voided by the high court's decision (even if flag abuse as a clear-cut act of vandalism might still be banned, Justice Brennan noted).

No doubt the ruling disturbs many Americans, who see the flag as a cherished and venerable symbol, not to be insulted or violated.

Yet the freedoms which it represents, as Justice Brennan wrote, are not enhanced by punishing those who don't share respectful sentiments. He also said:

"If there is a bedrock principle underlying the First Amendment, it is that the government may not prohibit the expression of an idea simply because society finds the idea itself offensive or disagreeable."

That's the underpinning of the constitutional guarantee of freedom of speech, that the unpopular, the oddball, even outrageous expressions must be tolerated and protected against governmental proscriptions.

"The hard fact is that sometimes we must make decisions we do not like," Justice Kennedy aptly pointed out. "We make them because they are right, right in the sense that the law and the Constitution, as we see them, compel the result."

As now has occurred in the flag-burning case.

## Lincoln Journal
*Lincoln, NE, June 22, 1989*

Man does not live by bread alone. Neither does a tribe or a nation or even a culture exist without transcending symbols.

If we want to be thoroughly candid, the uncomfortable truth is that the dollar sign is this country's single most unifying and important abstract symbol. That having been said, the national flag stands as the supremely mystical symbol of what this society is supposed to be about. For it — and this cannot be historically denied — people have died. What also is a fact is that the flag, from early on, has been execrably discredited and abused. It has appeared as a talisman to sell virtually every kind of market product, no matter how tawdry. It has been appropriated and brutalized by government authorities. It always has been a cynical refuge for scoundrels.

Now the U.S. Supreme Court, dividing 5-4 and with the majority including President Reagan's last two appointees, says a state cannot declare the political protest act of flag burning a criminal transgression.

The Journal respectfully disagrees — and is just as agonized in reaching that conclusion as the five Supreme Court members who prevailed Wednesday. For those with a commitment to First Amendment values, this is the closest of calls.

Of course Justice Anthony Kennedy is correct writing "it is poignant but fundamental that the flag protects those who hold it in contempt." That is one of the glories of this land. Tolerating the expression of views which are hateful is as basic as it is foreign to much of the rest of the world. For the freshest example of that, see China, where both people and symbols are crushed. Justice John Paul Stevens best captured the belief here in his passionate dissent:

A country's flag is a symbol of more than nationhood and national unity. It also signifies the ideas that characterize the society that has chosen that emblem as well as the special history that has animated the growth and power of those ideas.

It is a symbol of freedom, of equal opportunity, of religious tolerance and of goodwill for other peoples who share our aspirations. The symbol carries its message to dissidents both at home and abroad who may have no interest at all in our national unity or survival.

The value of the flag as a symbol cannot be measured. Conceivably that value will be enhanced by the court's conclusion that our national commitment to free expression is so strong that even the United States as ultimate guarantor of that freedom is without power to prohibit the desecration of its unique symbol. But I am unpersuaded.

The creation of a federal right to post bulletin boards and graffiti on the Washington Monument might enlarge the market for free expression, but at a cost I would not pay. Similarly, in my considered judgment, sanctioning the public desecration of the flag will tarnish its value — both for those who cherish the ideas for which it waves and for those who desire to don the robes of martyrdom by burning it.

# The Union Leader
*Manchester, NH, June 29, 1989*

The U.S. flag is important and we have nothing but contempt for those who say otherwise. Without our national pride, our dedication to this blessed country and all it stands for, we cannot survive, for the greatest danger to the United States comes from within, not from without. It is the apathy of a lazy, sated public that would rather beef about what is wrong than be responsible citizens trying to make things right. This is not what government by the people is all about.

There are those who say that compared with today's problems it is not important that some misguided protester burned the flag a couple of years ago. Of course it's important. There is nothing more important.

Unbelievably, our own Sen. Gordon Humphrey, of all people, is among those who make this "unimportant" argument. By some aberration, he has joined Ted Kennedy and Howard Metzenbaum as the three in the Senate who voted not to condemn the Supreme Court's decision.

The reaction of patriotic Americans is not "a bit of overkill," as Sen. Humphrey would have us believe. If we have just the "two or three" instances a year of desecration of the flag, as Humphrey says, that is two or three too many.

What is overkill is the fact that a decision by a single member of the court changes a 4-5 vote to a 5-4 vote and determines the law of the land in such a way that flag burning becomes no more than self-expression.

What is important is that the very people who enjoy our blessings of liberty could, by doing nothing about this outrageous decision, abandon our flag and the nation for which it stands.

# The Seattle Times
*Seattle, WA, June 23, 1989*

THE U.S. Supreme Court boldly endorsed free speech as it declared this week that burning an American flag was a protected form of political protest.

As galling as the 5-4 ruling will be for most Americans, the court decision was a courageous affirmation of liberty, a triumph of substance over a symbol.

The case involved a man who set fire to a flag outside the 1984 Republican National Convention in Dallas. A crowd chanted, "America, the red, white, and blue, we spit on you," as Gregory Johnson put a flame to the Stars and Stripes.

By every measure, the court majority spat right back in the crowd's face with its ruling to side with free speech. The message was plain that some Texas pissant with a lighter was not going to put a flame to principles that had withstood armed aggression.

Americans have fought and died to protect the right to disagree with their government. Blood was not shed or lives given for a symbol but for the rights behind the flag.

Johnson is a confused soul caught up in a radical pantomime. He says he is not an American but "a proletarian internationalist, a Maoist," and a member of the Revolutionary Communist Youth Brigade.

How would those cliched allegiances translate in Tiananmen Square? Would Johnson have been with the soldiers firing on unarmed protesters, or dying with the proletarian internationalists being run over by tanks?

Johnson obviously picked the safest turf for Maoist gibberish and pyrotechnic political expression.

The same day on which a majority of justices affirmed Johnson's right to burn a flag, some other followers of Mao ordered the deaths of 27 students and workers who cried out for democracy.

Sadly, this will be lost on Johnson, but such myopic heretics rightfully put democratic rhetoric to the test. They force us to re-examine values and, it is to be hoped, to stand behind them. As Justice Brennan wrote for a majority on the court that embraced Johnson's odious challenge:

"If there is a bedrock principle underlying the First Amendment, it is that the government may not prohibit the expression of an idea simply because society finds the idea itself offensive or disagreeable."

## Omaha World-Herald
*Omaha, NE, June 26, 1989*

Some of the defenders of the U.S. Supreme Court's ruling on flag-burning have suggested that the ruling makes America a better, freer or more reasonable nation. To judge from the reaction of the public and its representatives in Congress, a lot of Americans are having trouble swallowing that idea.

Understandably so. Consider some of the statements made in defense of the ruling:

— Justice William Brennan, the author of the opinion that struck down a flag-desecration law in a Texas case, said that to punish those who desecrate the flag is to "dilute the freedom that this cherished emblem represents."

— Syndicated columnist Otis Pike said the five justices who approved the decision "joined to keep our minds masters of our passions."

— Columnist Jeff Greenfield wrote: "The fact that our system permits the desecration of the symbol of our land is one reason why that symbol is to be treasured."

Some of those statements could have been written by George Orwell.

The idea seems to be that carrying a right or privilege to extremes makes it more meaningful. The sacred constitutional guarantee of freedom of speech, by the perverse way of thinking that applauds the flag-burning decision, becomes more sacred each time the courts discover another kind of behavior that can be reclassified as "speech" and crammed under the constitutional umbrella.

Now flag-burning is under the umbrella and Americans are being asked to believe that the decision demonstrates high regard for the flag, a triumph of reason over emotion and the dawn of a higher state of freedom after decades of something less.

It's no wonder that a lot of people are dismayed by the ruling. The explanations and defenses make it no more palatable than it seemed when announced.

To protect the flag is not to place unreasonable limitations on free speech. Political debate is not thereby stifled. The right to speak out on the issues — and to use the many other symbolic ways that have been developed to attract attention and make a point — is in no significant way abridged.

A nation must stand for something. To reserve one symbol for special status is a demonstration of the bonds that hold the people together and the self-respect that they have as a nation. A nation that looks on powerlessly as its flag is burned and spat upon has, in the moral sense, disarmed itself unilaterally.

## The Wichita Eagle-Beacon
*Wichita, KS, June 23, 1989*

I am the American Flag. Like the country that grew up around me, I was born in controversy. No one knows for certain what my origins were, though the legends are many. It is appropriate, for I am a legendary symbol. No other banner in the world's recent history has symbolized the virtues of the human race as I have. The swastika of Nazi Germany, the rising sun of wartime Japan, the hammer-and-sickle of the communist world — all elicit hatred, dread or, in the case of the last-named, pity for the inhabitants struggling under the rule it represents. I elicit universal admiration for the principles of liberty and justice — and a burning desire to emulate the country I represent.

I was at Fort McHenry when America's national anthem was conceived "by the dawn's early light." I was at Bull Run and Gettysburg and Pea Ridge and Shiloh — and I adorned the memorial photos of the "Great Emancipator," Abraham Lincoln. I was carried into battle at Belleau Wood and the Argonne Forest in one world war, and at Normandy, Sicily and Iwo Jima in another. I was at Heartbreak Ridge in Korea and the Mekong Delta in Vietnam — and I covered the caskets of tens of thousands of American fighting men. I was handed to their widows or their parents when the funeral services were over.

I was at Montgomery, too, and Birmingham and Selma and Memphis, when another great war was fought — this one against racism and bigotry and injustice in its every form. And I covered the casket of Dr. Martin Luther King Jr. when he was brought home to the "red hills of Georgia" for the last time.

More recently, the oppressed peoples of China, the Soviet bloc, Panama, Cuba and Nicaragua have looked to my country for inspiration and support, and I have been the symbol of freedom for millions. The pro-democracy protesters of Tiananmen Square didn't erect a hammer-and-sickle to express their fondest dreams, but the Goddess of Democracy — patterned after my sister symbol of freedom, the Statue of Liberty.

Because I am the symbol of freedom that I am, I represent freedom even for those who hold me in contempt. When the U.S. Supreme Court held this week that I could be defiled, even burned, as an expression of political views, the decision brought great sadness to many. As Justice William Brennan wrote for the court majority, however, "We do not consecrate the flag by punishing its desecration, for in doing so we dilute the freedom that this cherished emblem represents."

I am bigger than any who would dishonor me, though. I am the symbol of freedom and the hope of millions around the world. I am the banner of justice and equality and of the quest for a better life that have motivated those who have looked to me for more than 200 years. I am the symbol of America. I am the badge of human freedom. I am the Flag.

*(With apologies to the author of an earlier version of "I am the Flag.")*

## The Star-Ledger
*Newark, NJ, June 23, 1989*

From the beginning, it was considered patriotic to regard the American flag with reverence. That holds true today, having survived periods marked by the social progress of an enlightened civil rights movement and a darker passage of rites to the political turbulence that erupted on U.S. college campuses in the 1960s.

While it remains appropriate to exhort Americans to rally round the flag, it has now been decreed by the highest court in the land that state laws cannot prohibit the burning of the flag as an expression of political protest.

In a narrow 5-4 decision that is certain to stand as a landmark First Amendment interpretation, the Supreme Court found the flag desecration laws in 48 states and a similar federal statute constitutionally flawed in instances of peaceful political dissent.

The ruling was marked by a significant crossover in the court's usual ideological composition. Two of the court's most conservative justices—Antonin Scalia and Anthony Kennedy—joined liberal Justices William Brennan and Thurgood Marshall and moderate Harry Blackmun in the majority opinion.

The appeal evolved from a violation of the Texas flag desecration law. As a protest against the 1984 Republican National Convention in Dallas, a demonstrator doused an American flag with kerosene and burned it. The case was taken before the Supreme Court after the conviction was overturned by a Texas appellate court on constitutional grounds.

The sharply differing stands among the justices were evident in the emotional majority and dissenting opinions. Writing for the majority, Justice Brennan said, "We do not consecrate the flag by punishing its desecration, for in doing so we dilute the freedom this cherished emblem represents."

In his dissent, Chief Justice William Rehnquist alluded to the broadly based legislative bans on flag-burning. The intent of these proscriptions, he held, was consistent with "one of the high purposes of a democratic society to legislate against conduct that is regarded as evil and profoundly offensive to the majority of people."

But in a democratic society, the rights of free expression and political dissent have a fundamental constitutional primacy; they should not be diminished, even in such regrettable instances where extreme protests are patently offensive to most Americans. The litmus test of democratic institutions is their resilience in reaffirming the principles of freedom that the flag symbolizes.

## Houston Chronicle
*Houston, TX, June 22, 1989*

The U.S. Supreme Court says there is a First Amendment right to burn the American flag as a form of expression.

We want to use our First Amendment right to express the opinion that even if burning the American flag is legal, it is contemptible.

Justice William Brennan wrote: "If there is a bedrock principle underlying the First Amendment, it is that government may not prohibit the expression of an idea simply because society finds the idea itself offensive or disagreeable."

Free speech must be protected. But defiling the flag that so many died to defend is more than offensive and disagreeable. It is beyond contempt, and society retains the right to say so in the strongest of terms.

## Chicago Tribune
*Chicago, IL, June 23, 1989*

The foundation of the American Constitution, wrote Oliver Wendell Holmes Jr., is "free thought—not free thought for those who agree with us but freedom for the thought we hate." Rarely has the Supreme Court endorsed that view more emphatically than in Wednesday's decision overturning the conviction of a man for burning an American flag.

The verdict will not be popular, but it is the only one worthy of the ideals the flag represents.

The 1st Amendment to the Constitution guarantees freedom of speech. The court and legal scholars have long acknowledged that speech includes not only spoken words but also "symbolic" speech such as pictures, artistic performances, emblems and the like.

Few symbols are more potent than Old Glory. Americans stand respectfully when it ascends, fly it from their front porches on patriotic holidays, lower it to half-staff at times of national tragedy, shroud their veterans' caskets in it. Enemies of what this nation stands for burn it or stamp on it to dramatize their contempt.

One of those is Gregory Lee Johnson, convicted of torching a flag at a 1984 protest at the Republican National Convention in Dallas. But the Supreme Court said the statute he violated is unconstitutional because it attempts to suppress unpopular opinions, in defiance of the 1st Amendment.

The lawyers defending the law argued the need to preserve the flag as a symbol of the nation. Justice William Brennan, writing for the majority, pointed out that the special protection could hardly stop there: "Could the government, on this theory, prohibit the burning of state flags? Of copies of the presidential seal? Of the Constitution?"

The flag ought to be treated as a symbol, not an idol. If the ideals it embodies may be abused, the flag itself can't be made inviolable. The point should not be lost on the Illinois General Assembly, which is considering a bill to punish those people, like the notorious student at the School of the Art Institute of Chicago, who deliberately place the flag on the floor. Like the Texas law at issue here, that bill runs afoul of the Constitution.

Chief Justice William Rehnquist, in his dissent, found the court's decision at odds with the American system of government. "Surely one of the high purposes of a democratic society is to legislate against conduct that is regarded as evil and profoundly offensive to the majority of people—whether it be murder, embezzlement, pollution or flag burning," he wrote.

But the chief justice misses the point of the Bill of Rights, which is precisely to deny the majority the right to legislate on certain matters. The government can forbid murder and punish pollution because the Constitution gives it broad latitude to protect citizens against each other. It can't ban flag burning for the same reason it can't censor books, imprison criminal suspects without a trial, or search homes on a whim: The Constitution limits its power.

Some observers were surprised at the unusual coalition of justices voting to strike down the law, which included the court's most liberal members (William Brennan, Thurgood Marshall, Harry Blackmun) and two staunch conservatives appointed by Ronald Reagan (Antonin Scalia and Anthony Kennedy). Despite their seemingly opposite ideologies, these justices share a deep respect for the limits the Constitution imposes on majority rule.

"We do not consecrate the flag by punishing its desecration," wrote Justice Brennan, "for in doing so we dilute the freedom that this cherished emblem represents." The sometimes bitter paradox of a free society is that freedom extends to those who revile it. The highest tribute we can make to Old Glory is the faithful observance of our highest ideals. By upholding freedom, the court honored the flag.

## MILWAUKEE SENTINEL
*Milwaukee, WI, June 23, 1989*

Although it probably sent Francis Scott Key spinning in his grave, the US Supreme Court Wednesday was correct in its ruling that the willful burning of an American flag was protected as a political statement under the right of free expression granted by the First Amendment to the US Constitution.

That does not make less reprehensible the action taken by Gregory (Joey) Johnson, who was convicted of violating a Texas law after setting fire to a flag to protest the Republican National Convention in Dallas in 1984.

This was no prank on the part of the New York City native and member of something called the Revolutionary Communist Youth Brigade who doesn't consider himself an American.

Rather, it was clearly a renunciation of the government for which the flag he desecrated is a symbol. And it is unfortunate that he could not be sentenced to the fate of Philip Nolan, the fictional Army officer who got his wish of never wanting to see the United States again by being sentenced to spend his life in isolation aboard a ship at sea.

First Amendment advocates will be heartened by the fact that two conservative justices, Antonin Scalia and Anthony M. Kennedy, supported the five-member majority opinion written by veteran Justice William J. Brennan, which said that outlawing desecration of the flag would only "dilute the freedom that this cherished emblem represents."

If nothing else, this case will teach plaintiffs not to take the court for granted on the basis of ideological stereotypes.

In retrospect, local authorities in Dallas might have done their duty adequately had they treated Johnson with the dignity he deserved by arresting him for disorderly conduct and treating him to a free night's lodging in the county jail.

Those of us who have fought for Old Glory and protected the rights of the First Amendment over the years obviously don't see this as a joyous victory in any sense but as a matter of "bedrock principle," as Justice Brennan put it.

In any case, both the flag and the Constitution have been dragged through the mud before without any damage to the moral fabric of the nation. Their made-in-America quality assures that they will survive this controversy, too.

## The Hutchinson News
*Hutchinson, KS, June 23, 1989*

The U.S. Supreme Court has joined the "If it feels good, do it" crowd.

With a 5-4 vote Wednesday, the court ruled that you can burn the American flag at will, because you'd only be showing some of your First Amendment-guaranteed rights of "expressive conduct."

That is legal twaddle.

The court's idea that any nauseating action can be excused as an expression of opinion is a distortion of civilization and a capitulation to the mindless selfishness displayed by a Me generation.

Would the U.S. Supreme Court accept as constitutionally protected "expressive conduct" some kook's defacing of the Statue of Liberty because he didn't like to pay income taxes?

Would the U.S. Supreme Court accept as constitutionally protected "expressive conduct" the actions of some nut who took a pick ax to the Supreme Court building and chipped off the corners of the columns because he didn't like what the court thinks about abortion?

Based on this week's ruling, the U.S. Supreme Court might.

For once, Chief Justice William Rehnquist was right in his dissent. He was on the losing side, but argued correctly, that flag burning "is the equivalent of an inarticulate grunt or roar that, it seems fair to say, is most likely to be indulged in not to express any particular idea, but to antagonize others. Surely one of the high purposes of a democratic society is to legislate against conduct that is regarded as evil and profoundly offensive to a majority of people."

An amendment to the Constitution would appear to be the only possible way to fix the nauseating flag-burning decision. An amendment should be adopted promptly.

An amendment also might persuade the court not to allow other outrageous or destructive actions to be viewed as mere "expressive conduct."

## The Philadelphia Inquirer
*Philadelphia, PA, June 23, 1989*

Say you come upon a flag-burner at an antiwar rally. You flush with anger. Maybe your father stormed the beaches of Normandy beneath Old Glory, the same proud banner you've saluted on the wall of your elementary school or passing in the July Fourth parade or draping the casket of a Vietnam veteran.

What to do, this being a free country? Nine Supreme Court justices sorted through their own angers and confusion for an answer. And this week, splitting 5-4, they delivered it: Even if burning the flag seems outrageous, it is nonetheless legal. In so ruling, they struck down laws in 48 states that make flag-burning a crime.

If the burning is "expressive conduct," the court's majority said, then the Constitution's free-speech provisions protect it. Instead of punishing flag-burners, the court told lawmakers, "persuade them they are wrong."

How so? "We can imagine no more appropriate response to burning a flag than to wave one's own; no better way to counter a flag-burner's message than by saluting the flag that burns...." And so forth.

Chief Justice William H. Rehnquist, in dissent, found the whole exercise smacked of a "regrettably patronizing civics lesson."

Indeed, maybe the court needn't have spelled out correct decorum for a flag-burning. But the suggested responses beat Mr. Rehnquist's remedy, which would allow anti-flag-burning laws as an expression of the majority's desire to outlaw conduct it sees as "evil and profoundly offensive." Isn't that what democracy is about, he argues?

But flag-burning to protest government policies is not the same as murder, embezzlement or pollution, the other activities the chief justice cites as evil and offensive and thus criminalized by popular demand. Those crimes actively deny other citizens their rights. Burning the flag doesn't.

What Mr. Rehnquist forgets in his majoritarian paean is the stuff about individual rights, the things that make America vital, zesty and often messy and contentious. No dogma or symbol is sacred, at least under the law. In America, as Justice Wiliam J. Brennan reminds in his opinion, everything, including the flag itself, is fair game in the marketplace of ideas.

It's not easy being free, watching symbols you may hold dear go up in smoke. But poignant as it seems, conservative Justice Anthony M. Kennedy wrote in eloquent and courageous support of the liberal Mr. Brennan, it remains "fundamental that the flag protects those who hold it in contempt."

Long may it wave, over the land of the free and the home of the brave.

## The Providence Journal
*Providence, RI, June 23, 1989*

On Wednesday, the U.S. Supreme Court handed down what is certain to be one of its most controversial rulings when it declared unconstitutional any laws which prohibit political demonstrators from burning, or otherwise desecrating, the American flag.

The issue is entangled in a complex web of legal and historical factors, as was amply demonstrated by the court's own handling of the matter: The narrowness of the 5-4 decision; the unusual disruption of the customary liberal-conservative split among the justices; and the extraordinary passion behind the written and oral presentations of both the majority and minority viewpoints.

The specific case at hand, *Texas v. Johnson*, involved a demonstration at the 1984 Republican National Convention in Dallas, when Gregory Johnson exhibited his opposition to the GOP and its policies by dousing a flag with kerosene and setting it aflame (as his fellow protesters chanted, "America, the red, white and blue/We spit on you").

Mr. Johnson was convicted under a Texas statute prohibiting such intentional desecration of the flag — although not, of course, barring the accompanying chants, ugly as they may have been. The federal government and 48 of the 50 states, including Rhode Island, have similar legislation on the books. Now these laws are null and void, except as they apply to cases where the desecration threatens to lead to serious injury or acts of violence.

In his majority opinion, Justice Brennan declared that Mr. Johnson had been prosecuted "for his expression of dissatisfaction with the policies of this country," and that, he declared, was a violation of the First Amendment's free speech protections.

We confess we find this to be a dubious and unconvincing argument. As Chief Justice Rehnquist noted in his dissenting opinion, nobody was seeking to block Mr. Johnson's freedom of speech. The flag desecration statute "left him with a full panoply of other symbols and every conceivable form of verbal expression" with which to articulate and express his views.

In any event, the court has ruled, and its decision stands — at least, for the time being. Conceivably a future court, with a more realistic view of the issues involved, will reverse Wednesday's narrow majority.

Meanwhile, it is only fair to acknowledge that while Justice Brennan's opinion may have been wrongheaded in its constitutional interpretation, nevertheless it was animated by his own deep sense of patriotism and respect for the flag. Along these lines, he expressed a sentiment which all Americans may wish to bear in mind: "We can imagine no more appropriate response to burning a flag than waving one's own."

## The Chattanooga Times
*Chattanooga, TN, June 27, 1989*

Few cases can provide such a test of personal ideology and interpretation of constitutional principles as the United States Supreme Court found in the flag-burning case decided Wednesday. In a case involving a man who burned the flag in a political protest at the 1984 Republican national convention in Texas, the court had to determine whether the nation has any supreme symbol worth protecting from desecration, or whether the First Amendment right to free speech reigns in the most offensive circumstance.

Ultimately, in a necessary ruling sure to evoke both outrage and appreciation, the court protected the most odious political protest and gave new landmark weight to the First Amendment. Still, no one who reads the court's opinion can fail to appreciate the whole court's love of the flag, the predicament the case presented, and the eloquence on both sides of this difficult issue.

The 5-4 ruling cut across ideological lines, joining two stauch conservatives, Reagan appointees Antonin Scalia and Anthony M. Kennedy, in the majority. And a traditional liberal, John Paul Stevens, joined the dissent. Not surprisingly, both sides articulated arguments that hardly anyone could fault.

There was no dispute as to whether use of the flag as a communicative vehicle constituted the sort of expression traditionally contested on freedom of speech turf. Rather, the court's conflict was over whether any limit should be imposed on conduct involved in that sort of expression.

"If there is a bedrock principle underlying the First Amendment, it is that the government may not prohibit the expression of an idea simply because society finds the idea itself offensive or disagreeable," wrote Justice William Brennan in part of the majority opinion. He wisely questioned how society would define which symbols were sufficiently special to warrant the unique icon status urged for the flag by the court's dissenting minority. In conclusion, he said, "We do not consecrate the flag by punishing its desecration, for in doing so we dilute the freedom that this cherished emblem represents."

In ringing dissent, Chief Justice William Rehnquist declared, "Surely, one of the high purposes of a democratic society is to legislate against conduct that is regarded as evil and profoundly offensive to the majority of people — whether it be murder, embezzlement, pollution or flag burning."

Even more compelling, Justice Stevens noted how the flag has come to symbolize national values of liberty and equality. He asked how, if those ideas are worth fighting for — as this nation has — "it cannot be true that the flag that uniquely symbolizes their power is not itself worthy of protection from unnecessary desecration."

This emotional case need not be divisive to proponents of either side, however. Justice Brennan argued that the way to preserve the flag's special role is not to punish those who feel so differently that they would burn the flag, but to persuade them that they are wrong. This worthy goal would unite us by enhancing our listening and focusing our vision to solve problems that divide the most bitter among us. If there is a good outcome to a flag-burning case beyond protecting the precious right of free speech, we can make it this.

## New Flag-Burning Law Struck Down

The Supreme Court June 11, 1990 struck down as unconstitutional a federal law enacted in 1989 forbidding desecration of the American flag.

The decision touched off an immediate political and constitutional debate over the issue.

The high court, decision in a 5-4 split decision, reaffirmed a 1989 ruling that had invalidated a Texas law against flagburning, on the ground that such a symbolic gesture was protected by the First Amendment's guarantee of free speech. The 1989 court ruling had led to enactment of the Flag Protection Act of 1989, written in broader terms than the Texas law and prohibiting all forms of flag desecretion for any reason, not only as a gesture of protest.

The court divided the same as it had in the Texas case. Justice William J. Brennan Jr., writing the majority opinion, quoted from the previous ruling: "'If there is a bedrock principle underlying the First Amendment, it is that the government may not prohibit the expression of an idea simply because society finds the idea itself offensive or disagreeable.' Punishing desecration of the flag dilutes the very freedom that makes this emblem so revered and worth revering."

The opinion was joined by Justices Thurgood Marshall, Harry A. Blackmun, Antonin Scalia and Anthony M. Kennedy.

The dissent, written by Justice John Paul Stevens, said the government had the right to protect "the symbolic value of the flag."

The flag "uniquely symbolizes the ideas of liberty, equality and tolerance – ideas that Americans have passionately defended and debated throughout our history...," Stevens said. "Thus the government may – indeed, it should – protect the symbolic value of the flag without regard to the specific content of the flag burners' speech."

Making flag-burning a criminal act, he said, did not unduly interfere with protesters' ability to communicate their ideas.

The dissent was joined by Chief Justice William H. Rehnquist and Justices Byron R. White and Sandra Day O'Connor.

The ruling, *U.S. v. Eichman*, upheld lower federal court rulings in Seattle and the District of Columbia in the case of a protester who had been arrested for putting the 1989 law to an immediate test.

Republicans, led by President George Bush and bolstered by public opinion polls, called again for an amendment to the Constitution to protect the flag. Democratic congressional leaders supported the court's decision upholding the First Amendment right to free speech.

### THE SAGINAW NEWS
*Saginaw, MI, June 14, 1990*

Just in time for today's celebration of Flag Day, the U.S. Supreme Court has given our flag a salute.

A 5-4 court majority struck down a law — enacted in the wake of a similar ruling last summer — prohibiting the burning of the flag.

That's a salute? Not even some of the most liberal politicans, such as U.S. Sen. Carl Levin, think so any more. But then, it's an election year. Righteous outrage at the very idea of permitting the desecration of the flag is no doubt the popular political thing to do.

And burning the flag is an outrageous, despicable act.

That's the whole point — and idea.

Flag-burners are telling America where they stand: Against the values, traditions and beliefs of this country. Yet, one of those values is the right of citizens to express their political viewpoints. It is not abrogated just because the view and its expression are repugnant.

If the flag stands for the United States, it stands first for the Constitution. By allowing it to be burned, we rise to its defense. The flag is a cherished symbol. The Bill of Rights is very real, a living, enduring gift of freedom that has lasted through all the election years for 200 years.

The flag-burners cannot take that away from us; if anything, they give themselves away. But we should beware of letting them tempt us into surrendering our own freedoms — because that would give them the victory they really seek.

Sometimes Americans have to endure a lot: Vile language on stage — to preserve the right of free speech. The possibility that hate groups may meet in our schools — to permit Christian students to meet in prayer. And the burning of the flag — to keep intact the Bill of Rights.

If we endure, so will our freedom, and our flag. That is the Supreme Court's tribute to liberty, and it needs no amendment.

## The New York Times
*New York, NY, June 14, 1990*

To the Members of Congress:

There could be no finer moment than this Flag Day, in this year of democratic upheaval around the world, on which to register the nation's devotion to the Stars and Stripes. We Americans really love our flag; and when we stop to think about it, we know that, precisely because of that devotion, the flag cannot be burned.

A few misguided publicity seekers set fire to one copy of it on the Capitol steps last fall to protest something or other and to get their names on a Supreme Court case. Yet the flag flew on that day, and flies on now, unsullied, high above the Capitol, and everywhere else.

Americans — We the People — also love our Constitution. It remains a model for the world, still working splendidly after two centuries. The Constitution is not perfect and was not expected to be; it has been amended 26 times. But the Bill of Rights, those first 10 amendments that spell out so many precious liberties, has never been altered.

Why, then, are so many of you Members so eager to make Americans choose between their Constitution and their flag? The higher patriotism lies in protecting and defending both.

•

Many Americans are so infuriated by flag burners they let their judgment, too, go up in smoke. In their rush to defend the flag, they forget the Bill of Rights. Perversely, they would mar the charter that lists the liberties of the people by adding to the power of government.

A little leadership and understanding can change that, but the public is getting precious little of either from President Bush or many other elected officials. Many politicians, some sincerely and others cynically, contend that an amendment is the only way to protect the flag. The cynicism is so thick that it's deplored even by the four Supreme Court Justices who dissented on Monday and voted to uphold last year's flag-burning law.

They denounced "those leaders who seem to advocate compulsory worship of the flag even by individuals whom it offends, or who seem to manipulate the symbol of national purpose into a pretext for partisan disputes about meaner ends."

The First Amendment, the one that the Supreme Court says invalidates the 1989 law, commands that Congress shall make no law abridging the freedom of speech. You *could* write a law outlawing the abuse of the flag in situations calculated to incite violence. That would be helpful; otherwise, one of these days, somebody's going to get hurt. To pass such a law would protect the flag without touching the Constitution. To do more would dilute the Constitution and thus the values that the flag represents.

Americans of passionate patriotism, knowing how irresistible is the temptation here for demagoguery, implore you: Don't yield to it. Leave us the flag we love and the liberty for which it stands.

copyright © The New York Times 1990

## The Arizona Republic
*Phoenix, AZ, June 12, 1990*

WITLESS though it may be to reason, as the Supreme Court reasons, that the framers had so-called "symbolic speech" in mind when they threw the First Amendment around political discourse, a flag-burning amendment would be equally witless — or nearly so.

Yesterday the Supreme Court reiterated its rubbery view of "free speech," striking down 5 to 4 the Flag Protection Act of 1989 — a congressional attempt to safeguard the national emblem. Writing for the majority, Justice William J. Brennan argued that the right to burn Old Glory was a "bedrock" principle of the Constitution.

That this is a nonsensical view of the First Amendment goes without saying. The framers, whose intentions should not be entirely irrelevant, plainly had something in mind other than protecting flag burners, cross burners or even wearers of obscene T-shirts. They had in mind protecting verbal discourse, and their intentions almost certainly did not extend much beyond the spoken word, for otherwise it would have been unnecessary to provide separately for a free press.

These were not, let us keep in mind, products of 20th century public schools, but literate men educated in the classical tradition and quite at home with the English language and with legal and philosophical abstractions. If they had intended for the First Amendment to include symbolic protest, they would have used some other word than "speech" for the activity they meant to describe — "expression" or "communication" perhaps.

Be that as it may, the Supreme Court has held flag burnings constitutionally protected, albeit by the slenderest majority, and the question now on the agenda is whether Congress, inflamed by political passions, ought to try to remedy the court's action through constitutional amendment. The temptation should be resisted.

Principally it should be resisted because, except for major surgery (prohibiting slavery, providing for presidential succession, that sort of thing), the Constitution should be left alone. In 199 years the language of the First Amendment has remained unchanged, which is a good argument for letting it stand now.

It is not as though American flags were being hauled down and burned coast to coast. Flag desecrations are isolated incidents staged by political cranks and marginal "artists" hoping to call attention to themselves, as in the case of last year's flag-stomping exhibit in Chicago.

The proper response to such silliness is not to rewrite the national charter. The proper response is to deny the offenders serious notice, which is what they crave, while keeping the Constitution intact.

## St. Petersburg Times
*St. Petersburg, FL, June 12, 1990*

The decision by a U.S. Supreme Court majority Monday that the First Amendment means what it says puts forth a hard test for today's Americans.

Do they value their freedom of speech as much in 1990 as did their forebears in 1790? Will they respect free speech even when the exercise of it desecrates a beloved symbol, the American flag? Can they separate the symbol from the speech?

The justices stood Monday just where they had earlier when they ruled that Texas could not outlaw flag burning because it was an act of free speech. A firestorm of protest swept across the country, led by some politicians who exploited the public's reaction and called for a constitutional amendment.

Realizing the danger of tampering with the Bill of Rights, Congress tried to find a statutory way to protect the flag. That's what the Supreme Court tossed out Monday. It was the right decision, but it seems certain to have dangerous results.

"Punishing desecration of the flag dilutes the very freedom that makes this emblem so revered," the majority opinion said. ". . . If there is a bedrock principle underlying the First Amendment, it is that the government may not prohibit the expression of an idea simply because society finds the idea itself offensive or disagreeable."

The conduct of President Bush on this issue has been particularly disappointing. Instead of using his office to educate citizens on the difference between the symbol and the act of speech, he has been leading the rabble rousers. Monday he said he would intensify his efforts to amend the Constitution.

This seems to be the worst of times for such a crucial decision. First, it will distract attention from the nation's real problems, such as the enormous budget deficit, the huge debt and the trade deficit. Freedom of speech already is under attack in several quarters. In Florida, Broward County deputies last week stormed a small record shop to arrest its owner on the charge of selling a recording to an undercover officer. Then members of the band that made the record were arrested for performing an offensive rap song from it in an adults-only club. The record in question already has sold 1.7-million

> **The Supreme Court Monday tossed out a law against flag burning. It was the right decision, but it seems certain to have dangerous results.**

copies, but the state is using every tactic to suppress it merely because some people find it offensive.

Ignorant or unscrupulous politicians always are eager to exploit emotions by calling for police-state suppression of offending speech.

Defenders of traditional American freedoms must take care that the representatives they send to Congress and to state legislatures share their views, for these are the people who will decide whether the First Amendment will be changed.

It is telling that the First Amendment, which has helped keep Americans and their democracy free since it took effect on Dec. 15, 1791, faces its gravest challenge two centuries later — from today's generation.

## The Phoenix Gazette
*Phoenix, AZ, June 12, 1990*

As expected, the Supreme Court has rejected the Flag Protection Act of 1989, a clumsy attempt to outlaw desecration of the American flag.

The issue is certain to be dragged into debate over a constitutional amendment now that this second attempt at penalizing flag desecrators — the Supreme Court struck down a Texas flag-burning law last year — has failed.

In its most recent 5-4 decision, the court said the government cannot prevent flag-burning, "simply because society finds the idea itself offensive or disagreeable." The justices said the law violated freedom of expression guaranteed by the First Amendment of the Constitution.

What's the solution? Change the Constitution. So, well-meaning but misguided flag protectionists will be spreading the gospel of patriotism as they push a constitutional amendment, something "content-neutral," something that ensures free speech while proscribing the burning of the flag.

We doubt the possibility of devising an amendment that ensures a citizen's right to speak against his country, while at the same time preventing him from making a gesture with the flag that carries the same message.

Like Justice William J. Brennan, we agree that desecration of the flag is an offensive act, so egregious that it almost reflexively clenches the fists of any American.

But, wrote Brennan in the majority opinion, "If there is a bedrock principle underlying the First Amendment, it is that the government may not prohibit the expression of an idea simply because society finds the idea itself offensive or disagreeable."

Nevertheless, the idea of protecting the flag against flame and other desecrations is too provocative for any politician to ignore. Thus a constitutional amendment, requiring approval by two-thirds of the members of the House and Senate and ratification by 38 states, is certain to elbow its way into public debate.

Perhaps the lengthy process will allow reason to prevail, and the drive will die away with the realization that, for all its heat, this is a "problem" that occurs so rarely it scarcely justifies amending the Bill of Rights.

## PORTLAND EVENING EXPRESS
*Portland, ME, June 13, 1990*

If more politicians in Washington chose to wrap themselves in the Constitution instead of in the flag, the nation would be a lot better served than is now the case.

The Supreme Court has predictably struck down a new federal law prohibiting flag desecration on the grounds that the First Amendment protects even offensive forms of political expression.

Just as predictably, the call for a constitutional amendment to prohibit flag burning has once again gone out from the White House.

This ignoble proposal is being greeted enthusiastically by Republican congressional leaders bent on turning the matter into an election year issue by calling the patriotism of their Democratic opponents into question.

There ought to be a better reason than pure partisanship — or political demagoguery — for rewriting the Bill of Rights. But both are clearly on the minds of political leaders — primarily in the GOP — eager to exploit the issue as successfully as George Bush did in his 1988 campaign against Democrat Michael Dukakis.

"It's a good issue to define your opponent," says Ed Rollins, head of the House Republican campaign committee. "If your opponent is for flag burning, he's got to go through a very sophisticated explanation of why he is."

This cynical view presumes that the average American is too stupid to understand that "protecting" the flag by undermining the very freedoms it represents is wrong.

As Senate Majority Leader George J. Mitchell puts it: "The issue is not the flag. The issue is whether we are going to amend the Bill of Rights."

Or is that too sophisticated an idea for Republican leaders to grasp?

## Richmond Times-Dispatch
*Richmond, VA, June 13, 1990*

"I have been flouted by pagans and distorted by the isms of ingrates who live under my protection. I have been subjected to questionable practices and smeared with the slime of petty politics. To such I give my charity but withhold my respect. I am the flag!"
— From "I Am The Flag," author unknown.

On Monday Justice William J. Brennan delivered his second U.S. Supreme Court majority opinion securing a right to burn or otherwise desecrate the American flag. The old liberal even read a portion of his work from the bench, a dramatic extra the justices reserve for those cases by which they are extraordinarily moved.

The case was actually two cases, against incendiaries named Eichman and Haggerty, who wasted no time toasting up a flag after Congress last year passed a law prohibiting such demonstrations. The vote was identical to that striking down a Texas flag statute last year — 5-4, with justices Antonin Scalia and Anthony Kennedy falling into bad company, joining Thurgood Marshall, Harry Blackmun and Mr. Justice Brennan for a fruit-salad majority unlikely to coalesce ever again.

Justice Brennan and others who share his visions like to make a lot of sophisticated arguments about First Amendment liberty, symbolic speech and flag desecration. The central tenet is always one or another expression of the radical freedom ethic. "Punishing desecration of the flag," he writes in his opinion, "dilutes the very freedom that makes this emblem revered." Serving up a slightly different formulation, the 9th Circuit judge in Seattle who struck down the law earlier wrote that "In order for the flag to endure as a symbol of freedom in this nation, we must protect with equal vigor the right to destroy it and the right to wave it."

In other words, all values and ideas are equal, with none to be judged good or bad, true or false. The First Amendment, written and adopted to ensure pursuit of truth, is turned on its head in an age when many judges and citizens come to believe there is no such thing. The flag controversy itself may be overworked, fueled by politicians seeking points for patriotism, but that underlying philosophical conflict is anything but trivial. All the high-minded constitutional talk about tolerance and First Amendment "values" holds little meaning for those whose own sense of value tells them that burning the flag is simply wrong.

Considered in this light the issue of flag-burning is far less a question of law than of values. At the present time there happen to be a lot of people, including five Supreme Court justices, who do not place enough value in the flag to support a law against burning it. The legal arguments are a bit of a sham. The bald eagle is a national symbol too, and there is a law to protect its destruction. If we were to blast one from its nest do you suppose we could plead in court that it was a political protest and beat the rap? Of course not, because in our environmentally sensitive age virtually everyone values the scarce and animate bird. But the values that once rallied Americans around their flag no longer make a consensus; they have fallen to the "isms of ingrates who live under my protection," of which the anonymous verse above speaks.

The president will now resume his push for a constitutional amendment to proscribe flag-burning (and if "tinkering" with the Constitution is such a horrible idea, then why did the framers devise an amendment process?) and this time the Joe Bidens in Congress will not be able to hide behind a statute they know will be found unconstitutional. If Congress does not want to pass an amendment, it could turn the same trick merely by exercising its Article III, Section 2 power to except flag desecration from federal court jurisdiction. That is a constitutional tonic that the activist and aged Mr. Brennan and friends should have tasted long ago, and if the flag ends up as the vehicle by which the thing is finally accomplished it will have inspired those who still honor and defend it to yet another victory.

## THE DENVER POST
*Denver, CO, June 12, 1990*

NOW THAT the Supreme Court has struck down the new federal law against flag-burning, the self-proclaimed guardians of Old Glory undoubtedly will rally 'round the notion that such behavior should be outlawed through a constitutional amendment.

This misguided, albeit understandable, attempt to circumvent the court's judgment — cheered on by President Bush — will subject the American people to a pointless election-year debate over the emotionally divisive issue of what constitutes patriotism.

Worse, it will divert public attention from the many problems that pose a much more realistic threat to the nation's well-being, such as the crushing burden of the long-term federal debt.

Nobody can deny that the desecration of the flag is a deeply offensive, even repugnant act in the eyes of most Americans. But as an expression of political belief, it must be tolerated in this free society — just as the rantings of extremists like Lyndon LaRouche or Louis Farrakhan must be tolerated.

Once the government begins suppressing people's legitimate right to speak their minds, either verbally or symbolically, it is undermining a First Amendment guarantee that has helped this country to endure for two centuries.

Moreover, a constitutional amendment would suggest wrongly that what is actually at stake here is not individual freedom, but the power of the state to command respect for a symbol of authority.

If the U.S. flag represents anything, it is certainly not this concept of imperial majesty. That's something that should be as revolting to Americans today as it was to the colonists more than 200 years ago. Rather, the flag symbolizes the nation's commitment to "liberty, equality and tolerance" — the ideals, ironically, that Justice John Paul Stevens cited in dissenting from the high court's majority opinion yesterday.

As Justice William Brennan put it so succinctly in writing for the majority, "Punishing desecration of the flag dilutes the very freedom that makes this emblem so revered."

The flag-wavers, bless them, should continue to decry any desecration of our nation's banner but, at the same time, try to understand how even a distasteful act sometimes must be tolerated by a free society.

## The Honolulu Advertiser
*Honolulu, HI, June 12, 1990*

Just in time for the Fourth of July and the election campaigns, the U.S. Supreme Court has returned the flag-burning issue to the political arena.

The court was expected to strike down the new federal law that made flag-burning a crime. It was a controversial stop-gap action engineered by congressional Democrats last year to hold off a Republican effort for a constitutional amendment against flag-burning.

Equally expected is the new political battle for such an amendment, which began right after the Supreme Court ruling yesterday. President Bush, who got elected with all-out flag waving in 1988, is leading the charge again.

What's less predictable is the attitude of the American people. As an adjoining analysis article notes, polls show them strongly for a constitutional amendment, but it's also possible some views may change when people think about the issues at stake.

Almost everyone abhors burning of the American flag. But the Supreme Court says such action is a legitimate form of free expression under the First Amendment. The answer is not to amend the Constitution to limit freedom, to suppress a view because it is distasteful.

In effect, the Supreme Court has reminded us that the Constitution, with its freedoms, is above the flag, which is only a symbol of those freedoms.

The American Bar Association and other groups feel the best legal action on the flag-burning issue is no action, no new law or constitutional amendment. We agree.

This country has survived its few flag burners. It will not survive as well if we start to limit freedom in the name of patriotism.

## The Washington Post
*Washington, DC, June 14, 1990*

PRESIDENT Bush declared the other day that the act of burning the American flag "endangers the fabric of our country." If that were true (and it's not), it would be hard to explain how the United States has survived for 199 years with the First Amendment in full effect, guaranteeing this allegedly dangerous and subversive freedom of expression.

Some of the congressional Democrats, inclined to oppose the president, are reportedly wondering how to explain themselves to their constituents. There is a simple answer: point to actual American experience. American history has not been a gentle process. This country has been through a terrible civil war, foreign wars, depressions and riots, times of great fear and confusion, without compromising its basic principles or finding it necessary to shorten the Bill of Rights.

Would you say that the fabric of society is in greater danger today than at the height of the Vietnam War and the demonstrations against it? In the violence of that moment, there was much abusive behavior, and the flag was desecrated many times. But the crisis has passed, and the fabric of the society has never been stronger than today. One leading reason for it is the preservation of constitutional freedom.

Mr. Bush has now made himself the first American president in some years to stand firmly and explicitly in favor of limiting the right to free political expression—for burning a flag or wearing it on the seat of your pants constitutes expression just as picketing or other symbolic actions do. The president argues that the law is already full of restrictions on expression, and he would only add another. But those present restrictions are the sanctions against libel, and revealing military secrets, and crying "Fire!" in a crowded theater and that sort of thing. They all involve speech that threatens real and specific harm to other people. To burn a flag is offensive, but it is a pure act of political expression. To enact a constitutional amendment restricting political expression would be something entirely new for this country, which has always taken a deep pride in a legal tradition that protects the right of all Americans, even small and unpopular minorities, to express their opinions.

The president's performance does not, in the view of the White House, constitute demagoguery. As one White House official generously explained to a reporter, Mr. Bush "is not going to demagogue on this. That's what he's got Dole for." This rather demeaning reference is to Sen. Robert J. Dole, the minority leader. But Mr. Bush seems to be making rapid progress in the demagoguery department without senatorial assistance.

## THE RICHMOND NEWS LEADER
*Richmond, VA, June 13, 1990*

The Congress of the United States of America didn't see it coming. But on Monday the Supreme Court did precisely what any student of junior-high civics would have predicted: It struck down the federal law that bans flag-desecration.

The debate opened last year when the court threw out a similar Texas statute. When the Bush administration called for a constitutional amendment to override the court's position, congressional leaders in effect said, hold on, let's not amend the Constitution; a sweet little bill will suffice. They spiked the proposed amendment and passed their doomed law instead. Whereupon some flags were burned, lower courts threw out the flag law, and the issue went to the Supremes.

The Court's decision ought to make it clear even to Senate Judiciary Committee chairman Joseph Biden that only a constitutional amendment can protect the flag. As long as the high court defines flag-desecration as an exercise of First Amendment rights to free expression, no statute to protect the flag will withstand scrutiny. During debate on the original amendment and bill, Senators and Congressmen draped themselves in Old Glory. Nevertheless, they refused to approve an amendment and passed a worthless bill instead. It ranks as one of the more cynical votes of a thoroughly disreputable Congress.

Now the pressure is on. Politicking for mid-term elections soon will begin in earnest. Will those who opted for an unconstitutional bill summon the courage either (1) to vote for an amendment or (2) to tell the voters why they oppose efforts to protect the flag? The issue will test the character of many members. The debate promises to be instructive and — well — fun.

## Portland Press Herald
*Portland, ME, June 12, 1990*

The First Amendment is alive and well, its vitality reaffirmed by the Supreme Court's decision striking down a new federal law banning flag burning.

Given a choice between protecting a symbol of freedom or freedom itself, the court chose the latter. And it did so for precisely the right reason: because, in Justice William H. Brennan's words, "punishing desecration of the flag dilutes the very freedom that makes this emblem so revered."

If politics were more rational, the court's 5-4 decision would be it. Heated emotions fanned by a brief rash of flag burnings last year have cooled. As they have, Americans have heeded the concept summed up by Brennan: "If there is a bedrock principle underlying the First Amendment, it is that the government may not prohibit the expression of an idea simply because society finds the idea itself offensive or disagreeable." The public has also rethought the wisdom of limiting an amendment which has served it superbly well for two centuries.

But politics is not always about reason, it's about winning elections. With the law struck down, some in Congress from both parties will move quickly to propose a constitutional amendment banning desecration of the flag. For reasons the court has outlined, such an amendment is both unnecessary and unwise.

Sadly, that won't stop it from playing a big role in the fall elections. Congressional candidates who should be assessed on their handling of critical issues — the federal deficit and savings and loan bailout, for instance — will instead wrap themselves in Old Glory.

Are we content with that? We shouldn't be.

## The Chattanooga Times
*Chattanooga, TN, June 14, 1990*

On Monday the Supreme Court pruned the fig leaf that Congress adopted last year to avoid having to confront a possible constitutional amendment to prohibit flag burning. Now that the Flag Protection Act of 1989 is officially unconstitutional, however, President Bush and some members of Congress are falling all over themselves to introduce such a constitutional amendment — just in time for the fall elections.

Of course burning the American flag is an offensive, thumb-in-the-eye way to protest government policy. But it is by no stretch of common sense a justification for tinkering with the Bill of Rights, specifically diluting the First Amendment. That part of the Constitution is too precious, and has served Americans well for too long, now to be vandalized by the politicized emotion masquerading as protection for the flag.

The proposed amendment is nothing less than an attempt to restrict the freedom of expression so that we can protect the symbol of that freedom. We surely hope that Tennessee Sens. Jim Sasser and Albert Gore Jr. will lead the fight against trivializing the nation's founding document.

This amendment is already becoming a political football, as the comments on Monday by two prominent Republican politicians prove. Said Ed Rollins, co-chairman of the National Republican Congressional Committee: "I think it's an excellent issue upon which you define your opponent, his character and values. And if Democrats choose to vote against a constitutional amendment, I think they'll pay a price." Senate Minority Leader Robert Dole chimed in that a vote against an amendment "would make a good 30-second (TV) spot."

Talk about irony: Here you have two politicians supposedly trying to protect the flag from abuse while simultaneously expressing their approval of another form of flag abuse: using it as a barometer of other Americans' patriotism.

In their wisdom the nation's founders deliberately made it difficult to amend the Constitution. They probably foresaw the likes of Sen. Dole shamelessly using the amendment process for partisan political advantage.

Nevertheless, the fact remains there has been no outbreak of flag burning, nor is one likely; the proposed amendment is a false solution to a non-existent problem. The flag does not need the amendment's "protection" for a simple reason: A single flag can be destroyed by fire, but the flag itself, the symbol of this country, cannot.

Our enemies have destroyed countless American flags in battles throughout our history. Yet the flag endures, as do the freedoms that it symbolizes. Those freedoms are enshrined in the Bill of Rights and are the envy of millions of people worldwide. Man's rights of freedom of speech, press and assembly, among others enumerated in the Bill of Rights, have been hallowed by the deaths of thousands of soldiers in the nation's wars. Now, one of those rights, freedom of speech, is threatened by members of Congress who are afraid, for political reasons, not to support the flag-burning amendment.

Make no mistake: A vote for this amendment is a vote to restrict the First Amendment's guarantees of free speech. A vote for this amendment is an admission that America is too weak to withstand the isolated protests of a few twits who resort to political theater to make a point. A vote for this amendment suggests a refusal to acknowledge that it could have far more calamitous results than flag burnings themselves.

Congress voted for the Flag Protection Act knowing it was unconstitutional, and hoping they wouldn't have to confront the amendment issue. Thanks to the court, they can no longer dodge the issue. But they must understand the seriousness of voting to amend the Bill of Rights, thus repudiating the founders who left us a brilliant founding document that protects our freedoms.

There is no reason whatsoever to circumscribe those freedoms simply because a few oddballs have expressed their public protest in an offensive way. Sens. Gore and Sasser can best signal their reverence for the flag by voting against a measure that would use the flag to bludgeon the First Amendment.

## LEXINGTON HERALD-LEADER
*Lexington, KY, June 13, 1990*

A year ago this month, the U.S. Supreme Court sparked a national controversy by declaring unconstitutional a Texas law that prohibited desecration of the U.S. flag. Monday, the court did it again, throwing out the law Congress passed in a wave of patriotic fervor after last year's court decision.

Each time, the court split along the same 5-4 line. In each instance, this emotion-charged issue prompted a justice to write a brilliant defense of individual rights to freedom of expression.

This time, oddly enough, the compelling case was not found in the majority opinion written, as it was last year, by Justice William J. Brennan. The opinion Brennan issued Monday was constitutionally correct, but was saved from boring dryness only by quoting his best line from 1989: "If there is a bedrock principle underlying the First Amendment, it is that government may not prohibit the expression of an idea simply because society finds the idea itself offensive or disagreeable."

It was in Justice John Paul Stevens' dissenting opinion that the most eloquent argument for free speech was found Monday. It was Stevens who said an individual's freedom of expression "is one of the critical components of the idea of liberty that the flag itself is intended to symbolize." It was Stevens who said that " ... the First Amendment embraces not only the freedom to communicate ideas, but also the right to communicate them effectively." It was Stevens who said the impact of burning the symbol of the nation is itself "purely symbolic" — assuming the protester owns the flag he burns.

Still, Stevens found reasons to argue that burning the flag is not protected by the Constitution — reasons that he presumably can rationalize against his own well-crafted arguments to the contrary. His right as a Supreme Court justice to hold such seemingly contradictory opinions is just as inviolable, just as constitutionally protected as the right of free expression.

## THE SPOKESMAN-REVIEW
*Spokane, WA, June 12, 1990*

To ban desecration of the American flag — whether by legislative fiat or constitutional amendment — is impractical, unenforceable and ultimately dangerous.

U.S. Supreme Court Justice William Brennan, in a ruling Monday striking down a new federal law that outlaws desecration of the American flag, cut right to the heart of the matter: "If there is a bedrock principle underlying the First Amendment, it is that the government may not prohibit the expression of an idea simply because society finds the idea itself offensive or disagreeable."

The Supreme Court, in a 5-4 decision, has settled the issue of legislative remedy by declaring the Flag Protection Act of 1989 in violation of the First Amendment to the Constitution. Now it is up to Congress to settle the issue of whether to amend the First Amendment.

The sight of an American flag torched by one of life's losers sickens, angers and provokes those of us who set great store on the principles this nation stands for. The flag burners disrespect Old Glory, but the flag's importance rests not in its symbolism but in the ideals that symbolism represents.

To threaten people who deface or mutilate the symbol with incarceration puts belief in this nation's ideals on shaky ground. Freedom of speech becomes freedom of acceptable speech. Both the flag-burning law and a constitutional amendment that would accomplish the same thing present a direct test. Is this nation's belief in the First Amendment lip service or a real commitment to an ideal, no matter how uncomfortable it sometimes makes us?

It is impossible to legislate against jerks — people who will resort to any despicable act simply to get a rise out of someone. And it would defy anyone to write an amendment that will cover all objectionable uses the flag can be put to. To attempt to do so is to invite demonstrators to find new, unique ways, to use the flag, or some other symbol, to get the nation's goat.

But the biggest danger arises from the fact that once the Bill of Rights has been tampered with, it becomes fair game for a host of further changes. That is a Pandora's box Congress should fear to open.

It is not by accident that this nation's founders made changing the Constitution difficult. Amending it requires approval by two-thirds of the members of the House and Senate plus ratification by 38 state legislatures.

In the nearly two centuries of its existence, the First Amendment has been spared the tinkerings of do-gooders eager to improve on a good thing. This time and this issue do not warrant such a precedent-setting step.

Despicable as flag-burning is, its practitioners have faded into obscurity along with their causes, powerless to weaken the country's moral convictions. Congress should not now become their instrument.

## ST. LOUIS POST-DISPATCH
*St. Louis, MO, June 12, 1990*

Consider these words from a Supreme Court justice in Monday's 5-4 decision that again upheld the rights of Americans to burn their flag in protest:

"The flag uniquely symbolizes the ideas of liberty, equality and tolerance — ideas that Americans have passionately defended and debated throughout our history. The flag embodies the spirit of our national commitment to those ideals."

This passage — not from the eloquent majority opinion of Justice William Brennan but from the impassioned dissent by Justice John Paul Stevens — shows precisely the dilemma that flag burning presents. Given the difficult choice between protecting the cherished American ideals of liberty, equality and tolerance or the flag that is the symbol of those ideals, the ideals must come first. If the ideals are weakened, the flag stands for nothing.

For the second time in less than a year, the Supreme Court issued a spirited defense of those ideals, what the court has called the "bedrock principle underlying the First Amendment." Freedom of expression cannot be limited merely to mainstream thoughts, those that don't make waves. The true test of the tolerance and the liberty that Justice Stevens feels the flag symbolizes comes when people freely tolerate thoughts they hate.

When the Supreme Court issued its first ruling on flag burning last summer, the response in Washington was a flurry of chest-thumping superpatriotism.

Too often, the debate was not over the principles that needed protection but over the best way to undermine the court. A new law was passed over the reluctance of President Bush, who preferred an amendment that would have placed an unprecedented and unwise asterisk on the Bill of Rights.

The new law quickly prompted flag burnings in protest, and the resulting prosecutions were put on a fast track by the Supreme Court. Now the issue has been joined again, just days before Flag Day, in time for this fall's election campaign.

President Bush says he will push again for an amendment, to accomplish a ban on flag burning that he feels is in the public interest. Many members of Congress will surely join him on that flag-waving bandwagon.

But before they take their crusade too far, they should consider this: Those who burn the flag destroy only a piece of cloth, symbolic though it may be. Those who tamper with the First Amendment weaken something much more precious.

Respect for the flag can't be strengthened by trampling the values for which it stands. Instead of wrapping themselves in the flag, those who want to protect it should instead work to make sure that its ideals — those values that Justice Stevens says "Americans have passionately defended and debated throughout our history" — remain as strong as ever.

## THE INDIANAPOLIS STAR
*Indianapolis, IN, June 14, 1990*

As another Flag Day unfurls, the pride felt by many Americans is tinged with dismay over this week's decision by the U.S. Supreme Court which struck down the federal statute against flag-desecration.

The court ruled 5-4 that flag-burning is a form of symbolic speech protected by the First Amendment. A lot of people, including the four dissenting justices, find the majority's logic hard to swallow. Burning is speech? Tut, tut, honorable justices.

If burning is really speech, and protected, then why can't those nuts burn down the Capitol, the White House, the Supreme Court building and anything else that enrages them because it symbolizes the United States of America, which they hate?

Let's face it — if they had a big enough match, some of them would burn down the country. After all, it is a symbol — of freedom, opportunity, hope and government with the consent of the governed.

> If burning is speech, look out for spoilers with matches.

It may be more a symptom of spinelessness than anything else that today these obnoxious and in some ways pathetic figures are able to command the attention of the president, Congress, the U.S. Supreme Court, state legislatures, front pages, national television and a large part of the public.

In dealing with such pesky characters, the rule used to be: Ignore them and they will go away. But the flag-burners keep winding up back in the spotlight.

Now President Bush is pushing for a constitutional amendment against flag desecration. It may be unwise to let the issue dominate public attention and debate to the detriment of much more important and potentially damaging problems. It may not even be necessary.

What is generally overlooked in the debate on flag-burning is the fact that there are enough ordinances against air pollution, illegal burning, disorderly conduct, inciting to riot, disturbing the peace, littering and so forth in any community to whisk such crackpots into court to face the same charges that would be faced by any other citizen who broke the law.

It is only natural for Americans who love their country and their flag to get red hot with anger and frustration when they see a flag dishonored. That is precisely the reaction the desecraters and the burners want. Without it, they can't get media attention and attention is what they hunger for.

Perhaps the calmer voices are correct. Ignore the creeps and they'll go away. Meanwhile, though, hit them with the laws that are already on the books.

## THE COMMERCIAL APPEAL
*Memphis, TN, June 14, 1990*

PRESIDENT Bush and many others were right about the federal flag-burning law on two counts.

First, the U.S. Supreme Court would find that the law was a violation of the First Amendment's protection of free speech.

Second, the only way to protect the flag is by a constitutional amendment.

The court has overturned the law. It's time for the amendment.

Perhaps the strongest anti-amendment argument is that criticism of the government or the nation, even by burning the flag, is covered by the right of dissent.

This society, however, does not have to be perfect to survive. It often makes compromises between conflicting ideals.

The Supreme Court, for instance, recently liberalized the use of evidence seized without a warrant, despite protests from purists who think police should treat a criminal's drug stash the same as they would a widow's piggy bank.

As President Bush pointed out, "The law books are full of restrictions on free speech and we ought to have this be one of them." Flag-burning, he said, "endangers the fabric of our country and I think it ought to be outlawed."

Most Americans, the polls indicate, deeply resent desecration of the flag. They don't argue the finer points of constitutional philosophy. To paraphrase a justice of the high court on the related subject of obscenity and pornography, they know an attack on the nation's honor when they see it. They consider flag-burning an obscenity and an incitement to disorder.

Brian Lunde, former Democratic National Committee executive director, had sound advice for anti-amendment Democrats.

"If we're smart," Lunde said, "we'll quickly support the amendment and say, 'If you can't spray-paint the White House why should you be able to deface the flag?' If we're dumb, we get caught up in the ivory tower too high."

The issue is not despotism vs. free speech, but permissiveness vs. patriotism.

## Omaha World-Herald
*Omaha, NE, June 13, 1990*

How regrettable it is that one more U.S. Supreme Court justice couldn't be found to uphold the 1989 flag desecration law. One more vote would have saved the law and denied constitutional protection for the contemptible act of flag-burning.

Now, instead, the door is open for more headline-seeking geeks to claim that they are making a political statement when they deface a symbol that most Americans hold sacred.

Now Congress is about to be forced into a potentially bitter battle over a constitutional amendment to protect the flag at the very time its members should be devoting themselves to restoring fiscal responsibility in Washington.

And now more weight has been given the questionable proposition that a wordless gesture has much the same constitutional standing as political speech.

The deterioration of political discourse into street theater continues.

There was a time when the purpose of political speech was to persuade. A person with an idea to sell was judged on the logic of his reasoning and the clarity of his presentation. The First Amendment provided a foundation for robust political discourse by prohibiting government from abridging unpopular ideas. Ideas rose or fell on their merits.

Dramatics have now replaced ideas in some of what passes for political discourse. Certainly flag-burning is not an idea. It is an act, the principal purpose of which is to shock and offend. It rips at the shared values of loyalty and mutual understanding that hold the country together. It showers contempt upon the sacrifice of veterans, the pride of immigrants and the hard work of millions of other law-abiding citizens. It ridicules the very system of government that permits it to happen.

To clothe that act in the protective garments of constitutionally protected speech exceeds any reasonable requirement of free and unfettered political debate.

The four protesters whose case the Supreme Court decided had contended that the flag desecration law unconstitutionally restricted their freedom to dissent. They had been charged in connection with a demonstration against the law in Seattle last October. They called it a "festival of defiance" — they hauled down an American flag belonging to the U.S. Postal Service and set it afire.

Now, as Flag Day approaches, they and their supporters celebrate by saying that the freedom to dissent has been preserved in time for them to observe "flag desecration day."

Their freedom to dissent was never called into question. The only freedom abridged by the flag law was the "freedom" to burn the flag without being arrested. As Justice John Paul Stevens, writing for the four-member minority, said, prohibiting flag-burning "does not entail any interference with the speaker's freedom to express his or her ideas by other means."

The flag is so important to so many people as a symbol of shared national values, Justice Stevens wrote, that government should protect it. It is unfortunate that he and his colleagues could not assemble a majority that would do so.

## Cartoon

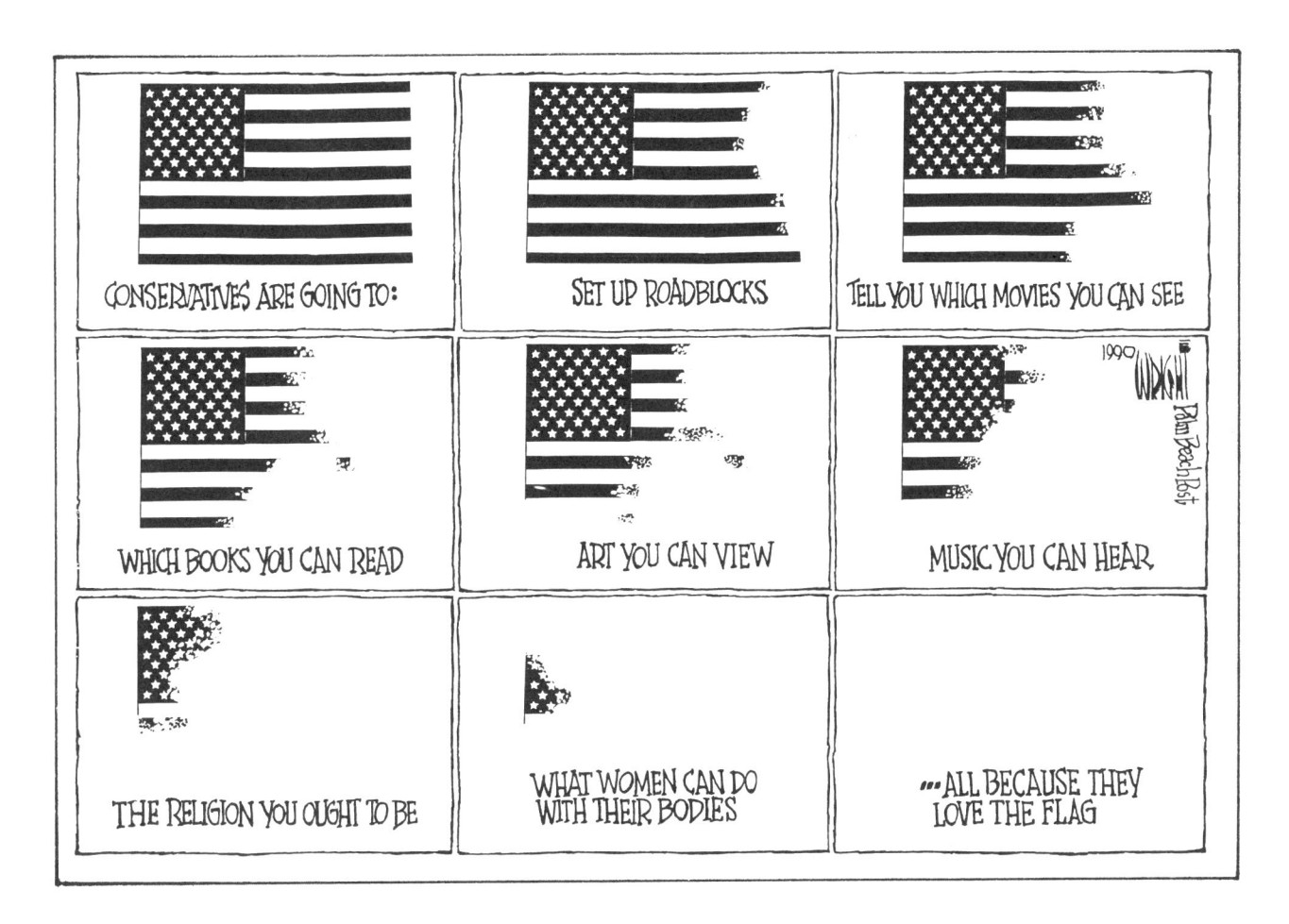

| CONSERVATIVES ARE GOING TO: | SET UP ROADBLOCKS | TELL YOU WHICH MOVIES YOU CAN SEE |
| --- | --- | --- |
| WHICH BOOKS YOU CAN READ | ART YOU CAN VIEW | MUSIC YOU CAN HEAR |
| THE RELIGION YOU OUGHT TO BE | WHAT WOMEN CAN DO WITH THEIR BODIES | ...ALL BECAUSE THEY LOVE THE FLAG |

— Wright, Palm Beach Post, 1990

## Newsday

*New York, NY, June 12, 1990*

The Supreme Court once again is right in deciding that burning the flag, however appalling to most Americans, is political speech properly protected by the First Amendment. Unfortunately, the court's 5-4 decision yesterday nullifying a new federal law that prohibited burning and otherwise defiling the flag has set off a new round of cheap politicking.

President George Bush declared that he would press to amend the Constitution — the Bill of Rights, in fact — to ban flag-burning. Bush and his Republican confederates are determined to make flag protection an issue in upcoming mid-term elections for the House and Senate by pushing the amendment — and bashing Democrats who vote against it. Bush should spare us this senseless stumping.

Of course, it was Bush's crass manipulation of the flag's symbolism during his 1988 presidential campaign that created the climate of political angst about flag burners. The Supreme Court's correct decision last year to void a Texas law under which a protester had been prosecuted for burning the flag prompted the president to make a campaign-style appearance at the Iwo Jima memorial. That sent shivers through Democrats mindful of the way Bush had made Gov. Michael Dukakis seem downright un-American because he once vetoed a bill to force Massachusetts teachers to lead the Pledge of Allegiance.

The result was the Flag Protection Act of 1989, crafted largely by Democrats and thrown out by the court yesterday. Associate Justice William Brennan's majority opinion makes it clear why the First Amendment cannot be compromised, even when it is used to protect an act many Americans find deeply offensive: "Punishing desecration of the flag dilutes the very freedom that makes this emblem so revered, and worth revering."

Bush and the Republican tacticians should read Brennan's analysis. But they should take special note of the dissent by Associate Justice John Paul Stevens. Reverence for the flag, Stevens laments, has diminished. And its integrity has been compromised by leaders "who seem to manipulate the symbol of national purpose into a pretext for partisan disputes about meaner ends."

## Fort Worth Star-Telegram

*Fort Worth, TX, June 14, 1990*

Before today ends, millions of Americans who are not everyday flagwavers will have unfurled Old Glory in tribute to the principles that are the foundation of this free nation.

Also, before this Flag Day ends, some Americans may have burned replicas of the Stars and Stripes, either to express their contempt for those principles or just to show that they have a constitutional right to perform such a contemptible act.

Sadly, on this Flag Day, thoughts about flag-burning distract millions of Americans from the usual exhilaration of flag-waving.

By correctly striking down a federal statute prohibiting flag-burning, the U.S. Supreme Court has set the stage for a drive to amend the Constitution to protect the flag against desecration.

In their zeal to protect the flag, the advocates of the constitutional amendment, including President Bush, would tamper with the Bill of Rights for the first time in the nation's history.

That would be a tragedy. By pandering to a wave of patriotic emotionalism and savaging the Bill of Rights, Congress and the president would be playing into the hands of the worst among the flagburners.

Those are the ones who despise what this country stands for and seek, through such outrageous acts, to stampede us into transforming this republic into a harsher, less-tolerant place.

If the First Amendment is diluted in a rush of politicized patriotic fervor, the flag that will be waved on future Flag Days will have lost an essential part of its meaning.

## House, Senate Kill Amendment to Bar Flag Desecration

The U.S. House of Representatives June 21, 1990 rejected a proposed constitutional amendment that would have permitted the prosecution of those who destroyed American flags. The amendment had been put forward after a 1989 federal law banning flag desecration was overturned by the Supreme Court earlier in the month.

The vote was 254 in favor and 177 against. The vote was 34 short of the two-thirds majority needed to pass a constitutional amendment.

The timing of the vote was controversial, with Republican supporters of the amendment charging that House Speaker Thomas S. Foley (D, Wash.) had brought the bill to the floor too quickly. Proponents of the amendment had asked that consideration be delayed in hopes of marshaling public support. Rep. Newt Gingrich (R, Ga.) said Foley "deliberately rushed this thing to the floor so the American people would not be heard."

Foley worked hard to defeat the measure, which he called a crass political maneuver to paint Democrats as unpatriotic. Foley took two untraditional steps for a speaker, joining in the debate on the measure and casting his own vote against it. He told the House that whatever the Senate did, the vote would be "the final...on this issue this year."

Opponents argued that the proposed amendment would be the first alteration of the First Amendment free speech guarantee in 200 years. In his speech from the Senate floor, Foley said, "We should not amend the Constitution to reach the sparse and scattered and despicable conduct of a few who would dishonor the flag and defile it." He said, "If we began the process of changing the First Amendment, we would be looking at more than just this vote. What about burning the Bible or the Constitution?"

But supporters insisted that an amendment was the only way to protect the flag. President George Bush, who had actively promoted the proposed amendment, June 13 said, "I am for free speech, but I am for protecting the flag against desecration. The law books are full of restrictions on free speech and we ought to have this be one of them."

House Minority Leader Robert H. Michel (R, Ill.) declared in the House debate, "Now's the time to take a stand. Everything – the arguments, the expert testimony, the heated debate – everything comes down to one question each has to ask for himself or herself: Do I want to protect our flag from physical desecration?"

Some members of Congress and political observers saw the amendment's defeat as a sign that public interest in the flag-burning controversy was waning. The 1989 federal flag law had passed both chambers of Congress by wide margins after a public uproar over a Supreme Court decision overturning a Texas flag-protection statute. But members reported relatively little outcry from voters after the most recent Supreme Court decision.

The Senate June 26 rejected a proposed constitutional amendment that would have permitted states to prosecute those who destroyed or desecrated American flags.

The vote count in the Senate was 58 in favor and 42 against, nine votes short of the two-thirds majority needed to pass a constitutional amendment. Voting "yes" were 20 Democrats and 38 Republicans. Voting "no" were 35 Democrats and seven Republicans.

Opponents of the amendment noted that the measure was dead after the House vote. They charged that supporters had insisted on Senate action for political reasons.

"We will take a meaningless vote so that some campaign operatives can try to bludgeon senators who are willing to stand up for the Bill of Rights and vote against this amendment," said amendment opponent Sen. Howard M. Metzenbaum (D, Ohio).

Senate Minority Leader Robert J. Dole (R, Kan.), a supporter of the amendment, said, "We're not going to give up, and we'll see what happens in the days, weeks and months ahead."

## THE INDIANAPOLIS NEWS
*Indianapolis, IN, June 23, 1990*

Hallelujah. The crisis is over.

After nearly a year of posturing and pontificating by its members, the U.S. House of Representatives held a vote last week on a proposed constitutional amendment that would prohibit flag-burning.

The measure failed, but that was almost beside the point. All the votes now are on the record. Battle-ready politicians know that they have sound-bites proclaiming their support for a) Old Glory or b) the First Amendment to use in this autumn's campaign.

With the flag-burning battle out of the way, however, the esteemed members of Congress are left with a new challenge: What other "crisis" can they hype out of proportion so that the American people will forget about the savings and loan scandal?

The search for a distracting crisis will be a desperate one, because smart politicians know that the S&L debacle has all the identifying signs of a campaign catastrophe. If Americans are allowed to think too long about the failure of the S&Ls and the federal government's decision to bail them out with taxpayer money, those Americans are likely to start screaming for blood.

And with good reason. Estimates of the cost of the bailout keep climbing. According to one numbers-cruncher in Washington, the S&L bailout will cost every American — on the average and including those, such as children, who don't pay taxes — $40 a month for the next 20 years.

It doesn't take a mental giant to calculate that the cost will be much higher to those Americans who *do* pay taxes.

Congress, however, doesn't want to give voters the time or even the information to do those calculations.

That's why the leaders in the House and Senate have fallen all over themselves getting their faces in front of the television cameras proclaiming their undying devotion to the flag and/or the Constitution. At the same time, they've been struggling mightily to keep the lid on the S&L mess by voting not to spend money to investigate who was responsible for the disaster and why the regulatory process "governing" — the word is used loosely — the S&Ls didn't work.

The members of Congress hope that they can keep Americans so distracted that they won't remember the S&L debacle until after the election in November. And the only way to do that is to have a summer of "crises."

## THE KANSAS CITY STAR
*Kansas City, MO, June 23, 1990*

The following members of the U.S. House of Representatives from Kansas and Missouri voted this week to carve a hole in the Bill of Rights: In Kansas, Jan Meyers, Pat Roberts and Bob Whittaker; in Missouri, Jack Buechner, Ike Skelton, Mel Hancock, Bill Emerson and Harold Volkmer.

Remember their names. Most are seeking re-election this year. If you get a chance, ask them why they are so keen to revise the Bill of Rights by passing a flag desecration amendment.

It might be a good idea, too, to ask whether there is anything else they don't like about American democracy in its current form. If they want to whittle down the First Amendment, it would be nice to know if there are some other constitutional protections and freedoms they want to whittle down as well.

The Bill of Rights has served this country well for many generations. Why are some people in the late 20th century — many of them self-described "conservatives" — so certain that they have found flaws in this marvelous document that have somehow escaped previous notice?

When you talk to the members of Congress who have voted to revise the Bill of Rights, try to pin them down on their thinking as much as possible. It's important. Historic American principles and freedoms could be at stake in the future, as they were this week.

"This will be the first time this portion of our Constitution has been amended in over 200 years," Meyers noted in a recent statement. But she continued:

"The flag is unlike any other symbol of our country. It is a symbol of high achievement, as when the astronauts placed our flag on the moon. And when men and women in our armed forces have died, we have draped their coffins with the flag. It is the symbol of our national identity and our national values."

This is all true. But as Meyers' own language makes clear, the flag merely symbolizes American freedom. It should hardly take precedence over freedom itself. Meyers, along with many of her colleagues, has it all backward.

Others in Washington are simply trying to score partisan points. Sen. Bob Dole of Kansas, for example, talks eagerly of the 30-second campaign ads that will be built around the flag amendment, then howls about the need to "come through for Old Glory."

If that isn't flag desecration, what is? Please, senator. Show some respect.

Much of the other rhetoric behind the flag amendment has been simplistic and shameless. Some of it, frankly, was offensive. There was certainly no need to drag in the war dead to serve as political props.

In a pleasant surprise, wisdom prevailed over haste, cynicism and misguided patriotism in the House. Supporters of the proposed amendment complain that the vote was rushed through before they had enough time to get the public riled up again.

This is typical of the nonsense this side has been dishing out. They have been clamoring about flag-burning for months and, in some cases, years. But the more voters hear about flag burning, the less concerned they seem to be about it.

This country has much more important things to worry about than a few idiots burning flags. It's about time some people in Congress — starting with a few people from Missouri and Kansas — figured that out.

## The Chattanooga Times
*Chattanooga, TN, June 26, 1990*

The Bill of Rights was attached to the U.S. Constitution to limit the power of the state and to secure for Americans the greatest possible individual liberty. This charter of freedoms is the glory of American democracy, and it is to the credit of a courageous minority in the House of Representatives that it will not be compromised by a constitutional amendment against flag burning.

The 177 members of the House who voted against the amendment proved themselves statesmen, willing to defend the foundational principles of this democracy despite threats of political retribution. Would that the defenders of the Bill of Rights had been a majority.

Nevertheless, the founders of this country recognized the danger of allowing a simple majority to rewrite the Constitution and wisely required a two-thirds vote in each congressional chamber to submit an amendment to the states. Proponents of restricting the Bill of Rights fell decisively short of mustering that two-thirds in the House.

Now the drama moves to the Senate, where a vote on the flag amendment is expected this week. It will be strictly for show. The House killed the amendment for this session of Congress, so a Senate vote will be meaningless — except for its political impact. Knowing that, some senators might be tempted to vote for a measure they oppose because it is the politically expedient thing to do. For the good of the country, they should reject that temptation and make their stand on principle.

The principle is this: The greatness of this country rests in its guarantees of individual freedoms. That greatness, those freedoms, must be defended not only against foreign enemies, but also against the enemy within, which in this case is a public passion for repression of political dissent.

That passion is born of an emotional reaction to the sight of protesters burning copies of the American flag. But for all the flames, protesters cannot burn the flag. *The* flag is a symbol of the ideals upon which this country was founded. It is something more than the copies of it which abound, and it is not damaged in the least by those who torch a replica. The symbol of American freedom does not need the protection of those who would limit liberty in its name.

Safeguarding the fundamental political freedom to protest one's government is a sign of the strength of our democracy. Chipping away at that basic freedom by amending the First Amendment would be a sign of weakened allegiance to the principles for which the flag stands.

So let emotions subside. Let the Bill of Rights stand unamended. And let the flag billow proudly in that wind which is the breath of freedom.

## The Phoenix Gazette
*Phoenix, AZ, June 23, 1990*

In a prudent move supported by 200 years of history, the U.S. House of Representatives rejected a proposed constitutional amendment that would have protected the American flag from "desecration" but would have jeopardized the constitutional freedoms the flag represents. The measure failed to win the necessary two-thirds majority to amend the constitution.

Americans should respect the common sense House members, including Arizona Democrat Morris Udall and Republican Jim Kolbe, who voted against this transparently political attempt to overturn two U.S. Supreme Court decisions on flag burning.

Like the high court, high-minded Americans should agree that the government cannot prohibit the expression of an idea simply because the idea is offensive or disagreeable. That is the fundamental principle of the First Amendment. If Americans don't hold that idea dear, then the flag itself symbolizes nothing. A nation is more than a geographical accident. It is a sharing of values, history, ideals and goals.

There is no flag-burning crisis in America today. There never has been. A few lunatic provocateurs have desecrated their own flags in a few isolated episodes. America has survived, prospered, even flourished as our freedoms have expanded.

Like Justice William Brennan, we agree that desecration of the flag can be extremely offensive, outrageous. But do those sad, angry, disillusioned minds really think America is so fragile, so fearful, it cannot withstand the burning of cloth or a barrage of angry words? If so, they know little about their country.

We hope that the members of the Senate and other political figures accept the House vote and move on to more important national issues. The advent of another election campaign will tempt some to inject super-patriotism into their races. That would be a disservice — to the flag and the Bill of Rights it represents.

## The Honolulu Advertiser
*Honolulu, HI, June 22, 1990*

If only this were the last we were going to hear about it!

The House of Representatives yesterday rejected a constitutional amendment to ban desecration of the American flag by a 254-177 vote. Although a majority favored sending the amendment on to the Senate and states, the tally was 34 votes short of the two-thirds required.

Sadly though, this is not the end. Some are intent on forcing a roll-call to get senators on the record, too. And with a Gallup Poll showing two-thirds of the public in favor of a flag-burning ban, it's a safe bet that the issue will come up this fall in many of the dreaded "30-second spots," the quickest, least meaningful political advertising.

It may even happen in the Senate race in Hawaii, where one contender, Republican Representative Pat Saiki, favors a constitutional amendment while the other, Democratic Senator Dan Akaka, is on record against it.

For Americans worried about the quality of political debate, it will be instructive to see which candidates flog the flag question and which spend their time on less trivial pursuits.

The irony of this year-long brouhaha is that there's no epidemic of flag burning to wipe out. The act is rightly so repugnant to the overwhelming majority of Americans that only a tiny minority use it — for its shock value, not to persuade.

But since the Supreme Court ruled that even flag desecration is protected by the First Amendment, some politicians have played on legitimate love and respect of country for the basest partisan purposes.

It seems not to trouble them that in protecting the flag — a great symbol, but only that — they were for the first time in 200 years threatening to tamper with the Bill of Rights and the basic freedoms that America is really all about.

## ST. LOUIS POST-DISPATCH
*St. Louis, MO, June 24, 1990*

In an election year, the sensible stand by the House of Representatives against a flag-burning amendment to the Constitution certainly won't be the last word on the issue. But it was just as certainly the right one. The momentum created by the amendment's failure to get a two-thirds majority should carry the day through the coming campaign.

Thursday's debate featured the typical appeals for protection of the symbol of the flag rather than the unique rights and protections the flag represents. But the issue was decided by the realization that the public furor ignited by last year's original Supreme Court flag-burning decision has not been matched following this year's rerun. Democratic Rep. Don Edwards of California, a leading critic of the amendment, said his mail ran as much as 30-1 against his position a year ago but now is 50-1 in favor. "The American people are actually moving toward understanding better what they have in the Bill of Rights every day," he said.

That movement didn't stop emotional speech-making by his colleagues, of course. Flags were waved and representatives took refuge in them, trying to overcome reason with rhetoric. But in the end, House Speaker Thomas Foley won the day, with the amendment coming up 34 votes short of the majority it needed. Rep. Foley summed up his argument well in a rare floor speech: "We should not amend the Constitution to reach the sparse and scattered and despicable conduct of a few who would dishonor the flag and defile it."

House members who agreed with him and voted no included Missouri Democrats William Clay and Richard Gephardt and Illinois Democrats Glenn Poshard and Richard Durbin. Those voting in favor were Missouri Republicans Jack Buechner and Bill Emerson, Missouri Democrat Ike Skelton, Illinois Democrat Jerry Costello and Illinois Republican Lynn Martin, candidate for the Senate. Their constituents should recall how they voted.

Incumbents who bravely decided to preserve freedom may worry that their vote will be misrepresented in one of Sen. Bob Dole's threatened "30-second spots," but they should recall the words of Rep. David Skaggs, a Colorado Democrat. Hailing the "many individual acts of political courage" on the House floor, he added: "Men and women have literally risked their political future on behalf of the Constitution and the Bill of Rights." Few aspects of government are more worth taking such a risk.

## THE BUFFALO NEWS
*Buffalo, NY, June 23, 1990*

THE HOUSE of Representatives served American freedoms wisely when it defeated a misconceived effort to amend the Constitution in order to protect the flag from desecration.

Trying to protect the Stars and Stripes may be understandable. But approval would have given undeserved momentum to the attempt — backed by President Bush and many Republican legislators — to undermine First Amendment guarantees of personal liberties for the first time since the Bill of Rights was adopted nearly 200 years ago.

It would be uncommonly bad judgment to revise the Bill of Rights because of a few crazies who defile the flag. It is a symbol strong and sturdy enough to withstand that.

The Supreme Court has twice ruled — sensibly — that desecration of the flag, repugnant as it is, represents a form of speech. It is important to remember that one need not agree with what someone says in order to respect his or her right to say it. Indeed, for free speech to carry true meaning, it must apply to very unpopular ideas and sentiments as well as popular ones.

Fortunately, this reasoning appears to have gained ground over the past 12 months since the high court's first flag-burning decision. The reaction to this year's similar court decision, voiding a statute enacted last fall that made defiling the flag illegal, seemed more restrained. Apparently, many had pondered the deeper issues involved and concluded that the substance of their freedoms was more important than symbols of them.

A majority of House members did vote for the amendment. But the Framers of the Constitution, the James Madisons and Alexander Hamiltons, intentionally made it difficult to upset their handiwork. Though attempts are often tried, the Constitution has been revised only four times in two centuries to overturn unpopular Supreme Court rulings.

So the 254-177 House vote Thursday fell short of the two-thirds majority required to approve constitutional revisions. The Senate could still pass the amendment, but both houses of Congress must approve it for any revision to go to the states for ratification.

Those who get credit for turning back this misguided effort must include the Western New York delegation, where four of the five members voted no. Only Rep. Bill Paxon, R-Amherst, supported this symbol over the substance of individual liberties.

Rep. G. V. Montgomery, D-Miss., lead sponsor of the amendment contended that "we owe it to the brave Americans who have died for this country."

Not really. What we owe those brave people who sacrificed their lives for America is a set of personal freedoms kept fresh and undiluted. That, after all, is what they really fought for.

## SYRACUSE HERALD-JOURNAL
*Syracuse, NY, June 21, 1990*

Rep. James Walsh prides himself on being an independent thinker — a man who can peer through the veil of party politics and clearly discern right and wrong.

But on the issue of tampering with the Constitution to protect Old Glory from flag burners, he is a groupie. Opposition to flag burning is fashionable and our congressman wants to be a member of the "in" crowd.

In defense of counting himself among those politicians who have elevated flag burning to crisis level, Walsh says that nothing is absolute.

He acknowledges the First Amendment grants free speech. He then reminds us you can't shout "fire" in a theater.

The Second Amendment, he says, grants the right to bear arms, but still leaves room for gun control.

Weak arguments for amending the Constitution.

The restrictions on free speech and the right to bear arms exist to protect all of us — from the crackpots, the mean-spirited, the insane. The only thing flag burners hurt is our feelings.

Most of us can't even recall having seen a flag torched. Yet Walsh is convinced flag burning poses so great a danger it is worth weakening the First Amendment provisions of freedom of speech and expression.

If his logic is followed to its end, then attention should be focused on the Second Amendment, not the First. Guns do pose a real threat. People are mowed down in the streets with them every day. Gun are used in crimes of passion and crimes for money. They are toted by mad people who kill everyone in sight because their cars were repossessed. They are the weapons of choice for street gangs, drug dealers and anyone else for whom killing is an option.

But there is no clamor in Congress or in the White House for the prohibition of the sale of guns in this country. No gun-waving politician has called for an amendment to the Constitution.

Why not?

Surely Walsh and other lawmakers must know that being blown away by a semiautomatic offends our sensibilities more than the thought of a smoldering flag.

Flag burning is feel-good politics. It's a distraction meant to tug at our heart strings, to whip us into a frenzy. Lawmakers hope the tears that form in our eyes when we think about Old Glory will temporarily blind us so we can't see what's really going on. And it's a fine campaign issue. Only America-haters are against the flag, right?

We thought Jim Walsh was above all that.

## The Washington Post
*Washington, DC, June 23, 1990*

IN THE 1988 campaign, the Republicans beat the Democrats at manipulating patriotic symbols. With the flag amendment in the House of Representatives this week, they tried again—but this time they lost. It would be a mistake to see the House vote as a turning point in the nation's recent stagy, nasty politics. But the 177 House members—160 Democrats, 17 Republicans—who preserved the First Amendment by blocking the proposed codicil on the flag performed a noble service at perhaps considerable risk. They are owed a greater debt than is likely to be soon recognized. Who knows? They may even have transferred some backbone to their rabbity fellows.

The national legislature has better things to do than debate flag burning. The issue is a retreat from reality, and perhaps no wonder. The deficit approaches $200 billion, the paths to its reduction are uniformly painful, national defense policy waits to be rewritten, the health care system is in financial crisis, income inequality is at a modern high, the savings and loan industry is in ruins—and the vote of the week is on whether Congress and the states should be empowered, contrary to the free-speech clause, to prevent the physical desecration of the flag.

Everyone understood what kind of vote this was. No sooner was the tally in than the National Republican Congressional Committee was faxing press releases into the districts of Democrats who voted no, cutely accusing them of "flag wavering." The Republican operatives are trashing the values they are pretending to champion even as, in a new twist on the tactic of the big lie, they accuse their opponents of besmirching the values the opponents are struggling against press release and 30-second spot to uphold.

The victory was a tribute partly to Tom Foley. Some in his party have sniffed of late that he and his counterpart in the Senate, George Mitchell, have not been vigorous enough in their leadership. But on this most basic of issues and tests Mr. Foley bought time when he needed it a year ago, marshaled his troops, helped provide them with cover, above all took the right position on the merits—and won. George Bush's position on this issue will not help him in the history books. Nor may it turn out to help him as much in the short run as the supposed shrewdness of some of his handlers would suggest. The only danger the flag-burners represent to the country is if they provoke precisely what Mr. Foley's House has now sanely and courageously prevented.

## Omaha World-Herald
*Omaha, NE, June 24, 1990*

The voters should reject any attempt that might materialize to make flag-burning the main issue of this year's political campaigns. To impugn the character or patriotism of a senator or congressman because of sincerely held views about the proper role of the Constitution and Bill of Rights would be wrong, and the public shouldn't stand for it.

Decent, honorable people are to be found on both sides of the congressional debate. Four of the nine members of the U.S. Supreme Court felt that flag desecration could be punished by law without violating the Constitution. That doesn't make the other five flag-burners.

Nebraska's two Democratic U.S. senators have split on the issue, with J. James Exon voicing support for a constitutional amendment and Bob Kerrey coming out against an amendment. Rep. Doug Bereuter of Nebraska, a moderate Republican, voted for the amendment that died in the House of Representatives Thursday. Rep. Fred Grandy of Iowa, also a moderate Republican, voted against the amendment, as did Democrat Peter Hoagland of Nebraska.

Such splits in no way suggest that one side loves the flag more than the other. Bereuter was right when he said that "patriotic Americans can certainly disagree on the merits of a constitutional amendment to protect the American flag."

This is not to say that a congressman's position on the flag amendment should be off-limits in the campaign. How an official votes is always the public's business. Political candidates are always entitled to point up the differences between their positions and those of their opponent.

It is one thing, however, to point up a number of differences in positions and qualifications and quite another to wrap oneself in the flag, exploiting that issue above all others with attack commercials suggesting that the other person is unpatriotic.

We don't know if that kind of campaign is being planned anywhere in the country. We hope it isn't.

But if a single-issue campaign is attempted, the public shouldn't be shy in showing its disapproval. Candidates in every congressional district should be held to their responsibility to address the broad range of issues that the next Congress will have to deal with.

## Arkansas Gazette
*Little Rock, AR, June 28, 1990*

As the House of Representatives had already disposed of the flag-burning amendment, there was no need for the Senate to consider it. But the Republicans pushing the amendment are more interested in politics than flags and they demanded a vote, which they believe can be used against Democrats. So the Senate gave them their vote Tuesday, and honorably. Like the House, the Senate rejected the amendment.

Arkansas can be proud that both its senators, Dale Bumpers and David Pryor, voted against the amendment. Courage was required; only four other Southern senators voted no. Though the amendment is actually an attack on freedom of speech, it is thought to be politically popular.

The forcing of a vote in the Senate was another shameful display of partisanship over patriotism, in line with the whole flag-amendment campaign. The amendment's backers in Congress and the White House were willing to undermine the Bill of Rights, which guarantees Americans' most precious freedoms, in exchange for political gain. Senate Minority Leader Bob Dole, R-Kan., had gloated publicly that a senator's vote against the amendment would make a great TV spot for the senator's opponent. Dole and fellow conspirators insisted Tuesday that they were sincere about protecting the flag, but Dole has had trouble keeping a straight face throughout this whole business. Remember the picture of him waving the tiny flag to celebrate the president's birthday? He has a sense of humor, if not of responsibility. Sen. Edward Kennedy, D-Mass., had it exactly right when he said the only reason the Senate was voting was "because of a partisan campaign to misuse the flag and abuse the Bill of Rights for political advantage."

With this diversion out of the way for another year, Congress can turn its attention to real issues, especially the federal deficit. If this crushing problem is approached with the same selfish factionalism that powered the flag-burning amendment, there is no hope of resolution.

## THE BLADE
*Toledo, OH, June 26, 1990*

THE House defeat of a proposed flag-burning amendment to the Constitution came as a considerable and pleasant surprise to opponents who only days earlier had all but given up on turning back the anti-flag burning tide.

The vote was 254 in favor and 177 against, 34 votes shy of the two-thirds vote necessary for a constitutional amendment. One would be hard-pressed to see this as a ringing endorsement of the First Amendment's protection of free speech. After all, a majority of House members obviously believe that putting flag-burners in jail is quite reasonable. But the action effectively kills chances of passing any such measure this year, even if the Senate approves it.

What the action does suggest is that an increasing number of congressmen refuse to be stampeded either by emotional rhetoric or the fairly blunt threats that anyone who doesn't want to punish flag desecrators will pay for that view when seeking reelection. In fact, many Capitol Hill watchers are beginning to believe that the issue is no longer the emotional dynamite it once was, even though President Bush mousetrapped Michael Dukakis over the Pledge of Allegiance in the presidential campaign two years ago and has been in the vanguard of the free speech assault again this year.

This is not a liberal vs. conservative matter by any standard. Twice in less than a year, ideologically conservative U.S. Supreme Court justices have sided with the few remaining liberals to strike down flag-burning laws, the first one passed by the Texas legislature and the second one — the Flag Protection Act of 1989 — passed late last year by Congress in an attempt to override the High Court. Conservative as well as liberal legal scholars, including former Supreme Court Justice Lewis Powell, urged Congress to reject the amendment as an invalid restriction upon the Bill of Rights.

Yet flag amendment proponents continue to let their anger about insults to the flag outweigh what should be their deeper concern for protecting the Constitution. For example, Illinois congressman Bob Michel, House minority leader, said that those who would burn the flag still have "an all but infinite number of ways to continue expressing themselves." In other words, Congress will just remove one of them, and maybe two, or three or four ... or more.

We can just imagine James Madison penning the words "Congress shall make no law ... abridging the freedom of speech except when Congress doesn't like what someone is saying."

First Amendment rights to free speech exist exactly to prohibit that kind of thinking and to protect those whose views are unsettling or distasteful, no matter how contemptuous of those people one may be. As Justice William Brennan said in his majority opinion a few weeks ago, "... punishing desecration of the flag dilutes the very freedom that makes this emblem so revered and worth revering."

May lawmakers get that message during the moratorium that the House vote has provided.

## DAILY NEWS
*New York, NY, June 23, 1990*

The House of Representatives' vote to reject a flag-burning amendment leaves an essential question: Is there a way to stop flag burning without diluting the Bill of Rights? Some people think so: Amend the federal flag code to require that all official American flags be made from fireproof cloth. You might chuckle, but the idea isn't all that silly. And it sure would avoid the pitfalls of tampering with this nation's fundamental document.

The suggestion has been made by various folk. Vermont state archivist Gregory Sanford says: "If anyone was burning a flag, you'd know it wasn't the official flag because the official flag wouldn't burn. Then we could get back to more burning issues like the S&L scandal and the budget deficit."

Of course, there'd still be a bunch of pre-amendment flammable flags out there, but they'd eventually be retired. There's also nothing to prevent some radical Betsy Ross from hand-crafting a version solely to condemn it to the flames — but odds are that wouldn't happen often and the "flag" would be a poor facsimile. Flag-burners are good at striking matches, but their needlework skills aren't necessarily all that hot.

## Birmingham Post-Herald
*Birmingham, AL, June 23, 1990*

The men who drafted the U.S. Constitution in 1787 deliberately made the amendment process difficult. They knew — and feared — what was likely to happen if each and every issue that stirred public passions resulted in an amendment to the charter of the federal government. They wanted amendments to be adopted only after thorough study and debate.

The wisdom of the founding fathers was proven Thursday when the U.S. House of Representatives failed to muster the two-thirds vote needed to send a proposed amendment to ban desecration of the American flag on to the U.S. Senate. The shortfall — 34 votes — was greater than expected, indicating that the initial passions aroused by the U.S. Supreme Court's June 11 ruling on flag-burning are cooling.

Supporters of the amendment are claiming that they lost because House Speaker Tom Foley rushed the issue to a vote, preventing them from bringing public pressure to bear. Aside from the fact that House members have actually had a year to think about the issue — last week's ruling simply reiterated what the court majority said a year ago — we doubt that a delay would have increased the vote for the amendment.

It is inconceivable that even the densest of politicians is unaware of how the overwhelming majority of his or her constituents feels about flag and those who would treat it with disrespect. A larger percentage of politicians feel the same way — there aren't many, if any, places in this country where you can get elected while showing contempt for the flag. The pressure to pass an amendment has been intense from the time the court's ruling was released.

What took more time to develop was the realization that an attempt to protect the flag by a constitutional amendment would, by its nature, destroy a very important part of the freedom that the flag symbolizes. Supporting the proposed amendment is not a conservative position, it is a radical one.

For example, until the day before the House vote, moderately conservative Rep. Tim Valentine, D-N.C., was a sponsor of the proposed amendment. He joined the opposition because, "I finally heard the voice of my own conscience."

A similar conversion happened last year when Sen. Bob Kerrey, D-Neb., a Medal of Honor winner in Vietnam who originally thought the court was wrong, sat down and read what the justices actually said. Kerrey became a strong opponent of an amendment. He was persuaded by words such as these from Justice William Brennen: "If there is a bedrock principle underlying the First Amendment, it is that the Government may not prohibit the expression of an idea simply because society finds the idea itself offensive or disagreeable."

The American flag and all that it symbolizes is not endangered by the actions of a few childish individuals who can think of no better way to attract attention then by burning flags.

Justice John Paul Stephens, who thinks flag-burning can be outlawed by statute, pointed out the greater danger to what the flag symbolizes when he wrote in his dissent, "... the integrity of the symbol has been compromised by those leaders who seem to advocate compulsory worship of the flag even by individuals whom it offends, or who seem to manipulate the symbol of national purpose into a pretext for partisan disputes about meaner ends."

Now that 177 members of the House have prevented passage of the flag amendment, perhaps the Bill of Rights and the freedoms those first 10 amendments to the Constitution protect are out of immediate danger from that source. At least we hope so.

## THE SACRAMENTO BEE
*Sacramento, CA, June 23, 1990*

Asked to choose between protecting the flag and protecting the liberty for which it stands, 177 members of the House of Representatives, Democrats and Republicans alike, stood by the Bill of Rights. In doing so they marked themselves as patriots every bit as sturdy as those who waved the flag.

What separated the two sides in the debate was not love of nation or the flag it represents. Instead, they were divided between those who, following President Bush, believe the flag needs special protection even at the expense of amending the Bill of Rights for the first time in two centuries, and those who have confidence in the power of liberty and democratic values to prevail over the insults of a few flag-burning kooks.

In the end, confidence triumphed: in part because the founders wisely made it difficult even for passionate majorities to tamper with the nation's basic liberties; but mostly because, for all the nervous patriots' posturings, the nation was not moved to panic. When Bush issued his call for a flag protection constitutional amendment after the latest Supreme Court ruling, the phones did not ring on Capitol Hill or the mail pour in. And the House heard that message.

The House vote kills the flag protection amendment but won't end the shouting. Politicians with nothing else to say will rush to exploit Old Glory. But wrapping oneself in the flag for a 30-second campaign commercial is speech as crude and inarticulate as burning it. The House members who voted against rewriting the Bill of Rights showed a commendable faith that good ideas and articulate speech will win out over both forms of flag abuse.

## THE ASHEVILLE CITIZEN
*Ashville, NC, June 23, 1990*

So that's what it has come to, has it? Used to, conservatives cherished the American Constitution and upheld our Bill of Rights. Most of us were proud to call ourselves "conservative" when it came to protecting our fundamental freedoms.

But listen to Rep. Newt Gingrich of Georgia, House minority whip and firebrand of the Republican right wing. Those who oppose diluting the First Amendment to accommodate flag laws represent a "Hollywood-San Francisco-Greenwich Village value system," he said.

Right. Anyone today who wants to protect citizens against the awesome power of government surely is not an average American citizen. He must be a flake, homosexual or weirdo, if you follow Gingrich's rationale.

How far some so-called "conservatives" have fallen from the principles that made this nation great.

## THE EMPORIA GAZETTE
*Emporia, KS, June 25, 1990*

THE wave of political "patriotism" that threatened to clutter the Constitution has subsided just in time.

Good judgment prevailed Thursday when the U.S. House defeated a proposed Constitutional amendment to protect the American flag from harm. The vote moves the flag debate from Congress to the campaign trail, where it is sure to become a major issue.

The flag-burning amendment was proposed in reaction to two U.S. Supreme Court rulings that said destruction of the flag as an act of political protest is protected by the First Amendment right of free speech. One court ruling struck down a Texas flag-burning law, and the second, earlier this month, rejected a revived Federal statute.

Soon after the second ruling, the proposed Constitutional amendment surfaced again, with wide public support and strong support in both houses. The proposed amendment said, "The Congress and the States shall have the power to prohibit the physical desecration of the flag of the United States."

To become part of the Constitution, the amendment would need 289 votes in the House and 67 in the Senate. Then it would have to be ratified by 38 state legislatures.

The decisive House vote on Thursday was 254 in favor to 177 against.

Last week, as the vote approached, Congress was divided bitterly over the flag issue. Then passionate support for the amendment began to wane. Some Congressmen said their mail was beginning to contain fewer letters of support for the amendment.

Supporters said Old Glory should be protected by the Constitution. Opponents said the amendment would weaken the First Amendment's protection of free speech.

The American flag is a grand symbol of the freedoms we enjoy in this country. It is sad that our fellow countrymen would burn or desecrate it. But it also is sad that many Americans are homeless and starving, children are abused and minorities must continue to fight for equality.

The Constitution protects our right to think and act as free people. It does not protect us from bad judgment or bad taste.

We cannot let emotions and political opportunism clutter up the Constitution and pare away our freedoms. — N.H.

## The Atlanta Journal AND THE ATLANTA CONSTITUTION
*Atlanta, GA, June 28, 1990*

The vote in the Senate was meaningless. The House already had killed the proposed constitutional amendment that would intrude into the Bill of the Rights for the first time ever, just to get at a handful of fringey flag-burners.

For the record, however, it was disappointing to see both of Georgia's senators, Sam Nunn and Wyche Fowler, go with the Constitution-burners. The disappointment is particularly sharp in Mr. Nunn's case. No one has a safer seat. If Mr. Nunn had stood against the panic and political opportunism of the amendment, his position would have provided shelter for other moderates to take a similar stand.

Presumably, Mr. Nunn's vote was sincere. Sincerity in the sour business of diminishing the Bill of Rights is no virtue.

## Rockford Register Star
*Rockford, IL, June 24, 1990*

The cause of freedom won a victory over political pandering last week when 177 courageous members of the U.S. House of Representatives successfully staved off an effort to rewrite the Bill of Rights just to punish a few miscreants who would burn the American flag.

With this attempted assault on the Constitution behind us, at least for a while, now we'll see which politicians will try to use the flag issue to impugn the patriotism of their opponents in the fall campaigns.

The demagogues should first consider, however, that such a strategy is fraught with political peril, as the electorate is not necessarily so simpleminded as to equate opposition to changing the First Amendment with sympathy for flag-burners. Indeed, the thoughtful voter will take offense at the candidate who dares to desecrate both the flag and the Constitution with phony patriotic posturing.

None of this is to say, we should emphasize, that all those lawmakers who voted in favor of the flag-protection amendment were insincere. On the contrary, many were eloquent in their heartfelt explanations of why they thought an exception to the First Amendment should be made for physical abuse of the flag.

But too many in Congress have made no bones about the delight with which they anticipate slinging mud at those who opposed the amendment questioning their loyalty to this country, lumping them with the lunatic fringe, implying that they don't respect the sacrifices of America's fallen military warriors.

There's a word for such political poison: fascism. It exalts a false loyalty, and it is inimical to the most basic American principles of freedom. It doesn't honor the flag; rather, it dishonors what the flag represents.

As for this district's representative in Congress, Republican Lynn Martin, we don't question the ingenuousness of her vote in favor of the flag-protection amendment. Nor do we doubt that a sizable segment, perhaps even a majority, of her constituents agree with her on this issue.

But we are uncomfortable with recent signals from Martin's campaign staff that the flag matter might be used to cast aspersions on the patriotism of incumbent Democrat Paul Simon, her opponent in the contest this fall for the U.S. Senate.

That's gutter stuff, and we trust that Lynn Martin is too classy to resort to it.

## RAPID CITY JOURNAL

*Rapid, City, SD, June 17, 1990*

We'd like to think that Alexis de Tocqueville was wrong about freedom of thought in America, but the debate over flag burning makes it difficult to argue that case.

"In America the majority has enclosed thought within a formidable fence," Tocqueville wrote in 1835. "A writer is free inside that area, but woe to the man who goes outside it." The fence Tocqueville described was a social, psychological and political barrier. Its fence posts — public condemnation and ridicule — were strung with the wire of ostracism. "I know of no country in which, speaking generally, there is less independence of mind and true freedom of discussion than in America," he wrote.

Surely this Frenchman's jaded 19th-century analysis overstated the case.

Or did it? Congress, by seeking to amend the Bill of Rights in order to ban flag burning, would include the Constitution itself in Tocqueville's fence. If this happens, a type of political expression would be banned, not because it endangers public safety but because the idea itself is repugnant to the majority. Flag burning would be prohibited not just by the force of public scorn but by the Constitution itself. Such a ban goes beyond even Tocqueville's criticism.

On the other hand, the political dialogue on the issue would come as no surprise to Tocqueville.

Conservatives, who should be fighting for individual freedom and against government control of our lives, are leading the charge to reduce our freedom. Liberals, who should be sticking up for the minority, are so afraid of losing elections, they are joining the stampede.

Fortunately, there are a few heroes who refute Tocqueville's thesis. Sen. Bob Kerrey, D-Neb., who said he was "ashamed" of President Bush's manipulation of the issue, has been a consistently strong voice of opposition. Kerrey lost a leg in Vietnam and won a Congressional Medal of Honor there, so it's difficult for political opponents to question his patriotism. Sen. John Danforth, R-Mo., who lacks Kerrey's dramatic "advantages," deserves even more credit for his warnings against the proposed amendment and his stand against fellow conservatives.

Tocqueville was right about one thing. There does tend to be a "tyranny of the majority" in democracies. That's why the Bill of Rights is such an important part of the Constitution. It protects unpopular ideas. Amending the Bill of Rights to prohibit a certain type of political expression would ratify one of Tocqueville's harshest criticisms of the United States.

We still think Tocqueville was wrong about freedom of thought in America. Congress or the state legislatures or the American people themselves can prove us right by rejecting this proposed constitutional amendment.

## ALBUQUERQUE JOURNAL

*Albuquerque, NM, June 25, 1990*

The wisdom of the giants who framed the Constitution has been demonstrated once again. That document requires an extraordinary majority — two-thirds of the members of both chambers — for the lesser mortals that followed to amend the Constitution.

Why not make it easier? Why not the 50 percent plus one vote it takes to enact the ordinary laws prompted by mundane motivations like political posturing, pandering to polls, maneuvering for partisan advantage and lust for re-election?

Because the Constitution is not ordinary. The Constitution is supposed to stand above political tides and popular currents, a timeless beacon.

That's what it is supposed to be. What it has been lately is just a way for Republicans to leverage some short-term political advantage over House Democrats.

Thursday's House vote to kill the amendment will become the campaign year refrain: Those unpatriotic congressmen who voted against fiddling around with the Constitution to end flag-burning should be hounded from office. And the issues that really smolder — the deficit millstone around the nation's economic neck, education, the savings and loan debacle, persistent poverty and illiteracy — can be obscured once again.

The flag-burning issue is just a red cape to be waved in front of voters to distract and maneuver them until election day. At that point, the GOP can fold up the flag issue and put it on the shelf until the next election.

Like the Constitution itself, politicians of both parties need to look behind the flag and beyond the next election.

## CHICAGO Sun-Times

*Chicago, IL, June 24, 1990*

The 11 Illinois congressmen who voted against a constitutional amendment to prohibit desecration of the flag did so against a tide of emotionally potent public opinion on the other side.

They would have risked virtually nothing politically in voting for the proposal, but they were willing, for the sake of fidelity to their own convictions and to the values of the Bill of Rights, to risk political disfavor for taking an unpopular position.

For that, a salute here to: Republican John E. Porter and Democrats Terry L. Bruce, Cardiss Collins, Richard J. Durbin, Lane Evans, Charles A. Hayes, Glenn Poshard, Dan Rostenkowski, Martin A. Russo, Gus Savage and Sidney R. Yates.

## Van Gogh, Renoir Works Set Records

*Irises*, a painting by Vincent van Gogh that had set the current record for the most expensive painting ever sold when it was auctioned for $53.9 million in 1987, had been resold for an undisclosed sum to the J. Paul Getty Museum in Malibu, Calif., it was reported March 22, 1990.

The Getty purchased the painting from Australian financier Alan Bond, whose business empire had been experiencing financial difficulties.

Sotheby's, the auction house that handled the record-breaking sale, subsequently revealed that it had loaned Bond half the money needed to purchase *Irises*, using the painting itself as collateral. The auction house said it had taken "control" of the painting after Bond failed to repay the loan.

After receiving widespread criticism following the disclosure of its lending arrangement with Bond, Sotheby's had announced in January that it was ending its service of providing "margined" loans to art purchasers.

A painting by van Gogh and another by Pierre Auguste Renoir became, respectively, the most expensive and second-most expensive paintings ever sold at an auction.

The van Gogh canvas, *Portrait of Dr. Gachet*, which was painted just six weeks before the artist committed suicide in 1890, was sold for a record $82.5 million May 15, 1990 at Christie'e auction house in New York City to Japanese art dealer Hideto Kobayashi. (The price included a standard 10% "buyer's fee," or commission, to Christie's.)

It was revealed May 17 that Kobayashi had purchased the *Portrait of Dr. Gachet* on behalf of a Japanese businessman, Ryoei Saito, 74, who was the honorary chairman of Daishowa Paper Manufacturing Co., the second-largest paper manufacturer in Japan.

Two days after the van Gogh sale, a painting by Renoir, *Au Moulin de la Galette*, became the second-most expensive painting ever sold when it was auctioned for a total of $78.1 million (including the 10% auction house commission) at Sotheby's in New York. The painting was the smaller of two versions of the same open-air dance-hall scene that Renoir had painted in 1876. The larger version hung in the Musee d'Orsay in Paris. It was revealed May 18 that the buyer once again had been Saito.

Saito stated that "for paintings like that, the price was cheap."

The sales capped two weeks of mixed auction activity at Christie's and Sotheby's spring sales of Impressionist and Modern art in New York City and London. Although record prices were paid for paintings and sculptures by some artists, other works went unsold or were purchased for prices below their pre-sale estimates.

## Richmond Times-Dispatch
*Richmond, VA, April 2, 1987*

Some works of art are beyond the understanding of ordinary mortals, and so are some financial decisions about art. Such as an unidentified purchaser's willingness to pay $39.8 million for a painting of sunflowers in a pot.

To be sure, it was not an ordinary painting of ordinary sunflowers in an ordinary pot. The artist was Vincent van Gogh, whose reputation has the effect of gold-plating whatever his name appears on. But was the painting worth the fortune it brought?

The price, wrote John Russell in The New York Times, "is best regarded in the context of the even larger lunacies that arise when too many people suddenly have more money than they know how to get rid of. It bears no relation whatever to any rational scale of values, to the status of this particular painting within van Gogh's total output or to its present condition." Which seems to be another way of saying a fool and his money are soon parted.

John Wilmerding, deputy director of the National Gallery of Art, told The Washington Post that the painting "now may be too famous and too valuable to put on view anywhere" largely because insurance and transportation costs would be prohibitive. Which suggests that whoever bought the painting will have to keep it in the same vault that used to hold the $39.8 million he paid for it.

Van Gogh no doubt would be astounded. During his life, which he ended himself a year after he painted "The Sunflowers" in 1888, van Gogh sold only one painting. He suggested to his brother that "one of these Scots or Americans" might be willing to pay as much as $30 for "my sunflowers," which he apparently would have considered a good deal.

A good deal obviously is what the purchaser of The Sunflowers believes he or she got for the $39.8 million. And that, after all, is what matters, whether the rest of us understand or not.

## Omaha World-Herald
*Omaha, NE, April 2, 1987*

What is the value of a work of art? The 19th century Dutch impressionist painter Vincent van Gogh hoped to sell his painting "Sunflowers" for the equivalent of $125. Several days ago, the painting sold for more than $39 million.

When van Gogh died, he left 200 paintings in the care of his sister-in-law. They were valued at about $40 apiece. Two years ago, his "Landscape With Rising Sun" brought $10 million.

The success of van Gogh's paintings after his death is an ironic sequel to the tragic story of his life. An emotionally disturbed man, he was crushed by loneliness that was both physical and spiritual. As a painter, he boldly sought new forms and colors, a new way of seeing the world. But he couldn't support himself by selling his paintings. He killed himself in 1890 at age 37.

Why is the world sometimes so blind to an emerging talent? It seems that pioneers in new artistic technique, whose peculiar genius demands that they reject safe, academic painting and acceptable styles, must often struggle against rejection. Charlatans of pop art are honored today with income and attention beyond the dreams of van Gogh, a true artist.

The true value of van Gogh's paintings can't be measured in dollars, or in millions of dollars. The value of his work is its ability to touch the imagination of generation after generation of art lovers.

## The Washington Post
*Washington, DC, April 2, 1987*

VINCENT VAN GOGH made practically nothing off his paintings. When he ended his unhappy life by his own hand in 1890, most of his works were still stacked up unsold in the home of his brother, an art dealer. This week, one of those works—a little picture of some sunflowers for which van Gogh had thought he might get 50 francs—was auctioned off in London for $39.9 million. Some art lovers might well argue that that's not such an outrageous price for a masterpiece when you consider the mundane nature of the other things $39.9 million could purchase: one mile of interstate highway, two F-16 fighter planes or the Seattle Mariners baseball team, which not only can't paint masterpieces but can't play baseball very well either.

Most of the art world, however, was somewhat alarmed if also thrilled by the spectacle at the Christie's auction: jittery guards bringing forth the painting as if it were a holy relic; anonymous bidders in distant parts of the world raising the ante $805,000 at a time via telephone hookups; a fancy, jaded crowd growing feverish with excitement as the price mounted quickly to more than three times the previous high for a work of art.

Van Gogh painted a half-dozen pictures of sunflowers, and some are in better shape than the one sold this week, whose original vibrant yellows are said to be darkened by age. Nevertheless, someone—known but to Christie's, for like most of the highest-priced works of art these days, this one went to an anonymous buyer—valued it very highly.

"There is an enormous pressure of money and a declining number of works of art that can come on the market," said a London art dealer after the sale. "It can go too far; it can create an almost explosive situation." Ronald de Leeuw, director of Amsterdam's van Gogh museum, agreed. "Prices like this not only put the pictures out of reach of the average museum, they could also influence insurance premiums, possibly making staging exhibitions prohibitively costly." So in time perhaps, many of van Gogh's best works, which once sat unsold and unseen in his brother's home, will sit unseen and uninsurable in the homes of various anonymous multimillionaires.

After the auction, Christie's held a little party in honor of van Gogh, whose birthday it was. "He was a strange man" said the auctioneer, Charles Allsopp. "He wasn't very good at marketing. . . ." Van Gogh, for his part, might find today's art handlers to be a bit strange themselves: far from being poor at marketing, they are so good at it that they may be marketing his masterpieces right back into obscurity.

## The News and Courier
*Charleston, SC, April 7, 1987*

It was Vincent Van Gogh's failure to sell his paintings that drove him to madness. Yet it never crossed his mind to change his style — one so ahead of his time that he was doomed to be rejected by the art market of his day.

Were he alive and painting today, Van Gogh would be bombarded with advice. Change your style, he would be told.

Had he given in and turned his hand to paintings that would have been snapped up by the fashionable art dealers of the late 19th century, he would have failed the final test of greatness.

The $39.9 million that was paid at Christie's in London for Vincent Van Gogh's painting of a vase of sunflowers last week indicates that the world, as Oscar Wilde noted, is still dominated by people who know the price of everything and the value of nothing.

It is a neat paradox. The multi-million dollar sums that Van Gogh's paintings fetch today are proof that his genius cannot be measured by money. We know today's monetary worth of that vivid painting of sunflowers. The canvas, worthless when he finished it in 1889, now has a price tag of $39.9 million.

Worth means nothing. Value that is above money is what counts. Van Gogh's sunflowers were always — and always will be — priceless.

## THE SUN
*Baltimore, MD, April 12, 1987*

A century after painter Vincent van Gogh dashed off his seventh and darkest "Sunflowers" and failed to sell it for 50 francs, Christie's auction house of London has made $3.6 million just as its commission on the impressionist painting's sale to a Japanese insurance company. The $40 million worth that the Yasuda Fire & Marine Co. has put on one work by a relatively prolific artist of the late Nineteenth Century creates myths, not all of which are true:

*All artists who are unappreciated will be recognized in time.* Wrong. Most unknown artists deserve it. Some who don't deserve it are stuck with it.

*Dirt-cheap art is a good investment.* Wrong. Some is overpriced. You might speculate successfully on unknown art. You might even win the Maryland Lottery.

*Still-lifes are back in.* Wrong. Those sunflowers aren't still. They wiggle and writhe. That is van Gogh's charm.

*Madness helps.* Wrong. It sometimes coincides with greatness, but it never helps.

*Post-Impressionists fetch as much as High Renaissance masters.* Wrong. Anyone who can now predict a price for an extant Leonardo da Vinci oil painting would probably understand the federal budget.

*The art world is crazy.* Wrong. It does not always behave rationally.

*Too much money is chasing too few objects of great intrinsic worth.* Right. This raises their prices prohibitively and creates the need for lesser objects to be collected, inflating their prices as well. For this, art lovers suffer while artists do not gain. That is the way of the world and always was.

## AKRON BEACON JOURNAL
*Akron, OH, April 9, 1987*

A GROWING attitude in the civilized world — that wealth is the highest measure of human achievement — burst into full flower last week in two auctions in Europe.

Thursday and Friday, the jewelry and other baubles given to the late Duchess of Windsor by her husband were auctioned off to the assembled rich in Geneva, New York, and throughout the world via telephone hookups. The New York Times described the scene as a "garage sale from Never-Never Land."

The Duke, of course, was the man who gave up the English throne to marry not only a commoner but an American. But if he gave up the throne, he did not relinquish the trappings of royalty. And his love-gifts to his wife were sold for $50 million.

Another auction the previous Monday, at Christie's in London, saw a fading van Gogh painting, *Sunflower,* become the most expensive ever sold as two anonymous bidders took the price to $39.9 million before the matter was settled.

Both Vincent van Gogh, who sold but one painting in his lifetime, and the Duke of Windsor, who forfeited the chance to be more than a footnote to history, still enjoy celebrity status and still attract attention as only fame and/or fortune can.

The van Gogh was sold to pay inheritance taxes on an English estate. The Duchess' jewels went for a better cause — to benefit the Pasteur Institute in Paris. Both, however, celebrate wealth: the joy of being rich and the spectator sport that is involved for the rest of us in following the antics of the rich.

… Van Gogh

# The Star-Ledger
*Newark, NJ, April 1, 1987*

Can a price really be placed upon a work of art? Some true believers will answer that there is a falsity about all such efforts. Art is a work of the spirit, they say, and the human spirit cannot be measured in terms of dollars and cents.

But, false effort or not, there is a very real market in works of art, a market quite as tangible as the stock exchange or the diamond mart. Works of art are regularly bought and sold, with little concern for the spirit but a great deal of concern about what the traffic will bear.

Just as the Dow-Jones industrial average hits record highs, so does the art market. A painting by the 19th Century Dutch artist Vincent van Gogh was sold in auction at Christie's in London at a price of nearly $40 million, almost triple the previous highest price paid at an auction for a painting.

There is a deep and bitter irony that many will feel at the news of this enormous price. The artist killed himself in 1890 at the age of 37 in disappointment at his inability to sell his paintings. He had hoped to receive $125 for his work. After the sale of the painting, Christie's threw a party that highlighted a cake decorated with a replica of the painting in honor of Van Gogh.

There is perhaps a fundamental economic injustice in this wide discrepancy between what a collector can make from art and what an artist receives. Some have suggested laws be changed to allow an artist to realize something from the resale of his art—but even this would obviously not have helped Van Gogh. Perhaps the only real consolation for the artist was the self-realization of his talent and the words of a great poet, 200 years ago: "Art is long, life is short."

# THE BUFFALO NEWS
*Buffalo, NY, April 6, 1987*

VINCENT VAN GOGH would have been proud. He was able to sell only one of his paintings during his lifetime — and that was for a pittance. He committed suicide at age 37, a failure. But last week, one of his paintings, "Sunflowers," was sold at the fashionable Christie's auction house in London for $39.8 million.

Appropriately, the painting was sold on March 30, the 134th anniversary of the birth of the tortured Dutch artist. Van Gogh once described his painting as "magnificent," saying "it has the effect of a piece of cloth with satin and gold embroidery." He painted five similar sunflower pictures that express an emotion that Van Gogh described as "tremendously keyed up."

Van Gogh epitomized the popular view of the struggling, impoverished artist whose work is recognized only after his death. His work is now seen as an important part of the revolutionary Impressionist and Post-Impressionist movement, but to his contemporaries it had an unfamiliar, jarring effect.

But how can a painting, once considered worthless, be worth $39.8 million? Can any painting be worth that much? A painting is worth, of course, exactly what people are willing to pay for it. Great art works have soared in value in the past few years as museums and private collectors have competed to purchase them at prices beyond a king's ransom.

All of the 10 most expensive paintings ever sold at auction were sold in the past seven years. The price for "Sunflowers" was four times the price of another Van Gogh in the top 10, which was auctioned in 1985. Is it four times as good — especially today, when the ecstatic chrome yellow quality has started to fade?

One is reminded of the tulip craze in the 17th century, when tulip bulbs prices soared to outlandish levels only to collapse. But recognition of Van Gogh's genius will never collapse.

One only regrets that the picture may now disappear into the home of the anonymous purchaser. However, the public can still view the other four sunflower masterpieces in museums in the United States and Europe.

JAPANESE BUY "SUNFLOWERS"

## Edmonton Journal
*Edmonton, Alta., April 1, 1987*

**NOTE:** An anonymous buyer has paid $52 million for a Vincent van Gogh painting titled Sunflowers — a painting the artist had hoped to sell for $160 in 1890, but couldn't.

It just goes to show that in the world of art, today's junk can be tomorrow's masterpiece. Imagine — 50 years from now, art collectors may be clamoring for pastels of Elvis painted on black velvet. There's no accounting for taste.

## THE RICHMOND NEWS LEADER
*Richmond, VA, July 12, 1989*

The gift by Pamela Harriman of Vincent Van Gogh's still-life, "Roses," to the National Gallery of Art has set the art world a'twitter. And well it should: The gift of this painting, valued at $60 million or more, qualifies as a real windfall for the public in a volatile art market and under current tax laws.

For many art museums, what they now have in their collections is just about what they are going to get. The supply of classical art is dwindling, and works by masters now fetch prices on the open market well beyond a museum's ability to pay. The last Van Gogh to be sold, for instance — his "Irises" — went for almost $54 million in the fall of '87. These multi-million-dollar purchases are vanishing into private collections, to be available to public view only if the owners can be prevailed upon to lend them for special exhibitions.

The 1986 tax-reform law also is wreaking havoc with the donation of privately owned artworks to public facilities. It is not known what Mrs. Harriman's late husband, Averell, paid for the Van Gogh in 1930, but say he bought it for $50,000. That purchase price is the maximum tax deduction now allowed by the tax law; a donor is not permitted appreciation in value or current market value in determining a tax deduction. Mrs. Harriman's generous gift thus will enjoy no realistic tax treatment, even for a painting worth $60 million. You can bet, however, that had she sold it instead of donating it, the IRS would be pounding at her door for its cut of her profit.

The tax law has hurt museums far and near. A study by the American Association of Museums recently found that the value of donations dropped by almost $31.5 million in 1987 — the year the tax law took effect — or a one-third decline from 1986. The value of appreciated property, which gained tax breaks under the old tax law, fell by more than half. Items donated to museums dropped in number by more than 160,000. The trend continues, as donors conclude that even if they have to pay taxes on appreciated value, they benefit more by selling artworks than by donating them. They are not thinking about a few thousand — but millions — of dollars.

It is well and good for Congress in its infinite wisdom to suppose that philanthropy is based on altruism, in which the tax system plays no role. That supposition, however, is largely stupid. Economists constantly warn that tax laws determine economic activity and rule private decisions, but few on Capitol Hill pay attention. Thanks to Congress' idea of tax reform in 1986, many valuable works of art have disappeared from public view, perhaps forever, robbing our culture of a priceless heritage.

Mrs. Harriman's gracious gift may be one of the last of its kind. Her donation will not cost the IRS any lost revenues through a charitable donation based on the current value of Van Gogh's "Roses," and the IRS will continue to clean up on sales of other important artworks that originally were bought for a song. Only museums — and the public — will pay in losses beyond price.

## Newsday
*New York, NY, April 1, 1987*

The sale of a celebrated painting of sunflowers by Vincent Van Gogh on Monday has provoked a fair amount of astonishment and even some anger among our friends and associates. What, they wonder, can possibly make a painting worth $39.9 million?

The answer, of course, is simple: A painting — like a piece of jewelry, an acre of land or an employee, for that matter — is worth precisely as much as someone is willing to pay.

Is Dwight Gooden worth $1.5 million for six months or so of pitching one day out of five for the Mets? Of course he is — probably because the Mets' management has calculated how many fans Gooden is likely to draw to Shea Stadium and how much TV money he's likely to attract and has decided he's worth the price.

Similarly someone — for whatever reasons of vanity, investment acumen or genuine love of art — thought the Van Gogh painting was worth $39.9 million, thus establishing the current value of this particular work of art and probably elevating the price of everything else Van Gogh painted during his tormented life.

And here lies an irony. While Van Gogh lived, about a hundred years ago or so, his paintings were regarded as worthless. During his entire lifetime, he managed to sell only one. He was financially dependent on his brother and ended his life by committing suicide in what was then called an insane asylum.

What a shame that this poor man, while he was alive, could not have had just a shred of the recognition — and cash — his paintings now bring. And why didn't he? Because, according to the auctioneer who sold the $39.9 million painting in London, he "wasn't very good at marketing" his work. In other words, in this fellow's view — and he's an expert — it's not enough to be merely an artistic genius. You have to be a good salesman as well.

That's a sad commentary — not so much on Van Gogh's failing as on some of the standards and values of western civilization.

## Lincoln Journal
*Lincoln, NE, June 28, 1989*

The country is permanently enriched by the gift of a Vincent van Gogh still life to the National Gallery of Art by the widow of Averell Harriman.

Experts believe van Gogh's "Roses" could have commanded up to $60 million, if put on the auction block. Of the work, the gallery's senior curator of paintings, Charles S. Moffett, said:

"This picture is so beautiful that when you look at it, you don't think of money, you don't think of the market value today, you just think of the extraordinary power and beauty of the painting. It's one of the artist's greatest statements. The pure visual pleasure that you take from standing in front of this thing is — I don't know what to say. It almost defies words. It's one of those pictures that when you stand in front of it, you never forget it."

Van Gogh did the painting in 1890, the year of his suicide. Harriman acquired it exactly 40 years later. Now it will be a treasure for unlimited sharing.

## Record Theft at Boston Museum

Two thieves disguised as policemen broke into the Isabella Stewart Gardner Museum in Boston, Mass. early March 18, 1990. After overpowering two museum guards, they stole 12 priceless artworks, including paintings by Vermeer, Rembrandt, Degas and Manet.

The stolen works, were believed to be worth at least $100 million, making the robbery the largest known in the art theft world.

Previously, the largest theft had been the robbery of three van Gogh paintings from the Kroeller-Mueller Museum in Otterlo, the Netherlands in 1988. Those paintings, worth an estimated $72 million to $91 million, had since been recovered.

The Gardner Museum revealed March 19 that it had not carried any insurance against theft because the annual premiums would have been higher than the museum's $2.8 million operating budget. In addition, under the terms of the will of Isabella Stewart Gardner – the wealthy Boston socialite who had founded the museum in 1903 in the mansion that had once been her home – the museum was barred from purchasing new paintings or replacing any that were lost to damage or theft.

In a highly unusual arrangement, the auction houses of Christie's and Sotheby's announced March 20 that they would underwrite a $1 million reward for information leading to the recovery of the 12 stolen art works.

The stolen works included:

■ *The Concert* by Jan Vermeer – one of only 35 Vermeer paintings known to exist.

■ Two Rembrandt paintings – *A Lady and a Gentleman in Black* and *The Storm on the Sea of Galilee* – his only seascape – together with a self-portrait etching.

■ Several works by Edgar Degas, including *La Sortie de Pesage* and *Cortege aux Environs de Florence*.

■ *Chez Tortoni* by Eduard Manet.

■ A Chinese vase from around the 12th century B.C.

### The Providence Journal
*Providence, RI, March 25, 1990*

Last Sunday's theft from Boston's Isabella Stewart Gardner Museum is sad indeed.

Among the stolen works were *The Concert*, one of only 32 that survive by the Dutch painter Jan Vermeer, and the only one in New England, and *The Storm on the Sea of Galilee*, Rembrandt's only seascape. Also lost were two more by Rembrandt, five by Edgar Degas, single works by Edouard Manet and Govaert Flinck, a bronze beaker made in China three millennia ago, and a gold eagle flagpole cap from Napoleon's army. Together, they are valued at $200 million, the biggest art heist in history.

The works are really priceless. The museum's treasures were donated in 1903 by Mrs. Gardner, a *grande dame* of Boston in whose mansion they are housed. Originally from New York, she enjoyed tweaking the Brahmins of her adopted city, so her will characteristically barred them from adding to, subtracting from, lending out, or rearranging her collection in any way. The result is a very intimate, eccentric museum. (The Boston Globe editorialized on Thursday that the theft presents "an unsought opportunity for the museum to renew itself." We hope the museum will resist.)

Stolen art is often recovered — the *Mona Lisa* was taken from the Louvre in 1911 and found two years later. Perhaps the Gardner's lost trove will also be found. Meanwhile, the remaining collection is still a public treasure, amply rewarding the drive to Boston. After all, many great works were *not* taken, including paintings by Rubens, Botticelli, Raphael, Van Dyck and Fra Angelico.

We hope the museum will bolster its security to protect the masterpieces that remain. In fact, *all* museums should make sure that their security arrangements reflect not only the market value of their collections, but also act to calm the fears of private collectors so that they will continue to lend their works for the enjoyment of the public.

Art thievery will grow more brazen as long as the market value of art escalates. But if people could purchase a copy of a painting as easily as they can buy a book or a musical recording, this crime might decline.

That may soon come to pass. At the Chestnut Hill Mall, outside Boston, we recently viewed copies of paintings by Claude Monet, originals of which are on display at the Boston Museum of Fine Arts. These were not just your ordinary prints; they were "painted" by computer. Such copies, reproducing even the texture of brush strokes, are quite expensive, but prices could decline if consumer demand creates a lucrative market.

This could revolutionize the art world: Aside from making virtual duplicates of art available to hang in the average aesthete's living room, this process could moderate the value of original works. The biggest losers might be the wealthy art speculators whose craving has bid up the price of art so high that many museums can no longer afford to make acquisitions, or to lend out what they have to other museums.

And the next biggest losers might be art thieves.

### THE CHRISTIAN SCIENCE MONITOR
*Boston, MA, March 23, 1990*

INSTANCES of art theft have increased to between 5,000 and 8,000 a year over the past decade. This is not surprising, considering that classics such as works by Van Gogh can command $50 million in an auction.

But the theft of 13 pieces of fine art at the Isabella Stewart Gardner Museum in Boston this week is not only the biggest art haul ever. At more than $200 million in value it is the biggest criminal heist in US history.

The works were uninsured. Works of such value are, at today's prohibitive rates, uninsurable. How do you protect such art against theft or loss? How do you protect art in a world flooded with narcotics cash, in which financial transactions leave no trace?

The thieves came in the night, dressed as police. They took five Degas, three Rembrandts, a Manet, and a priceless Vermeer – one of only 35 in the world. Rembrandt's "Storm on the Sea of Galilee" was the only sea-theme the Dutch master ever painted.

The high-tech, state-of-the-art security system was useless once the guards – who at $6.85 an hour make the same as kids at Burger King – were conned and tied-up. Then the thieves had the place to themselves. They cut and stripped the paintings from the frames, damaging them. How are the masterpieces now being treated?

Great paintings are a record of the best visions of the best minds. Such crimes are crimes against history.

The paintings could soon be recovered. More than half the fine art stolen each year is recovered.

We are often unmindful of our greatest treasures until they are taken from us. The Gardner Museum theft has made all the world's museums immediately more vigilant.

# The Washington Post
*Washington, DC, March 21, 1990*

WHAT DID they hope to get out of it? Two days after thieves made off with a spectacular haul of art masterpieces from the Isabella Stewart Gardner Museum in Boston, the biggest art theft in recent history, no plausible theory of the criminals' motive has been put forth. Money, of course, and yet the only consensus so far seems to be that money is what such a crime cannot possibly bring. The stolen works, including a Vermeer, several Rembrandts and a Chinese beaker from the second millennium B.C., are so well-known worldwide and have belonged to the museum for so long that they are, in a practical sense, priceless: no one could plausibly sell or resell them for anywhere near their real value, anywhere in the world. Only the totally uninformed could hope to pass them off as legitimately acquired works or works of lesser but still substantial value.

That leaves the field open for a whole range of more lurid, spy-novel scenarios: Was it ransom? A rich, crazed private collector? The "Asian connection" conspiracy theory, which whispers about prominent works showing up in Japan? Unlikely prospects all, but no stranger than the event. True, the art world (and underworld) have become vastly more fluid and fast-moving in the past decade, and art theft has been on the rise, mostly because of the dizzying, much-publicized ascent of art prices. But at the same time international computer networks and tracking mechanisms have become more sophisticated, and dealers are savier and more inclined to worry about acquiring "hot" goods.

The disposition of this case will help give a reading on the progress of these changes—maybe to the surprise of those who carried off this theft with such evident ease and careful planning. "It's possible," says Constance Lowenthal of the New York-based International Foundation for Art Research, "that whoever it is woke up this morning with something less than elation." Hence, perhaps, a best-case scenario: ordinary thieves, drawn to the prospect of fantastic profits and now taken aback, maybe intimidated by the breadth and volume of outrage they have unleashed. Pricelessness is a concept not often encountered in the normal round of public business. And yet the emotional outpouring from Bostonians and others goes well beyond the monetary value of these works on some legitimate or illegitimate market. The Gardner Museum has stood far outside the whirlpool of art market changes in the '80s—by the terms of its eccentric founder's will, the collection could be neither sold, added to nor rearranged—and this adds in many minds to the general sense of affront and violation.

There has been some hand-wringing over the museum's admission that the stolen paintings were uninsured. But in a sense the whole matter of insurance is beside the point: what good is an insurance company's reimbursement when the object in question is, by definition, irreplaceable? The thieves may have hoped to exact some kind of ransom. But it makes no more sense to bargain with the kidnappers of paintings than with any other kind of hostage-takers. The museum yesterday announced a $1 million reward for information; as this implies, the real answer is detective work, and a happy ending is by no means implausible.

# St. Petersburg Times
*St. Petersburg, FL, March 20, 1990*

Sunday's theft of 12 famous works from a Boston museum has been labeled the biggest art heist and the most costly burglary in American history. A preliminary estimate of $200-million is considered conservative, because art experts can't put easy pricetags on such masterpieces as Jan Vermeer's *The Concert*, sadly counted among the losses.

"Incalculable," one expert on the 17th century Dutch master told the *Boston Globe*.

Visitors to the Isabella Stewart Gardner Museum may feel another loss as well, intangible but no less poignant than the blank stretch of wall so recently occupied by Manet's *Chez Tortoni*, another stolen masterpiece. Built as a mansion by its namesake at the turn of the century and open to the public as a "house museum" since 1925, the Gardner has become a timeless refuge from the deterioration and escalating violence of the streets outside.

The chill was clearly felt by stunned visitors who spoke to the *Globe* after finding the museum unexpectedly closed on Sunday.

"I feel like someone has kicked me in the gut," remarked a student upon learning that thieves had made off with her favorite painting.

"This is more than a theft," another visitor was quoted as saying. "They are stealing our chance to see good art."

Good art remains to be seen elsewhere, of course, but rarely in such an accessible setting. Isabella Stewart Gardner built her house museum in the style of a Venetian palace, with a beautiful courtyard in the middle and 15 galleries filled with 2,000 paintings, sculptures and other treasures. Mrs. Gardner lived upstairs until her death in 1924, and in her will she specified that the objects she had arranged could not be moved, on pain of auctioning off the entire collection.

Thus the personality of a rich eccentric has reached out across the decades, offering harried city dwellers the impression that their gracious hostess has just stepped out for a moment, if they would care to look around while they wait. Even those who know nothing of the artwork can enjoy the setting without feeling intimidated or overwhelmed.

Now people fear that security consciousness will rob the Gardner of its accessibility, and with it, the gift of a healing respite from an urban environment where 35 children and adults have already been murdered this year.

"The reason that we have these places is so that people can enjoy culture in the inner city," a wistful would-be visitor to the Gardner told the *Globe*. "This is one of a kind, you don't find a beautiful palace in the inner city."

> **The Gardner museum in Boston has offered the gift of a healing respite from an urban environment where 35 children and adults have already been murdered this year.**

# The Evening Gazette
*Worcester, MA, March 22, 1990*

The shivers started by the theft of 12 priceless, uninsured works of art from Boston's Isabella Stewart Gardner Museum will ripple through the art world for a long time. Security, already a burdensome budget item, is bound to divert even more money from art preservation and display.

The protection of art treasures has concerned museum directors for years. The Gardner has a new, sophisticated television security system. The brazen theft from the Gardner, carried out after thieves gained entrance by tricking personnel, is a reminder that any security is only as good as its weakest link.

Often, that is the human factor. The thieves, evidently professionals with a "shopping list," used the ruse of being Boston police officers investigating a disturbance.

Once inside the museum — a former private home better described as a palace — they went swiftly to their goal.

The world-famous paintings and artifacts they took cannot be sold on the open market; they are too well documented.

They can be held for ransom. More likely, they will be interred in a private collector's hoard or exchanged as payment among drug kingpins and other nefarious characters.

In all probability the treasures are gone for generations.

Few institutions will talk about their security systems, but you can be sure many of them are checking and updating procedures.

Since it was the human element that failed at the Gardner, many museums will wisely consider retraining personnel. Legitimate private collectors will also become more wary.

Well they should. Sad to say, the Gardner raid will force private collectors and public institutions to commit even more money and effort to protect art treasures from thieves.

# Part III:
# Publishing & Pornography

Communication has long been subjected to control. The two phenomena are linked in mutual adversity and as communication has proliferated so have the means of control. The invention of movable-type printing was paralleled all across Europe by the elaboration of the means of its suppression – first by the church, militant against heresy and new faiths; then by governments, fearing sedition within and treason without; and, in their wake, by the successive campaigns of self-appointed moralists, dedicated to an imposed purity.

The first cultural censor was the Roman Catholic Church which dominated Europe until the Reformation, although its determination to suppress heresy derived as much from a desire to maintain its political power as to propagate true belief. The early Indexes of Prohibited Books dealt in ideology, not obscenity. But the very nature of the church as the arbiter of public morality meant that these lists soon expanded to encompass the sins of the flesh as well as those of mind.

The wider moral censorship that was to come as a product of the 18th and 19th centuries abandoned any connection with a breach of the peace. Instead it saw its purpose as simply to maintain control of "dirty books" – ushering in the modern concept of "obscene publications."

More recently, there have many individuals and groups arose, maintaining their own moral status quo by attempting to emasculate the written word in its various permutations. Because of their pressure, plays, poetry and prose have all had the censor's knife taken to them.

In the United States the First Amendment provides the fundamental guarantee to U.S. citizens of freedoms of speech and expression and stands as the basis of all subsequent legislation in these areas. It reads: "Congress shall make no law respecting an establishment of religion, or prohibiting the free exercise thereof, or abridging the freedom of speech, or of the press; or the right of the people peaceably to assemble, and to petition the government for a redress of grievances."

Civil liberterians argue that this phrase outlaws a national system of censorship. But in the federal system of government, obscenity laws vary widely and the prominence and power of various pressure groups can mean that in the short term local prohibitions have greater force than do the pronouncements of federal authorities.

The current test for obscenity, as set down by the U.S. Supreme Court, derives from the case of *Miller v. California* (1973). It requires that all these conditions be satisfied: the "average person," taking contemporary community standards, would find a work, taken as a whole, appeals to the prurient (sexually arousing) interest; the work depicts or describes sexual conduct in a patently offensive manner; the work taken as a whole, lacks serious literary, artistic, political or scientific value. The Supreme Court further defined patently offensive representations or descriptions of intimate sexual acts, normal or perverted, actual or simulated, or patently offensive sexual or excretory representations. The general effect of such definitions is for all cases dealing with obscene publications to be restricted to allegedly hard-core pornography. State laws generally ban all trafficking in obscene materials, but the compulsion under *Miller* to define such materials by a specific test has forced some states to reenact old laws or create new ones for their own use.

The Attorney General's Commission on Pornography was established in February 1985 by then-U.S. Attorney General William French Smith. Its final report was delivered in July 1986 to his successor, Edwin Meese III, by its chairman Henry E. Hudson, the U.S. attorney for the Eastern District of Virginia. The findings of the 1,960-page, two volume report were based on public hearings in six cities, a review of published articles relating to pornography, the work of staff investigators and the views expressed in more than 3,000 letters from the public.

The 11-member panel acknowledged that its conclusions were diametrically opposed to those of the 1970 President's Commission On Obscenity And Pornography, which said erotic material was not a significant cause of crime, delinquency, sexual deviancy or emotional disturbances. The new panel claimed that times had changed, the problem of pornography had grown much worse and the conclusion of the earlier report were "starkly obsolete."

The panel concluded that "there is a conection between the pornography industry and organized crime." The panel also concluded that there was a "casual relationship" between certain kinds of pornography and acts of sexual violence. On this, and on other important points, the panel was not unanimous, and two of its members issued a dissenting statement, pointing out that the printed and video materials presented to the commission as evidence "were skewed to the very violent and extremely degrading." They also stressed that efforts to "tease" the current social science data into "proof of a casual link" between pornography and sexual crimes "simply cannot be accepted" and claimed that there had not been enough time for "full and fair discussions of many of the more restrictive and controversial proposals."

The commission rejected proposals to broaden the legal definition of obscenity, which embraces some but not all pornographic material, and said that current laws were basically adequate but woefully underenforced by federal, state and local prosecutors. The cited the Supreme Court's *Miller* decision, suggesting that judges can can apply "contemporary community standards" to determine what is obscene, and called for much more vigorous enforcement of laws against obscene materials.

In the news media arts, beleaguered authors find themselves under attack from the government and a multitude of private groups and organizations. Prior to the mid-20th century, the major threats to free expression by authors in the U.S. came from the government. Whether it was prosecution of unpopular political writings or censorship of books and movies, the limiting action was taken by governmental agencies. Since then, boards of censors have been abolished by judicial decision or simply been permitted to expire. Their place has been taken to a large extent by ad hoc citizen groups and organizations. The groups seek to censor books in school libraries, dictate the choice of textbooks and promote boycotts of films and dramas. Pressure is being exerted on those who write, publish, teach and perform. Though some teachers may be protected by tenure and some performers by contract or union rules, the vast majority of creative people have few legal remedies against private interference and censorship.

## Attorney General's Panel Links Pornography, Violence

The Attorney General's Commission on Pornography July 9, 1986 released the final draft of a report claiming that violent pornography probably led to sexual violence. The report called for a crackdown on obscenity by federal, state and local authorities. The report contradicted the findings of the 1970 President's Commission on Obscenity and Pornography, which had found no danger in circulation of pornography.

Response to the new report ranged from praise to heated denunciation. The 1,960-page report had been prepared by an 11-member commission appointed in May, 1985. The group, working with a budget of $500,000, commissioned no new scientific research but reviewed current findings, held public hearings in six cities, heard testimony from "victims of pornography" and other witnesses, read or viewed samples of pornography and visited "adults only" emporiums.

The commission report said it identified pornography as "sexually explicit" material "intended primarily for the purpose of sexual arousal." It listed three types: pornography that featured violence or its threat, pornography that did not show violence but did show one sex partner's degradation by another, and pornography that featured only simple nudity or sex acts engaged in by apparently willing and equal partners.

The report said commission members were divided on the effect of the violent pornography. It reported "no persuasive evidence to date" linking it to violence but said that the material did in all probability encourage promiscuity.

In the months preceding the release of the report, several scientists whose research was cited by the panel complained that complex and often inconclusive evidence had been willfully misread. One, Edward Donnerstein of the University of Wisconsin, was quoted May 19 as calling the draft report "bizarre."

Attorney General Edwin Meese 3rd repeatedly declined to comment on the report's proposals, saying he had not read them. But he assured listener's that "this department, as long as I am attorney general, is not going to engage in any censorship that violates the First Amendment."

### Los Angeles Times
*Los Angeles, CA, July 10, 1986*

The kindest thing that can be said about the 2,000-page report of the Attorney General's Commission on Pornography is that it's a joke. Not funny, but a joke. The commission's scholarship is ludicrous, its conclusions unsupported, its methodology zany.

In 1984 President Reagan declared, "It's time to stop pretending that extreme pornography is a victimless crime." Then Atty. Gen. Edwin Meese III, no fool, carefully selected an 11-member commission that spent a year and $500,000 chasing around the country, listening to crackpot testimony and reaching the conclusion that the President had ordained. The report is a miasma of misplaced morality and prudishness masquerading as social science.

Henry E. Hudson, the commission's chairman, was a county prosecutor in Virginia who made a name for himself waging war on adult businesses there. Just the right person to head this group. In releasing the report on Tuesday, Hudson disclosed his real agenda. "I, as well as all the other commissioners, believe that sexual promiscuity . . . is not something that should be socially condoned," he said.

The commission's "hearings" were scenes out of a Fellini movie. The majority of witnesses were cops, victims of sexual abuse and spokesmen for anti-pornography groups, who told the commissioners lurid tales of harm that started with pornography. There were also field trips to red-light districts and private screenings of X-rated films.

The commission's main conclusion—based on the flimsiest of evidence, none of it original—is that sexually explicit material, whether violent or not, can cause violence and other social harm. Even Hudson acknowledged that the case had not been proved. "If we relied on scientific data for every one of our findings, I'm afraid that all of our conclusions, or all of our work, would be inconclusive," he said Tuesday.

Fortunately, two of the commissioners would not go along with this. Ellen Levine, editor of Women's Day magazine, and Judith Becker, a Columbia University psychologist, said that "efforts to tease the current data into proof of a casual relationship" between pornography and sex crimes "cannot be accepted." They said that no "self-respecting investigator" could reach these conclusions.

Nonetheless, the panel recommends 92 tough steps that governments and citizens should take to quell the plague of pornography. For his part, Meese assured everyone that "there will be no censorship . . . in violation of the First Amendment." Meese wouldn't know a First Amendment violation if it bit him.

The commission has already done harm. In February it sent letters to two dozen retail chains encompassing 10,000 stores that sold Playboy and Penthouse magazines, telling them that they had been identified as smut peddlers. The letter threatened to name the retailers in the commission's final report. Many stores have withdrawn the magazines. Last week U.S. District Judge John Garrett Penn in Washington ruled that such a blacklist would be unconstitutional.

Now that this silly episode is over, it should be quickly forgotten. The commission's report should be consigned to the trash.

### Detroit Free Press
*Detroit, MI, July 12, 1986*

A FEDERAL COMMISSION has spent one year and half a million dollars producing a report on pornography that is, at bottom, a sham. Though the report does focus on some important issues — including the sexual exploitation of women and minors — it doesn't offer much credible evidence to justify a crackdown on pornography that might approach censorship.

Many Americans will applaud the 11-member Attorney General's Commission on Pornography for proposing that citizens' groups begin working more vigorously to shut down pornographers. The report urges citizens to guard against the sale of sexually explicit material, including magazines, videotapes and even cable television programming, by setting up "citizens watch groups." It also calls for tougher enforcement of existing obscenity laws, a crackdown on child pornography, and stronger and better co-ordinated attempts by local, state and federal enforcers to break up the porno industry.

The most controversial part of the report, though, is its claim that exposure to sexually explicit material portraying the violent abuse of women by men can cause some people to commit "anti-social acts of sexual violence," sometimes including sex crimes. But where is the social science research to back up such a claim? No one has yet conclusively proven that a presidential commission was wrong when it decided in 1970 that erotic material was not a significant cause of crime or sexual deviancy.

The conclusion seems inescapable that some members of this current panel had difficulty separating their strong feelings about pornography from the actual facts. Six of the panel's 11 members had publicly stated their anti-pornography views before their appointment, and discouraging sexual promiscuity among Americans seems to have been one of the panel's goals.

The commission's report does raise some important issues, especially the need for stronger laws against child pornography in some municipalities. Its attempt to categorize the relative impact of sexually violent, degrading but not violent, and neither violent nor degrading sexually explicit materials also may turn out to be useful to researchers in the future. But it's hard to take too seriously a report that urges that the doors be removed from the peep show booths in "adults only" stores to discourage sexual activity in those booths. "The need for research remains as compelling as ever," the panel acknowledged. That is surely the case.

## The Miami Herald
*Miami, FL, July 11, 1986*

ALARMISTS view findings of the Attorney General's Commission on Pornography as tantamount to roving bands of vigilantes snooping in theaters and book stores and finding obscenity in every film, book, and magazine therein. Civil libertarians fret over potential First Amendment abuses if certain commission recommendations are enacted. Many religious leaders applaud the report as a return to decency. And the average citizen, what does he think?

Not much, probably. Quite often, high-level commissions' reports on national problems are news today, dust collectors tomorrow. This panel, established by former Attorney General William French Smith in 1985, studied pornography and decided that, no surprise, it is bad. Specifically, the 11 commissioners found child pornography pernicious in the worst sense. They recommended stringent enforcement of current laws and enactment of a few new ones such as making possession of child porno a felony. Agreed.

Agreed, too, that pornographic material portraying violence linked with sexual arousal is true depravity, as the commission states. But there is no scientific evidence that this obscenity and rape are directly connected, as the commission alleged while admitting that it had no proof.

A "Well, we *know* it but we can't *prove* it" reasoning is dangerous because it *would* jeopardize First Amendment rights if accepted as fact. One hopes that Attorney General Edwin Meese III sticks to his pledge that the Justice Department "is not going to engage in any censorship that violates the First Amendment."

The panel also alleged that "non-degrading, nonviolent" sexually explicit material causes promiscuity. Here the commissioners are way out of line, again cloaking mere opinion as fact. A sample of their moralizing: "There are undoubtedly many causes for what used to be called the 'sexual revolution,' but it is absurd to suppose that depictions or descriptions of uncommitted sexuality were not among them." Proof? None.

When the commission came down from the pulpit and stuck to analyzing the actual facts gathered during its hearings, it came up with the soundest recommendation — that the U.S. Justice Department vigorously enforce existing anti-pornography laws, which are plenteous. As to its other suggestions, such as forming local watchdog committees to seek out hard-core porn, let the average citizen — whose viewing and reading tastes are his own concern — make these private choices.

## The Salt Lake Tribune
*Salt Lake City, UT, July 11, 1986*

The report of the Attorney General's Commission on Pornography holds no surprises. The commission did exactly what was expected of it: Conclude that pornography can cause sexual violence. It didn't, however, provide much scientific evidence that its conclusion is correct.

The conclusion was pre-ordained the day the commission was appointed. Its 11 members included six people who had previously taken strong, public anti-pornography positions. Two other members, both academics, had done work that could be used to defend censorship of sexually explicit material.

Additionally, the commission was created in response to pressure on the Reagan administration from the religious right in America, elements of which have been sharply and stridently critical of government, at all levels, for failing to move more aggressively against pornography.

A further suggestion that the commission was a sop to the religious right are the limited resources of time and money granted the commission. It was given only a year to do its job, on a budget of a scant $500,000. That is half the time and one-sixteenth the money that the commission's 1970 predecessor was allowed.

Such severe restrictions of money and time automatically precluded the commission from conducting sound, independent and objective scientific research into the effects of pornography.

Instead, as it turned out, the commission had to rely extensively on such shaky information as the subjective testimony of law enforcement officials.

It is not surprising that two of the commissioners, Ellen Levine, editor of Woman's Day, and Judith Becker, a Columbia University psychologist, dissented from the report's central findings, deploring "efforts to tease the current data into proof of a causal relationship" between exposure to pornography and the commission of sex crimes.

"No self-respecting investigator would accept conclusions based on such a study, and unfortunately the document produced reflects these inadequacies," they wrote.

The document that has been produced is exactly what the Reagan administration, and its friends on the religious right, effectively ordered; a lopsided, unsubstantiated attempt to connect sexual violence with pornography. But what else could be expected from a biased, demonstrably anti-pornography commission predisposed to censorship that only had a year and a half-million dollars to do its job?

What the American public has received is a 2,000-page, two-volume, $35 a copy, sermon instead of the superior, scientific study it deserved.

## The Forum
*Fargo, ND, July 11, 1986*

Pornography got a black eye from the Attorney General's Commission on Pornography this week.

A 2,000-page report links hardcore porn to sex crimes and contains 92 recommendations for federal, state and local governments to crack down on pornography.

We haven't read the report, but what we've been reading about pornography lately would make the Marquis de Sade blush. Pornographers have pushed too far, and as with any other kind of threat to civilized existence, there is a backlash by society.

We cannot put up with pornography that uses children, with depictions of sexual sadism against women, with showings of bestiality — most of it done exploitively to make a buck, or billions of bucks, as the pornography report states.

It calls pornography an $8 billion a year business.

There are those who say that pornography does not cause sex crimes. Well, when we get into cause and effect and whether or not certain sex crimes would have been committed anyway, we are dealing with hypotheses that could consume hours of debate and analyses.

The commission researched it, and came to the conclusion that hard core pornography — such as perversions and sadism — does endanger those who are depicted as the objects of sex crimes.

The commission states that, with regard to state and federal obscenity laws, there is "under-complaining, under-investigation, under-prosecution and under-sentencing."

Only 160 people have been indicted under the federal obscenity law since 1978.

The report has been condemned by civil liberties groups as a move toward censorship.

Attorney General Edwin Meese says, "I'm not concerned about any censorship being fostered by this. I can guarantee you there will be no censorship ... in violation of the First Amendment."

The U.S. Supreme Court has ruled that community standards define what is obscene and that action can be taken legally against obscenity.

Of course, there can be no pre-publication action against publications, whether they be movies or printed matter or any kind of taped or recorded material.

Once there is publication, then charges can be filed, and there is a time-honored, well-established, Supreme Court-validated procedure for this.

The fact that little has been done against pornography indicates that the public at large is broadminded and in no mood to interfere with the choice by adults of what they read or view.

The pornographers, though, have pushed beyond tolerable limits, and the call for action is justified.

## The Star-Ledger
*Newark, NJ, July 11, 1986*

Predictably, the findings of a year-long national study on pornography have stirred a sharp, emotional controversy between conservative elements and civil libertarians. There are broad divisions reflecting concern over the potentially deleterious social implications of hard-core pornography and the possible unsettling intrusion of censorship raised by the tough law enforcement remedies proposed by the federal inquiry into pornography.

One point of difference involves a major conclusion of the commission, which found a direct causal relationship between pornography and violent sex offenses. This conclusion conflicts with findings by a presidential commission on pornography in 1970 and scientific studies that could find no such link.

Another troublesome factor in trying to address this volatile social issue was underscored by the inability of the commission even to define pornography, a dilemma that also has frustrated the nation's court system. In this void, a determination of what constitutes pornography essentially becomes a matter of community standards, creating a confusing melange of conflicting regulatory constraints on the multibillion-dollar pornography industry.

In this regional concept, there is a potentially inflammatory issue of vigilantism inherent in the commission call for citizens to act unilaterally against stores and other establishments that deal in adult materials. This is a responsibility better left in the hands of law enforcement authorities.

There is little doubt, however, that rigorous enforcement measures can be justified against pornographic entrepreneurs who prey on children for illicit gain. But a more reasoned, balanced official overview should be taken in government anti-pornography initiatives, given the ambiguities in trying to definitively ascertain what is pornography.

But what is clearly—and distressingly—apparent is that there have been radical changes in pornography in the 16 years since the presidential commission study. It not only has become markedly widespread, but it has taken on disturbingly darker forms of violent child pornography and sadomasochism. Sadly, there is a thriving market for this type of filth.

Unfortunately, the current panel has not made needed distinctions between erotica and hard-core pornographic materials. This kind of demarcation could have provided guidelines for effective law enforcement in checking the proliferation of the pornography commerce.

## THE ATLANTA CONSTITUTION
*Atlanta, GA, July 11, 1986*

Forget for a moment the academicians and civil libertarians. The general public may have offered the most eloquent response to the overheated screed released this week by the Attorney General's Commission on Pornography: Z-z-z-z-z.

Employees of the Government Printing Office bookstore had expected brisk sales Wednesday when the panel's final report came out. Instead, they sold a measly 75 to 100 copies in three hours. People got more excited over copies of the president's budget. The reasons are plain enough.

At least the budget had an element of surprise and some anchor in reality. The porn report has neither. Its findings are about what one would expect from a panel tilted from the beginning to favor anti-porn crusaders. The 2,000-page tome serves mainly as a call to action.

The question is, against what? While the report rattles off scores of recommendations on how to curb "the spread of pornography," it never bothers to say what it believes "pornography" is. The panel must hail from the know-it-when-we-see it school.

The commission said the "centerpiece" of its report is this: "Obscene publications which depict child pornography and violent and degrading behavior toward women are socially harmful." OK, but what is new about that? The link between depictions of violence and acts of violence is something of a given. As for child pornography, there are laws against it now.

Interestingly, two dissident panelists charged the examples of pornography put before the panel "were skewed to the very violent and extremely degrading." That notwithstanding, the majority went on to say (in a notably vague passage) that materials showing sex between consenting adults, even those without any hint of violence or degradation, harm society. That contradicts volumes of real research, and some researchers have protested that the commission twisted their conclusions.

Oh, well. The administration set out to give the religious right a buzz, and it did. But the results were not entirely harmless.

For example, the commission convinced the owners of some 8,000 convenience stores they shouldn't sell mainstream publications like *Playboy.* How? It threatened to identify them (arbitrarily and unfairly) as distributors of pornography. It was a distinctly un-American bit of censorship-by-intimidation.

It is only reasonable to ask at this point. If the dread porn scourge has had its way in our society, what is the result? Do citizens clamor for relief? Do police reel from the struggle? Do judges beg for more authority?

Uh, not exactly. The report finds "under-complaining, under-investigation, under-prosecution, and under-sentencing."

*Under-complaining?* Well, at least the public is consistent. Z-z-z-z-z.

## The Birmingham News
*Biringham, AL, July 13, 1986*

The furor that liberals, led by the American Civil Liberties Union, have created following release of the Attorney General's Commission on Pornography report is a manufactured tempest in a teapot.

In view of Attorney General Edwin Meese's pledge that the study will not be used to promote an attack on the First Amendment, the shrill cries from liberal strongholds seem bogus and designed to distort Meese's intent as well as deform his character.

By inference, they also distort the First Amendment. Do liberals actually believe that the First Amendment was designed to include protection for the bestial fantasies contained in the kind of pornography the commission deplored?

Do liberals actually believe that the 10 words guaranteeing free speech and press were meant to include protection for the creators and dealers in pictures of children explicitly engaged in the sex act?

Do liberals actually believe that the amendment protects the publication and distribution of sadistic and masochistic, violence-ridden garbage that demeans all of humankind, especially women and children, and sex itself?

Do the outraged liberals believe the First Amendment was intended to work to provide organized crime with income with which to finance drug smuggling, prostitution and a host of other crimes?

Of course not. And censorship is not the real issue here. The real fear in the liberal camp is that Meese, the commissioners and their report will mobilize public opinion to suppress this outrageous transgression of the public good, not through censorship, but through expressions of public outrage.

Perhaps hard-core pornography does not encourage sex crimes, such as rape and molestation of children. But in view of the vast increase in these crimes since pornography became so widespread and readily accessible, the public will need more than the carping of psychologists to convince it that brutalized sex displays have played no part.

While this newspaper deplores any attempt to censor any political discourse, written or otherwise, news events or legitimate literature, we believe society has an obligation to defend itself against forces that tend to corrupt it or dissolve the glue which binds it together.

If Americans want to register their protest against hard-core pornography, they have every right to do so — through boycotts, picketing or critical comment, as Americans have done for numerous liberal causes — as long as they avoid violence and any illegal activity directed at the people who sell hard-core pornography.

And it can be argued that under the general welfare clause of the Constitution government is empowered if not obligated to warn the nation when it is on the wrong track. Is censorship involved in such a warning? How about the legislated warning on tobacco? Is the free speech of cigarette manufacturers compromised when they are prevented by law from advertising their products on television and radio? And what about the other numerous warnings issued by various government agencies on a variety of diseases, foods and consumer items?

The truth is, Meese is no threat to the First Amendment. Neither are groups which pressure stores to eliminate hard-core pornography from their shelves.

[Cartoon: Two panels. Left panel caption: "THE REPORT OF THE COMMISSION ON PORNOGRAPHY WILL CAUSE NO CENSORSHIP..." Right panel caption: "NEXT QUESTION." Signed AUTH, 7/11/86, Philadelphia Inquirer.]

## CHARLESTON EVENING POST
*Charleston, SC, July 15, 1986*

As syndicated columnist Andrew J. Glass reminds in an article on this page, pornography has a long history. So have concerns about it and attempts to control it. In consequence, the recent report by the Attorney General's Commission on Pornography is likely to be regarded by the record-keepers as just another brief footnote on the subject.

The commission report, which concluded that some forms of pornography cause sexual violence, has been criticized for leaping to conclusions unsupported by scientific findings. It has been assailed as a "lopsided, pro-censorship report." It also has been praised by feminists and hailed by religious groups as "the death knell for the criminal pornography industry."

Even though it runs to almost 2,000 pages, the report is unlikely to be even half the things some say it is. It can be said without fear of argument that the report offers no new data (because, the commission said, there wasn't money for original research). It likewise can be said that it plows no new analytical or philosophical ground, although it does its share of moralizing.

The report does, however, contain 92 recommendations for federal, state and local crackdowns on pornography, including that most loathsome aspect some label "kiddie porn." In discussing child pornography the commission recognized what law enforcement agents are up against. There are more amateurs engaged in the production of "kiddie porn" than there are professionals, which makes policing difficult. Even so, that's no reason to relax efforts to counter child pornography.

In setting priorities for combating pornography, we suspect most Americans would favor letting adults (including consumers) fend for themselves so resources can be concentrated on (a) curbing porn's most repulsive aspect, the sexual exploitation and abuse of children, and (b) keeping pornographic material out of young hands.

## San Francisco Chronicle
*San Francisco, CA, July 11, 1986*

PERHAPS ONE of the most incisive criticisms of the $500,000, two-volume Meese Commission on Pornography report is contained in the report itself. The 11 members concluded that they could not define pornography. We're not sure what it is, the commission said in effect, but we're sure agin it.

Pornography can, indeed, be defined. But it cannot be defined in a way which is acceptable to all people, just as the conclusions of this wasteful and useless study will not be accepted by all people.

The commission was rigged at appointment. More than half of its members were veterans of anti-porno campaigns and the commission was obviously designed to appease conservative fundamentalists in general and smutbusters in particular.

ITS FINDINGS have led the commission to encourage picketing and boycotting of a variety of enterprises: book stores, video shops, sex theaters and magazine racks dealing in sexually explicit material. It is difficult to understand this declaration of holy war against an enemy which cannot be defined to the commission's satisfaction. The report advocates federal, state and local censorship, but we doubt this has much popular support.

The commission's conclusion that pornography is linked both to sexual violence and sexual discrimination runs contrary to the findings of a 1970 presidential commission which relied more heavily on expert testimony. We do not believe that such a casual relationship can be demonstrated scientifically. We do know one other thing about the report. It lists plot outlines of hundreds of blue movies with great explicitness; that is bound to help the sales of the report to the interested public.

## Attorney General Meese Vows Pornography Crackdown

Attorney General Edwin Meese 3rd Oct. 22, 1986 said he would launch an "all-out campaign against the distribution of obscene material." As part of the effort, he said, the Justice Department would create a special task force to aid the prosecution of pornographers.

For his proposals, Meese drew heavily on a report by his Attorney General's Commission on Pornography. He also endorsed the report's controversial finding that obscene materials probably led to sexual violence.

As the commission had recommended, Meese called for Congress to "proscribe" sexually explicit cable television programming and limit so-called dial-a-porn telephone services. He would also ask that anybody under age 21 be legally barred from appearing in "sexually explicit visual depictions." Retailers and producers of the material would be required to keep records showing that the models were not under age.

As had the commission, Meese said organized crime loomed large in the pornography industry, and he echoed a commission call for laws that would require the forfeiture of profits by convicted pornographers.

Meese ignored some of the commission recommendations, such as the call for mandatory prison sentences in obscenity convictions. But the Justice Department antipornography task force he planned had first been urged in the commission report. Meese said the group of prosecutors would augment a planned Justice Department "center for obscenity prosecution" that would act as an information clearinghouse and provide training and assistance for prosecutors at all levels of government.

Meese did not say how many people would be involved in these projects, or how much money would be required. He did say the funds would come out of other department operations.

Antipornography groups reacted favorably to the announcement. "I think they're modest proposals, but at least it's a beginning," said Rev. Donald Wildmon, who was leader of the National Federation for Decency.

The American Civil Liberties Union (ACLU) denounced the proposals. Barry Lynn, a lawyer with the ACLU, said the "fanfare" of the Meese announcement was "designed to frighten producers and retailers out of the business of selling sexually oriented materials."

### Los Angeles Times
*Los Angeles, CA, October 28, 1986*

Attorney General Edwin Meese III's latest foray into legal theory finds him asserting that opinions of the Supreme Court of the United States apply only to the parties in the case in court and are not the "supreme law of the land that is binding on all persons and parts of government, henceforth and forevermore."

To be sure, in the course of two centuries the Supreme Court has many times reversed itself or changed direction as conditions changed or as a new generation re-examined a theory of law. Members of Congress can vote against a bill because they think it is unconstitutional, and the President may veto an act of Congress on those grounds. If that is all that Meese meant to say, he could perhaps be excused for a careless choice of words.

But Meese was being very careful, and the political message he sent was the message he intended to send: "If you don't like the Supreme Court's opinions, you should ignore them. After all, it is the Constitution, not the Court that is the law." As a practical matter, this notion is exactly wrong.

Since 1803, the Supreme Court has been recognized as the interpreter of the Constitution. Its rulings are indeed the supreme law of the land, and it is the obligation of every citizen, every judge and every agency of government to heed them.

It is particularly distressing that Meese chose to criticize the court's opinion in the 1958 case of Cooper vs. Aaron, which was the first segregation case following Brown vs. Board of Education. At a time of great turmoil, when many people wanted to defy the court, the justices unanimously reaffirmed their decision in Brown and declared, "Article VI of the Constitution makes the Constitution 'supreme law of the land.' In 1803, [Marbury vs. Madison] declared the basic principle that the federal judiciary is supreme in the exposition of the law of the Constitution, and that principle has ever since been respected by this court and the country as a permanent and indispensable feature of our constitutional system."

The justices were forced to make this declaration in 1958 because Gov. Orval Faubus of Arkansas had made an assertion similar to the one that Meese made last week. The Arkansas schools did not have to be desegregated, Faubus claimed, because Arkansas had not been a party to Brown vs. Board of Education, and Supreme Court decisions apply only to the parties in the case. Not so, said the justices in Cooper vs. Aaron, and all nine of them personally signed the opinion—the only time in the history of the court that that has occurred.

Legal scholars have long debated the source and scope of the court's authority, which presents an interesting intellectual and philosophical discussion. Meese, however, is out of his depth in that league. Even if he were up to the task, it is inappropriate for the nation's highest law-enforcement officer to make such pronouncements, for they encourage lawlessness in a society that values the rule of law.

### LEXINGTON HERALD-LEADER
*Lexington, KY, October 25, 1986*

A daring way to cut the value of a state's marijuana crop, a brave new insult and the terrorizing of the United States — possibly by the Internal Revenue Service or the Soviet Union or both — highlight this week's collection of truly thoughtful tidbits of talk.

• Oklahoma has hit upon an innovative way to cut in half the value of the state's crop of illegal marijuana: Cut in half the value you place on it. It used to be that each marijuana plant confiscated was valued at $1,000. Now, quicker than you can say "a pox on pot," it's $500.

"The old figures gave a distorted picture of the marijuana economy in Oklahoma," said Tom Soosbee of the Oklahoma Bureau of Narcotics and Dangerous Drugs. "And people were always trying to compare it to the wheat crop."

• When U.S. Attorney General Edwin Meese delivered himself this week of the opinion that Supreme Court decisions are valid only as far as the front door of the Supreme Court, the American Civil Liberties Union was shocked and appalled.

That must be why Ira Glasser, ACLU executive director, claimed that Meese "is fast establishing himself as the most dangerous public official since Richard Nixon."

That Glasser. He knows how to make a guy wince.

• Asked if those listed in Forbes magazine as the nation's 400 wealthiest people fear that they'll be targeted for terrorists plots, publisher Malcolm Forbes said that only a few lose sleep about such matters.

"I think the terror most people are concerned with is the IRS," Forbes noted.

• Discussing the ABC television miniseries "Amerika," for which the great allure appears to be the idea that the Russians have taken over the United States and things are not exactly nifty, a program executive contends that the show isn't meant to alarm anybody.

"The Soviet takeover of America in no way is intended to imply that this is either possible or even what the picture is about," said Donald Wrye, writer, director and executive producer of the series. "It's not intended to be taken literally. It's not intended to express any Paul Revere alarm that the Russians are coming."

OK, Donald, so the show isn't really about the Soviet Union running the Super Bowl, the Final Four and the Toyota deal. What is it about? On second thought, never mind. We'd just as soon not know.

## The Hartford Courant
*Hartford, CT, October 29, 1986*

Maybe Attorney General Edwin Meese III is just twitting us when he implies that Supreme Court decisions deserve little more respect than comedian Rodney Dangerfield says he gets. But if he's serious, he's bent on nothing short of revolution. That's a peculiar role for an ostensible conservative to be playing.

Mr. Meese, speaking at Tulane University, acknowledged that Supreme Court rulings must be obeyed by the parties in cases, and that the executive branch, if necessary, has to enforce the court's rulings. But a high court decision, he said, "does not establish a supreme law of the land that is binding on all persons and parts of government, henceforth and forevermore."

The word "forevermore" turns this remark into a simple truism. The fact that the Supreme Court has reversed itself so many times demonstrates that no decision can be expected to stand "forevermore."

But the rest of the statement and similar ones in the attorney general's speech suggest more than truisms. They unmistakably imply that the country's chief law enforcement officer believes that even a fresh Supreme Court opinion need not be heeded by anyone not a party in the case before the court.

There's no harm, Mr. Meese said, in legislators' passing bills that contradict Supreme Court opinions because the court's decisions "do not necessarily determine future public policy." Approvingly, Mr. Meese quoted a historian's assertion that "it is ... the Constitution which is the law, not the decisions of the court."

In both statements, the attorney general is half right. The future of public policy is indeed unpredictable, and the Constitution is of course supreme in the hierarchy of the law. No one says otherwise.

What's troubling, and particularly strange for a conservative, is Mr. Meese's apparent scrapping of the idea of legal precedent. He seems to be suggesting that government officials who daily make, interpret and apply the Constitution and laws at all levels shouldn't feel in any way guided by what the Supreme Court says.

If a legal system like ours is to function smoothly, some governmental entity must decide, at least for the moment, what the Constitution and laws mean. Without such authoritative decision-making, legal disputes could be endless. To reject this principle, as Mr. Meese seems to be casually doing, is to blaze a trail toward legal chaos.

The agent selected to make these decisions in the United States is the Supreme Court. There has been little serious disagreement with that choice since 1803, when Chief Justice John Marshall wrote, in the case of Marbury vs. Madison, that "it is, emphatically, the province and duty of the judicial department to say what the law is." Comes now the attorney general to add a footnote: "But what the law is can also just as well be decided by anyone else."

Perhaps we misread Mr. Meese. Perhaps all he meant was what his spokesman said he was trying to say — "that when one believes a constitutional decision was wrong, one should not feel shy or inhibited about responding to it in a responsible fashion." There's nothing objectionable about that.

But if the attorney general is advocating free-for-all constitutional and statutory interpretation, in which no judicial opinion settles anything, even temporarily, and every basic principle of law is completely open to question from moment to moment, he's talking about a government that few Americans would tolerate.

## The Cincinnati Post
*Cincinnati, OH October 24, 1986*

In a mischievous statement, Attorney General Edwin Meese has said Supreme Court interpretations of the Constitution are not "the supreme law of the land" and do not bind all public officials.

The attorney general's view is dangerous, but it has historical backing. It was shared, among others, by Presidents Madison, Lincoln and Franklin Roosevelt, especially when the high court interfered with their policies.

But it has been accepted since 1803 that Supreme Court interpretations of the Constitution are binding on the entire country, and one wonders what Meese was up to by seeming to encourage defiance of the court.

He did so by suggesting that its rulings had to be followed only by parties to particular cases, while other officials should be guided by their own views of the Constitution.

Meese has written a prescription for chaos: Each of the branches of government interpreting the Constitution on its own and officials everywhere ignoring high court rulings with which they disagree.

This raises disturbing specters: Legislators repeatedly passing laws that the court has struck down; Nixon-like presidents defying court orders to surrender documents; a school board in one city adopting a desegregation plan that the court has declared unconstitutional in another.

The administration's response to intolerable court decisions should be to work within the system by rewriting the law or amending the Constitution. It should be to appoint justices who put the Constitution above their personal agendas.

But no cabinet member, especially an attorney general, should speak as if to foment rebellion against an institution that has served the nation well.

## The Boston Globe
*Boston, MA, October 25, 1986*

Opponents of a Justice Department plan to create a special pornography-prosecution team should consider it from another perspective. Instead of criticizing the plan, it may be better to encourage Attorney General Edwin Meese to redouble his personal anti-pornography efforts and oversee the operation.

For all his ramblings on social ills, Meese seems genuinely concerned about what he calls the "cancer of obscenity." Meese's commission on pornography came up with a recommendation that would allow the attorney general to substitute action for outrage.

If "illegal" obscene materials are as pervasive as the commission report suggests, the matter is worth Meese's attention. Of course, he will probably have to curtail some of his other activities, but that, too, can be looked upon as a public service.

America has been unable to reach a consensus on what material is obscene and, therefore, beyond the protections guaranteed by the First Amendment. The Supreme Court has suggested that such material is without socially redeeming value. That led only to a continuation of a debate that has been going on for ages, with the civil libertarians on one side and the Ed Meeses on the other.

Now, Meese has an opportunity to dig up and show Americans what he means when he refers to material that is not "entitled to First Amendment protection" and that is "unlawful under any reasoned and reasonable interpretation." It would be worth the time and the expense to the taxpayer if Meese can finally settle the pornography debate by bringing about agreement on what is obscene.

Rooting out pornography and prosecuting its purveyors could take years – two at least. But the nation must spare Meese for this mission. Engaging him in a war on pornography also might hamper his campaign to curtail liberties and rights that are spelled out in the Constitution and numerous court decisions.

**"ED MEESE, DOING WHAT HE DOES BEST ... YOU'VE GOTTA LAUGH TO KEEP FROM CRYING!"** — Sneaky Previews

Bill Day, Detroit Free Press

An outrageous black comedy of an attorney general pretending to represent blacks, who guts the civil rights laws and the Constitution!

**SOUL MAN**

## The News and Observer
*Raleigh, NC, October 25, 1986*

Attorney General Edwin Meese's attack on the authority of the Supreme Court presents the Reagan administration at its radical worst. Instead of displaying a true conservative's devotion to tradition and precedent, Meese tries to sabotage the Supreme Court's historic role as the ultimate arbiter in constitutional disputes.

Meese advances the outrageous notion that only the actual parties to a federal case, as well as authorities with enforcement responsibilities, are bound by a specific Supreme Court ruling. Think about the implications. Every time the court decided that a certain government practice violated someone's constitutional rights, only the people who had brought suit would be entitled to relief. All others, even if they were victims of the identical injustice, would have to fight their own expensive and arduous legal battles.

The entire American legal landscape would be far different today if such a doctrine had been in effect in recent years. Such vital protections as the right of an indigent defendant to have a lawyer and the right of a suspect to be notified that his statements can be used against him might never have been extended nationwide.

In his speech at Tulane University, Meese singled out a Supreme Court decision that was instrumental in finally halting a national disgrace — racial segregation in public schools.

The court in 1954 had prohibited segregated classrooms in the epic Brown v. Board of Education ruling. When some states that had not been parties to the case balked in complying, the nine justices in 1958 issued a unanimous follow-up decision affirming that their desegregation ruling must be regarded as "the supreme law of the land," binding on all the states, under legal principles dating back to the nation's early years. Meese rejects those principles, which the court itself called "a permanent and indispensable feature of our constitutional system."

There certainly is a legitimate legal issue in how the executive and legislative branches of government — which are co-equal with the judiciary — properly may express disagreement with Supreme Court decisions. Gerald Gunther, a Stanford University law professor who is among a host of legal experts reacting to Meese's speech, agrees that the court cannot "quiet a constitutional debate simply by issuing a particular ruling." However, Gunther says, "The system would break down if every mayor, every state and local official insisted on being dragged into court" before they would treat a clear Supreme Court precedent as law.

Meese makes the obvious point that since the court sometimes overrules itself, its opinions should not be regarded as binding "henceforth and forevermore." But that truism fails to bolster his argument that the court's opinions need not be honored as the law nationwide while they are in dispute. Eugene C. Thomas, president of the American Bar Association, notes that both Supreme Court decisions and acts of Congress can be tested in the courts, "but unless and until they are overturned, they are the law of the land."

Meese's court-bashing is part of a Reagan administration pattern that has seen the federal bench stacked with right-wing ideologues and unprecedented public criticism of individual Supreme Court justices. It reveals the attorney general's role as point man on a political commando squad whose mission is to undermine the federal judiciary's defense of average citizens' constitutional rights.

## THE ASHEVILLE CITIZEN
*Asheville, NC, October 26, 1986*

Attorney General Edwin Meese sure has some strange ideas about the law. It was Meese, you may remember, who suggested that police really needn't concern themselves much with the rights of criminal suspects, such as by allowing them to have a lawyer present when they are questioned.

And why not? Well, because only innocent people need their rights protected by lawyers, said Meese. Criminal suspects are not innocent, or else they wouldn't have been arrested.

If that seems contrary to 200 years of American law, it was nothing compared to the doctrine Meese advanced in a speech at Tulane University. He said that Supreme Court rulings on the Constitution do not determine what the law is nationwide. Such rulings apply only to the parties in the case at hand.

A Supreme Court decision "does not establish a 'supreme law of the land' that is binding on all persons and parts of government, henceforth and forevermore," said Meese. A ruling "binds the parties in the case and also the executive branch for whatever enforcement is necessary" — but not others.

TV evangelist Pat Robertson offered a similar view a couple of months ago, but no one took it very seriously. You might expect someone like Robertson to propose so extremist a notion, but the attorney general of the United States?

Meese specifically criticized a 1958 decision by the Supreme Court, Cooper vs. Aaron, which referred to the landmark school desegregation case four years earlier, Brown vs. Board of Education, as "the supreme law of the land."

It was no such thing, Meese said. Neither the court nor anyone else should elevate the court's decisions "on a par with the Constitution itself." Prevailing opinion in the country changes, and so do ideas of what is constitutional and what is not. The Supreme Court sometimes overturns its own rulings. Therefore, we should not take court decisions as the final word. Congress, state legislatures and other government agencies should feel free to propose laws and policies at variance with constitutional rulings in specific cases. To do otherwise is to "submit to government by judiciary."

Whether Meese likes it or not, Supreme Court decisions do establish the "supreme law of the land." Occasionally the court does reverse itself, but that does not mean we can ignore its rulings in the meantime.

When the court decrees that a particular policy or practice violates the Constitution, the decision must be binding upon everyone. To have it any other way would lead to chaos in the law.

If Brown vs. Board of Education had applied only to schools in Topeka, Kansas, school systems everywhere else could have remained segregated. To gain redress, blacks in each of thousands of school districts in the country would have to bring their own cases before the court. It would take decades, and the federal court system would be overwhelmed.

This year the court ruled that it was constitutional for Renton, Wash., to use its zoning powers to keep "adult" theaters and bookstores out of residential neighborhoods. Are we to suppose that every other city adopting such an ordinance must fight a case all the way to the Supreme Court before it can enforce its ordinance?

Multiply this by the scores of widely applicable rulings the Supreme Court makes every year, and the impossibility of what Meese suggests becomes apparent.

The argument over whether Supreme Court rulings on the Constitution establish the supreme law of the land, to which everyone is bound, was settled long ago. Like most of our legal traditions, it came into being for good reason.

Anyone who would destroy that tradition is not a conservative, but a radical.

## Arkansas Gazette
*Little Rock, AR, October 26, 1986*

Attorney General Edwin Meese III is engaged in a curious enterprise, which is to reduce the Supreme Court of the United States to the level of an ordinary government bureau. In his latest pronouncement, Mr. Meese said Supreme Court rulings shouldn't be observed as "the supreme law of the land." The attorney general thinks government officials should feel free to ignore decisions with which they disagree as long as they are not enjoined in the specific case.

His example was that the decision of the Supreme Court in a Topeka, Kan., suit in 1954 that segregated public schools were unlawful should not have been regarded as binding on the rest of the country. Mr. Meese called it "astonishing" that the Supreme Court declared in the Little Rock desegregation suit in 1958 that the 1954 decision was the law of the land and was binding on the country.

It no doubt was "astonishing" to some in 1803 when the Supreme Court first undertook to declare the intent of the federal Constitution against a piece of legislation by the Congress. But the Supreme Court's pre-eminent authority to state the meaning of the Constitution has been the doctrine since *Marbury v. Madison*.

Mr. Meese's doctrine would turn the judicial system into chaos. Think what would happen if separate suits had to be brought to enforce compliance in each instance with an interpretation of the Constitution. Carried to the state level, it would mean that after the Arkansas Supreme Court struck down a Hot Springs bond issue because the Constitution required an election first cities would go on issuing bonds without an election until separate suits were brought to stop each one.

Mr. Meese's attack on the supremacy doctrine of the court is more curious than threatening. Even if it should be stacked with like believers, the Supreme Court of the United States will not sacrifice its jurisdiction to declare what the law means. It would declare a different meaning but protect it just as jealously. What Mr. Meese is up to is a little court-bashing at election time. We may be wrong. And it may be only coincidence that he chose New Orleans, a city of the Deep South, to espouse his doctrine and its specific application to Southern school desegregation.

## AKRON BEACON JOURNAL
*Akron, OH, October 28, 1986*

EDWIN MEESE'S ideas on American law and justice sound like the uninformed pronouncements of a radical who, unsatisfied with the balance in the American system, would do away with basic judicial review. Unfortunately, Mr. Meese is U.S. attorney general, so his ideas must be taken seriously.

In a recent speech at Tulane University, Mr. Meese said that U.S. Supreme Court decisions should not be considered the "supreme law of the land," and are not "binding on all persons and parts of the government, henceforth and forevermore." To illustrate the point, he criticized a 1958 court decision that unanimously held that the 1954 school desegregation ruling was, indeed, binding on Arkansas Gov. Orval Faubus, who sought to defy the law in 1958.

In a remarkable gesture, all nine Supreme Court justices signed the 1958 opinion, which, among other things, reaffirmed the legitimacy of the 1803 *Marbury v. Madison* decision, which was the first time the court overturned a federal law. The reasoning then and now is that the judiciary is supreme in its "exposition of the law" and that its decisions *are* the "supreme law of the land."

That's the way the system is designed to work. The judiciary is the final, best and least political check on other branches of government. When it interprets law, that law applies in similar cases. It's ridiculous to think, for instance, that school desegregation cases must be brought from every school district in the nation before the law applies to all.

And though Mr. Meese and anyone else may disagree with and criticize any Supreme Court decision, that decision is the law until the court overturns it. It's surprising that the attorney general of the United States doesn't seem to realize that.

Mr. Meese has a point in claiming that the Constitution, not the court, is the actual supreme law of the land. This might be seen as a simple disagreement over semantics except that Mr. Meese's latest pronouncement is part of a pattern in which he, as point man for the Reagan administration, has attacked gains in civil rights, personal freedom, and other liberties.

His radical group seems to see the judiciary as one more enemy standing in the way of the group's efforts to remake America in its own, narrow image. Their views have nothing to do with conservatism or strict interpretation of the Constitution. They are merely wrong.

## Pornography Laws Debated Across U.S.

The Supreme Court Feb. 24, 1986 struck down as unconstitutional an Indianapolis ordinance that defined and penalized pornography as discrimination against women. The court affirmed, without issuing an opinion, lower federal court rulings that the statute violated First Amendment right of free speech.

The high court cited an the appellate court decision in Chicago that the Indianapolis law was an attempt at "thought control."

The law defined pornography as "the graphic sexualy explicit subordination of women, whether in picture or in words" if it showed them enjoying "pain or humiliation" or in "positions of servility or submission or display," among other things.

Three members of the high court – Chief Justice Warren E. Burger and Justices William H. Rehnquist and Sandra Day O'Connor – disagreed with the majority on handling of the case. They wanted to hear oral argument. But they offered no opionion on the correctness of the ruling.

The case, *Hudunt v. American Booksellers Association Inc.*, drew an unusual alliance of support from feminists and religious conservaitves for the Indianapolis law. Opponents of the law included civil liberties groups, booksellers and librarians.

The Supreme Court upheld by a 7-2 vote Feb. 25 a zoning law adopted by the city of Renton, Wash. that prohibited adult movie theatres within 1,000 feet of a school park, church or residential areas.

Justice William H. Rehnquist's majority opinion said the restriction, instead of an outright ban, did not violate the First Amendment's free-speech guarantee.

Justices William J. Brennan Jr. and Thurgood Marshall, dissenting, said a zoning law based on the content of films being shown did violate the First Amendment.

The ruling, in *City of Renton v. Playtime Theatres*, reversed a decision by the federal appeals court in San Francisco.

Southland Corp. April 10 announced that its national chain of 7-Eleven convenience stores would no longer welcome Playboy, Penthouse and Forum magazines. Southland was thought to be the largest retailer to act against so-called magazines.

Playboy and Penthouse were the country's largest-selling adult publications; Forum was the sister publication of Penthouse. The 4,500 7-Eleven stores that Southland directly owned would stop selling the magazines as of May. The company would advise the 3,600 stores it had franchised to the same.

Rev. Jerry Falwell praised the company for "putting principle above financial gain." His Liberty Foundation (a group that included the Moral Majority) and the separate National Federation for Decency had both organized boycotts of 7-Eleven stores to protest the magazine sales.

Antipornography activists said that Southland's decision brought to 10,000 the number of stores that had barred such publications.

The Supreme Court Feb. 21, 1989 ruled unanimously that an anti-racketeering law could not be used to close an adult bookstore without prior court determination that the material for sale were obscene.

Closure without the obscenity finding ran afoul of the First Amendment's guarantee of free speech, the court said in a unanimous opinion combining two cases, *Fort Wayne Books, Inc. v. Indiana* and *Sappenfield v. Indiana.*

The cases involved police action against bookstores whose owners were charged under state laws with engaging in a "pattern of racketeering" by repeated sales of obscene material.

"While a single copy of a book or film may be seized and retained for evidentiary purposes based on a finding of probable cause," Justice Bryon R. White wrote for the court, "the publication may not be taken out of circulation completely until there has been a determination of obscenity after an adversary hearing."

### The Record
*Hackensack, NJ,
January 30, 1987*

Memo to Attorney-General Edwin Meese III: If you want a lesson in how to fight pornography, talk to the owners of the Queen Anne Theater in Bogota, N.J. This old movie house showed hard-core porn films for almost two decades. Now it's closing. The reason: lack of customers. Video cassettes now enable those who enjoy this type of voyeurism to do so in the privacy of their own homes, cutting down the number of potential customers at the box office.

The Queen Anne was the last movie house in Bergen County to feature pornographic films. Only three are left in all of North Jersey. If this trend continues, it won't be long before the real-estate value of these movie houses is a lot greater than their box-office intake. Then they'll shut their doors, too.

By contrast, anti-pornography groups have rarely succeeded in their efforts to close or restrict theaters like the Capitol and Montauk in Passaic. Such crusades usually run aground in the courtrooms of sensible judges, who recognize that one person's "pornography" is another person's art — that any restriction on freedom of expression endangers everybody's right to say or write what he thinks.

But while cries for censorship rarely work, box-office quarantine always does. No theater continues to show X-rated films after its patronage fades away. That's the highest form of censorship. The beautiful part is, it's constitutional.

## The Atlanta Journal AND THE ATLANTA CONSTITUTION
*Atlanta, GA, February 2, 1987*

The recent admission by Attorney General Edwin Meese III that he has read Playboy and Penthouse magazines and doesn't consider them obscene makes the harassment of those publications last year by the Justice Department's pornography commission all the more cynical and inappropriate in retrospect.

The Attorney General's Commission on Pornography sent letters last February asking several convenience-store chains to respond to testimony by the Rev. Donald Wildmon, head of the National Federation of Decency. Wildmon had told the commission he considered Playboy and Penthouse "porn" magazines and called the retail chains that sold them "major players in the game of pornography."

Several chains stopped carrying the magazines, and although the Justice Department has contended that no intimidation was intended, U.S. District Judge John Garrett Penn ruled last July that the letter was designed to "discourage distributors" from selling the magazines. The letter had indicated that the chains might be named in the final commission report if they continued selling Playboy and Penthouse. The letter, Penn found, "does appear to contain an implied threat."

Meese, in remarks after a recent speech to law clerks of federal court judges, not only acknowledged that he once read Playboy and Penthouse but said they are tame by today's standards.

A conclusion that seemed likely last year seems even more likely now: Meese's commission was using muscle to harass publications against which it had no plausible legal case. The political clamors of conservative activists and the religious right were put before the high imperatives of the U.S. Constitution. For shame.

## the Charleston Gazette
*Charleston, WV, March 28, 1987*

SIXTEEN years ago a pornography study commission appointed by President Nixon concluded that sexual materials are harmless and should be legalized.

But last summer, a new commission under Attorney General Edwin Meese concluded the opposite — that pornography may cause rape and should be suppressed.

Why did two supposedly authoritative panels contradict each other? Because the second was a stacked deck, a vehicle to confirm prejudices of the administration and the fundamentalist New Right.

Not long ago, the *Los Angeles Times* commented:

"The kindest thing that can be said about the 2,000-page report of the Attorney General's Commission on Pornography is that it's a joke — not funny, but a joke. The commission's scholarship is ludicrous, its conclusions unsupported, its methodology zany."

*Publishers Weekly* said the report "speaks for a large number of generally right-wing fundamentalist groups and their supporters, who in turn have been supporters of the current administration...."

*The Daily News* of New York warned that "the public should not be fooled by the veneer of authority. The fact of the matter is that the commission has not proven any such link between pornography and sex crimes, nor has it demonstrated that pornography presents a threat to society. Government censorship, however, presents a very real danger to a society that allows free expression and respects the right of privacy."

The Meese commission was dishonest in reporting its own evidence.

For example, commission researchers examined 13 best-selling sex magazines and found that less than 1 percent of their content was violent. But this data was omitted from the report.

So was research by Ohio University's Joseph Scott, who studied movies in four categories — PG, PG-13, R and X — and found that X had the least violence.

The report doesn't mention psychological studies which found that movie violence, but not movie sex, induce aggressive responses in viewers. In fact, no scientific study ever has found that pornography is a contributor to sex crimes.

Thursday night, ABC's news magazine *20/20* demonstrated once again the hostility some Meese Commission members have to any moral viewpoint other than their own. One member, asked why the commission didn't criticize the violent content of many R-rated films, merely responded that violence in movies wasn't their concern.

As for the commission's focus on child pornography, a two-year U.S. Senate study recently concluded that this field involves only a few pedophiles, and that no child pornography has been produced in the United States since a tough federal law was passed in 1984.

Two members of the Meese Commission, Dr. Judith Becker of Columbia University and *Woman's Day* Editor Ellen Levin, refused to sign the report. They filed a dissent saying the commission majority harbors hostility to sex, that evidence before the panel was "skewed to the very violent and extremely degrading," and that "some of the commissioners are simply attempting to legislate their own personal morality."

All Americans are entitled to espouse their beliefs — but it's dishonest to warp a government study in an attempt to impose one group's belief on everyone.

## The Washington Post
*Washington, DC, February 21, 1987*

THE IMPACT of a report issued last year by a national commission on pornography was considerably blurred when Attorney General Meese briefed the press on its contents while standing in front of a colossal statue of a seminude woman in the Justice Department lobby. The general hilarity that greeted a published photograph of the occasion temporarily distracted the public from the substance of what was being recommended. This may happen again, for this week another set of government officials put out a set of regulations containing a howler that will keep Johnny Carson and Mark Russell supplied with material for weeks. As part of a program to test federal workers for drugs, the water in certain federal toilets will be dyed blue. This is supposed to prevent the surreptitious dilution of a urine sample with plain water. The Tidy-Bowl jokes have already started.

For a million or more federal civil servants, however, these regulations are no laughing matter. Under a directive issued by President Reagan last fall, agency heads may order random or blanket drug tests of persons in sensitive positions without having any probable cause to believe an employee is using drugs and without any special finding that a test is necessary to protect the public safety. The proposed regulations are supposed to protect privacy—the urine police will be present in the restroom but not in the stall—and to ensure accuracy the temperature of the sample will be taken immediately to prevent a substitution. But does anyone believe that these steps are going to make a shy young typist or a distinguished elder policy analyst feel any less humiliated?

These precautions may be fine for dealing with people arrested on drug charges, civil servants who mumble, nod and snort their way through the day or certain highly restricted classes of workers such as railroad engineers and deputy sheriffs whose drug habits can kill others. If tests must be given—and in some cases that is prudent—rules that promote privacy and ensure accuracy are welcome. But the wholesale testing of a group that could exceed a million workers is constitutionally suspect and obviously unwarranted. One civil-liberties lawyer compared the policy to an order authorizing the search of a million civil servants' homes in order to find the few who have been stealing government paper clips. The drug testing program, equally intrusive, is not amusing. Litigation challenging the new policy, not giggles, is the best response.

# THE DAILY HERALD
*Biloxi, MS, November 9, 1988*

The Federal Communications Commission sent the multimillion-dollar dial-a-porn industry an obscene message Monday: Keep that material inaccessible to minors or pay dearly for the transgression.

One California company that didn't had to pay the first FCC fine for not restricting access by minors to their trashy offerings. The fine against Audio Enterprises Inc. and operator Wendy King totaled $50,000.

Other companies offering similar services should take note of the size of the fine. It's bad enough that this filth is allowed in the telephone system. Restricting access to it by minors is the least the FCC should do.

In one of its better moments this year, Congress passed a law banning obscene and indecent commercial messages, but the law is being challenged in court. The challenge would make a distinction between indecent messages, which porn phone services say are permitted under the First Amendment, and obscene messages, which the Supreme Court agrees can be banned.

Dial-a-porn is obviously lucrative, producing revenues of $54 million annually. Without restrictions, it will continue growing. The FCC is to be commended for stepping in to make those smut peddlers shield their material from minors.

# the Charleston Gazette
*Charleston, WVA, November 19, 1988*

WE'VE NEVER understood why fundamentalists react so fiercely against sex. The Bible makes no fuss over Solomon's 700 wives and 300 concubines — so why are born-again people endlessly on the warpath against lovemaking?

Mainline churches generally ignore *Playboy* magazine, R-rated movies, and even hard-core porn. If *Penthouse* doesn't upset Presbyterians, why does it drive evangelicals into a frenzy?

This week, born-again churches held a censorship rally in the Raleigh County Armory Civic Center and heard dire warnings.

Larry Braidfoot, a Nashville lawyer, spoke grimly about a "13- or 14-year-old boy looking at the picture of a body of a female and becoming excited. There's a chemical in his body system that burns into his brain, into his memory as if by a hot poker."

Patrick Trueman, head of the Justice Department's Obscenity Task Force, advised the 450 Beckley believers how to "wipe out obscene material" by swearing out warrants and prosecuting magazine sellers and video renters.

The Beckley rally was organized by the Rev. Howard Miller, who led a petition drive that caused the Raleigh County Commission to pass a law imposing 30-day jail terms and $500 fines on sellers of sexual materials. Miller declared that "freedom doesn't give you the right to do what you want. It gives you the right to do what you ought."

What he means is that West Virginians should have no rights to do anything except what fundamentalists allow.

Educated mainline faiths — Methodists, Lutherans, Presbyterians, Episcopalians and the like — oppose censorship. Why don't they speak up, so America will know that some churches have other views? Why do they sit silent and let the sex haters be the only voice of Christianity in this issue?

# Chicago Defender
*Chicago, IL, October 1, 1988*

Some people have a strange way of giving nice-sounding names to vile things. Consider the phrase "kiddie porn." Phonetically, it does not assault the ears. If it were a musical chord, it would have ressonance, consonance, sounding so pleasant that it just might generate a state of relaxation and peace within the listener. But in reality, child pornography is a repugnant, and sometimes violent thing.

Fortunately, members of the U.S. Senate don't choose to deal with child pornographers in a tender manner. The legislators recently voted 97-0 for a provision that would increase the fines and penalties for anyone involved in producing, distributing, and possessing child pornography. Way to go, senators!

Pedophiles, those adults who sexually exploit children, don't necessarily lurk in alleys, wear weird clothes, or exhibit any signs that could readily identify them to society. They are be difficult to identify since they may look like any other average Joe or Jane.

As a nation, we must let it be clearly known that we will not take a soft stand against adults who so abuse our children. We must not submit to those who would make moral trash of our youth.

America has to really get tough with these child molesters since the perverts are developing new ways, through technology, of exploiting our youngsters. Now computers are being used. In fact, Sen. Paul Trible (R-Va.) reportedly was told of one exploiter who was using his home computer to network with other pedophiles. One of his computer printout sheets showed contacts in 33 states and seven foreign countries. Some of the major supermarket chains don't have such an extensive network.

After the pedophile's arrest, authorities seized approximately 30 video tapes and dozens of photos of grown people being involved with children ages six to 15. For all we know, the offender and his new technology may be more the norm than the rarety today. If so, that truly is frightening and it is even more reason why the Senate was right in structuring the get tough law.

It's bad enough when adults are sexually exploited but the crime truly sinks below sewer level when it is perpetrated against children. Victims range from toddlers to teenagers. None of them are legally old enough to make lucid decisions about getting involved in such activities. Many of the children are kidnapped, tricked, forced and otherwise intimidated into becoming victims. Some of the abuses are too sordid to mention here.

Authorities report that sellers of child pornography are sometimes involved in inventive public relations while peddling their wares to an underground clientele. Tantalizing words like "sexy, kinky, thrilling, exciting, breathless, etc." are used to market the so-called product. It must be stressed here that the wares do not always consist of literature, photos and tapes of the children. Sometimes, they include the youngsters themselves. That is truly shameful and must be stopped. Therefore, we at the *Defender* enthusiastically support the senators on this one.

## LEXINGTON HERALD-LEADER
*Lexington, KY, October 4, 1988*

When the U.S. Supreme Court ruled a few years ago that pornography is defined by community standards, it did an injustice to constitutional law. The nature of that injustice was apparent in last week's raids on two Lexington adult bookstores.

First, the "community standards" decision indicated that constitutional freedoms — in this instance, freedom of press — vary according to locality. Imagine what such a selective recognition of rights would mean when applied to other civil liberties. For instance, by this criteria, lunch counters, restrooms and schools in the South might still be segregated.

If constitutional rights do not apply equally to all Americans, no matter where they live, those rights are not rights at all. They become privileges held by the few and denied to the many.

Equally important, the court's murky decision gave local law enforcement officials leeway to abuse the legal process. And that is what makes last week's raids troubling.

Were Fayette County's police and prosecutors really trying to rid the community of obscene books and films? Or were they merely using obscenity laws to harass two bookstores into closing — and in the process, stopping other *alleged* activities that the law enforcement officials have not been able to prove?

During the raid, police confiscated 700 sexually explicit magazines, 13 adult videos and a variety of "sexual toys." Other bookstores in Lexington sell sexually explicit publications. Other video stores rent or sell some of the same adult videos that police confiscated at 2004 Video Store and The Bookstore.

So why were these the only two places that were raided? The comments of Assistant County Attorney Joe Famularo give some indication:

"I've lived in Lexington since 1964 and regard it as a conservative city, and I was surprised by it — not so much by the literature but by the activity they (the police) told me was going on there."

This gives a somewhat clearer view of this raid. The raid seems to have been aimed not so much at the books and movies as at the "activity" that goes on at the bookstores. And what is this alleged activity? According to police, it includes prostitution, solicitation of prostitution and people having sex in the video viewing ("peep show") booths.

There's no question that prostitution and solicitation are crimes. If law enforcement officials believe prostitution and solicitation are going on at the two bookstores, they ought to gather evidence and prosecute the alleged offenders. But no one was charged with prostitution or solicitation as a result of these raids. No charges were made in relation to sex in the booths.

The only charges filed were for the distribution of obscene materials, some of which are available at numerous other locations around town. And if the same sexually explicit materials are available all over town, what does that say about those nebulous "community standards" that have supposedly been violated?

It is interesting to note that Vice Mayor Barkley Blevins' plumbing business is located across the street from one of the bookstores and that one of the people who complained about the other store was Martha Wilkinson, the governor's wife.

When the Supreme Court set the "community standards" test, the justices surely did not mean that the standards of leading citizens should determine what is and is not permissible. Yet that seems to be what is happening in this case. That's no way to interpret the Constitution.

## Congressional Legislation Bans "Dial-A-Porn" Services

The Senate April 20, 1988 approved by voice vote a bill extending federal education programs for the next five years. The legislation, which included an amendment banning so-called "dial-a-porn" telephone services, had passed the House of Representatives April 19 by a vote of 397-1. The entire package was sent to the White House for President Ronald Reagan's signature.

The bill, known as the Hawkins-Stafford School Improvement Act, authorized maximum spending of $8.3 billion on elementary and secondary education programs for fiscal 1989, an increase of about $1.6 billion from the current fiscal year.

Attached to the education legislation was an amendment banning pornographic telephone messages. The measure, sponsored by Sen. Jesse Helms (R, N.C.), would make it illegal to use obscene and indecent speech over the telephone. Many legislators questioned the constitutionality of the ban and predicted that it would be challenged in the courts.

The Senate Nov. 19, 1989 added an amendment to the so-called "dial-a-porn" legislation offered by Sen. Helms. The amendment redrafted a previous ban on dial-a-porn telephone services to conform with a Supreme Court decision in June that upset the congressional ban on obscene ones.

## SYRACUSE HERALD-JOURNAL
*Syracuse, NY, May 24, 1989*

The impending intrusion of dial-a-porn into our state has created a golden opportunity for our elected officials. Most have climbed aboard an extremely popular anti-porn bandwagon. Those who have not simply have not figured out an angle yet, or are not as politically adept as the others.

The imminent disaster that has served to mobilize many of the state's political soldiers into action is the availability in New York state of direct telephone lines to sexually explicit messages. You dial the number and listen to a lot of heavy breathing ... and much, much more. The first of the month, you get a bill that tells you a sex fiend and his money are soon parted, at the rate of somewhere between 50 cents and $2-a-minute.

Unfortunately, it is not always the caller seeking the thrill who pays the bill. Opponents of the dial-a-porn calls claim, and we would not argue with them, that it is one more opportunity for our children to be exposed to the kinds of smut we would rather they did not have access to. It is assumed Mom and Dad don't know about the calls until the bill arrives in the mailbox.

The telephone companies say they would love to save their customers from the scurrilous sound tracks, but they are bound by law to keep the lines of communications open, regardless of the message. What they don't make a point of telling us is that the calls are a giant money-maker for the telephone companies.

Our own state Sen. Tarky Lombardi has introduced a somewhat complicated measure in the Senate to keep the wrong ears from hearing the phone filth. His bill would require those consenting adults who wish to listen to sounds of smut to sign up for identification numbers. Whenever they want to make such a call, they would have to give the number to the operator at the other end. Presumably, nobody under the age of 18 would have such a number or would have access to one.

There are a couple of things wrong with this legislation. First, it seems to us a person determined to steal such a number will find a way to do it.

Second, while the vast majority of us have no interest in paying to listen to recordings of sex, the thought of a list somewhere of those who do, along with their identification numbers, is frightening. Frankly, as long as it is legal to listen to dial-a-porn, it is none of the government's business who does it.

No, we have a better way. Let the telephone companies and those who offer the dirty talk tape service take the responsibility for keeping our phone lines from being misused. We should be able to call our phone company and tell them to block out the smut from our lines ... at no cost to us.

The same should go for those other telephone company money-makers, like the Saturday morning cartoon characters who invite the young viewers to call and run up big tabs on Mom and Dad's bill.

## Minneapolis Star and Tribune
*Minneapolis, MN, June 28, 1989*

Alexander Graham Bell likely never imagined that his invention would be used to transmit gutter talk. But every year, millions of Americans pick up the telephone to listen to sexually explicit messages. The $2-billion-a-year dial-a-porn industry is an illustration of the American appetite for cheap thrills. But as the U.S. Supreme Court observed last week, it is also a legitimate exercise of the constitutional right to free speech.

The controversy over dial-a-porn is a modern twist in an old tale. For decades, porn vendors have sought to satisfy the salacious with explicit books, magazines and movies; time and again, the high court has rebuffed government attempts to censor such material. Yet that history did not keep Congress from trying to squelch the new and booming business in phone sex. Troubled by the impact the vulgar messages might have on underage dialers, lawmakers voted in 1988 to entirely outlaw all interstate dial-a-porn services.

No go, said the court. Though messages deemed "obscene" by community standards can be censored, the court said, material that is merely "indecent" cannot be squelched. As Justice Byron White wrote for the court, the law "has the invalid effect of limiting the content of adult telephone conversations to that which is suitable for children to hear." That setup, observed White, "is another case of burning up the house to roast the pig."

Congress could have roasted the pig more effectively by severing youngsters' access to dial-a-porn services. As White remarked, the Federal Communications Commission has endorsed requiring phone-sex services to assign passwords to adult users or to secure payment only through credit cards. Or, as Michigan Rep. John Dingell urged last week, Congress could require that access to dial-a-porn lines be limited to adults who specifically request it.

But censoring all explicit phone messages is the wrong way to attack dial-a-porn's potential evil. The First Amendment protects the expression of honorable and offensive ideas alike. If Americans are to think for themselves, they must decide for themselves what they wish to see and hear. Last week's ruling makes clear that not even the seaminess of dial-a-porn can justify an exception to the First Amendment.

## DESERET NEWS
*Salt Lake City, UT, June 24, 1989*

With its unfortunate vote that Congress cannot outlaw the so-called "dial-a-porn" industry — a $2 billion-a-year sleazy business — the U.S. Supreme Court this week once again left the nation and its children at the mercy of smut peddlers.

Congress last year banned all sexually explicit telephone dial-up messages, making it a crime to use a telephone to make "obscene or indecent" communications for commercial purposes. A major thrust was to protect children from making such calls.

In its verdict, the Supreme Court once again jumped into the old question of "obscene" versus "indecent" — a distinction that has never been satisfactorily spelled out.

While it upheld the right of Congress to forbid "obscene" messages, the court said the ban could not apply to "indecent" communications. Obscene has been identified as speech that appeals to the prurient interest, is patently offensive and has no serious literary, artistic, political or scientific value.

What outrages many people is that this definition has been defined in such a way as to exclude much sexually oriented, highly explicit and offensive material.

The Supreme Court justices agreed that such material is not desirable for children, but said protecting children did not justify banning the entire dial-a-porn industry.

The justices said certain steps — some proposed earlier by the Federal Communications System — can be taken to limit access of such phone services to children. These include the use of access codes, scramblers and credit card payment.

Justice Byron R. White admitted there may be "no fail-safe method of guaranteeing that a minor will never be able to get access to the dial-a-porn system." But he insisted that technological restrictions would probably prove extremely effective in most cases.

Dial-a-porn companies make their services available through 976 exchanges and AT&T's long distance 900 lines. The telephone companies charge callers on various per-call rates, keeping a portion of the charges and giving the rest to the dial-a-porn company.

How big is the industry? Recent figures are not available, but in 1983, 800,000 calls were made to dial-a-porn services in the New York telephone system in one month alone. In 1984, of the 27 million recorded phone message calls on the Pacific Bell System, 12 million were to dial-a-porn services.

It's bad enough that the Supreme Court has given this abscess on society new life, but the ruling could embolden dial-a-porn companies to expand their operations and become even more vulgar and indecent. It was the threat of congressional action that caused several such companies to give up some of the awful things they had been doing.

Even worse, the court's decision will likely mean the abandonment of future attempts to quash this growing filth, even though dial-a-porn may gradually move from "indecent" to blatantly "obscene." Morality and good sense took a beating in this case.

## DAYTON DAILY NEWS
*Dayton, OH, June 28, 1989*

The U.S. Supreme Court has said that Congress can outlaw dial-a-porn businesses that peddle obscene talk, but not ones that stick to conversations that are merely indecent. On the latter point, the court was unanimous.

The word "indecent" has come in court to refer roughly to sex that is not all-out explicit.

These issues have been thrashed out again and again in court, so often that Congress should have known it couldn't do what it tried.

Basically, what's obscene and what isn't is decided by courts. The Supreme Court holds that obscenity is a matter of community values. The main worry of the pornographers now is that local communities might try to restrict them. For example, while a dial-a-porn message emanating from New York might not be considered objectionable there, it might be defined as obscene in Boise. The Supreme Court said this predicament isn't its problem, and that dial-a-porn operators would have to find ways to keep certain messages out of certain communities, if those communities object.

The court also left open the possibility that the Federal Communications Commission could enact rules that would make it more difficult to access dial-a-porn numbers, with the intention of keeping children off the lines. In some communities, kids have learned about the dial-a-porn numbers and have run up thousands of dollars in bills calling the numbers without their parents' consent. The F.C.C might try to require the use of credit cards to access dial-a-porn messages, or Congress might require phone companies to block customers' access to the numbers unless they requested it.

There may be constitutional ways to make business difficult for dial-a-porn outfits. Congress and phones companies shouldn't be shy about doing that, but they can't throw out the First Amendment in the process.

## The Washington Post
*Washington, DC, June 24, 1989*

DIAL-A-PORN, like flag-burning, has few defenders. Customers, yes. The service in New York City, for example, receives 6 million to 7 million calls a month. But few are likely to stand up in a public forum and praise an industry that makes a lot of money providing cheap thrills over the phone lines. Nevertheless, unpopular, controversial and even revolting activities are not necessarily unconstitutional. Earlier this week the Supreme Court ruled 5 to 4 that burning the flag cannot be prosecuted as a crime. And yesterday, the same court—unanimous this time—held that at least some kinds of dial-a-porn messages are protected speech.

The government has a legitimate interest in protecting children from pornography. To this end, Congress, the FCC and the courts have been grappling with restrictions that would keep these phone messages from youngsters without unconstitutionally restricting the rights of adults to hear what they will. A number of parents, by the way, were doubly offended when they discovered that Junior was dialing the junk message line and the phone company was billing them at a rate roughly comparable to the monthly grocery bill. After a number of false starts, the FCC proposed regulations that would require the porn purveyors to use access codes, insist on payment by credit card and send scrambled messages that would be unintelligible without the use of a decoder. All this was designed to keep children from hearing the trash, and by all accounts the regulations were successful.

Enter Congress. No longer content to focus on youngsters, legislators passed a bill last year to prohibit indecent and obscene interstate commercial telephone communications directed to any person regardless of age. Obscene speech is not protected by the First Amendment. It has been defined by the Supreme Court as that which appeals to a morbid interest in sex, is patently offensive and, when taken as a whole, has no serious literary, artistic, political or scientific merit. But indecent speech—patently offensive references to excretory and sexual organs or activities—cannot be restricted where adults are involved. Three justices believe even obscene speech is protected, but yesterday's ruling extends only to the indecent.

The dial-a-porn people are taking a chance with every message they provide that it will be judged obscene. It is hard for laymen to make these fine distinctions—which vary from community to community—and even justices of the Supreme Court have been known to invoke an "I know it when I see it" standard. But that risk is their business. As for the average American, his right to spend a lot of his hard-earned money to listen to heavy breathers, bathroom banter and sex at a distance has been upheld. The government cannot be in the business of supervising speech between adults, whether or not the speech consists of grunge and squalor.

## The Chattanooga Times
*Chattanooga, TN, July 10, 1989*

When the Supreme Court unanimously overturned Congress' clumsy attempt to outlaw so-called dial-a-porn telephone messages, it reiterated the crucial distinction between what is likable, and what is constitutional and thus permissible. The court's decision should be helpful in guiding Congress away from legislation that ignores the First Amendment's free speech guarantees.

There's little question that some people like to spend their dime dialing those services and listening to heavy breathing, dirty words and fantasy sex; dial-a-porn is a billion-dollar-a-year business. Neither is there question that many people consider such services a blot on the constitutional landscape.

But the court drew a crucial distinction. It left in place a ban on obscene messages that must meet the community standards test. The court has defined obscene speech as whatever appeals to a morbid interest in sex, is patently offensive and, taken as a whole, is devoid of any serious literary, artistic, political or scientific merit. Indecent language, however, mostly consists of what are, for lack of a better term, "dirty words." And although three of the justices would have given the services the right to use obscene messages, the court unanimously agreed that "sexual expression which is indecent but not obscene" is entitled to the Constitution's protection.

Obviously, government has a responsibility to protect children from pornography. Accordingly, Congress, the courts and the Federal Communications Commission have spent a lot of time devising restrictions to keep young people away from those recorded messages but without restricting the right of adults to hear what they want to hear. To that end, the FCC finally came up with regulations requiring dial-a-porn entrepreneurs, among other things, to use access codes and receive payments by credit card.

But Congress overstepped passing a law last year to ban indecent and obscene speech via interstate telephone lines, no matter what the caller's age. Sable Communications sued, arguing that given the protections already put in place by the FCC, it should be constitutional to provide the dialed porn messages to adults who want them and are willing to pay.

The court has not given the dial-a-porn crowd free rein. They have to live with the risk that "indecent" expression might go too far and thus be judged obscene. True, many will consider such fine distinctions obtuse, even destructive of a community's values, to the extent they can be clearly defined. The point to be kept in mind is that in the effort to keep the government from overstepping its bounds in supervising talk between adults, better to err on the side of permissiveness than to diminish the precious protection of the First Amendment.

## THE DAILY OKLAHOMAN
*Oklahoma City, OK, June 30, 1989*

SMUT peddlers for years have been hiding behind the protections of the U.S. Constitution's First Amendment to distribute their filth to anyone willing to pay the tab — including youngsters.

The Supreme Court — in another of its recent decisions that defy logic — has extended that protection to the billion-dollar "dial-a-porn" industry.

The justices ruled Congress was not justified when it passed a law last year banning all sexually explicit telephone dial-up message services. The court said Congress may outlaw obscene telephone messages only, not indecent ones. Such a ban violates free-speech rights when applied to "indecent" messages, the court ruled.

The court thus rejected the Justice Department's argument that a ban on the dial-a-porn is needed to protect the nation's children from hearing "patently offensive speech." It upheld a lower court ruling that acknowledged the phone messages may be inappropriate for minors, but stated outlawing them violated the Constitution.

In writing the Supreme Court decision, Justice Byron R. White conceded there may not be a fail-safe method to prevent a minor from accessing the dial-a-porn system, but he said technological restrictions might prove "extremely effective, and only a few of the most enterprising and disobedient young people will manage to secure access to such messages."

If laws requiring a jillion things to protect children from unsafe toys are constitutional, it seems logical to protect them from filthy, indecent messages.

## The State
*Columbia, SC, July 6, 1989*

LAST YEAR Congress caved in to ultraconservative forces and passed legislation outlawing all dial-a-porn services. Predictably, the Supreme Court ruled last week that the ban violates the constitutional right to free speech.

In May, 1988, Congress, led by Sen. Jesse Helms, R-N.C., approved a law making it a crime to use the telephone for any "obscene or indecent" communications. But the total ban was never imposed because a California district judge ruled it could be applied only to obscene — not indecent — phone messages.

The high court unanimously agreed. "Sexual expression which is indecent but not obscene is protected by the First Amendment," wrote Justice Byron R. White.

In supporting the total ban, the U.S. Justice Department argued that it was needed "to protect children from hearing patently offensive speech."

But Justice White, while conceding that there is "no fail-safe method" for excluding minors from dial-a-porn, said technological restrictions on industry should prove effective. "Because the statute's denial of adult access to (indecent) telephone messages far exceeds that which is necessary to limit the access of minors," he wrote, "... the ban does not survive constitutional scrutiny."

In fact, phone-blocking methods already are available in most areas of the country. Most phone companies — including all those that serve South Carolina customers — retain strict control over all dial-in services and block 976 and 900 exchanges at the customer's request. There are no dial-a-porn services in this state, although in some states, like New York, they still do a thriving business.

But with the high court ruling, dial-a-porn businesses are now at risk of criminal prosecution if they cross that fine line that demarcates obscenity — a line that may vary from community to community.

When Congress approved the dial-a-porn ban, it bypassed compromise legislation to require telephone companies to block access to pornographic messages unless an adult customer specifically requested that they be made available. That sensible alternative makes far more sense and should pass constitutional muster.

## DAILY NEWS
*New York, NY, June 30, 1989*

A bill to straighten out the dial-a-porn mess has passed the full Senate but is hung up in an Assembly committee. It deserves to be brought out and given full passage.

The bill responds to the U.S. Supreme Court ruling permitting all but the most obscene recorded phone messages. Parents would be able to apply to local phone companies for personal identification numbers (PINs) so they could have access to recorded information but keep their children from dialing the dirty stuff. Phone companies would also be able to reject messages they deem damaging to their reputations. It's a sensible way to protect children and let the marketplace, not Big Brother, decide what's acceptable to the community.

## Omaha World-Herald
*Omaha, NE, July 5, 1989*

Congress, according to the U.S. Supreme Court, has the authority to ban "dial-a-porn" messages that are obscene. But it doesn't have the authority to stop adults from receiving telephone messages that are merely indecent. Once again the court has come up with an interpretation of the Constitution that defies easy understanding by ordinary people.

A dictionary is of little help. One definition of "indecent" in "Webster's Third New International Dictionary" is "tending to be obscene," while one of the definitions for "obscene" is "inciting or designed to incite to . . . indecency."

The dial-a-porn opinion didn't shed much light on the difference between obscene and indecent, either. Written by Justice Byron White, it included this sentence: "The case before us today does not require us to decide what is obscene or what is indecent but rather to determine whether Congress is empowered to prohibit transmission of obscene telephonic communications."

White, referring to previous court decisions, said materials that are obscene in some communities might be acceptable under contemporary standards in others.

The Supreme Court in 1973 said a work is obscene if it appeals to a morbid interest in sex, is patently offensive and, when taken as a whole, lacks serious literary, artistic, political or scientific value. Four years later, for broadcasting purposes, the court accepted a definition of indecency as consisting of "patently offensive references to excretory and sexual organs or activities."

Does that mean a dial-a-porn message that appeals to a morbid interest in sex can be banned while a message that appeals to a morbid interest in "excretory activities" must be permitted? We don't know. White wrote that the government can pass laws to protect children from messages that are indecent but not obscene, whatever that means. But a flat ban on such messages, he wrote, violates the constitutional rights of adults.

Considering the inventiveness of some young people in getting around other age-based restrictions, where is the rationale in that? The point has now apparently been reached where it is all right for regulated industries to be conveyors of filth, or at least some filth, so long as it doesn't reach young people or go into communities where it might, by local standards, be considered obscene.

In effect, a person's right to be entertained by a pornographic telephone message is contingent on where he lives and how old he is.

The law, finally, should make sense. In this decision, instead of clarifying the issue, the Supreme Court has produced something reminiscent of the medieval debate over how many angels can dance on the head of a pin.

## ST. LOUIS POST-DISPATCH
*St. Louis, MO, June 28, 1989*

By unanimously striking down Congress' ban on so-called dial-a-porn services that delivered indecent messages, the Supreme Court once more drew the crucial but often blurred distinction between what is likable and what is constitutional. Just because the indecent telephone messages included in such services are anathema to many people, Congress had no reason to disregard the First Amendment by declaring them illegal as well.

Friday's ruling upheld the ban on obscene messages, continuing the legal distinction between obscene expression, which a community judges graphic, offensive and without redeeming value, and indecent expression, which is primarily "dirty words." Three justices said they would allow dial-a-porn services to use obscene messages as well, but the unanimous majority extended constitutional protection to "sexual expression which is indecent but not obscene."

The case began last year when Congress, to limit the growing popularity of explicit telephone recordings, outlawed both indecent and obscene messages. Sable Communications, a company involved in dial-a-porn, sued, claiming that existing technology and other methods such as requiring credit-card payment effectively keeps explicit recordings away from children. Providing them to adults who want them should be constitutional, Sable said.

In his majority opinion, Justice Byron White agreed that for keeping indecent messages away from children, such techniques are "extremely effective, and only a few of the most enterprising and disobedient young people will manage to secure access to such messages." Banning such messages altogether to thwart such enterprising youngsters is too high a price to pay.

## Chicago Tribune
*Chicago, IL, June 16, 1989*

The 1988 "dial-a-porn" law was a grandstanding over-reaction to a small problem. The problem arises from the spread of commercial telephone services that allow callers to hear sexually oriented messages for a fee. Parents have had a legitimate complaint against services that expose curious juveniles to hard-core audio pornography. The government's interest in protecting children demanded some kind of action.

Congress could have shielded kids while preserving the freedom of adults to indulge in this degrading but hardly dangerous commerce—for example, by requiring telephone companies to grant access to dial-a-porn only to customers who affirmatively request it. Instead, Congress decided this kind of material should be available to no one.

Even given that dubious goal, Congress easily could have tailored its approach to the demands of the 1st Amendment. Obscenity has been defined by the Supreme Court as prurient, patently offensive material that lacks serious social value, and unlike most forms of expression it has no constitutional protection. Congress simply could have outlawed those messages that meet the definition of obscenity.

But this would allow dial-a-porn services to offer less explicit sexual fare, which lawmakers weren't willing to tolerate. So they banned any commercial communications that are "indecent." That term is conveniently vague. Any provider who guesses wrong about its meaning could be punished with six months in jail and a fine of $50,000.

Last week the Supreme Court agreed to review a lower court ruling that struck down the ban on indecency while upholding the one on obscenity. A decent respect for the Constitution will oblige the Supreme Court justices to turn back Congress' gratuitious attack on free expression.

## Supreme Court Extends Protection To Satirize Public Figures

The Supreme Court Feb. 24, 1988 unanimously reaffirmed and extended the constitutional protection of criticism of public figures. "At the heart of the First Amendment is the recognition of the fundamental importance of the free flow of ideas and opinions on matters of public interest and concern," Chief Justice William H. Rehnquist said in an opinion joined by all the participating justices except Byron R. White, who wrote a brief concurring opinion. Justice Anthony M. Kennedy who was seated the week before, did not participate in the 8-0 decision.

The ruling overturned a jury's $200,000 award to Rev. Jerry Falwell for "emotional distress" over a *Hustler* magazine parody that depicted him as an incestuous drunk. While the jury did not believe the parody was libelous, since it could not be believed, it held *Hustler* publisher Larry C. Flynt liable for "intentional infliction of emotional distress."

The federal appeals court in Richmond, Virginia sustained the jury's findings. The parody was "sufficiently outrageous" to justify the damage award, it said, even though it was not libelous because it was not represented by *Hustler* or understood by readers to be factual.

Rehnquist strongly reaffirmed the court's 1964 opinion in the *New York Times v. Sullivan* that public figures in suing for libel, must prove "actual malice" on the part of the publisher with knowledge that it was false or with reckless disregard for the truth. In this case, *Hustler v. Falwell*, Rehnquist said the parody did not purport to be factual and thus did not contain statements involving reckless disregard of the truth or awareness of false statements of fact. The question was whether the First Amendment protected citizens from "intentional infliction of emotional distress," Rehnquist said. While the material was "doubtless gross and repugnant in the eyes of most," Rehnquist said, even "outrageous" statements of opinion must be protected under the Constitution. "Outrageousness in the area of political and social discourse has an inherent subjectiveness about it which would allow a jury to impose liability on the basis of the juror's tastes or views or perhaps on the basis of their dislike of a particular expression," he said. Rehnquist said there was no "principled standard to separate" legitimate political cartoonists and Flynt's crude efforts. Reviewing the role of political cartoonists throughout American history, he cited their frequent resort to "slashing and one-sided" attacks that injured the feelings of those caricatured. "Our political discourse would have been considerably poorer without them," he said of the lampooning.

## The Washington Post
*Washington, DC, February 25, 1988*

WHILE A POLITICAL cartoon may be offensive, the Supreme Court declares in its unanimous opinion, the First Amendment nonetheless protects it. Chief Justice Rehnquist's decision reaffirms the traditional defense of expression and removes the cloud that a terrible appellate decision had placed over it. Had the Supreme Court accepted the appellate court's view, cartoonists would have suffered. Written and spoken satire and caricature of every sort would have had to be fuzzed and softened, from newspapers and magazines to television, the theater, night clubs and soapboxes. The needle would have been out, the powder puff in. Anything that might create emotional distress in the mind of its target would suddenly have become, in legal terms, very dangerous.

The case began with a parody of an advertisement in Hustler magazine—a gross and vile parody—in which Jerry Falwell, the clergyman, was supposed to have described a drunken and incestuous encounter with his mother. Mr. Falwell sued for invasion of privacy, libel and emotional distress. The trial judge ruled out the assertion of privacy. The jury rejected the libel claim, on grounds that no one could possibly have believed that the parody was describing actual facts. But the jury found for Mr. Falwell regarding his emotional distress and awarded him damages. More startling, the U.S. Court of Appeals for the Fourth Circuit in Richmond upheld that verdict.

But now the Supreme Court has firmly and explicitly restated its longstanding position that a public figure such as Mr. Falwell is entitled to damages only when he can show that he was injured by a false fact. A public figure, it held, is not entitled to compensation for emotional distress alone. Mr. Falwell's lawyer urged the court to establish a separate category of parody that is "outrageous . . . and loathsome." But as the chief justice replied, a standard of outrageousness gets very subjective and invites a jury to impose its own tastes and opinions.

The court has maintained the cherished freedom of expression—even to the point of excess—in good working order. That is a profound service not merely to people like ourselves who write and draw but also to people who read, watch and listen—to anyone who thinks that caricature and satire are a vital part of the open political discussion that is the essence of democracy.

## ST. LOUIS POST-DISPATCH
*St. Louis, MO, February 26, 1988*

The case of *Hustler vs. Falwell* had the potential of radically redefining American libel law and critically damaging the constitutional protections of our free press. But the Supreme Court's 8-0 ruling overturning a $200,000 award to the Rev. Jerry Falwell was a ringing endorsement of the First Amendment.

The case was an emotional one. Publisher Larry Flynt ran a vile parody in his raw pornographic magazine, *Hustler*, lampooning the Rev. Jerry Falwell as a hypocritical, incestuous drunkard. The Rev. Falwell responded with a $45 million libel suit. The jury rejected the libel charge, but it did award the founder of the Moral Majority $200,000 for "emotional distress." The federal appeals court upheld the award.

If the Supreme Court had concurred, it would have set a revolutionary precedent to allow other public figures to sue for emotional distress any publication or individual that satirized or attacked them. Such a precedent would have driven a wedge between regular news stories and editorials, which are protected under the landmark 1964 *New York Times vs. Sullivan* ruling, and cartoons, parodies and satire. The chilling effect on the press would have brought a new ice age.

The Supreme Court, however, wisely ruled that even the most crude satire was protected by the First Amendment because such "graphic depictions and satirical cartoons have played a prominent role" in American political history and that even "vehement, caustic" attacks are protected by the First Amendment. The court also found that "an 'outrageous' standard," for which the Falwell attorneys had asked, "runs afoul of our longstanding refusal to allow damages to be awarded because the speech in question may have an adverse emotional impact on the audience."

## St. Paul Pioneer Press & Dispatch
*St. Paul, MN, February 29, 1988*

What Larry Flynt did to the Rev. Jerry Falwell was morally wrong. He published a disgusting ad parody slurring Mr. Falwell and his mother. Mr. Falwell had every right to feel insulted and hurt. However, the U.S. Supreme Court properly concluded last week that Mr. Falwell's wounded feelings must go uncompensated.

The Supreme Court could not find a standard that would allow retribution for some sorts of expressions of opinion that also would not jeopardize desirable public debate. So it decided that injured feelings must be part of the price of a free society. It's too bad that the degenerate Mr. Flynt had to benefit directly.

In his lawsuit against Mr. Flynt, Mr. Falwell was trying to expand the rights of public figures to penalize opinions intended to inflict emotional distress. Remember, public figures *can* recover money damages from someone who knowingly or recklessly spreads falsehoods about them. But the Constitution protects opinions. A jury had found that Mr. Flynt's ad parody was opinion — not an assertion of fact. The jury, however, tried to make Mr. Flynt pay for insulting Mr. Falwell. The Supreme Court overruled that jury.

The Supreme Court might have allowed compensation for "outrageous" opinions calculated to make public figures feel bad. To do so, the court would have had to define "outrageous." But the court worried that no definition of "outrageous" could be limited adequately. Better that some outrages go unpunished than that juries be able to declare merely unpopular views "outrageous" — and therefore punishable — because the juries disagree with them, the court decided.

Inevitably, some things that need to be said hurt the feelings of some people in the public eye. The trouble is, people disagree about what things need to be said, or what is offensive. Freedom of expression would flounder if people had to fear that they might — depending on the makeup of a jury — have to pay a civil fine for venting their opinions about public figures. The Supreme Court did the nation a great service with its ruling.

## Honolulu Star-Bulletin
*Honolulu, HI, February 25, 1988*

Although the First Amendment guarantee of free speech and press does not protect libelous material, it does protect outrageous material. That is the reasoning employed by the Supreme Court in unanimously overturning a $200,000 award won by evangelist Jerry Falwell against *Hustler* magazine and its publisher, Larry Flynt.

The magazine's treatment of Falwell was certainly outrageous. After the full-page "ad parody" appeared, Falwell sued the magazine and Flynt for libel, invasion of privacy and intentional infliction of emotional distress. He asked for $45 million in damages.

A federal jury ruled that the ad did not libel Falwell, and the presiding judge threw out the invasion-of-privacy allegation. However, the jury ruled for Falwell on his emotional-distress claim, and awarded him $200,000. An appeals court upheld the award, but the Supreme Court threw it out.

Writing for the court, Chief Justice Rehnquist said, "Outrageousness in the area of political and social discourse has an inherent subjectiveness about it which would allow a jury to impose liability on the basis of the jurors' tastes or views, or perhaps on the basis of their dislike of a particular expression. An 'outrageous' standard thus runs afoul of our long-standing refusal to allow damages to be awarded because the speech in question may have an adverse emotional impact on the audience."

The American democratic system requires the fullest possible leeway for comment, even comment that is unfair and in the worst taste. That description applies to the *Hustler* spoof. Because it could not have been reasonably interpreted as stating facts about Falwell, his claim of libel failed. At that point the First Amendment took over.

Many of us committed to the First Amendment would feel more comfortable rallying behind a worthier champion than *Hustler* magazine. But great principles of justice can sprout from unseemly roots. The Supreme Court, by extending constitutional protection for parody and satire, has advanced the cause of freedom.

## THE BILLINGS GAZETTE
*Billings, MT, February 29, 1988*

Politics makes strange bedfellows and so does the freedom of the press.

Hustler magazine and its publisher Larry Flynt spell journalism S-L-E-A-Z-E.

Most journalists wouldn't touch a copy of the magazine or shake hands with Flynt without first donning rubber gloves.

But ... Flynt is entitled to the same protections as the legitimate press in America, and a recent Supreme Court ruling upheld that premise, much to the relief of everyone who comments about the public's business.

The case goes back to an "ad" in Hustler depicting Moral Majority leader Jerry Falwell as a drunkard who had had an incestuous relationship with his mother in an outhouse. At the bottom of the page in fine print was a disclaimer stating that the ad was a parody and "not to be taken seriously."

Falwell, of course, was furious. Any of us would have been. He filed suit against Flynt and his magazine, asking $45 million in damages for libel, invasion of privacy and infliction of emotional distress.

A federal jury in Roanoke, Va., found that the ad did not libel Falwell, and the presiding judge threw out the invasion of privacy allegation.

But the jury found that Falwell was entitled to legal redress because of emotional distress he had suffered due to the "ad." Jurors awarded him $200,000.

And that opened a pandora's box.

Falwell has thrust himself into the public eye as certainly as politicians and entertainers and network newscasters have. He is subject to public criticism.

A democratic institution like the United States cannot survive if its citizens are not allowed to criticize the high and mighty among us. Political cartoons, and public speakers and reviews of books and movies and music, all rely on that premise.

The right is limited, of course. We cannot libel — maliciously lie about public persons — but we can freely comment.

The Falwell decision jeopardized that right. The jury ruled that public figures could collect damages simply because they were upset by the comment, not because the comment was libelous.

One example of how insidious this ruling was can be found in a comment by Falwell after the ruling:

"No sleaze-merchant like Larry Flynt should be able to use the First Amendment as an excuse for maliciously and dishonestly attacking public figures as he has so often done."

"Sleaze-merchant?" "Maliciously and dishonestly attacking public figures?"

If the Falwell decision had been applied to those comments, Flynt might have been awarded damages — not because the comment was libelous — but because the publisher suffered "emotional distress."

Each time we step on someone else's rights, we are stepping on our own. As sleazy as Flynt is, he is entitled to the same rights as the rest of us. That's the American way.

We must be thankful the Supreme Court recognized that.

## The Wichita Eagle-Beacon
*Wichita, KS, February 26, 1988*

A unanimous U.S. Supreme Court demonstrated restraint and common sense this week when it declared that the Rev. Jerry Falwell couldn't punish a magazine publisher who hurt his feelings.

The result of the lawsuit against sleaze merchant Larry Flynt, publisher of Hustler magazine, is no surprise. The court had little choice, for deciding otherwise quite literally would have erased 200 years of American freedom.

It is clear from the opinion that the justices' patience and sense of decency are pushed to the brink by the likes of Mr. Flynt. So is ours.

But decency and taste are not appropriate criteria for limiting the precious right of free speech. To adopt such criteria, as the court noted, "would allow a jury to impose liability on the basis of the jurors' tastes or views, or perhaps on the basis of their dislike of a particular expression."

In public debate about public figures, the case is clear. Our democracy was forged in robust, even unfair or injurious debate, and its survival is dependent upon that open conflict of ideas.

It must extend, yes, even to a satire in which a Jerry Falwell is depicted as a drunken hypocrite having sex with his mother in an outhouse.

The additional supportive news in the decision is the court's continued adherance to the 1964 standard that a public figure, in order to win a libel suit, must prove the statements not only were false but were made with reckless disregard as to whether or not they were true.

Mr. Falwell sought to establish a different standard: that it was sufficient simply to show he was caused personal pain and anguish by the publication and that Mr. Flynt meant to inflict that pain and anguish.

In the simplest terms, the court told Mr. Falwell that the imperatives of free speech outweigh his personal feelings.

To decide otherwise would have recognized nationally what some states now recognize, a kind of "tort of anguish" available to those who seek and benefit from the public limelight. Comforting as that might be for them, our democracy could not survive limitations on the right of every person to comment, however outrageously by normal standards, on those public people and activities.

On Wednesday, Jerry Falwell described Hustler magazine as malicious and dishonest. If he was right on the first count, he was definitely wrong on the second, which is why the Supreme Court, in a major victory for freedom of speech and of the press, unanimously threw out a $200,000 judgment he had won in lower court against Hustler publisher Larry Flynt.

Mr. Falwell won the judgment because of a captioned photograph the magazine ran in 1983. Based on the well-known Compari ad series, the photo showed the leader of the Moral Majority discussing how his first sexual encounter occurred while he was drunk with his mother in an outhouse. This was certainly gross and offensive, as Mr. Falwell's attorneys had no trouble convincing a jury in Virginia.

But Mr. Falwell also successfully argued that it was libelous and constituted intentional affliction of emotional distress, even though he made no effort to prove dishonesty or contempt for the truth, the usual basis for a libel award. He didn't try for the simple reason that the magazine, self-evidently, was not dishonest. The reason: beneath the photo, in small but readily discernible letters, appeared an all-important disclaimer: "ad parody — not to be taken seriously." If Hustler had tried to pass off the material as legitimate news, it would have been indefensible. But it didn't. It clearly and properly labeled the work the fiction that it was. The Compari takeoff may have been malicious. But, *pace,* Mr. Falwell, it was in no way dishonest or deceitful.

## The Record
*Hackensack, NJ, February 26, 1988*

This is what made the $200,000 judgment against Hustler dangerous and the Supreme Court, conservative as it is these days, unanimous in striking it down. If Jerry Falwell had gotten away with punishing Hustler for the crime of bad taste, whose turn would have come next? Don Novello, also known as Father Guido Sarducci, for his satirical assaults on the Catholic Church? Garry Trudeau for his disrespectful treatment of some of our leading political figures in "Doonesbury"?

It wasn't so long ago (21 years, to be exact) when one of the big hits on Broadway was Barbara Garson's "MacBird," a takeoff on "Macbeth" that accused Lyndon Johnson of nothing less than murdering John F. Kennedy to take over the White House. Some thought the play was funny and properly rude. Others, like the New Yorker, sniffed that it was "libel thinly disguised as a high-spirited undergraduate prank." Yet if the Falwell rule had applied, the play never would have opened. LBJ, sensitive as he was to criticism, would have slapped it with a lawsuit before the producers had finished with auditions.

The moral is that sleaze, like beauty, is very much in the eye of the beholder, and the judiciary has no business setting standards for good taste. In democratic political debate, there most be room for both the high-toned and polite as well as the rude and raucous. If Mr. Falwell can't understand this, he should abandon public life and begin looking for another line of work.

## The Arizona Republic
*Phoenix, AZ, February 25, 1988*

NO matter how loathsome *Hustler* huckster Larry Flynt and the filth he peddles, the Supreme Court was correct yesterday in siding with Flynt, a man without redeeming social value, against the Rev. Jerry Falwell, the former Moral Majoritarian.

The case involved more than Falwell vs. Flynt. It raised important constitutional principles, and raised them in a troubling way. Troubling because Flynt, in his reprehensible magazine, had published an obscene spoof portraying Falwell as losing his virginity to his mother.

Rightly offended, a Roanoke jury awarded Falwell $200,000 on grounds that, though he had not been libeled, since no reasonable person would have thought the portrayal of him was literally true, he certainly had suffered emotional distress.

In an 8-to-0 decision, the Supreme Court overturned the judgment, holding that political satire, even though it deliberately inflicts pain, enjoys wide First Amendment protection. The court had no choice. Had it ruled otherwise, the nation would have been assured of an epidemic of "emotional distress," as public figures found themselves subjected to parody, satire and criticism.

This is not what the framers had in mind. As Chief Justice William Rehnquist observed, "the sort of robust political debate encouraged by the First Amendment is bound to produce speech that is critical of those who hold public office or those public figures who are intimately involved in the resolution of important public questions or ... shape events in areas of concern to society at large.

"The art of the cartoonist," he added, "is often not reasoned or evenhanded, but slashing and one-sided." Even so, he said, it has "played a prominent role in public and political debate."

Raunchy, vile, disgusting, crude and tasteless — the Falwell spoof was all this and worse. In the words of the court, it was "gross and repugnant," but to be gross and repugnant is not necessarily to be libelous, and simply to have produced anguish is not actionable.

"Were we to hold otherwise," said Justice Rehnquist, "there can be little doubt that political cartoonists and satirists would be subject to damage awards without any showing that their work falsely defamed a subject."

Learning of the decision, Falwell remarked that the Supreme Court must have had to hold its nose, and no doubt he was right. But holding the nose is a small price for being able, on most occasions, to breathe free.

## Portland Press Herald
*Portland, ME, February 27, 1988*

This week's unanimous Supreme Court decision overturning a damages award to the Rev. Jerry Falwell for "emotional distress" over a Hustler magazine parody is not simply a victory for publisher Larry Flynt. It is rather another resounding affirmation of the First Amendment right of all Americans to speak out freely and critically.

The ruling — written by the court's most conservative member, Chief Justice William H. Rehnquist— said the First Amendment extends even to "outrageous" criticism such as Hustler's parody portraying Falwell as an incestuous drunk.

In criticizing the decision, Falwell said it gives the "green light" to a "sleaze merchant like Larry Flynt."

Actually, that green light has been there right along. But it is a green light which extends upward from "sleaze merchants" to encompass all Americans who may choose to criticize public figures through ridicule.

As Rehnquist noted, "Graphic depictions and satirical cartoons have played a prominent role in public and political debate" throughout the nation's history.

The price we pay for the constitutional protection of free speech is that it covers even — perhaps especially — the expression of ideas we find hateful.

The court wisely refused to start down a dangerous path: attempting to define public expression which may be "too offensive" to enjoy constitutional protection.

The decision left Flynt and Hustler free to indulge in the sleazier brand of satire, true. But that judgment left intact a fundamental liberty enjoyed by every American.

As the late Justice Hugo Black once put it, "Freedom to publish means freedom for all and not for some."

You don't have to like Hustler to support this week's Supreme Court decision.

## The Burlington Free Press
*Burlington, VT, February 29, 1988*

Manure comes with a herd of Holsteins along with their river of milk. Get rid of the stink, and you lose the nourishment, too.

Chief Justice William Rehnquist put the matter a bit more elegantly, but that's what he said in last week's U.S. Supreme Court decision on Hustler magazine.

The First Amendment guarantees Americans a right to criticize public figures, the court held, even if the criticism is "outrageous" and offensive.

The broad and ringing language of the decision was especially sweet coming from a justice who's take a cramped view of the First Amendment in the past.

Led by Rehnquist, a unanimous court overturned a $200,000 jury award to the Rev. Jerry Falwell for a Hustler parody that depicted him as an incestuous drunkard. The jury decided the parody wasn't libel, since it made no claim to be factual, but awarded Falwell $200.000 anyway, for "emotional distress."

The high court saw the jury award for what it was — an end run around libel rules designed to protect free speech.

"Vehement, caustic and sometimes unpleasantly sharp attacks" are the price of vigorous political debate, Rehnquist wrote. If Falwell suffered emotional distress at the hands of a cartoonist, so have politicians from Abraham Lincoln to Franklin Roosevelt.

It might be nice, Rehnquist implied, if there were a standard to separate conventional political cartooning from its "poor relations" like Hustler's.

"But we doubt that there is any such standard and we are quite sure that the pejorative description 'outrageous' does not supply one," Rehnquist concluded.

In other words, if Americans want Oliphant and Doonesbury and the freedom to shoot their mouths off about those scalawags in Washington, they must live with Larry Flynt's magazine manure as well.

The court's decision reaffirms its faith in the public's ability to distinguish one from the other.

# THE DENVER POST
*Denver, CO, February 26, 1988*

HUSTLER publisher Larry Flynt has a fly-crawling garbage can for a mind. But his 9-0 victory in the U.S. Supreme Court ensures the right of legitimate satirists to practice their barbed craft in the honorable tradition of Jonathan Swift.

Flynt was sued for a tasteless parody of an ad that painted the Rev. Jerry Falwell as a drunk who committed incest with his mother in an outhouse. The parody included a small disclaimer saying it was "not to be taken seriously."

Falwell claimed he was libeled. The jury members rejected the libel claim because they recognized that satire cannot be taken literally. But the jurors did award Falwell $200,000 after finding the magazine had intentionally caused him emotional distress.

If that decision had stood, American satirists ranging from cartoonists such as Mike Keefe and Steve Benson to writers like Art Buchwald and Mike Royko would have been out of business. There is no doubt that effective mockery can cause "emotional distress" to the target, whether the victim is Ronald Reagan or Mikhail Gorbachev. But if all political commentary had to be pleasing to its subjects, you'd be reading a sterilized editorial page right now. And the First Amendment — including your right to voice an opinion — would have ceased to exist.

The Supreme Court ruling doesn't mean that Falwell is a bad person or that Flynt is a good one. It simply recognizes that bad taste often must be tolerated as the price of freedom of speech, which underlies and safeguards all our other rights as Americans.

# Richmond Times-Dispatch
*Richmond, VA, February 26, 1988*

*Hustler Magazine Inc. vs. Reverend Jerry Falwell* was the title of the landmark case that the Supreme Court decided this week. But only secondarily did the unanimous verdict represent a win for the raunchy magazine and its publisher Larry Flynt, and a defeat for the famous television evangelist from Lynchburg. Of far surpassing significance is the victory that has been won for continued free and robust expression under the First Amendment.

The high court had constitutional principle to decide, not questions of individual probity or good taste. The November 1983 Hustler parody of Mr. Falwell as an incestuous drunkard was conceded, in Chief Justice William Rehnquist's words, to be "gross and repugnant in the eyes of most." But the critical legal issue was whether a public figure who had been distastefully lampooned could short-circuit (and effectively enlarge) the libel law by collecting damages for "intentional infliction of emotional distress" under an obscure tort doctrine. In saying that he could not, the court basically reaffirmed libel standards that give writers or artists considerable latitude, but not absolute license, in discussing public figures. To recover damages, a public figure must prove "actual malice" — that is, that false material was knowingly presented as factual truth or that it was disseminated with "reckless disregard" of its truth or falsity.

A Roanoke federal jury found that the Hustler parody could not reasonably be read as a literal, factual account of Mr. Falwell's life and a blight on his reputation; thus it was not libelous. However, the jury did rule that the plaintiff was entitled to $200,000 in compensatory and punitive damages under the "emotional distress" tort, which originated in common law as a remedy against abusive debt collectors and the like. A divided 4th U.S. Circuit Court of Appeals in Richmond affirmed that judgment, holding that the "actual malice" standard need not be satisfied before damages could be collected. The panel concluded that the parody was so "outrageous," it deserved no protection as opinion and rhetorical hyperbole.

Had the Supreme Court upheld that view, the chilling effect on satire and caricature could have been enormous. Juries would have been called on to decide by some subjective standard when hyperbole reached "outrageous" proportions. By claiming wounded feelings, politicians and others in the public limelight might have been able to collect for being portrayed unfavorably, say, in a "Saturday Night Live" skit, or a satirical column, or a political cartoon. As Mr. Rehnquist noted, "graphic depictions and satirical cartoons have played a prominent role in public and political debate," from early portraitures of George Washington "as an ass," down to the present. As we noted in criticizing the Roanoke jury's verdict in 1984, Thomas Jefferson endured the vilest sort of personal attacks in the public prints, yet he never abandoned his faith that a free press, with all its imperfections, is vital to democracy.

Chief Justice Rehnquist appeared to draw heavily from an incisive historical analysis 4th Circuit Judge J. Harvie Wilkinson III, a Richmond native, had penned in arguing for a rehearing of the case. Thus, as often happens, a "great dissenter" winds up contributing to constitutional protections.

It is necessary, said Mr. Rehnquist, to give adequate "breathing space" to freedoms protected by the First Amendment. All Americans should breathe a little easier about their democratic freedoms as a result of the court's unambiguous, unanimous decision.

# Minneapolis Star and Tribune
*Minneapolis, MN, February 29, 1988*

The Rev. Jerry Falwell is not the first butt of a bad joke to try to get even. But he is likely to be the last to sue his lampooner for hurt feelings. Last Wednesday, the U.S. Supreme Court declared that the right to poke fun cannot be curtailed — even when the poking irks the poked. That ruling should cheer not only comedians and cartoonists, but anyone with a sense of humor.

It takes a twisted mind to see the humor in Hustler magazine's jab at Falwell, a phony ad that portrayed the preacher as an incestuous drunkard. In a grim search for the last laugh, Falwell sued Hustler publisher Larry Flynt for libel. A jury shrugged off that claim, ruling that a parody so plainly fictitious would not be believed — and hence was not defamatory. Yet the jury agreed with Falwell that Hustler had meant to get his goat and ordered Flynt to fork over $200,000 for intentionally inflicting "emotional distress."

But taunting a public figure is no crime, and shouldn't be. Writing for a unanimous Supreme Court, Chief Justice William Rehnquist explained that satire, by nature "slashing and one-sided," is one indispensable exercise of the First Amendment "freedom to speak one's mind." Satirists exercise it by rocking political pedestals and taking shots at the men who stand on them. Without their sharp aim, Rehnquist says, "our political discourse would have been considerably poorer."

It's hard to swallow Pat Oliphant's salty jests in the same gulp with Hustler's bitter barbs. But Rehnquist could find no "principled standard to distinguish savory satire from tasteless. For readers who know enough to avoid Hustler, this ruling is sure to taste sweet.

## The Hutchinson News
*Hutchinson, KS, February 25, 1988*

So much for the "emotional distress" of Jerry Falwell.

With a resounding 8 to 0 vote, the Reagan-Nixon Supreme Court decided Wednesday that a loudmouth like Jerry Falwell can't run to the courts for compensation for the "emotional distress" caused when a scum bag attacked him in print.

The court tossed out a $200,000 award that an unthinking jury had levied against Hustler magazine for its pornographic parody of Falwell.

"Outrageousness in the area of political and social discourse has an inherent subjectiveness about it, which would allow a jury to impose liability on the basis of the jurors' tastes or views, or perhaps on the basis of their dislike of a particular expression," Chief Justice William H. Rehnquist wrote.

"An 'outrageous' standard thus runs afoul of our longstanding refusal to allow damages to be awarded because the speech in question may have an adverse emotional impact on the audience," he said.

The Hustler parody was outrageous. It also was disgusting and vile, like most of the stuff in the miserable magazine.

However, if all the material that causes "emotional distress" to somebody, somewhere, someday were suppressed in American life, there would be precious little printed or broadcast.

If the court had ruled otherwise, it wouldn't be long before you wouldn't even see satires about pigs in Hutchinson.

## The Union Leader
*Manchester, NH, February 29, 1988*

What kind of country would we be living in, anyway, if a pornographer couldn't even smear a clergyman as an incestuous drunk having sex with his mother —and call it harmless parody?

Well, in effect, the U.S. Supreme Court ruled last week that it wouldn't be much of a country at all. By an 8-0 vote, the high tribunal overruled a jury that had awarded the Reverend Jerry Falwell $200,000 in damages for emotional distress flowing from a controversial ad published in smut merchant Larry Flynt's Hustler magazine. And, we are supposed to believe, every newspaper cartoonist and satirist in the country who ever wanted to savage a local clergyman as an incestuous drunk ravaging his mother danced rejoicingly in the streets.

Porn-peddler Flynt was so delighted with the court's ruling that, pandering to the preacher-bashers, he went out and celebrated by launching another attack on Falwell. Sort of like the scumball calling the skillet black.

Jane Kirtley, executive director of the Reporters Committee for Freedom of the Press, exulted that the court's ruling "sends a message to public figures and public officials that you can take the heat or get out."

**Regrettably, that's not the only message the ruling sends them. It informs them that, for openers, each of *them* can be parodied as an incestuous drunk having sex with his mother.**

This is not to suggest that the court's ruling is indefensible on constitutional grounds. On the contrary, one must concede that, on balance, as painful as are the ramifications of this ruling in terms of encouraging journalistic depravity, it does constitute a powerful blow for freedom of expression, for robust public debate. The court faced a dilemma. Falwell is probably correct in his assumption that "the justices, in view of Larry Flynt, were holding their noses while making the ruling." It's just that the alternative was so uninviting.

**So, once again, the court rejected a crabbed view of First Amendment rights, just as it did in its heralded Sullivan ruling expanding the right of the press to criticize public officials and personalities and placing on plaintiffs a difficult burden of proving malice. But with this latest expansion of freedom of expression should come a heightened sense of *responsibility*. For the news media to hide malice behind parody is as cowardly as taking cheap, reputation-ruining shots at public personalities under the protection of the Sullivan ruling.**

But both will continue to happen. What last week's Supreme Court ruling means — bottom line — is that only the consumer has the power to punish hit-and-hide cowards such as Larry Flynt by treating them as social lepers.

## THE PLAIN DEALER
*Cleveland, OH, February 26, 1988*

This was a good week for cartoonists, satirists and caricaturists, those people whose job it is to distort and exaggerate to make a point. The U.S. Supreme Court on Wednesday upheld their right to produce and publish their biting commentary, even if it produces emotional distress in its intended targets. As such, the decision also made it a good week for an underlying tenet of democracy—the robust, free and uninhibited exchange of ideas and views, even those that may be offensive to many people.

"Offensive" may be too mild a term for Hustler, the magazine, once based in Columbus, that is one of the raunchiest on the newsstands. In 1983, Hustler produced a parody ad—clearly labeled as such—depicting the Rev. Jerry Falwell as a hypocrite and a drunkard and, in a takeoff on an advertising campaign for Campari Liqueur, said that Falwell's "first time" was with his mother in an outhouse.

Falwell sued for libel, invasion of privacy and emotional distress. But he could not prove any actual damages: in fact he cleverly used the ad to raise $800,000 for the Moral Majority and the "Old Time Gospel Hour." As to emotional distress, Falwell did not seek counseling and maintained a strenuous work schedule. He told the court that after seeing the ad he felt like crying, but did not.

The lower court jury disallowed the libel claim and the judge threw out the invasion of privacy argument. But incredibly, the court awarded Falwell $200,000 on the emotional distress claim, a decision upheld by a U.S. Appeals Court in Richmond. Clearly, the jury and the Appeals Court judges were blinded by the thought of coming down on the side of Hustler and its publisher, Larry Flynt.

The Supreme Court avoided that emotional trap. Its unanimous decision made clear the role of cartoonists and satirists in the public debate. "From the viewpoint of history it is clear that our political discourse would have been considerably poorer without them," wrote Chief Justice William H. Rehnquist. Some of their work may be outrageous, Rehnquist noted, but as the court long has held, the fact that society may find some speech offensive is not reason enough to suppress it.

The very role of political cartoonists and satirists is to poke, to jab and to punch, and expose, to the ridicule they deserve, those public officials who violate the public trust. Sure, when the cartoonist hits his target, the wound stings. Shouldn't it?

People holding public positions have every right to seek damages when libelous information is distributed knowingly and recklessly, the Supreme Court standard that has been followed for two decades. But democracy will not stand for long if those people are allowed damages for satire that almost makes them weep.

## The Chattanooga Times
*Chattanooga, TN, February 26, 1988*

Few Americans have a high regard for Larry Flynt, who glories in his reputation as publisher of the gratuitously raunchy *Hustler* magazine. But with its unanimous ruling Wednesday overturning a $200,000 "emotional distress" judgment against Mr. Flynt, the Supreme Court gave Americans something more valuable: a strong reiteration of First Amendment freedom, even when the subject matter is an expression of outrageous opinion.

The principals in this case could hardly be more different. On one side was Mr. Flynt, publisher of sexually explicit magazines; on the other, the Rev. Jerry Falwell, a Baptist minister and founder of the political action organization Moral Majority. But again, a clash of values involving individuals poles apart in values has produced a valuable court decision.

The Falwell-*Hustler* case originated as an "ad parody" which featured a photograph of Mr. Falwell in a takeoff on a then-current advertisement by Campari liqueurs. The parody purportedly quoted Mr. Falwell discussing a sexual relationship with his mother and describing himself as a drunkard. At the bottom of the ad, however, was printed this disclaimer: "Ad parody — not to be taken seriously."

Mr. Falwell took it very seriously and sued *Hustler*. A jury decided he had not been libeled because the ad's message was not portrayed as factual. It agreed, however, that he had suffered "emotional distress," and awarded him $200,000. The Supreme Court's ruling on Wednesday overturned that award, which had been upheld on appeal.

But the Supreme Court, in a decision written by Chief Justice William Rehnquist, has now extended First Amendment protection to "outrageous" statements of opinion that lampoon public figures, which Mr. Falwell surely is. That protection is not absolute. The court said, as it has in the past, that a public figure can hold a speaker or writer liable for damages to his or her reputation by a defamatory falsehood — if, that is, the statement was made with the knowledge that it was false or with a reckless disregard of whether it was false. That was not the case in the *Hustler* parody.

Few would disagree that the parody was outrageously offensive to Mr. Falwell; it certainly reflected what might loosely be called Mr. Flynt's level of taste. But the issue is neither Mr. Flynt's taste or lack thereof, nor Mr. Falwell's sensitivities. Rather it is the need, as the court said, to be "particularly vigilant to ensure that individual expressions of ideas remain free from governmentally imposed sanctions."

First Amendment guarantees aren't worth much if they only protect "safe" opinions that offend no one, or provoke no counterarguments. The First Amendment's real value is proven when it protects controversial speech, whether written or oral. It is easy to criticize the court's Falwell ruling because of the circumstances of that case, but the justices had a larger purpose in mind: to ensure continued robust debate of public issues and public figures. The Falwell-Flynt case just happened to be a good, albeit controversial, vehicle.

## The Honolulu Advertiser
*Honolulu, Hi, February 25, 1988*

The hardest test for our prized civil liberties is whether they protect the likes of Hustler's Larry Flynt. Much that passes for humor and satire in his "ragazine" is at best outrageous bad taste and at worst simply repugnant.

But all eight sitting members of the U.S. Supreme Court, across the spectrum from liberal to conservative, wisely and properly ruled that the Rev. Jerry Falwell cannot collect damages for "emotional distress" over a Hustler parody portraying him as an incestuous drunkard.

Falwell, who as a television minister and former Moral Majority chief is certainly a public figure, had also claimed libel and invasion of privacy. A lower court threw those out, but awarded him $200,000 from Flynt for emotional distress.

The great danger was that if the high court had upheld the award, other public figures would avoid hard-to-prove libel suits by seeking damages for emotional distress when hard-hitting political commentary or cartoons were not to their liking.

No doubt the parody distressed Falwell. Political cartooning and satire are often intentionally harsh and discomforting to their targets. While Flynt may or may not have had a high purpose in attacking Falwell — and Flynt's style was on the level of juvenile bathroom humor — the First Amendment protects his right to free expression of opinion.

Hard though it may be to swallow spreading the Constitution over someone like Flynt, he can not be condemned without also restraining worthy commentators and muckrakers using strong language and images to drive their points home. That would leave political discussion in this country as dull and drab as a high-school civics book, and far less meaningful.

## THE INDIANAPOLIS NEWS
*Indianapolis, IN, February 26, 1988*

*We must not make public debate soft and comfortable.*
— **Robert Bork**

Chief Justice William Rehnquist surely took little pleasure in letting smut lord Larry Flynt off the hook in his Supreme Court opinion Wednesday. The court, however, was right to uphold Flynt's claim to First Amendment protection.

TV evangelist Jerry Falwell sued for libel and intentional infliction of emotional distress after Flynt's Hustler magazine satirized Falwell as a drunk who lost his virginity to his mother in a Virginia outhouse. Flynt had been ordered by a lower court to pay Falwell $200,000 in damages.

The Supreme Court unanimously overturned that decision and ruled that political satire — even if it is outrageous and designed to cause its subject pain — must be protected.

"We think the First Amendment prohibits such a (verdict) in the area of public debate about public figures," Rehnquist wrote of the $200,000 award. "Were we to hold otherwise, political cartoonists and satirists would be subjected to damage awards without any showing that their work falsely defamed its subject."

The ruling is important in the constant struggle to defend free speech and a free press against the rising tide of litigation. It doesn't go as far as some would like, however. Note Rehnquist's careful reference to "public debate about public figures."

The court has historically shied away from the absolutist view of the First Amendment represented by former Justice Hugo Black's statement that, "All I know is that it says there shall be no laws abridging the freedom of the press; not some, not just a few, but no laws."

This nation's founders had faith in the people's ability to sort out truth from falsehood and fair commentary from vicious attacks. They wisely left these decisions out of the hands of government officials, recognizing that public debate in a free society is bound to hurt sometimes and that public figures often get hurt the most.

"The test of accepting the true meaning of the press provisions of the First Amendment," writes New York Times columnist A.M. Rosenthal, "is willingness to see them protect the right of some 'journalists' to be vulgar lying scoundrels."

Or, as Decatur County Court Judge George R. Watts so aptly puts it, "The Constitution does not require TV or newspapers to be truthful or fair. We must zealously protect the right of the news media to lie and misinform the public."

Unsightly as it may be, the road of press freedom must remain open to all — even garbage truck owners like Larry Flynt.

## FORT WORTH STAR-TELEGRAM
*Fort Worth, TX, February 25, 1988*

The U.S. Supreme Court had no choice but to overturn lower-court decisions that had awarded $200,000 to evangelist Jerry Falwell on the grounds that he had been libeled by a smutty parody in *Hustler* magazine that reached new lows in bad taste.

That is because constitutional protection of the freedom of expression does not carry an asterisk excluding those examples that are in poor taste or that most people would find repugnant.

There will be no attempt here to defend the item in question — for it was a shabby example of satire at its most repulsive level — or *Hustler* Publisher Larry Flynt's decision to publish it. But freedom-loving people everywhere must recognize the necessity of defending the magazine's *right* to publish it.

Falwell's lawsuit was in response to a full-page "ad parody" that appeared in two separate issues of *Hustler*, a sexually explicit magazine. The ad featured a picture of Falwell and "quoted" him discussing a sexual encounter with his mother and admitting that he was a drunkard. At the bottom of the page, in small print, readers were told that the ad was a parody and was "not to be taken seriously."

Falwell, however, took it seriously, as did the jury that originally awarded him $200,000 and an appeals court that upheld the decision. Fortunately, the highest court in the land has taken more seriously the U.S. Constitution, which guarantees that citizens' right to express themselves will not be stifled even if that which they choose to express is unpopular and disgusting.

## Los Angeles Times
*Los Angeles, CA, February 25, 1988*

Wednesday was a red-letter day in the U.S. Supreme Court for cartoonists, satirists, parody writers, caricaturists and all those other rascals who amuse us all until one of them happens to gore our personal ox. The high court unanimously extended to them the same First Amendment protection already granted to more sober-sided members of the media—and made it clear that the protection applies even when they're outrageous.

We confess that the press celebrations would be louder if the victors in the case were some publication other than Hustler magazine and someone other than its publisher, Larry Flynt. The parody that inspired the lawsuit, a phony advertisement depicting the Rev. Jerry Falwell engaged in what the court delicately called "a drunken incestuous rendezvous with his mother in an outhouse," was just as tasteless as anything that appears in that magazine.

But Chief Justice William H. Rehnquist's opinion recognized that public figures like Falwell have ample ways to defend themselves against tasteless parodies, against vitriolic criticism, even against sleaze, without suing their critics. That reasoning underlies more than two decades of First Amendment decisions by the court, all affirming that public officials and public figures must show actual malice before they can collect for defamation.

Falwell, claiming that Hustler's parody almost made him cry, had urged the high court to exclude outrageous statements from First Amendment protection as long as they intentionally cause emotional distress, even if no one believes them.

His argument has been echoed in other courtrooms as other famous people have tried to get around the broad First Amendment shield that the Supreme Court has erected in defamation cases by suing for emotional distress, a common-law tort.

But Rehnquist wasn't buying. Outrageousness, he said, is such a slippery standard that it would allow jurors to impose liability on the basis of their own likes and dislikes. The chief justice could not bring himself to say that Hustler magazine itself added much to the robust political debate that the First Amendment is supposed to foster. But he could find no logical difference between the Hustler parody and the work of Thomas Nast and other splendid cartoonists and satirists. He acknowledged that such humor is "outrageous," "slashing" and "one-sided," but concluded that "our political discourse would have been considerably poorer" without it.

Anyone who doubts that people like Falwell can look out for themselves ought to keep in mind what he did with the Hustler parody. After the ad had twice appeared in Hustler, he shared his emotional distress by mailing hundreds of thousands of copies of it to his supporters to raise money for Moral Majority, which he headed at the time, and Old Time Gospel Hour. He netted $800,000 for his efforts.

As for Larry Flynt and Hustler, their victory is a vivid reminder that the real test of our commitment to the First Amendment is whether we can accept gracefully the idea that it shields even those who personally offend us.

## The Hartford Courant
*Hartford, CT, February 28, 1988*

Not in nearly a quarter-century has the U.S. Supreme Court done as much to encourage vigorous public discussion of public figures as it did Wednesday when it rejected a jury's monetary award to the Rev. Jerry Falwell for what he claimed was "emotional distress" caused by a magazine parody.

The court's unanimous decision in this landmark case provides strong and welcome assurance that Americans' freedom to exchange opinions about prominent people and public issues is virtually unlimited. A healthy democracy requires nothing less.

The trigger for Mr. Falwell's lawsuit, a Hustler magazine parody of an advertisement for Campari liqueur, seemed almost calculated to test the limits of expressive freedom. The ad depicted the minister as drinking excessively and having sexual intercourse with his mother in an outhouse. It clearly was meant to cause emotional pain.

At the trial, Mr. Falwell's invasion-of-privacy claim was dismissed, and the jury found that the parody — which included the warning "ad parody — not to be taken seriously" — couldn't reasonably be seen as purported truth. That finding scuttled his libel argument, because an obviously false statement can't hurt anyone's reputation. The jury, however, decided that Mr. Falwell had been the victim of intentional infliction of emotional distress, and awarded him $200,000.

The importance of this case is best measured by considering what an opposite ruling by the Supreme Court would have meant. Had Mr. Falwell won, public figures seeking to retaliate for verbal or pictorial attacks could have sidestepped the high hurdles involved in libel litigation and instead simply have begun suing their critics for emotional distress.

That would have made publishers, cartoonists, writers, broadcasters, public speakers and other purveyors of commentary vulnerable to large jury awards based not upon reckless defamation of public figures' characters but simply upon the fact that their feelings had been hurt. In such a hostile legal climate, public debate would rapidly become lifeless.

The Supreme Court did much to ensure the vitality of that debate in 1964 when, in a case involving The New York Times, the justices declared that public officials and other public figures could successfully sue for libel only if they could show that a statement was false, defamatory and made "with knowledge that it was false or with reckless disregard of whether it was false or not."

The decision in the Falwell case seems no less significant, in part because the opinion, written by Chief Justice William H. Rehnquist, quotes repeatedly and approvingly from the Times opinion and others that have bolstered First Amendment rights. It even reached back to 1944, recalling Justice Felix Frankfurter's assertion that "one of the prerogatives of American citizenship is the right to criticize public men and measures." Added Chief Justice Rehnquist: "Such criticism, inevitably, will not always be reasoned or moderate."

A disappointed Mr. Falwell, referring to Hustler's publisher, said he thought the court had "given the green light to Larry Flynt and his ilk to print what they wish about any public figure at any time with no fear of reprisal." That's an exaggeration; several restrictions, including the laws against libel, will continue to restrain expression.

But the high court has made it clear that harsh, even malicious, commentary about public figures is almost always constitutionally protected, and that's a declaration that all Americans should applaud. Uninhibited discussion of public figures and public affairs is the best prescription for a democracy's well-being.

## The Boston Globe
*Boston, MA, February 25, 1988*

The seamy squabble between evangelist Jerry Falwell and sleaze merchant Larry Flynt, resolved yesterday by the Supreme Court, was really a trial of the First Amendment – and the First Amendment won. The resounding 8-0 decision vacating a $200,000 tort award to Falwell for Flynt's tawdry, tasteless parody of the preacher firmly reinforced the principle of a free press.

Anyone contemplating statutory restrictions on that freedom will do well to contemplate the court's reasoning. Chief Justice William H. Rehnquist, who chose to write the opinion himself, emphasized what may be the most troubling aspect of the case for those offended by the apparent vindication of Flynt's pandering to the basest of impulses.

"[Falwell] would have us find that a state's interest in protecting public figures from emotional distress is sufficient to deny First Amendment protection to speech that is patently offensive and is intended to inflict emotional injury, even when that speech could not reasonably have been interpreted as stating actual facts about the public figure involved. This we decline to do," Rehnquist wrote.

In pointing out the impossibility of drawing a line between caricature that is merely slashing and caricature that is coarse and in terrible taste, the court has affirmed wide boundaries for parody and satire and for political commentary. Crudity, the court found, is neither a crime nor cause for the awarding of tort damages.

The case illustrates a common misconception about penalizing coarseness in print or other media. Falwell had sued on charges that Flynt's parody had libeled him and invaded his privacy, seeking damages for pain and suffering.

The judge threw out the invasion-of-privacy charge, and the jury found no libel but awarded Falwell $200,000 for his claimed suffering. Whether or not Falwell enjoyed the publicity attendant on the whole affair, the jury seems to have felt that a figure like Flynt should not get off lightly. The court has properly found that free speech, however coarse, cannot be penalized on such grounds.

## Buffalo Evening News
*Buffalo, NY, February 26, 1988*

THE U.S. SUPREME COURT struck a solid blow for freedom of speech with its unanimous ruling in the Falwell-Hustler case. By overturning a $200,000 award won by the Rev. Jerry Falwell against Hustler magazine, the high court made it clear that the protection of the First Amendment extends to parody and satire, even when they are outrageous.

Mr. Falwell had sued the sex magazine over a vicious ad parody that it had published concerning him. A jury held that Mr. Falwell was not libeled since the material was not understood by readers as being factual, but it nevertheless awarded him damages on the grounds that the parody had caused him "emotional distress."

Mr. Falwell had every right to be angry about the Hustler item — which portrayed him as an incestuous drunkard — but the Supreme Court correctly ruled that even vulgar commentary must be accorded First Amendment protection in the interest of preserving free speech.

The ability of Americans to engage in robust debate and criticism on public issues would be seriously threatened if they could be forced to pay monetary damages simply for causing public figures hurt feelings. Editorial cartoons and opinion columns frequently engage in biting satire and ridicule, and a victory for Mr. Falwell in this suit would have had a chilling effect on all such criticism.

In saying this, The Buffalo News certainly holds no brief for an offensive magazine like Hustler, and we recognize that the parody of Mr. Falwell vastly exceeded the bounds of elementary good taste practiced by most publications.

Still, as the Supreme Court indicated in its ruling, there is no way to try to distinguish between degrees of outrageousness and still maintain true freedom of speech and the press in this country.

"Outrageousness in the area of political and social discourse has an inherent subjectiveness about it which would allow a jury to impose liability on the basis of the jurors' tastes or views, or perhaps on the basis of their dislike of a particular expression," Chief Justice William H. Rehnquist wrote for the court.

The decision held that even pornographic spoofs about a public figure are constitutionally protected as long as it is apparent that they are indeed satirical, and not implying actual facts. As Rehnquist affirmed, even "vehement, caustic and sometimes unpleasantly sharp attacks" fall under the First Amendment mantle.

What makes the ruling particularly significant is that it was unanimous, uniting high court liberals and conservatives alike in a strong statement of support for free speech in the public arena.

Nothing in this decision, of course, upsets the basic libel laws. Public figures like the Rev. Falwell may still obtain judicial relief from the reckless publication of false facts about them.

But when it comes to mere satire and ridicule, people continue to be constitutionally free to express themselves as they see fit, even if they do so in ways most Americans would find utterly gross.

That's the essence of the present ruling, and it's a principle everyone concerned with preserving free speech should support.

## The Charlotte Observer
*Charolette, NC, February 26, 1988*

As its unanimous decision indicated, the U.S. Supreme Court had no choice but to rule that Hustler Magazine's sleazy cartoon attack on Jerry Falwell was not illegal.

The cartoon was plainly labeled an "ad parody, not to be taken seriously." Lower courts had ruled that it did not libel Mr. Falwell. The award of damages came under a Virginia law that permits recovery of damages when satire hurts its subject's feelings even if it is not libelous.

Leave aside, for the moment, the fact that Jerry Falwell did not consider the cartoon too offensive to use in a fund-raising mass mailing, thereby exposing it to thousands of people who would no sooner look at Hustler than they would drink Lysol. Simply consider the impact of such a law. It would either put an end to any political satire more pointed than a Mickey Mouse cartoon, or it would create a court-supported gold mine for thin-skinned public figures. George Bush, for example, once remarked that parodies of him in the "Doonesbury" cartoon strip made him "a basket case" for the rest of the day. Could he sue and collect? If so, satire would be riskier than sticking up banks.

Satire is an ungentlemanly enterprise. But the First Amendment was not written to protect only gentle speech, or fair speech, or reputable speech. It was written to protect the free interchange of ideas and opinions. The authors of that amendment knew that any law strong enough to protect responsible speech would also protect a lot of irresponsible speech. Yet they considered freedom of speech to be so vital to the success of representative government that they accepted that bargain. So did the Supreme Court in its decision in the Falwell case.

The Hustler cartoon was a disgusting example of the disgusting nature of the magazine and its publisher, Larry Flynt. Mr. Falwell chose to react to it by (1) using it to raise money, and (2) suing. We can think of at least two other ways to react. The first is to ignore it, on the theory that Hustler is a cesspool and everybody knows what cesspools are full of. The other would be to load a 50-gallon can with garbage, take it to the Hustler offices and dump it on Larry Flynt. Not a jury in America would do anything but applaud Jerry Falwell if he did so.

## Houston Chronicle
*Houston, TX, February 26, 1988*

One of the most heartening things about the U.S. Supreme Court's latest affirmation of freedom of speech was its unanimity.

It was no close issue, no divided judgment, that Hustler magazine could not be punished by being forced to pay "emotional-distress" damages for distastefully parodying evangelist Jerry Falwell. The high court, by 8-0 vote, overturned a $200,000 award to Falwell for emotional distress stemming from the parody.

This was no small matter. Riding on its outcome was the future of America's traditionally robust and satirical political cartooning and social satire. Equally at stake was the effective undermining of libel law which protects strong opinion about public figures.

Hustler magazine would offend the Marquis de Sade. True to its sexually explicit and unrelentingly repugnant style, it published a full-page parody ad of Falwell, labeled as such in small type, which purportedly quoted him discussing a sexual encounter with his mother and describing himself as a habitual drunkard. In a word, it was awful.

Falwell sued for libel, invasion of privacy and asked damages for intentional infliction of emotional distress. A jury ruled Falwell was not libeled and the lower-court judge threw out the invasion of privacy charge. But the jury also awarded the emotional-distress damages. The Supreme Court reversed that.

Chief Justice William Rehnquist, writing for the court, may have best explained what was at stake here and why it had to be protected: "There is no doubt that the caricature of (Falwell) published in Hustler is at best a distant cousin of the (traditional) political cartoons, and a rather poor relation at that." But he then noted that there is no way the law can punish one and let the other flourish.

Just so. As for the damages for emotional distress, it takes no legal genius to know that vigorous opinion is by definition distressing to the public figure involved. If vigorous opinion is protected speech, but that protection can be undermined by damage awards nevertheless, then there is effectively no protection.

Just as the Supreme Court's unanimity in protecting free speech was heartening, the fact that it had to be done in a case involving Hustler magazine was depressing.

It is not pleasant to have to protect the likes of Hustler in order to protect everyone else. Unfortunately, no one has ever found a way around that dilemma.

## AKRON BEACON JOURNAL
*Akron, OH, February 26, 1988*

THE SUPREME Court's unanimous decision in the Jerry Falwell-Hustler magazine case was *not*, as some may think, a defense of smut. It was instead an important landmark decision upholding freedom of speech and expression, and upholding political dialogue.

Clearly, the way in which Larry Flynt's scuzzy magazine characterized the Rev. Falwell was unfair and irresponsible. Who among us would enjoy being depicted, even in satire, engaging in incest with his mother?

In ruling against Falwell, and against a lower court award of damages to him for emotional distress, the Supreme Court said that the advantages of having a free and open society, where political debate is vigorous, outweigh the momentary pain caused by a slimeball like Flynt.

Significantly, the court's decision was written by Chief Justice William H. Rehnquist, who noted that the First Amendment protects "vehement, caustic and sometimes unpleasantly sharp attacks." Elsewhere in the decision, he made this key point: "At the heart of the First Amendment is the recognition of the fundamental importance of the free flow of ideas and opinions on matters of public interest and concern."

In this unusual case, a lower court had dismissed Falwell's libel claim, noting that the offensive Hustler cartoon of 1983 was labeled an "ad parody — not to be taken seriously," and thus could not be understood to be based on actual events. A lower court jury then awarded Falwell $200,000 for emotional distress because the caricature was so "outrageous."

Chief Justice Rehnquist said that to establish a standard of "outrageousness" would be impossible, and would leave the appropriateness of political criticism and debate subject to the individual whim. What might not be "outrageous" to one person could well be so judged by another.

An analogy is the time many years ago when Boss Tweed and his Tammany Hall gang ruled New York City and stole millions from the public treasuries. Before the Tweed gang was finally brought to justice and jailed, one voice against the Tweed ring was that of the cartoonist Thomas Nast. From Tweed's perspective, Nast's biting cartoons would have been just as "outrageous" as Hustler's depiction of Falwell.

So the Supreme Court opted for the free flow of debate and discourse rather than the uncertain limits implied by the earlier court judgment in Falwell's favor. Acknowledging the distress that can be caused by someone like Flynt, the court properly ruled that democracy works best when debate and criticism are not muzzled.

## Chicago Tribune
*Chicago, IL, February 26, 1988*

The unmistakable message of that parody magazine ad in a 1983 issue of Hustler magazine was that evangelist Jerry Falwell had his first sexual experience in a drunken outhouse rendezvous with his mother.

The unanimously approved message from the U.S. Supreme Court on Wednesday was that however repugnant, gross and emotionally distressing that parody was to Rev. Falwell and the rest of society, it was nonetheless a legitimate expression of opinion protected by the 1st Amendment to the Constitution of the United States.

For the court, whose balance has shifted with appointments by President Reagan, it was a strong and courageous stand in favor of the kind of free and unbridled political debate vital to democracy. All eight justices who heard the case, including those alleged enemies of the press William H. Rehnquist and Antonin Scalia, deserve a standing ovation.

This one was not easy. If ever there was an opportunity for the Supreme Court to step in and gag the press, this was it.

Rev. Falwell, darling of right-wing press bashers, had been viciously attacked by loony smut peddler Larry Flynt in a manner beyond all bounds of decency. A federal appellate panel had upheld a lower court's award of $200,000 in damages to the preacher on the theory that even though the parody was not libelous, it was "outrageous" enough to justify a payment for "intentionally inflicted emotional distress." If that decision had been allowed to stand, it would have successfully undercut constitutional guarantees of free speech, specifically political satire as practiced by editorial cartoonists, columnists and editorial writers.

The case had forced a nervous legitimate press to hold its nose and stand beside Larry Flynt, because anything less than a Hustler victory would have sent politicians everywhere into court to silence their critics. If causing emotional distress to politicians becomes illegal, we all would be imprisoned before dark, either by the Chicago City Council or the Illinois legislature.

Obviously, the magnitude of their ruling was not lost on members of the high court. The justices reaffirmed and extended rules protecting criticism of public figures even when it is offensive and "outrageous."

No doubt the court was holding its nose, too, because the kind of political free speech that needs preserving in this country is not the gutter language of Larry Flynt's pornography. His taunting antics and deliberate abuse of press freedom remain the greatest enemy of the 1st Amendment.

Still, the press should well remember that this case has not thrown open the doors for anything-goes journalism. What the court gives and protects one day, it surely can take away the next.

## Iran Offers Reward for London Author's Death

Iranian leader Ayatollah Ruhollah Khomeini Feb. 14, 1989 urged Moslems throughout the world to execute the Indian-born British author of a novel perceived to be blasphemous to Islam. The next day an aide to the religious and political leader offered a million-dollar reward for the killing of the author, Salman Rushdie. The Iranian pronouncements came amid widespread condemnation of Rushdie's novel, *The Satanic Verses*, in the Islamic world, particularly among fundamentalists.

Six people died in Islamabad, Pakistan after police Feb. 12 fired on a crowd protesting the book at a U.S. cultural center. Another three protesters were killed in Srinagar, India, Feb. 13, according to the *New York Times*. Moslems in London had protested against *The Satanic Verses* Jan. 28, and two weeks earlier copies of the book had been burned at a rally in Bradford, England, where many Moslems lived. Some Islamic leaders there Feb. 14 backed Khomeini's call for Rushdie's death. Among other countries where the book was banned were Pakistan, Bangladesh, India, Egypt and South Africa.

The growing protests over the book led the Waldenbooks Inc. unit of K-Mart Corp. Feb. 16 to order the removal of *The Satanic Verses* from its store shelves. The company, the largest U.S. bookseller, cited concerns over employee safety for its action.

Rushdie was born to a Kashmiri Moslem family in Bombay in 1947. He was educated in England and was a British citizen. He had won Britain's prestigious Booker Prize in 1981 for the book *Midnight's Children*. *The Satanic Verses* had been short-listed for that prize. In the novel, one of the characters underwent a dream sequence involving a character resembling Mohammed, the founder of Islam. The sequence appeared to challenge basic tenets of Islam (such as that the Koran was the absolute word of God), and it portrayed the Mohammed-like character in an irreverent manner.

Rushdie himself contended that the book was not blasphemous and charged that those protesting against it had little knowledge of the work. He was reported to be in hiding with police protection in England Feb. 15. That day he canceled a publicity tour to the U.S. scheduled to begin Feb. 17. Some commentators compared the protests over *The Satanic Verses* to those by Christians against the movie *The Last Temptation of Christ*.

An international furor continued to mount Feb. 16-24 over *The Satanic Verses*. Rushdie issued an apology, but Iran's Khomeini spurned it and reiterated his death threat against the novelist. European nations responded by calling their diplomats from Teheran.

Meanwhile, the affair had developed into the biggest uproar in literature and publishing in recent years. Initially, major U.S. booksellers removed the novel from their shelves and several European publishers suspended plans to print it. But some of the companies reversed themselves in reaction to a growing chorus of outrage from writers, intellectuals and the press.

Iran's responses to the controversy were not uniform, lending support to the theory that the death edict against Rushdie was largely a product of domestic Iranian politics. Specifically, it was seen as an effort by radicals within the regime – led by Interior Minister Ali Akbar Mohtashemi and Premier Mir Hussein Mousavi-Khamenei – to undermine the pragmatic faction led by parliament speaker Ali Akbar Hashemi Rafsanjani and President Ali Khamenei. The radicals opposed the pragmatists' efforts to repair Iran's ties with Western nations and seek foreign loans for postwar reconstruction.

The U.S. response to the Rushdie affair was relatively low-key. Secretary of State James A. Baker 3rd said Feb. 19 that Khomeini's death threat was "intolerable."

---

### The Chattanooga Times
*Chattanooga, TN,
February 20, 1989*

Few of us are immune from fear; still, it is sometimes surprising to discover its dimensions. It can reach from far abroad — from a fanatical Iranian leader's call to Moslems to murder a British author — to produce censorship in our own backyard. Try to find a copy of *Satanic Verses* in Chattanooga.

The book by Salman Rushdie has occasioned widespread and sometimes violent Islamic protest. Condemned as a blasphemy against Islam, it was banned in several countries, including Mr. Rushdie's native India. Then Iran's Ayatollah Khomeini took the protest to terroristic heights, calling for the murder of Mr. Rushdie and his publishers. That led three major U.S. book chains, including Waldenbooks, to order the book off their shelves as a measure to protect employees and patrons from potential violence.

Indeed, as of last Friday morning the book was off Waldenbooks' shelves here, and would-be purchasers were told no copies were on order. Fear inspired by fanatical zealots won this battle over the freedom to exchange ideas under American democracy. And similar circumstances apply in other Western countries, in some of which plans to publish the book have been dropped.

Meanwhile, Mr. Rushdie is in hiding somewhere in Great Britain under police guard. His hopes that a narrowly scripted apology would be enough to lift the ayatollah's "death sentence" against him collapsed Sunday. On Friday Iranian President Khamenei said if Mr. Rushdie apologized for insulting Islam and Moslem believers, "it is possible the people may pardon him." In response, Mr. Rushdie issued a statement Saturday that did not apologize for the book but expressed regret for "the distress" it has caused.

On Sunday, however, Ayatollah Khomeini rejected the very idea of accepting an apology. "Even if Salman Rushdie repents and becomes the most pious man of time," he said, "it is incumbent on every Moslem (to) employ everything he's got, his life and wealth, to send him to hell." The Iranian leader thus underscored the execution orders which some observers believe were issued to raise his profile and promote his sagging political fortunes.

Regardless of motive, the ayatollah's calls for murder, the $5 million "reward" offered for the execution of Mr. Rushdie and the bomb threats that have closed the Manhattan offices of Viking Penguin publishers are inexcusable, outrageous examples of state-inspired terrorism. They cast serious doubt on Iran's supposed desire for improved international relations.

But the serious threat to Mr. Rushdie's life and the potential for violence to his publishers are not the end of the costs. Iran is attempting — with an unfortunate degree of success — to impose what one official at Viking Penguin called "censorship by terrorism and intimidation." Everyone who cannot now obtain a copy of the book, including interested Chattanoogans, is as directly affected by the ayatollah's terror as is the concept of free speech.

Apparently, Islam accepts no dividing line between the spiritual and the secular, which creates difficulties for the Western view of democratic free speech. We should seek to understand Moslems' interests and concerns and to exercise responsible sensitivity for their religious views. But mutual respect dictates as well that Moslems learn to refrain from terrorism against freedom of speech in democratic societies.

## Wisconsin State Journal
*Madison, WI, February 15, 1989*

Salman Rushdie's novel, "The Satanic Verses," was published in England a year ago, well before it was published in America by Viking Penguin. Indian-born Rushdie lives in London, and he has received major British writing awards. So why have throngs of angry people rioted outside the American cultural center in Islamabad, the capital of predominantly Moslem Pakistan?

Also, why are Pakistanis so upset by a book that is not for sale there, and that has not even been translated in Urdu, the language of Pakistan and northern India?

The reasons may be far too complicated for most Westerners and non-Muslims to understand, but an explanation offered by UW-Madison Professor Muhmammad Memon seems to make as much sense as any offered thus far. Why not attack the British Embassy instead of the American cultural center? Memon says the protesters are trying to reach the U.S. news media.

"Look, if it didn't happen outside the American (information office), it wouldn't have been in all the newspapers and on CNN," said Memon, noting that religion and politics are almost inseparable in Islam.

This protest should be seen for what it is — an excuse for Islamic fundamentalists to deliver an anti-Western (not specifically anti-U.S.) message, to air some legitimate gripes and to work against Prime Minister Benazir Bhutto's attempts to democratize Pakistan. As for unofficial Pakistani demands that "The Satanic Verses" be banned in America and all existing copies be burned, they are showing that they understand our culture even less than we understand theirs.

## Calgary Herald
*Calgary, Alta., February 15, 1989*

When he isn't holding public executions in the streets of Tehran, Iran's Ayatollah Khomeini spends his busy days calling for the murder of foreigners who have earned his wrath.

Just this week, as hundreds of alleged drug dealers were being strung up in public, Khomeini took time out to call for the death of author Salman Rushdie and all those connected with the sale of Rushdie's latest book.

Apparently it isn't good enough that the book Satanic Verses has been banned in such Muslim states as Pakistan, Egypt and Iran, and even burned in merry old England by obedient followers.

Now, according to the Ayatollah, Rushdie and a sizable number of people in the printing, ink, paper and book trade must pay with their lives for the perceived blasphemies contained in a book which few Islamic fundamentalists have read.

This is all par for the course for religious fanatics who have a deep and abiding fear of everyone who does not accept everything they say without question. Everyone, that is, who dares to think for themselves.

When thoughtful dissidents are discovered, the priest-kings call for them to be crushed, not only to silence them but to maintain fear and obedience among the faithful.

That's why as many as 12,000 educated Iranians have been executed in the last few months by Khomeini's followers. That's why the Ayatollah issued his latest cowardly contract to kill Rushdie. It is simply the literal fundamentalist's way of attempting to kill the messenger.

Where will he stop?

## StarPhoenix
*Saskatoon, Sask., February 17, 1989*

The violent protest by Pakistani Muslim fundamentalists over Salman Rushdie's novel, The Satanic Verses, recalls the furore in North America over a film which ventured to re-interpret the Bible.

A key difference is that the Christian fundamentalists who criticized The Last Temptation of Christ weren't calling for director Martin Scorsese's head.

In the riot Sunday in the Pakistan capital, Islamabad, five people were killed by police gunfire, and 65 protesters were wounded. In the aftermath, Iranian patriarch Ayatollah Ruhollah Khomeini exhorted his fundamentalist Muslim followers to track down and kill Rushdie, a Muslim now living in England.

The award-winning novelist has described The Satanic Verses as a satire. It has been banned in Pakistan and India because it implies the prophet Mohammed was fallible, and that there are female gods as well as Allah.

The rioters were marching on United States government offices to demand that the U.S. ban the book, too. The protest may have also signified some criticism of Prime Minister Benazir Bhutto's perceived liberal leanings.

The episode is a devastating reminder of the power of the printed word, particularly when that word conflicts with deeply-held beliefs. It's appalling, though, that people should be killed over a work of fiction.

## The Seattle Times
*Seattle, WA, February 15, 1989*

AUTHOR Salman Rushdie has garnered a dubious literary distinction for his latest novel, "The Satanic Verses." It has earned him a death warrant from Iran's Ayatollah Ruhollah Khomeini.

If "banned in Boston" guaranteed sales, will "condemned to death in Tehran" simultaneously move the book and its writer to the head of the best-seller list and the obituary page?

Khomeini claims the Moslem faith and faithful are defamed by Rushdie's allegory of good and evil. Particular offense is taken at a dream sequence that likens the wives of the Prophet Mohammed to prostitutes, later punished for their immorality.

In this country awhile back, a movie depicting a dreaming, sexual Jesus Christ provoked pickets, boycotts and angry letters. But "The Satanic Verses" has led to bloodshed. Riots in Pakistan and India have claimed several lives.

For Rushdie, who was born in India and resides in England, the furor is both puzzling and infuriating. He finds selective passages denounced by people who are forbidden to read his book in countries where the sale of "The Satanic Verses" is outlawed. He wonders whether there is more exploitation of emotion at work than theological outrage.

Pakistan's prime minister, Benazir Bhutto, is fearful that protests fueled by the book are a ruse to undermine her new government. An American cultural center was attacked after plans for the book's U.S. debut were announced.

In the ayatollah's theocracy, there is no difference between religious affairs and affairs of state. In Pakistan, sacred smoke and mirrors may be used to obscure gritty secular motives. Bhutto's ascendancy is an affront to fundamentalists.

In such an environment, free expression of ideas is not compatible with the expression of religious faith. True believers stand ready to visit their pure vision on others, while denying any deviations.

"You have a situation where a handful of extremists are defining Islam," Rushdie said in a New York Times interview. "And what makes it even sadder for me is that they are simply feeding the Western stereotype: the backward, cruel, rigid Muslim, burning books and threatening to kill the blasphemer."

Khomeini has sent 12-year-old boys to their deaths on the battlefield. Now, he invokes a death sentence for an author and those associated with the publication of his book.

But if Rushdie is an infidel in Khomeini's eyes, the writer is not about to change his ways: "You cannot let something like this take over your life," he says, "or you have lost."

## Rockford Register Star
*Rockford, IL, February 20, 1989*

The fragility of our First Amendment freedoms in this country is amply demonstrated by the current de facto banning of a controversial new book by numerous American bookstores. This disturbing precedent virtually guarantees similar incidents in the future.

The book at issue, of course, is Salman Rushdie's fanciful novel, *The Satanic Verses,* at which the Islamic world takes great offense over purported blasphemies in the work. Since the Ayatollah Khomeini has put a price on Rushdie's head, booksellers around the world have grown nervous about offering his book.

Even in America, where intellectual freedom is a cornerstone of our system, several big chains have removed *Verses* from their shelves. Some stores are afraid even to peddle the book on demand from under the counter. Such is the frailness of freedom. The threat of terrorism can effectively ban a book.

This lesson doubtless will not be lost on others who don't want certain books, films or art works to gain any wide circulation. It's a slippery slope, and it's the same slope that was charted last summer by those who sought to bar the showing of the film *The Last Temptation of Christ.* Their intolerance is now mirrored, albeit in a much more menacing image, by the current Islamic uprising against the Rushdie book.

What is required in these cases is that those who cherish freedom rise up and defend the rights of Americans to read or sell whatever books they want and to see or exhibit whatever movies they want. Censorship through terrorism must be resisted.

## St. Paul Pioneer Press & Dispatch
*St. Paul, MN, February 17, 1989*

The cultural gulf between religious politics in the Islamic world and the secular-governed Christian West underlies the firestorm over "The Satanic Verses." That people would riot and incite to murder over passages in a novel the protesters are forbidden to read is like, well, bad fiction here.

Yes, the protest of what is viewed as sacrilege in art is well-known in the West. Most recently, the film "The Last Temptation of Christ" drew highly visible demonstrations in the Christian world. "Jesus Christ Superstar" was wildly offensive to some Christian groups. Boycotts and book-burnings in the name of orthodoxy are no strangers here. But those outcries are mere whispers against Iran's screams for the murder of author Salman Rushdie; riots that result in death; stone-throwing at a British diplomatic mission; threats against a book publisher, and threats to blow up airplanes.

Moslems have every right to be offended by passages in Mr. Rushdie's book that the devout believe blaspheme the prophet Mohammed. Words, even fictional, that probe at the foundations of faith offend the faithful. Mr. Rushdie, a Moslem, knew this. But he is a great novelist who wanted to write some sophisticated things about pluralism in society.

In hiding and in fear of his life, Mr. Rushdie is paying far too much for the right to tell his story.

The riots over the book and the bloodthirsty rhetoric have come from the other side of the cultural gulf between the West and Islam. There, the line between secular and eccelesiastical fades; in that grayness comes political violence dressed up as truth. There, Pakistani riots over Mr. Rushdie's book left six people dead; Prime Minister Benazir Bhutto's opponents capitalized on the uproar. There, Iran's Ayatollah Khomeini plucked "The Satanic Verses" issue to feather his theocratic nest at the expense of improved relations with Britain. Never mind that Islamic scholars say the ayatollah's theology is muddled because an apostate must be given the chance to repent.

The hatemongers devalue thoughtful objections of reasonable Moslems and leave other honest people in fear of their lives. Would that all concerned would awake and find that the chaos surrounding "The Satanic Verses" is the dream of an insane character in a novel.

## The Wichita Eagle-Beacon

*Wichita, KS, February 27, 1989*

LIKE Vlad the Impaler destroying his enemies one by one, the Ayatollah Khomeini apparently thinks he can eliminate all who oppose him simply by killing them. It has worked so far for the thousands, or tens of thousands, of political opponents he has murdered inside Iran. So what is one lowly author to him?

Sadly, when he ordered the execution of Salman Rushdie, author of "The Satanic Verses," some of those who should have been outraged quaked in fear instead. The American book-sellers who removed the volume from their shelves, even temporarily, must not have realized what happens when one backs down to a bully.

If Khomeini had succeeded in keeping the Rushdie book off bookstore shelves in America and elsewhere, it is certain he wouldn't have stopped there. Before long, there would have been other volumes to which he would have objected, and other titles that would have had to be yanked from bookstores' inventories.

Fortunately, the Western democracies for the most part have denounced the Ayatollah's latest madness, the entire 12-nation European Community leading the way.

But what of the nations that have knuckled under to the book-burning — supposedly democratic India and (under Prime Minister Benazir Bhutto) Pakistan being among them? Suddenly they have a Fanatics' Board of Censorship, nominally headed by a terrorist ayatollah, determining their people's reading habits.

Khomeini said the controversy over Mr. Rushdie's book showed it was pointless to pursue moderate policies with the West. He's got that partly right, at least. It does show it's pointless for the West to pursue moderate policies with Iran as long as there are madmen at the helm of its government.

As a group of 21 American writers said at a protest meeting in New York, a threat to the safety and freedom of one writer anywhere is a threat to every writer everywhere. The way to meet such threats isn't through quiescence but through a unified resistance to the despotism that spawned them.

## Los Angeles Times

*Los Angeles, CA, February 15, 1989*

If no one had been hurt, reasonable people might simply ignore the disturbances surrounding publication of Salman Rushdie's novel, "The Satanic Verses." But people have been killed and injured in this senseless tumult, and that awful fact reminds us that the intolerance of free expression ought to be opposed always and everywhere.

Rushdie is a gifted British author who was born into a Muslim family in Bombay, India. His new book, a fanciful meditation on the origins of belief and Britain's attitudes toward its Indian immigrants, takes its name from the lines that Mohammed is said to have omitted from the Koran because they were inspired by the devil. Some devout Muslims see Rushdie's allegory as an insult to their faith.

Already banned in India, Pakistan and South Africa, the book also has been the target of public protests in England. Booksellers who stock it have been threatened. Over the past two days, five Pakistanis and an Indian have been killed in rioting touched off by the novel's impending publication in the United States. The affair took an even more sinister turn when Tehran radio announced that the Ayatollah Ruhollah Khomeini had pronounced a "sentence of death" on Rushdie and his publishers.

Such squalid goings-on have as little to do with religion as they have with literature. What they have to do with is fear and intolerance, and the way in which those in thrall to them can be manipulated by the cynical and the callous.

Open societies often appear to be chaotic, threatening places. But there is no safety behind the wall of censorship. To the contrary: The rioting in Pakistan was in fact fomented by opponents of Prime Minister Benazir Bhutto; their casualties were not martyrs to religious truth, but unwitting victims of sordid political deception. The Ayatollah Khomeini is no more a religious leader than was the Borgia Pope. He is a garden-variety tyrant whose apparently irrepressible impulse to evil mischief expresses itself in a religious vocabulary. People expose themselves to exploitation by Khomeini and his kind when they delude themselves into thinking that the security of their own values depends on denying others the right to express their opinions.

Those who believe that this is a lesson to be learned only in Islamic societies need only recall the West's recent convulsions over Martin Scorsese's film "The Last Temptation of Christ."

That this latest controversy has nothing to do with Islam itself was brought home to us on Tuesday during a conversation with Dr. Maher Hathout, the erudite spokesman for the Islamic Center of Southern California. He pointed out that tolerance of differing opinions derives its sanction in Islamic tradition from the fact that the Koran itself records the criticisms directed against Mohammed by his contemporaries.

Hathout said that he had just finished reading "The Satanic Verses" and that, personally, he found its language "crude" and its appropriation of Islamic scripture "discourteous." He recommended that those of similar sentiment read Rushdie's earlier novels. "They are more interesting," he said, "and are discounted on the bargain tables at local bookstores."

There speaks the voice of reason, as well as faith.

## THE INDIANAPOLIS NEWS

*Indianapolis, IN, February 23, 1989*

Iran is a nation still at war — at war with itself as well as with a growing number of nations revulsed by Ayatollah Khomeini's recent foray into "literary criticism."

It is exceedingly interesting, however — and perhaps significant, too — that while the ayatollah was issuing death threats to authors, his "designated successor" was making contrasting noises in commemoration of the 10th anniversary of the Islamic revolution in Iran.

In a speech last week Ayatollah Hossein Ali Montazeri said, "On many occasions we showed obstinacy, shouted slogans that frightened the world. The people of the world thought our only task in Iran was to kill people."

Montazeri said his country should strive to recapture the early days of the revolution and to "create coordination, optimism and confidence among the people, just like the beginning of the revolution."

He lamented in a second speech that the revolution had failed to meet the promises it made in 1979 when the shah was ousted. Costly mistakes, he said, had been made in the eight-year war with Iraq.

"Let us see," he continued, "how many forces did we lose, how many towns were destroyed . . . and then repent after realizing we made those mistakes."

Montazeri said he favored an open society and that he also favored making it easier for Iranians who fled the revolution and the slogans, to return to their native land.

The question, then, is who speaks for Iran today — Khomeini or his successor? Or, perhaps a more pertinent question is: Will the designated successor ever get to be the successor after making such speeches?

## The Honolulu Advertiser
*Honolulu, HI, February 21, 1989*

Western leaders are right in condemning and retaliating diplomatically against Iran's Ayatollah Khomeini for his order for Moslems to kill India-born British author Salman Rushdie.

Rushdie's novel "Satanic Verses" is controversial with many more moderate Moslems because they feel it blasphemes the Islamic religion. There were strong protests for months before the aged Iranian leader got in the act with his own religious and political agenda.

But Khomeini has elevated religious protest to contract murder. That is a form of terrorism the world cannot abide. And unfortunately he has been abetted by some of this country's biggest booksellers who practiced self-censorship by hastily pulling Rushdie's book off their shelves.

So this is an issue that involves artistic freedom and our First Amendment on one side, and terrorism and a totalitarian response on the other. But it is also about religion, and, as an adjoining column notes, history has seen other extreme responses.

Americans may ask themselves how they would react if this were a novel deemed anti-Semitic or anti-Christian. While the author and his rights would be protected and death threats denounced, there would also be more mixed feelings.

Islam is a rich and varied religion embraced in degrees by a quarter of the world's people. Thomas Jefferson said we need to have "a decent respect for the opinions of mankind."

Therefore, we must stand up to Khomeini's tactics and for our own values, while realizing this is about more than his extremist beliefs.

## The Washington Times
*Washington, DC, February 22, 1989*

The Ayatollah Khomeini's death sentence on British author Salman Rushdie has turned the world upside-down. It inspired Europe to embrace American-style tolerance for free speech and intolerance of extortion. American publishers, booksellers and diplomats on the other hand have curled into a fetal ball. It enraged the Yugoslavian government, whose newspapers began printing exerpts of the book on the eve of Iranian President Ali Khameini's visit to the country. It scared booksellers in Japan and America and publishers in West Germany into halting distribution of the novel. Americans who boldly defend the rights of people to sell things like Screw magazine have fallen silent, as if the mullah had gotten their tongues.

All this was caused by the publication in America of Mr. Rushdie's novel, "The Satanic Verses," which depicts Mohammed's wives as harlots and the Koran as anything but divinely inspired. Certainly such a novel ought to stir up a complex and furious debate about the proper ways for societies to express respect for serious religions.

But the ayatollah's obscene death decree has made such debate impossible for now. It doesn't matter that the aging mullah may have pulled the stunt to rebuild popularity in a demoralized Iran. It doesn't matter that he didn't get alarmed about the book, which was published five months ago in Britain, until it was printed in America. What matters is that people have taken his decree seriously, and Iranian clergy have put a bounty of nearly $6 million on Salman Rushdie. The ayatollah's form of literary criticism assails the freedom of religion and expression upon which Western civilization rests.

European governments recognized this and fought back. The members of the European Economic Community withdrew their ambassadors from Iran on Monday (the British closed their consulate entirely), inspiring the ayatollah to recall his ambassadors to the 12 Common Market capitals the following day. The EEC also has begun considering tough sanctions on Iran, especially if any harm comes to citizens of common market countries.

Back in kinder, gentler America, however, little has taken place. Secretary of State James Baker couldn't work up any more fury than to warn that the ayatollah's decree would defer Iran's re-entry into the club of civilized nations. And his boss, the leader of the free world, didn't say a thing until pressed on the issue yesterday. Even then, he could say no more than Mr. Baker.

In short, the man Americans most hate thus has repealed the constitutional amendment they most revere: the First. The ayatollah's act and America's response have sent the message that our fundamental freedoms have become contingent upon the goodwill of terrorists. If the bad guys get angry, we roll up the Constitution.

Civilized nations fall when they cease defending the principles upon which their societies rest. Teddy Roosevelt, who helped make America a credible world power, certainly understood that when he cabled the Moroccan chieftain responsible for kidnapping American citizen Ion Perdicaris. He wrote, "Perdicaris alive or the Raisuli dead."

Before George Bush and James Baker jet away today for Emperor Hirohito's funeral, they ought to send the ayatollah a similar love letter: "If your threat harms any American, you and your country will pay the price."

## THE CHRISTIAN SCIENCE MONITOR
*Boston, MA, February 17, 1989*

RARELY in the modern era has a novel been the cause of international incidents, including violent demonstrations. But the Muslim world is in upheaval over a book that has been published in Britain and is about to appear in the United States.

The book is "The Satanic Verses," by Salman Rushdie, who was born in Bombay to Muslim parents but now lives in London. A capacious, complex interweaving of realism and fantasy – and the winner of a prestigious literary award in Britain – the novel has provoked wrath throughout the Islamic world.

Muslim opinion leaders have denounced as blasphemous dream sequences suggesting that the wives of the Prophet Muhammad were prostitutes and that the Koran is not God's infallible word. (Mr. Rushdie says the detractors are distorting his work.)

The book has been banned in Egypt, Saudi Arabia, Bangladesh, and India, which, though predominantly Hindu, has a large Muslim minority. Last month Muslim protesters in Bradford, England, publicly burned the novel and demanded that it be withdrawn from booksellers. This month a mob in Islamabad attacked an American cultural center, ostensibly to protest against the imminent release of the book in the US (the book has not been distributed in Pakistan). Most recently, Iran's Ayatollah Ruhollah Khomeini condemned Rushdie to death and called on Muslims to carry out the sentence.

To Western observers, this frenzy of censorship, culminating in a barbaric death threat, is perplexing, even frightening. The battle for freedom of expression has largely been won in democratic countries (which makes the action of the Indian government particularly disturbing). To most Westerners, moreover, freedom of expression is a universal value, not one rooted in a peculiar culture. They hold that every voice is entitled to be heard, that truth is best gleaned in a free "marketplace of ideas," and that protests should be made through the media of civil discourse.

But Westerners should not be glib in their – quite proper – denunciation of censorship. For one thing, many Christians also are sensitive to what they regard as misinterpretations of received truth or, if you will, revelation. This lay behind the recent outcry in the US over the film "The Last Temptation of Christ."

Westerners must also bear in mind the troubled history of dealings between the Western/Christian world and Islam, in which neither culture is blameless. More is going on in the Muslim turbulence than just hostility to a single book. The upheaval must be viewed as part of a backlash against what many Muslims see as cultural imperialism.

Even so, the hysteria and intolerance that have been unleashed against Rushdie's book are deeply disturbing. Whether motivated by religious zeal or, as some in India and Pakistan have suggested, by political opportunism, fanaticism should not supplant reason in public discourse. Iran offers an example of what excesses can be perpetrated in the name of religious purity.

## THE ARIZONA REPUBLIC
*Phoenix, AZ, February 18, 1989*

IN fundamentalist forms of religion, the Devil is nearly as important as God. The ethos of fundamentalism is deeply rooted in a dualistic view of the world, a contest between equal and competing forces — darkness and light, good and evil, God and Satan.

For fundamentalists, shades of gray are missing. Their palette consists of stark blacks and brilliant whites, no sense of irony, only truth and falsehood. The fundamentalists' *idee fixe* is the existence of an arch-adversary. This is the theological reference point — "the devil made me do it" — that comprehends the universe and all the vagaries of life.

Demagogues have an intuitive sense for the spiritual disposition of the true believer. They know how to manipulate the fundamentalist tendency to simplify existence into one epic struggle, turning the contest to political ends. Hitler did it with the Jewish arch-enemy, Stalin demonized the *kulaks*, Christian fundamentalists blame godless communism and secular humanism for the nation's ills.

The Ayatollah Khomeini is a master of the art. Just as it appeared that the tide of his fundamentalist Shiite Islamic revolution had been turned back — having failed to push itself beyond Iran into Iraq in the Persian Gulf War — along came Salman Rushdie, award-winning author and back-sliding Moslem, with his bizarre, convoluted novel, *The Satanic Verses*. The furor has been a godsend for the Iranian imam, and for the sale of the book.

Seizing the opportunity created by an upwelling of popular Moslem protest against Islamic religious themes in the previously obscure novel, the ayatollah has used the furor to reassert his claim to the unofficial title "Defender of the Faith." The ayatollah called on the faithful to hunt down and kill the apostate Mr. Rushdie, promising instant bliss for the assassin should he be sent to his reward.

Just in case assurances of heavenly felicity proved an insufficient incentive, the ayatollah posted a reward of a few million dollars. One cannot, it seems, always depend on sincere, but often inept, martyrs. Occasionally it is necessary to call upon professionals.

The ayatollah is manipulating the popular hysteria over the Rushdie novel — not one Moslem in a million has read it — to offset the recent gains by some of the more pragmatic leaders in Iran (parliamentary speaker Hashemi Rafsanjani, for one) who have been nudging Iran closer to the West and even to the Great Satan itself, the United States. When forces of moderation threaten to bank the fires of fanaticism, the ayatollah regularly fine-tunes his revolution in this way.

Moslem extremists elsewhere also are exploiting the Rushdie book. Fundamentalist leaders in Pakistan have whipped the people into a frenzy in an attempt to undermine the administration of President Benazir Bhutto, doubly despised for being a woman and a moderate Moslem.

The ayatollah is a cunning old mountebank who has caught other Moslem leaders napping in the game of one-upmanship. His bold stroke in the face of the silence from other Moslem spokesmen has at once endeared him to the fundamentalist masses and cooled the warming relationship between Iran and the Western powers. Rather than calling for his execution, the ayatollah should have bestowed on Mr. Rushdie a reward for services rendered.

## The Hartford Courant
*Hartford, CT, February 24, 1989*

The furor over the Ayatollah Ruhollah Khomeini's threat against the life of author Salman Rushdie did not bypass Hartford.

Earlier this week, Dr. Ali Imran Hashmi, president of the Islamic Center of Hartford and director of respiratory therapy at Manchester Memorial Hospital, was reported to have agreed with the ayatollah's assassination order. Nafees Rahman, the center's director of religious affairs, reportedly also concurred that the killing of Mr. Rushdie would be appropriate.

Now, however, Dr. Hashmi denies ever saying that the author of "The Satanic Verses" deserves to die. The doctor objects to the novel, but doesn't believe in punishing the writer with death.

Having been embroiled in the controversy, it would be appropriate for Dr. Hashmi and Mr. Rahman to speak more clearly than they have. Let them issue a written statement, or hold a news conference.

Sadly, some American Moslems have made statements in support of the ayatollah's kill-the-author order. By doing so, they have maligned Islam and shown contempt for basic humanitarian values.

Most Americans respect the constitutional guarantee of free speech. They tolerate, and many enthusiastically embrace, the concept of the marketplace of competing ideas. All but the fanatical among us recoil in horror at the notion that an author should be put to death for writing something, no matter how unpopular or offensive.

Mohammad Zaheer, a professor of economics at Manchester Community College and a member of the Islamic Center, asked about Dr. Hashmi's original reported comments, said that if you live in America, you have to believe in the freedom to publish. Dr. Hashmi, who admitted to being "emotional" about the Rushdie book when he was interviewed last week, now is quoted saying he does not "follow Khomeini and I am not for killing" the author. He also said the book should not be banned. Those comments show a more tolerant face of Islam.

Ironically, some people who were critical of Dr. Hashmi based on the original stories called for him to be fired from his job at Manchester Community Hospital. They forgot, perhaps, that the First Amendment is an umbrella that covers all.

## THE DENVER POST
*Denver, CO, February 22, 1989*

AYATOLLAH Ruholla Khomeini's death threat against novelist Salman Rushdie attacks the most sacred political beliefs of the world's democracies — freedom of religion, freedom of expression and freedom of dissent.

Initially, Khomeini's murderous words likely were aimed at appeasing religious radicals within Iran. Faced with a faltering economy and continued internal strife, Khomeini needed an external scapegoat to bolster his hometown popularity — and Rushdie provided a convenient target.

Many Moslems genuinely were angered by Rushdie's writings. But many were more appalled by Khomeini's call to commit murder. Khomeini simply does not represent all of the world's 600 million Moslems, who consider themselves peaceful people. Most Moslems are devout, but few are fanatics.

Yet Khomeini's threat of violence against a British citizen has widened the gulf of misunderstanding between his Islamic nation and the world's democracies. The U.S. denounced Khomeini's threats, and 12 European nations recalled their envoys from Tehran. At the time Iran most needs Western aid simply to care for its people, Khomeini's rhetoric resurrected the specter of medieval intolerance.

Unfortunately, Khomeini's virulent words forced Rushdie into hiding and compelled many American bookstores to pull his novel from their shelves. But at bottom, this dispute isn't over a book. It's over whether the world's democracies will let a religious fanatic terrorize them into surrendering their beloved beliefs. If Khomeini does succeed in silencing Rushdie, he will have won a terrible victory against freedom of thought.

## THE RICHMOND NEWS LEADER
*Richmond, VA,*
*February 22, 1989*

The news brings two items reflecting yet again the infamous Liberal double standard.

(1) The literary and political communities rightly rose up in wrath over the Ayatollah Khomeini's death threat against novelist Salman Rushdie. Khomeini ought to be informed that the U.S. and its allies will consider a personal attack against Rushdie as an attack on their countries — thereby justifying military and economic retaliation against Iran.

But even as European countries protested the death threat by removing their diplomats from Tehran, a Czech show trial received scant attention. A noted playwright and some friends were sentenced to nine months in jail for discussing truths that the Communist regime finds unpalatable. Indeed, in every Eastern Bloc country writers are imprisoned for refusing to submit to Party censorship.

When will the Western countries remove their diplomats from Moscow, Warsaw, Prague, and elsewhere? If they can pull their people out of Iran, why can't they pull them out of Eastern Europe?

— (2) David Duke's election to the Louisiana legislature has embarrassed the GOP. Duke, a former leader of the KKK, ran as a Republican (he defeated a mainstream Republican to win), and now the national GOP is told that it must censure him, that the refusal to do so will suggest the party is racist. The GOP plans to repudiate Duke. It is worth noting that the primary issue in the Louisiana campaign was not race but taxes.

The pious denunciations of Duke ring hollow. Robert Byrd, one of the Senate's most powerful Democrats, is a former Klansman: The Democratic Party hasn't censured him. Harry Truman consorted with Klansmen, but the Party has not retroactively repudiated him. Hugo Black, who became one of the Supreme Court's great voices for civil rights, was member of the Klan, too.

And during the Forties and early Fifties, Democratic Congressman George Crockett of Michigan made common cause with Communist sympathizers. Will the organs of enlightened opinion demanding Duke's censure by the Republicans similarly demand Crockett's censure by the Democrats? Will they demand that the Democrats repudiate any Senators, Congressmen, or state officials who had ties to the smarmy Leftist outfits that proliferated during the Sixties?

If not, why not?

## The Times-Picayune
*New Orleans, LA, February 17, 1989*

How is the world to deal with a fanatic like Ayatollah Khomeini, a modern-day Old Man of the Mountain who publicly dispatches martyr-assassins to murder such as British-Indian author Salman Rushdie for alleged disrespectful treatment of the Prophet Mohammed in a novel of philosophical fantasy?

Simply ignoring him is not possible since his followers, though they are a minority even among fundamentalist Moslems, are a disruptive group against whom the world is forced to take measures to protect itself.

Some no doubt would prefer to reply in kind with a "Get Khomeini" squad. But that would only lower us to his depth and not solve the larger problem of violent anti-Western Islamic fundamentalism.

This is a movement that has brought occasional turmoil to Islamic nations throughout Islam's history and was revitalized in a particularly virulent form by the Khomeini takeover in Iran in 1979. Islam does not require a separation of religion and politics, and political movements more often than not assume the form of religious reform or revival.

The ayatollah turns up the fundamentalism when he wants to direct his followers' attention away from something — the losing war with Iraq, a shambles of an economy. Perhaps this time he wants it understood that he is still in charge and as great a defender of the true faith as ever even though his more pragmatic associates are working to mend foreign fences and reduce Iran's isolation.

So there is at least as much politics as there is religious umbrage involved in the Rushdie affair, and the world should deal with it as a political matter. When the effective leader of a state publicly orders the murder of a citizen of another state — and even offers a bounty payment or an eternity in paradise, whichever turns out to apply — he removes his country from the company of civilized nations.

Iran has not been improving its relations with other countries, particularly Western countries, because of any mellowing of its belligerence. It needs good relations to reduce political tensions and particularly to gain access to the economic resources of the prosperous democracies.

During the dark Khomeini night in Iran, the rest of the world has managed to live without normal relations with Iran. It can continue to do so.

All the countries Iran is now courting should so inform the Iranian government. No further efforts toward regularizing relations, particularly economic relations, should be made until the ayatollah publicly calls back his assassins.

And the Iranian government should be further informed that if terrorist actions attributable to the ayatollah's call to arms are taken — against foreign airlines, as already threatened, or government facilities or personnel — the civilized world will find ways to hold outlaw Iran accountable.

## THE PLAIN DEALER
*Cleveland, OH, February 17, 1989*

What will it profit Salman Rushdie to have written a best-seller if he has to remain in hiding the rest of his life? Vengeful Muslims, led by the unspeakable Ayatollah Ruhollah Khomeini, already have inflicted severe punishment on Rushdie for his novel "The Satanic Verses," which they say blasphemes the Prophet Mohammed. By calling for his murder —and putting a price on his head—Khomeini and his fellow clerics have practically guaranteed that at all times, even in the distant future, Rushdie will have to be wary of hit squads of Muslim fanatics, or even lone assassins, eager to kill him in the name of Allah.

Khomeini and his brother zealots may also have succeeded in extending their brand of censorship beyond Islam's borders to countries that admittedly, in the past, have experienced outbreaks of bigotry in the name of one brand of Christianity or another. Rushdie's book is selling well in Britain, where he lives, and in the United States—a heavy demand was reported in Greater Cleveland; but publishers in France and Italy regrettably are hesitant to release the novel. Rushdie himself decided to cancel a promotional tour of the United States, a wise move under the circumstances, but deplorable because it is necessary.

The most outrageous aspect of this dismal affair is Khomeini's resort to raw invocation to assasination. Not far behind in reprehensibility is the exploitation of the issue for ungodly purposes by politicians and clerics in Iran and Pakistan. Demonstrations that included burning copies of the book in England and marching elsewhere were disheartening for what they said about the closed mentality that inspired them. But they did not directly threaten the well-being of the author or publishers who dared to print his book.

Khomeini's intervention, and that of other Muslim spokesmen who have suggested Rushdie deserves to be killed, is not only dangerous to the author, but an affront to the very notion of free societies hospitable to a panoply of ideas. Iran's representatives, and those of other nations that have ganged up so despicably on Rushdie, should be told as much.

As well, it is a warning to democratic governments, especially those that have been attempting to rebuild ties to Khomeini following the end of the Persian Gulf war; the ayatollah simply is not to be trusted. Not least, it is a warning to guard against over-optimism when assessing political developments in countries where Islam is dominant. Pro-Western moderates may be not only in short supply, but may have a low life expectancy as well.

## The Washington Post
*Washington, DC, February 18, 1989*

IN A REMARKABLY craven response to a vague threat, many of this country's biggest book dealers have hastily pulled Salman Rushdie's book off their shelves. It is a shameful performance. The first to go was the Waldenbooks chain, the country's biggest bookseller.

The book, "The Satanic Verses," is beginning to be hard to find. The holy war declared on it by Moslem fundamentalists has increased interest in it, and some stores are genuinely sold out. Others, like some of the Waldenbooks branches, occasionally have it under the counter to be produced surreptitiously on request. And some, in a panic, have carted their copies off to the basement. It seems to be chiefly the smaller independent bookstores that have shown the courage to keep the book on display. It's another reason to think warmly of the independents, and to be grateful that the chains do not entirely dominate the book trade.

"This is not a freedom of speech issue," a Waldenbooks official is quoted as saying, "the sole reason is the protection of our employees." But Waldenbooks is mistaken about that too. It is obviously and inescapably a freedom of speech issue. Waldenbooks, and the many other stores that have done the same thing, are engaging in what's known as self-censorship. No one has forced them to hide the book. They are avoiding attack by a preemptive surrender.

The American publisher, Viking Penguin, is bringing out a second printing of the book. When it arrives, booksellers will no longer be able to claim that it's unavailable. But perhaps by that time Waldenbooks and the others will have had an opportunity to reflect on the dangers of self-censorship.

If it's wrong for the stores to cave in to the current protests, it's far worse for a government to join them. But Canada's customs service yesterday began seizing imports of "The Satanic Verses."

Canada? The Canadian edition is printed abroad, and the government said stiffly that it is acting on a complaint by a Moslem group. It will hold the books until it determines whether they violate the law against the distribution of hate literature.

That's truly grotesque. Those laws proscribe material that incites to genocide or to the hatred of specific people or groups. They have nothing to do with the kind of religious dispute that Mr. Rushdie's book has ignited. The government says that it hopes to have the question settled in a day or two. Since there's only one possible answer, it's unlikely that any enduring threat to free expression will emerge. But since Canadians are sophisticated readers, and since the book has been on sale there for four months, the border seizures certainly suffice to make the Canadian government look very foolish.

One of the purposes of literature is to cause readers to reflect on human weakness and cowardice, as well as on courage and wisdom. Mr. Rushdie's book is succeeding in that respect to a degree that its author could never have imagined.

## The News and Observer
*Raleigh, NC, February 21, 1989*

Americans cherish their First Amendment right to read what they choose. But what good is that freedom if the books they want to read have been withdrawn from the market because of a bully's threat?

That's why the Ayatollah Khomeini's death threat against Salman Rushdie, author of "Satanic Verses," should repel even those Americans who have no interest in a fictional treatment of Moslem lore. The ayatollah has managed to curb freedom of expression not just in his own land, but in the nation that sees itself as the world's bastion of intellectual freedom. Fears of terrorist attacks have led three of America's largest book chains to pull the novel from their shelves.

In a column on the opposite page, William Safire explores troublesome aspects of this affair. The growth of giant chain book retailers has given enormous power to the chains not just to distribute books, but to suppress them for whatever reason is deemed appropriate. And there is the enormous gulf that becomes apparent between Judeo-Christian and Islamic cultures.

In the United States, books, plays and films that offend certain groups are regularly denounced, often in harsh terms. Recall, for example, the recent film "The Last Temptation of Christ." Suppression and death threats to authors of course are not acceptable options. Among the Shia Moslems of Iran, however, no experience similar to the Western Enlightenment has prepared them to be tolerant of what they see as blasphemy.

So what is to be done? The Iranian regime may appear immune to American pressure, but the Bush administration must take a strong stand, if only for the symbolic value. The Rushdie affair again brings home the truth that there can be no compromise with tyranny or terrorism — whether it is blowing up airplanes or restricting a nation's freedom to read what it chooses.

# The News Journal

*Wilmington, DE, February 21, 1989*

THE fundamental fact about the fierce old fellow is that any mentions of forbearance or forgiveness in his holy book are in chapters that he has managed to avoid reading throughout his long lifetime of study.

The Ayatollah Ruhollah Khomeini, religious and temporal head of the Islamic Republic of Iran stands firm on his demands for the execution of Salman Rushdie, a subject of another state, because of the latter's book, "The Satanic Verses."

Many expressions of indignation and outrage over the novel have been heard recently from the Islamic world.

The ayatollah and those closest to his fundamentalist approach to Islam, however, are those responsible for the death threats against the author and his associates.

They also are the sources of the offers of large monetary rewards for anyone, believer in Islam or not, who would kill Mr. Rushdie for his offense.

Some other voices from worldwide Islam stress the teachings of the Koran on the subject of tolerance, of the need for discussion and dialogue.

There is no doubt of the serious nature of the ayatollah's original threat. It was enough to send Mr. Rushdie into hiding under the protection of authorities in the United Kingdom, where he lives as a British subject.

There is no doubt, either, that the ayatollah continues to mean his threat. Mr. Rushdie apologized to Islam for any offense. No matter what apology was issued, or what repentance shown, or what amends made, even if the author "becomes the most pious man of time," the ayatollah said, it still would be incumbent on every Moslem to bend every effort to "send him to hell."

We cannot avoid comparing the fundamentalist fury over the Rushdie book to the furor generated some months ago, mainly in the United States, by the film, "The Last Temptation of Christ."

In that controversy there also was a great deal of outrage, a great deal of failure to communicate, a great refusal to understand the positions of those on the other sides of the arguments.

There was talk of boycotting the film, of buying every copy so as to incinerate it.

There was, however, no public discussion of executing the author, director, producer or actors involved. That difference lies partly in the name of the nation over which the ayatollah, at least ostensibly, presides.

Iran is an "Islamic Republic." In a situation where a state and a state religion are so related, it is not unheard of to have recourse to extreme measures in the name of such a thing as censorship.

Others speaking in the name of Islam but from outside Iran suggested that theirs was a faith for the devout, but not for the fanatic.

The ayatollah's fanaticism resembles that of others who have gained dominion over secular affairs in the name of this or that religion.

Stories of death threats and of rewards of millions of dollars to carry them out are the sorts that would have been carried in newspapers of the Middle Ages, if there had been newspapers then.

# DAILY NEWS

*New York, NY, February 16, 1989*

"I inform the proud Moslem people of the world that the author of the 'Satanic Verses' book, which is against Islam, the Prophet and the Koran, and all those involved in its publication who were aware of its contents, are sentenced to death. I ask all Moslems to execute them quickly wherever they are found so that no others dare to do such a thing. Whoever is killed doing this will be regarded as a martyr and will go directly to heaven."

To begin with, it's important to remember that there are millions of Moslems throughout the world who do not follow the orders or the reasoning—if that word can be used—of Ayatolla Ruhollah Khomeini, author of the jolly little declaration printed above these words. A second thing is well to bear in mind: In more primitive, bygone times, all sorts of sects and societies, including many that ostensibly were Christian, have ordered and imposed death, dismemberment and other horrors on people perceived to have been blasphemous. And a third: The author of "The Satanic Verses," Moslem-born Salman Rushdie, insists "the novel is not an attack on Islam or any other religion, but an attempt to challenge preconceptions and to examine the conflict between the secular and religious views of the world."

With all that said, a lesson remains: Anyone who continues to regard Khomeini and other leaders or implementers of Islamic fundamentalism as civilized or susceptible to civilized values or persuasions is wrong. Dead wrong.

# The Clarion-Ledger Jackson Daily News

*Jackson, MS, February 21, 1989*

Terrorism has taken a new twist in the past week, this time focusing its violence on a book, *The Satanic Verses*, by 41-year-old Indian-born British writer Salman Rushdie.

Book burning, of course, is not new, and the world should be far from shocked that these two types of intimidation have been fused. But even with this age-old attempt at censorship comes a rather novel threat: Not only to burn the book but to "burn" (kill) the author — no, even worse, "to send him to hell," in the words of Iran's Ayatollah Ruhollah Khomeini.

Iran's fundamentalists can rail against the book all they want to — Moslems say it blasphemes their religion, among other offenses — but their effort to export its repression abroad is reprehensible.

The governments of the United States, Britain, Spain and West Germany are right to condemn the campaign against Rushdie and to stand up to the threats and call Khomeini's bluff.

Unfortunately, and surprisingly, some of the large bookstore chains have stopped displaying or selling the book. Unsurprisingly, that has triggered a frenzied demand for the book and shortages at independent stores.

One Jackson store has sold all its copies, and may all local bookstores cash in on it. May the book sell and sell and sell — if, for no other reason, to show that Mississippians and other Americans are not afraid of ideas or those who would try to restrain or hold them down. The book may be praiseworthy or contemptible, but people have a right to form their own opinions.

The rest of the world can ill afford to quake every time an Iranian suicide squad is dispatched. The sooner Iran's dictatorial government or that or any other nation employing terrorism learns it will firmly resisted, the safer the world community will be.

Secretary of State James A. Baker III's declaration that the United States will oppose such "state-sponsored terrorism" should help persuade Iran's leaders that this form of taking hostages will not be tolerated and is not the thing to do if Iran is really serious about rejoining the community of civilized nations.

The British should be supported in protecting Rushdie, who is in hiding under Scotland Yard guard. Iranian fanatics must accept the fact that extraordinary measures will be taken to protect freedom of speech and conscience.

## THE ANN ARBOR NEWS
*Ann Arbor, MI, February 23, 1989*

It's not every day the nation's top chain bookstores take a bestseller and pull it off their shelves because of intimidation.

And it's not *any* day that the Ayatollah Khomeini should have veto power over America's reading choices.

It's certain Salman Rushdie's novel is offensive to many Muslims. And it may be that employees of bookstores which stock "The Satanic Verses," are at risk. But booksellers shouldn't hide behind "protecting the safety of employees" to knuckle under to the mad mullah.

Many Christians were equally outraged by Nikos Kazantzakis's novel "The Last Temptation of Christ" when it came out and even more outraged by the movie of the same name. Despite the furor, the film played in cities across America and then the uproar died.

The larger issue is not the literary value of Rushdie's book but whether he has the right to express his views without intimidation or censorship. It's no credit to chain bookstores B. Dalton, Waldenbooks and Barnes & Noble that they yielded with such unseemly haste to bullying tactics from abroad.

The book apparently was "too hot" and the international shock waves too much for the booksellers. But if anybody needs to stand up to the threat of terrorism, censorship and Gestapo-like tactics, it should be men and women associated with the free traffic in words — publishers, journalists and book dealers.

In the minds of many people overseas, the U.S.A. is, for better or worse, the land of free speech and tolerance for the other fellow's point of view.

When we compromise ourselves on those important issues, we lose face and respect. The Ayatollah doesn't call the shots in this country. And fear of his death squads, while a threat to be taken seriously, isn't the threat that suppression of books poses to a free people.

That's why it's important for the bookseller chains to show courage and put "The Satanic Verses" back on their shelves. And it's equally important that the government, as President Bush finally did Tuesday, condemn as outrageous and unacceptable the Iranian government's reckless disregard for international law and civilized behavior.

Here is one occasion for America to speak up for what it stands and at the same time, tell the fanatic in Teheran where to get off.

In the Rushdie affair, it's also important to avoid stereotyping Islam. Just as the Moral Majority doesn't speak for all Christians, the Shiite Muslims don't speak for all of Islam, which is a religion sharing many of the values Christianity and Judaism hold.

Also, America would do well to reflect upon the danger that religious intolerance holds for a political democracy. If a foreign despot can almost succeed in "purifying" *our* bookshelves of viewpoints hostile to his own, a homegrown version of such intolerance could try the same thing. The mischief potential should not be taken lightly.

Free speech in America means exposure to the widest possible range of viewpoints, including that which is objectionable. Trying to muzzle opinions and free thought by protest only tears at the very fabric that has made our society so strong.

## The Birmingham News
*Birmingham, AL, February 18, 1989*

The mercurial Khomeini this week denounced the novel *The Satanic Verses* as blasphemy against the Islamic faith and urged Moslems around the world to execute its author, Salman Rushdie, and the book's publishers.

Iran offered a $2.6 million reward for Rushdie's killer.

This is a calculated political move, not a spontaneous outburst of religious zealotry.

In fact, protests against Rushdie's book had been raging in the Moslem world for days before Khomeini issued his outrageous order. The ayatollah surely knew its contents long before he spoke.

Iran's stumbling conduct of its decade of war with Iraq, and its about-face toward peace in that conflict, have tarnished Khomeini's image with Moslem leaders. Iran's recent efforts at closer ties with some Western countries have caused many to wonder if the Islamic revolution is running out of steam.

And the internal economic chaos in Iran dictates that some drastic move be made to get the people's eyes toward heaven and away from their pocketbooks.

Thus, to shore up prestige, Khomeini is one-upping the other Moslem leaders.

Seen against that backdrop, his very serious threat on Rushdie's life takes on even more sinister shadings.

Khomeini is openly ordering a political assassination against a citizen of a foreign country, and perhaps against publishers here in the United States.

At the very least, the warming trend in relations with Iran should quickly turn cold. The ayatollah has to be shown that civilized nations will not tolerate such thuggery.

If harm comes to Americans because of the ayatollah's demogoguery, it should be treated as we would treat any nation's encouragement of a terrorist act against us. An appropriately forceful response would be required.

None of which is to say that Moslems don't have the right to protest Rushdie's book. They certainly do, just as Christians in this country had the right to protest against the controversial film *The Last Temptation of Christ*.

But murder is no less damnable when ordered under the banner of religion.

## St. Louis Review
*St. Louis, MO, February 24, 1989*

Some years ago, an author's sure key to successful promotion of his work was to have his book banned in Boston. More recently, successful promotion is directly proportional to the amount of salacious gossip, derogatory anecdotes, calumny, detraction, and outright lies directed at celebrities in the political, entertainment and religious fields.

During the past year, Christians were appalled by the scurrilous depiction of Jesus in the film "The Last Temptation of Christ." In many cities, demonstrators picketed the theaters where the movie was being shown. The threat of boycott was raised against the producers and sponsors of the movie. All of these actions fall within the legitimate expression of opposition in Western society.

The now-famous book Satanic Verses clearly contains material offensive to devout Moslems. The reaction by the Ayatollah Khomeini and fundamentalist Moslems, calling for the murder of the author and his publishers, has shocked the Western world. Yet, it is in keeping with the creed and the society that reveres the concept of holy war and the utter destruction of the enemy.

Authors, publishers and producers ought to recognize that there are deeply held convictions and values that should not be trampled on gratuitously. The restraints of Christian morality and democratic feedom of speech should not be interpreted as a license to ridicule and attack cherished values.

In the short run, the threats of the Ayatollah have been effective. The offending author as well as his publishers and book dealers have been intimidated. Nevertheless, the vengeful, murderous invective from Iran has done more damage to worldwide respect for Islam than could ever have been accomplished by the book. In the Satanic Verses incident all have behaved badly.

[Editorial cartoon: figure labeled "SATANIC VERSE" depicting Ayatollah Khomeini with speech bubble listing: TERRY ANDERSON, TERRY WAITE, THOMAS SUTHERLAND, WILLIAM BUCKLEY, PETER KILBURN, FRANK REED, JOSEPH CICIPPIO, EDWARD TRACY, ROBERT POLHILL, ALANN STEEN, JESSE TURNER... — Palm Beach Post, Wright, 1989]

## The Seattle Times
*Seattle, WA, February 22, 1989*

AFTER a moment of stunned silence, civilized nations have recovered from the sheer audacity of Iran's death sentence on novelist Salman Rushdie to rise and condemn the act.

Britain and the 12 members of the European Community have called their diplomats home from Tehran. If the Ayatollah Ruhollah Khomeini is bent on Iran living in hard-scrabble isolation, exasperated nations are ready to accommodate him.

After a decade as an outlaw nation, Iran had been inching back toward a gritty acceptance. Eight bloody years of pointless slaughter with Iraq had created such desperate economic straits that Iran would be forced to mind its manners. Or so it seemed.

Ten years ago the world was slow to recognize the malevolent power behind the so-called students who swarmed over the U.S. embassy compound in Tehran. Over the next decade, the ayatollah's fingerprints would be found on the bombing of a U.S. Marine barracks and numerous kidnappings.

Throughout all of this, Khomeini's personal power has been as important as his revolution of Islamic fundamentalism. He has combined the flair of a showman with the visceral instincts of street-wise activist to protect himself and his cause.

Lest there be too much focus on his country's economic condition, the ayatollah found another foreign bogeyman: a 41-year-old writer living in London.

Rushdie, author of "The Satanic Verses" is a convenient foil. He was sentenced to death for blaspheming the Prophet Mohammed. The author denied any intent to offend, but nonetheless issued an apology, which Khomeini brushed aside.

Civilized nations must condemn Khomeini's manipulations in the strongest terms.

Khomeini's shameless exploitations in the name of religion mock the heritage of a faith that honored learning and preserved knowledge of science, philosophy, history, literature and the arts during the Middle Ages.

## Edmonton Journal
*Edmonton, Alta., February 20, 1989*

By suspending imports of Salman Rushdie's novel, The Satanic Verses, the government of Canada demonstrates the moral bankruptcy of its hate-literature laws.

By allowing one complaint to block distribution of the book, pending investigation of the hate-literature allegation, Canada allows free expression to be held hostage; the policy carries a presumption of guilt rather than innocence.

If the government wanted to investigate the complaint against the novel, it could have gone out and bought a copy. Instead, it imposes a censorship that is arbitrary.

The very premise of the hate-literature law is offensive enough: it says that the power of the state should be used to block the flow of unsavory ideas.

A healthy society rejects repugnant ideas and has an obligation to denounce them. Yet that is an individual obligation — it goes with the individual right of freedom of expression.

When that power passes to the state, the right of free speech is unduly subject to the arbitrary interpretation of the state.

The law as it stands enables any interest group to practise censorship, and to use the government as its agent.

The law is intended principally to block the import of hard-core pornography and of material that incites hatred against a particular group. It is not intended to block the distribution of prize-winning novels that are the object of controversy.

At any rate, it is not Rushdie's novel that is inciting hatred and violence. Violence against the author, and the publishers of the book, is being stirred up by the leader of a militant theocracy.

What's most untenable about the government position is that the book already is widely distributed in Canada. Blocking further imports cannot undo the offence, if there is one, done to some Muslims who object to the book.

Nor would copies of the book already in circulation be seized, if the novel is deemed offensive by the government.

Clumsy laws serve no useful purpose. The hate-literature law, if it should exist at all, must be rethought — to narrow its application and to uphold the presumption of innocence.

## The Des Moines Register
*Des Moines, IA, February 21, 1989*

Freedom of speech, among the most fundamental rights in a democracy, has become the latest victim of terrorist attack by Iran's Ayatollah Khomeini.

Three leading U.S. book retailers have played into Khomeini's hands by pulling from their shelves the book "The Satanic Verses" by Salman Rushdie.

Khomeini has threatened Rushdie's life, as well as those of anyone who cooperated in the publishing and sale of the book, which many believe is a thinly veiled attack on Islam.

In response, B. Dalton, Waldenbooks and the Barnes & Noble chains have removed the novel from their shelves, saying they fear for their employees. Publishers from France, Greece, Turkey and West Germany canceled plans to publish the novel.

Far greater courage has been shown by independent U.S. bookstores continuing to sell the book, as well as publisher Viking Penguin, which has vowed another printing, condemning "censorship by terror and intimidation."

Americans have long fought, and died, protecting freedom. It's shameful that some would throw it all away by cowing to the threats of a terrorist thug.

## ARGUS-LEADER
*Sioux Falls, SD, February 22, 1989*

**EDITORIAL**

Last year, many Americans felt strongly about the movie, *The Last Temptation of Christ*.

The movie was both praised and condemned. Critics called for the film to be boycotted and, in some cases, banned.

Now, a book that ponders another set of sensitive religious issues has touched off a bigger and more dangerous turmoil.

Death threats, violent protests and diplomatic battles have accompanied the international controversy over the book, *The Satanic Verses*, by British author Salman Rushdie.

The Ayatollah Khomeini, spiritual leader of Iran, has declared that Rushdie's novel slanders Islam and has ordered Moslems to kill the author.

This is mostly England's fight. For Americans, if nothing else, the dangerous uproar reinforces the fundamental soundness and value of tolerance, free expression and this nation's practice of separating matters of church and government.

U.S. officials, like English officials, rightly consider Khomeini's threat intolerable.

For many Moslems, Rushdie's book is blasphemous. They complain that *The Satanic Verses* depicts the prophet Mohammed's wives as prostitutes and suggests that he, rather than God, wrote the Koran, Islam's holy book.

The title of Rushdie's book refers to verses Mohammed is believed to have removed from the Koran, thinking they had been inspired by the devil. *The Satanic Verses* has been banned in some countries, including Pakistan, Bangladesh, India and Egypt. The novel has also prompted Moslem protests around the world, including protests in Pakistan and India in which seven people were killed.

Elsewhere, book sales have soared. Khomeini's attempts to suppress *The Satanic Verses* and kill the author have turned the book into a hard-to-find best-seller.

Without all the controversy, Rushdie probably would have remained largely unknown outside of literary circles. Generally, book critics seem to consider him an important writer who takes on significant topics with a style that is difficult to read.

Rushdie, 41, was born into a Moslem family in Bombay, India, but he lives in London. The growing controversy over his book is distressing.

European Common Market governments have withdrawn their top diplomats from Iran to protest Khomeini's death order. England pulled out its entire embassy staff.

In response, Iran has recalled its ambassadors from Common Market countries.

For a while, it appeared that Rushdie might have an escape. Iran's president, Ali Khamenei, said an apology from Rushdie might lead to a pardon. Rushdie apologized, but Khomeini rejected the apology. So, Rushdie remains in protective hiding, and tensions elsewhere in the world increase.

Iran's foreign ministry called Khomeini's order for the death of Rushdie the "consensus judgment of all Moslem leaders throughout the world." That's difficult to believe, because not all Moslems want the author killed.

The United States, which severed diplomatic ties with Iran a decade ago, is not perfect. But at least no one in an official position of power called for the execution of the director of *The Last Temptation of Christ*.

## THE INDIANAPOLIS STAR
*Indianapolis, IN, February 17, 1989*

The international furor over the novel, *The Satanic Verses*, and the Ayatollah Khomeini's offer of a $5.2 million reward to any Iranian who kills the British-Indian author, sounds like a news report from the Dark Ages but is more ominous than any fantasy.

The Khomeini henchman who issued the assassination offer said $1 million would be paid to any foreigner who kills the novelist, 41-year-old Salman Rushdie. In England, where he lives, Rushdie was reported under armed guard.

Khomeini also ordered death for the novel's publishers. They include Viking Press in the United States, which has received bomb threats and a torrent of hate mail, and Viking Penguin in Britain. The book's French publishing house suspended publication, citing the danger to its employees.

The ayatollah is demanding an international ban on the book. Foreign Minister Ali Akbar Velayati said the regime will close cultural centers of all nations allowing its publication.

The uproar is global. In India and Pakistan, six people were killed and 180 injured in riots sparked by the book's U.S. release. In a Bradford, England, Islamic center, the book was burned. In Tehran Wednesday, an estimated 2,000 demonstrators staged a protest outside the British embassy.

Islamic fundamentalists say the novel insults their faith. One story in its complex plot is a satiric tale of the rise of a prophet and religion with irreverent parallels to Mohammed and Islam. This is what detonated the fury.

Demonstrations were staged by fundamentalist Christians in the United States who opposed the release of the film, *The Last Temptation of Christ*, which they branded highly irreverent, but no one ordered a hit on the producer, and no one was injured or killed.

*The Satanic Verses* is, after all, fiction. So intense and widespread is the furor that it appears to have been been orchestrated. The terror-mongers of the Khomeini regime are old hands at that kind of conspiracy.

Forcible denial of freedom of expression has been around for centuries and is common today in many lands. In our country in our time, many books that were once banned are now readily available. The trend in the civilized world has been steadily increasing freedom of expression, publishing, speaking and broadcasting, freedom to read, hear and see.

Islam will not be scarred by one novel any more than Christianity has been scarred by the attacks of thousands of atheists in millions of words or by the misdeeds of its backsliders, so the attack on Salman Rushdie can be misinterpreted.

What is really under attack is freedom.

## Murdoch Forced to Sell New York Post

In appropriating $99 million to the Federal Communications Commission for fiscal 1988, Congress Dec. 22, 1987 attached a condition that apparently ruled out Australia-born press baron Rupert Murdoch's continued ownership of both newspapers and television stations in New York and Boston. FCC rules prohibited cross-ownership of a television station and a daily newspaper in the same market, but the FCC had granted Murdoch temporary waivers from the rules to allow him time to come into compliance with them. Murdoch, meanwhile, was seeking permanent relief from the rules.

The restriction, which was not contained in the original Senate or House versions of the omnibus spending bill, was added in conference by Sen. Ernest F. Hollings (D, S.C.), at the request of Sen. Edward M. Kennedy (D, Mass.), a target of frequent criticism in the pages of Murdoch's *Boston Herald*. The restriction stipulated that none of the appropriations could be used "to repeal, to retroactively apply changes in, or to begin or continue a re-examination of the rules of the FCC with respect to the common ownership of a daily newspaper and a television station" where the station's primary signal "encompasses the entire community in which the newspaper is published."

Nor could the FCC, it added, "extend the time period of current grants of temporary waivers to achieve compliance" with the agency's rules.

Murdoch reportedly was the only person currently granted such waivers.

# THE BLADE
*Toledo, OH, January 10, 1988*

WE wonder if it is true, as more than a few have charged, that Sen. Edward Kennedy, just for spite, sneaked a rider onto the recent omnibus budget bill, forcing application of the FCC ban on media cross-ownership to publisher Rupert Murdoch?

The Australian-born Mr. Murdoch, now a U.S. citizen, is cast roughly in the mold of the early William Randolph Hearst. Like Hearst, Mr. Murdoch is something of a lowest-denominator populist, trashing the politicians in his paper and along with them most of the higher standards of journalism. But he is financially successful, and this has allowed him to buy some respectability, usually by acquiring respectable papers like the Times of London and the Chicago Sun-Times.

If anyone could prove to be Mr. Murdoch's nemesis, it would be Senator Kennedy. The Murdoch-owned Boston Herald has never said a kind word about the senator and has printed many unkind words, headlines, and photos. This scenario assumes that Edward Kennedy was at least partially driven by desire to avenge himself upon the Herald and not his abiding concern for enforcing anti-trust laws.

One has to wonder about this use of the law for vengeance by power brokers and about a legislative process that allowed the two New York senators, Daniel Moynihan and Alfonse D'Amato, to say they didn't know what was in the bill they voted for.

Then again, perhaps it was Mr. Kennedy who met his match. It took Teddy Kennedy to make Rupert Murdoch look good — even principled. The publisher now says that if relief is obtainable in no other way, he will make the ultimate sacrifice and sell his Boston TV station in order to keep his newspaper. Without an FCC waiver he cannot keep both properties in the same market.

Meanwhile, saving the New York Post, which is not much of a paper, has become a *cause celebre* in New York. Senator Moynihan will introduce a bill to allow the FCC to extend its waiver of the cross-ownership law. That would permit Mr. Murdoch to keep his TV station and his paper. And Mayor Koch will seek a bond issue that could ease capital investment for new printing plants for the Post and the Daily News.

Mayor Koch, a Democrat like Senator Kennedy, questioned the senator's character and no one blanched. Senator Kennedy has come to be known and accepted as one of the leading bullies in Congress — and one of the most cynical ones — when it comes to dealing with those with whom he disagrees.

# The Hutchinson News
*Hutchinson, KS, January 10, 1988*

Ted Kennedy is not only a vindictive coward, he's a lousy shot.

He set out to kill a Boston newspaper that he didn't like, but now it appears he may have killed a New York newspaper instead.

Kennedy and fellow senator Ernest Hollings conspired before Christmas to insert a vindictive piece of personal legislation in the massive 1,000-page national budget bill. At the time, they didn't have the courage to disclose what they were doing.

They put into effect a law that could, effectively, put the Boston Herald and the New York Post out of business, since both are losers, financially. The papers are owned by newspaper tycoon Rupert Murdoch, who would be required under the sneaky Kennedy law either to sell the ailing newspapers or sell the profitable TV stations in those cities.

Late this week, Murcoch surprised them all.

He said he'll keep the losing Boston Herald alive, and perhaps kill the New York Post. The Post is the nation's oldest newspaper in continuous publication, and employs more than 1,000 people.

Stay tuned to this one. It ought to make fascinating reading throughout the rest of the winter.

One thing is certain, already, however.

Don't ever be an innocent bystander when Ted Kennedy's around. He might get mad at somebody else, and you'd be in deep trouble. (Which is where all his senatorial colleagues should be today, for not having spotted his vindictive cowardice before.)

## THE SAGINAW NEWS
*Saginaw, MI, January 16, 1988*

The "omnibus" national budget bill is more like a little shop of horrors. You never know what deviltry will appear just around the next page.

Here's a provision, reportedly sponsored by Sen. Edward M. Kennedy, that might have the effect of killing two newspapers, the New York Post and the Boston Herald. The latter, as it happens, has been a harsh critic of one Sen. Kennedy of Massachusetts.

Here's another little gem giving states power to raise the speed limit on roads other than interstates.

If the year brings a rash of new business pull-outs from South Africa, chances are that goodness, in the sense of revulsion against apartheid, will have nothing to do with it. The bill calls for double taxation of such investments, even though principled employers can set highly visible examples of fairness and justice in that troubled land.

It's enough to make you afraid to look in the footnotes or check that rattle in the amendments. In a $600 billion piece of legislation, covering appropriations for 13 major programs, many such monsters might lurk, inserted literally in the dark of night at a conference to reconcile the House and Senate versions. It is an atrocious way to run a country when the 65 mph extension, for instance, does not bring even cursory review of evidence that the higher limit is costing hundreds of lives.

President Reagan has long sought authority, routine in the case of state governors, for a line-item veto. He has failed so far to communicate his argument to the country. But by its own failure, Congress is doing a pretty good job for him.

Absent the line-item power, a president has no choice but to reject everything, or accept everything, no matter how repulsive the special-interest or pork-barrel gremlins.

Even members of Congress can't bear to look. "Some of the most important questions of our time are reduced to a simple, binary question: yes or no," said Rep. Robert H. Michel, the House Republican leader. Rep. William H. Natcher, D-Ky., a senior member of the House Appropriations panel, agreed: "If I were the president, I'd feel the same way this one does."

Natcher's teammate on the committee, Democrat Vic Fazio of California, said many lawmakers felt "a revulsion against the process this year" and vowed not to repeat it in 1988.

That's a good New Year's resolution. Unfortunately, it depends on the individual as well as collective responsibility of Congress to avoid turning the nation's spending program into a midnight massacre. Given the recent record, that is a risky proposition.

A line-item veto would not deprive Congress of its own spending authority. Vetoes would remain subject to override. But when members know they may have to explain themselves in open debate, there would be much less temptation to play holiday havoc and loose budgetary Frankensteins upon the land.

## ST. LOUIS POST-DISPATCH
*St. Louis, MO, January 13, 1988*

Rupert Murdoch is a ruthless media baron, but that does not excuse the tactics used by Sens. Edward Kennedy and Ernest Hollings to block what they regarded as a Murdoch power play.

It is Federal Communication Commission policy to avoid having a single company controlling both a television outlet and a newspaper in the same city. Mr. Murdoch, however, was granted a temporary exemption from the rule and was seeking an indefinite extension so that he could save his profitable TV outlets in Boston and New York while keeping *The Boston Herald* and *The New York Post*. Sens. Kennedy and Hollings, fearing the FCC was going to allow the extension, added to a $606 billion federal spending bill a rider preventing the agency from making exceptions to its rule.

Sen. Kennedy is a regular target of the conservative *Herald*, which may explain his interest in media concentration. Also, there is a likelihood that the money-losing *Post* would fold as a result of the Kennedy-Hollings amendment inasmuch as there are few potential buyers. Most disturbing, however, was the backdoor method used by the two senators: The rider was surreptitiously added in the conference committee at the last minute without discussion or a vote by either house.

That's not the way to make policy. The FCC has established rules for dealing with the Murdoch request; they should be followed. If the worst fears of Sens. Kennedy and Hollings are realized and the FCC grants Mr. Murdoch the long-term exemption he seeks, then it would be time to introduce a bill to overturn the FCC action. That way the rules and the proposed law could be debated on their merits and the issue resolved by majority decision.

## The Star-Ledger
*Newark, NJ, January 11, 1988*

Sen. Edward Kennedy has emerged as the villain of a particularly distasteful abuse of political power. He is accused of pushing through a special, self-serving piece of legislation in the catchall budget measure recently passed by Congress and grudgingly signed into law by President Reagan.

It is doubtful whether more than a handful of Senate and House members knew that the Kennedy amendment had been inserted into the omnibus legislation, a likelihood which in no way condones what occurred.

The legislation had nothing whatever to do with the budget. It had no connection at all with the raising or spending of federal revenues. What it seemed to be doing was to silence a voice critical of Sen. Kennedy, who is the Democratic powerhouse of Massachusetts, a state where the Democrats have things pretty much their own way.

Under the Kennedy amendment, the Federal Communications Commission was stripped of any right to moderate its rules prohibiting the cross-ownership of newspaper and television stations within a single market area. Rupert Murdoch, a media giant whose holdings include the Boston Herald and New York Post, as well as TV stations in both cities, said the "Kennedy measure clearly targets these newspapers based on their editorial opinion."

Although protecting the First Amendment right of publications to speak out freely is a pillar of the liberal citadel, it doesn't seem to have troubled Sen. Kennedy, one of the acknowledged leaders of the liberal movement in America, as he pressed ahead, with the help of a Democratic colleague, Sen. Ernest Hollings of South Carolina, to gain passage of the amendment.

Another leading liberal Democrat, Sen. Daniel Moynihan, announced his intention to seek repeal of the Kennedy mischief, and New York Mayor Edward Koch said the Kennedy maneuver exposes a flaw in Sen. Kennedy's character.

Beyond the misuse of power, the Kennedy gambit calls attention to the indefensible way Congress has been going about the business of legislating a budget. The budgeting process desperately needs a complete overhaul. As things stand, Congress must accept full blame for the failure of the existing irrational plan—and only Congress can reform it.

## Chicago Tribune
*Chicago, IL, January 7, 1988*

Rupert Murdoch is a press lord on three continents. As such, he seldom has hesitated to use his vast newspaper and television holdings to seek special treatment from governments on all three. And he is accustomed to getting his way, to being treated specially. Although it seems almost fitting, he is now being singled out by government for attention he may seem to deserve, but to which in all fairness he should not be subjected.

In the rush of appropriations legislation pushed through Congress and signed by the President just before Christmas, a rider was attached to a catchall spending bill that would forbid the Federal Communications Commission to change its rule prohibiting cross-ownership of television stations and newspapers in the same market except where they were grandfathered in when the rule was adopted.

That part of the new law that prevents further extensions of waivers already in force is aimed solely at Mr. Murdoch. He already is under orders to divest himself either of the Boston Herald and the New York Post or of television stations in their home cities, and holds the only current waivers. Sen. Edward Kennedy of Massachusetts has said he sought the law because he believes cross-ownership is not in Boston's interest. Mr. Murdoch's representatives have accused him of conducting a political vendetta against the Boston Herald, which often has criticized the senator. He denies the charge. New York's senators, who overlooked the passage of the provision, now say they will try to exempt at least the Post.

It is usually difficult to agree with Rupert Murdoch. But much as he likes special treatment and as nice as it would be to see him get what he deserves, he should not be singled out as the target of legislation. In fact, Congress should stay out of anything that smacks of regulation of the press. Even the FCC rule, which is not a law but a policy, makes no sense in this age of broad diversity of the press and television. There is no question the rule should be changed, but not by congressional fiat. Until it is changed, however, Mr. Murdoch and his News America Corp. should be required to abide by it just as other media companies have.

What could stand some changing is Rupert Murdoch's arrogance of presumed power. Newspaper people, Mr. Murdoch not excepted, have no rights or privileges that exceed those of any other individual.

Sometimes folks in the business forget that. Sometimes they get taken by the notion that people who buy ink by the barrel and paper by the ton are formidable enough to walk mean and tall right into the best seats in any house. That's not the way it works.

What special treatment is due newspapers, the only special treatment they should be accorded, is bestowed by the First Amendment to the Constitution of the United States. That amendment has but one purpose as it applies to newspapers. It establishes the press as the people's representative, eyes and ears of a democracy too numerous to be everywhere, to see and hear events upon which informed judgments are based, to be the people's watchdog over government and courts.

Newspaper people who seek special favors for themselves or for their businesses are sadly confusing who they are with what they merely represent. What is worse, they are at least implying to those they court that a *quid pro quo* may be forthcoming.

Let's hope Rupert Murdoch remembers enough about his native Australia to recognize the boomerang effect in clout.

# DAILY NEWS
*New York, NY, January 9, 1988*

TO BEGIN WITH, THIS NEWSPAPER has a competitive interest in what happens to Rupert Murdoch's control of the New York Post. The Tribune Company owns the Daily News and WPIX-TV, Channel 11, in New York and thus has a financial interest in what affects Murdoch's holdings. The cross-ownership of the Daily News and WPIX existed before establishment in 1975 of a Federal Communications Commission rule that prohibits such cross-ownership in any city after that date.

It is only fair that the Daily News' readers be aware of those interests in considering this newspaper's position on Murdoch's problems. Those problems, in brief:

On the night before Christmas recess, the U.S. House and Senate passed a budget bill. On page 34 of 1,194 pages was language that prohibits the FCC from reconsidering, reversing or waiving the 1975 cross-ownership rule. That "rider" was attached in the final frantic hours of the congressional year. It was not subject to public hearings, or even closed-door consideration, in any subcommittee or committee. It was not debated on either floor.

BECAUSE NO OTHER COMPANY HAS a temporary waiver, Murdoch is the only one affected by that legislation. If it stands, he must sell either the Post or WNYW-TV, Channel 5, in New York by March 6, and either the Herald or WFXT-TV, Channel 25, in Boston by June 30.

The principal people responsible for the rider are Sen. Edward Kennedy (D-Mass.) and Sen. Ernest Hollings (D-S.C.). Hollings acted on Kennedy's request.

Kennedy has been often and vigorously attacked in the columns of the Herald under Murdoch's ownership, but he claims his motives were based on the principles of the First Amendment and U.S. anti-trust laws. He argues that if he had not moved with swiftness and stealth, Murdoch's lobbying efforts with a sympathetic FCC would have enabled Murdoch to evade both those principles.

When the FCC established the cross-ownership rule in 1975, the stated intent was to nourish variety and thus vigor among news media voices. Cross-ownerships that existed in major markets at the time the rule was written were exempted. A retroactive prohibition would have been economically disruptive and almost certainly unconstitutional.

In the ensuing 13 years, a substantial number of individuals and companies have had to choose between newspaper and television ownership, selling one for the sake of owning the other or forgoing attractive purchases.

MURDOCH BOUGHT THE POST in 1976 and WNYW-TV in 1986; The Boston Herald in 1982 and WFXT-TV in 1986. At each of those times, the FCC rule was in force and clear. Today, no other cross-ownerships exist in the U.S. except Murdoch's and those that were in place before the rule was established in 1975 and therefore exempt. Murdoch acquired both television properties under FCC waivers that were presumed to have been granted only to allow him two years to find buyers.

Now, unless the Kennedy measure is rescinded, Murdoch will have to divest himself of one property in New York and one in Boston. The Boston paper is profitable and salable. The Post is far from profitable, but the attractiveness of having a public voice in New York may be strong enough to draw in buyers able to carry the Post's losses.

Kennedy's method, to move in secrecy, is offensive—and would be whatever the legislation's aim. Any measure of wide national importance should be deliberated in full legislative daylight and voted on in knowledge of its consequence. Congress must have a warning mechanism to prevent such surreptitious back-door legislation.

IT IS PROPER FOR THE FCC to reconsider and update its policies. It was beginning the process for such a consideration when its power to do so was curtailed. Kennedy argues that any revision of the cross-ownership rule ought to be done by Congress, not a bureaucratic agency.

Between 1975 and the present, other individuals and companies—including the Tribune Co.—abided by the rule and sold or divested one property or another. Murdoch knew the rule was in force and unequivocal, affecting others. Simple fairness demands that he, too, abide by it.

Media industry economics and public perceptions have changed since 1975. Serious people now argue that the cross-ownership rule is wrong for major markets. Others argue that doing away with the prohibition would encourage owners to swap properties to create monopolies.

All that should be debated, exhaustively and in daylight. But consistency demands that any change in the rules or the law must apply to *future* cases only. The rule wasn't retroactive. Changes must not be retroactive. Murdoch cannot fairly be given exemptions all others were denied.

# Honolulu Star-Bulletin
*Honolulu, HI, January 15, 1988*

The same omnibus appropriations bill that contained Senator Inouye's controversial $8 million for schools for North African Jews in France had another fascinating item that was slipped in on behalf of Sen. Edward Kennedy. The purpose of the measure was to force media magnate Rupert Murdoch to dispose of either his newspapers or his television stations in Boston and New York.

Now it happens that Murdoch's Boston paper, the *Herald*, has been a fierce critic of Kennedy. The senator seemed to be trying to silence his antagonist by the simple expedient of forcing him to sell.

That's not what the Federal Communications Commission had in mind when it adopted a rule in 1975 aimed at breaking up media monopolies. The rule prohibits a company from owning a newspaper and either a television or radio station in the same city. The FCC is currently considering whether the rule should be revoked.

The measure inserted in Congress' continuing resolution, without benefit of hearings or floor votes, forbade the FCC to use appropriated funds to re-examine the cross-ownership rule or to grant permanent waivers from it. Kennedy claimed it was in "the best interest of Boston and the best interest of the First Amendment."

Fellow Democrat Edward Koch, the mayor of New York, who has been supported by Murdoch's *New York Post*, had a different view. He said: "What Senator Kennedy and Senator Hollings (chairman of the subcommittee that handled the amendment) have done rivals the worst in a totalitarian country that still professes to have a parliamentary structure." Both of New York's senators say they will sponsor legislation to revoke the Kennedy measure.

One difference between the Boston and New York situations is that the *Herald* is profitable and the *Post* is not. If Murdoch were forced to dispose of the *Post*, he might have to close it down for lack of a buyer. That would not advance the cause of increasing diversity of ownership in the news media.

The FCC rule still has its defenders as a way to prevent companies from controlling news dissemination in a community. Critics argue that it's no longer needed because of the rapid growth of cable television and electronic information services, which provide a host of alternative sources of news. Some add that by forbidding newspapers to buy profitable television stations that can subsidize newspaper operations, the rule may even be helping to kill newspapers.

Kennedy's action has added another dimension to the debate by showing how the rule can be used to threaten a hostile newspaper with extinction.

Even if the cross-ownership rule were worth retaining, sneaking this measure into the omnibus bill without the knowledge of Kennedy's colleagues, much less of the public, was the wrong way to do it.

## The News and Courier
*Charleston, SC, January 8, 1988*

Weep not for Rupert Murdoch. He is big enough and mean enough to fend for himself in the rough and tumble of Washington politics. Weep instead for honor, fair play and ethical behavior in what was once "the world's greatest deliberative body."

The story from Washington is an all too familiar one, heavy with the smell of special interest and vindictiveness. A key figure, we are sorry to say, is one of our senators from South Carolina, Fritz Hollings.

Acting apparently at the behest of Sens. Edward M. Kennedy and John Kerry of Massachussets, Sen. Hollings, chairman of the Commerce Committee, inserted a last-minute amendment in the $600 billion appropriations bill, an amendment that some say will force Mr. Murdoch to give up ownership of The Boston Herald and The New York Post. The Herald is a frequent and, we might say, refreshing critic of the two Massachusetts senators.

Sen. Hollings, of course, insists that his motives are pure. His amendment, he says, is simply meant to require that the Federal Communications Commission carry out a policy forbidding publishers from owning newspapers in cities where they also operate television stations.

The practical effect of Hollings' action, however, is that an obnoxious publisher most likely will be removed from the backs of two liberal senators in Massachusetts, and that yet another New York City daily newspaper will fold.

The latter likelihood has enraged New York's two senators, who were asleep at the switch, and New York City Mayor Koch. The mayor accused Sen. Hollings and Sen. Kennedy of acting "in the dead of night without alerting their colleagues, who became unwilling collaborators."

There are right ways and wrong ways to legislate. Ends do not necessarily justify means. Fair-minded senators should know that; but fair-mindedness is becoming an increasingly rare quality among those who work and deal on Capitol Hill. It's doubtful that anyone could find a stronger argument for giving the president a line-item veto than the one illustrated in this sorry example of the politics of you-scratch-my-back-and-I'll-scratch-yours.

## The Cincinnati Post
*Cincinnati, OH, January 8, 1988*

Rupert Murdoch owns media properties in his native Australia, in Britain and here in his adopted land. He is a billionaire and can look out for himself. Nevertheless, we think it is shameful the way Sen. Edward Kennedy mugged him.

In recent years Murdoch bought television stations in Boston and New York—cities where he also owns daily newspapers, The Boston Herald and The New York Post.

The TV purchases broke a Federal Communications Commission rule against the same person owning a broadcast station and a daily newspaper in the same market. Dual ownership was allowed to continue in cities where it already existed before the rule was adopted.

If forced to dispose of the newspapers or the stations, Murdoch would keep the latter. They are profitable, and useful to his Fox television network. Meanwhile, the Post loses gobs of money and the Herald is only a break-even operation.

Murdoch asked for and the FCC sensibly granted waivers letting him own the stations and the newspapers while he sought buyers for the properties he would divest. The waiver on the Post ends March 6 and on the Herald June 30.

Enter Ted Kennedy, who believes in his family credo: Don't get mad, get even. The feisty, conservative Herald has angered Boston's liberal barons—Kennedy, Sen. John Kerry and Gov. Michael Dukakis—by criticizing them.

So as lawmakers conferred behind closed doors on the $600-billion catchall spending bill, Kennedy and his friend Sen. Ernest Hollings inserted what may be the Post's death sentence. Without debate, hearings or sunlight, they got Congress to order the FCC not to extend Murdoch's waivers.

Since the publisher probably can't get the Post in strong hands by March, we may be witnessing a liberal senator throwing 2,000 union members out of work and silencing a newspaper that traces its lineage back to Alexander Hamilton.

The Herald may survive. Several lawmakers have vowed to undo Kennedy's damage. But if a powerful politician, acting secretly, can threaten to kill one newspaper and force another into the "right" hands, this nation's press freedom is in some jeopardy.

## WINSTON-SALEM JOURNAL
*Winston, NC, January 11, 1988*

U.S. Sens. Kennedy and Hollings have come in for a good deal of well-deserved criticism for their behavior in a case involving press mogul Rupert Murdoch. Some have objected to their motives, others to their methods. Neither will bear much scrutiny.

Murdoch owns both newspapers and broadcast outlets in two markets — Boston and New York. FCC rules forbid such ownership on the grounds that it may tend to an unhealthy monopoly on the news. The logic is the same as that contained in the famous A.J. Liebling remark to the effect that freedom of the press is a wonderful thing so long as you are lucky enough to be among those who own one.

Many, however, feel the FCC rule is an antique. Once upon a time it might have been possible for one media company to control virtually all news flowing into a community. But information, like money, has been globalized. Satellites, cable television, and new publishing technologies have made such monopoly fears obsolete. Particularly in large markets like New York and Boston, alternative news sources have proliferated.

Kennedy and Hollings apparently felt that an appeal by Murdoch to the deregulation-minded FCC might have met with a friendly hearing. The FCC might have decided to drop its ban on multiple ownership in a single market.

To prevent such a change, they chose to put the ban into law. But here critics of their methods raise objections. The senators attached the ban at the last minute to the budget bill. By stealth, critics say. In the dead of night. Such tactics are commonplace, but that doesn't make them any more admirable. They are one good argument against last-minute legislating, unwieldy omnibus bills and clotted grab-bag continuing resolutions.

In this case, at any rate, the ban passed without most legislators even being aware that they were voting for it. This undoubtedly pleased Kennedy for several reasons, one of which is the fact that the Boston paper owned by Murdoch has been consistently anti-Kennedy. It might not have been so under new ownership and certainly wouldn't have been if forced out of business.

Now that the truth is out, New York senators who don't want the paper in their state to die and oppose the ban will attempt to retract it. More power to them. Both the ban and the legislative means used to enact it are antidemocratic.

# The Union Leader
*Manchester, NH, January 10, 1988*

Warren Rudman tells the Washington press that he might not seek reelection — in 1992. Careful, senator, somebody back here in New Hampshire might take you seriously.

In fact, judging from some of the junior senator's recent actions, more than a few Granite Staters — and one Presidential candidate — might be happy to see Rudman make good on that thought right now.

The Presidential candidate, of course, is Bob Dole, for whom Rudman serves as state campaign chairman. To paraphrase Sam Clemens, Dole might be thinking these days that were it not for the honor of the thing, he'd just as soon not have Rudman's "help."

When Rudman gets back, tomorrow, from his Persian Gulf fact-finding trip, he has a lot of explaining to do about some facts found out much closer to home.

Those facts concern his role in a sneaky, back-door deal to help Teddy Kennedy and to deny the Boston Herald a fair and public hearing on its owner's request not to have to sell it.

The Herald has been giving the liberal Boston Globe a tough time in the Boston circulation market of late. It has been giving Kennedy a tough time for years. Its owner, Rupert Murdoch, expected a hearing this year on his appeal of a law that bans ownership of both a newspaper and TV station within the same market.

But Teddy the K. feared such a hearing. So he concocted a secret amendment to a federal spending bill. His amendment effectively prohibits the Federal Communications Commission from giving the Herald its hearing.

There was no public hearing — no public notice, even, — of Teddy's dead-of-night maneuver.

So much for fairness, so much for the public's right to know and its right to have a say on such matters.

And so much for Warren Rudman. For it was Rudman, as a leading budget conference subcommittee Republican, whom Kennedy and his chums sought out to get the wink and the nod needed to have the amendment attached to the spending bill. Had Rudman protested, an aide in the affair says, it is doubtful whether the deal would have made it.

Campaigning in New Hampshire last week, Sen. Dole criticized the Kennedy tactic and called the amendment "a lot of junk." He politely declined comment on the role played by his campaign chairman, Rudman.

Warren Rudman has a reputation for playing straight with people. We're mightily disappointed in his role in this and we welcome his explanation.

# The Record
*Hackensack, NJ, January 10, 1988*

The battle between Ted Kennedy and Rupert Murdoch over Mr. Murdoch's ownership of newspapers and TV stations in the same city is a matter of wrong versus wrong.

On one hand, we have an international press lord who, in 1986, purchased TV stations in New York and Boston, where he also owns newspapers, knowing perfectly well that the Federal Communication Commission formally bars such "cross-ownership." Now he is hollering that his constitutional rights are being trampled because Senator Kennedy is seeing to it that the ban is enforced.

On the other hand, we have a powerful Democratic senator who doesn't like Mr. Murdoch's brand of right-wing sensationalism, who has been personally stung by Mr. Murdoch's Boston Herald, and who, in a late-night budget conference last month, hit upon a neat parliamentary maneuver for sticking it to his old enemy. Mr. Kennedy inserted in the final appropriations bill a line directing the FCC to force Mr. Murdoch to get rid of either his newspapers or his TV stations.

Finally, in the middle, we have the FCC, which adopted the rule against cross-ownership 13 years ago. The antitrust provision might make sense in a small town with one newspaper and one TV station. But it seems increasingly pointless in a large urban market like New York, with its four daily newspapers, seven VHF stations, and countless cable channels — not to mention a profusion of special-interest magazines, political journals, neighborhood newspapers, etc. The notion of anyone cornering a news market as sprawling and unruly as New York's is farfetched. The FCC rule is decidedly out of date, which is why no one was very enthusiastic about enforcing it.

So where does that leave us? Right in the middle of a raging battle between the sneaky and pettily vindictive Senator Kennedy and the unscrupulous and hypocritical Mr. Murdoch over the pointless and obsolete FCC cross-ownership ban.

The best thing for honest citizens is to settle back and enjoy the show, knowing that it doesn't really matter who wins in the end.

# The Register
*Santa Ana, CA, January 5, 1988*

Last Sunday we commented on a law that Congress included in the omnibus spending bill passed in December. The law forces publisher Rupert Murdoch to sell two of his newspapers, the *New York Post* and the Boston *Herald*, in direct violation of the First Amendment protection of freedom of the press. The law, if upheld in the courts, might kill the *Post* and force the *Herald*, profitable for the first time in many years, to be sold at a fire-sale price.

*The New York Times* has now discovered which congressmen perpetrated this assault on liberty: Sen. Teddy Kennedy of Massachusetts, the prime target of the *Herald*'s news stories and editorial barbs, and fellow leftist Sen. John Kerry. It seems that Sen. Ernest Hollings, who sponsored the bill, was put up to it by his Massachusetts cohorts. Hollings admits that the bill was aimed directly at Murdoch. "I was glad to do it," said Hollings, who in 1984 campaigned for president on a good-government platform.

Columnist William Safire writes, "The impetus for this circumvention of deliberation" — the bill was never debated in Congress — "came from influential backers of Kennedy and Kerry. ... Was anybody involved who wants to buy the Boston *Herald* at a forced-sale price?"

Let's also remember the pose Teddy took during the recent hearings that considered Judge Robert Bork for the Supreme Court. Teddy insisted that Bork would attack the First Amendment and led the campaign that resulted in Bork's defeat. How ironic that it's Teddy who is now assaulting the First Amendment.

But suppression of press freedoms isn't a new sport for Teddy. In the early 1980s he got the Federal Election Commission to sue *The American Sentinel*, a conservative newsletter. The Teddy/FEC axis insisted that the *Sentinel*'s unfavorable reports on Teddy were actually political activism and thus under the FEC's purview. (The fact that many constitutional scholars consider the very existence of the FEC unconstitutional is another matter.)

Fortunately, a federal judge ruled against Teddy and the FEC and upheld the *Sentinel*'s First Amendment rights. But the newsletter incurred great legal expenses.

Maybe Rupert Murdoch and the *Herald* will likewise defend their First Amendment rights against the assault of Teddy Kennedy, John Kerry, and all other would-be tyrants.

# Part IV:
# Music in America

Popular music has perhaps reflected the real state of America more clearly than any other cultural idiom because, despite everything, it offered diversity. But when Elvis Presley, Bill Haley and Chuck Berry successfully launched the "Rock 'n' Roll Revolution" in the mid-1950s with their anthems, both urgent and carefree, a definite line was drawn between the emerging youth culture and their horrified elders. All aspects of the music – its heavy beat, loudness, self-absorbed lyrics and raving delivery – indicated a teenage defiance of adult values and authority.

Essentially a hybrid in origin, rock music includes elements of several black and white American music styles: guitar accompanied blues, rhythm and blues, gospel, country-western and doo-wop.

As rock 'n' roll became a financial success, record companies that had considered it a fad began to search for new acts. But as the commercialization of the music transpired, rock 'n' roll was robbed of much of its gutsy quality by the end of the 1950s.

Rock music surged to popularity again in 1962 with the emergence of The Beatles, an infectious group of four lads from Liverpool, England. They were initially acclaimed internationally for their energy and appealing individual personalities rather than for any innovations in their music, which was derived from Presley and Berry. But as their musicianship improved and the quality of their compositional concepts broadened, recognition in these areas followed. The Beatles popularity inevitably produced other groups, the most important of which was the Rolling Stones. The Stones were influenced by the American blues tradition and, in contrast to the Beatles, were raunchy and overtly sexual.

An important transformation of rock occurred in 1965 at the Newport Folk Festival when Bob Dylan, noted as a composer and writer of poetic folk songs of social protest like "Blowin' in the Wind," appeared backed by a rock band. A synthesis of the folk revival and rock subsequently took place. As a result the verbal content of rock songs turned even more toward rebellion, social protest, sex, and increasingly, drugs. Many groups, among them the Jefferson Airplane and the Grateful Dead, tried to approximate in music the aural experience of psychedelic drugs, producing tunes with abtruse lyrics and marked by long, piercing lead guitar solos.

From about 1966 on, the rock festival was regarded as the ideal context in which to hear rock music with thousands of fans attending. "The Woodstock Music and Arts Festival," held in upstate New York in August 1969, was the most successful and peaceful of these gathering and has gained legendary status in the years since its presentation. Later in the year, however, a similar festival was held in Altamont, Calif. Featuring the Rolling Stones, the festival was marked by several violent incidents, including a murder.

Altamont signaled the end of an era in rock. Within a year, several of the genre's top performer's, including Jimi Hendrix, Janis Joplin and Jim Morrison, were dead, the victims of drugs.

By the 1980s rock had firmly planted itself as the popular music of America with a host of varying classifications. Punk, new wave, ethno-pop, heavy metal, hard core, hip-hop, rap and reggae were just some of the styles that impacted popular culture. But many of the elements of the music that disturbed Middle America in the 1950s, particularly violence and sexual innuendo, continued to stir controversy. Two of these forms, rap and heavy metal, have been the focus of particular concern and action.

Essentially the domain of Black urban America, rap began in New York basement clubs in the 1970s when disc jockeys kept dance rhythms going by seamlessly cutting back and forth between snatches of the same record on two separate turntables while chanting rhymes that both celebrated themselves and offered angry social commentary as well as inspiring the dancers on the floor. Rap's recent wild popularity has provoked questions of its responsibility to the community and given it a new urgency.

Pioneered in the early 1970s by the band Led Zeppelin, heavy metal has grown to become hugely popular, mostly among white adolescent blue-collar males. Featuring hard-driven and deafening guitars, heavy metal's lyrics darkly echo many of rock 'n' roll earliest themes: lost love, class frustration and unformed teen-age anger.

But because some of the biggest rap and heavy metal acts include sexually explicit lyrics in their songs (not to mention racism and misogyny) they have put themselves in the center of a cultural and political storm.

Although many Americans may never have heard of them, these are not obscure bands playing in garages and afterhours clubs. In the 1970s, urban rappers performed in parks and on the street, plugging loudspeakers into lampposts. Now they fill major arenas – although more and more venues won't present rap concerts any longer, because of fear that violence can spill over from the stage to the crowd. The rap groups Public Enemy, 2 Live Crew and N.W.A. all have had platinum albums, with more than a million in sales. The heavy metal group Guns N' Roses sold more than four million copies worldwide of the "G N' R Lies" record, whose lyrics insult blacks, homosexuals and "immigrants" inside 10 lines. Major record companies are behind them: Public Enemy's releases for the Def Jam label are distributed CBS/Columbia Records; Guns N' Roses parades its prejudices on Geffen Records, headed, ironically enough, by the noted AIDS philanthropist David Geffen.

Every era of rock music has brought with it an organized backlash. Today there entire organizations devoted to keeping the music and its attitudes under control, most notably the Parents' Music Resource Center in Arlington, Va. The center has an extensive file of lyrics in rap and heavy metal music, describing every imaginable perversity from unsafe sex to devil worship. The center's executive director Jennifer Norwood was quick to point out that they take "no position on any specific type of music." But the center does support printing song lyrics on album jackets for the information of parents – although such a step might also make it easier for kids to learn them – and a warning label, which some record companies already apply voluntarily, about "explicit lyrics."

As the debate surrounding rap and heavy metal enters the legal arena, a major question seems again to be: Are the attitudes expressed in these genres protected by the First Amendment? But baby boomers who grew up with rock in the '50s and '60s may have another, perhaps more pertinent, cultural query: What ever happened to the idea that rock 'n' roll would save the world?

## Record Warning Labeling Set

The Recording Industry Association of America, a trade group that represents the major record companies in the U.S., had agreed to place uniform new warning labels on records, tapes and compact discs that contained potentially offensive lyrics, it was reported March 29, 1990.

The National Association of Independent Record Distributors, which represented many smaller record labels, also urged its members to adopt the labels.

The industry's action was an attempt to avert passage of state legislation that would require mandatory warning labels on records that contained explicit lyrics dealing with sex, violence or illegal drugs. Such legislation had been considered by 19 states across the U.S. Thirteen of those states had to drop their efforts in response to the voluntary plan, it was announced April 5.

The music industry had agreed in 1985 to place warning labels on records in the wake of an antiobscenity campaign spearheaded by the Parents' Music Resource Center, a group led by Mary (Tipper) Gore, wife of Sen. Albert Gore Jr. (D, Tenn.), and Susan Baker, wife of Secreatry of State James A. Baker 3rd.

The agreement called for record companies to place a warning label on the cover of records that contained offensive lyrics, or to print the lyrics on the record jacket.

However, critics complained that the labels were insufficient, because they often blended in with the album cover design and because compliance with the rule was erratic.

The new labels would all carry the same wording ("Explicit lyrics – parental advisory") as well as the same design, and would be placed in the same position on the covers of records, tapes and CDs.

The new plan was hailed by the Parents' Music Resource Center as an improvement over the 1985 agreement.

## Omaha World-Herald
*Omaha, NE, April 6, 1987*

Who would have guessed that 1987 would bring a pop song in which teenagers sing the praises of sexual abstinence? Not only that, but who would have guessed that the song would become a best seller in Latin America, which has one of the highest birthrates in the world?

Finally, who would have guessed that such a thing could be carried off by government bureaucrats?

Improbable as it might seem, that is precisely what the U.S. Agency for International Development has accomplished with "When We're Together."

Some songs glamorize sex. Why not have a song that glamorizes abstinence? The agency was willing to put up $300,000 to pay a composer to write such a song and to cover the cost of producing and marketing it.

The singers, Tatiana Palacios and Johnny Lozada, have become celebrities in Mexico. Their version of "When We're Together" has sold 500,000 copies in Mexico alone and is a best seller in other parts of Latin America.

The song became so popular a similar tactic is being planned for use in other Third World nations. As an additional dividend, the royalties from the record sales are being donated by the singers to Johns Hopkins University, which was chosen by the agency to carry out the project, which is aimed at urging responsible sexual conduct.

Whether the song has reduced sexual activity among young people is another matter. But the message has been delivered in a bright, original and appealing way. A relatively small investment of U.S. foreign aid has had an impact on the teen cultures of developing countries. It is a triumph in communication that seems to hold promise.

## THE INDIANAPOLIS NEWS
*Indianapolis, IN, May 26, 1988*

Her husband is out of the presidential race, but Tipper Gore continues her own campaign to warn about the trash in rock records and videos.

She's been accused of censorship and all kinds of other crimes.

But First Amendment defenders are coming to her side to point out that what she wants is more information, not less, when it comes to the contents of music for young people.

She started the Parents Music Resource Center in 1985 after her 11-year-old daughter brought home an album with lyrics featuring women wrapped in barbed wire.

The center's main proposal for warning labels has been accepted by a number of recording companies. She also has suggested that the companies print the lyrics on the record jackets or video containers, to help customers selecting music.

For such radical notions, though, she has been trashed as a "cultural terrorist" by rock star Frank Zappa, who ought to look in the mirror when he hurls such an accusation. Danny Goldberg has complained that she "sounds more like Jimmy Swaggart each day."

More consistent advocates of the First Amendment have come to her defense. "She's not for censorship — she's sensitive to First Amendment issues," says New York attorney Victor Kovner, who specializes in First Amendment cases.

"She's for full disclosure — more speech, rather than less — and that's consistent with the First Amendment," Kovner added in an interview in Quill magazine.

"I just want to have some influence over the raising of my children, and the least the industry can do is to put a warning on records or print the lyrics," sums up Mrs. Gore.

Her husband's presidential campaign is over for 1988, but it's good news to learn that another Gore campaign goes on.

## The Providence Journal
*Providence, RI, September 19, 1988*

Why have so many music concerts this summer turned violent? And what, if anything, can be done?

Last weekend's stabbing death of a concertgoer at the Nassau Coliseum in New York prompted officials to ban rap concerts there until the murder inquiry ends. But the problem is not limited to rap music. At a Michael Jackson concert in Liverpool last weekend 40 people were hospitalized and 1,500 more were injured in a crush near the stage. At concerts by Kiss and Slayer in Madison Square Garden last month, audiences tore seats apart and hurled cushions at one another.

It seems fair to wonder whether promoters and authorities are losing their grip on crowd control. The diversity of violent incidents suggests that banning a particular kind of music is not as effective as reviewing security procedures. Performers, promoters, security guards and audiences can all work to make concerts safer.

Stars should not encourage fans to rush the stage. It inevitably results in injuries to the people in the front who are crushed by the human wave from the rear. Should it become apparent that the crowd is surging forward, a performer who cares about the safety of his fans can do a lot by urging everyone back to his seat. Set designers can help, too, by making it difficult for audiences to reach the stage.

Security guards should be hired in sufficient number to protect lives and property. The Nassau concert had 100 guards inside for a crowd of 10,000 — clearly not enough, despite numerous police officers patrolling outside the coliseum. And too many weapons are getting through. The Nassau guards used hand-held metal detectors, but the number of weapons inside suggests that the system is faulty.

Guards argue that it's impossible to get a crowd of 10,000 inside in a timely fashion if entry security procedures take any longer. That brings us to the next suggestion. Why must promoters seek to maximize the number of people? Economic arguments are not entirely persuasive. If crowds cannot be controlled, why not raise prices for tickets, and/or schedule more performances for smaller numbers? If violence becomes routine, many concertgoers will stay away anyway. Or cities may begin banning certain performers or kinds of music, which is presumably the worst economic consequence of all.

Music fans themselves can help by cooperating with officials. Police suspect that robbery was a motive in much of last weekend's violence, saying that a gang of eight to 12 organized young men roamed the arena, snatching gold chains, bracelets and watches from the unsuspecting audience. Better to leave the jewelry at home.

The iconoclastic air of pop, rock and rap music can be enjoyed without the accompanying mayhem. People should be able to enjoy their favorite performers without becoming victims.

## SYRACUSE HERALD-JOURNAL
*Syracuse, NY, May 30, 1988*

The rappers RUN-DMC and rock groups Los Lobos and Aerosmith will be on tour this summer. At their concerts will be the usual paraphernalia — T-shirts, buttons, posters, programs, etc. The unusual item will be job information booths.

The three groups have joined forces with corporate leaders to promote the theme "Work Works" through the booths and in public service announcements and news conferences in concert cities. They will encourage kids to stay in school and to be ready and willing to go to work.

William H. Kolberg, president of the National Alliance of Business, reasons that kids are more likely to listen to musical groups than to business leaders.

He is right. As effective as Nancy Reagan has been in telling kids to "Just say no," her words don't have the impact they would have if they were uttered by RUN-DMC.

The rappers, who are expected to draw more than one million young people to their concerts this summer, warned about the dangers of drugs in promotions for the Drug Enforcement Administration.

Maybe other musical groups will follow the example of the three. The stay-in-school and work message needs to be heard by as many young people as possible.

Kolberg estimates that every year dropouts cost this country $240 billion. Dropouts don't have skills. They don't have jobs. They abuse drugs and alcohol.

We applaud the efforts RUN-DMC, Los Lobos and Aerosmith. They obviously care enough about their audiences. We hope the audiences will listen to what they have to say.

## Newsday
*New York, NY, September 13, 1988*

As an art form, rap music is a blend of intricately crafted rhymes spoken over African-based rhythms, usually amplified at maximum volume. Its poetry is unlikely to be understood by the uninitiated: anyone not attuned to the streets — especially the streets of the Bronx and other black and Hispanic neighborhoods, both inner-city and suburban.

It's partly because rap is so widely misunderstood that there's a temptation to blame its fans and impresarios for the violence that occurs at rap concerts, apparently with some regularity. Assaults at the "Jam '88" at Nassau Coliseum Sunday left one man dead and a dozen rap fans injured.

But officials are wrong to put a ban on rap concerts at the coliseum. As a solution to the violence, it overreaches the mark: It allows a handful of misfits to dictate how and when people can gather for what may be an otherwise rare opportunity to hear this kind of music.

A ban, moreover, takes an unfair swipe with a broad brush, wrongly portraying anyone who likes rap as violence-prone.

That certainly isn't true of most of the 10,000 people who attended Sunday's "Jam '88." About a dozen were among the victims, not the perpetrators, of the wolf-pack assaults.

The management of the coliseum has the primary obligation to protect concertgoers from the kind of viciousness that occurred Sunday. It's a responsibility shared by police. Both should have been more vigilant, notwithstanding the use of metal detectors which failed to turn up the knives and other weapons used in the attacks.

For the most part, rap speaks of struggles against drugs, teenage pregnancy, crime and homelessness and of aspirations for education, gainful employment and family stability — all pressing concerns for most of its fans.

Officials should be mindful of this and as one rap puts it, "Don't believe the hype." Instead of a ban, they should plan: Rap concerts may just need better security.

## Rap Singers Arrested; Record Ruled Obscene

Two members of the popular rap group 2 Live Crew were arrested on obscenity charges early June 10, 1990 following a performance at a nightclub in Hollywood, Fla. The arrests came four days after a federal district judge in Florida had ruled that the group's album *As Nasty as They Wanna Be* was obscene.

The two band members – producer and lead singer Luther Campbell and singer Chris Wongwon – were arrested on misdemeanor charges of violating state laws. If convicted, they each faced up to a year in prison and a $1,000 fine.

Legal experts said the arrests were an unusual occurrence in that they had apparently been made only in response to the band's lyrics, whereas most obscenity prosecutions in the U.S. were for nudity or indecent acts. 2 Live Crew's lyrics frequently used profanity to describe a variety of sexual acts. Some critics had also complained that the band's songs were demeaning to women.

U.S. District Judge Jose Gonzalez ruled June 6 in Fort Lauderdale, Fla. that *As Nasty as They Wanna Be* was obscene under state law. Florida's obscenity law followed the guidelines set down in a 1973 U.S. Supreme Court ruling, *Miller v. California*, that deemed a work to be obscene if it appealed to prurient interests, lacked serious artistic value and patently offended local community standards.

In an immediate response to the ruling, law enforcement officials from Broward County, Fla. June 8 arrested a Fort Lauderdale record store owner, Charles Freeman, who sold a copy of *As Nasty as They Wanna Be* to an undercover police officer. Freeman was charged with distributing obscene material, a misdemeanor that carried a maximum penalty of one year in prison and a $1,000 fine.

Civil liberties groups expressed outrage over Gonzalez's ruling and vowed to fight on behalf of Freeman and the 2 Live Crew members. Some charged that the prosecution of 2 Live Crew was racially motivated, since the band's members were black. No similar action had been taken against any white performers such as comedian Andrew Dice Clay, whose work was also the target of obscenity opponents, they noted.

## The Atlanta Journal AND THE ATLANTA CONSTITUTION
*Atlanta, GA, June 13, 1990*

The weekend arrest of two members of the rap group 2 Live Crew in Fort Lauderdale, Fla., has been portrayed by authorities there as an assault on indecency and obscenity. In truth it represents something more troubling.

In Florida, as in many other parts of the United States, video stores stock graphic, X-rated movies that show people actually doing the things that 2 Live Crew only talks about, and no one gets too excited. Well, maybe a few people do, but that's another story. The point is, the video stores aren't being busted. Neither are the convenience stores that peddle Playboy magazines, or the cable TV companies that provide a little late-night T and A for suburban America or the nude nightclubs.

No, the people who got busted are young blacks with an attitude.

It is that attitude, that anti-establishment, street-smart edge, that transforms sexually titillating and offensive language into something deemed socially threatening and deserving of repression. Seen in that light, the events over the weekend in Fort Lauderdale represent the crackdown of a dominant society against an aggressive, threatening subculture.

It is also important to note that the situation in Fort Lauderdale does not involve minors. The record-store owner who was arrested last week was charged not with providing obscene material to minors, but with having the 2 Live Crew album for sale at all. The concert at which the group so offended the Fort Lauderdale oligarchy was adult-only, and presumably everyone who walked through the front door knew what to expect from the group.

It is perhaps appropriate, as some have proposed, to mark sexually explicit recorded material to guide parents. It may even be acceptable to ban the sale of such material to minors.

But those issues have little to do with what has taken place in Fort Lauderdale, with the incomprehensible assistance of a federal judge who found the 2 Live Crew album obscene. That judge, Jose Gonzalez, ruled that the album "lacked any serious artistic merit," a conclusion that many would dispute.

The judge may not like the music; he may, as he said, find it personally offensive, as would millions of other Americans. But in this country offending a judge's musical taste is not a crime.

## THE TENNESSEAN
*Nashville, TN, June 12, 1990*

THE music group 2 Live Crew should thank law authorities in Broward County, Florida.

Broward County sheriff's deputies, by arresting members of the group on obscenity charges, have brought more publicity to 2 Live Crew's music than the group could have ever attained by conventional means.

The rap on 2 Live Crew is that their lyrics are dirty. There seems to be little argument about that. Their expression of freedom of speech is an "X"-pression.

After U.S. District Judge Jose Gonzalez declared the group's album *As Nasty As They Wanna Be* obscene, the Broward County sheriff sent an undercover detective to arrest a record store owner for selling the album. Later deputies arrested members of the group after a concert.

Crew's cuts off the album went unheard in Nashville recently when the group failed to show for a concert April 15 at the National Guard Armory. But the rap session in Florida got plenty of attention.

How comforting it must be to the citizens in Broward County that law officers there chose to spend their crime-fighting efforts by targeting a group of men who talk dirty. One assumes you would never hear a dirty word in a patrol car.

"This city has a lot greater problems to deal with than who is performing at Club Nu," said City Commissioner Bruce Singer before the recent show.

Thus far, 2 Live Crew has sold more than 1.7 million copies of the album. Thanks to the publicity generated by Broward County law authorities, that number might climb.

"Until this trial, we never could have booked this group on such short notice, with no time [to advertise] and still expect a full house," said Mr. Bob Slade, Club Nu promoter. "They're more popular than ever now."

The definition of obscenity has long been open to debate. But perhaps Mr. Bruce Rogow, an attorney for 2 Live Crew, has a good one. "To have a dozen sheriff's officers spending all this time over some dirty lyrics seems to me to be obscene," he said.

This case might be a bad rap, in more ways than one. ■

# The Miami Herald
*Miami, FL, June 9, 1990*

"THIS IS a case," the troubling opinion began, "between two ancient enemies: Anything Goes and Enough Already." With those words, Federal Judge Jose A. Gonzalez began a 62-page ruling that the 2 Live Crew rap album *As Nasty As They Wanna Be* is obscene. Thus is escalated a First Amendment free-speech battle that is by no means as nasty as it's gonna get.

The judge's finding is a reasonable application of the U.S. Supreme Court's obscenity rule — *whatever one thinks of that rule.* What's not reasonable, what's indeed odiously intrusive, is the Florida obscenity law that makes the state a morals squad to "protect" adults from their right to read, or see, or hear sexually explicit works that the thought police deem "bad for a person."

Judge Gonzalez's ruling means that anyone selling the album in South Florida faces criminal prosecution. Even so, the judge also found that Broward County Sheriff Nick Navarro committed unconstitutional prior restraint by threatening earlier to arrest record dealers if they sold the album.

Though Skyywalker Records, Inc.'s suit against Sheriff Navarro involved the album producer's rights under the U.S. Constitution, it required Judge Gonzalez to interpret a Florida obscenity law. He held that the album meets all three tests for obscenity set by the U.S. Supreme Court in 1973.

That is, the average person, applying the community's contemporary standards, would find that the work "appeals to the prurient interest"; "the work depicts or describes, in a patently offensive way, sexual conduct" deemed obscene; and the work "taken as a whole, lacks serious literary, artistic, political, or scientific value."

At several points, his ruling's language evidences Judge Gonzalez's discomfiture at having to be the arbiter of such a prickly issue. "The absolutists and other members of the party of Anything Goes should address their petitions to the Florida Legislature, not to this court," he wrote. "If they are sincere, let them say what they actually mean — Let's Legalize Obscenity."

In sum, Judge Gonzalez said, "obscenity is not a protected form of speech under the U.S. Constitution, with or without voluntary labeling. *It is a crime* [his emphasis]. If the people of Florida want to legalize obscenity, they have every right to do so. It is much easier to criticize the law, however, than it is to work to repeal it...."

That's an understatement. Yet if Judge Gonzalez's ruling is affirmed on appeal, Floridians who value free speech have a clear challenge. It is to make indelible the state's clear right to protect minors from smut, and to tell the state to butt out of adults' choices of what they prefer to see, hear, or read.

Clearly the law should protect minors from smut. Clearly it should prosecute fully those who produce or sell sexual materials involving children. Equally clearly, the law should allow adults free access to sexually explicit works, whether in their own homes or in commercial establishments where the customer unmistakably knows the entertainment's nature before entering.

All of that requires changing the law. Which undeniably is harder than criticizing a judge's interpretation of existing law.

---

*Miami, FL, June 14, 1990*

NOW PLAYING nationwide, yet another enlightening act from South Florida: Sheriff Nick Versus 2 Live Crew. Both are getting air time on network television that they never could buy, and for reasons hardly uplifting. Sheriff Navarro is boosting his political fortunes at the expense of more-pressing priorities in Broward law enforcement, while 2 Live Crew is netting a bankroll far beyond expectations for its meager talent.

That always has been the side effect of censorship. It gives more currency to the ideas of those who are censored, thus confirming some young people's specious notion that outrageousness bears rewards.

It is the young who now should be the focus in this case. Legal arguments aside, the album *As Nasty As They Wanna Be* is obscene as most people would define it. And while adults should have free access to *anything* that they wish to read, hear, or view, no parent should have to tolerate the ready availability of obscenity to children.

That issue is being skirted. The sheriff invested a huge amount of police power — some 30 officers — to attend an after-midnight 2 Live Crew performance that admitted only adults who wished to attend.

Also extraneous to this core issue is the argument that 2 Live Crew was singled out because of race, that the group is black, and that it is being heard by middle-class white youths. For society to tolerate obscenity because it is directed to black youths would be the epitome of irresponsibility.

Indeed, children loom large in legal discussions of obscenity. Writing for the majority in the key U.S. Supreme Court decision on obscenity, Chief Justice Warren Burger said: "States have a legitimate interest in prohibiting dissemination of obscene material when the mode of dissemination carries with it a significant danger of offending the sensibilities of unwilling recipients or of exposure to juveniles."

The movie industry's rating system tries to address that issue. Imperfect as that system is, it is an honest effort, and it does convey to children a sense of demarcation and levels of acceptance. The record industry promised cooperation in voluntary labeling but has done so only in fits and starts. Some producers argue that labeling merely attracts the local morals police.

In fact, that is one of the ironies in this case. 2 Live Crew does label its albums, and it makes "clean" versions. Still, there is no bar — except in South Florida now and other scattered areas — to a 13-year-old buying the "nasty" version.

The fact that the idea of labeling has sprung from the political Right and self-righteous does not make it wrong. What would make it right would be an effort that focused carefully on controlling what *children* buy. That is, if children, rather than making a national splash, truly are the issue.

# Chicago Tribune
*Chicago, IL, June 14, 1990*

Chicago's mettle is about to be tested in the war against raunchy rappers.

The controversial 2 Live Crew is scheduled to perform its rap music, if that is not a contradiction in terms, with several other rappers at the Chicago Amphitheater on Friday night.

Here's hoping cool heads prevail.

The Miami-based group has performed twice in Chicago without incident in the last eight months. But that was before two members' arrest Sunday in south Florida on charges of giving an obscene performance in an adults-only night club. It was before its album, "As Nasty As They Wanna Be," was ruled obscene by a federal district judge in Ft. Lauderdale, and before authorities there arrested a record store owner who refused to stop selling the album.

In San Antonio, Tex., police have warned store owners to stop selling the album or face obscenity charges. And the city council in Huntsville, Ala., where 2 Live Crew is to perform Sunday, expanded its obscenity ordinance to include live performances.

All of which should have founder Luther Campbell and the other members of 2 Live Crew crying all the way to the bank. Relatively unknown outside rap music circles before, they certainly are well known now—and they have booming record sales to prove it. No one is more responsible for their windfall than the man spearheading the drive to ban them, Miami anti-porn lawyer Jack Thompson.

That's what happens when you try to bring down the weight of America's criminal justice system on a set of words and ideas, no matter how vile or otherwise objectionable they may be.

And make no mistake about it: The uncensored lyrics of "As Nasty As They Wanna Be" are quite vile, graphically describing loathsome acts of degradation and brutality against women—an audio version of the video porn that many Americans routinely see on late-night cable television.

That's why the album has an adults-only label on its jacket, a signal to parents that it contains material they may not want little Johnny or Susie to hear. Some defenders of boundless freedom for recording artists have decried such labeling, charging that it smacks of censorship. Quite the contrary. It can effectively remedy parental concerns without trampling over the constitutional rights of performers.

That's why major record producers have decided to follow the movie industry's lead and implement a voluntary labeling program, if only to avoid the heavy hand of state governments that have threatened to impose labeling systems of their own.

Record labeling gives parents a fighting chance to keep filth out of their homes without subverting our Constitution. Clapping 2 Live Crew in irons is a remedy worthy of a totalitarian state, not the United States, a nation too good and strong to be shaken by a few raunchy rappers.

## The Pittsburgh PRESS

*Pittsburgh, PA, June 15, 1990*

Things must be pretty quiet down there in south Florida. No cocaine traffic, no kids toting assault weapons, no muggings or rapes or burglaries. How else to explain the man-hours spent by the Broward County Sheriff's Department to pursue a group of unsavory rap singers?

When a federal judge found "As Nasty as They Wanna Be," an album by 2 Live Crew, to be obscene, Sheriff Nick Navarro got the excuse to do what he clearly wanted to do anyway.

Members of the group performed the offending songs before an adults-only audience in his jurisdiction, so Sheriff Navarro dispatched deputies to arrest them. They were booked on obscenity charges.

No doubt the songs are as repulsive as sheriff and judge allege. And the singers' complaints of persecution sound hollow, considering that they designed their music to be offensive. Sure enough, people were offended, and it's no surprise that they flexed the long arm of the law to remove the offenders.

But can't the sheriff find better crimes to fight? Law enforcement everywhere suffers from meager resources. Busting pop singers should rank far down on its list of priorities.

## The Saginaw News

*Saginaw, MI, June 14, 1990*

A group called 2 Live Crew, which performs rap music — we're aware that may be a contradiction in terms — has run afoul, literally, of the law in Florida.

If it were only the Florida law, its legal problems would not hold much significance. That state has a checkered history of attention to legal niceties.

But the arrest of a record-store owner for selling 2 Live Crew albums, and of members of the group itself, had the sanction of a federal judge. That places the crackdown on nasty words on a national plane — meaning it could happen here.

It's hard to imagine Saginaw County sheriff's deputies pulling over a rock group outside the Civic Center because somebody didn't like the words or music. That's like arresting bookstore clerks or librarians because one person didn't think others should read "that type of material."

Well, now. As it happens, Michigan bookstores and libraries are worried. The Legislature is considering giving police the power, based on a single complaint, to not only arrest those selling "offensive" books, magazines or tapes, but also to destroy the whole business — before prosecution, never mind conviction. That would set the Supreme Court's "community standards" rule at the lowest Puritanical viewpoint of the Morality Police.

But wouldn't the authorities act reluctantly on such complaints? Not in Florida, where the sheriff in Fort Lauderdale dispatched six deputies to nab that dangerous record-seller, and then multiplied the absurdity by sending 30 officers against some performers armed with nothing more than lyrics.

The brutal anti-woman message of 2 Live Crew stinks. But the Bill of Rights does not protect only the words that uplift and edify. Obviously a lot of people want to hear that message; the group's current album has sold 1.7 million copies. That says something dismal about today's standards, but it's still an awfully large "community" for any judge, or any number of deputies, to disregard.

South Florida, like Mid-Michigan, has some problems considerably more serious than policing what someone says, on tape or on stage, to a willing, paying adult audience. 2 Live Crew's street language may come from the gutter. But these arrests reflect a system with priorities that are not much higher — and far more offensive to liberty.

## MILWAUKEE SENTINEL
*Milwaukee, WI, June 12, 1990*

"Look around."

We've used that beginning to several editorials lately dealing with American values. We've mourned their decline; we've raged at their corrupters.

Now, the spotlight's glare must expose the newest evidence of decline:

An album — filthy and degrading — put out by a rap group called 2 Live Crew.

They couldn't get a date in Milwaukee last year because promoters couldn't sell enough tickets. But that was only a stop in the crew's vault to national notoriety.

The group has reached its apogee: The album — "As Nasty As They Wanna Be" — has been declared obscene in a Florida case, a Florida record dealer has been arrested for selling the record and two crew members have been arrested for singing lyrics from the album in defiance of the ruling.

First Amendment lawyers are beating a path to Florida to challenge the ruling on constitutional grounds. And liberals are wringing their hands, mourning the federal court's intrusion onto hallowed ground.

The liberals are right in this case.

There is the adult right to hear and see anything. There is a First Amendment right to produce those things that offend and shock. There is even the right to publish or produce those things that twist minds and propel someone into an act of mindless cruelty.

But there also is the principle that some things, though constitutionally protected, make a mockery of free speech and open access to ideas.

There is nothing redeeming about the album in question. It's lyrics are foul, offensive to women and, worse, encourage attacks upon them.

It took no genius to devise the words or the melody. Melody? Pardon the choice of words.

All it took was a few dirty minds and a convenient excuse that this was an album with deep social and ethnic messages that could only be properly expressed with obscenity.

Oops. There we go, using the word "obscenity." Not even the courts know what it is, it seems. They've tried for years to come up with a definition that meets constitutional muster and have essentially failed.

But some things are "obscene." The word is in the dictionary, free to be used.

What 2 Live Crew and other purveyors of smut have done takes no great talent. They have taken taste and turned it into a constitutional issue. In the end, they probably will prevail. A free society demands it.

Still, there is the implicit understanding by a civilized people that some things are taboo.

That means the First Amendment does not protect groups such as 2 Live Crew from the contempt of others, or from the kind of consumer aversion that will make their careers "As Brief As They Wanna Be."

## THE TAMPA TRIBUNE
*Tampa, FL, June 12, 1990*

You have to wonder about Broward County Sheriff Nick Navarro, who has charged members of the rap group 2 Live Crew with obscenity. He had intended to arrest all the members of the controversial quartet but the several deputies attending the group's Fort Lauderdale concert managed to snag only two.

In any event, Navarro's action succeeded only in getting yet more publicity for the squalid entertainers.

2 Live Crew's sole talent, such as it is, is devoted to debasing women. Their lyrics are filth, but does such filth threaten the Republic? And why the concentration on black rap bands? There are white punk-rock bands whose songs are equally lewd.

Without all the fanfare, wouldn't interest in 2 Live Crew soon wither? After all, there are talented rap groups that offer more than just obscenity, groups that capture something of the anger and vitality of the inner-city environment.

But Sheriff Navarro appears intent on keeping 2 Live Crew in the headlines. Last week, he won a ruling from a U.S. district judge that one of their albums was obscene. Sheriff's deputies made arrests when the band sang songs from that album at a concert to which only adults were admitted.

Children, to be sure, should be protected from this foulest smut, and that's the job of parents. It would help, perhaps, if the record industry adopted a rating system similar to that for movies.

But grown-ups don't need Sheriff Navarro to decide what music they can listen to. And 2 Live Crew doesn't deserve any more valuable publicity. Exploitive, anti-social entertainers should be permitted to vanish into a well-earned oblivion.

## St. Petersburg Times
*St. Petersburg, FL, June 9, 1990*

Assuming the First Amendment hasn't yet been eroded as badly as the Fourth, it won't take long for an appeals court to overturn U.S. District Court Judge Jose Gonzalez's ruling that an album by the rap group 2 Live Crew is obscene.

Is *As Nasty As They Wanna Be* vulgar and artless? Most people probably would think so, but when vulgarity and artlessness are made illegal, our jails will be 10 times more overcrowded than they already are. The definition of obscenity is much stricter and narrower than that, unless Gonzalez and other pandering judges succeed in changing it.

In ignoring 100 percent of the expert testimony offered in the case, Gonzalez ruled that the album *As Nasty As They Wanna Be* meets the 1973 U.S. Supreme Court standard for obscenity. Among other things, those guidelines say that the material in question must be outside of contemporary community standards. Any album that sells 2-million copies, despite intense official efforts to make it hard to find, is by definition within the mainstream of a large segment of American communities. In this case, the community in question is Fort Lauderdale, where the standards historically have been far laxer than in the great majority of communities where 2 Live Crew and other rap groups haven't been subjected to harassment.

The court's 1973 guidelines also say that an obscene work must lack serious artistic, literary or political value. *As Nasty As They Wanna Be's* artistic merits are dubious, although several sociologists and music critics have extolled them.

However, the album's political value is undeniable. This trumped-up case has already proved its political value for politically ambitious Broward County Sheriff Nick Navarro and politically desperate Florida Gov. Bob Martinez.

On the list of serious crimes that should be commanding Navarro's and Martinez's attention, nasty rap lyrics surely rank near the bottom. The issue does make a handy diversion, though, for politicians who would prefer to keep the public from giving too much scrutiny to their success in controlling the infinitely more serious issues of murder, robbery, drug trafficking and organized crime. No wonder, then, that Martinez and Navarro are at the vanguard of the anti-2 Live Crew crusade.

There's always a whiff of political expediency at the center of our periodic blue-nosed obscenity hunts. In this case, there's a whiff of racism as well.

If judges, governors and sheriffs are going to be hypocrites, at least let them be equal-opportunity hypocrites, harassing the respectable middle-aged suburban consumers of X-rated films as well as the less respectable young urban consumers of rap music.

## Judas Priest Rock Group Cleared in Teen Suicide

A state district judge in Reno, Nev. ruled Aug. 24, 1990 that the British heavy-metal rock group Judas Priest was not responsible for the deaths of two youths who had shot themselves after listening to the group's album *Stained Class*.

Judas Priest and its record company, CBS Records, had been sued by the parents of the two dead youths, Raymond Belknap and James Vance. The parents, who had sought a total of $6.2 million in damages, claimed that their sons had shot themselves after being influenced by subliminal messages contained on *Stained Class*. Some of the messages, said to be clearly audible only when the record was played backward, were alleged to have included the repeated phrase, "Do it."

Lawyers for Judas Priest and CBS Records argued that Belknap and Vance had troubled lives marked by heavy use of drugs and alcohol, physical abuse at home, failure at school and problems with the law.

State district Judge Jerry Whitehead ruled that although hidden messages had been contained on *Stained Class*, Judas Priest had not placed them there intentionally. He also ruled that the parents had failed to prove that the subliminal messages had caused their sons to shoot themselves. But because CBS had failed to supply the court with an original master tape of the album, Whitehead ordered the company to pay $40,000 to the parents' attorneys.

Media and recording industry lawyers said they were pleased by the verdict but that they were troubled that Judge Whitehead had not rejected the notion of backward subliminal messages outright.

# THE DENVER POST
*Denver, CO, August 29, 1990*

IT TOOK a Westerner to inject some horse sense into the debate over roll 'n' roll lyrics.

The families of two Sparks, Nev., youths sued heavy metal band Judas Priest, alleging that subliminal messages in the group's music caused Raymond Belknap, 18, and James Vance, 20, to attempt suicide.

To non-lawyer types, this suit seemed to stretch the notion of product liability to the border of absurdity. But then, the law's no stranger in the land of the absurd.

That's why Washoe District Judge Jerry Whitehead, who heard the case in his Reno courtroom, spent 93 pages explaining his decision to side with the rock band's contention that the music did not provoke the suicide attempt.

Whitehead isn't a fan of the thumping, unimaginative noise Judas Priest calls music. It's just that he couldn't find any evidence that the band intentionally injected subliminal messages into its lyrics. Besides, he seemed unconvinced that such messages would provoke a young person to take his or her own life anyway.

Whitehead especially is correct about the latter point. Despite a couple of decades of debate, there's more evidence that subliminal messages *don't* work than data to show that they do cause behavioral changes.

Moreover, the particular Judas Priest album in question — Stained Glass — was cut in 1978. That's 12 years ago. Young people who bought the record when it first hit the market would be in their late 20s to early 30s today.

If the music contained messages telling young people to commit suicide, and these signals did spur them into action, there should have been an abnormal rash of self-induced deaths among people in this age group. There wasn't.

Therefore, a person with a half pint of common sense has to reject the notion that the band's music caused these two Nevada youths to take a very troubling step.

Young people are influenced by what their peers think and do, and by some outside forces, including television and music.

But the responsibility for preventing suicides among teenagers — which is a serious problem in this country — still has to reside with family, friends and other adults such as teachers and clergy.

Too often, that bit of horse sense gets lost in the sometimes overly strident debate about the evils — or virtues — of rock 'n' roll music and its contemporary offshoots.

# MILWAUKEE SENTINEL
*Milwaukee, WI, August 29, 1990*

The attempt by the families of two young men to blame a Judas Priest album for the men's suicides was not only a long shot. Given the circumstances, it simply defied all odds.

The victims had been smoking marijuana and drinking, so the story goes, before they entered a suicide pact and shot themselves on a church playground. They also had been listening — for six hours — to the band's "Stained Glass" album.

The allegation by the families in their $6.2 million lawsuit was that there were hidden messages in the album. "Do it" was the specific phrase that plaintiffs charged provided the impetus for the men, aged 18 and 20, to pull the triggers on themselves.

There was quite an argument in court over whether the phrase, indeed, was effective.

The families lost the case, but not because the band and CBS records proved that subliminal messages cannot affect human behavior. They lost, the judge said, because no one could prove the defendants intentionally placed subliminal messages on the album.

In the midst of all this, one band member took the stand to show that the "do it" phrase was merely his exhaling during the recording session.

Despite their loss in court, the families' attorney proclaimed that this will not be the last case and that "sooner or later, a case like this will win."

It's worth noting that little, if anything, was made of the youths' bout with drugs or the dangerous combination with alcohol on the day they shot themselves (one of the youths died three years later from his wounds).

Their mothers testified that their sons had both exhibited violent behavior at an early age.

A good case can be made that the youths, indeed, were prime candidates for suicide, and that they wanted a little mood music for accompaniment. But the notion that the music alone pushed them over the edge is far-fetched.

Independent of subliminal stimuli, they were candidates for tragedy.

## LAS VEGAS SUN

*Las Vegas, NV, July 25, 1990*

Judges are justifiably complaining these days about the overburdened courts. An ever-growing number of drug cases appears to be the biggest reason for the backlog of work in America's justice system.

But frivolous cases that judges agree to hear also are a major problem. There is no better example than the Judas Priest trial under way in a District Court in Reno.

The parents of two young men who attempted suicide in 1985 are claiming that subliminal messages in a song by the British rock band Judas Priest compelled the boys to shoot themselves.

Raymond Belknap, 18, died from a single shot from a sawed-off shotgun held to his chin. James Vance, then 20, attempted to do the same but managed only to blow his face off. He died three years later after an overdose of medication.

The parents are seeking to prove that hidden messages in a couple of songs on the Judas Priest's "Stained Glass" album encouraged the teenagers to shoot themselves.

That a judge would legitimize such a case by ordering a trial seems absurd. Blaming a record company and a rock band for the suicide of two unquestionably troubled teenagers does not make legal sense.

The subliminal lyrics specter has unjustly haunted rock music for years. But it has been extremely difficult to prove that they even exist, let alone that they are effective enough to convince teenagers that suicide is the answer.

Rock 'n' roll has been blamed for corrupting the morals of the youth since its beginnings in the mid-1950s. The gyrations of Elvis Presley would be considered tame today, but they were barred from television 35 years ago.

Most of the kids of that era seem to have turned out all right. In 1990, they run major corporations and sit in Congress. It is obvious that rock music has not turned them into sex fiends or devil worshipers.

While Judas Priest's heavy metal music certainly can be considered aggressive and militant at times, it seems inconceivable that it could be blamed for the deaths of two teenagers in Northern Nevada.

Evidence in the case has shown quite clearly that the two young men had many other problems that contributed to their decision to try to kill themselves. In addition to substantial alcohol and drug abuse, Belknap and Vance had turbulent family lives, had dropped out of school in the 10th grade and had criminal records.

The parents of the two young men should know better than to blame rock music for the unfortunate fate of their sons. Besides the obvious First Amendment arguments that should shield the band from prosecution in this matter, Judas Priest clearly is not to blame for the deaths of Raymond Belknap and Jay Vance.

This could have been decided long before taxpayer money was wasted to debate the matter in court.

## LAS VEGAS REVIEW-JOURNAL

*Las Vegas, NV, August 26, 1990*

Washoe District Judge Jerry Carr Whitehead did the right thing on Friday when he exonerated the British heavy-metal band Judas Priest in the celebrated "subliminal message" case in Reno.

The judge ruled that hidden words do, through happenstance, exist on a Judas Priest album — but they were not put there intentionally and did not cause two young Sparks men to try suicide. The families of the suicide victims had been seeking $6.2 million in damages from the band and CBS records, claiming hidden satanic lyrics on the 1978 "Stained Class" album drove the young men to suicide.

On Dec. 23, 1985, Raymond Belknap put the business end of a sawed-off shotgun under his chin and pulled the trigger. His buddy James Vance reloaded the gun and tried to blow his head off, too. Belkamp died instantly, but Vance, survived, horribly mutilated, dying of a drug overdose three years later.

Belknap and Vance both dropped out of school in the 10th grade. Belknap, an abused child, was a small-time thief who drank, smoked dope and "experimented" with cocaine and speed.

Vance, according to court records, "experimented" with marijuana, LSD, cocaine, heroin, angel dust, PCP and barbituates. In the two years before his suicide attempt, Vance checked into a drug rehab center, attended Alcoholics Anonymous and Narcotics Anonymous meetings, and ran away from home 13 times. Vance once tried to choke his mother and threatened her with a hammer and a loaded pistol.

Despite their children's obviously muddled lives, the parents blamed Judas Priest for their deaths and tried to squeeze more than six million bucks out of the well-heeled rockers. The judge last week killed that dream of riches — and he put a crimp in the families' transparent quest to censor music they don't like.

Aunetta Roberson, mother of Raymond Belknap revealed her motivation in an interview with the Los Angeles Times earlier this month, saying: "This case has brought so much public attention to the issue. The problems with heavy metal music are finally out in the open. Bands are beginning to be censored, and I'm happy about it."

Phyllis Vance, James' mother, also blamed her kid's problems on heavy metal music. She said before the verdict that, if she won, she planned to use the money to build a shelter where parents could bring allegedly imperiled heavy-metal fans to be "deprogrammed."

This, you see, was the plaintiffs' true objective: Not to punish the band for "subliminal messages" but to silence Judas Priest and other rock musicians they associate with their sons' miserable lives. One can sympathize to a degree with these troubled families, but when they try to exploit their tragedy to encourage unconstitutional censorship, that sympathy is sorely strained.

## 20th Anniversary of Woodstock Marked

Aug. 15-17, 1989 marked the 20th anniversary of the Woodstock Music and Art Fair. In 1969 the rock music festival, described as an "Aquarian Exposition, Three Days of Peace and Music," drew 400,000 young people to Bethel, N.Y. in the Catskill Mountains, creating massive traffic jams and extreme shortages of food, water and medical and sanitary facilities. Despite these conditions, which were complicated by frequent downpours, no incident of violence occurred. Eighty arrests were made, mostly on drug charges involving LSD, amphetamines and heroin. Marijuana smokers, estimated to be the majority of the audience, were not arrested. Three accidental deaths were reported.

The festival featured about 25 of the era's most popular rock and folk acts, including Richie Havens, Jimi Hendrix, Santana, The Jefferson Airplane, Joan Baez, Arlo Gutherie, The Grateful Dead, The Who, and Crosby, Stills and Nash. The festival had been scheduled to be held in Walkill, N.Y. But, after townspeople objected, it was moved to the 600-acre farm of dairyman Max B. Yasgur. The organizers of the festival, John Roberts, Michael Lang and Joel Rosenman, had originally estimated expenses, to be covered by admissions fees, at $750,000. The crush of spectators, however, caused ticket-taking to be abandoned.

Ultimately, Woodstock Ventures, Inc. spent $2.5 million while collecting only $1.5 million. The $1 million debt was to be offset by a film of the festival and recordings of the music.

In the years since the festival, Woodstock had grown to legendary stature as one of the significant events of the 1960s.

## The Washington Times
*Washington, DC, August 16, 1989*

In 1969, the same year that the Woodstock nation declared its independence from the cosmos, historian Theodore Roszak wrote in "The Making of a Counter Culture" that "it is the American young ... who seem to have grasped most clearly the fact that ... the paramount struggle of our day is against ... 'technocracy,'" which Mr. Roszak called "that social form in which an industrial society reaches the peak of its organizational integration." But whatever it was that the 350,000 children who gathered in an Upstate New York cow pasture 20 years ago this week were revolting against, technocracy wasn't it.

From all over the United States they came, down the highways built by President Eisenhower as much for national security reasons as for the closer economic integration of American industrial society. They rode on high-powered cycles, shared vans or hitchhiked with middle-class technocrats returning from Disneyland with their 2.3 children in tow. Without the automobile and transportation system and the technocracy that designed and produced it, Woodstock couldn't have happened.

Once they arrived, they enveloped themselves in rock music electronically produced, amplified, and played by multi-millionaire celebrities who were themselves the creatures of an entertainment industry based on high-tech smoke and mirrors and the celluloid manipulation of fantasies. The drugs the Woodstockers smoked, injected, sniffed or swallowed were products of a scientific industrial chemistry distributed through propaganda at least as fraudulent as the cigarette commercials on television or Defense Secretary Robert McNamara's promises of victory in Vietnam. Without the electro-narco-techno-system, Woodstock could not have existed.

When the Woodstockers O.D.'d on their chemicals, emergency medical units staffed by highly trained technicians took care of them. When they got hungry, mass-produced food imported and distributed by the National Guard fed them. When they wondered what to think, when to laugh, when to applaud or boo, electronic signals from the stage told them. When they threw away their garbage or excreted on the ground, technocracy was there to clean up after them. When they finally grew bored of being liberated, technocracy gathered them to its aluminum bosom, because technocracy had given the Woodstockers the money, the leisure and the appetites to buy what technocracy offered them. There's a sucker born every minute, and Woodstock was there to take them in.

The Woodstockers, and the generation they symbolized, were the captives of the illusion that they had liberated themselves from technocracy and bureaucracy. But all they had liberated themselves from was the internal disciplines that real liberation demands. Victorian England had very little bureaucracy or technocracy, but the Woodstockers wouldn't have liked it much.

Exactly one week before Woodstock, would-be rock star Charles Manson used drugs, sex and the mystical gobbledygook of the counterculture to manipulate his "family" into committing murder. Four months after Woodstock, Calif., at the next big music festival at Altamont, the Hell's Angels, high on bad dope, beat up fans and knifed a man to death on camera while the Rolling Stones sang "Sympathy for the Devil." You have to wonder why everyone this week is wallowing in nostalgia about Woodstock. It never went away.

## THE SAGINAW NEWS
*Saginaw, MI, August 14, 1989*

Latest and maybe last of the receding wave of 1960s anniversaries is the Woodstock festival that took place in mid-August 20 years ago.

This was an event where half a million young people with nothing better to do gathered in a New York field to listen to rock music, drink, smoke dope, take off their clothes, listen, and smoke some more. About 2 million others remained stuck outside on the roads.

While apprehensive old folks wondered, Golly, what next?, its citizens hailed their "Woodstock Nation" as a sure sign of peace upon the planet, because here we all are, kids proving that humanity can get mellow and live in harmony. It was the dawning of the Age of Aquarius.

That sunny sign never made it to high noon. The light began to dim when, pretty soon, "freeks" started killing each other at rock festivals, just like in Vietnam. Jimi Hendrix, Janis Joplin and other turned-on types fried their brains, Timothy Leary dropped out, and that's where all the flowers went.

Many of those who remember Woodstock, though, regard it fondly as the final flourish of a special, if short-lived, time. Amid the gross self-indulgence, excess and manipulation, they recall holding a faith in something better — a belief that finally proved only tragic delusion.

Well, it was fun while it lasted, and it did bring change to American society, if not politics or ethics.

That is, the crooks are still crooks, and everyone who was greedy then is greedy now. However, ever since, it has been quite common to curse vigorously in public, and especially in the movies. It is an individual judgment whether this victory of honest expression over 1950s hypocrisy has advanced or retarded civilization as we know it. Just don't ask Jerry Falwell.

One strong image that does remain from Woodstock is the huge photo in Life magazine of the festival grounds after the happy campers departed. It was a 600-acre expanse of trash. We just hope it is not a portent for the 1990s that those now growing into maturity and leadership come out of a generation that never learned to pick up after itself.

### The Dallas Morning News
*Dallas, TX, August 16, 1989*

No, this is not another of the Woodstock paeans that have saturated the media in these dog days of August. By now, we figured, you didn't need to be told once more about how a rock concert supposedly became the capstone for a decade of excess and experimentation and how the three-day event in Upstate New York crystallized the way a generation defined itself.

As the years have gone by and responsibilities have increased, the Baby Boom generation has become more and more wrapped up in the mystique of Woodstock: that a generation of youth found oneness in the mud and that everyone stood around grasping flowers and gushing about the karma. Well, maybe Woodstock was more than just a party, but was it really that great?

As Robbie Robertson of the Band recently put it, "Over the years, between the news footage and the movie, it's kind of foggy in my mind as to who was doing what to whom and where." At the risk of offending some former flower children, we thought we'd rummage through the Woodstock clip file and report on what we found. We'll leave it to the sociologists to draw conclusions.

■ Despite its peace-and-love motif, the festival spawned 80 lawsuits and countersuits. Two of the concert's partners sued the other two; the owner of a raceway sued because the traffic blocked his entrance; a farmer sued because his cows didn't give milk for three days; and a man filmed while making love sued because the movie showed him to be heterosexual, thus supposedly hurting his hairdressing business.

■ If the event were restaged, the performers would be fewer. Ten have succumbed to drugs (Janis Joplin, Jimi Hendrix, Keith Moon, Paul Butterfield, Tim Hardin, Al Wilson of Canned Heat), suicide (Richard Manuel of the Band), a heart attack (Bob Hite of Canned Heat), a liver ailment (Ron McKernan of the Grateful Dead) and gunshots (Felix Pappalardi of Mountain).

■ The Who was paid $6,250 for appearing at Woodstock; this summer, the group's tour is expected to earn approximately $70 million. The Grateful Dead made $2,500 at the festival; this year, when major groups were contacted about possibly playing at a Woodstock reunion concert this autumn (a plan that ultimately fell through), virtually all demanded fees in the mid-six figures.

■ And, finally, this often-overlooked gem: The festival's closing act, Jimi Hendrix, actually was an accident of sorts. The concert promoters originally had wanted Roy Rogers to sing *Happy Trails*, but somehow he declined the invitation. Maybe it was just as well. Trigger might have slipped in the mud.

### The Record
*Hackensack, NJ, August 13, 1989*

In the lexicon of the Sixties, it was a happening. Twenty years ago, 500,000 people from across the country gathered at Max Yasgur's farm for what was billed as a three-day music and arts fair. By the time it was over, the Woodstock nation had been born, and sex, drugs, and rock-and-roll would never quite be the same again.

Just what happened on that farm in the tiny town of Bethel, N.Y. on the weekend of Aug. 15 depends on who you talk to. A few came for the weekend and wound up as permanent residents. One woman rode to the festival on a motorcycle and had her baby delivered by the former president of the local chamber of commerce. One young man was killed when a tractor drove over his sleeping bag. For some it forever changed their lives. Others don't remember much.

Everyone remembers the rain and the mud, though. There was lovemaking and drug overdoses. Strangers became fast friends. Old friends never saw one another. Some remember it as a high point. Others say it was awful.

Looking back, trying to balance nostalgia and revisionism, Woodstock seems best remembered simply as a party. It was the summer of the moon landing, Ted Kennedy and Chappaquidick, Sharon Tate and Charles Manson, and the Vietnam war. It was time for a party, and what an event it was. Guests began arriving a month ahead of time. By the time the celebration was in full swing, the New York State Thruway had been shut down and turned into a parking lot. Originally, the guest list was to include 100,000 or so paying customers. When a half a million people showed up, promoters had no choice but to let eveyone in for free.

Like all good parties, this one had music. The Who, Richie Havens, Ten Years After, Santana, Joan Baez, Country Joe and the Fish, Joe Cocker. When it was time to go, Jimi Hendrix reminded everyone just where they were with a haunting rendition of "The Star Spangled Banner."

Maybe the most remarkable thing about Woodstock was the way people got along. Put a half million people, many of them high on drugs, in a pasture for three days in the pouring rain with not enough to eat and inadequate sanitary facilities, and you have a prescription for disaster. Instead, the hardships were a kind of bonding agent. People for the most part were kind and polite to one another.

Woodstock was supposed to be a rebellious statement. A counter-culture gathering. But was it? Who were these kids with long hair, wearing love beads, and in some cases nothing at all? They weren't revolutionaries. They were America's sons and daughters.

The final word on Woodstock, at least for five years until it comes time to commemorate the 25th anniversary, is that it will never happen again, at least not for the original members of the Woodstock nation. Drugs may once have seemed innocent, but that innocence is now long gone. Spontaneity has given way to family planning and plotting career paths. No gold card member of the plastic generation would give a thought to attending a Woodstock reunion, unless the promoters could promise jogging tracks, aerobics, whirlpools, and on-site day care.

The Woodstock party is over.

### The Miami Herald
*Miami, FL, August 17, 1989*

FOR TODAY'S teen-agers — nurtured on MTV and televised rock fests — the publicity is almost incomprehensible, the nostalgic ruminations excessive, and the music . . . well, save for a legendary exception or two, the music is simply uninteresting. Ah, but for many Baby Boomers, the 1969 Woodstock music festival still represents a bright mythical moment, an embodiment of life's limitless possibilities, a New Age whose birth they were midwifing.

Commercial enterprises of every sort — from the disastrous reunion of Woodstock veterans to a spate of testimonials — have sprouted around images of the farm in Bethel, N.Y., where the three-day festival was actually held. The media join the merchants' opportunism. The whole exercise preys upon our collective need for myths.

But why choose Woodstock for the myth-making? Because this reminiscence is a formless event with something in it for just about everyone. Festival devotees pine for lost youth, tribal ecstasies, and the absence of inhibitions. Cynics point to the influence of Baby Boomers in the media who, now engirthed by early middle age, endow Woodstock with significance. Dispassionate observers and skeptics focus on the muddy fields, the chaotic planning, and the fatuousness of an Abbie Hoffman declaring himself the citizen of "Woodstock nation." Adolescents complain about the hype and rightly say that many post-Woodstock groups are better than those that played there.

Still, Woodstock has become a point of reference, in retrospect the Sixties' lyrical coda to political assassinations and the Vietnam War. Yet it is a perfectly threadbare myth, a pleasure point in many people's youth that doesn't merit the meaning that some attempt to find in, or impart to, it.

Nothing of lasting significance — save for the odd song or two — has come of Woodstock. Abundant nostalgia has. But nostalgia can be an immensely egocentric emotion. It pillages the past for selfish ends while disparaging the present.

Like all nostalgia, that for Woodstock neglects the future. And at the threshold of the 21st Century, when famine, environmental menace, nuclear disaster, and economic ills of every sort still stalk the globe, mindless nostalgia is distracting. Encouraged by hucksterism, it negates the spirit of many of the kids who were lost in musical reveries 20 years ago this week.

# Newsday

*New York, NY, August 16, 1989*

Twenty years ago today it became clear to America that the giant traffic jam-mud bath-rock concert in Bethel, N.Y., was going to end up as a seminal event — Woodstock.

But even today it is not entirely clear what the long-term consequences were, or will be, of those three days when half a million rain-drenched people gathered to celebrate peace and music on Max Yasgur's upstate farm.

Consider these ironies:

• Designed to make profits for its organizers, Woodstock lost money after the crowd grew so big that gates collapsed. Yet, perhaps more than any other event, Woodstock defined a *market* that entrepreneurs have profited from ever since, a market that scarfed up LPs then — and Cuisinarts today.

• A showcase for rock 'n' roll, Woodstock was followed by a period of imaginative music that today has, sadly, run its course. Rock has split into categories, fragmenting listeners and making the Woodstock crowd's passionate unity seem weirdly antique.

• A friendly venue for the use of marijuana and LSD by middle-class and college-age kids, Woodstock made it seem inevitable that drugs like marijuana would be legalized. Instead, addiction is poisoning the underclass and a new Gallup poll says Americans view drug abuse as the nation's worst problem — a welcome and clear-eyed change of view.

Social trends are cyclical, so perhaps the changes in attitude about music and drugs were inevitable. Given the money the counter-culture had to spend, exploitation of that crowd was probably inevitable, too.

But not all attitudes popularized by Woodstock have been reversed. Consider antiwar activism, idealism. Kids at Woodstock hollered ribald antiwar chants. Yet America's peace movement succeeded in changing U.S. policy on Vietnam and the draft, and today's politicians still shrink from reawakening it: There's widespread consensus that "we don't want another Vietnam." Basically, good.

Woodstock itself — the hair, the mud, the music, the drugs — seems a surreal relic of the distant past. But don't count out its influence: Remnants of '60s idealism still surface like old love beads in Bethel's plowed fields. And Woodstock's hippies have become the Me Generation's yuppies. Who knows what mutation is next? Stay tuned.

# SYRACUSE HERALD-JOURNAL

*Syracuse, NY, August 18, 1989*

Was Woodstock a cultural watershed or a just muddy sex orgy for a few hundred thousand doped-up, self-indulgent brats?

Analyses of the rock music festival have ranged between both extremes as its 20th anniversary was marked this week. Whatever it was, nothing quite like it has happened before or since. Attempts to duplicate have fallen far short of the mark.

For good or ill, Woodstock reflected the rage and confusion of a generation in turmoil. It was an escape from a world that to many seemed to have gone mad. It provided a snapshot of anarchy — what the world might be like if there were no rules, no authority. Even those who remember Woodstock with fondness admit three days of it was about all they could stand.

Humorists have had a lot of fun the last few days with the image of graying, paunchy, clay-footed suburbanites hauling out the tie-dyes and Jefferson Airplane albums in a pathetic attempt to recapture their youth. More sober critics point to Woodstock as the event that gave us not peace and love, but the drug epidemic, guilt-free promiscuity, ethical and moral degeneration.

There's a kernel of truth in the drug argument. Drug abuse wasn't invented at Woodstock, but the event did serve to propagate the cruel lie that it was possible to use drugs and escape harm. It has taken society a long time to arrive at the consensus that drug abuse *always* has consequences.

But critics who blame the Woodstock attitude for all our current social ills are wrong. To hear them tell it, our society was perfect until those rabble-rousers and nihilists came along and ruined it for everybody. But take a hard look at that idyllic existence Woodstock-bashers seem to remember so fondly.

Maybe they miss the sight of unarmed people being tear-gassed, beaten with nightsticks and chewed by police dogs because they had the audacity to try to vote, or to use a public lavatory, or to apply for a job. Maybe they miss the nightly filmed reports of American teenagers and young men being killed and maimed by the thousands in a faraway war that had, at best, a vaguely defined purpose, a war that seemed to stretch on and on without a prospect of conclusion.

The kids at Woodstock didn't create those horrors, they were merely reacting to them. The world they had grown up in — the world of Camelot and Beaver Cleaver and Mickey Mantle — had been turned on its head. Where was the "liberty and justice for all" they had spoken of every school day of their lives? No one had told them this might happen. They felt betrayed.

Today the same people who made-love-not-war in the Woodstock muck and mire are engineering hostile takeovers instead of fomenting rebellion, driving BMWs instead of Volkswagen bugs. They no longer protest The System. They are The System.

Has the Woodstock generation betrayed its ideals? No more than any other. How many of us at 20 could have foretold what we would be at 40? We live our lives in minutes and hours, not 20-year chunks. We are mostly reactive, not proactive. Plans get changed — not because of any individual or collective character flaw, but because circumstances alter our outlook. Our attitudes are shaped by what happens around us.

Most members of the Woodstock generation are grateful that these are far more serene times than the summer of 1969. Still, the wave of Woodstock nostalgia reflects their longing for the excitement of it all — when dreams were not yet beaten down, when they defined themselves in terms of possibilities, not limits. It's worth remembering.

## DAILY NEWS
*New York, NY, August 12, 1989*

It's time to put Woodstock in its proper perspective. Yes, the crowd was half a million strong. Yes, for a short while Woodstock was the third largest city in New York. And yes, there was almost no violent crime during the three-day festival. But all this inane adulation isn't deserved. It wasn't the greatest rock show of all time. Some of the biggest names of the period — the Beatles, the Rolling Stones, Bob Dylan — weren't there. No R&B artists appeared. The only black performers were those who had been assimilated into the white counterculture — Jimi Hendrix, Sly and the Family Stone and Richie Havens.

The miracle of Woodstock was that it succeeded in spite of itself. There were too many people, too few toilets, not enough food and no real security guards. And it rained. Woodstock's success ended in that upstate field. When the crowd left, it was supposed to be the start of the "Woodstock Nation." An era of peace, love and happiness. It never happened.

Sadly, it's members of the Woodstock Nation who have perverted the memory of the event. They've changed it from a symbol of the counterculture to an over-the-counter product.

What's the true legacy of Woodstock? That for one brief moment, music, politics and the youth culture became one. But it was only a moment. It wasn't the future.

## The Seattle Times
*Seattle, WA, August 16, 1989*

ABOUT 12 million people attended the three-day concert held on a rain-soaked farm in upstate New York. That estimate does not jibe with the 400,000 figure from August 1969, but it roughly matches the number of people who claim to have been there.

On this anniversary, Woodstock takes a 20-year jump on being fat, flatulent and 40. The event survives as a generational experience that is burnished by time, like childbirth and military basic training.

Memories of bad drugs, scalper prices for food and water, monster traffic gridlock, overflowing toilets, and miserable weather were replaced with myth-making recollections.

Woodstock was one of a kind. Attempts to reproduce its spirit failed. Except, of course, on the double album and film.

Three days in the mud have been transformed into an age of innocence and charm. Woodstock's naiveté is its hokey legacy.

*Warner Bros. Inc.*

For all its exquisite, illicit pleasures, no one got away with a thing. Woodstock was also a symbol of a generation in over its head.

Two decades of pandemic drug problems, sexually transmitted diseases, and a reptilian-like shedding of any pretext of social awareness have mocked the idea that the Woodstock Nation was anything but a fleeting good time.

Woodstock's famous images have a curiously contemporary feel. But today's visions of wet, cold and miserable teen-agers are not young people on a glorious lark.

These waifs are living life on city streets without a movie sound track.

Most of the Woodstock revelers would throw a high-fiber fit if their children tried to have their own muddy bacchanal of drugs, sex, and rock 'n' roll.

OK, maybe if the snacks weren't too sugary, Waterpiks were available for cleansing orthodontic braces, everyone wore bike helmets to and from the festival, and there were complimentary parental seating so Mom and Dad could share the experience.

Woodstock nostalgia is pure kitsch. By the 25th anniversary everyone ought to be hooting with laughter.

## LAS VEGAS SUN
*Las Vegas, NV, August 16, 1989*

It was 20 years ago that the late Max Yasgur ignored warnings from his neighbors and offered his 30-acre dairy farm in Bethel, N.Y., for a cozy little outdoor rock festival.

More than 350,000 journeyed to the tiny farming hamlet in the Catskill Mountains. They stayed three days. They shared their food, and when they ran out, many turned to pot and pills.

Conservative leaders screamed about all those "hippies" taking drugs, taking off their clothes and frolicking in the mud.

The youths never heard the conservative voices, just as they shrugged off the rain. As Yasgur said with tears in his eyes, "You've proven to the world that a half-million young people can get together and have nothing but fun and music."

But even Yasgur had no idea how big that rock festival would become. The name of the festival really is a misnomer: Woodstock actually is 50 miles northwest of Yasgur's farm in Bethel.

But after August 1969, Woodstock no longer was just a place. More than anything else, it became the symbol of a movement.

It's the symbol of the "love and peace" generation. It's the symbol of turning on and dropping out. It's the symbol of protest — and of a time when some national leaders started to listen to the young people.

In one respect, Yasgur was correct. Woodstock was nothing more than some muddy fun in "the garden" to the sounds of the likes of Richie Havens, Janis Joplin, John Sebastian, Jimi Hendrix and a new foursome called "Crosby, Stills, Nash and Young."

But it was also so much more. The music symbolized the eruption of protests on college campuses throughout the nation. The rock rhythms served as an eerie funeral dirge to the Kent State shootings and the My Lai massacre. It played as background to the end of the Vietnam War, the downfall of the Nixon administration, and the end of a long period of public trust in our national policies and goals.

Admission to the concert was $20, but because several turnstiles were not erected, many got in free. For that weekend in August, there was free music, free love and a carefree attitude.

But in years to come, most in the Woodstock generation would change their carefree attitudes. More than 90 percent of the heart of the Woodstock generation — 40-year-olds — indicate in polls that they believe marijuana is a harmful drug. They also believe in monogamy and individual financial success.

These ideas probably were not bandied around very much during the rock festival.

We surely have changed a great deal. But that doesn't prevent some of us from taking a break and remembering what it was like "back in the garden."

At the time, it was a lot of fun for a lot of people. But quickly, it developed into an avalanche that captured the hearts and minds of a generation.

For years, Woodstock symbolized the division of the young and not-so-young. But today, the hippies have grown up. Many have graduated from yippie to yuppie. Most learned the pratfalls of dropping out of society and have since become part of its mainstream.

Perhaps that's the most valuable lesson we have learned since Woodstock.

# INDEX

## A

ABC—*See* AMERICAN *Broadcasting Company*
ACLU—*See* AMERICAN *Civil Liberties Union*
ACQUIRED Immune Deficiency Syndrome—*See* AIDS
ACTOR'S Equity
   Miss Saigon casting controversy 114–117
ADVERTISING
   'Amerika' TV film controversy 28–31
   Children's TV bill veto 22–27
   Screenwriters' strike 50–53
ADVOCATE, The (Los Angeles newspaper)
   Andy Rooney 60 Minutes suspension 42–43
AIDS (acquired immune deficiency syndrome)
   NEA grant rejections 104–107
ALLEN, Woody
   Film colorization controversy 54–63
ALLIANCE of Motion Picture and Television Producers
   Screenwriters' strike 50–53
AMERICAN Broadcasting Company (ABC)
   'Amerika' TV film controversy 28–31
AMERICAN Civil Liberties Union (ACLU)
   Meese porn crackdown 156–159
AMERIKA (TV film)
   Broadcast controversy 28–31
APPLE Computer Inc.
   FCC HDTV guidelines 48–49
ARPNET (Advanced Research Projects Agency Network)
   Computer virus controversy 84–89
ART—*See* PAINTING *& Sculpture*
AS Nasty as They Wanna Be (recording)
   2 Live Crew arrest 200–203

ASSEMBLIES of God
   Swaggart sex scandal downfall 78–81
ATTORNEY General's Commission on Pornography
   Meese crackdown 156–159
   Violence linkage 152–155
AU Moulin de la Galette (painting)
   Record art sale 144–147

## B

B. DALTON Booksellers (of Barnes & Noble)
   Satanic Verses controversy 178–189
BAEZ, Joan
   Woodstock 20th anniversary 206–209
BAKER, Susan
   Record warning label debate 198–199
BAKKER, Rev. Jim
   Sex scandal downfall 68–77
BAKKER, Tammy Faye
   Sex scandal downfall 68–77
BARRIE, Dennis
   Mapplethorpe photo show debate 108–113
BELKNAP, Raymond (1967-85)
   Judas Priest teen suicide case 204–205
BENNETT, William
   'Amerika' TV film controversy 28–31
BETHEL, N.Y.
   Woodstock 20th anniversary 206–209
BOND, Alan
   Record art sale 144–147
BOOKS—*See* LITERATURE
BOSTON, Mass.
   Media double ownership rule annulment 190–195
   Record art theft 148–149
BOSTON Herald, The (newspaper)
   Media double ownership rule annulment 190–195

BRANDENBURG v. Ohio
   Flag-burning ruling 118–127
BROADCASTING
   'Amerika' TV film controversy 28–31
   Andy Rooney 60 Minutes suspension 42–43
   Bakker sex scandal downfall 68–77
   Children's TV bill veto 22–27
   FCC 'fairness doctrine' debate 4–13
   FCC HDTV guidelines 48–49
   FCC indecency debate 14–17
   Film colorization controversy 54–63
   Keillor radio show retirement 82–83
   Media double ownership rule annulment 190–195
   Screenwriters' strike 50–53
   Senate live TV coverage 44–47
   Swaggart sex scandal downfall 78–81
   TV talk show sensationalism 32–41
BUSH, George Herbert Walker (President of the U.S.)
   Art censorship opposition 100–103
   Flag-burning rulings 118–135
   Swaggart sex scandal downfall 78–81
BYRD, Sen. Robert Carlisle (D, W. Va.)
   Senate live TV coverage 44–47

## C

CALIFORNIA, University of
   FCC indecency debate 14–17
CAMPBELL, Luther
   2 Live Crew arrest 200–203
CAPITAL Cities/ABC Inc.
   'Amerika' TV film controversy 28–31
CBS News
   Andy Rooney 60 Minutes suspension 42–43

CBS News
    Andy Rooney 60 Minutes suspension 42–43
CBS Records
    Judas Priest teen suicide case 204–205
CHEZ Tortoni (painting)
    Record art theft 148–149
CHICAGO, Ill.
    Porn legislation controversy 160–163
CHILD Protection and Obscenity Enforcement Act (1988)
    Porn legislation controversy 160–163
CHILDREN
    Kiddie TV bill veto 22–27
    Porn legislation controversy 160–163
    Record warning label debate 198–199
CHRISTIE, Manson & Woods International Inc.
    Record art sale 144–147
    Record art theft 148–149
CHRYSLER Corp.
    Amerika' TV film controversy 28–31
CINCINNATI, Ohio
    Mapplethorpe photo show debate 108–113
CINEPLEX Odeon Corp.
    Last Temptation of Christ debate 64–67
CITY of Renton v. Playtime Theatres
    Porn legislation controversy 160–163
CIVIL Rights
    2 Live Crew arrest 200–203
CLAY, Andrew Dice (Andrew Silverstein)
    2 Live Crew arrest 200–203
COMPUTERS
    Virus controversy 84–89
CONCERT, The (painting)
    Record art theft 148–149
CONGRESS, U.S.
    Bush art censorship opposition 100–103
    Children's TV bill veto 22–27
    Dial-a-porn debate 164–167
    FCC 'fairness doctrine' debate 4–13
    Film colorization controversy 54–63
    Flag desecration bill rejection 136–143

Media double ownership rule annulment 190–195
    Meese porn crackdown 156–159
    Porn legislation controversy 160–163
    Senate live TV coverage 44–47
    Senate obscene art ban rejection 92–99
CONSTITUTION, U.S.
    Children's TV bill veto 22–27
    Congressional flag desecration bill rejection 136–143
    Dial-a-porn debate 164–167
    FCC 'fairness doctrine' debate 4–13
    Flag-burning rulings 118–135
    Meese panel porn, violence linkage 152–155
    Porn legislation controversy 160–163
    Public figure satirization protection 168–177
CONTEMPORARY Arts Council
    Mapplethorpe photo show debate 108–113
COPYRIGHT Office, U.S.
    Film colorization controversy 54–63
CORCORAN Gallery of Art (Washington, D. C.)
    Mapplethorpe photo show debate 108–113
CORTEGE aux Environs de Florence (painting)
    Record art theft 148–149
CRIME
    Meese porn crackdown 156–159
    Record art theft 148–149
CROSBY, Stills & Nash (singing group)
    Woodstock 20th anniversary 206–209
CURRENT Affair, A (TV show)
    Broadcast sensationalism debate 32–41

# D

DAFOE, Willem
    Last Temptation of Christ debate 64–67
DAISHOWA Paper Manufacturing Co.
    Record art sale 144–147
DANCE
    NEA grant rejections 104–107

DEFENSE, U.S. Department of
    Computer virus controversy 84–89
DEGAS, Edgar (1834-1917)
    Record art theft 148–149
DIGITAL Equipment Corp.
    FCC HDTV guidelines 48–49
DINGELL, Sen. John (D, Mich.)
    FCC 'fairness doctrine' debate 4–13
DOLE, Sen. Robert J. (R, Kan.)
    Congressional flag desecration bill rejection 136–143
    Senate live TV coverage 44–47
DONAHUE, Phil
    TV talk show sensationalism 32–41
DONNERSTEIN, Edward
    Meese panel porn, violence linkage 152–155
DOWNEY Jr., Morton
    TV talk show sensationalism 32–41

# E

ENTERTAINMENT Tonight (TV show)
    Broadcast sensationalism debate 32–41
EUROPE
    FCC HDTV guidelines 48–49

# F

FAIRNESS Doctrine
    FCC debate 4–13
FALWELL, Rev. Jerry
    Bakker sex scandal downfall 68–77
    Porn legislation controversy 160–163
    Public figure satirization protection 168–177
FAMILY Worship Center
    Swaggart sex scandal downfall 78–81

FBI—*See FEDERAL Bureau of Investigation*
FCC—*See Federal Communications Commission*
FEDERAL Bureau of Investigation (FBI)
    Computer virus controversy 84–89
FEDERAL Communications Commission (FCC)
    Children's TV bill veto 22–27
    'Fairness doctrine' debate 4–13
    HDTV guidelines 48–49
    Indecency debate 14–17
    Media double ownership rule annulment 190–195
FINLEY, Karen
    NEA grant rejections 104–107
FIRST Amendment Issues
    Congressional flag desecration bill rejection 136–143
    FCC 'fairness doctrine' debate 4–13
    Flag-burning rulings 118–135
    Meese panel porn, violence linkage 152–155
    Porn legislation controversy 160–163
    Public figure satirization protection 168–177
FLECK, John
    NEA grant rejections 104–107
FLORIDA
    2 Live Crew arrest 200–203
FLYNT, Larry C.
    Mapplethorpe photo show debate 108–113
    Public figure satirization protection 168–177
FOLEY, Rep. Thomas S. (D, Wash.)
    Congressional flag desecration bill rejection 136–143
FORUM (magazine)
    Porn legislation controversy 160–163
FOWLER, Mark
    FCC 'fairness doctrine' debate 4–13
FOX Broadcasting Co.
    Children's TV bill veto 22–27
FREEMAN, Chris
    2 Live Crew arrest 200–203
FREE Speech—*See FIRST Amendment Issues*
FROHNMAYER, John
    Bush art censorship opposition 100–103
    NEA grant rejections 104–107

# G

GARDNER Museum, Isabella Stewart
    Record art theft 148–149
GERALDO (TV show)
    Broadcast sensationalism debate 32–41
GETTY Museum, J. Paul
    Record art sale 144–147
GINGRICH, Rep. Newt (R, Ga.)
    Congressional flag desecration bill rejection 136–143
GLENN, Sen. John (D, Ohio)
    Senate live TV coverage 44–47
GONZALEZ, Judge Jose
    2 Live Crew arrest 200–203
GORE, Mary (Tipper)
    Record warning label debate 198–199
GRATEFUL Dead, The (singing group)
    Woodstock 20th anniversary 206–209
GRUTMAN, Roy
    Bakker sex scandal downfall 68–77
GUTHRIE, Arlo
    Woodstock 20th anniversary 206–209

# H

HAHN, Jessica
    Bakker sex scandal downfall 68–77
HAVENS, Richie
    Woodstock 20th anniversary 206–209
HAWKINS-Stafford School Improvement Act
    Dial-a-porn debate 164–167
HDTV—*See HIGH-Definition TV*
HEFLIN, Sen. Howell (D, Ala.)
    Senate live TV coverage 44–47
HELMS, Sen. Jesse A. (R, N.C.)
    Dial-a-porn debate 164–167
    Senate obscene art ban rejection 92–99
HENDRIX, Jimi (1943-70)
    Woodstock 20th anniversary 206–209

HERITAGE USA
    Bakker sex scandal downfall 68–77
HERSHEY, Barbara
    Last Temptation of Christ debate 64–67
HEWLETT-Packard Co.
    FCC HDTV guidelines 48–49
HIGH-Definition TV (HDTV)
    FCC guidelines 48–49
HOLLINGS, Sen. Ernest F. (D, S.C.)
    FCC 'fairness doctrine' debate 4–13
    Media double ownership rule annulment 190–195
HOLLYWOOD, Fla.
    2 Live Crew arrest 200–203
HOMOSEXUALITY
    Andy Rooney 60 Minutes suspension 42–43
HOUSE of Representatives, U.S.—*See CONGRESS, U.S.*
HUDUNT v. American Booksellers Association Inc.
    Porn legislation controversy 160–163
HUGHES, Holly
    NEA grant rejections 104–107
HUSTLER (magazine)
    Mapplethorpe photo show debate 108–113
    Public figure satirization protection 168–177
HUSTLER v. Falwell
    Public figure satirization protection 168–177
HUSTON, John (1906-87)
    Film colorization controversy 54–63

# I

IBM—*See INTERNATIONAL Business Machines*
INDIANAPOLIS, Ind.
    Porn legislation controversy 160–163
INFINITY Broadcasting Corp.
    FCC indecency debate 14–17
INSIDE Edition (TV show)
    Broadcast sensationalism debate 32–41
INSTITUTE of Contemporary Art (Philadelphia, Pa.)
    Senate obscene art ban rejection 92–99

INTERIOR Department, U.S.
  Senate obscene art ban rejection 92–99
INTERNATIONAL Business Machines Corp. (IBM)
  FCC HDTV guidelines 48–49
INTERNATIONAL Radio Consultative Committee
  FCC HDTV guidelines 48–49
IRAN, Islamic Republic of
  Satanic Verses controversy 178–189
IRISES (painting)
  Record art sale 144–147
ISLAM
  Satanic Verses controversy 178–189
ITT Corp.
  FCC HDTV guidelines 48–49

# J

JAPAN
  FCC HDTV guidelines 48–49
JAPAN Broadcasting Co.
  FCC HDTV guidelines 48–49
JEFFERSON Airplane (singing group)
  Woodstock 20th anniversary 206–209
JUDAS Priest (singing group)
  Teen suicide case 204–205
JUSTICE Department, U.S.
  Meese porn crackdown 156–159

# K

KCSB-FM
  FCC indecency debate 14–17
KEILLOR, Garrison
  Radio show retirement 82–83
KEITEL, Harvey
  Last Temptation of Christ debate 64–67
KENNEDY, Sen. Edward M. (D, Mass.)
  Media double ownership rule annulment 190–195
KHAMENEI, Ayatollah Mohammed Ali (Iranian president)
  Satanic Verses controversy 178–189

KHOMEINI, Ayatollah Ruhollah (1900-89)
  Satanic Verses controversy 178–189
K-MART Corp.
  Satanic Verses controversy 178–189
KOBAYASHI, Hideto
  Record art sale 144–147
KPFK-FM
  FCC indecency debate 14–17
KRISTOFFERSON, Kris
  'Amerika' TV film controversy 28–31

# L

LABOR & Employment
  Miss Saigon casting controversy 114–117
  Screenwriters' strike 50–53
LADY and a Gentleman in Black, A (painting)
  Record art theft 148–149
LANG, Michael
  Woodstock 20th anniversary 206–209
LAST Temptation of Christ, The (film)
  Opening protests 64–67
  Satanic Verses controversy 178–189
LEAHY, Sen. Patrick (D, Vt.)
  Film colorization controversy 54–63
LEIS, Sheriff Simon
  Mapplethorpe photo show debate 108–113
LIBERTY Foundation
  Porn legislation controversy 160–163
LIBRARY of Congress
  Film colorization controversy 54–63
LITERATURE
  Satanic Verses controversy 178–189
LONDON, England
  Miss Saigon casting controversy 114–117
LOS Angeles, Calif.
  FCC indecency debate 14–17

# M

MACKINTOSH, Cameron
  Miss Saigon casting controversy 114–117
MALTESE Falcon, The (film)
  Colorization controversy 54–63
MANET, Edouard (1832-83)
  Record art theft 148–149
MAPPLETHORPE, Robert (1946-89)
  Bush art censorship opposition 100–103
  Photo show debate 108–113
  Senate obscene art ban rejection 92–99
MAYER, Roger L.
  Film colorization controversy 54–63
MEESE 3rd, Edwin
  Porn, violence linkage 152–155
  Porn crackdown 156–159
  Porn legislation controversy 160–163
METRO-Goldwyn-Mayer (MGM)
  Film colorization controversy 54–63
METZENBAUM, Sen. Howard (D, Ohio)
  Congressional flag desecration bill rejection 136–143
MGM—See METRO-Goldwyn Mayer
MICHEL, Rep. Robert (R, Ill.)
  Congressioanl flag desecration bill rejection 136–143
MILLER, Tim
  NEA grant rejections 104–107
MILLER v. California
  2 Live Crew arrest 200–203
  Senate obscene art ban rejection 92–99
MISS Saigon (play)
  Casting controversy 114–117
MOHTASHEMI, Ali Akbar
  Satanic Verses controversy 178–189
MORRIS Jr., Robert T.
  Computer virus controversy 84–89
MORTON Downey Show, The (TV show)
  Broadcast sensationalism debate 32–41
MOTION Pictures
  'Amerika' TV film controversy 28–31
  Colorization controversy 54–63

Last Temptation of Christ debate 64–67
NEA grant rejections 104–107
Porn legislation controversy 160–163
Screenwriters' strike 50–53

MOTOROLA Inc.
FCC HDTV guidelines 48–49

MOUSSAVI-Khamenei, Mir Hussein (Iranian premier)
Satanic Verses controversy 178–189

MOVIES—See MOTION Pictures

MURDOCH, Rupert
Media double ownership rule annulment 190–195

MUSE Hi Vision
FCC HDTV guidelines 48–49

MUSIC
Judas Priest teen suicide case 204–205
2 Live Crew arrest 200–203
Record warning label debate 198–199
Woodstock 20th anniversary 206–209

# N

NADER, Ralph
FCC 'fairness doctrine' debate 4–13

NARCOTICS & Dangerous Drugs
Bakker sex scandal downfall 68–77
Judas Priest teen suicide case 204–205
Record warning label debate 198–199
Woodstock 20th anniversary 206–209

NATIONAL Association of Broadcasters
Children's TV bill veto 22–27

NATIONAL Association of Independent Record Distributors
Record warning label debate 198–199

NATIONAL Coalition Against Pornography
Mapplethorpe photo show debate 108–113

NATIONAL Council on the Arts
NEA grant rejections 104–107

NATIONAL Endowment for the Arts (NEA)
Bush art censorship opposition 100–103
Grant rejections 104–107
Mapplethorpe photo show debate 108–113
Senate obscene art ban rejection 92–99

NATIONAL Federation for Decency
Meese porn crackdown 156–159

NATIONAL Public Radio (NPR)
Keillor departure set 82–83

NATIONAL Security Agency (NSA)
Computer virus controversy 84–89

NEA—See NATIONAL Endowment for the Arts

NEW York City
Media double ownership rule annulment 190–195
Miss Saigon casting controversy 114–117

NEW York State
Woodstock 20th anniversary 206–209

NIGHTLINE (TV show)
Bakker sex scandal downfall 68–77

NPR—See NATIONAL Public Radio

NSA—See NATIONAL Security Agency

# O

OBSCENITY—See PORNOGRAPHY

OLD Time Gospel Hour (TV show)
Bakker sex scandal downfall 68–77

OPRAH Winfrey Show, The (TV show)
Broadcast sensationalism debate 32–41

# P

PACIFICA Foundation Inc.
FCC indecency debate 14–17

PAINTING & Sculpture
Record sale 144–147
Record theft 148–149

PALM Springs, Calif.
Bakker sex scandal downfall 68–77

PARENTS' Music Resource Center
Record warning label debate 198–199

PENNSYLVANIA, University of (Philadelphia)
Senate obscene art ban rejection 92–99

PENTHOUSE (magazine)
Porn legislation controversy 160–163

PEOPLE That Love—See PTL Club

PERFORMANCE Art
NEA grant rejections 104–107

PHILADELPHIA, Pa.
FCC indecency debate 14–17

PHOTOGRAPHY
Bush art censorship opposition 100–103
Mapplethorpe show debate 108–113
Senate obscene art ban rejection 92–99

PLAYBOY (magazine)
Porn legislation controversy 160–163

POLITICS
Congressional flag desecration bill rejection 136–143
FCC 'fairness doctrine' debate 4–13
Flag-burning rulings 118–135
Public figure satirization protection 168–177

POPE v. Illinois
Obscenity rules clarification 18–21

PORNOGRAPHY & Obscenity
Dial-a-porn debate 164–167
FCC indecency debate 14–17
Legislation controversy 160–163
Mapplethorpe photo show debate 108–113
Meese crackdown 156–159
Meese panel violence linkage 152–155
NEA grant rejections 104–107
Obscenity rules clarification 18–21
Record warning label debate 198–199
Senate art ban rejection 92–99
2 Live Crew arrest 200–203

PRAIRIE Home Companion, A (radio show)
Keillor retirement 82–83

PRAISE The Lord—*See PTL Club*

PRESIDENT'S Commission on Obscenity and Pornography
    Meese panel porn, violence linkage 152–155

PRYCE, Jonathan
    Miss Saigon casting controversy 114–117

PTL Club
    Bakker sex scandal downfall 68–77

PUBLISHING
    Media double ownership rule annulment 190–195
    Meese panel porn, violence linkage 152–155
    Meese porn crackdown 156–159
    Porn legislation controversy 160–163
    Public figure satirization protection 168–177
    Satanic Verses controversy 178–189

# R

RACISM
    Andy Rooney 60 Minutes suspension 42–43
    FCC indecency debate 14–17
    Miss Saigon casting controversy 114–117

RAFSANJANI, Ali Akbar Hashemi
    Satanic Verses controversy 178–189

REAGAN, Ronald Wilson (U.S. president; replaced Jan. 20, 1989)
    Children's TV bill veto 22–27
    Dial-a-porn debate 164–167
    FCC 'fairness doctrine' debate 4–13

RECORDING Industry Association of America
    Warning label debate 198–199

RELIGION
    Bakker sex scandal downfall 68–77
    Last Temptation of Christ debate 64–67
    NEA grant rejections 104–107
    Satanic Verses controversy 178–189
    Senate obscene art ban rejection 92–99
    Swaggart sex scandal downfall 78–81

REMBRANDT Hermenszoon van Rijn (1606-69)
    Record art theft 148–149

RENO, Nev.
    Judas Priest teen suicide case 204–205

RENOIR, Pierre Auguste (1841-1919)
    Record art sale 144–147

RENTON, Wash.
    Porn legislation controversy 160–163

RIVERA, Geraldo
    TV talk show sensationalism 32–41

ROBERTS, John
    Woodstock 20th anniversary 206–209

ROBERTS, Oral
    Bakker sex scandal downfall 68–77

ROBERTSON, Rev. Pat
    Swaggart sex scandal downfall 78–81

ROCK 'n Roll—*See MUSIC*

ROGERS, Ginger
    Film colorization controversy 54–63

ROONEY, Andy
    60 Minutes suspension 42–43

ROSENMAN, Joel
    Woodstock 20th anniversary 206–209

RUBIN, Judge Carl B.
    Mapplethorpe photo show debate 108–113

RUSHDIE, Salman
    Satanic Verses controversy 178–189

# S

SAITO, Ryoei
    Record art sale 144–147

SANTA Barbara, Calif.
    FCC indecency debate 14–17

SANTANA (singing group)
    Woodstock 20th anniversary 206–209

SATANIC Verses, The (book)
    Salman Rushdie controversy 178–189

SCORSESE, Martin
    Last Temptation of Christ debate 64–67

SENATE, U.S.—*See CONGRESS, U.S.*

SERRANO, Andres
    Bush art censorship opposition 100–103
    Senate obscene art ban rejection 92–99

7-11 Convenience Stores (of Southland Corp.)
    Porn legislation controversy 160–163

SEX & Sex Crimes
    Bakker downfall 68–77
    Swaggart downfall 78–81
    **Homosexuality**—*See Homosexuality*
    **Obscenity**—*See Pornography*
    **Pornography**—*See Pornography*

SHERMAN Antitrust Act
    Children's TV bill veto 22–27

SIAS, John B.
    'Amerika' TV film controversy 28–31

60 Minutes (TV show)
    Andy Rooney suspension 42–43

SORTIE du Pesage, La (painting)
    Record art theft 148–149

SOUTH Carolina
    Bakker sex scandal downfall 68–77

SOUTHEASTERN Center for Contemporary Art (Winston-Salem, N.C.)
    Senate obscene art ban rejection 92–99

STAINED Class (recording)
    Judas Priest teen suicide case 204–205

STERN, Howard
    FCC indecency debate 14–17

STODDARD, Brandon
    'Amerika' TV film controversy 28–31

STORM on the Sea of Galilee, The (painting)
    Record art theft 148–149

SUPREME Court, U.S.
    Congressional flag desecration bill rejection 136–143
    FCC indecency debate 14–17
    Flag-burning rulings 118–135
    2 Live Crew arrest 200–203
    Obscenity rules clarification 18–21
    Porn legislation controversy 160–163
    Public figure satirization protection 168–177

SWAGGART, Rev. Jimmy
    Bakker sex scandal downfall 68–77
    Sex scandal downfall 78–81

# T

TEKTRONIX, Inc.
    FCC HDTV guidelines 48–49
TELEPHONES
    Dial-a-porn debate 164–167
TEXAS
    Flag-burning protection 128–135
TEXAS Instruments Inc.
    FCC HDTV guidelines 48–49
THEATER
    Miss Saigon casting controversy 114–117
    NEA grant rejections 104–107
TURNER, Ted
    Film colorization controversy 54–63
TURNER Entertainment Co.
    Film colorization controversy 54–63
2 LIVE Crew (singing group)
    Arrest on obscenity charges 200–203

# U

UNITED Nations
    'Amerika' TV film controversy 28–31
UNIVERSAL Pictures
    Last Temptation of Christ debate 64–67
URICH, Robert
    'Amerika' TV film controversy 28–31
U.S. v. Eichman
    Flag-burning protection 128–135

# V

VANCE, James
    Judas Priest teen suicide case 204–205
Van GOGH, Vincent (1853-90)
    Record art sale 144–147
    Record art theft 148–149
VERMEER, Jan (1632-75)
    Record art theft 148–149

# W

WALDENBOOKS, Inc.
    Satanic Verses controversy 178–189
WHITEHEAD, Judge Jerry
    Judas Priest teen suicide case 204–205
WHO, The (singing group)
    Woodstock 20th anniversary 206–209
WILDMON, Rev. Donald
    Meese porn crackdown 156–159
WINFREY, Oprah
    TV talk show sensationalism 32–41
WONGWON, Chris
    2 Live Crew arrest 200–203
WOODSTOCK Music Festival
    20th anniversary 206–209
WRITERS Guild of America
    Screenwriters' strike 50–53
WYSP-FM
    FCC indecency debate 14–17

# Y

YASGUR, Max
    Woodstock 20th anniversary 206–209

# Z

ZENITH Electronics Corp.
    FCC HDTV guidelines 48–49